The black lamb was a sacrifice offered up at a pagan rite Miss West attended on St. George's Eve among the mountains not far from the Greek frontier. The grey falcon is the symbolic bird in a celebrated Serbian folk poem. Together, these creatures stand as a symbol of why the Balkans have become the "tinder-box of Europe." The black lamb of the tortured dark Slav soul and the grey falcon of the invaders represent a land that Miss West has loved and pitied and admired, and which, through the pages of her book, will live forever.

"That it is Miss West's *magnum opus* goes without saying, but I am almost as sure that, of its sort, it is also one of the great books of our time."
—CLIFTON FADIMAN, *The New Yorker*

"It tells the story, essentially, of what has happened to our world. In an excitingly new form, in language which is at the same time precise and rich, it is an analysis of our culture, the world of ideas and emotions in which we live.... The timing of its publication, at one of the great climaxes in the story of Western European culture, matches the scale on which it is told and the skill with which Miss West tells it."
—JOSEPH BARNES, *New York Herald Tribune*

Juarez

AND HIS MEXICO

Other Books by Ralph Roeder

SAVONAROLA

THE MAN OF THE RENAISSANCE

CATHERINE DE' MEDICI AND THE LOST REVOLUTION

Juarez
AND HIS MEXICO

A BIOGRAPHICAL HISTORY BY

Ralph Roeder

NEW YORK · THE VIKING PRESS

1947

To My Wife

Contents

Grateful acknowledgment is made to Señor Pedro Hurtado, Lic. Pablo Prida Santacilia, and Arq. Carlos Obregon Santacilia for access to the personal archives of Benito Juarez in their possession and for generous assistance in the preparation of this book.

PART ONE

Education

I

THE road rises steeply, and we nose our way slowly around the shoulder of the mountain, hugging the treacherous curves, and halting wherever a brook breaks through the underbrush to water the white-hot engine and to rest the human machine. The engine wears out in four months, and though the Indian who drives the truck has been trained from time immemorial not to tire, habit has not made the haul easy, and the passengers help the ascent by their silence: every word is a weight, and not one is spoken until we reach the crest. Then they look back and bid us take our leave of Oaxaca. Below, infinitely far below, lies the floor of the valley with its fertile farm lands and the distant domes of the city, where the presence of man has made some impression upon nature; before us, and no less far below, opens a vast basin of valleys and mountains multiplying, in labyrinthine confusion, in every direction—the land of the man whose fame has risen from the wilderness in which he was born and whose origin we have come to seek—the Sierra Juarez.

The road runs along a ridge that divides two worlds, and here, level with the eagle, the one ahead seems to be completely uninhabited, but our destination is already in sight, and our companions lean forward and point to something, visible to them at least, halfway up one of those far slopes, we are not sure which, which is San Pablo Guelatao. Why we are going there is a mystery to them, but, being sensible people, they suppose that we are going to look at the lake. The lake is enchanted and one of the natural wonders of the region. Man is not, and the memory of the one who was born there, or of any man, means so little that when we mention it they relapse into silence. So we slip into the other world. One by one our companions, who have been our fellows for an hour or two, drop away and set off afoot for some solitude of their own in the mountains. The road winds on and on, dipping, rising, disappearing, skirting an occasional settlement indistinguishable from the mud of which it is made and the green into which it grows, and fading immediately into the vacant immensity that dwarfs it. Once we pass through a village deserted by day and pause to drop provisions for a woman, who stands by the wayside taking leave of a man; as he swings away, she retreats into her doorway and stands there weeping,

3

and indifferent to the food laid at her feet. The Sierra is poorer by one more man, and she clings to her memories while they last.

After six hours on the road the truck drops us in another vacant village and winds its way on up the mountain to the mines at the end of the run. There is no one in sight, and we are free to wander at will; and we discover with surprise that the place is conscious of the man. A statue of him stands in a diminutive garden; a plinth marks the site of the hut in which he was born; an official portrait hangs in the municipal office. But by-and-by the people appear, and we discover that the cult has been imported and imposed on a community that has only a remote and casual connection with it. Three of his kin come in from the fields, and we make their acquaintance. They are willing to talk of their famous ancestor, but bewildered to know what we want and pained to find nothing to say. "We were not in the world then," they plead in apology of their ignorance, and we stand rebuked for disturbing it. They are of the sixth generation, and after so long a lapse of time, in a people without memory, immersed in an everlasting and unvarying present, there is not even a thread of family tradition by which to recover the trace of that distant kinsman who left his people one hundred and twenty-nine years ago, and who has returned to them in the form of a statue on a pedestal in the village green. The continuity lies in their ignorance, and curiosity breaks the connection. Time has long since severed the tie, and so has the statue standing there, a stranger like us, scanning the horizon like a solitary bronze tourist.

So they send us to school. The school is a better memorial than the statue, for it honors by a living return the memory of the boy who fled the wilderness in search of knowledge: here some eighty young men have come from all parts of the Sierra to gain some consciousness and control of life; but by its very progress the school marks the passage of time no less irrevocably than the statue. What the students know of Juarez is what we know ourselves—the conventional knowledge drawn from books—and that we should have come so far to borrow or to better it by some intimate truth out of the mouths of his own people seems to them a strange foreign notion, as it is; but they humor it. After nightfall, when the work of the day is done, masters and pupils troop with us to the municipal office, where the whole community assembles to satisfy our curiosity and to wonder at it. The mayor lights a lamp and opens a ledger and waits patiently while we read the few lines in which one of his predecessors transcribed, in 1902, the little that could then be gleaned from local tradition; for our notion is neither new nor original; others before us have burrowed in the placid oblivion of San Pablo Guelatao for some hint of his forgotten humanity, and left their meager findings to satisfy and silence all future intruders. We close the book, convinced that our curiosity is cloud-mining, and willing to admit that we have come to look at the lake.

The meeting breaks up, and on our way to bed we are shown a little cattle pool which we had noticed before without suspecting that we were looking upon wonders.

No. To know is to be, and here where his being began all that remains of the man is the statue that he has become, the metallic cast from which the living substance has long since fled. The road to San Pablo Guelatao leads nowhere; and not until we turn back and follow it, as he did, in the reverse direction does the journey make sense and the road remember the traveler.

2

BIOGRAPHY being a composite of what a man thinks of himself and what others think of him, we should begin with a blank but for an autobiographical fragment left by Juarez himself. Late in life he began a memoir for his children, which is valuable less for the information it contains than for that self-revelation which in the case of any man, and above all of one so bitterly disputed, will always be the most veracious of truths. The *Notes for My Children,* however, were written by one who had long since lost all connection with his origin, and who recalled his childhood with the detachment of maturity: it is a bare record of facts, and its self-revelation lies in his reticent and matter-of-fact recital of them.

Two dates lingered in his memory. The first was borrowed from the parish register. His birth on March 21, 1806, would have passed as unnoticed as the birth of an animal, had he awakened to it with no other witness than the spring equinox; but on the following day his father, his godmother, and his grandparents carried him up the mountain to Santo Tomas Ixtlan, where the vicar baptized him and entered the name of Pablo Benito Juarez in the book of life. The material facts that followed the end of his prenatal sleep were equally remote from his ken. "I had the misfortune," we are told, "not to have known my parents, Marcelino Juarez and Brigida Garcia, Indians of the primitive race of the country, for I was hardly three years old when they died, leaving me and my sisters, Maria Josefa and Rosa, to the care of our paternal grandparents, Pedro Juarez and Justa Lopez, Indians also of the Zapotec nation." He knew his nation, and that was enough. A few years later his grandparents died, his sisters married, and he was left to the care of an uncle. Here were the common facts of Indian life—birth and death, baptism and burial, dispersal and adoption, where the burden of fertility was borne by everyone in turn—but within the immemorial pattern the will to escape it was also born, and with the awakening of that urge his own memories begin.

"As my parents had left me no patrimony and my uncle lived by his own toil, as soon as I could reason I applied myself, so far as my tender years would permit, to the work in the fields. In some idle moments my uncle taught me to read and impressed on me how useful and helpful it was to learn the Spanish tongue, and as it was extremely difficult then for poor people, and especially for the native class, to pursue any learned profession other than the ecclesiastic, he wished me to study for ordination. These promptings and the examples of some of my countrymen who knew how to read and write and speak the Spanish tongue, and who exercised the sacred ministry, awoke in me a vehement desire to learn, so much so indeed that when my uncle called me to take my lesson, I myself brought him the whip to punish me if I did not know it; but his occupations and my application to the daily toil thwarted my desires, and I made little or no progress in my studies. Moreover, in a little village like mine, where there were hardly twenty families, and at a time when little or no attention was paid to the education of youth, there was no school; the Spanish tongue was not even spoken, so that fathers who could afford the schooling of their children took them to the City of Oaxaca for that purpose, and those who could not pay the fees put them into service in private homes on condition that they be taught to read and write. This was the only method of education generally in use, not only in my village, but in the whole district of Ixtlan, so that it was a remarkable fact in that period that most of the servants in the houses in the City were young people of both sexes from that district. Because of these facts which I felt, rather than by any mature reflection, of which I was yet incapable, I came to the conclusion that only by going to the City could I learn, and indeed I often begged my uncle to take me to the capital; but whether because of the affection he felt for me or for some other reason, he came to no decision and merely gave me hope that he would take me there some day."

The accuracy of his memories is fully confirmed—save for one small detail—by the recollections of his oldest living kin collected in 1902 in the municipal ledger. Centenarians or near-centenarians, they remembered that even at that remote period their *pueblo* boasted a school, run by a native, and that the boy attended it every morning before leaving for the fields. If there was some disagreement as to the school, there was none as to the scholar. He was very much devoted to study and showed application and profit in his letters. "His character was obedient; he was reserved in his thoughts and usually shy; he had friends, but few, and to them he showed formality and good sense." He practiced his chosen vocation even in the fields while he was minding his flocks, and it was not uncommon to see him "mount a tree and harangue his sheep in his native Zapotec tongue."

The day when he would exercise his vocation in Oaxaca, however, was indefinitely deferred, his uncle being a man of small means "whose interests were limited to a small flock of sheep and a parcel of ground by the lake." With little to do but to count sheep or convert them, the most unsleeping ambition may well have nodded, and the boy was obedient. The years wore away uneventfully, their even tenor unbroken save by a single adventure, and that inadvertent. One day, or once upon a time, he fell asleep on the shore of the enchanted lake and woke to find himself adrift in the dark, on a clump of bushes, under a driving downpour of rain, wind, thunder, and lightning. It was the most terrifying experience in his life. He spent the night on the treacherous waters, where long ago another shepherd had fallen asleep and been drowned, and his body never found, unless by the water-witch down below; but whether she was asleep, or dead, or did not want him, he drifted safely ashore in the morning, and her legendary haunts became once more what they had been the day before, a standing lure no larger than a cattle pool in his back yard.

In his twelfth year he was no nearer Oaxaca. His uncle was loath to part with him, and the lad with his uncle. Had it been left to them, the decision might never have been made. But a sheep made up their minds for both of them.

The second date that lingered in his memory was indelibly imprinted on it—the year, the month, the day of the week, and even the hour of the day. "It was Wednesday, December 16, 1818. I was in a field, as usual, with my flock, when some muleteers chanced to pass, at eleven in the morning, leading their mules on the road to the Sierra. I asked them if they came from Oaxaca. They replied that they did, and at my request they described some of the things they had seen there and went on their way." Fatal curiosity! for when he went back to counting his sheep he found that one of them was missing and, worse yet, "another boy, who was much older than I and whose name was Apolonio Conde, approached and told me, on learning the cause of my grief, that he had seen one of the muleteers make away with the sheep." Weighing what his uncle would or would not do, he anticipated the worst, and "that fear and my natural desire to amount to something decided me to walk to Oaxaca."

Then and there the boy discovered himself. Of that mishap no mention is made, however, in the memoir: what the man chose to remember was the compunction it cost him to part with his uncle. "For my part," he wrote in the notes for his children, "I was loath to leave his side and to forsake the house that had harbored me as a child and an orphan, and to abandon the tender companions of infancy with whom one always forms profound ties and affections that suffer by absence, which withers the heart. Cruel was the conflict between these feelings and my desire to go to another society, new and unknown to me, to secure my education. Nevertheless, the desire was stronger than the sentiment, and on the 17th day of December of 1818, and at twelve years of age, I fled from my home and walked to the city of Oaxaca, where I arrived the same night."

The brevity of the account of his childhood sufficiently testifies to its truth. His birthplace was the background of his being, and his first twelve years of life merely a prelude to the day when he obeyed the lure of the road and followed it out of the cramping immensity of the mountains, through the echoless solitude of the valleys, across the crest that divides the two worlds, and down to the City, where a society new and unknown to him quickened his self-consciousness, and he became aware at last of us. San Pablo Guelatao was the point of departure; the starting-point was Oaxaca.

3

A RRIVING in Oaxaca on the night of the fatal day that followed the theft of the sheep, he found shelter in the house of Don Antonio Mazza, where one of his sisters, who had tired of marriage, was working as a cook. Here he earned his keep by watching the grain, which could not run away anyway, while he looked about for a place. Three weeks later he found one—thanks to the time-honored system by which young people from the Sierra secured an education in return for domestic service, and the charitable householders of Oaxaca an abundant supply of cheap labor—in the home of Don Antonio Salanueva. His employer was a bookbinder by trade, and by vocation a lay brother of the Third Order of Saint Francis. "Although very much addicted to devotion and religious practices, he was fairly unprejudiced and a friend to the education of youth," and was familiar with the books which he bound. His favorite reading was the Epistles of St. Paul and the collected works of Feijoo—who? no matter, he, too, promised to teach the heathen to read and write. A pious and honorable man, Dr. Salanueva fully lived up to his side of the bargain. He adopted the boy, body and soul, became his godfather, and gave him the benefit of all the educational facilities available in Oaxaca in 1818.

Before long the lad discovered their limitations. In the primary schools of New Spain, Spanish grammar was not taught at that period, reading, writing, and reciting the catechism of Padre Ripalda being hard enough to learn by heart; and as Juarez spoke what was still a foreign tongue to him, "without rules and with all the faults of the vulgar," he himself soon became dissatisfied with his progress, which was slow and imperfect. He applied, accordingly, for admission to a higher institution. Here the headmaster set him a task and he formed a page, which was faulty of course, "since I was a pupil and not a professor"— but the master, not knowing the pupil, lost his temper and, "instead of showing me my mistakes and how to correct them, merely said that it would not do and ordered me to be punished." Now, this would not do, not at all, not with Pablo Benito Juarez. "This injustice offended me profoundly, and so did the inequality with which instruction was dispensed in that institution, which was called 'The Royal School'; for while the master taught a certain number of so-called respectable pupils correctly in a separate apartment, I and the other poor boys like myself were relegated to another room, under the direction of a man who called himself the Assistant, and who was as little fitted to teach, and of a character as harsh, as the master himself." Class consciousness was all that he learned in the Royal School, and as his native handicaps were aggravated by those of being a charity pupil, he took his education in hand himself. "I was disgusted with this wretched method of instruction, and, since there was no other establishment in the City to which I could go, I decided definitely to leave school and to practice the little I had learned by myself, so as to be able to express my ideas in writing, although the form might be poor, as it still is today."

His ideas developed rapidly. The mechanics of schooling he mastered by slow and solitary application, working late into the night by the light of a stump of resin which a woman in the next courtyard lent him. Though the lad had exhausted the elementary facilities of Oaxaca so quickly, he was ill fitted to teach himself; but within less than three years he was ready for the next step. He had noticed many young men of his age going in and out of the Seminary every day, "which reminded me of the counsels of my uncle, who wished me to be an ecclesiastic" —counsels that might have been forgotten but for another fact which spurred him at fifteen. "Moreover, it was an opinion generally accepted then, not only among the vulgar but in the upper classes of society, that clerics, and even those who were merely students without being ecclesiastics, knew a great deal, and I noticed that they were respected and considered for the knowledge attributed to them. This circumstance rather than any thought of becoming a cleric, for which I felt an instinctive dislike, decided me to beg my godfather to let me study in the Seminary, offering to do everything to make the fulfillment of my obligations in his service compatible with my devotion to the study to which I was going to consecrate myself."

Dr. Salanueva not only agreed but encouraged him to adopt a calling in which he could turn his deficiencies to excellent account, explaining that, as he possessed his native Zapotec tongue, he could be ordained by right of it, under the ecclesiastical law of America, without having to possess some patrimony as well, as was required of other boys while they were waiting for a benefice. This consideration carried some weight with Salanueva and increased the satisfaction with which he welcomed the choice of a sacred career by his charge. As the motives that led the boy to embrace it were religious only in the candor with which he confessed them to himself, a mutual understanding was reached. On October 21, 1821, he donned a mantle larger than his little body and, carrying a copy of his birth certificate, joined the other young men flocking into the Seminary.

The memoir, up to this point, gives us a picture of solitary youth exclusively devoted to study; but though it is true to the dominant motive of his development, it is incomplete. In Oaxaca, as in Guelatao, his habits were noticed by the neighbors, and what is wanting is supplied by other witnesses. The nearest was the woman next door who contributed a stub of resin to his progress; the farthest, an old lady living down the block, who spent a long life there and who could still remember in her nonage that the houseboy of Dr. Salanueva was "very humble, very much devoted to study, and always to be seen with a book in his hand." These habits, she supposed, were part of his housework, since she had never seen him going to school or anywhere else for that matter, except down the street on days of religious processions. Dr. Salanueva kept in his house a figure of Christ carrying the Cross, and every day, when it went out, out came the houseboy clad in spotless linen, book in hand, reciting the *Via Crucis*. What the women saw, as they sat in their windows, was limited, however, by their powers of observation: the boys on the block saw something more, and in the reminiscences of one of them we catch a glimpse of other habits. "Although Juarez was very timid," we are told, "he was also very lively. He would buy apples and distribute them, not to eat but to pelt people buying and selling in the shops that we passed. On nights of religious exercises, and in moments of discipline, he would do the same thing when the churches were darkened, and we would throw apples until we were discovered by Salanueva and punished; but we played the same prank the next time, only more carefully." This habit was as incorrigible as his inability to distinguish between a shop and a church. Exercise of some sort was a necessity, and while Dr. Salanueva was nodding over St. Paul or Feijoo, or both at once, Juarez would slip out and join his friends around the corner. Their favorite sports were running and jumping, and he excelled in them to his cost: one day he dared the crowd to run down the Street of the Bells leaping the gutter, and with a single bound he fell in and had to be hauled out, "and though he was not soiled, since there was no filth, he made himself thoroughly wet and for that he won his whipping."

Among these larks some were more memorable than others. Most memorable of all were the outings which they made beyond the bounds of the City, across the River Atoyac, to the Lake of Montoyac. This lake was not enchanted, and here he built a springboard of his own invention, with barrels, turf, and timber borrowed from some work-men near by. Like his copybooks in school, the experiment "produced the picture we expected, not quite perfect, but nearly so." Before test-ing it the boys studied one another, "for a bold spirit was needed to make the jump." Anyone would follow the leader, and "finally Juarez made up his mind with all the courage of a good seaman, but as he came to the center of the plank or the end, both tipped and went over-board; fortunately the plank fell short and the body fell far, and he was not crushed by it." Undrowned, he was undaunted. On their next holiday he led them back to the swimming hole and repaired the con-traption with the help of a clever friend who knew the mechanics of springboards. This time it worked perfectly. The spirit of enterprise developing, he charged the boys who collected around them three or four pennies a jump, and with the profits he fed his own crowd fruit candy. Then came philanthropic cravings. "Juarez had an aversion for the strong and always favored the weak, and often he would say to us, 'When I have money I shall give it to that poor man—and some day I shall have it.'" But at fifteen, fruit candy came first.

Rambles were rare, however, and at the end of the day the road led back to the beaten path. "On the nights when we went to chapel early, Salanueva would read to us from the book that explained the mysteries of religion, the mystery of the Trinity, and the preservation of the Church and the destruction of Jerusalem, and I forget what else. When Salanueva wearied of reading, Juarez would take up the lesson, and he explained it to us fairly clearly. Then came the Rosary, or whatever office fell on that day, until eight or a quarter past eight at night." By then everyone was nodding, and curfew concluded the accustomed routine. So the memorable but dateless days of his boyhood ended, for "all this happened in our last years, about the year '20. Juarez changed his clothes and I left the chapel of Salanueva never to return, since it had been decided that I should enter the Seminary."

The reminiscences of his boyhood friend were written on the margin of the main theme: in the memoir the dominant motive develops with-out digression. His formal education was slow. When he entered the Seminary he was as ignorant of Spanish grammar as when he left the

Royal School, but this was not a serious drawback since the other students were equally deficient. In the Seminary, however, he mastered Latin grammar; four years were spent on this study, and in August 1825 he passed or, as he said, suffered, the statutory examinations with the rating of "Excellent." He was now qualified for the higher learning; but a serious difficulty arose with his godfather. The course in Philosophy, which followed the mastery of grammar, was not to be given that year, and Salanueva decided that Juarez might very well dispense with it, take up the study of Moral Theology at once, and be ordained the following summer. "This suggestion was very painful to me, both because of the repugnance which I felt for an ecclesiastical career, and because of the bad opinion which people held of priests who studied nothing but Latin grammar and Moral Theology, and who were ridiculed for that reason and called 'Mass-and-Meal Priests' or *Larragos*. The former nickname was given them because in their ignorance they sang Mass merely as a means of subsistence and were not permitted to preach or to exercise any other function requiring learning and ability; and the latter because they studied Moral Theology only in the manual of Padre Larragos." Having embraced an uncongenial calling for the sake of social advancement, Juarez meant to make the best of a bad bargain and had no mind to be cheated of four years of domestic servitude for the sake of a small curacy and the life of an ecclesiastical menial somewhere in the mountains.

In his haste to hatch his charge, Salanueva made a serious mistake. As an employer of native labor, he might have known that a discontented domestic, however docile, devoted, and obedient, always ends by having his way, and that he would have done better not to begin what he could not finish; for Juarez had a will of his own and was not to be hurried into holy orders. As best he could, he defended his claim to a complete education, explaining to his godfather that he was too young yet for the Presbytery and that nothing would be lost by taking a course in Arts. As they were both reasonable beings, who had lived under the same roof for seven years, the difficulty was overcome by mutual agreement. Arts it was.

Thereafter the youth advanced at his own pace. He managed to prolong the reprieve for two years more and to stretch the persuasive appeal of immaturity well beyond the age at which it lost all legal validity. His years of schooling in Oaxaca wore away slowly, like the years of his ignorance in Guelatao, and the plodding pace of the narrative eloquently testifies to their dreary aridity. The calendar is dated by the curriculum, the milestones are the opening and closing of courses, and the record is as narrow and confined as the corridors of the convent and the dwindling vista of doors opening and closing on his adolescence. The outer world never intrudes, no companions appear. The memoir is a monologue, and the self-portrait is painted in monochrome. Dr. Salanueva is not even mentioned; his guardian had been tamed, and the greatest difficulty under which he labored was himself, for despite his distaste for his chosen profession he displayed a marked aptitude for his studies and could not deny his abilities or defer the dreaded day indefinitely. In 1827 he suffered and passed the statutory examinations in scholastic Philosophy, sustaining two theses in public with the rating of *Excelente nemine discrepante,* and winning the unanimous commendation of his synodics. He was twenty-one, it was impossible to stall any longer, he was a man, and the next term he began the study of Moral Theology.

It was the beginning of the end, and his dilemma now became acute. He knew that he was not fitted for the Church, and he knew that there was no escape from it. The secular professions were inaccessible, since they could be pursued only in the capital or in foreign parts, and "for poor people like myself there was no hope." The monopoly of education exercised by the Church left him no choice. He was trapped by his own essential needs and the limited opportunities for satisfying them, which had driven him from Guelatao nine years before; his plight was repeated on a larger scale in Oaxaca and aggravated by the knowledge he had picked up since then of a society no longer new and unknown to him. He had found a place, and a privileged one, in Oaxaca, adopted by a sympathetic patron and given all the advantages that the philanthropic facilities of the provincial capital provided for his people. There was no further to go, and he could not go back to Guelatao. He had enjoyed all the benefits and exhausted all the resources of the City, from the Royal School with its class distinctions to the Seminary, which offered the refuge of religious equality to those who renounced the world for it; and he found himself in an impasse, advancing consciously toward a dead end. The dilemma was cruel, but it was of his own choosing, and he could not complain. The Church it was.

So his last years in the Seminary slipped away. He was bored, he was listless, he found the principles of Moral Theology incomprehensible, but he completed his contract. Nothing less than a direct intervention of Divine Providence, or a change in the whole social order, could break it, and he knew too little of Moral Theology to believe in miracles. Before the year was out, however, something happened in Oaxaca that completely altered his destiny. Here the narrative breaks off in a digression that is an integral part of the chronicle and necessary to explain how it was that in the course of time he was able to write those notes for his children.

4

"IN THAT period great events had already occurred in the Nation." The words with which the digression begins read like the belated acknowledgment of a debt; and so they were. The Nation is a new word in the narrative, and a new fact in his consciousness, and it is introduced at the precise moment when it begins to have a meaning for him. Born in 1806, he grew up in the period during which a Crown colony of Spain was gradually transformed into an independent people. His childhood coincided with the birth throes, and his adolescence with the growth, of the movement for national emancipation, but between that development and his own there was no connection until he reached manhood and reaped its benefits in 1827. The debt was acknowledged when he was ripe to appreciate it; but the great events of that period were too familiar to require more than a passing mention in the memoir, and the brief allusion which he makes to them there deserves some enlargement because of the far-reaching effect which they exercised on his destiny, recasting it and foreshadowing the forces that determined his future.

The separation of the colony from the mother country had long been foreseen by the Spanish themselves as a natural phenomenon foreordained by its very constitution and born in the bowels of the world. Predestined by political geography, the distance of one continent from the other, the remote control of the colony by the mother country, and the detachment of the offspring from the parent—nature and human nature combined to make it inevitable. Geopolitical generalities are less important, however, than the specific factors—the time, the place, and the human agents—that produced the foregone conclusion. The *why* was foreseen, but not the *how* and the *when*. Like other fatalities, though the rupture could not be prevented, it could at least be postponed by the normal precautions of human prudence; and no safeguard was neglected to defer it. The colony was isolated and preserved in hermetic seclusion from the outer world, and for two centuries after the founding of New Spain the policy was applied with success, breeding a race of political minors and a dependent mentality in the colonials, which provided the best means of perpetuating their bondage; but eventually the parental hand slipped.

The process of emancipation was common to the whole continent and contagious, and for New Spain it began with the rebellion of the British colonies in North America. When the peace treaty was signed in Paris in 1783, France and Spain were parties to it, as they had been to the revolt, which they abetted to cripple a rival empire. The Conde de Aranda, who signed the treaty in the name of Spain, improved the occasion to read his royal master a lesson. "The independence of the English colonies has been recognized, and this fact is for me an occasion of sorrow and fear," he wrote. "France has few possessions in America, but she should have considered that Spain, her closest ally, has many, and that henceforth they will be exposed to dreadful convulsions. From the first France has worked against her own interests in favoring and stimulating this independence. I have said as much more than once to the ministers of that nation. I shall not dwell on the difficulty of preserving our domination in America. Never have possessions so extensive and lying at so great a distance from the metropolis been successfully preserved for any length of time. Without entering into such considerations, I shall confine myself to what concerns us now, the fear of finding ourselves exposed to the perils that threaten us from the new Power that we just recognized in a land where no other State exists to check its advance. This Federal Republic was born a pygmy, so to speak, and needed the support of two Powers as mighty as Spain and France to achieve its independence. A day will come when it will become a giant, a colossus to be dreaded in those parts. It will then forget the benefits it received from both Powers and will think only of its own aggrandizement. The first step of this new Power, when once it begins to grow, will be to gain possession of the Floridas to dominate the Gulf of Mexico. After thus hampering our commerce with New Spain, it will aspire to the conquest of that vast empire, which we shall be unable to defend against a formidable Power established on the same continent and adjoining it as well."

The prophet of doom, however, was also a statesman determined to outwit it, and he crowned his complaint with a remarkable recommendation. Since the loss of the colonies was inevitable, and the proximity of the new nation certain to speed it, either by example or conquest, it was obviously the part of wisdom to yield to necessity and to forestall it gracefully. Startling as his advice seemed, what the Conde de Aranda had in mind was no wanton flight of reason, but a completely hardheaded scheme: he proposed to abandon all the overseas possessions of Spain with the exception of Cuba and Puerto Rico and some islands to the south to serve as a route and a storehouse for colonial trade, and to convert the dominions into a commonwealth of autonomous American monarchies bound to the mother country by an issue of Bourbons who would sit, one on the throne of Peru, another on that of New Spain, and a third on the coast of Costa Firma.

Nor was the shadow of sovereignty to be the sole compensation for abandoning its substance. The condition of this great cession was that the transatlantic kings should recognize the King of Spain as the head of the family and pay tribute to him in kind—gold from Peru, silver from New Spain, and colonial commodities from Costa Rica; trade would be conducted on a basis of complete reciprocity, binding the four thrones together in a close defensive and offensive alliance for their mutual protection and prosperity. Since the factories of Spain could not meet the demand in America for manufactured articles, France would be invited as an ally to supply the shortage, to the absolute exclusion of England, and the boycott against the British would be embodied in formal trade treaties. The contributions of the three kings would be more valuable than all the silver currently drawn from America, Aranda believed; the population would increase, emigration from Spain would be checked, and the power bloc would be strong enough to prevent the aggrandizement of the Anglo-American colonies or of any other competitor in that part of the world. "In short," he concluded, "we shall enjoy all the advantages of the possession of America without suffering any of its drawbacks."

The admonitions of the Conde de Aranda have often been cited for the accuracy of his forecasts; they are no less notable as the statement by a contemporary of the causes which were already apparent in 1783 for the imminent dissolution of the Spanish empire. Spain at the close of the eighteenth century was no longer the nation that had colonized a hemisphere in the sixteenth, but a weakening world Power barely able to maintain its position on the old continent, and incapable of retaining its possessions overseas without adapting its colonial system to the changing times. The consciousness of that fact pervades the recommendations of Aranda, and the best advice he could offer under the circumstances was necessarily senile. The proposal to transform the colonies into a protectorate and to lend a new lease of life to the decrepit Spanish empire by an act of fraudulent political bankruptcy was one of those schemes, dear to the minds of lawyers and chancellors alike, which had the merit of professional shrewdness but which could not cheat the facts; it was an accommodation to change which merely encouraged the delusion of past grandeur. The proposal to form an economic bloc between France and Spain against Great Britain was inspired, on the other hand, by a clear grasp of the forces which were to determine the future and, speeded by the industrial revolution, to tip the balance of power.

With his long view of history and his limited means of controlling it, the Conde de Aranda was a typical *fin-de-siècle* statesman, looking backward and forward in impotent perception of a dilemma which could be met only by makeshifts. His whole scheme might be described as the daydream of a senile realist, had it not influenced the course of independence and caught the fancy of later and no less level-headed statesmen who tested it in the nineteenth century. At the time, it was taken seriously by no one but its author. His warning was addressed to an enlightened monarch; but not even a liberal Bourbon could transcend his regal limitations and the settled inertia of two centuries of colonial empire. Institutions, and not men, govern such situations, and Carlos III, a liberal, a Bourbon, but not an anomaly, found no better means of postponing the loss of his dominions in America than to tighten his grip on them, increasing the garrisons and adopting all the traditional precautions best calculated to produce the traditional results of repression. The real interest of the recommendations of his minister lies in the forlorn attempt, one of the first and not the last of its kind, to foresee historic processes, to anticipate inevitable defeats, and to avert unnecessary conflicts. As such, it fully demonstrated the futility of sparing humanity and the impossibility of writing history painlessly.

Of the two partners to the mutiny in North America, France was the first to suffer the consequences of her reckless philanthropy. The Rights of Man, discovered in America and the first colonial commodity to be exported abroad, were proclaimed in Paris in the thick of a revolution and weakened the control of the metropolis over the Crown colonies in the Caribbean. As the conflagration progressed, the sparks crossed the ocean. In Haiti, the French portion of Santo Domingo, where the accumulation of class, caste, and race conflicts lay packed and inflammable, a series of social explosions followed, of such intensity that slaveholders all over the world, and above all in the New World, saw in the column of smoke rising from the tropical island a warning to redouble their vigilance and tighten the rigor of repression, so plainly warranted by the reprisals to which they were exposed if they weakened. The upheaval in Haiti brought the danger measurably nearer to New Spain; but the Spaniards were not disturbed by the troubles of their neighbors, and their indifference was the more remarkable in that the proximity of Santo Domingo to New Spain, as close politically as it was geographically, heightened the hazards of contagion.

Both provinces were ruled by the Colonial Compact; by the terms, that is, of a code to which that misnomer added the final touch of absurdity, since it involved no reciprocity and was designed to secure the complete exploitation of the colony by the mother country. The Colonial Compact embodied the mania of monopoly in its most senseless forms and developed it to the highest degree to which human ingenuity could carry it: monoply of trade to the exclusion not only of foreign nations, but of intercolonial commerce; monopoly of industry, to the suppression of any local commodity that might compete with the exports of the home market; monopoly of office by Europeans, to the exclusion not only of the natives, but of their own offspring born in the colony, who, thus disqualified, formed a class apart, the anomalous Creoles, Europeans by blood and natives by law, belonging neither to one world nor to the other; monopoly of privilege, with the consequent division of families into classes and classes into castes, according to color and origin, each jealous of the other and all destined to support the ruling caste by their divisions; and lastly, monopoly of education, entrusted to the Church and enforced by censorship—though the last was not a serious privation, perhaps, in tropical countries where the climate provided the best censorship, all the labor essential to life was performed by illiterates, and the need for mental exertion was unknown to their betters. On those broad principles all the possessions of France and Spain were run and the structure of colonial society was built. They had the rational merit, at least, of reducing to their simplest terms and revealing in their crudest forms the natural relations governing all empires and all colonies, without attenuating compensations to make them tolerable to the colonials themselves, and were admirably adapted, therefore, to provoke them to revolt. Although the rules had been relaxed in some respects by contraband trade and administrative laxity by the end of the eighteenth century, these involuntary concessions to necessity had merely served to adulterate the system with the contagious dram of delivery.

While the regime was identical in Santo Domingo and New Spain, some social differences there were which explained the indifference of the Spaniards to the upheaval in Haiti. There the bottom class, which supported the structure of colonial society, was composed of black slaves, and slavery was an institution repugnant to the Spaniards in the raw form of human bondage. Without it, they obtained the same labor from their serfs, bound to the land by feudal service and aboriginal habit, and the submissive Indian of the mainland was not the same breed of primitive as the jungle-bred black of the islands, nor liable to the same ferocity that marked the insurrection in Santo Domingo. What happened there showed very clearly, nevertheless, that the initial danger lay not in the lowest, but in the upper, strata of the community. The insurrection began at the top between Europeans and Creoles, in the friction of fathers and sons who were foreigners to each other under the terms of the Colonial Compact. It spread with the natural virulence of a family quarrel to the subordinate castes and half-castes, degenerated rapidly into the aboriginal rages of race war, and brought the whole structure crashing to the ground in a complete demonstration of human brotherhood. The servile class was not the first danger but the last; and the saving difference between the Negro and the Indian was a feeble safeguard against a duplication of the Haitian experience in New Spain, in a Crown colony bound by the same practices, the same monopolies, the same discriminations, and the same servitudes to the parent Power.

Nevertheless, the Spaniards preserved their immunity. They trusted in God: a special Providence protected the land that they had covered with convents and churches, and in New as in Old Spain the Church had performed its social mission and subdued a heterogeneous population by divine precept to the security of the State. They trusted in man: the docility of the native and his hermetic seclusion had preserved him in a state of political innocence so incorruptible that in two and a half centuries only five small flares of revolt betrayed his original depravity. And the confidence of the Spaniards was warranted. After five years of conflagration the insurrection in Santo Domingo flickered out without affecting the Spanish dominions either on the island or on the mainland. The French Revolution, from which it caught the spark, also burned itself out, and the years of crisis abroad passed without disturbing the settled peace of the colony. It was not until France turned against Spain that the ties with the mother country became actually strained.

Out of the embers came the phoenix. It was Napoleon who, by diverting the energies of the French Revolution to the conquest of Europe, finally relayed, indirectly and inadvertently, the impulse of colonial emancipation to Spanish America. By 1808 his armies had overrun Spain; the Bourbons were his captives; his brother sat on their throne; the defense of the peninsula was carried on by popular insurrection and patriotic committees; and the dismemberment of the old country created a dilemma for the Viceroy of New Spain. To whom or to what was his allegiance due? To the dynasty represented by a captive monarch? Or to the nation represented by the self-constituted regional bodies? Each horn of the dilemma was worse than the other, but he hit upon a solution that evaded them both. He decided to hold the colony in trust, under temporary self-government and in a state of suspended animation, until the return of normal times. While professing absolute loyalty to the sovereign, he met the emergency by adopting the example of the patriotic committees, which also swore allegiance to Ferdinand VII, and summoned an assembly of the local administrative bodies—the Audiencia, the Archbishopric, the Municipality of Mexico, the Delegates of the Tribunals, the secular and ecclesiastical bodies of the Nobility, the leading citizens, and the military commanders—which ratified his decision, declared for the sovereignty of New Spain, and invested him with supreme authority. To protect the colony against the possibility of foreign attack, either by the English who were tampering with the integrity of the empire in South America, or by the French or the Dutch who were based on the islands of the Caribbean, the Viceroy mobilized the military forces on an unprecedented scale and put them through imposing maneuvers between the capital and the coast.

Sensible and loyal as the solution was, it alarmed the conservatives of the colony, always more orthodox than those of the old country, and now deprived of their protection. To the party of Old Spaniards, as they called themselves, self-government, even as a provisional measure, spelled a dangerous precedent. Suspecting the Viceroy of ulterior aims and personal ambitions, they formed a conspiracy to nip them in the bud. He was deposed, deported, and replaced by one of their own choosing. The coup was approved by the provincial authorities in Spain, who claimed jurisdiction over the colony, and who profited by it, collecting fourteen million pesos from the coffers of New Spain for the defense of the peninsula, and appointing their own regents in Mexico. These changes, and the confusion and uncertainty of the situation, inevitably produced an unsettling effect on the colony, and the party of Old Spaniards kept a close watch over the lower orders, lest they improve on the precedent. The masses did not move; they had not moved for centuries. It was in the higher classes that the danger lay, and there the damage was done. The name of self-government had been pronounced, and by a Viceroy, sanctioned by legitimate authority and fostered by his forcible overthrow; the idea had been sown, the precedent set; and the seed settled among the Creoles. Fretting to free themselves from the inferiority to which they were condemned by the accident of colonial birth, they were not slow to perceive the favorable opportunity which the flux of the times offered them, but they were themselves confused by it. The inferiority was fictitious, class barriers had become blurred, they were favored with wealth and position, the driving motive was feeble, and if the Creoles, as a class, were restless, they were not rebellious, being by nature and training both indolent and mercurial, and the vigilance of the Old Spaniards held them in check. The colony remained quiet—for a year—for two years—and vigilance had already relaxed when the outbreak came.

Belated as it was historically, the long-awaited revolt was nonetheless premature. In September 1810 the military commander of Queretaro was informed of a seditious conspiracy by one of its members, who, alarmed by its consequences, denounced himself. In an access of conscience he betrayed one of its leaders, a captain of Dragoons stationed in the neighboring town of San Miguel el Grande and well known as a scion of the Creole aristocracy of the region, by the name of Ignacio Allende. Warned by his confederates in Queretaro, where he was spending the day, Allende made his escape, carried the alarm to his friends in San Miguel, and galloped on to the village of Dolores to take counsel with the parish priest, who was the head of the movement. Arriving after nightfall, Allende lost a precious hour in locating him in the home of a local Spaniard, where a dance was in progress, and in inducing him, after some dallying, to withdraw to his own house and hear him out. There Father Hidalgo insisted on sitting down to a cup of chocolate while he sent for their confederates in Dolores.

About nine, when they were assembled, came another cavalryman, Captain Aldama, from San Miguel, with a message from the Colonel of the Regiment for Allende and his friends to escape. The offer was warmly welcomed and hotly debated until Father Hidalgo forbade them to discuss it, reminding them that it would be an unpardonable crime to desert the cause and their comrades who were compromised and defenseless. "Forget it," he said, "for such an idea is neither honorable nor, far less, great." But what else could they do? someone protested. Die, he replied; when men had sworn as highly as they to redeem their country. . . . The company was not convinced. The classic cry of the patriot seemed to be aimed at posterity, not at them. It was then that the priest displayed his peculiar generalship. "An idea occurs to me, gentlemen, and it will be our real salvation," he said. "Come on, Valleza. Now, and without losing time, you are going to arrest the *gachupin* priests. You, Mariano"—turning to his brother—"the *gachupin* traders. You too, Aldama, and Don Santos Villa. To prison with all of them, without touching their interests."

The company stood aghast, protesting that they were unprepared and would be the sole victims of their temerity. "That is how children talk," he replied, "who never measure the circumstances of a situation nor calculate that the most insignificant details, if one has the skill to combine them, will form a strong and terrible whole. With the cry against the *gachupines,* tomorrow we shall have all and more than we need. Pocket your fears and to work, without losing a moment." Every man to his trade—soldiers were trained to be commanded and men of action to be occupied—and without leaving them time to think, Hidalgo sent them out to round up the local Spaniards. "This bold feat, carried out by eleven men," says the account of one who witnessed it, "will appear fabulous, and some may consider it such, but it is entirely true." A silent patrol made the rounds of the *pueblo,* collecting the sleeping *gachupines* one by one. By five in the morning the last one had been bagged and put behind bars. The intervening hours were spent by Hidalgo and Allende in mapping their next move—a one-sided conference, for the problem so precipitately created could be met only by the qualities of inspiration peculiar to the priest, and he had yet to conceive his next step when he took the first.

So, in the small hours of September 16, 1810, a new nation was forced into being in the brains of a country curate and a few fugitives who followed his lead unquestioningly, hypnotized by his self-possession and obeying it blindly. The idea was not new—Hidalgo had nursed it for years and matured it patiently with a little group of initiates; but the original plan called for a concerted uprising by selected troops in December, and its premature disclosure compelled him to modify it in a manner which profoundly altered its character. Captain Allende had sought converts in his regiment and in those with which he had come into contact in the capital during the maneuvers ordered by the Viceroy two years before, and had declared himself ready to draw the sword as soon as he could find five hundred. But he found his countrymen deaf to the idea of independence, and to go off at half-cock before so vast a movement could be organized was so obviously foolhardy that he would have abandoned it, no doubt, but for his partner. The adventure so recklessly begun, without adequate preparation and against great odds, could survive only by consistently attempting the impossible. Hidalgo guided it accordingly, step by step, himself always well ahead of his lieutenants.

The next day was a Sunday. By five in the morning the *pueblo* was swarming with the usual crowd of Indians from the surrounding countryside, gathering for early Mass, market, and gossip. When word spread that there might be no Mass that morning, and no market, as Señor Hidalgo had spent the night locking up the *gachupines,* they assembled before his house to learn what remained of their only occupations in life. Their numbers increased with their uncertainty, and "seeing them swell," says the chronicle, "that estimable priest thought that the time had come to address a few words to the crowd and to explain his reasons for so novel and unknown a movement." The words were few but effective. He informed them that there was no longer a king, nor tribute to be levied, that the shameful tax, which was the badge of their slavery and which they had paid for two hundred years, was abolished, that the day of deliverance was at hand, and that the cause was holy and God would protect it. Raising a shout for America and the Virgin of Guadalupe, he bade them march. Accustomed to unquestioning obedience and the responses of the liturgy, the crowd caught up the cry and carried the day by acclamation. By ten o'clock, when Hidalgo reappeared on horseback, he was surrounded by thousands of men, armed with knives, cudgels, poles, slings and stones.

The hold which Hidalgo had over his flock was not due to his cloth alone, nor even to his war cry; for he was one of those rare priests in New Spain who brought his religion out of doors and applied it to the relief of the native. Fostering his crafts, extending his industries, and cultivating the prohibited vine of the Colonial Compact, he introduced into his district potteries and tanneries, beehives and silkworms, vineyards and distilleries. He could always be found, after Mass, at the silk works or the pottery, supervising the output or sitting in a corner, on call. He had advanced ideas. "He wanted every industry to be protected by societies," says the chronicle, "which would supply it with sufficient funds, every member holding one or more shares; the officials and workers would co-operate with the value of their labor, being given an advance to allow them to subsist until the utility was divided in which they were all to have a proportionate part. He was opposed, in short, to the tyranny of capital. He said also that every stranger who established himself in the country would have to belong to a society of industry, either as a shareholder or by means of his knowledge and labor, otherwise he could not live in the country. In sum, he wanted everyone to be useful to all. Theories these were which would have had some modification in practice; but at bottom there was an abundance of good intentions which aimed at the general good, since even our men of means in the whole Mexican country would have had to belong to the commercial or industrial societies, for he was opposed to the softness of our powerful men. Sometimes he would be heard to cite the aphorism of Hippocrates, 'To know the evil is half the cure.'" It was. If not the technique, Hidalgo created the habit of co-operation and the spirit of self-help in his community, and he reaped the fruits in the multitude that mustered to his call on the morning of September 16.

Long before he preached his subversive sermon, he had endeared himself profoundly to his charges; and when he took leave of his potters to whom he recommended the care of the silkworms and the beehives, "which formed a great resource for the poor, and the flax-seed of which he had high hopes, even of deriving something substantial from it," he gathered an abundant harvest and resowed it. Those whom he left behind were not the least in his sight. "Uniting them all, he embraced them and begged them to attend to their tasks. There were some tears, and he consoled them, saying that he would return soon," for they were the root. Thus, out of the root and the fruit of his pastoral labors, the curate of Dolores conjured up a movement revolutionary in its promise, its mass character, its contagious scope. The individual roles were still indistinct: leadership belonged by right to the man who provided the inspiration and the manpower, and the professional soldier fell inevitably into the background.

The crowd poured forth from Dolores, and the flock became a herd on the highroad, heading for San Miguel el Grande, gathering recruits on the way and growing prodigiously with the parade of the captives, for the *gachupines* under guard of Allende brought up the rear, and it was they, according to all accounts, "who provided the impulse for so colossal a revolution." Halfway to San Miguel, which was reported to be arming in haste, a halt was called while Allende with a hundred horsemen galloped ahead to reconnoiter the town. In the public square he found two companies, in fact, under arms, and was accosted by a subordinate who upbraided him and clutched his bridle, but he rode him down, and the troops broke ranks and joined him. An enthusiastic crowd followed them to the doors of the *Casas Reales,* where the Spaniards had taken refuge after appealing in vain to the military authorities for protection. Colonel Narciso Maria Loreto de la Canal bore a name that was synonymous with San Miguel, his family having endowed the town with churches and palaces of fabulous wealth, but he was a passive sympathizer with the movement, and he left the defense to his sergeant-major, who found less than fifty loyal men to face the oncoming flood. The Colonel himself, hoarse from haranguing the crowds that gathered under the windows of his palace shouting *"Viva la Religion," "Viva Fernando Septimo," "Viva la Patria y muera el Gobierno de los Gachupines,"* and imploring them to keep the peace, advised the Europeans to lock themselves up.

Summoned by Allende to surrender, the Spaniards came out and found protection in prison from a mob that would have massacred them but for the guard of Dragoons at the gate and the expostulations of the humane Colonel. There they were visited, later in the day, by Hidalgo, who promised that no harm would come to them, explaining that their captivity was a necessary precaution for the present and that they would fare better by-and-by, and left them in the dark to find food and lodging for his followers. By four in the afternoon the little town of San Miguel el Grande, great only by grace of the Archangel and big with rebellion, had been overrun by a horde that stripped it of its pretensions to size and importance, eating the inhabitants out of house and home, sleeping in the streets, but looting only one shop. The miracle could not be repeated, and the problem was unsolved two days later when, to the great relief of the Colonel, the insurgents moved on to Celaya, with twenty-five Spaniards in tow.

In Celaya also, the tactics of speed and surprise paralyzed the authorities, who succumbed after a feeble attempt at resistance and rallied to the cause. Here ten days were spent in attempting to organize the marchers. Before advancing against Guanajuato, Hidalgo preferred to try his powers of persuasion on the Intendant. "You already know the movement that took place in the *pueblo* of Dolores on the night of the fifteenth of this month; beginning with the insignificant number of fifteen men, it has grown prodigiously in so few days," he wrote after drilling his raw recruits for two days. "I am surrounded at present by more than four thousand men, who have proclaimed me their Captain-General. They and I, at the head of them and obeying their will, wish to be independent of Spain and to govern ourselves." Only one Spaniard had been wounded and one shop looted so far, he pointed out, and "hence Your Lordship will see that my intention is merely that the europeans leave the country at present. Their persons will be guarded until they embark, without fear of any violence, their interests will be in charge of their families or some trustee. The Nation assures them the proper protection; in its name, I pledge myself to provide it religiously." But in case of stubborn resistance, he could not answer for the consequences. "There is no help for it, Señor Intendente; the present movement is great, and much greater when it is a matter of recovering Sacred rights, granted by God to the mexicans and usurped by a few cruel conquerors, unjust and illegitimate, who with the help of the ignorance of the natives and accumulating Sacred and venerable pretexts have succeeded in usurping their customs and properties and vilely reducing free men to the degrading condition of slaves. The step I have taken will be considered immature and isolated by Your Lordship; but this is an error. It is true that it has happened before the time set for it, but this does not change the fact that a large part of the Nation holds the same sentiments. Soon, very soon, Your Lordship will hear the voice of many *pueblos* responding anxiously to the indication of liberty. The national movement increases every day in great proportions; its attitude is threatening; it is no longer possible for me to contain it, and only Your Lordship and the thoughtful europeans hold in their hands the means of moderating it, by means of a prudent condescension. If, on the contrary, they decide on resistance, the consequences in such cases are so disastrous and dreadful that they should be avoided even at the cost of great sacrifices. As events are moving more rapidly by the moment, I can wait only four or five days to learn the favorable or adverse result, in consequence of which I shall take my decisions." David talking up to Goliath spoke no differently.

The summons to surrender was rejected. Hidalgo wrote the "Nation" with a capital letter and the "mexicans" with a small one. That was the difference with which he had to reckon in Celaya in September 1810: the Nation was an abstraction, and the mexicans were a mere deduction from it. The Intendant Riano recognized the difference and, ignoring the advice of Hidalgo to consult "the principal classes and the europeans of most influence," made his decision without consulting anyone but himself. The city was the center of a rich mining region and the capital of the local Creole aristocrats, who, by exporting silver to Spain for centuries, had accumulated titles for themselves and treasure enough to guarantee the loyalty of Guanajuato; so that consultation was superfluous. Trenches were dug, barricades were built, and the whole population was mobilized, without distinction of classes, for the common defense; but at the last moment the Intendant withdrew into the public granary with the troops, the food supplies, the silver, the Europeans, and the Municipality. The move was made at night, and without consulting the townspeople, who besieged him in the morning with frantic appeals not to abandon them; but he was safe, and so was the silver, and he refused to budge.

On the morning of September 28, when the insurgents entered the city—the same raw and undisciplined force that had left Celaya in search of the food and fighting that alone could make an army of it— they met with no resistance until they reached the Alhondiga de Granaditos, where the Intendant had sent word that he was awaiting them. Here the first battle was fought. The building, a solid block-house built on a steep slope, was an impregnable position that defied the very idea of storming it.

The siege which the insurgents set to it with volleys of slingstones would have lasted indefinitely, or until the arrival of relieving forces, but for the feat of an individual who detached himself from the mass and whose exploit remained famous. On the slope above the citadel, Hidalgo commanded a clear view of it and nothing else, when he was informed that a miner had volunteered to burn the gate with the loss of no more than one life. He sent for him. A sickly little man, consumed by a chronic disease in the mines, appeared, explained his plan, and was permitted to try it. All that he needed was a big flagstone to cover his back, a rope, and a fuse, and off he went, downhill, slowly but steadily, like an invalid Atlas, under a hail of missiles that missed him, straight to the gate and fired it. As the door crumbled, the Intendant was seen behind it, repairing the damage; a slingstone killed him. Amid the crying confusion within, the besiegers swarmed in and massacred the garrison before Hidalgo and Allende could climb through the breach and proclaim the laws of civilized warfare.

The citadel was conquered, but the townspeople had still to be won. In Guanajuato Hidalgo had many friends. They came to call on him in the barracks where he set up his bed. The room was small, the affluence was great, and as there were only two chairs they sat on the cot or the floor, while one spoke for all. "Well, sir," said Hidalgo, after the preliminary compliments had been exchanged, "what do you think of my visit?"—"It is not like the others that you deigned to make me," was the reply.—"What is the difference?"—"The difference is that you come accompanied by much blood and destruction, and followed by much mourning and by no less fear, which we still feel." The speaker was his most intimate friend.—"You may be right, Señor Licenciado," Hidalgo replied, "but what is remarkable is that you were not alarmed by the terrible destruction which the Lion of Spain made, without pity and in cold blood, of the country, the life, and the welfare of our ancestors, ending with the people and forcing them into a shameful and humiliating situation which still exists, and which the backs of the mexicans have borne without murmuring for the long term of three centuries. By this destruction was formed the foundation of that terrible power, and the cement which our conquerors used to form and raise the structure of their abominable domination which is wet with the blood and tears of our elders, and though it is still very strong and high, all that you have seen, and that surprises and terrifies you, is no more than the first blow; it will not fall by it, because it is solidly built; but the blows to come will make it tremble and destroy it, perhaps. It is very high and it must fall, for its shadow or bulk prevents the rays of liberty from penetrating to fertilize the small grass that surrounds it.

Consult France in her revolution and you will see that we are mere pygmies and cannot compare with those terrible events; but the motives are not unlike ours. Courage, then Señor Licenciado, you shall see more, much more, we are only in the prologue."

The words which he put into the mouth of his friend remained there, however, and seeing him stand tongue-tied and embarrassed, Hidalgo changed the subject and asked him whether he had suffered any harm in his interests. "No, not yet, nothing but a great fear," the lawyer admitted, "and in spite of it I have come out into the street to beg a mercy."—"And of whom do you expect it?"—"Of you, in favor of some europeans who have been arrested, and their interests embargoed." The favor was readily granted, Hidalgo referring them to the offer which he had made to the Intendant and of which his friends were thus informed for the first time. But the terms of capitulation which he offered them would have made no difference, as it made none now, in their attitude: they showed their political instinct by petitioning him for the release of his European prisoners. The response was the same when he called a meeting of the Town Council to explain the aims of the movement and rally their support: the members sat speechless and dumfounded. When it came to organizing a government, he could find no one willing to accept a post of responsibility, not even to maintain law and order. They had seen him distributing silver bars to the men who made them and who neither needed nor waited for his permission to take them. The storming of the Alhondiga and its capture barehanded by a horde of half-armed rebels was a portent of what an aroused people could accomplish; and the fall of the local Bastille confounded, without converting, the bureaucrats. Since no one spoke up, Hidalgo said that he regarded their silence "either as a vague fear that his plans and ideas would not be realized for lack of imitators or as a real and pronounced neutrality, which, as it was so harmful in the present circumstances, he would punish as a declared partiality." They tried to reply but could not; before they could open their mouths he made the appointments, which were proclaimed and cheered by the populace celebrating the fall of the citadel.

Independence was two weeks old. Though word came that many places had declared for it, or would soon do so, in the immediate vicinity, Hidalgo was worried by the silence of his partisans in San Luis Potosi, where the preliminary organization of the conspiracy had been carried furthest and men of high position and powerful influence had pledged themselves to promote the movement. He decided to march there without delay. Guanajuato was not a guarantee but a warning. The respectable classes were not the only ones to be shocked by the license and alarmed by the success with which they were liberated by the lower orders. The reduction of the Alhondiga was a revolutionary feat, or a freak of fortune, too unscientific to satisfy the military mind:

an accident from which nothing could be argued and upon which folly alone would presume to found further operations; and a strong royalist force was reported to be assembling at San Luis Potosi. Allende took time out, therefore, to complete the training, interrupted by the triumph, of his nondescript troops. The miners made good shock troops; two wooden cannon were built and tested without exploding; they were of small caliber, but they were made to prove, as Hidalgo said, that "any people can be free that wants to be." But there were still, there would always be, more Alhondigas to burn.

Time was pressing, and Hidalgo started ahead with six thousand men. The march was made through the Sierra by night, with thousands of torches dispelling the solitude, if not the gloom, of the mountains. In the morning they passed through Dolores, where he was welcomed with sincere affection by his flock, his friends, his co-operatives. His return fired their faith in his other promises. But beyond Dolores it was different. The radius of confidence had not reached San Luis Potosi. Halfway there, he received a message from his confederates urging him to turn back and attack the capital first and promising, for their part, to follow up his success and cover his rear. San Luis Potosi was also a mining town. He hesitated; he turned back.

Returning to Guanajuato, where his reappearance restored public confidence for four days, he left it again on the fifth with his whole army and hurried on to Valladolid. One month after it had begun, the insurrection was still tentative, a magnified reconnaissance movement, a rising of the masses, but not yet a popular revolt. Possession of the capital was indispensable to its success, to catch the imagination and determine the loyalty of the country at large; and whatever the value of the advice from a military point of view, politically the partisans in San Luis Potosi did Hidalgo a service by restoring him to his inspiration and the giant strides of his instincts. Formidable in numbers, for the original five thousand had multiplied tenfold, the teeming multitude advanced on Valladolid and overran it. Here Hidalgo was on home ground. In the ancient University he had been student, teacher, and rector, in turn. In the citadel of books he had dipped into the forbidden volumes of French revolutionary literature and had drawn the blood of books with which he returned at the head of fifty thousand barefooted disciples, acclaimed by Indians, Creoles, and ecclesiastics alike. The reward of abounding in boldness was a triumphant entrance into the calm academic town—a triumphant entrance, not a triumphant welcome. Furious preparations had been made for defense; the Bishop had fled, casting excommunications behind him, the priests had rallied all the villages of that levitic valley; but as the shadow fell across it and the spell of an army of victorious and veteran vagrants spread, all resistance was abandoned and the excommunications were lifted at the point of the sword. There was some irregular looting, promptly suppressed by Allende, and Hidalgo helped himself to a million pesos from the coffers of the Cathedral; but the best of the booty was the garrison, which went over to the insurgents and supplied them with their first professional leaven. Thus fortified, Hidalgo started for the capital at the end of October; but with the increase in numbers and the difficulty of controlling them, his self-confidence clouded. Challenged by a critic to justify the upheaval, he replied that he knew what it ought to be but not what it was.

His best friends now were the enemy. The enemy knew what it was and what it ought to be from the day it began. His house in Dolores had long been called *la Francia chiquita,* and everyone foresaw what was coming when he left "little France" with his hordes of land-hungry insurgents: the movement for independence was at the same time a social revolution. The one was inseparable from the other and indispensable to its triumph. In Valladolid he issued a decree abolishing slavery, ignoring the legal fiction that there was no such thing in New Spain, and followed up his Emancipation Proclamation with decrees abolishing castes and tributes, reducing taxes and landed estates, and proscribing the accepted servitudes that were its substance.

The authorities anticipated his next step; they thought as he did, and faster. The Bishop of Valladolid had once been a reformer himself. Recognizing "the ignorance and misery of the Indians," which placed them "at an infinite distance from a Spaniard," he had recommended long ago the free distribution of some acreage among the castes and the Indians, the division of the communal lands in each *pueblo,* and an agrarian law, like that of Galicia or the Asturias, allowing the people to settle gradually, over a period of twenty or thirty years, upon the uncultivated lands of the great proprietors. But the reform remained on paper, and when the revolution came rolling to his door, he hurled anathemas at it, protesting that in this part "the plan of the Curate Hidalgo constitutes a private civil war, of anarchy and destruction, efficient also and necessary, between the Indians, Castes, and Spaniards, who compose all the children of this Country." The cry traveled. Another bishop discovered another danger and warned the country that, if the revolt succeeded, they would all be at the mercy of the first maritime Power that appeared off their coasts. Everyone knew that British, French, and American agents were trying to revolutionize the colony —everyone, that is, but Hidalgo. The authorities were better informed.

As the embattled farmers approached the capital, panic prevailed there. The Inquisition exorcised the leader, and the Archbishop of Mexico exhorted his followers. "Hidalgo errs," he warned them, "and his plan of reconquering America for the Indians is not only anti-Catholic but chimerical, extravagant, ridiculous, and supremely prejudicial to the author who proposes it. Even supposing that the plan of casting off the Europeans could be accomplished, would not a cruel war be kindled between the Indians and the Spanish-Americans for the estates, the mines, the riches wrested from the subjects of Spain and those of the Americans? And what would the length and outcome of such a war be? Who would be the gainers by it, and who the losers? Would not the Indians insist, as they are now being told by Hidalgo, that they are lords and masters of the land of which the Spaniards despoiled them by conquest?" Across the narrowing gulf between Indian and Spaniard, Creole called to Creole in supreme appeal, and the Indians were cautioned against the tempter. "Be not deceived, my sons, be not seduced! The Curate Hidalgo is on trial for heresy. He seeks not your fortune but his own, as we already said in our exhortation of the 24th of September. Now he flatters you with the attractive lure that he will give you the land. He will not, he will break faith with you, he will impose tributes and personal services, because otherwise he cannot subsist in the elevation to which he aspires, and he will shed your blood and the blood of your children to preserve and increase it, as Bonaparte has done. You are already free of tributes; enjoy this blessing in peace; shun the man whose doctrines are reproved by Holy Scripture and our blessed Mother Church, and that would put an end to the world, if they were practiced, yourselves being the first victims. Long live Religion!—as it will not with those who oppose the teachings of Holy Mother Church! Long live the Virgin of Guadalupe!—as she will not with him who decries her virginity, or those who subvert and overturn the lands of that Lady! Long live Ferdinand VII!—as he cannot with the independence of his vassals!" Hidalgo and the Archbishop came within shouting distance of the end of the world; and the protests, the appeals, the persuasions of an enemy already reduced to reason were the best proof that he was on the right road.

From Valladolid the unseen congregation of the Archbishop pressed on to Toluca; and on the last lap of the road to the capital, in a winding defile of the descent to the valley of Mexico, they met the troops hastily assembled by the Viceroy. These numbered no more than two thousand, but they were regulars, entrenched on high ground with cannon, commanding the winding road, on which the rebels lost the value of numbers and were raked, hour after hour, with accurate fire. The generalship of Allende rose to the test: hour after hour, he flung an inexhaustible supply of raw human material, or matter, against the guns overhead, while he mounted a single cannon above both, directing flank attacks by his few trained troops and head after head of the huge herd, with which he drew and drained the fire of the enemy. The slaughter lasted from ten in the morning until four in the afternoon. Finally, falling, scattering, and scrambling back for yet another and another rush, by sheer weight of numbers and uncounted sacrifices, the victims dislodged and overwhelmed the regulars and carried the day. The road lay open, and the victors followed it to within sight of the promised land. There it was learned that royalist troops were advancing by forced marches from San Luis Potosi. The position was critical. Caught between fresh troops and the unconquered capital, Hidalgo called a council of war. The roles were reversed: Allende recommended an immediate attack on the city, but Hidalgo decided on a tactical retreat. His inspiration was spent, he had stretched the movement as far as the momentum of improvisation could carry it, and within sight of the goal he faltered and fell back.

From that day disaster ensued. His star deserted him, his followers hugged his heels, and the retreat was a series of irresistible reverses. When they passed the Monte de las Cruces, where they had fought the battle that marked the crest of their advance two days before, the dispirited thousands broke ranks to bury their dead, and they were still disheartened when they were overtaken at Aculco by the troops from San Luis Potosi, whom they were trying to avoid. Neither side dared to engage the other, but a runaway horse, dragging a headless rider, stampeded the rebels, who abandoned the field without battle. Allende managed to bring the bulk of his best troops back to Guanajuato, where weeks were wasted in drilling men and casting cannon for a new stand, for when the government troops appeared, he found himself outflanked and abandoned the town, falling back on Guadalajara, which had declared for the cause and where Hidalgo had gone ahead to raise a fresh army. And at the gates of Guadalajara a great battle was lost, unfought, by another accident. Hidalgo had mustered an army of seventy thousand men. They were drawn up on the plain, awaiting the attack of the enemy, when the munitions exploded, the stubble caught fire, and the plain became a sea of flame, blown by a strong north wind against the rebels, who melted away in confusion and terror.

With a few officers, Hidalgo and Allende made their way northward, gathering recruits, ready, as one of them said, "for a long and perhaps eternal migration," their destination being their distance from the enemy. An agent whom they had sent to the United States to secure support and conclude an alliance was caught and shot, but they themselves eluded pursuit, although the local authorities were on the alert to prevent any contact with the fatal constellation of seventeen northern stars. Their worst enemies were the heat and thirst that retarded their progress as they worked their way slowly northward through the burning wastes of Coahuila. There they were overtaken by the final disaster, and not by accident. At a waterhole in the desert they walked into a trap laid by a traitor, and were captured on March 21, 1811. The lesser confederates, after rotting in the torrid jail of Monclova and corrupting their keepers, were farmed out for forced labor to the great landowners of the region. The ringleaders were sent to

Chihuahua, where they were shot four months later. Hidalgo died hard. Seated in a chair, and blindfolded, he pointed to his heart to guide the firing squad, but they were trembling "like whipped men," as the sergeant said, and their aim was poor. The first volley broke the belly and one arm; the second smashed the guts and one shoulder; the blindfold slipped, and the sight of his tears troubled the marksmen, who fired a third round without finding the heart. Not until the muzzles were placed on it, was he fit to be shown to the public. His head was sent to Guanajuato, with those of his three captains, Allende, Aldama, and Jimenez, and the trophies were suspended in cages from the four corners of the Alhondiga, where they remained for years, while time gave them new bodies.

The uprising had lasted six months. But it was not over. Between the autumn and spring equinoxes Hidalgo sowed the seed of a movement destined both to die and endure. Conservative historians have laid two charges on his tomb: that the enterprise which he initiated was premature and without plan. Premature it undoubtedly was, as he himself admitted, and in the conditions in which it was undertaken it could not have been anything else; and it was premature by more than three months. When he carried his cause to the people, he gave a revolutionary turn to the promotion of independence, which prejudiced it at the start, antagonizing the upper classes and converting the nebulous dream of national liberation into the dread, and the foretaste, of class war. The depredations of the rebels spared neither Creole nor Spaniard: the rich were all *gachupines;* and the resistance which he encountered and could not break compelled Hidalgo to countenance reprisals which he could not control against both. Marauding and massacre loom larger in the books of historians than they do in history; but the inevitable excesses of a servile insurrection were sufficient to determine the loyalty of the propertied classes. They rallied to the government or remained neutral; and to this position they clung for ten years, until independence was won without them. In this respect, the rising would have been premature at any time; but in another, and deeper one, it also suffered from precipitation. The masses were the one element ripe to receive the inspiration with which Hidalgo fired them, but they were incapable of sustaining it against trained troops. Despite the exceptional triumph at the Monte de las Cruces, Hidalgo himself was convinced by that costly success, and bowed to the dictates of common sense in beating his retreat from the capital. But the movement was not born of common sense and could not survive it, and he sacrificed at the same time the imponderable power, the unreckoning onrush, that made it possible. When he left Dolores a woman shouted after him, "Where are you going, Señor Cura?"—

"To free you of the yoke," he replied. —"Worse if you lose even the oxen," she cried. The woman was right. When he failed, the masses relapsed into their age-old submission and the apathy of abject disillusionment.

The second charge is of a piece with the first. The pace of events was too swift for the plan. What the conspirators originally contemplated is uncertain: Hidalgo himself compressed his creed into one word, *Independencia,* and his followers into a hue and cry against *gachupines;* but it was to have been carried out by the army and the educated classes. At first loyalty to the throne figured among the slogans, and the cry of "Long live Ferdinand VII!" among the flags of rebellion, a fluttering rag of Creole conscience, soon abandoned with the development of the movement; for his ideas developed with his motive power. The Emancipation Proclamation he issued in Valladolid, the promise of a Constitution and of the redistribution of the land, were picked up in the capital and re-echoed with enormous resonance in the excommunications of the Inquisition and the exhortations of the Archbishop. A movement which inspired such panic could hardly be said to have suffered from the want of a political plan; but whatever the ultimate aims of the heretic may have been, they were swept away in the whirlwind which he raised and could not ride.

A pioneer, he fulfilled the design of the pathfinder. He was the wind in the wilderness, but he was also the trail-blazer. He performed the function of every forerunner of revolution, advancing it against insuperable odds, by example and sacrifice. Premature, experimental, visionary, invertebrate, the enterprise he launched was doomed from its inception to disaster—but not to extinction. Even in retreat, and with a defeated following, he struck a spirit wherever he made a stand; and six months of mutiny precipitated changes that quickened the pulse of past and present and cheated time of its tenses. In Guanajuato, where the return of the rebels redoubled their ruin, the people fight for the honor of manning the guns and the women drag them to battle with songs "in the manner of the Marseillaise." In Guadalajara, where he raised an army twice as large as the one he had lost, he kindles a spark that is unquenched by the blazing field that scatters his battle. Fleeing northward, he still meets friends on whose faith he rests the burden of defeat and finds them willing and able to bear it. Defeat advances the cause; and knowing that no one else can kill it, the authorities extract a recantation from his corpse and drum it up as his testament. But they cannot undo his work, and the dead heretic himself cannot deed a doubt of his faith. His was merely the first wave of a seminal and unseasonable urge; and between the autumn and spring equinoxes the new seed has been sown. The insurrection is crushed; the resurrection begins.

The second wave also fell short of the goal, but it was deeper, more enduring, and incomparably more efficient than the first. Instead of six months, the next upsurge lasted for four years and was carried forward by a conspiracy of forces as well as of men—the spread of its ideas, the development of its spirit, the formation of its following, and the capacities of a leader fully equal to the test. José-Maria Morelos was also a priest, of the same militant temper as Hidalgo, endowed with the same social vision, and gifted with military talents and organizing ability in which he far surpassed his master. A pupil of Hidalgo at Valladolid, he became his disciple in the first days of the insurrection and was sent south to muster support for it. Cast on his own resources by the collapse of the revolt in the north, he abandoned the old methods of reckless dash after an unsuccessful raid on Acapulco, dug himself into his territory, and built up a body of partisans to repair the defeat of the cause. Starting with scarcely a score, he collected three thousand recruits, with whom at Cuautla, in 1812, he stood off a siege by government troops for two months. Though the besieged were finally reduced by hunger, the besiegers were reduced to offering them an amnesty and the honors of war, which Morelos ignored, beating his way out with flying colors and the garrison intact. Thereafter he took the offensive, and in a series of successful campaigns, which forced the Viceroy to describe him as "the genius of greatest strength, resourcefulness, and cunning" among the rebels, he held the enemy at bay and harassed him in his stronghold, threatening and at times cutting the trade routes to the capital. Swinging around from coast to coast, alternating periods of intensive training with well-timed blows, and adding new names to the patriotic rosary—Acapulco, Tehuacan, Orizaba, Huajuapam, Oaxaca—he dominated the south for two years with a force whose mobility compensated for the small numbers with which he controlled so large a territory.

Brilliant episodes without strategic plan, these sporadic successes have been called; but they followed a plan carefully laid and consistently pursued. What Morelos accomplished was to make good the defects of Hidalgo and to supply the movement, after a false start, with the preparation that should have preceded it. Instead of a mass rising, blind, chaotic, and blundering to destruction, he produced, without the help or hindrance of professional soldiers, an organized insurrection. Early in his progress he was joined by a few influential landowners with their *rancheros,* men of feudal fidelity and fighting traditions developed in the clanlike communities of the great estates; and out of these embattled families he formed the backbone of a compact and flexible force well adapted to the conditions of the struggle and the country. Less than an army, more than a guerrilla band, and transformed at will into the one or the other by the fortunes of war, this tenacious and elastic militia enabled Morelos to retrieve the failure of the first insurgents, to start anew with fresh methods in fresh territory, to gain experience and to secure credit, and to return to the north to recover the ground his forerunner had forfeited. In December 1813 he was ready, and two years after starting his mission he laid siege to Valladolid. There he was attacked in force by the troops of the Viceroy and disastrously defeated. After two years of fugitive efforts to recover, he was captured and shot in December 1815.

As a military leader, the function of Morelos in the development of independence was to redeem and discipline the crude initial impulse. But he was not merely a military leader: in the field of ideas he was also an emancipator, and here he extended the aims of the movement far beyond those of his master. Recognizing that the principal impediment to its progress lay in the latent conflicts of class interests and patriotic loyalty, he exploited social forces not merely as makeshifts imposed by expediency, but consciously and deliberately as revolutionary levers of popular insurrection. "All the rich, the noble, and the civil servants of the first class, *creole* and *gachupin* alike," he wrote in his instructions to his lieutenants in the field, "must be considered enemies of the nation and addicted to the party of tyranny, since they find sanction for their passions and vices in the system and legislation of Europe, the plan of which comes down in substance to severely punishing poverty and stupidity; that is to say, the lack of money or talent, the only crimes recognized by the Magistrates and Justices of our corrupt Courts." His officers were directed to confiscate the property of the bureaucracy, half the proceeds going to the war chest and half to the relief of the poor, to lay the same levies on the wealth of the Church, and to expropriate the great estates wherever the arable lands exceeded two leagues and were uncultivated, breaking them up into small holdings for the benefit of the landless peons. Military expedients were transformed into social strategy, and in the agricultural provinces of the south, where he operated, the land might have supported him, had his triumphs not been too transient to test his policies. The masses, hypnotized by Hidalgo and magnetized by Morelos, remained passive, sobered by the collapse of the master and slow to trust the disciple. His program succeeded merely in neutralizing the propertied classes, already shocked by the casual and unscientific looting that had followed the progress of Hidalgo, and the movement remained equally isolated socially; but he drove a furrow in the wilderness.

Conscious of the mortality of his cause, and unwilling to be indispensable to it, Morelos provided for the future as soon as he was master of his territory. In 1813 he called a Congress in Chilpancingo to draft a Constitution and create an embryo of national life capable of surviving him. Here he showed his full measure. In this prenatal Constitution Morelos developed a democratic conception of independence, which marked the growth of national consciousness since he caught the impulse from Hidalgo, and the advance he had made over the hazy ideals of his model. The claims of Morelos began with the sole eligibility to office of Americans, and the exclusion of foreign immigration, except for skilled artisans likely to be socially useful; but they went far beyond protective restrictions and attacked the alien elements within the nation and the settled institutions incompatible with the existence of a free people. He proclaimed as cardinal principles and indispensable conditions of independence the abolition of slavery in all its forms, not only of bestial bondage and caste distinctions, but of class privileges and legal immunities of every kind, including those of the military and ecclesiastics, the extinction of the Inquisition, the disestablishment of the Church, and the moderation of poverty and opulence by measures providing rates of pay and means of subsistence for the poor to protect them against the vices of their class, "ignorance, rapine, and theft."

As superior to Hidalgo in social insight as he was in military talents, Morelos was even further ahead of his time; but he spoke of times present in terms of times to come, and belonged to the future because he believed in it. The importance which he attached to the preservation of his ideas and the survival of their custodians was such, indeed, that it cost him his life: it was while he was protecting his Congress from capture and shepherding its flight that he fell, a hunted outlaw, into the hands of the enemy.

His trial was conducted by the Inquisition, and that Court, which he had so lightly vowed to extinction, consecrated the occasion and fully manifested its vitality as the guardian of colonial society. For two hundred years the Holy Office had fed on a small diet of relapsed converts, blasphemous slaves, and Jewish recreants without encountering a case worthy of the functions for which it had been founded until Hidalgo and his disciple fell into its lap and supplied it with legitimate fare. The indictments brought against the first and second insurgents were the best measure of how far the subversive movement had progressed by 1815. Hidalgo was arraigned as a religious rather than as a civil schismatic, and was condemned for his heretical views on a variety of canonical questions—Hell, auricular confession, the virtues of the Eucharist, for every reason, in short, but the real one for which he was brought to book and defrocked by the Church before he was handed over to the secular arm. So strenuous was the conspiracy of silence and the determination to stifle his ideas that not only was a recantation wrung from his shroud, but the recantation itself was buried. After his death a campaign of espionage was conducted by a force of monastic police in a systematic attempt to efface every vestige of his memory, and so thoroughly that no authentic portrait of him survived.

The first count brought against Morelos, in fact, was that he had defied the ban against "all persons who approve the sedition of Hidalgo or receive his proclamations, keep his portrait and epistolary correspondence, lend him any manner of aid or comfort, harbor his revolutionary ideas, and in any way promote and propagate them," and that he had used the paper on which it was printed for his cartridges. In the case of Morelos, however, the Inquisitors came directly to the point and condemned him frankly for his secular offense. They attacked his Constitution and denounced the self-determination of peoples, "which is as much as to say that law is an expression of will and not of necessity; whence comes the habit of considering Man independently of God, of His eternal Justice, and of Nature, Reason, and Honor. As human society in the system of this libertine is neither necessary nor natural, he has decided in his abominable constitution that rational beings have no other obligations than those which they assume by reason of the social contract or the expression of the general will deriving from general representation, as the impious authors already cited declare, and as is categorically stated by this infamous man in Article 18 of his perverse and preposterous Constitution. . . ."

An attempt was made to secure a recantation from Morelos as well—and before he died—but the Court was reduced to parading as such an admission which he made in the course of his questioning that his charter was hastily drawn and impractical. Morelos could not recant, not only because of the strength of his convictions and his character, but because the power of the movement could no longer be repudiated. The pressure of time was beginning to tell, and the behavior of the Court demonstrated it: its frankness in facing the issue, its condescension in arguing as well as its fury in denouncing it, and the expostulation of panic and recrimination, betrayed an insecurity that transformed every item of accusation into another of self-defense; for, indeed, the days of the Inquisition were counted, and the Inquisitors knew it. The trials of Hidalgo and Morelos were not only the first but the last cases with which the Holy Office justified its existence in New Spain. In 1815 it was already doomed to extinction by another Constitution, upon which Morelos modeled his own, equally profane and equally implacable, and coming, moreover, from the mother country. An ally had appeared on the horizon; merely by carrying on the movement for four years, Morelos had advanced it immeasurably.

Morelos was shot close to the capital, as he deserved, for his doctrines had penetrated to the heart of the citadel.

The second wave also fell short, but it came within sight of the goal. The third wave reached it. It lasted longer, but it was also weaker; and it crossed the mark muddied, adulterated, diluted, and drained of its original power.

Reporting to the Viceroy, who wished to muffle the death of Morelos, the Inquisitors justified the publicity which the trial had given to his ideas and the fair hearing he had received, "because of the good effect produced on the innumerable disciples whom he had made, since many have ceased to pity him and have even received his death well, and others have been convinced of the bad cause of the rebels, seeing it cemented with such perverse principles and sustained by leaders so wicked." But Inquisitors are notoriously men of limited acquaintance and accustomed by their activities to a conformity of opinion which affects their judgment. Conversely, they convince no one but themselves. The movement continued, beaten, broken, but stubborn, for six long years after the death of Morelos. It was reduced in scale, however, and in scope, scattered and dispersed, localized, isolated, and confined to spasmodic flares of guerrilla warfare by fugitive lieutenants of Morelos, of whom the foremost was Vincente Guerrero. Without the same talent but with no less tenacity, the third champion of insurgency operated in the south, in the territory which Morelos had made his own and by his tested methods, with a small following of impenitent patriots, repeatedly routed and repeatedly re-forming, whose campaigns roused the people in the only way in which the cowed and the inert could be convinced, by slow unrelenting example and seemingly useless sacrifice. By heroic drudgery Guerrero managed to keep the movement alive, but he could do no more; he succeeded in harassing the government, but at no time was he strong enough to challenge it seriously; and there is no doubt that independence would not have been achieved had it been left to the efforts of Guerrero and his fellows alone. Help came, however, and from an unexpected quarter—from the mother country itself.

In 1812, the last free corner of the Spanish peninsula was held, and the last shred of sovereignty claimed, by a Cortes sitting in Cadiz, which wrote a liberal Constitution born of the boldness of extremity and the freedom of disaster. When the French were driven out and the Bourbons returned from exile, the Constitution was imposed on the King, Ferdinand VII, who accepted it provisionally and repudiated it as soon as he was securely restored to the throne. For the next few years absolutism resumed its old unfettered sway in Spain; but in 1820 a military revolt compelled the King to restore the Constitution. The effect of these events on the colony was a series of reflex actions. In 1812 the Constitution of Cadiz, emanating from a proscribed parliament without authority either to promulgate or enforce it, could be safely ignored overseas; countenanced by the King, it was accepted officially but disregarded in fact; but when a copy of it was produced by Morelos, the authorities became alarmed, and the native version was banned by the Church and its author hunted down by the military with the blessing of the absolutists abroad. In 1820, however, when the Constitution of Cadiz became the basic law of the realm, a crisis was precipitated in the colony. The growing power of liberalism in the old country could no longer be ignored, and steps were taken to check the spread of its ravages to America.

The interested parties comprised all the privileged classes in the colony—the great landowners, the official bureaucracy, the military, the magistracy, the ecclesiastics—and they found their natural center in the most comprehensive and powerful of all the privileged bodies, the Church. The Constitution of Cadiz contained most of the charter principles of liberalism obnoxious to the Church—freedom of opinion and of the press, popular elections, national sovereignty invested in the Cortes—and, in addition, it included provisions directly affecting its interests and curtailing its sovereign attributes as a temporal power.

In Spain ecclesiastical reform had long been recognized as a social necessity and had recently been attempted by a Minister of the Crown. He failed, but he made the name of Manuel Godoy memorable merely by grappling with the problem of the most priest-ridden country in Europe, where the revenues of the Church cut into those of the State, and the impoverishment of the people required drastic reforms of the one or the other. "I thought it possible, if not to cure it completely, at least to prevent it from developing gangrene," he wrote in apology for his failure. "This sacred industry was all the more exacting because of the immense competition, for it was not limited to a few: the Order of Saint Francis alone, with its various families and colors, already reduced from its former estate, still counted in Spain (I do not mention the colonies) seven hundred and twenty-five thousand inmates living on charity, with no other industry but religion and no property but the purse of the people. And then there were the other mendicant orders, shod and unshod, which supplement their income with the offerings of the faithful, although most of them possess property. . . . It was a difficult, a very difficult matter to reform them, but not impossible." Not impossible, that is, as long as there were colonies to relieve the congestion of the mother country; but this solution had already been tried with disappointing results. "Look at the statistics of the American regions, and one is amazed by the neglect of the propagation of the Gospel with two or three million pagans at our door, while here, overcrowded and superabundant and pernicious, we have so many home-keeping apostles and sedentary prophets."

To dump the surplus population of parasites on the colonies was a cure worse than the disease, for the colonies suffered from the same complaint in an even more acute form. There the plethora of churches, the competition of convents, the culture of drones, the manipulation of piety and the milking of faith, magnified by the extent of the territory, the ignorance of the people, and the opportunities of the religious market, eclipsed the conditions prevailing in Spain. The quality of emigration that the colony drew was determined by the function for which the colony was founded and the New World providentially created. Fortune-hunting was not confined to the Crown, and in the course of centuries the ecclesiastics had built up a society there thoroughly mercenary and theocratic, with a tax-gatherer in every village collecting the first fruits for the Church, with a confessor in every household molding opinion, and with half the wealth of the country in the hands of the hierarchy. Such a society could be revolutionized, it could not be reformed, as Manuel Godoy discovered. "Laws are nothing when they touch abuses only in the branch and not in the root. Laws are powerless against those numerous bodies that govern conscience and manipulate opinion at their pleasure." He failed. Nevertheless, another attempt to regulate the position of the Church was made by the liberals when they framed the Constitution of Cadiz. The features directly affecting the Church ranged from the suppression of monastic orders, the reduction of convents in proportion to population, and facilities for the secularization of nuns and friars at the expense of the State, to the abolition of ecclesiastical immunities in penal cases under civil jurisdiction, and the extinction of the Inquisition. Though these reforms lopped off the branches, they cut closer to the root. If this was not yet disestablishment, it was not far from it; and the Constitution of Morelos and his proscript Congress proposed the next step.

Accordingly, when the Constitution of Cadiz was restored in 1820 and the interested parties met to consult on its consequences for the colony, it was in the backroom of a fashionable Oratory that they assembled, and under the direction of an ex-Inquisitor. Dr. Monteagudo had been one of the judges who convicted Morelos and one of the abductors of the Viceroy who recommended local autonomy for the colony in 1808—a record which placed his loyalty to Spain beyond question and allowed him to propose solutions which would have cost anyone else his head. The workings of his mind were never more professional than in this predicament. He first proposed to the Viceroy that all knowledge of the Constitution be suppressed in New Spain, or if this was impractical, to ignore it as they had done in 1813, and for the same reasons, the sovereign being a prisoner of the liberals and not his own master. But the Viceroy, though no liberal, was a responsible functionary, and not only published the Constitution, but put some of its provisions into effect, including the expulsion of the Jesuits and the extinction of the Inquisition.

Thereupon Dr. Monteagudo dispensed with the Viceroy and took counsel with his congregation. The time for drastic measures had come; the Church was a power which had overruled more than one Viceroy in the past; and as the emergency called for heroic measures, Dr. Monteagudo ruled that the only way to preserve the colony from contamination was to sever its connection with the metropolis—to proclaim its independence, in short. The idea, advanced by a man who had deposed a Viceroy and convicted an insurgent to prevent that very consummation, won the approval of his confederates. Their qualms were settled by a letter from Ferdinand VII, lamenting his captivity to the liberals and suggesting that he might emigrate to the colony to recover his independence; and with the sovereign as a prospective accomplice, the consultations rapidly developed into a conspiracy.

To engineer the separation only a tool remained to be found. Among those who frequented the Oratory was a young Creole officer of good family, Agustin Iturbide, who had distinguished himself by defeating Morelos at the siege of Valladolid in 1813. Since then he had also distinguished himself by fleecing the traders who supplied the army, and it was in consequence of their complaints that he landed his historic mission. Summoned to the capital to answer their charges, he frequented the right people, attended the Oratory, and cultivated the acquaintance of Dr. Monteagudo. The spiritual director of aristocratic society quashed the charges of embezzlement, initiated him into his scheme, and secured him the command of an army which the Viceroy was raising to crush the lingering mutiny of Guerrero in the south. Iturbide was not equal to this assignment; victory in the field eluded him, but he secured the desired result by diplomacy. Overtures were made to Guerrero to combine with him in the common cause of colonial liberation, and though his advances were rebuffed at first, his emissaries persisted and his adversary, simple-minded, suspicious, but wearied by years of fruitless struggle, and aware of his weakness, agreed to a compromise. It was the meeting of two infirmities, and in the Plan of Iguala they coalesced.

By the terms of this compact, independence was proclaimed on the basis of three principles: union of Europeans and Americans, preservation of the Catholic faith without toleration of any other creed, and the establishment of a moderate monarchy to be known as the Mexican Empire, the throne to be offered to Ferdinand VII or one of his relatives. The army flocked to the banner of the "Three Guarantees," and on September 21, 1821, the combined forces of Guerrero and Iturbide entered the capital in triumph. The Viceroy vanished, relieved of his office and his responsibility by the arrival of his successor, who landed just in time to witness the accomplished fact, to ratify it by treaty, and to return to Spain with the loyal troops.

So ended a decade of struggle. Eleven years after Hidalgo launched the movement, independence was achieved by intrigue. A new nation was born, but under such conditions as to raise the question whether it was a birth or an abortion. Independence had been won by its enemies, and the aims of the original insurgents had been completely defeated by the Three Guarantees: union instead of separation of Europeans and Americans by the first; reversion of the colony to the Crown by the third; and between them, connecting and explaining them, the guaranteed supremacy of the Church. Independence had been won—but of what? The answer to that question was Mexican history. When the successors of Hidalgo and Morelos realized that what had happened on September 21, 1821, was not the culmination, but the contradiction, of what had occurred on September 16, 1810, a new phase of the insurgent movement began. The struggle for political independence ended, the struggle for social liberation began, with the meretricious triumph of the Plan of Iguala, and thenceforth Mexican history was governed by its results. Two congenital conditions determined its course. The false start condemned the country to a revolutionary development, and to follow foreign movements, as the pathfinders had done, with a time lag that further retarded its progress. The realization came slowly, and the new movement was long in forming. The rebels who came to power in 1821 were incapable of correcting the swindle, and the task of redeeming it fell to another generation. Of that generation of social insurgents Juarez was one. A month after Iturbide entered the capital, he entered the Seminary.

5

THE muddled beginnings of national life cleared with the first attempts to reconstitute the colony as an independent country. The antagonistic elements which combined to proclaim the Plan of Iguala were soon winnowed by its application. The Mexican Empire was proclaimed by a provisional Governing Board, in which none of the old insurgents was represented, and a Constituent Congress, elected by professional representation, ratified the assumption of the Crown by Iturbide, who substituted himself for the Bourbons with the backing of a barracks revolt and a popular demonstration. The parvenu Emperor rapidly lost popularity and political support, however, by plundering the Spanish plutocracy and dissolving Congress and arresting its recalcitrant members, and in 1823 he was overthrown by a military revolt, banished, and on his return to the country a year later captured and shot. The ephemeral reign of Iturbide abolished the Third Guarantee. Monarchy answered the needs of the classes which had engineered independence and which desired a mere modification of the colonial regime to secure their vested interests, and was readily accepted by the people at large, the popular patriots being so devoid of political experience and self-confidence that even Guerrero and the old guard rallied to it enthusiastically; but after the fall of Iturbide republican sentiment gained strength, and the experiment in domestic monarchy was followed by an experiment in self-government. Another Constituent Congress proclaimed the Republic in October 1824, and the first President and Vice-President, Guadalupe Victoria and Nicolas Bravo, were both old insurgents. A Constitution was drawn on the best available model, borrowed from the United States; but the basic charter of 1824 was also a compromise, like the declaration of independence, between incompatible partners. Modeled on the American Constitution in its administrative structure, it recognized popular sovereignty and some of the corollaries of that principle, but none of the radical features embodied in the prenatal Constitution of Chilpancingo, save for the abolition of slavery, and it reasserted the principle of religious intolerance and ecclesiastical supremacy proclaimed in the Plan of Iguala.

The republicans who came to power in 1824 gradually eliminated the Spaniards and abolished the First Guarantee; but the Second remained inviolable. Though the flag of Spain was furled, the structure of colonial society over which it had ruled for three centuries remained intact; and in the liberating tricolor of the new nation, between the green of Hidalgo and the red of Morelos, it was the white flag of truce that still represented the national colors. Within a few years of the False Independence of 1821, as it came to be called by political coroners, the rulers of the Republic were forced to recognize the miscarriage of the insurgent movement in their relations with the midwife. During the decade of insurgency the Church had shown its colors: though the movement had been led by two priests, and many members of the lower clergy had rallied to it, the Church as an institution had consistently opposed it until the day when it appropriated the cause for its own protection and condoned independence conditionally. The hierarchy resigned itself to the Republic and accepted a situation which offered some appreciable compensations for the status of the Church in the colony, the most valuable of which was the reversion to the Church of the right of ecclesiastical appointment and patronage hitherto exercised by the Spanish Crown; and it was over this right that the first difference arose between the two powers. As an attribute of sovereignty, inherited from the Spanish Crown, this prerogative was claimed by the government, but it met with such resistance that the attempt was abandoned. During the debate in Congress and the press, however, public attention was focused on the relations of Church and State, and the dispute created intense feeling on both sides, aggravated by the appearance, in the midst of the crisis, of a Papal Encyclical reserving recognition of the Republic and urging the late subjects of Ferdinand VII to return to their allegiance. Though the question of patronage was a minor and debatable issue, the spirit which it aroused and the contention which it raised were neither negligible nor negotiable; and the controversy cleared the air. Henceforth it was manifest that, of all the liabilities under which the infant Republic labored, the greatest, because the most organic, was the existence of a huge, hard, impenetrable foreign body embedded in its very constitution, defying its control and defeating its functions at will. To master that impediment was too formidable a task for the government of the day; but the passionate concern of a small group of liberals was enlisted, within and without Congress, who applied themselves to the task in an independent campaign. Few but farsighted, they realized that the contest would be long and unequal and that it would require time, patience, preparation, and a power more compelling than official initiative, unsupported by the pressure of public opinion. The skirmish over the patronage question was followed by a flank attack on the main issue and the start of a long-range political strategy. They bent their efforts to circumventing the monopoly of education held by the Church and emancipating the coming generation by founding lay schools. They undermined the Second Guarantee, and here and there they succeeded.

Thus it was that, after describing so long an arc, far beyond the horizon of Oaxaca, the rainbow of independence finally reached Juarez. The red and green and white of the national colors spanned a world beyond his ken, luminous with the afterglow of sun and storm, and beyond his reach until the long concatenation of events and remote connection of forces, the delayed action of ideas and indirect urge of their agents that combined to create a new nation—the revolt of the British colonies, and the French Revolution, and the Napoleonic Wars, and the weakening of colonial bonds, and a decade of battling to break them, and the belated but foreordained conclusion—resulted in one more school.

In 1827 a Liberal majority in the local legislature created a Civil College in Oaxaca and provided Juarez with the opening for which he had been unconsciously waiting and which the transformation of his country alone could supply. As soon as the Institute of Arts and Science opened its doors, desertions from the Seminary began, and though he did not commit himself immediately, he went so far as to attend the inaugural ceremony. "Whether because of this example, or of curiosity, or of the impression that the speech of Dr. Canseco made on me, or of the boredom which the study of Theology caused me because of its incomprehensible principles, or of my natural desire to pursue some career other than the ecclesiastic," he confessed, "the fact is that I found no pleasure in following the course of Theology." The variety of his motives reflected as yet nothing more than an unsettled state of mind. In deference to his godfather, he completed the course

in Theology; and it was not until a year and a half later that, haunted
by the rainbow, he entered the Institute. Dr. Salanueva consented, as
usual; and with that final concession, his name fades from the record.
Henceforth, having completed his contract, Juarez transferred his allegiance to the State; whatever his obligations to his benefactor may
have been for the past, he was now bound to the nation of which he
was the ward.

Boredom, ambition, curiosity—whatever the motive that drew him
to the Institute, conviction was not among them as yet; that was to
come as a consequence of the others. For the flight from the Seminary
was in itself a political step. The first announcement of a secular school
created less opposition than might have been expected in Oaxaca. The
somnolent provincial town was becoming accustomed to progress.
Thirty years before, paving had been introduced, and the great square
before the Cathedral, which every rain turned into a quagmire, consolidated; street-lighting began about the same time; and in 1824 a
normal school opened, unnoticed, without anyone being the worse for
these costly conveniences. Material improvements were assimilated,
and mental advances survived. But Oaxaca was slow, slow in the pace
of life, slow in public perceptions, slow to realize the implications of
the latest innovation; and it was not until the Institute actually functioned that its significance as the seminary of a new world was recognized. Then the protests arose, and the constancy of the pupils was
tested, and Juarez discovered his convictions. "The Director and the
instructors of the new establishment were all liberals and took part,
naturally, in all the political questions that arose in the State. For this
reason, and for a truer one, the clergy, knowing that this new nursery
of learning, where no trammels were placed on the mind in the search
for truth, was bound to become in time, as it has, the ruin of its power
based on error and interest, declared a cruel and systematic war upon
it, employing the very powerful influence which it then exercised over
families, the civil authority, and the whole of society. They called the
Institute 'a house of prostitution,' and the teachers and pupils 'heretics' and 'libertines.' Parents refused to send their sons to it, and the
few students who attended classes were ill considered and excommunicated by the immense majority of that ignorant, fanatical, and miserable society. Many of my companions deserted, terrified by the powerful enemy that persecuted us. A few, but a very few, continued to
support the house by attending classes daily."

Man and boy, Juarez was no backslider. For a young man born
beyond the pale, with no family to blush for him, and with no social
standing to maintain but that of a favored domestic, persecution and
ostracism were a less trying ordeal, perhaps, than for other libertines;
but for one who had worked his way through the Seminary with the
sole aim of improving his prospects in life, it was sufficiently severe to

test his stamina. He had the advantage, however, of being an orphan—with all due respect to Dr. Salanueva—and he had the most compelling of all reasons to persist, for in the Institute he discovered his latent capacities and grasped the true bent of his mind; and from that satisfaction there was no turning back.

So his re-education began, at the age of twenty-two. It was late to make a fresh start, but he was old enough to appreciate the necessity of beginning anew. The native ignorance which he had brought to the Seminary had been refined and developed there into the dogmatic ignorance indispensable to the sacred calling; and whatever else might be said of the knowledge he acquired there, it was completely divorced from actual life and calculated, as an intellectual discipline, to prepare the adept for a purely contemplative existence and a passive and unproductive part in the activities of the world. That education as a social function was limited by the society which it served was an axiom which he had spent seven of the best and most formative years of his life in learning; but they were not wasted. He had been an apt pupil and had improved his opportunities to the satisfaction of everyone but himself; if the result was unprofitable, the fault clearly lay elsewhere. Where, he discovered in the Institute. What he learned there was not anticlericalism or incredulity, for the Director was a churchman and there were priests on the staff, but the limitations which the Second Guarantee imposed on the growth of his ignorance.

The education provided in the Institute represented only a relative advance over that dispensed in the Seminary. The professors were not far ahead of their pupils, and some of the novices acted as their substitutes, doubling between the bench and the platform, so that the whole enterprise resembled a common adventure, teachers and taught beating out the untrodden paths of knowledge together; but the spirit was progressive. What made the Institute so subversive a departure was the approach to knowledge—the appeal to experience, the untrammeled search for truth, and the range of studies. A ferment of fresh wine was poured into the old bottles: instead of the curriculum laid down by the Council of Trent and confined to four courses in the Seminary—Latin grammar, Philosophy, Elementary Physics, and Theology—the qualifications for contemporary life in the nineteenth century; instead of Latin grammar, living languages and free access to foreign thought; instead of scholastic Philosophy, Political Economy; instead of elementary Physics, taught as a branch of dialectics and as a metaphysical exercise, experimental science itself; instead of a small scale of sterile accomplishments, a broad range of socially useful knowledge, above all in the branch which Juarez elected to pursue. In the study of Jurisprudence the Institute offered, besides Canon Law, courses in Natural, Civil, and Constitutional Law, undermining the concept of dogmatic authority by the comparative study of various systems of law, all deriving from the concept of society as a contract and a partnership, imperfect, experimental, progressive, and all developing the exciting and abstract sense of justice as a science advancing by trial and error. The proficiency which Juarez showed in his studies in the Institute was as marked as in the Seminary; and with the widening of his mental horizon and the confidence of manhood awakening, he felt for the first time the full pulse of a mind that was positive, active, and rational.

His progress was rapid and marked by recognition more conspicuous than the honors bestowed on him in the Seminary. In 1830, a brief year after entering the Institute, he substituted for the Professor of Physics while he continued his law studies; and in 1831 he was sufficiently qualified to enter a local law office and practice his profession. The law, however, was even then an overcrowded profession, which supported very few of its members and which was adopted, therefore, by many of them as a passport to politics. In the same year he stood for public office and was elected to the Municipality as an Alderman, a success which was associated in his mind with another of no less weight. In 1831 he presided over the examination in Physics, which one of his pupils submitted to the Seminary scientists. The two triumphs were not casually coupled—they were the arms of a compass which described his point of view in public life. For a young law student with a bent for physical science, taking his first step in politics, his profession and his avocation combined to provide an excellent education in political science. The facilities which the period offered for investigation and survey were unlimited. The nation was a laboratory of political experiment, and a law student who was also a physicist could discover the principles of self-government by observing daily the action and reaction, computing the natural forces, and analyzing the physical properties by which a new social body constituted itself. The demonstration developed during his student years, at the most propitious moment, with an elementary clarity which made the nature of the process visible to the naked eye.

New nations not being born in the laboratory, but wrested from the bowels of old ones and carrying over the constitution of the parent in the throes of release, the problem was to transform the structure of colonial society into a self-sustaining organism and to create an independent identity and a unified entity out of the heterogeneous mass of raw material, divided by race, color, caste, and class, left over from the paternal regime and molded and cast by the Spaniards for the confusion of their successors. With the consummation of political independence, the internal conflicts generated by its development began to appear. The simplicity of the insurgent movement was succeeded by the complexities of reconstruction; and in the second and creative phase of nation-building the effort of bringing forth a new synthesis of the same elements brought forth at the same time the organic laws governing the creation of any consistent society. Of the hereditary handicaps to genuine independence, diversity of race was the least, all nations being the outcome of a fusion of strains, though the process might require centuries for its completion, and the Spaniards had systematically cultivated cross-breeding for three hundred years. The elaborate caste system which they had created to divide and control the amalgam could be abolished, as it had been, by law, though the prejudices created under it were bound to endure. Ethnic fusion was guaranteed by a common culture, and this was the crux of the question. Social culture and economic interest were synonymous, and the economic interests that determined the formation, the disintegration, and the reconstitution of the colony were the basic obstacle to its complete emancipation from the past.

If human societies were the product of planning and foresight, planning and foresight would be the first instead of the last problem to engage political science and the rational study of self-interest, but being the reverse, the natural order is also reversed, and civilization the continuous process of correcting its origin and revising and unraveling its development. The rule was proved by the exception in Mexico. There indeed nothing had been neglected to anticipate and defeat independence and its inevitable consequences. Planning and foresight distinguished the administration of the colony by the Spaniards, who drained its resources for the benefit of the mother country. Planning and foresight also distinguished the beneficiaries of the independence, who opposed and adopted it, in turn, for the protection of their property and privileges; and planning and foresight were conspicuous by their absence in the Republic, which had done nothing to redeem these liabilities except to borrow abroad without benefit for the economic recuperation and political consolidation of the country. The Spaniards had been supplanted by the Creoles, who preserved intact the structure of colonial society, under a transfer of title to themselves. The propertied and privileged classes, by whose grace a nominal independence had been won for the others, were the arbiters of national development. The wealth of the country was concentrated in their hands and hoarded improvidently and unproductively by a caste without public spirit or responsibility; and this economic autocracy gravitated by natural affinity toward the Church, whose culture protected their common interests, and which was the greatest and most powerful monopolist, mentally and materially, of Mexico. To break that monopoly, to purge that culture, and to recover and control the natural resources of the country was the essential condition of national existence, and political independence carried with it, implicit and implacable, the mandate, the necessity, the physical law of social reform.

Planning and foresight also distinguished one of the students of the

Institute, to whom the destiny of the nation was a topic of burning interest. A Zapotec Indian from the Sierra, who had followed the traditional road to education from Ixtlan to Oaxaca, passed through the Seminary, deserted to the Institute, and joined the staff, Miguel Mendez had made a brilliant name for himself as an agitator of advanced ideas. Endowed with a driving eloquence, which made his convictions contagious, he was in the habit of holding meetings in his rooms, where he held forth freely and feverishly fashioned plans for the future—for he was a prey to consumption—charging his hearers to carry the liberal cause to its logical conclusion and to create a state completely independent of ecclesiastical control. Juarez fell under his influence. On one occasion, according to local tradition, young Mendez, flushed with his mission, impatient for the millennium, and familiar with the capacities of his other disciples, singled out Juarez with the words, "And this one whom you see here, so serious and reserved, this one will be a great politician. He will rise higher than any of us, and he will be one of our great men and the glory of our country."

Foresight certainly, and planning perhaps, were required to divine the coming man of the country in the one on whom Mendez laid his finger and who had barely set his foot on the lowest rung of the political ladder. But Mendez combined the faith of a missionary with the born agitator's insight into men. If time, patience, preparation, and public support were essential to the coming struggle, here was his man, for these were the features that distinguished his chosen messiah at that period: Juarez knew how to listen and to stand and wait, grasping the ladder and biding his time. And it was by way of practical politics, and not by the studied approaches of political science, that the students of the Institute were drawn into the national destiny.

Principles there were none but those of self-preservation to distinguish the two parties—Liberal and Conservative as they called themselves, vinegar and oil as they called each other—that divided the country in the first years of the Republic. The meaning of independence penetrated slowly in Oaxaca, which had barely been touched by the battlers of the insurgent period and had temporized until the turn of the tide, and where the cult of independence followed, instead of preceding, its triumph. In 1828, when Guerrero stood for election to the Presidency, feeling ran high in Oaxaca and nowhere higher than in the Institute, where the fevers of the decade were revived in a fever of retrospective patriotism, and the students turned out in a body to support their hero with a zeal all the more burning for being belated. Bloodshed and rioting marked the primaries—a foretaste of what was to follow throughout the country. Guerrero lost the election; his partisans broke it. One rising led to another: in the south by Juan Alvarez, a veteran of the wars of independence, who came to his rescue; in Veracruz by the governor, General Antonio Lopez de Santa Anna, who followed suit. Marching to join forces with Alvarez, Santa Anna entered Oaxaca in search of support, occupied a convent, and stood a siege without finding any, and was relieved only by the success of another revolt in the capital, where a cowed Congress declared Guerrero President in the autumn of 1829. The success was celebrated in Oaxaca. General Santa Anna was wined and dined in liberal circles, and at a supper given in his honor by a professor of the Institute he met Juarez—without recognizing him as the coming man of the country. Many years later he recalled that meeting bitterly, for he had the flair of an expert politician for names and faces, and all that he remembered was that Juarez was waiting on table at the time, and barefoot. But foresight was not among the faculties of Santa Anna: he was a fortune-hunter, and not a fortune-teller; and being one of the coming men of the country himself, he saw only the feet.

The triumph of Guerrero was costly to himself and the country. By breaking the elections and breaching the machinery of free institutions which they created, his partisans set a precedent by which their opponents profited and on which they improved. Within two years of his imposition by force, he was deposed by the same methods, compelled to flee with a price on his head, captured and killed. The closing scenes of his tragedy occurred in Oaxaca, where he was brought after his capture and confined in the convent which had served Santa Anna as a fortress. Santa Anna deserted him; Alvarez could do nothing; and his sympathizers in the city were a helpless minority of silenced civilians. The public tragedy surpassed his personal fate, for the appeal from ballots to bullets raised a fundamental and recurring issue, to which public moralists—and in that period of political immaturity moralists were in the ascendant—pointed as the coming curse of the country. The imposition and murder of Guerrero made a breach in the machinery of self-government and public confidence in it, opening the way to chronic violence, inveterate lawlessness, and public demoralization. The question of determining the popular will by ballots or bayonets was settled for the moment: justice of a sort had been done— the rudimentary justice of retaliation, which settled nothing for long— and both parties had outlawed themselves, breaking the compact upon which the Republic rested, and leaving power to be disputed without curbs by the parties, and arbitrated by the military.

The moralists were right, as they always are, but not for the correct reasons. More than one moral could be drawn from the facts—for one, whether it was more important for the nation that legality be respected or that the popular will be determined by that revolutionary law which dictates and discards codes, because it is the source of them. That issue had been raised by Guerrero, although nothing more important was involved in his election than his personal triumph. The last of the great trio of original insurgents, he was the symbol of the popular struggle for independence, and his partisans were determined to repay his services with the Presidency. They claimed power as a patriotic right and as a token of popular triumph; and when their idol was outvoted, they flew to arms to enforce their right to self-preservation. These were the motives, blind and instinctive, sentimental and unreasoning, which fired old insurgents like Alvarez, loyal to the man who typified their compromised cause, to take up arms against their class enemies; and the Conservatives recognized them in a revolt that they repressed with equal unscrupulousness, as a flare of class warfare that broke the truce on which the Republic was founded. Like the dispute over ecclesiastical patronage, the minor and ostensible question of the elections foreshadowed the larger conflict latent within it. The political moral of the tragedy lay not in the methods, which were common to both parties, but in the correctness of the cause that produced them.

Such were the working conditions under which Juarez entered public life. He was elected to office and took up legal practice in Oaxaca in the same year in which Guerrero was killed there—a conjunction of circumstances singularly favorable to his political education. The memory of Guerrero was passionately cherished in the Institute, where he was honored as the last martyr of independence and as the ultimate symbol of the movement, falling blindfolded before the muskets of triumphant reaction. The firing squad shattered the legal conception of the State as a social contract and reduced it to something more closely approximating a scientific demonstration of physical forces. The State was not a coherent whole to be studied and planned *a priori* even in theory; in reality, it was a chronic condition of violence, static or active, of the classes that composed it, a conflict alternately arrested and aroused, constantly compounded, controlled by the master class and to be mastered only by correction and experiment. Preconceived concepts of the State were a theological notion carried over from the Seminary and only slightly modified by the scientific revisions of the Institute. Mendez, who had shed the moral bias both of the Seminary and the Institute, had a clearer conception, perhaps, of the nature of the coming struggle when he put his finger on Juarez to lead it, but both views were, in fact, academic. Juarez found his bearings slowly in the crude school of practical politics. His future, and the future of the nation, lay not with Mendez, but with Santa Anna.

6

FOR Santa Anna was unquestionably the coming man of the country. He was the portent, the product, and the personification of the period. The years that followed the elimination of Guerrero and the old guard from public life were a dreary and static stretch of confusing, incurable, and insignificant turmoil, of governments set up and overthrown by military mutinies, of transient adventurers dogging one another without aim or policy, and so monotonously the same under the ever-recurring ferment of seething instability that foreign observers, and Mexicans themselves, were convinced of the congenital incapacity of the nation for self-government—a verdict based on superficial evidence, for the agitation, shallow and stationary itself, was the symptom of an unlocated infirmity, and if any one phrase could synthesize that age of national colic, it might be described as "the reign of Santa Anna." His was the figure that returned again and again, in one guise or another, through all the veering vicissitudes of those teething times, the constant element in their mutability, the arch adventurer, the persistent opportunist, the perpetual turncoat, trimming his principles to every wind, steering by instinct and without compass, speculating on any program to gain power. Buoyant, ambitious, callow, and self-confident as he was inconsistent, he was the consummate creation of a period which he bestrode like a colossus and straddled like a politician; and because he was both its creature and its creator, he was a social phenomenon.

Antonio Lopez de Santa Anna Perez de Lebrun was the scion of a Spanish family located in Veracruz and Jalapa and established in trade and society by a respectable income: his father was a mortgage broker in Veracruz and a landed gentleman in Jalapa. At the age of sixteen Santa Anna declared for a military career, was sent to the Military Academy, and graduated in time to serve in 1810 and to join in hunting down Hidalgo and his fugitive followers in the north. The culminating year of independence found him still loyal to Spain, but only a captain; for in consequence of a scandal arising out of his gambling debts he had been assigned to chasing bandits in his native state; but thereafter his promotion was rapid. One day in March 1821 he made three grades in twenty-four hours. In the morning he routed a column of rebels and was commissioned lieutenant-colonel; in the afternoon the rebels were reinforced and raised the bid to a full colonelcy; and he declared for independence at the end of the day. The motley was in his blood, but he wore it with epaulettes. Iturbide made a brigadier-general of him, and when Iturbide was overthrown he declared for the Republic. All that he knew of republics at that time was, he said later, what a lawyer in Jalapa had told him, for his education had been confined to barracks; and though he subsequently acquired a nominal acquaintance with political systems, he remained to the end of his life politically illiterate. As opportunities for advancement under the Republic were few, he proposed to liberate Cuba, but found no support for this scheme in Mexico, and after fretting for action and aging in harness for four years, now as governor of Yucatan and now of Veracruz, he seized the first opportunity of resuming his career and revolted in favor of Guerrero.

Up to this point his record presents nothing remarkable—the common career of a pushing young officer bent on reaching the top and indifferent to the means of promotion, whose change of colors betrayed his ignorance of the issues involved, and who tested every cause by its effect on himself. It was not until the individual type was transferred to public life and encountered there the conditions which enabled it to wax and flourish that his career became significant and his promotion portentous. He was the typical Creole, whose mercurial loyalties were the result of his anomalous station under the colonial regime, emancipated by independence but also uprooted by it, for whom his native land remained his adopted country, to be exploited for his personal profit, and whose patriotism remained that of an emancipated opportunist. The motives which impelled him to champion Guerrero were the antithesis of those which fired Alvarez, but they had one element in common—both pinned their faith on popular heroes. In a time of political immaturity, tension, and insecurity, the tendency to look to men rather than principles, and to personal instead of party leadership, was pronounced throughout the country. Here the career of Santa Anna crossed that of the country with contagious effect. Equally indifferent to both parties, but not to the hero-worship which Guerrero inspired and the popularity which he commanded, Santa Anna gambled on Guerrero and won, and a run of political luck was converted into a system which he worked, after the fall of Guerrero, for his own benefit. In the meanwhile he had covered himself with glory by repelling a Spanish expedition sent from Cuba for the reconquest of Mexico in 1829 and had been acclaimed a national hero himself. Thereafter the history of the country was his.

Less than a year after the death of Guerrero, Santa Anna led a successful revolt against the government and, after a short interval, was elected President in 1833. Conscious of his inexperience, he retired to his country estate, leaving the government in the hands of the Vice-President, Dr. Valentin Gomez Farias. Under the provisions of the Constitution the Vice-Presidency fell to the defeated candidate, and as his opponent was a Liberal who had missed the Presidency by a margin close enough to indicate considerable popular support, Santa Anna showed his sagacity in entrusting him with responsibility, while he stood and observed the results.

Gomez Farias was a physician with radical ideas, which he lost no time in testing, with the tacit consent of Santa Anna, who gave him a free hand to experiment. Besides Santa Anna, he had another partner, though an unofficial one, in Dr. Mora, a Doctor of Philosophy who became his mentor and collaborator. Between them the two doctors administered a profound shock to the country by initiating a program of sweeping reforms. For ten crowded months measure followed measure, each more unsettling than the other: education was secularized; the University of Mexico disestablished; civil coercion in the collection of ecclesiastical tithes and the enforcement of monastic vows suppressed; the right of ecclesiastical patronage appropriated by the State; the right to control the sale of Church property claimed; and interment in temples prohibited on sanitary grounds. The invasion of sacred ground by what was no more in reality than a program of civic sanitation was pressed forward rapidly and relentlessly by Mora and Farias and a friendly Congress, but the Reform Laws of 1833-34 so clearly presaged the separation of Church and State that they created consternation among the conservative classes and aroused agitation in the most remote reaches of the country, where the rising generation was provided with a dangerous example of how much could be accomplished, and how quickly, by determination and daring. A halt was called again and again by the offended parties during the ten months; indignation was ignored, remonstrance redoubled, denunciation deepened into the rattle of revolt, and then the situation was saved by Santa Anna, who returned to the capital, dismissed Farias, and restored the confidence of the country in an established order in which such experiments could not be lightly repeated—and lightly they were not.

The reverberations of these events were felt in Oaxaca, where the Liberals breathed freely with Farias in power and elected their best barristers to the local Congress, Juarez among others. Here he distinguished himself by initiating, with two other sponsors, a motion to honor the memory of Guerrero. The motion was carried unanimously, and Oaxaca showed its colors in a solemn ceremony in which the entire community united to make what amends were still possible to the dead hero. A long procession, escorted by troops and headed by the civil, military, and ecclesiastical authorities, wound its way slowly through the countryside to the site of his execution, where the parish

priest pronounced an unqualified eulogy, and the remains were disin-
terred and emptied into a silver urn, which was then brought back in
parade, at the same solemn pace, pausing every quarter of an hour for
a salvo of musketry, to Oaxaca, where it was displayed, amid the booming of cannon and bells, in the Cathedral and, after a Requiem Mass,
transferred to the convent in which he had been imprisoned and sentenced, a trophy of time imposed on eternity. The participation of the
clergy in these rites, as conspicuous as it was politic, honored them, the
only dissenting voices being those of the Dominicans in whose convent
he was laid to rest, and who murmured but submitted.

The participation of Juarez, whose motion was responsible for mobilizing public sentiment, was not forgotten. The gesture by which he extended his hand to this protomartyr of Independence and caught the
consecrating touch definitely placed the young deputy. But where?
About the same time he introduced a bill into Congress to confiscate
the estate of Cortés for the benefit of the State. Both motions were
commemorative gestures linked with the past, and he was engaged in
pious exercises of retrospective patriotism when the country had already
been overtaken by the hurrying call of the future. Farias and Mora,
catching up the heritage of Independence and replacing hero-worship
with reform, had begun their iconoclastic attempt to create that purely
secular state which Mendez had impressed on his disciples as their
common duty; but Mendez was dead, and Mora and Farias were short-
lived, and far away.

The impression which their crusade made on the rising generation in
Oaxaca was remote and faint. Agitation it aroused, but an agitation
confined to scandal, tale-bearing, backbiting, and gossip. A group of
women, signing themselves the "Mothers of Oaxaca," wrote to the papers in the capital, protesting against the corruption to which their sons
were exposed in the Institute; and the conduct of the Institute under
their attack would no doubt have made Mendez turn in his grave. The
faculty met in high agitation to consider whether to ignore or to answer it, elected the latter course, but could not decide how to clear their
good name, whether by a joint statement rehearsing the respectability
of their members and the orthodoxy of their opinions—the venerable
Dominican who had been their first Director, the honorable magistrate
of the Supreme Court their second, the choirmaster of the Cathedral
their third; or by citing the magnificent altar presented to the Virgin
of Guadalupe by the Institute; or by appealing to the neighbors; or by
citing the women to court—and whether to the civil courts or to the
Tribunal of the Faith; or by hiring a lawyer to sue them to expose
what lay behind the tendentious complaints of the pseudo-mothers, for
the charges were certainly concerted and inspired; or—and—if but and
how—until finally, flustered and confused and exhausted, they resolved
to publish the minutes of the meeting as their best defense. The solu-

tion was suggested by Juarez, who sat with the faculty as Professor of Physics.

Six years after its foundation, institutional timidity had fallen upon the house, leaving little distinction between Sadducee and Pharisee, and making it a safe and inoffensive seminary where salvation could be gained by words without works. Fortunately for Juarez himself, however, he had an experience at this time that sharpened and riveted his convictions, one of those saving disgraces which are revelations in disguise, and the value of which he recognized by the extended account he gave of it in his mcmoir.

"The clergy were still in full enjoyment of their privileges and prerogatives, and their close alliance with the civil power gave them a well-nigh omnipotent influence. The rights which exempted them from the jurisdiction of the common courts served them as a shield against the law of safe-conduct and allowed them to indulge in every excess and any injustice with impunity. The rates of the parish dues were a dead letter. The payment of obventions was governed by the will and the greed of the curates. There were, nevertheless, some honest and upright pastors who confined themselves to legitimate charges without fleecing the faithful; but few were those really evangelical men whose example, far from deterring the bad from their abuses, led to their own censure on the charge that they were 'misleading the people and undermining the curacies.'"

It was with the rule, and not the exception, that Juarez came into contact, since his law practice lay with the poor. A typical case was presented by the villagers of Loricha, who appealed to him for protection against the extortions of their curate. He accepted the case and appeared on their behalf in the ecclesiastical court. "Undoubtedly, by reason of my position as a deputy and because a Liberal administration then governed the state, for this occurred in the beginning of the year 1834, my petition was accepted and the priest was ordered to appear and to answer the charges against him, and was forbidden to return to his parish until the trial was over; but unfortunately a few months later, the administration fell"—and the case collapsed. The accused returned to his parish, secured the arrest of all those who had informed against him, held them incommunicado in the county jail, and obtained orders from the City to imprison the delegation which had made the complaint. "I was then, at the close of 1834, substituting in the chair of Canonical Law in the Institute, and being unable to regard with indifference the wrong done to my wretched clients, I obtained leave of absence for a few days and went to the village of Miahuatlan, where the prisoners were held, to obtain their release." On his arrival he was allowed to communicate with them, but on the following day the local judge started trial against him as a vagrant, and fearful of further outrages he returned to Oaxaca and accused the judge in the

state court. There too the curate had forestalled him, securing a writ
for his arrest on the charge of inciting the people against the authorities. Juarez was imprisoned with another advocate who had been
taken into custody for the same reason. He complained to the Supreme
Court, but it was not until nine days later that he was released on bond,
"and no action was ever taken on my complaints and charges against
the judges who injured me."

"These blows which I suffered, and which I saw suffered daily by
the disabled, who complained against arbitrary acts of the privileged
classes in concert with the civil authority, dimly revealed to me that
society could never be happy with the existence of the former and their
alliance with the public powers, and confirmed me in my determination to work constantly for the destruction of the baneful power of the
privileged classes. And I did so insofar as I could, and so did the Liberal party; but, unfortunately for humanity, the remedy that was attempted at that time was not a radical cure for the evil, for although
retrograde administrations were repeatedly overthrown and replaced
by Liberal ones, the changes were only of persons, while laws and constitutions continued to retain the ecclesiastical and military immunities,
religious intolerance, a State religion, and the possession by the clergy
of that abundant wealth of which they abused to encourage the causes
that cemented their pernicious power. Thus it was that hardly had a
Liberal Administration been established than it was overthrown in a
few months and its partisans were persecuted."

Of such experiences living convictions are made: the curate of Loricha completed what Miguel Mendez began. When Juarez took the
case, he was a professor, a deputy, and a magistrate just appointed to
the bench; when he dropped it, he was a reformer for life. But he was
not yet an active one. Gomez Farias had fallen, the Liberal fling was
over, Juarez was politically out and no match for the ubiquitous curate
of Loricha. "Implacable in his vengeance as the latter was, and as the
sectaries of any religion usually are," he served, however, to put Juarez
on the highroad to Damascus. The results of the "dim revelation" were
long in manifesting themselves, but they had lodged deep in a man
who had the memory of an animal and the patience of an immortal to
wait for an opportunity to strike at the peculiar institution he abhorred.

The failure of Mora and Farias made it clear that they lacked sufficient public support and were still ahead of the times; but their success
proved that they had merely anticipated it and that the attempt would
be repeated; that the opportunity would return was guaranteed by
their wreck, though how and when were unknown terms of the equation. The period between the birth and rebirth of Reform was a long
hiatus, during which the occasional return of a relatively Liberal regime served merely to vary without violating the dominant combina-

tion of Conservative powers, producing the improvisations of persons without jarring the institutions of the privileged classes. Nevertheless, it produced something more than the monotonous intervals of major and minor counterpoint. The *status quo ante* was preserved for another, and yet another, decade, steadily weakened by its very security, before the discovery was made that in political as in physical life an organism that fails to develop tends to decay. Though the succeeding years were filled with the superficial agitations of politics, socially and economically the country remained at a standstill, a prey to the ravages of arrested development. The progressive enfeeblement of national life was abruptly revealed by its first collision with foreign powers, in 1836. What the reforms of 1834 failed to accomplish, the pressure of the outer world and the internal weakness of the nation combined to bring about.

Mora and Farias went into exile, pursued by the execrations of the clerical press. "Yesterday," ran a leader in its loudest organ, "the execrable Farias finally left this capital, laden with the just imprecations of a whole city, the foremost in the New World of Columbus, upon which his frightful excesses will forthwith weigh." An epidemic of cholera, which coincided with the crisis, raged in the oratory of press and pulpit as a divine visitation: "Gomez Farias attracted, like an ominous comet, cholera and misery, immorality and tyranny, treason and espionage, ignorance and sacrilege, the uplifting of criminals and the degradation of honorable men, the triumph of the filthy rabble and the fall of the chosen few, the terror and affliction of families, proscription, mourning, and death under a thousand and more horrible forms," including the death by default of Ferdinand VII—"Ferdinand VII was ashamed to see that his former colonies could produce a monster surpassing him in scandals and terror, and descended to the sepulchre satisfied that his presence was no longer needed on the face of the earth to afflict humanity."

The danger was over, but not the shock, for there was no security that the danger had passed. No revolution is ever lost, however abortive, no reform ever fails completely. Its results may be abolished, but a residue remains. The movement returns pendulum-wise by the very momentum of reaction; and though the reform laws were annulled, they remained on the statute books, a dead letter, blotted, void, overwritten, with erasures, but alive in the popular consciousness, from which they could not be completely effaced. At the opening session of the new Congress the carefully chosen ecclesiastics and Conservatives who composed it were dumfounded to hear one of their own ministers read a memorial on the right of patronage, defending the claim of the State to control it. It was supposed that he had read by mistake a paper dropped by his predecessor, but he persisted in his error and upheld it in the press; and a little later the question of exclaustration was raised by a public scandal, when a nun was abducted in the heart of the capital to the applause of a sympathetic crowd and the approval of some Conservative papers. No less a mouthpiece than the organ which had puffed so hard against Gomez Farias a few months before now declared that "there is no lock strong enough to prevent the progress of the world." Whatever else the reformer had done or left undone, he had left confusion behind him.

But there was always Santa Anna. Convinced by the experience of his colleague of what would not work, but not yet by his own of what would, he jammed the helm hard to the right and filled his administration with Conservative persons and centralist tendencies. This touched off an inflammable issue. Conservatives and Liberals had identified themselves with two mechanical principles, Centralism and Federalism, the former seeking effective control of the country through a centralized administration and the latter ample latitude for local autonomy to preserve their independence in a loose federation that favored states' rights—principles which were of more actual interest to the country at large than social reform at that period when the regional basis of national life was a pronounced feature of its amorphous beginnings. The abrupt reversal excited the centrifugal and separatist forces associated with Federalism and was felt with peculiar acuteness in the remote extremities of the country, where it created other domestic complications. Meeting with active resistance in Zacatecas, the native province of Gomez Farias and a hotbed of reform, Santa Anna led a punitive raid into that state. The agitation spread to the adjoining state of Coahuila and thence to Texas, where it kindled yet another brand of contention in the alien population of the frontier. The American colonists flew to arms to defend the local autonomy guaranteed them by a succession of Mexican governments as their privilege for settling the territory, and the fuse thus lighted developed rapidly into the blaze that ended with the secession of Texas.

The Texan crisis provided Santa Anna, when it began, with a martial diversion from social reform and the opportunity to unite the country and increase his prestige by the suppression of what promised to be an insignificant revolt; but it ended in disaster for himself and a cruel exposure of the condition of the country. In the brief campaign which he conducted against the colonists (December 1835 to May 1836) he displayed his soldiership at its best and worst and fully in both: his organizing ability in putting an army into the field practically without funds; his public spirit in pledging his personal property to raise them; his leadership in the long burning marches across the desert; his gallantry in the capture of the Alamo and his savagery in the slaughter of the prisoners there and at Goliat; his incompetence on the field of San Jacinto, where he was defeated by a beaten foe; his cowardice after his capture and his bravado in recognizing the independence of Texas on his own responsibility, and by a secret agreement, to secure his release. Through every phase of the campaign one factor in his conduct remained constant: he managed the war as a personal enterprise, and the genuine devotion to his adopted country which he displayed when he fought for it was matched by the facility with which he disposed of it when fortune deserted him. Psychologically he was an alien still, sovereign and irresponsible; and while anyone else would have been completely discredited by such a defeat, he returned to Mexico in 1837 and settled down on his estates to recuperate from it.

The disaster to the country was more serious. The inability of the government, with all the material and moral resources of the country at its command, to suppress an insignificant revolt was an admission of weakness which clearly indicated that something was radically wrong with Mexico. What those resources were worth was revealed when Santa Anna was forced to mortgage his own property to outfit an army and to levy forced loans and to resort to makeshifts of all kinds to keep it afoot. The Texas crisis caught the country unawares in its chronic conditions of disorganization and poverty, conditions which went back to Independence and before it. The formation of the nation was from the outset an economic problem which remained untouchable. In 1821, when the colony which Cortés described as containing the most vast and varied wealth ever bestowed upon a single people in a single area declared itself independent, it was cast on its own resources; and after three hundred years of exploitation, which had drawn off all the exportable wealth, prohibited or neglected native production, and forbidden foreign trade, those resources were what might have been expected: they were undeveloped, or disorganized, or exhausted. The mines, which had been worked to the exclusion of every other field of natural wealth, had been abandoned because of deterioration of yield or antiquated methods of extraction, and by the end of the eighteenth century the industry was in a state of chronic slump. Agriculture, in a land whose greatest potential asset was the soil, was unprofitable to the great landowners, in whose hands the largest and most fertile tracts lay idle, because the colonial regime supplied them with no incentive to develop them, and cultivation was confined to the local and immediate needs of a class that was actually land poor and that operated on loans from the Church. It was the threat of foreclosure, when these mortgages were taken over by the Crown shortly before the outbreak of revolt, that eventually led the gentry to join it. Commerce and industry, deliberately restricted by the monopolies of the motherland, were virtually nonexistent.

Everything remained to be done, therefore, when the new nation came into being: roads had to be built, mines rehabilitated, agriculture developed, industry created, trade fostered; but the task was rendered well-nigh impossible by the classes which called the nation into being for their own benefit. With the expulsion of the Spaniards, capital fled the country. Besides capital, economic reconstruction required an initiative of which the native plutocracy was equally devoid. The greatest capitalist in the country was the Church: it was the sole banker, controlling the land-poor *haciendados* by its mortgages, and directly interested in the mines, which built its temples and supplied their treasure; it was rich in its own right, in real estate, in pious legacies, in the accumulated revenue of the centuries; and it was proportionately poor in public spirit. An institution independent of the State, immobilizing one-third of the national wealth in mortmain, it recognized no obligation to contribute to the commonwealth. Theoretically a partner to the State, it took no part in government problems except when they menaced its interests; and in every such crisis the antisocial attitude which it invariably displayed, and in which it was supported by its economic vassals, demonstrated beyond a doubt that the monopoly of the material and moral resources of the country by the Church constituted the greatest single obstacle to the integration of the country.

The new nation began life, accordingly, by borrowing abroad, and to all its other liabilities were added those of a foreign debt which accumulated swiftly and fruitlessly, for the money was dissipated in meeting the running expenses of a government always in arrears. The loan produced none of the economic benefits for which it was made, while the claims incurred by it promoted the infiltration of foreign capital, the appropriation of the natural resources by alien enterprise, and the alienation of the national revenues. Nor were these the only penalties of the failure—the organic and organized failure—of the ruling classes to provide the country with a living. While the overwhelming majority of the population sank to the bottom, submerged in poverty, apathy, and crime, a restless minority struggled to the top and snatched a precarious means of livelihood from the State. The competition for public office produced those furies for which a special word had to be coined —*empleomanía*. Politics for employment attained the proportions of a social obsession in Mexico and reproduced those periodic upsets of the government, led by ambitious generals and backed by hungry bureaucrats, which kept the country in continuous commotion and gave it a bad name with investors abroad. The persistence of these conditions, unimpaired by Reform, from 1836, made them so habitual and accepted that the infirmity they bred was not generally recognized until the collapse of the Texan campaign. Nor was it admitted then, for public opinion was controlled by a conservative press, in the service of a party interested in laying the blame elsewhere, and as far from home as possible.

Trouble with Texas had long been anticipated as an inevitable problem: the problem of a vast stretch of frontier territory, sparsely populated, lying between two countries, one of which failed to settle it while the other was rapidly expanding. Nature abhors a vacuum, and the Americans to the north were a natural people; and as long as the people to the south neglected to make good their claim to the land, their legal title to it weighed as little as an injunction against the law of gravity. Sooner or later the pressure of population was certain to settle the problem. If the question of rights was involved at all, it resolved itself into the right to let a great area of uncultivated territory lie idle indefinitely. One Mexican government after another, recognizing the force of facts, legalized it by allowing that vast outlying domain to be colonized by American homesteaders and sought to assure their loyalty by liberal treatment, nominal allegiance, and loose control of their local autonomy—obligations faithfully observed on both sides, but feeble guarantees against the effects of isolation and virtual independence, the difficulties of assimilation, the proximity of the settlers to the land of their origin, to which they remained bound by consanguinity and easy commercial access, and their remoteness from Mexican markets and the central government. The crisis had long been anticipated, but nothing had been done, or could be done, to avert it, and the result was none the less bitter for being expected. The secession had been foreseen, but so had the secession of Mexico from Spain, and it was the particular time and circumstances in which it occurred that made the inevitable break important. The ease with which the Texans consummated their revolt constituted an indictment of the debility and mismanagement of the Mexican Government, which the holders of power hastened to deflect in another direction—the inevitable direction foreseen by the Conde de Aranda when he pointed to the infant Republic to the north as a focus of infection destined to lead sooner or later to the disintegration of Mexico.

Like their forebears, the Mexicans read the handwriting on the wall. The war in that no-man's-land to the north had not been waged in a void; it had been fought along the frontier, and in the fear, of a neighbor whose shadow had fallen on that territory long before. The first contact between the two peoples established after independence had not been fortunate. Aranda had predicted that the approaches of the other would be made either by propaganda or conquest, and the Mexicans were on their guard against both. The first American Minister to Mexico had made friendly advances, in fact, and had advocated republican ideals with a zeal which antagonized the Conservatives and led to his recall on the complaint that he was meddling in internal politics. The second made himself objectionable to both parties by pressing with all the means at his command—bribery, intrigue, bluster, and cajolery, and in spite of repeated rebuffs—a bid for the sale of Texas and a strip of the California coast; he was also recalled. Thereafter the problem of Texas was allowed to lapse; but when the revolt broke out, in spite of the strict neutrality of the American Government, it was easy to believe that neither its inception nor its issue was spontaneous, and credulity throve on the shadow.

Though the war was unpopular in Mexico, and the upper classes were indifferent at first to its complications, their patriotism awoke with defeat and manifested itself in post-mortem mourning and national alarm. The designs of the adjacent Republic, so plainly advertised by its first two ministers and so suspect after the loss of Texas, were recalled and woven into those of the ruling oligarchy. If the Texan war provided a timely diversion from internal reform when it began, it served that purpose far more effectively when it was over; patriotism covered a multitude of political sins. A pointed comment on the state of the nation was supplied by a famous Mexican who rent the seamless mantle in twain. Lorenzo de Zavala, a disappointed reformer, threw in his lot with the Texans, preferring the prospect of freedom under a foreign flag to the certainty of degeneration under his own—a conception of patriotism that was neither the popular one nor that of the ruling class: theirs was the common variety, springing from the instincts of possession and satisfied with territorial integrity. It was sufficient to cover the loss of Texas with a cloud of popular sentiment, to wrap a republic land-poorer in the ample folds of the national flag, and to nurse mistrust of American ambitions into a fixed idea which deepened with the passage of time. For the secession of Texas remained an unsettled question and a strain in the relations of its neighbors. The independent Republic of Texas, recognized by the United States but not by Mexico, which refused to relinquish and was incapable of enforcing its claim to sovereignty, was too feeble to sustain its position as a buffer state and became a source of agitation on both sides of the border; the strain was sustained for eight years, and in 1845 the inevitable solution was reached. The United States annexed Texas, and the settled question, infinitely aggravated by time, plunged Mexico into an internal and external crisis far surpassing that of 1835, which it reproduced and magnified.

For the Mexican Bourbons had learned nothing from the warning in 1835. The fresh crisis found the country as unprepared as the first, paralyzed by endemic poverty, shiftlessness, and instability. The Conservative forces remained in control of the State, to the accompaniment of those conventional mutinies, revolutionary only in name, which shuffled persons and programs but left the foundations intact. Political ferment was as incessant as it was futile, the bubbling and choking of a stagnant society whose resources, monopolized by the top-heavy and parasitic organizations of Church and Army, made relief impossible. Agriculture was still feudal; mining, commerce, and industry were controlled by foreigners, who exported the country and maintained its governments by supplying their main source of revenue through the customs, which became increasingly crippled with debt service; while government provided the sole national industry for the countless qualified or unqualified unemployed who filled its berths, in a thriving competition of climbers and outcasts taking their turns, on any change of program, to oust one another. A government operated by successive shifts of fortune-hunters, for the protection of the propertied classes, on an ever-deepening national deficit, under the liability of a rising foreign debt and a mounting bill for damages to foreign nations incident to its turbulent functioning—such was still the condition of the Mexican Republic ten years after the Texas war. Yet it was under those risks that the Arandas of Mexico challenged the annexation of Texas as a question of national pride and committed themselves to war with the United States.

But still, as always, there was Santa Anna. During that dreary decade he had gradually recovered from his disgrace of 1835; but it had taken him a decade to do it. In 1838 he lost a leg in action defying a French squadron, sent to collect damages for injuries to French nationals in a riot: the leg was preserved by a grateful country. But he was not yet ready for a political return, and though he served as Acting President for a few months in 1839, he nursed his reputation on his estates until 1841, when he returned and overthrew the government, assuming power as President-Dictator with the support of the clergy. Before long he found it as impossible to govern with the Church as without it—an experience which had ruined most of his predecessors. The reluctance of his backers to foot the bills frustrated and infuriated a dictatorship which could exercise itself only in the ostentation of authority, the persecution of opponents, and an orgy of extravagance and corruption; and in 1843 he was overthrown and fled the country under a storm of obloquy that recalled all the causes he had served, abused, and betrayed. When he escaped to Havana, his career appeared to be irreparably closed, but his buoyancy defied bankruptcy, and his star began to glow again through the war clouds that gathered with the annexation of Texas. The crisis offered a favorable opportunity for another patriotic return. Knowing that a war with the United States was hopeless, he weighed the prospects coolly. Was it not better, was it not the part of true patriotism perhaps, to strike a bargain instead of a blow? Unpopular as such a solution was certain to be in Mexico, it had been contemplated there and abandoned in the face of popular feeling; but Santa Anna had more courage in Cuba, and sent an emissary to Washington with a proposal to sell all the territory north of the Rio Grande and the Colorado of the West for thirty million American dollars. The response was favorable, provided the offer were made by the recognized authorities in Mexico: the agent objected that no government could make such an offer and remain in office and suggested that the proper course, in the opinion of his principal, was for the United States to bring pressure to bear by sending a sufficient force to the Rio

Grande and a strong naval detachment to Veracruz. Upon this basis a preliminary understanding was reached. Santa Anna agreed to negotiate in return for American support, and sent back specific military suggestions for the maneuver. The understanding offered a fair degree of insurance, something to fall back upon in case of defeat, while it left him free to prosecute hostilities in earnest as long as he could do so successfully, and it was merely a gentleman's agreement. Everything was contingent upon his return to Mexico, and his credit was so low there that he was forced to take the first bid from any quarter. The bid came from another bankrupt, Gomez Farias.

During that deadly decade the reformer had not recovered from his defeat of 1834, but neither had he accepted it. "When one has undertaken and started a social change, one must not look back until it is completed, nor halt until one has overcome those who oppose it, whoever they may be. Otherwise one must bear the responsibility for the innumerable evils of an attempt for which a people is made to suffer and from which they derive none of the benefits expected of success." The maxim, coined by Dr. Mora after the manner of Marcus Aurelius but with revolutionary composure, was peculiarly applicable to the past decade in Mexico. The compassionate intransigence, the reasonable ruthlessness, of a classic truism had been repeatedly proved by the patient in that invalid interval and fully appreciated by Gomez Farias. The counsel of the philosopher had not been wasted on the physician, and the prescription had gained a force which compelled its application in 1846. The imminent conflict with the United States roused all the helpless resentment, the patriotic pride, the fear and mortification and confusion, and the desperate resolutions of a country conscious at last of its weakness, to fighting pitch; it also broke the hold of a self-centralized government, and the elements flew apart in wildly careening chaos. In the turmoil the old radical reappeared, determined to recapture power from the bankrupt incompetents who had controlled it so long. Alone, he was too radical to be more than a minority leader; an ally was needed of commanding personal prestige, and such was the poverty of spellbinders in 1846 that the only one who answered the specifications was Santa Anna. Overtures were made and accepted. The risk of such an association was self-evident, but it was no time to be squeamish. In May 1846, two months after the outbreak of war, Gomez Farias raised a revolt against a commander who had employed his troops to capture the government, deposed him, and paved the way for the return of Santa Anna, who slipped through the American blockade by agreement with Washington and landed in Veracruz in July. In December he was elected to the Presidency, with Gomez Farias once more as his Vice-President. Thus twelve years after its collapse Reform reappeared in the persons of the same crippled team, by one of those combinations which sum up a period, and in the teeth of foreign invasion, as a desperate, belated, but supreme effort to save the integrity of the nation. Mora was missing, and so was the game leg of Santa Anna.

It was in the midst of this crisis that Juarez came for the first time to the capital of his country, drifting helplessly toward the vortex of war, bankruptcy, and liquidation. Too late for social cures, some of the principles of the original program were hastily applied to the emergency, and though these measures were not a rebirth of Reform, they were a flare in the dark, a signal of distress that restored the vision of those who had caught it dimly in 1834 and were ripe to receive it twelve years later.

And Juarez was ripe, overripe indeed, for though his vision had not failed, that arid decade of national life had been a barren stretch in his own as well. The failure to advance carried penalties of stagnation in public life from which no one escaped, and least of all those who suffered from shallow living; and his reputation has suffered with posterity for his common share in the miseries of this period. After his brush with the curate of Loricha he eschewed political activity, retiring to private life and the practice of his profession. In the subsequent years he accepted appointments, professional and political, from the prevailing regime, which have scandalized his critics and pained his apologists. One of his clerical critics has tabulated the various administrations which he served to prove the pliability of his convictions and to conclude that he was no better than the vulgar office-seekers of the time; a statistical triumph. The charge, advanced all the more eagerly by his enemies because it was the only one that could be brought against his recognized probity, has been aggravated by his friends who have admitted it regretfully; and it has thus grown into an imputation exaggerated out of all proportion to its importance by a partisan spirit which has reduced critics and champions alike to the provincial scale which the question occupied at the time, and which remains the true measure of its merits.

Whatever political inconsistencies were involved in his conduct were more apparent than real, and were shallow concessions to expediency and temporizing. He had to live—a vulgar motive, no doubt, but sufficiently compelling, if not to his posthumous enemies, to a struggling lawyer who specialized in poor clients and who belonged to an overcrowded profession and a politically outlawed party. Appointed to the bench in 1841, he turned a political favor to public account and served the community well in his judicial capacity. In 1843 he married; and the vulgar motive acquired increased force and perfect respectability. For he married well: from a social point of view, brilliantly; and from a personal one, fortunately. His bride was the daughter of the house in which he had found shelter twenty-four years before as the runaway brother of the cook. The Mazzas ranked among the *gachupin* families of Oaxaca in point of respectability, although they were of Italian origin, and the match was a remarkable example of the freedom from racial prejudice, which was one of the few benefits bequeathed by Spanish civilization to its colonies. His courtship was accepted by society as unquestioningly as by Margarita Mazza herself, and she described her suitor in two words, which honored them both. "He is very homely but very good," she wrote, and the comment conveyed her whole heart, which was conscious of nothing else.

Definitely established in the middle-class world of Oaxaca by his marriage and his professional standing, he now had a position to keep up. Everything tended to reconcile him to the existing order, to make him amenable to its advantages, and, like many another middle-aged idealist, to reduce him to a sensible appreciation of the possible. It was possible, for instance, a year later, to accept a position as secretary to the government, although the Governor was a satellite of Santa Anna, who was then in full blast of his clerical dictatorship. How compromising it was is clear from the satisfaction of his critics, who have cited his signing of an invitation to the unveiling of a portrait of Santa Anna as serious evidence of his political servility. When it came, however, to signing an order from the Governor to the courts directing them to prosecute those who refused to pay ecclesiastical tithes, Juarez resigned. Yet he did not suffer for his stand; he was returned to the bench and seated shortly after on the Supreme Court of the state.

Nevertheless, though the concessions to security and propriety were few and small, they were damaging. A decade of timeserving was deadening, the sands of expediency drove the living springs of faith underground, and the dust continued to accumulate and settle on his late youth. The mere passage of time was a setback: middle age was upon him, not the active maturity of a vigorous prime but the thickening flesh, the slackening fires, the sedentary wisdom of the forties, and he had done nothing to redeem the high hopes with which he had been invested by Mendez so many years ago. Marriage was sobering, his was happy and fruitful, and the birth of children tightened his bonds. In 1845 he was elected to the Departmental Assembly, as the conservative version of the local legislature was called, and universally recognized as a safe man. But new times were at hand. With the coming of war in 1846 the Conservative grip on the government was broken in Oaxaca as well as in the capital. A local mutiny seconded the revolt of Gomez Farias, and a triumvirate of Liberals was set up to administer power provisionally. It was a tribute to his past that Juarez was one of them; but it was also a comment on it that the nomination for a new governor went to one of his colleagues who had been both Liberal and active. Some penalty had to be paid for expediency.

Out of his compromises he was suddenly caught, however, by the national crisis, lifted by the national peril, and swept out of his provincial sphere into the vortex of the struggle for national survival. Elected to the Congress called by Santa Anna to meet the emergency, he arrived in the capital when the nation itself was facing the crushing test of foreign war with the preparation of a backward province.

7

THE "terrible year" of '47, as it came to be known in Mexican annals, was terrible above all as a test of the patriotism of a people deprived of every other resource with which to face a foreign war. When Congress convened in January the war had been in progress for nine months; the invasion had overrun the north and was pushing toward the capital; the Mexican forces had lost one battle after another; Santa Anna was mustering a fresh army, pledging his personal property, conjuring up resources out of nothing: drastic measures were required to produce them. In 1835, under less stress, he had pinched the Church; in 1847, under a national warrant, he was driven to the same extremities, but he delegated the duty to Gomez Farias and Congress while he went to the front, and the actual brunt of the business was borne by the deputies from Oaxaca, who introduced into Congress a motion empowering the government to mortgage a portion of Church property, to the value of fifteen million pesos, for the prosecution of the war. The motion was carried, but it was a costly victory for the government. Six weeks later a crack regiment, suborned by the clergy, rebelled as it was about to leave the capital for the defense of Veracruz, paralyzing the government for three weeks. The deadlock was broken by the return of Santa Anna from the front, defeated, but welcomed as a victor by the clergy and the unruly regiment. He dismissed Gomez Farias and repealed the assessment.

So ended once more the brief chimerical combination of reformer and adventurer, wrecked by the same power and for the same reasons as in 1834, but under infinitely more serious circumstances. The lengths to which the Church was willing to go to protect its property were so cynically revealed by the revolt that outraged patriots pressed the charge further; for on the same day that mutiny broke out in the capital, Santa Anna lost the battle of Buena Vista, missing victory by so narrow a margin that, instead of a familiar blunder, the defeat seemed to be a deliberate foul. Rumors of his treasonable relations with Washington were rife, and suspicion gained a grim plausibility because, in a sense, the whole campaign was a conscious sham. Resistance, as everyone knew by now, was being prolonged to preserve the popular fiction of national honor, and betrayal, more bitter to the sentiment than to the interest of the nation, became a joint guilt and prompted a common defense: so that the most suspicious patriots rejected the rumors of his collusion with the enemy as incredible, and though his proposed deal was disclosed by an American paper, it was discounted in Mexico as enemy propaganda. Denied in one form, the accusation appeared in another.

That a major engagement was lost on the field at the same time that a mutiny in the capital paralyzed the defense of the country was a coincidence which no longer seemed accidental when Santa Anna was welcomed home by the clergy and the rebels and promptly complied with their demands. If it was equally shocking, it was less difficult to believe that the battle of Buena Vista had been lost for the benefit of the Church. After the revolt nothing appeared impossible; and anticlericals could henceforth claim, as they did, that if the nation met the crushing test of foreign war with the preparation of a backward province, it was because the nation was in reality no more than a province of the Church.

The revolt of the *Polkos,* as the devout dandies and dashing ballroom dancers who manned the mutinous regiment were called by an outraged people, was a passing scandal and a lasting stigma that cost the Church more money than it spent on it, for the mutiny was too crude a maneuver in wartime, and the hierarchy hastily retreated from the harsh glare of public opinion and covered its miscalculation by supplying Santa Anna with sums well in excess of those they had refused to Gomez Farias. The cost in moral authority was even more prejudicial to the clergy, for the credit of a corporation that acknowledged no civil obligations sank in public respect past recovery. None of those thwarted by the incident recovered from it completely. Gomez Farias was finished. As for Santa Anna, success alone could dispel his discredit, and victory fled his every approach to it, as he fled the reproaches that pursued his repeated defeats. But the chief sufferer was the country at large. Public confidence called for new leaders, and there were none. Congress presented its customary spectacle of parliamentary impotence, absorbed in an oblivious fury of factional wrangles as if there were no war on the agenda—a morbid condition of which the members were well aware and from which, like sick men or men in a nightmare, they were unable to awaken. As the months passed all the forces that had frustrated national unity in the past were brought to the surface and exposed to public view by the pressure of foreign conquest: the congestion of the two great parasitic bodies at the top, a

Church engrossed in self-service, an Army trained to revolt; a bankrupt government bargaining with both; a minority of hopeless critics below; a demoralized mass at the bottom; and over and above all a Santa Anna struggling to galvanize the whole by personal spellbinding; and the progress of military collapse followed its course spasmodically.

The war was lost at great length, however, and with ample time between blows for reflection. What it meant to an average public-spirited but not party-minded Mexican may be seen epitomized in the running comment on its significant symptoms made by an independent observer, whose correspondence with others of his kind traced the arc traveled by the public mind during the terrible year with the graphic accuracy of a fever chart. The name of José-Fernando Ramirez was generic for a type of mind sufficiently educated, indeterminate, and catholic to be affected by many contradictory influences and to reflect in a sensitive medium the daily zigzags, the broad curve, and the concluding ellipse of the public temper in his reaction to it. For Gomez Farias he felt nothing but impatience. "The most compact, the most organized party is that of Farias, a party of immense basis but small elevation," he admitted; but it was composed of fanatics and had succeeded in antagonizing everyone and attaining the last degree of exaggeration. For the *Polkos* he felt nothing but contempt. "The scapularies, medals, chaplets, and bags of religious relics by the dozen that adorned the chests of the rebels, and especially of the soft and sybaritic young men who form our fashionable class, might have convinced anyone ignorant of our customs that here was a camp of martyrs ready to a man to sacrifice everything for the inviolability of religion"—if it had not been common knowledge that they continued the mutiny only as long as they could blackmail the Church. For the clergy he felt the kind of tolerant contempt of one accustomed to the religious cant with which they sanctioned and subsidized revolt, and a bitter relish when they overreached themselves and were duped by their improvidence. As for Congress, its conduct convinced him of the impossibility of the representative system. Unless it improved, "despotism pure and simple awaits us; that is, supposing that we still have a country." For Santa Anna he had both contempt and pity when he was told that, convinced of his unfitness to command, he proposed to enlist Spanish officers from among the Carlist *émigrés*—the final touch to the countless absurdities of independence. "We have all awakened late, all of us in our various fields, to the hard fact that we are unfit for command! If at least we profit by the discovery, all will not have been lost. What the end of the war will be it is not easy to say, for the sad truth is that no preparation has been made even for peace, but I believe that peace will be made soon, although probably only to renew our old civil wars."

When he was offered an honorable escape from his country—the best post in the diplomatic service abroad—Ramirez refused it. "My pride as a Mexican," he said, "is greater than our degradation, than which no more can be said, and I could not bring myself to represent a people which by its inane quarrels, its puerile petulance, and its senselessness, has been unable to defend itself, inferior in this to dumb brutes."

Counting the months to capitulation, and the dismemberment of the country which he foresaw as its inevitable consequence, he noted the progress of internal disintegration with growing fatigue and comments more and more fragmentary. In April Santa Anna led another army to the slaughter at Cerro Gordo, where "a small number of our troops fought and died heroically; the rest threw down their arms and fled without a fight. We must regard the morale of the soldier as lost, for even his race instinct is at work in the fear he feels of the foreigner." In May Puebla was surrendered by the clergy, the inhabitants having fled as soon as Santa Anna proposed to defend them, and some high dignitaries of the Church declared that, if the Yankees respected their faith and their property, nothing would be lost by the invasion. After the fall of Puebla the American Commander himself was said to be using his secret funds to influence Congress to bring the war to a swift and humane conclusion, but "the first to speak of peace will lose it, and hence none dares to pronounce the fatal word." In June the capital was invested, and a last stand for honor made at all its approaches, amply redeemed at Chapultepec where a score of boys young enough to believe in it bit the dust, and by their elders at Churubusco and Molino del Rey, and by countless feats of isolated courage. The zigzags became more and more erratic and desperate in the convulsive confusion of the culminating battle lost by Santa Anna, whose flight finally relieved a city that had been waiting for weeks to expel the army which it dreaded more than the Americans. Throughout the last hectic phases Ramirez remained there until the day of defeat, the day of delivery, dawned, and after it when the formal war was finished and a private war was waged by the populace against the Americans, whom they lured to death in obscure dives, and against the pest which followed the troops ridden with dysentery and relieving their disease in the sewerless streets.

Then, as peace settled over the extinct but still seething city, he fell to reviewing the past and casting up accounts for the future. He drafted utopias of what he would do, were the history of his country his to rewrite. He cited with approval "an old and neglected political saw which says that it is men rather than systems that determine the welfare of peoples and lend a high renown to nations." Yet that was no solution: the system of personal leadership had been played out by Santa Anna; politics was a science of averages. He laid out plans for reforms, too general to be good, and when he reduced them to cases, he was willing to make any concession for the sake of national unity. He noted the indifference of the people during the ceremonies of Holy Week in 1847 as a feature "which the false philosophy of our revolutionists will hail as a symptom of social progress," but which dismayed him as "one of death and destruction, for when our people reach the point of believing in nothing they will respect nothing." For the sake of self-preservation he was prepared to compound with idolatry and corruption. "I hope that you will do me the justice to believe," he wrote in one of the last and most revealing of his letters, "that when I refer to the reform of abuses, I do not propose to break a lance with the clergy or with any other class of society, as might be supposed from the senseless vulgarities and gross slanders that have been spread against me. The well-founded reputation that I enjoy as an aristocrat should make it clear that that quality is incompatible with class hatred." His conception of aristocracy was superior, but it led him in practice to very ordinary conclusions. Rather than risk a repetition of the penalties of the past, he was willing to return to the past: he surrendered to society, such as it was, his scorn, his disgust, his despair, his dreams of reform, for the sake of peace. He was beaten by his own observations, and in this, though he touched the nadir of nihilism, there is no doubt that his views reflected those of the average Mexican, in varying degrees, after the war.

Such was the conclusion to which Juarez also was driven by the same experience. His comment was quiet but nonetheless emphatic, and he expressed it not in words but in acts. Throughout the war he had played an inconspicuous part in public affairs. By his colleagues in Congress he was remembered only for his "sphinx-like silence," and, in that Congress whose clamorous incompetence was denounced by Ramirez, silence had all the effect of a sentence. Those were the days when a man could make his mark simply by holding his tongue, and it was noticed that Juarez took his seat only to pronounce a laconic yea or nay on the business of the day. He never mounted the tribune, where deputies made a pastime of insulting one another "with the adolescent fury of schoolboys." Silence in the wind—meaning in the mind; and though he left no trace on the public scene, he carried away from it conclusions of his own and a profound sense of the drift of national life, by which he was guided when he finally found an opportunity to act on it.

The revolt of the *Polkos* was seconded by a reflex movement in Oaxaca which captured the local government. With his fellow deputies Juarez initiated a motion in Congress to depose the usurping authorities, and by dint of pressure, parliamentary bargaining, and the influence of a prominent leader, secured its adoption; but as Oaxaca provided the Federal government with a steady flow of supplies and as

Congress had no means of enforcing its decrees, the resolution remained a dead letter until Juarez returned to Oaxaca in August 1847 and joined his friends there in ousting the "intruding authorities." They were successful, and for his part in the push he was appointed provisional Governor in November 1847. With this position he assumed a national responsibility. "The decision with respect to Oaxaca may be of immense importance, depending on the turn that matters are beginning to take at this time," wrote Ramirez when Congress adopted the resolution, for the turn which matters were taking then ran counter to national cohesion. A marked tendency to assert their local autonomy at the expense of the center had appeared among the states during the closing of the debacle, when the Federal powers were, in fact, no more than a conventional fiction, with one honorable exception recognized by Ramirez: "A single state, Oaxaca, has shown itself firm, consistent, and even heroic by providing everything, money and men, amid its own troubles." If the conduct of Oaxaca was conspicuous during the disintegration of the national defense, it was of far greater consequence that it should feed the nation with patriotic example after the war, when the motion of the vortex in reverse, whirling away from center, threatened the country with internal as well as external dismemberment. To counteract that tendency was important, and to begin the work of reconstruction there, preserving the part for the whole and rallying the nation to the example of a pivotal state, was possible, and the only thing possible then for practical patriotism, and it was the course Juarez adopted. He applied himself to his task with the benefit of the experience he had gained in the capital, and in a conservative spirit which would have won the approval of Ramirez, had he noticed it; avoiding controversial issues, superior to class hatred, and proving the truth of the proverb that it is men, and not institutions, that determine the welfare of peoples and lend a high renown to nations. But it was long before the average Mexican recognized the importance of what was happening in Oaxaca.

8

ASSUMING power in the wake of the American war, the first and
most pressing test which Juarez faced was the conquest of
peace, and the conservative character of his government was
determined by the conditions in which it began. After the fall of the
capital it was feared that the invasion might spread to the south, and
preparations were hastily made for the defense of the state—preparations which gave him the initial advantage of public spirit and spontaneous co-operation, and in which he mustered the full support of the
community, including the ecclesiastical authorities, who contributed
patriotic sermons from their pulpits and bells from their temples for
the casting of cannon. The phantom alarm had not passed when a real
one appeared. Santa Anna, fleeing southward, forsaken and disowned
wherever he turned, sought asylum in Oaxaca, and, as his approach revived the agitation of the local *Polkos,* Juarez took the precaution of
closing the state to that wandering germ of civil war.

Santa Anna never forgave him. Years later he recalled that rebuff as
the most bitter of all those which he had suffered because he could not
explain it. With the taste still bitter on his tongue, he wrote, rinsing
his mouth of the name of Juarez: "He could not forgive me because
he had waited on me at table in Oaxaca, in December 1829, with his
bare feet on the floor and in his linen smock and trousers. . . . It is
amazing," he added, "that an Indian of such low degree should have
figured in Mexico as we all know. . . ." Hardened as he was to the reverses of fortune, he was baffled by the unaccountable career of that
upstart, except as a freak of fortune. But then Santa Anna never could
explain anything, and to the end of his days he continued to wander
unknowing through the mysteries of the world and the maze of his
Mexican memories—one world which he thought he knew thoroughly,
and by which he was bewildered in 1847. Memory, the one faculty
which never failed him, and foresight, which always did—the two limitations of the typical Creole—made it equally impossible for him to
understand his rebuff by the native in that terrible year. He still saw
nothing but the feet waiting on table in 1829 and missed the face waiting on time to clear it. The time had come, the tables were turned, and
Juarez had shut one more door in his face. That was all. With the

ground giving under his feet wherever he turned, without a foothold on his native soil, escaping from it like a volatile gas, Santa Anna felt this final abuse all the more bitterly because the hunter and hunted of fortune was unable to realize that fortune was a deity of primitive peoples, that the era of political personalities was passing in Mexico, and that one in which men embodied forces was beginning to emerge. Like all tendencies that outlive their time and the needs which they served, the tradition of personal leadership was long in dying, however, and Santa Anna waited his turn, trusting to the perennial mutability of his fortunes, to settle his account with the upstart who, a nobody in 1829, was everybody in 1847. Santa Anna knew how to return; and life itself knows no more.

Between the beginning and the end of his government in Oaxaca five years elapsed, and what Juarez accomplished there in that time was the antithesis of everything that Santa Anna represented and understood. The administration of Oaxaca by Juarez became an example for the country, in fact, of how much could be accomplished by mere public spirit, honesty, thrift, and sound management. For it was by virtue of such qualities, and on his record as a provincial Governor, that Juarez came to figure "in Mexico as we all know," and the amazing result was accomplished quietly, inconspicuously, patiently—and permanently.

Beginning under the heavy liabilities of national ruin, he not only overcame but turned them to account in his own area, mobilizing the patriotic fervor and fusion of wartime, harnessing their driving power to the tasks of peace and reconstruction, holding them at high pitch, and winning the confidence of all classes so completely within less than a year that when his provisional term expired in 1848 he was re-elected without question to a post in which he had captured the popular imagination. He took a legitimate pride in the result. "Fortunately," he said at his inaugural, "neither a faction, nor favoritism, nor intrigue, but the free and spontaneous choice of the people has placed me in this position. There is no danger, therefore, that any class will be oppressed by my government, nor any portion of my fellow citizens." These were no idle words or conventional pledges: for fortune itself had been reconstructed in his hands, no casual deity or clay fetish, but a rational force formed and controlled by man. Social conciliation inspired his policy from the start, and he kept his comprehensive pledge to the end, despite more than one temptation or provocation to depart from it.

Temptation of a kind to which he was susceptible by nature, the natural temptation of partiality to his own race, came when his people tramped down from the mountains for his inauguration and presented him, together with their congratulations and their small offerings of fruits, fowl, and corn, their large tribute of trust and a common petition. "You know what we need and you will give it to us," said their spokesman, "for you are good and will not forget that you are one of us." He responded in kind, assuring them that he knew their needs and had not forgotten his origin. With his promise to do what was good for them he gave them the run of his house, where they spent the night, sleeping on the floor in the corridors; in the morning they tramped back to the Sierra, each with a peso as token payment on his pledge. The Governor's mansion, an imposing colonial building with courts, columns, and suites of rooms of stately solidity, was well fitted to foster delusions of grandeur in his callers, who, remembering that his father, on a trip to market, had died in a corridor of the Municipal Palace, claimed for themselves the son whom they saw installed in the seat of the mighty. The appeal was compelling. Since Independence the native masses had relapsed into silence and submission to an order which, however it changed, remained the same for them; and only at long intervals was their presence felt in a rare voice of protest.

In 1827 a social satirist wrote in his *Political Testament:* "I leave the Indian in the same state of civilization, freedom, and felicity to which the Conquest reduced them, the most notable fact being the indifference with which our Congresses have considered them"; and in later years the grim jest of the satirist was repeated in sober earnest by Dr. Mora, who drafted philanthropic plans of reform for their benefit. But these were the voices of white men, and it remained for an Indian to voice the passionate resentment and repressed aspirations that underlay the apparent resignation of his race. In 1828 there appeared in the back streets of the capital a leaflet bearing the title *The Indians Wish to Be Free, and Will Be Free,* by an anonymous author who revealed himself only in the words, "I am an Indian; for them and with them I propose to expose truths stripped of all foliage," and who rehearsed the grievances of his people as no outsider could do. All their disabilities he laid to the original loss of "our dear earth, which we have never doubted would be restored to us in its full extent: this being the common feeling of all the Indians who populate this vast continent. The Indians are in the most grievous depression and degradation. Our color, our ignorance, and our poverty place us at an infinite distance from those who are not in our condition, and the protection of the laws avails us so little that their effect is negligible." Their communal lands shrinking under the encroachment of the great estates, without property and without initiative, they were an alien element in the country. "Isolated by their language and form of government, which they do not understand because no one takes the trouble to explain it to them, they continue to live within their own customs, habits, and gross superstitions, which are mysteriously maintained in every village by five or six old Indians who live off the sweat of the rest, ruling them with the harshest of despotism. This combination of causes, known to all and by all lamented, preserves them in an inert and apathetic condition of indifference to the future and to virtually everything that does not serve the gross passions of the moment."

Of what they were capable they had shown when Hidalgo raised the cry of "Land and Liberty"; but Hidalgo had fallen, Morelos had fallen, and in 1828 their hopes were set on Guerrero. "Five million Indians rightly look to him alone for their fortune and prosperity. We want no more revolutions for which we, and we alone, pay the cost without any fruit whatsoever. . . . An Indian is, for our good fortune, the first man on this continent, and henceforth all those who govern us will be Indians, because it is just. We shall not appeal to the barbarous arbitrament of revolutions, which are the remedy of the desperate. Let those remain in their posts who now hold them; but let vacancies be filled hereafter by educated Indians, of whom there is no lack. In this manner we shall write an end to those political convulsions, promoted by the very same men who have caused the Nation incalculable evils in the past; in this manner, realize the predictions of our famous men, who foretold the reconquest of this soil by its legitimate masters; and in this manner, finally, fulfill the will of that good God who bade us give unto Caesar what is of Caesar and to God what is of God."

All these high hopes and profound rancors, wavering between racial assertion and social conciliation, between ancestral pride and Christian mansuetude, and so artlessly argued, sank with Guerrero, however, and were heard no more in the land until they were revived in 1848 by the rise in Oaxaca of another blood-brother, about whom his people gathered to claim him as their cacique and to appeal to the atavistic promptings of his blood. The temptation might have been great, had it not been misleading. He answered their plea, precisely as Providence answers the prayers of men, in ways which they do not recognize, not by special favor or land reforms or racial vindication, but by promoting their assimilation into the community, raising the general level of life, and trusting that the benefits would seep down to the bottom and redeem his token peso.

That level was his whole system of government. Education, of which he was so outstanding an example, lay close to his heart, and here he held out his hand to his people. "Myself a son of the people, I shall not forget them," he repeated at his second inaugural. "On the contrary, I shall provide for their education and see that they grow and make a future for themselves and forsake the career of poverty, vice, and disorder to which they have been reduced by men who only in words have called themselves their friends and liberators and in practice have proved their most cruel oppressors." He was as good as his word. Popular education was the branch of government in which he made the most progress, spreading it into the rural districts, adding fifty new schools to the four hundred and seventy-five already in existence, subsidizing the Institute and establishing two branches of it in the back country, and fostering the education of women as an indispensable part of the whole system. "To form women," he insisted, "with all the qualifications required by their necessary and lofty mission is to form the fertile seed of social regeneration and improvement."

That he fell short of the mark, however, he was the first to recognize, and in his reports to the legislature he insisted again and again on the fallacy of considering education as a popular panacea and the cause of his shortcomings. "That cause is the poverty of the people. The man who lacks the wherewithal to feed his family considers the education of his children a very remote benefit or an obstacle to providing their daily bread. If that man had some advantages, if his daily labor were of some little value to him, he would provide his children with solid instruction in some one of the branches of human knowledge. The desire to learn and improve is innate in the heart of man. Relieve him of the fetters which poverty and despotism impose on him, and he will awaken naturally, even without direct protection."

If education was not to be a fetish or a cure-all, what was the remedy? Not revolution, but road building. "I find that the sources of this poverty are easy to destroy. Let us facilitate our communications with foreign parts and with the other states of this Republic, opening our ports and our roads; let us allow fruits and effects of prime necessity, of common utility, and even of luxury, to enter without charge or check, and we shall have accomplished everything." A program of public works was undertaken for this purpose. In this direction his advance was marked by two milestones, the rehabilitation of an abandoned port on the Pacific coast and the building of a highroad to Tehuacan. The latter was abandoned for lack of funds to complete it; but the road to the Pacific was pushed through amid a remarkable display of public spirit. The parish priests co-operated with the local authorities and recruited volunteers all along the way; the peons built the road of their redemption in return for exemption from military service; and prosperous individuals shouldered a share of the costs.

It was a proud day when the port of Huatluco was opened, not the least sign of progress being the presence of the clergy assembled to bless the occasion. Mass was sung in the open, under the heavens overhead and not underfoot, and the official reporter struck a lyrical note in describing the supreme moment when "for the first time in almost three hundred years the Blessed Host was again raised in this place, and in sight of the sea, which in admirable calm seemed to render adoration and respect to the Author of Nature. Jesus Christ Himself made His power to shine upon it." Like pioneers on a peak in Darien, marveling at the illimitable prospects opening before them, the little group of official sightseers surveyed the dazzling scene, and no one noticed what a landmark the Governor had already passed in breaking through the isolation of the Church from civic service. For such works there was no amazement to spare: they were taken for granted. On the same day a church and a school were simultaneously consecrated on the shores of the sounding Pacific, and on his return to Oaxaca the Governor was congratulated by the Bishop and the Chapter on his "characteristic efficiency" in completing an advance with which they gladly associated themselves.

Besides mountains and roadbeds, however, there were other obstacles to be overcome in opening Oaxaca to the world. The antiquated and strangling system of internal customs, dating back to the days of the colony, was one which, despite his repeated appeals for free trade, he was unable to remove. But within the limits laid down by tradition and inertia he continued to persevere, cultivating every patch of the possible. In an agricultural state, paralyzed by the prolonged depression that followed the American war, he introduced rotation of crops, supplementing the flagging staples of cotton and corn with tobacco, and revived the mining industry by the foundation of a local mint, blocked by a foreign concession, after prolonged pressure on the Federal government. His failures and his advances were in the nature of feelers, tentative and groping, which fell short of the goal but which he irrepressibly renewed. The constant attention he gave to economic progress in his official reports testified to his concern with material improvements as the only alternative to social friction; and the most sensitive index of his progress was his financial record.

When he assumed office in 1847, the resources of the state were exhausted; when he retired in 1852, the deficit had been almost extinguished; and a favorable balance would have been shown but for unforeseen charges incurred in suppressing military revolts—the inevitable accompaniment of a return to normal conditions—and in combating an epidemic of cholera morbus. Acts of God and man could be discounted, however, when a government's record is judged by the average, and the average was high. The state was solvent. Corruption was attacked at the root. The plague of *empleomanía* gradually yielded, and something like a cure was insensibly accomplished by the simple device of introducing standards of fitness and efficiency into civil service in place of appointments by political favor. Here he was favored, as he knew, by hard times: the spoils of office lost their lure, because there were none. "In any period but one of transition and trial, I would have declined the distinguished honor with which I am overwhelmed, even at the risk of being branded an egotist," he declared when he first assumed office. "But now that power no longer has the attractions and charms that flatter one's self-esteem in days of peace and plenty, now that the resources of the Treasury are exhausted and the bonds

of obedience relaxed by our intestine revolts, the first magistracy of the
state is no more than an advance post of imminent peril and a heavy
burden, which offers nothing but vigils, fatigue, and bitter fruits."

He had nothing else to offer his subordinates then or thereafter, and
economy, discipline, efficiency, were impressed on them by an example
which silenced complaint. Punctually at nine every morning the clerks
set their clocks by his appearance at the Palace, and the long laborious
hours passed in unremitting industry, the whole force keeping pace
with the timekeeper. The old casual incompetence of the past, the
sociable heel-swinging, the interdepartmental chats, the official idleness
which relieved the tedium of official activity, the time out for under-
pay, were curtailed to keep in the grace of the taskmaster. A bureaucracy reorganized under stiff qualifications and adequate wages
acquired a new sense of civil service from a manager who made the
machine run, and for the first time in many decades of rule and misrule
the community had the novel experience of being actually governed.
If he had accomplished nothing else, he would have deserved well of
his country, but he would have passed into history as a master bureaucrat. He managed, however, to turn out innovations possible only
under a completely nonpartisan administration. His willingness to employ men of all parties was a source of strength, the coefficient of his
own weakness in serving any administration in the past. His very
timeserving bore fruit: he was a safe man, and as such he was able to
rally public support and conduct it toward goals which remained unsuspected until they had been passed. The changes which he introduced would have been refused to a professed radical and were not
recognized as inroads into established order, for they left accepted
institutions untouched and skirted insurmountable obstacles. He attempted nothing impossible; but slowly pressing forward what was
possible, he steadily enlarged the limits of the feasible.

All this was accomplished by the simplest and most obvious methods.
There was nothing radical, or spectacular, or original in the periodic
statements which he made to the public on work in progress: nothing
but elementary sense and homely morality. Neither his program nor
his record was revolutionary, and doctrinaire radicals of a later day
have attacked it on that score. In particular, they have been scandalized by his relations with the Church. These were of the most orthodox
character, as the correspondence that passed between them, stamped
on the one hand "Government of the State of Oaxaca" and "Ecclesiastical Government of Oaxaca" on the other, constantly recognized; and
they were governed by the conciliatory policy imposed on him by the
nature of his task. Progress, even in the modest measure which he
proposed, would have been impossible had he antagonized the ecclesiastical power; it was greatly facilitated by the collaboration of the
Church in every important phase of his advance. The other govern-

ment responded when he called for cannon and patriotic sermons; it responded when the curates mobilized their communities to build his roads; it responded by sanctioning his seaport and bestowing its blessings on his own; it responded by supplying teachers for his colleges in the Sierra; it responded, above all, during the epidemic of cholera by providing hospital facilities and nursing and shelter for the stricken; it responded, it responded, it responded to all the changes rung on it; and the result was to restore the Church to its original function and to revive something of the faded glory with which it had performed its evangelical mission in the strenuous days of the founding of the colony, before the zeal of sowing civilization had been corrupted by success and forgotten in the fatty degeneration of inactivity and sloth.

The association was of mutual benefit to both governments, and the Church gained in moral prestige by the stimulation of its dormant energies, even when the flush of health was quickened by friction. For friction there occasionally was, and at such times the Governor met the challenge by recalling the spiritual power to its high responsibilities. Provoked by the refusal of a confraternity to permit him to convert an unused wing of their convent into a workshop for convicts whom he wished to rehabilitate, he forced the issue and carried it to the public. "Society," he said, "and civilization will place the blame where it belongs." Society as God, the manifestation of the Creator in the creation of man, was not yet a creed which he professed consciously; but he worked on it consistently, within the limits and with the compromises imposed by social convention. For, of course, there was an obverse to the medal. The co-operation of the Church carried a price—and he paid it. Such concessions as he made to convention were usually of a formal and ceremonial character. When the cholera struck Oaxaca, he led religious processions through the streets and attended solemn services of intercession in the Cathedral—perfunctory compliances with custom cruelly derided by one of his critics as crass catering to superstitious practices; but when religious and sanitary observances conflicted, he set a different example. In deference to one of the Reform Laws of Gomez Farias, forbidding interment in churches—a law nullified "by prejudice to the detriment of public health"—he buried one of his children whom he lost in the plague in the public cemetery. Sometimes, however, he carried complaisance so far as to enforce ecclesiastical censure of a prohibited book. But the most serious of these accommodations was the support which he lent the other government in the collection of parochial obventions, a convention which he justified by appealing to statute and custom and demonstrating, with a great display of Seminary learning, the legitimacy of the claims of the clergy, "since as cultivators of the vine, they must feed on its fruits, and as laborers in the spiritual sphere, they are entitled to sustenance in the temporal." The words literally reproduced those of the Governor from whom he had parted three years before over that very issue; but "a democratic and eminently liberal system, such as that which now governs us," he declared, "is based on a strict observance of the law. Neither the caprice of one man nor the interests of certain classes of society form its essence . . . the most profound respect and observance of the law reveals the character of the true liberal, of the best republican." The publicans approved. The circular stating his position, stamped with the official formula, "God and Liberty," was gratefully acknowledged by the Bishop of Oaxaca, who concurred in all its conclusions, professed his faith in the Federal system, which, "as conducted by the sure and efficient hand of Your Excellency, is capable of leading us to felicity," and repeated his approval of roads and ports, "which I shall second for my part by repeating to the parishes in the mountains my advice to aid in so important a work." If the price was high, so was that of road-breaking.

"In all that has been published under the signature of Juarez from his birth until 1859," says his critic, "there is not one word to prove that his mind projected great social transformations. There is nothing in him that reveals the ideas of a revolutionary, the temperament of a reformer, the philosophy of a missionary of any great cause. On the contrary, following the development of his thought in his writings in Oaxaca (if they are his, for he was never very brilliant), one feels the placid movement of his official ideas, the apathy of his conscience, devoid of all rancor against the past, its monuments and its institutions. For Juarez there is no need of reforms in the State Constitution, nor in Federalism, nor, far less, in religion or the perfect union of Church and State. Whatever exists at that historic moment is good, whatever is rising is worthy of respect. All that the Oaxaqueños need to be happy is to cease their dissensions, to love one another, to unite in the good and the beautiful here and now, and to recognize the plain and easy duty that bids them never to disturb the peace for any reason whatsoever, and to be ready to give their lives when the country is in danger of foreign invasion. . . . Juarez reached the age of forty-six without being more than a good man, an amiable bureaucrat with patriarchal leanings, an affectionate sheep much attached to his wool in the flock of the Good Shepherd. . . . His mind was mediocre, his education insignificant, and hence instead of being ahead of his time he was to be one of its most conspicuous mollusks."

Ahead of his time he was not; he kept pace with it punctually. On the question of ecclesiastical tithes he marked time. That it was a sore point he admitted by arguing it; and that it was a weak one by the reasons which he adduced for his ruling: the "continued complaints" of the curates, the "resistance or sullenness of the flock to pay," and the sanctity of the law, which, if it covered his responsibility as an official, was a feeble defense for moral evasion of a vital issue. While he refused to countenance abuses, he also refused to countenance evasions of the parochial rates, and though he attempted to induce the ecclesiastical authorities themselves to regulate them, he left the correction of irregularities to their discretion. The curates of Loricha triumphed, in fact, all along the line. The battle given and the pledge taken by Juarez over that issue so many years before, the dim revelation of a revolutionary mission awaiting him, the conviction that society could never prosper by the alliance of the public powers and the privileged classes, the resolution to eradicate their complicity when his time came, and the token peso and the promise to his people when he came to power—all were compromised by the triumph of social conciliation, the *status quo,* and superiority to class hatred, which left the system intact and the little foxes free to feed on the vine. And by a cruel coincidence, while he bestowed his blessing on the curates of Loricha who worked within the law, the pulse of the time was beginning to quicken, and his stationary position was sharply accentuated by an incident which occurred beyond the borders of his state and which struck the changing hour.

In Michoacan the same issue was agitated in 1851 by a bitter controversy between a country curate and an ex-Governor of the state, Don Melchor Ocampo. The origin of the quarrel was a small and commonplace incident. The curate refused burial to a body which in life had been that of a penniless peon and in death belonged to a widow who could pay neither the legal nor the illegal rates for interring it; and when it became necessary for sanitary reasons to dispose of the remains, he did so by a bad joke, advising her to salt and eat what was left of her late bedfellow. The case came to the notice of Ocampo, who paid the fees but did not let the offense rest until he had brought it to public attention and made it the base of a petition to the legislature to regulate and reform the whole system of parochial obventions. Thereupon the curate rushed into print. The ensuing controversy went far beyond personal polemics and the bounds of the state, and in the course of it Ocampo made a national name for himself.

So common an instance of clerical callousness and rapacity would have passed unnoticed, had it not excited the crusading zeal of a superior character. Melchor Ocampo was a great landowner and a philanthropist who took a quixotic interest in the living conditions of his peons, and for him it was no small incident that pitted the subsistence of the poor against the subsistence of the priest. The priest took the same view of it; and both carried the dispute to its logical conclusion. The antagonists were ill matched: on the one hand, a pillar of society, a man of property with a distinguished political record as deputy, senator, and governor of his state; and on the other, a country curate. But the curate, cornered and fighting for his livelihood, was more than a match for his opponent in the conditions in which they fought. When the consequences of his little joke became serious, the curate became serious and a pillar of society himself. The reform of parochial obventions was not a minor, nor a local, nor a lay issue: it involved the very constitution of the Church and touched the heart of its organization. A blow to the meanest of its members was a blow to the whole mystic body of Christ, and the curate, hard-pressed and resourceful, rose to the challenge in his corporate character, denying the right of the State to invade the sovereignty of the Church, and raising at once the untouchable question of the relations of the two powers. "Reformers," he wrote, "know very well that the favorite method of attacking the Church is to impoverish the clergy. Away with abuses, they begin by saying, and then away with the ministers, and away with the Church. . . . Let Michoacan see whither Señor Ocampo is unwittingly leading it: to *freedom of faith* and *freedom of conscience,* two programs as impious as they are fatal, and that serve as the standard of socialism in Europe. If, as a scourge of God, they should succeed in settling among us, it is certain that universal destruction would be our end."

Ocampo's curate was of the same genus as the curate of Loricha, but not of the same species. A Liberal before he entered holy orders, he combined the zeal of a convert with the mentality of a renegade and the guilt of a turncoat fighting for his livelihood, and knew how to protect it by playing on the fears of the propertied classes on whom his self-preservation depended. He spread the alarm to the laity, pointing to the danger of a social upheaval in the backwash of the American war, and letting his tongue run to great lengths. "And what shall we say, sir, if it is not the barbarians that rob us, but the hungry masses of Mexicans whom we have among us, and who are the victims of the misfortunes of the country, because of a well-nigh total lack of markets for their former products? These masses may say to justify their depredations: 'Our industry is no more, we labor in vain, and a vain labor must be abandoned, but in the meanwhile we must not perish, the other classes must maintain us, and if they refuse we shall use force. Our methods will be the natural promptings of self-preservation. . . . Hand over those properties, hand over those treasures, hand over those estates. . . . Why is there such inequality in possessions? Why such abundance for some and such poverty for others? Why must our degradation serve to nourish the welfare of the mighty?' . . . These, Señor Ocampo, are but a small part of the pestilential doctrines that derive from your false reasoning."

Ocampo indignantly denied the revolutionary implications of his petition, himself shocked by them. "No one until now has ventured to publish anything so dangerous in Mexico," he retorted. But the appeal to the fears of his class was not lost, and he contributed to them by broadening the scope of the discussion himself and dwelling on the conditions of the peons and the debt slavery which bound them to the great estates as well as to the Church. The inequality of the contest was not on the side of the curate: he counted on the whole weight of the community, while Ocampo engaged it singlehanded. The contest ended in a draw, but it was a test of strength which attracted the attention of the country, and when it was over Ocampo was a marked man —marked by the curate for a bad end, marked by the conservatives as a dangerous crank, marked by the radicals as a man on whom they could rely to fight their battles for them.

The legislature took no more action on the petition to regulate parochial obventions in Michoacan than the Church did in Oaxaca, but the fact that Ocampo raised the issue was sufficient to quicken the pulse of the time. His skirmish with the curate of Maravatio produced a reaction among the conservative classes, whose dread of social disorders following the American war was still acute four years after its end because of the prolonged economic slump of the country, and the word socialism, because of events occurring abroad during that period, increased their insecurity and led them to take precautions for their protection to which, two years later, both Ocampo and Juarez fell victim. The same law, and the same sentence, overtook a marked man like Ocampo and a safe one like Juarez, sweeping together two men widely separated in revolutionary standing and temperament, and the reasons for their common fate were not fortuitous: they were the outcome of the movement of political life during the years following the American war carried to a point where the alternative of revolution or counter-revolution became inescapable, and the middle way was eliminated.

9

THE nation was long in recovering from the shock of the American war. In its wake came not only an economic but a moral depression that was severe and prolonged. Materially mutilated by the dismemberment of its territory, morally shattered by the demonstration of internal debility, the Republic recoiled upon itself in a double defeat; and the second was a worse disaster than the first. The physical liquidation of the war cost the country almost half its original heritage, California, Arizona, and New Mexico being the fine for forfeiting Texas, and the price was paid in national pride. From that shock the nation never recovered: its subsequent history was governed by a morbid complex of feelings—humiliation, hatred, fear, a rankling sense of inferiority, an incurable loss of self-confidence—that settled in the public mind with the force of an obsession and made patriotism pathological. The first effect of this state of mind was a complete prostration of public life; there was a prolonged pause, and it was part of the slow process of readjustment that action gave way to reflection and heart-searching, and the first symptoms of recovery took the form of self-criticism. It was time, it was high time, to stop and take thought and determine the causes of so crushing a disaster; and public-minded men who had tried and failed to make the history of their country turned to writing it.

Two major versions were presented to the public: the Liberal diagnosis of Dr. Mora, whose work, written ten years before, only now began to be generally read, and the Conservative analysis of Lucas Alaman, which was produced under the impact of the American war. Antithetical in their doctrines, there were fundamental affinities, nevertheless, between the ideas of the two historians and a significant parallel in their careers. Each had served a brief apprenticeship in practical politics, followed by a long and melancholy retirement, and each wrote his autobiography in the guise of Mexican history.

As a young man, Lucas Alaman made a brilliant debut in politics as minister and mentor to one of the early presidents of the Republic, but he was turned out of office by the coalition of Gomez Farias and Santa Anna in 1833, and his debut was distinguished by the fact that it was followed by no career. Discouraged by his first reverse, he forsook public life for the study and devoted the next fifteen years to the cultivation of his fortune and his ideas, which, based as both were on the stability of the traditional order, or at most on its slow and peaceful evolution, were repeatedly shocked by the violent developments of the years between the birth of Reform and the breakdown caused by the American war. A veteran amateur in 1833, he was an inveterate one in 1847. In the interval he collected material for a history of his country and began to write it, but the pace of events overtook him, and when the American war threatened to annihilate his subject, the history emerged, under pressure, full grown.

Appearing on the morrow of the debacle, the History of Alaman recapitulated the History of Mexico in a spirit exactly suited to the sober temper and the dull headache of the morning after a long debauch. His aim, he said, was to be accurate, objective, and impartial; but that was the statement of an aim and the delusion of an amateur. Actually his History was colored by conscious class bias, and its conspicuous features were a dominating preoccupation with property, the timidity that derives from it, and an intense search for security. With less reticence than is common with writers of his school, he wrote: "An essential condition for the perfect enjoyment of any possession is the certainty of enjoying it forever." And starting from this premise, he plotted the course of history accordingly. "You ask me what effect the publication of my History of Mexico and the Dissertation has had in Mexico," he wrote to a Spanish grandee whose estates in Mexico he administered. "The effect has been to change completely the idea held, as a result of revolutionary statements, about the Conquest, the Spanish domination, and the manner in which Independence was achieved. The Conquest was believed to be a real robbery, and hence your possessions were regarded as part of the theft, the nation entitled to recover them. . . . All this has been completely changed; you have only to see some of the speeches this year in which the Conquest is presented as the means by which civilization and religion were established in the country and Don Hernan Cortés as a remarkable man, appointed by Providence to accomplish these objects. . . . The advantages to you are obvious, since this has affected the odium with which your name and property were regarded and has secured you in their possession."

Himself a Creole aristocrat and hence not very far removed from his employer, Alaman deplored the course which Independence had taken in the hands of Hidalgo. He had grown up with the movement and was still haunted by the war cry against the *gachupines*—"a cry of death and desolation, which, after hearing it a thousand times in the first days of my youth, still rings in my ears with a terrifying echo!" Hidalgo was an incompetent visionary, whom he scolded for initiating a revolution which he could not control, rousing the rabble with the lure of plunder, and compelling the Creoles who would otherwise have joined it to combine against it, so that "the war became, not a struggle between those who wanted independence and those who opposed it, but the natural defense of those who did not wish to be despoiled of their property, against those who, following the direction which Hidalgo gave the revolution, had no other aim than to rob everyone to the tune of independence. . . . "No!" he concluded. "If independence could not be promoted by other methods, it should never have been attempted."

He preferred to date Independence from Iturbide, but when he scanned the years that followed it, his heart failed him. The grim and unrelenting progress of anarchy and impoverishment which they revealed was too much to stomach; and before attempting an account of those years he gave up and cursed the day on which his country was born. "This terrible Revolution, nevertheless, is what it has been sought to make the Mexican Republic recognize as its cradle," he exclaimed. "Divine Providence seems to have wished to inflict an exemplary punishment for that solemnity when it permitted, in the year 1847, in the very days in which I write these lines, the army of the United States, of that nation to which Mexicans looked in the beginning of their liberation as a natural friend and ally, to occupy the capital on the 14th of September and to wreak, and to allow the people to wreak, a terrible sack on the 15th and 16th, as if in reminder and imitation of the one Hidalgo made in Dolores and San Miguel on that same date." Trusting that a time would come when good sense would prevail over prejudice, and the original begetters of Independence would be recognized as the authors of all the evils of the country, he ended his account of the insurgent period despondently. "In the next volume we shall see other men, of different capacities and greater courage and fortune, follow the career that Hidalgo began with such ill success." But Alaman carried the history of Mexico no further. The next volume was life.

He returned to politics, flushed with the heat of battle among the shadows and insecure of success over the dead, to write the History of Alaman across the History of Mexico in one brief but remarkable page. The case of Alaman was the case of Mexico—an acute attack of heart failure—and he devoted himself to the recovery of his country with the knowledge he had acquired as an historian of their common infirmity. The cure was forecast in the arrested development of Volume One, in his nostalgia for the mother country and the characteristic craving of a class incapable of independence, and worsted by life, to return to the womb; since that was impossible, he could only approximate it in Volume Two. The cure was unpopular, and even the approximation required long and careful preparation; and he laid down the pen with the words: "If my work should have the effect of making the coming generation more cautious than the present one, I might flatter myself that I had produced the greatest benefit that can result from the study of history."

It would be too much to say that Alaman wrote his History to recommend that of his rival, though that was perhaps its most important result; but he did recommend the work of Dr. Mora to his friends, and not merely from professional generosity. After the collapse of his political debut in 1834, Dr. Mora had also passed into eclipse. The next twelve years of his life were spent in Paris, in exile and obscurity. Suffering from every kind of privation, secluded by a poverty that began by being genteel and that became monastic because it could not be bohemian, and that degenerated into such bare need that he begged the Legation for work at the wages of a menial; wasted by consumption and homesickness; subsisting on small remittances from his friends in Mexico; starving for the company of his intellectual equals and refusing that of his inferiors; solitary, proud, and fastidious, he was driven in on his mental resources, which were rich but unrewarding. In 1837 a French publisher brought out the first part of a projected work on *Mexico and Its Revolutions,* and in the following year a small sheaf of his *Collected Works,* both abandoned for lack of sale. These two fragments, which comprised the whole of his literary output, found no public in Paris, where the revolutions of Mexico were as remote as those of Saturn as a topic of popular interest; and none in Mexico, where the phenomena were too familiar to merit attention, save from a small circle of connoisseurs, particularly his political opponents, and above all from Alaman, who gave them the respectful attention due to a member of his class who had deserted it. For Dr. Mora had been born into the Creole aristocracy and, despite his radical views, retained one of its privileges—authority. The critical success which he won in 1838 remained the secret of a coterie, however, until the crisis of the American war led to a general reassessment of the past. Then his work was rediscovered and read as the Liberal antidote to the theses of Alaman and his party.

In their methods the two men had something in common. Alaman set himself an ideal of sobriety and moderation and was determined to be scrupulously scientific and impartial; but in practice his prepossessions violated his principles, and even when he observed them he produced an account of the Independence movement which depreciated and falsified it. The result was tame—a tone of flat and perfunctory justice, devoid of the sympathy and insight essential to the truth, and an estimate based on an obvious fallacy: a dispassionate account of any revolution was bound to misrepresent it. Dr. Mora made no such mistakes. He did not pretend to write history impartially; but he did write it scientifically. His habits of mind were analytical, and his logic, his objectivity, and his conscientiousness gave his work genuine weight and detachment; and his measure and sobriety were the result of judgment and experience, not of a covert desire to depreciate. Of revolution he wrote as a revolutionary, retired but not in retreat, and undismayed by the brute facts that alarmed Alaman; he never forgot that his country was condemned by its very origin to a revolutionary growth. Writing, moreover, against a European background, he brought to bear on his subject a universal perspective, a grasp of historical processes, and a capacity for broad and fundamental generalizations, in overwhelming contrast to the parochial bias that cramped the judgment of his rival. Time and distance had confirmed and sharpened his convictions; but they had also refined and qualified them and made him so discriminating in their application that at times his ideas seemed to touch those of his opponents, and thus it was that he could be read with appreciation by Alaman. A successful antidote contains, after all, an effective dose of the original virus; and the vaccine supplied by Dr. Mora was no exception.

Mora was still the reformer bent on completing the emancipation of Mexico, and his history was a militant analysis of the miscarriage of the Independence movement. Believing no less absolutely than Alaman in the sanctity of property, he deplored the looting and carnage of the uprising, but put them promptly in their place. "The revolution which broke out in 1810 was as necessary for the attainment of Independence as it was pernicious and destructive to the country," he argued, because it was indispensable to interest the popular classes in the insurrection, and this could not be done by the sole promise of remote and unknown benefits to follow, or by abstract ideas of justice. "It was necessary to cater to the prejudices of the multitude in order to secure their co-operation." Hidalgo he judged as severely as Alaman did, because he had failed to plan the result for which he was responsible—the gravest charge that a systematic ideologist like Mora could bring against the first begetter of that chaos which he called his country. What prejudiced the whole subsequent history of Mexico, however, was not the beginning but the end of the movement, which had left the social structure of the colony intact and its correction to future generations, themselves unprepared for the task. Under the name of a republic there had emerged something incompatible with it, or with public spirit, or patriotism, or national life—a corporate state. Whether by accident or design, Spain had bequeathed to its offspring the feudal infirmity from which it suffered—a tendency to create corporations, to accumulate upon them privileges and exemptions from the common law, to enrich them with donations from living or testamentary legacies, and to endow them, in short, with every requisite for independence. Not only the Church and the Army, but the Inquisition, the Universities, the Mint, the *Majorats,* the Confraternities, and even the Guilds, had their privileges, property, and corporate existence; and the mentality which they bred was fatal to national life and prosperity, public peace and morality, and judicial and administrative order. Had Independence been achieved forty years earlier, a man born in the territory would have attached no value to the name of "Mexican" and would have considered himself completely alone in the world, if he had nothing else to support him: his interests and his loyalties lay with the body, or bodies, to which he belonged; and this habit still subsisted. As Mora said, when social conscience or civil authority conflict with the *esprit de corps,* "the principal aim is to vindicate the corporation, to establish its exclusive jurisdiction, and to depress the civil authority. If these purposes can be reconciled with the punishment of the criminal and the observance of the criminal and penal laws, no obstacle is raised to the one or the other, but if, as frequently happens, the course of justice is, or is believed to be, in opposition to the corporate interests, the former will infallibly be sacrificed to the latter." And the damage to the civil authority did not end with moral disabilities, to which men adapt themselves easily. "The greatest obstacle against which the prosperity of nations has to contend is the tendency to interdict, accumulate, and unite lands and capitals eternally. From the day that society allows a given fortune to accumulate indefinitely, with no need of dividing it, it is clear that nothing is needed but the passage of a few centuries for the means of subsistence to become very difficult or fail entirely for the mass. The result is solely and exclusively due to *political corporations,* and a nation in which they succeed in multiplying or, even though they be few, in spreading throughout society, has already broached the abyss in which the public fortune is certain to be lost."

Independence, then, had produced a corporate state which tolerated and controlled the civil authority, and which was the negation of national life. The epitome of the whole system was the Church, which had created a theocratic state within the nominal one, and which Mora indicted, count by count, as an antisocial body by its constitution: because the clergy were composed "of men who are only materially in society and in accidental co-existence with their fellow citizens"; because they were educated to value none but heavenly interests and to identify them with the supremacy of their corporation; because by their celibacy they were without the bond of family, "the first and principal tie of man to society"; because they were forbidden to engage in lucrative enterprises, "and thus are extinguished the love of labor and the betterment of fortune which are the necessary consequence of individual industry and which create the second link with society"; because of their invincible aversion to religious toleration and freedom of thought and of the press, since these principles weaken their hold upon consciences; because of their opposition to legal equality," which eliminates their privileges and hierarchies and the power and consideration which these confer on their class"; because they were a permanent obstacle to the increase of population by defeating foreign immigration, lest it carry the germ of religious toleration; because of the monopoly and sterilization of the national resources, which they controlled and immobilized; and because their monopoly of education was responsible for the ignorance not only of the masses but, more important, of the classes. Here Dr. Mora spoke from bitter experience. He recalled, with the same horror with which Alaman remembered the vandalism of the insurgents, the years of his youth, which he had spent in the College of San Ildefonso. Here he had won honors and knowledge and had seen the effect on the average mind of an education which unfitted the ruling classes for their functions, because its unworldly character debauched them for life. "He who has been educated in a College has seen with his own eyes that, of all that has been told and taught him there, little or nothing is applicable to the uses of ordinary life; that the latter lies under other laws, which are unknown to him, of which no one has spoken to him, and the foundations of which are those common and ordinary needs that are never made the subject of study but are abandoned to *routine*. . . . This is the origin of the charlatanism of Mexico and of the people who have undertaken to govern it, graduates for the most part of our College. Accustomed to talk of improvements merely to display what are called their talents, and never attempting to realize them since they hold them to be ideal and impossible, they cling to the routine which, whether good or bad, is what has served them as a rule of practical conduct."

So, foreshortened, Dr. Mora traced the history of Mexico during his time, but he was not dismayed by his findings. He reiterated the prescriptions of his original program: confiscation of Church property, abolition of clerical and military privileges, diffusion of secular education among the popular classes, suppression of nunneries, absolute freedom of opinion, and equal civil rights for natives and foreigners. But if he retracted nothing and disavowed nothing, he did qualify and refine some of his leading ideas. Confounded himself by the incompetence of his countrymen, which he had so lucidly demonstrated, he found himself asking how far liberty was compatible with equality. "The mischievous meaning given to the principle of *legal equality* has almost always been the source of innumerable disappointments and pernicious results among those peoples that have adopted the representative system. The greatest of the evils caused in our Republic by this dangerous and fateful word has lain in the scandalous profusion with which we have lavished political rights, extending them to the lowest classes of society. . . . To restore the political structure, Congress should determine the conditions for exercising the rights of citizenship throughout the Republic, and these should exclude all those who can inspire no confidence: that is, the non-proprietors. . . . As a general rule, the owners of property alone have genuine civic virtues; beneficence, dignity of person and manners, love of the public good, are virtually the exclusive attributes of property-owners. . . ."

So wrote Mora, and not Alaman. Such a formula for freedom was not very alarming to his Conservative opponents who could read him, as they did, with the calm assurance that, despite his radicalism in some directions, he was essentially sound. And to the Liberal youth who turned to him as an antidote for Alaman it was sobering to find the lifelong enthusiast for freedom reducing liberty to a privilege, available to anyone who could put up a bond for it, and denied to those who lacked the necessary property qualifications.

Nor was this the only sobering conclusion of his History. For the heirs of the Mexican revolution he had some cooling reflections to make on the cost of revolution. Revolutions had their own routine. He drew a didactic distinction between those which arose from a direct cause and produced an immediate effect—"these are the fortunate revolutions: people know what they want, all move toward a

recognized aim, and when it is attained everything returns to rest"—
the English and American revolutions, for example; and those "that
derive from a general movement in the spirit of nations. By the turn
that opinions take, men tire of being what they are, the prevailing
order irks them in every way, their minds become suffused with an
extraordinary ardor and activity; everyone feels dissatisfied with the
place which he occupies and longs to change his condition, but no one
knows precisely what he wants, and everything resolves itself into discontent and unrest. Such are the symptoms of those long crises to
which no direct and exact cause can be assigned . . . and which would
be an endless chain of disasters, revolutions, and crimes if chance, and,
even more than chance, general exhaustion, did not bring them to a
close"—the French Revolution for example—a warning example for
Mexico, which derived its inspiration from it. "An impatience all the
more hasty in its attacks that it is vague in its desires is what produced
the first upheaval. . . . Everyone abandons himself to that sensation
without reserve or remorse. Everyone supposes that the equilibrium of
society is so firmly grounded that nothing can destroy it and forgets
that the interests and opinions of the many cannot be fermented with
impunity." Anarchy, and the natural ferocity of man, make short work
of the brief boast of civilization, "and then it is that fearlessness of
judgment begins to weaken, the dread of deceiving oneself increases,
and the confidence with which one risked everything on the frail securities of human reason ceases. But before these saving deceptions
come, one must pass through all the succession of calamities that *idealism* brings with it."

The brute realities of revolution alarmed him no less than Alaman,
when its scope could no longer be localized, limited, and controlled,
when purpose and plan were dissolved in indefinite restlessness, when
the partial dislocation of society threatened the whole, when the safeguards of reason and the tight system of idealists were swept away by
the relentless momentum of nature, and the revolution became, in a
word, a revolution of Saturn. Then Mora found himself facing a void
in which the heavenly bodies and the celestial corporations overhead,
and the corporate state and the state of nature below, were all beyond
control; and his heart failed him. The very vagueness of his words revealed the vertigo with which he contemplated such convulsions.
Clinging to the confines of his world, he traced with undisguised dismay the phases of the French Revolution in a long downward spiral:
from the philanthropists who began it, to the doctrinaires who followed them, to the cranks repeating "literally and without social modifications what certain books say about 'liberty' and 'equality,'" down
to the parvenus who parroted and the idealists who depraved them,
down to the fanatics and the freethinkers, whose errors were excusable
because they were blind to their spawn, down to the self-seekers, the

cynics, the demagogues, to the Terror, to the Reaction. "When matters have come to this point," the homily ended, "and men have grown weary of suffering, they profit by any favorable opportunity to bring about a change, and then things recede by the same stages but in reverse order. Happy the people that does not return to its point of departure, for then, without having bettered its condition in any way, it will have had to pass through all the horrors of a revolution."

What was this? a caveat or a confession? the morphology of revolutions or of Dr. Mora? Had he carried the History of Mexico as far as the History of Mora could go? Had the clear-sighted scientist finally been baffled by his vision of revolutionary routine, and forsaken the dictates of reason for the promptings of fatality? His counsel was clear, his state of mind ambiguous. The oracular utterance was open to any interpretation, and his work was crowned by the tongueless mask of tragedy. If this was his last word, a Conservative might well mistake it for a retraction; while the Liberals might equally feel that the labors of Mora, like those of Alaman, were addressed to the coming generation as a caution.

But neither man had spoken his last word when he laid down the pen. In 1847, when Gomez Farias returned to power for a few months, Mora was appointed Minister to London. In this war post—for in the crisis of American invasion it was such—he was called upon to defend his country against another foreign danger, the English debt.

This question was as old as Independence, and a growing mortgage upon it. The origin of the nation and of the debt were so closely related, indeed, as to be inseparable: both were the settlement of old scores with Spain. Spain paid for her part in promoting the revolt of the British colonies in North America when her own empire broke up, for British diplomacy was everywhere directed to aiding, abetting, and promoting the movements of secession in her colonies in the southern hemisphere. "I have called a new world into being," Canning boasted, taking a leaf out of Genesis and fanning himself with it. Though he took no part in the emancipation of Mexico, he extended his protection to the infant Republic when it was threatened by the Holy Alliance, and his was the first foreign government to recognize it—favors that were followed by the contraction of the debt. Two loans were floated in London to enable the new nation to begin life and to open a new market and a fresh sphere of influence for English trade, investment, and enterprise. The money sank into the quicksands of Mexican politics. Ten years passed before the mines, into which British capital was pumped, could be restored; trade languished under high protective tariffs, which fostered nothing but contraband; political turbulence and instability cooled the confidence of English investors.

The benefits evaporated, the obligation remained; and the debt accumulated under periodic conversions, which afforded only a fleeting relief to one party and growing irritation to the other, while successive administrations in Mexico ignored the liability, which each passed on to the next.

The first serious attempt to deal with it was made by Mora and Farias in 1834, when they proposed to liquidate it by confiscating Church property—a measure which failed to materialize but which prompted the clergy to liquidate some of their assets in anticipation of its passage: a nervous financial leak quickly dried by the dismissal of the reformers. "Then it was," Mora wrote, "that the depths of the abyss into which the Republic was insensibly sinking began to be suspected. 'Suspected' is the proper word to describe the state of neglect in which the parliamentary tribune, the public authorities, and the periodic press had left matters requiring urgent settlement and a branch of administration of the foremost and most vital importance." No ordinary resources were available: territorial property was bankrupt, the mines had not yet recovered from the slump in which the Spanish had left them, industry was embryonic, commerce was overtaxed, and the national revenues were overhypothecated. The confiscation of Church property was the only alternative to financial collapse and the abyss at the bottom of which lay blind revolution.

Thirteen years later, when Dr. Mora was called upon to deal with the debt again, the problem remained where he had left it, but in the meanwhile it had been aggravated by neglect and improvidence, and the economic debility of the country had been demonstrated in the two collisions with the United States. These conflicts affected the protector as well as the people of Mexico. Along with the commercial empire of Spain, the English had fallen heir to the fears of its former masters, and when the American war defeated and dismembered a country which British capital had transformed into a virtual dependency of the British empire, the bad debt became a matter of official concern in London, where the credit of Mexico, diplomatic and financial alike, reached a new low.

Dr. Mora saved it. He succeeded in negotiating yet another conversion of the bonds, whose accumulation for over a quarter of a century, and with it of periodic lapses, conversions, and defaults, had given his country a bad name and made its future problematical in the financial center of the world. And the feat was accomplished with nothing more substantial than promises. His success was facilitated, however, by the expectation that some part of the millions which the United States agreed to pay Mexico as indemnity for conquered territory would be applied to the British debt. As the British government by no means desired •the extinction of a claim which guaranteed its control of a dependent people, it was possible for Mora and the creditors to come to an understanding—the soundness of nations being rated, like that of individuals, by the amount of indebtedness they can bear.

By this transaction Dr. Mora benefited as much as Mexico. What his country gained was another reprieve; what he gained was fresh confirmation of the necessity of a radical reform of Mexican economy, if the crisis which he had averted were not to recur in an aggravated form in the future. In the counting-houses of London the historian of Mexico gained a better perspective on his country than in his study in Paris. He was now in a position to supply the element lacking in the philosophical sketch which he had begun and abandoned there, and which was indispensable to complete the account of a feudal colony born into the contemporary world of expanding capitalism and compelled to contend with it for national survival. All the weaknesses which he had analyzed in Paris gained fresh point in London, where they carried their inevitable penalty in the growing drain of foreign debt, foreign exploitation, foreign claims, and the risk of foreign complications based on those titles. Henceforth the history of Mexico had to be written internationally: it could no longer be isolated from the world and studied apart from its context. The American war marked a turning point in its destiny. Until then it had been possible to chronicle it partially and retrospectively: from now on it was necessary to relate it to the future and to chart its course scientifically as part of a comprehensive and developing process common to the whole Western world, where the social and political forces active in any one part excited a sympathetic reaction in every other, because the commonwealth of nations was a corporation controlled by the same economic system, and a nervous complex in which the weakest and most vulnerable members were liable to the most violent reactions. As the world went, so would Mexico go, once it was involved in its movements, and all the more readily because of its remoteness, and all the more blindly because of its backwardness. By 1848 that fact was appreciated even in Mexico.

If 1847 was a grim year for Mexico, 1848 was an alarming one for Europe: the year in which revolutions broke out at one point after another on the Continent with a contagious agitation that seemed to presage another of those epidemics that Dr. Mora dreaded—a general movement in the spirit of nations—an indefinite unrest, uncontrollable urges, and universal subversion—another peevish cycle of Saturn, perhaps. In 1848, however, the symptoms were specific and consistent with a definite disorder, which they revealed in various degrees, ranging from nationalism and the insurrection of oppressed minorities in Italy, Hungary, and Poland to socialism and the insurrection of oppressed masses in France and Germany: recognizable symptoms of a period of expanding capitalism whose promises of freedom inspired the movements of national liberation on the one hand, and whose practices of exploitation provoked popular revolts on the other.

The bearing of these events on Mexico were discussed by Mora and his friends with acute concern. "You are quite right in your observation," one of them wrote, "that because of the excesses which the revolution in Europe has committed, we must fear a reaction that will set things far back again; but I believe that will not happen for some time and not without much trouble and bloodshed. When the peoples are not controlled by a religious principle and respect for the higher classes, and aspire to share or possess the property of the rich, they will not readily give ground." The February revolution in Paris, which overthrew the monarchy of Louis-Philippe at the behest of the bourgeoisie which had created it, only to be transformed by the revolutionary proletariat into the insurrection of June against the middle class, alarmed them particularly. "As soon as I saw that the revolution in France, after destroying the monarchy, threatened property and the family," his correspondent continued, "I feared a reaction. And will not the reaction reach us?"

Precisely. The disorders in France were followed, in fact, by a reflex movement in Mexico, all the more dangerous because resistance was weaker and revolution endemic there. "Here the *Santannists* and the *Puros,* who are our socialists, are making extraordinary efforts to bring about a revolution," Mora was informed—a symptom which would have been insignificant but for the troubles in France, which gave irresponsible politicians and inexperienced reformers a pretext to hitch to foreign issues the casual disorders which were called revolutions in Mexico. The danger lay not in a rising of a revolutionary proletariat, since no such thing existed in Mexico, but in the fear of it which had haunted the upper classes there ever since the days of Hidalgo, and of a reaction to anticipate it.

Symptoms of this tendency appeared with the development of a monarchist party, which had begun to emerge before the American war and which gained momentum after it, when the slump favored two fears upon which the propaganda of the party played: the specter of foreign socialism and the dread of another American invasion if the country relapsed into disorder—both fictitious but sufficient to make them look to Europe for support. Mora was warned by Palmerston that bids were being made in Paris for a pretender, and though they were arrested by the February revolution, the movement was resumed under another name, but with the same latent aims, by a group of conservatives whose mentor was Lucas Alaman. The counterpart of the foreign crisis was already discernible in Mexico, albeit in embryo, and both tendencies bore watching in a defeated and demoralized country peculiarly susceptible to the promptings of postwar revolution and counterrevolution. Their morbid significance was recognized by Mora and his friends. "As for our internal questions, all of them founded on the basis of nationality," they warned him, "there are two parties which are fortifying themselves in silence and which tend, one to a foreign monarchy and the other to aggregation to the United States; and what seems incredible, both these parties derive from the same idea, our inability to govern ourselves."

Once again his friends turned to Mora for guidance. His position in London was a post of observation which commanded a broad view of the world and a clearing-house of accurate information where he could detect at once the connection between a commotion on one side of the water and its seemingly unrelated counterpart on the other. But his friends placed him in a cruel predicament. For socialism he had no sympathy; if a reaction provoked by it threatened to set things far back in Europe, how much further would a similar movement carry them in a backward country like Mexico! To press his radical ideas in the treacherous situation prevailing there after the American war, at the risk of foreign complications and an incalculable setback to the progress of his country, was a responsibility from which he shrank; and his friends turned to him for advice in vain. The situation was critical and complicated and called for just such leadership as with his courage, his clarity, and his intimate knowledge of European and Mexican politics he was fitted to give; but the call came too late. History had overtaken him, and he had reached the end of his revolutionary development. Morally he was paralyzed, and physically he was stricken. Consumption, the lifelong companion which had fattened on his years of privation and exile, now compelled him to abandon all his activities. He returned to Paris and entered a nursing home. In his last weeks of life he found himself almost at home under that Second Republic, which with its murky intrigues and multitudinous political combinations seemed to be Mexicanizing France. His friends continued to consult him. They were relieved by the triumph of the liberal bourgeoisie and the Constitution which had been worked out for France under the formula "Property, Religion, Family, and Order," but uncertain of its stability and worried by the election of Louis Napoleon to the Presidency of the Republic and rumors that he was planning a *coup d'état*. But their questions remained unanswered, for these matters were now of very remote interest to Dr. Mora. On July 14, 1850, with the echoes of some sort of a national celebration ringing dimly in his brain, he died.

The last word which Dr. Mora did not live to speak was his legacy to the coming generation. To the liberal youth who looked to him for guidance he left an example of fearless independence and a clear-cut plan of reform, clouded at the last by the difficulties which delay had raised to its application. But where was the coming generation? Where, in 1850, were the liberal youth old enough to embrace his cautious and contracting counsels and young enough to fight for them? That generation had been long in coming and was now middle-aged, and it had produced no outstanding men. Here and there a promising name appeared, and whenever a likely disciple crossed his path the master welcomed him, but few of them were affluent enough to travel and none of them sufficiently formidable to be forced into exile. In 1840 Melchor Ocampo had come to Paris and paid his respects to the famous expatriate, but the meeting was not fortunate and the visit was not repeated. "He is as sententious as a Tacitus," Ocampo wrote home, "as partial as a reformer, and as arrogant as an ecclesiastic." The comment illumined both men. Mora had been subdued too long, perhaps, to the element in which he worked, his mind was steeped in it and his soul dyed by it, and Ocampo had no pretensions to be a reformer himself at that time. Ten years later he modified his opinion, when he served for a few months as Minister of Finance in Mexico, and wrote a sympathetic note to the invalid, dilating on his own difficulties. But in 1850 Mora was a dying man, and Ocampo a beginner. The mantle went begging.

And stature was needed to fill it. The specifications for a successful reformer were laid down by Dr. Mora in a self-portrait. Being modeled on himself, they were exacting and, like everything he laid down, hard to meet: "Cold in his passions and invariable in his designs," he began; a broad culture, above all in the moral, political, and economic sciences, he added; a superior character, independent, disinterested, courageous, unassuming, human—moral aristocracy, in a word. On these virtues he prided himself. But where in Mexico was the man who could lay claim to such qualities and not be buried by them? Mora had written his own obituary. And if the candidate had the vocation, he could claim only half the succession; for who could combine the call, the character, and the training, with the ripe experience which Mora had gained and the mature understanding of cosmopolitan conditions necessary to further the cause of reform after the American war? With Mora the great breed seemed to have died and the cause to have come to a halt. The dead end the nation had reached was manifest in the prostration of public life; exhaustion and war weariness were so general that the succession went unclaimed. The old men, accordingly, continued to rule, despite their tragic incompetence, and the old thinkers returned to the scene.

But the old thinkers returned in a radical role. Alaman was timid by nature, and fear was the foundation of his political philosophy, but fear forced him to take a bold position when he returned to political life, and the apprehension which dictated his activities drove him to adopt an erratic defense of a radical reaction. He became the mentor of a party that was monarchical in all but name. The name was anathema in Mexico; the first propagandist to advocate monarchy in Mexico—a man by the name of Gutierrez Estrada—had been forced to emigrate in 1840; and though the idea had gained some ground since then and had been openly agitated before the war, it still provoked riots at political rallies. When Alaman ran for office, he was abused as an "absolutist," a "Bourbonist," an "antipatriot," an "enemy of Independence," and these epithets continued to be hurled at him despite his denials; for the historian who had written the history of Mexico as an apology for Cortés and a dirge for Independence and closed it with a tribute to Iturbide as the real founder of the nation had shown too clearly where his heart lay to conceal the umbilical vein that made it beat. He denied that he was a monarchist, and truthfully; for after the bids made for a pretender in Paris were nipped by revolution in France, they were dropped in Mexico. The year 1848 was unfavorable to monarchy everywhere, and Alaman adapted himself to the times, following the advice of Mora that "the wisest and surest way of preventing the revolutions of men is to appreciate the revolution of time, and to grant what it demands." He won a seat in Congress, but his party was beaten at the polls and compelled to mark time. The more they gave ground, the more there was to give. In 1851 the first socialist paper appeared in Mexico, and the first strike; the economic slump fermented in a flare of race war, and Melchor Ocampo caught the attention of the country by his polemic with the curate of Maravatio—straws in the wind that indicated the drift of the times to men possessed of foresight and fear. In Mexico they were drifting helplessly with the trend of the times, while in France the feeble figment of the Republic was abolished by the *coup d'état* of Louis Napoleon. "We call ourselves Conservatives because we wish to preserve the feeble life still left in this poor society," they declared in their profession of faith; but how much longer could they do so by remaining on the defensive? how much longer before they applied the caustic touch to tears? With every passing year the choice of revolution or counterrevolution became more pressing, the middle way more difficult, and marking time more dangerous.

Mora and his friends had predicted that the reaction to '48 would not come for some time in Europe, that it would be bitterly contested, and that it would reach Mexico. In the tail of their deductions they were correct. In Mexico the truce lasted as long as the American millions stabilized the government; when they gave out the reaction came. But it came not as a result of any revolutionary upsurge, but as a counterrevolution to forestall it. Promoted by fear and prompted by a state of mind which by no means corresponded to the state of the nation, the effect of the prophylactic was to provoke the actual revolution against which the preventive had been invented. The last word which

Mora did not live to speak was brought forth by Alaman, and it was
Absit omen!

In 1853 the government was overthrown by a mutiny, and Alaman
and his party came to power uncontested. The mutiny would have
been insignificant but for the driving forces that rallied behind it. It
began as a mere barracks revolt and was already failing when it was
adopted by the clergy and the landowners as a protection against their
premonitions of a coming wave of reform. They bought into it on a
falling market, in a panic so acute that the slightest alarm was sufficient to stampede them, and it was a very small threat that started
them. The sponsors were many, but who was responsible for the movement was less important than what—a state of mind that was prepared
for any extremities and a wave of panic that demanded strong measures, and strong men, to check it. A plan was drawn by Alaman, but
Alaman was an ideologist, and strong men were so scarce at that moment in Mexico that neither the scent of the scholar nor the instinct of
the herd could uncover one. But there was always Santa Anna. Santa
Anna, accordingly, was recalled from exile to put the plan into effect.
The conditions of his return, and the origins and aims of the movement, were explained to him by Alaman in a letter which laid bare
the melancholy anatomy of society and the feeble life left in it in 1853.
The responsibility for the reaction was allowed in equal shares to
three men. The author of the plan was Alaman himself; the authority
to enact it was entrusted to Santa Anna; and the credit for it went to
Ocampo, to whose parochial feud with the curate of Maravatio Alaman attributed the whole movement. "The one who really began the
revolution," he wrote, "was the Governor of Michoacan, Don Melchor
Ocampo, by the impious principles which he developed in matters of
faith, the reforms which he attempted in parochial fees, and the alarming measures which he announced against the landowners and with
which he aroused the clergy and the proprietors of that state. Once the
revolution had been begun by Bahamonde, by a chance accident that
of Guadalajara broke out, but it would not have progressed had the
clergy and the proprietors not declared for the plan, and from then on
one thing conspired with another, as happens in all revolutions when
there is great discontent, until it ended in your recall and election to
the Presidency in the hope that you would come and put an end to the
general dissatisfaction which the whole nation feels. This, and this
alone, is the revolution through which you are returning to the soil of
your country."

It was in the tone of a master that Alaman explained the aims of a
movement upon which he had grafted his ideas, and of which he remained the mentor and the guide. "The first is the preservation of the

Catholic religion, because we believe in it and because, even if we did not consider it divine, we regard it as the only common tie that binds all Mexicans now that all others are broken, and the only one capable of maintaining the Spanish-American race and saving it from the great danger to which it is exposed. We believe also in the necessity of maintaining the cult in splendor and supporting the property of the Church and in settling everything pertaining to ecclesiastical administration with the Pope. But it is not true, as some papers have said to discredit us, that we desire the return of the Inquisition or persecutions, although we believe that the circulation of impious or immoral books should be prohibited by public authority." The creed was adapted to the times: no Inquisition, no persecutions, but also no republican nonsense. "We are against the Federation; against the representative system by means of elections as they have been hitherto practiced, and against everything that goes by the name of popular elections until they rest on a different foundation. . . . We are convinced that nothing of all this can be accomplished by Congress and we want you to do it, assisted by a few advisers who will prepare your work. These are the essential points of our political faith. We have explained it frankly and loyally, for we make no mystery of our opinions, and to realize these ideas we count on general opinion, which is decidedly in favor of them and which we direct through the leading papers of the capital and the states, which are all ours. We rely on the moral force of conformity among the clergy, the proprietors, and all sensible people. . . . We believe that you will be in favor of these ideas, but if not, we fear that it will go ill with our country and even with you. In that case, I beg you to burn this letter and to give it no further thought."

Santa Anna returned and not only conformed, but put the program into effect with a gratuitous force which nothing but the fear of a genuine revolution could justify. There was no opposition; the pseudo-revolution was directed against imaginary enemies, and real ones were invited and created by men who suffered from a sense of persecution themselves and who were endowed with excessive caution and foresight. Measures of public safety were taken, and Santa Anna added his own to them. His first step was to rid the country of undesirable persons: a list of proscriptions was drawn up, but it was short and insignificant, for strong men were few in the ranks of the enemy as well as in those of the prosecution. Only two men seemed sufficiently dangerous to be invested with the mantle of Mora. One was Ocampo, who was expelled from the country without explanation or delay. The other was Juarez.

After completing his term as Governor of Oaxaca in 1852, Juarez had returned to the Institute as its director and to his law practice. His clients were still the poor, and his cases took him into the Sierra. He had just completed one in Ixtlan and started another in an outlying *pueblo* when he was arrested there, on May 27, 1853, and escorted out of the state with a picket of cavalry, but without explanation other than a passport specifying as his destination the town of Jalapa, capital of the State of Veracruz and seat of Santa Anna's ancestral estates. Here he was held under police surveillance for seventy-five days, his arrest still unexplained and his destination still undetermined, baited by conflicting orders to proceed to other points and bluffed by official uncertainties and despotic delays. Despite his repeated protests, the authorities remained inscrutable until the seventy-sixth day, when he was put into a coach by the son of Santa Anna and driven to Veracruz. There he was confined with the same studied mystery in the fortress of Ulua, and after spending twelve days in a cell below sea-level, he was told to pack, handed a passport for Europe, and placed on board the English packet. No provision had been made for his passage, and as he was penniless, the passengers took up a collection and paid his fare to the first port of call. He landed at Havana and made his way to New Orleans; and there he found a little group of fellow exiles ready to reconstitute the country from which they had been driven. In their company Juarez discovered his destination at last.

IO

THE designs of Santa Anna were as mysterious as those of Providence; but in the designs of Providence it was reserved for Santa Anna, himself so lacking in foresight and spurred by men oversupplied with it, to determine, in a supreme triumph of improvidence, the destiny of Juarez. The proscription of Ocampo was the logical consequence of his activity as an agitator—he was a plausible peril; but the name of Juarez carried no revolutionary challenge in 1853. He was an inoffensive Liberal known only for his model government of Oaxaca. In his own community he was a man of some consequence, but not until he was deported did he belong to the world and begin to make his way in it as an outcast. He was forty-seven and he had done little to redeem the high hopes with which he had been hailed in youth as the coming man of the Liberal cause; the promise so long deferred had grown dim, and though his faith had not failed, it had lost much of its driving power in the prudence, the timeserving, the compromises with which it had been applied. He was a safe man, and he had reached an age when most men have already revealed themselves and the habits of life have set, and with every passing year the setbacks accumulated: the settled ways of maturity, the satisfaction of a little success, the bonds of family, the claims and the comforts of security, the sedative marriage of the depths and the shallows—everything conspired to dull the slackening fires of youth. Then suddenly the blow fell: picked up overnight and dragooned out of the country, cut off from all his securities and cast into the unknown, he was uprooted and restored to his mission by the implacable memory of Santa Anna.

For if the designs of Santa Anna were mysterious, they were not inscrutable. It was no casual whim but the logical mind of a man for whom politics and personalities were inseparable that drove Santa Anna to settle old scores with the upstart who had expelled him from his state six years before. That motive remained a mystery to Juarez, who attached so little importance to the incident in 1847 that he saw no connection between it and his banishment in 1853. He attributed his proscription to the normal upset of politics and the intrigues of local foes and friends eager to ingratiate themselves with the new shift, "ambitious and vulgar men," as he said, "who made a place for themselves by sacrificing a man whose sole interest in government was to do his duty without injuring them." And it was in a spirit of injured innocence that he bore a blow that he sincerely believed he had done nothing to deserve. "I resigned myself to my fate," he wrote, "without uttering a complaint, without committing a humiliating action." These were not the words of a rebel, and they proved his political innocence.

But besides Santa Anna, there was the party. So far from suspecting that his fate had any political significance, however, he minimized it as a purely personal misfortune. He was known as a conscientious official and it never occurred to him that the combination might be as dangerous as the iconoclasm of Ocampo. How could he suppose that the good government he had made there in a nonpartisan and even conservative spirit might be as menacing to the reaction as a deliberate provocation? He was a sensible man; and it would have required uncommon credulity to believe that so safe an example might be challenging to a party obsessed by its own insecurity, or that so conservative a success would be considered subversive merely because it was achieved by a Liberal. He realized the psychology of reaction so little that he believed himself to be the victim of a political accident instead of a political rule. He had yet to learn that all his years of conformity were wasted, that compromise with reaction was impossible, and that in times of social tension no man was innocuous or inoffensive. That lesson was learned fully and finally, however, in exile, where he fell in with a group of refugees who had suffered the same fate and who were determined to profit by it and finish what Santa Anna had begun. None of them was remarkable minus his misfortune except Ocampo, whom he met there for the first time and with whom he formed a fruitful friendship.

Ocampo was not a rebel by nature. Bred in the closed world of the Creole aristocracy, he had acquired many of the mental habits of his class and the moral bent of a sheltered life before he broke with them. Of a lucifer he had no brand but an obscure origin. He was the adopted or natural son of a lady celebrated under the colonial regime for the great luxury, the great retinue, and the great charity which she displayed once a year, when she drove up from her estates in Michoacan to spend Holy Week in the capital. His father was reputed to be a patriot who found refuge under her roof during the years of insurgency. Whatever his origin, the boy had good blood and honored it at an early age. His mother died before he reached his majority. With her estates he inherited her habits of prodigal charity, and within a few years was so deep in debt that one day in 1840 he disappeared, mystifying his guardian by a wild tale of having been mistaken for a political enemy of Santa Anna, beaten, abducted, and shipped off to Europe. But on arriving in Paris he confessed the truth. "Without means to cover my debts, I was certain soon to appear in my real character," he wrote, "that is, as a lunatic who, partly because of a foolish vanity and partly because of injudicious bounty, had preferred for the past three years to discharge the obligations his prodigal promises had contracted rather than to attend to the sacred ones of his real duty. I had insensibly acquired such a reputation for generosity that not a week passed, nor a day in the seven, when I was not approached with a fresh request. . . . Weak and unable to say no, I could not cure the disease at the root and I could see nothing ahead but bitter mortification, belated remorse, and merited shame. . . . It was imperative to avoid all this in time, and the only means that my overwrought imagination could find was flight. . . ." He ran away with himself no further, however. He vowed to reform and to acquire the habit of work, "which has never been very deep-rooted and which the false prosperity of the last few years had led me to lose," and when he improved, to return to his country and to serve it with what he had learned by self-discipline. "There is no worse torment, sir," he concluded, "than merited self-contempt."

In Paris the young spendthrift spent several months of penitential poverty, steadfastly refusing relief from home lest his critics, as he said, "might take my poverty for a refined hypocrisy and all my actions as so many falsehoods." He practiced his privations, moreover, with a sharp eye on his motives. "Although my need was great," he admitted, "I think that the sense of vanity which prompted me to prove those stories untrue was stronger than hunger, nakedness, and my unwilling-

ness to cause you any further embarrassment." Vanity! the word was
always under his pen and the thing under his foot, and though he was
always on guard against it, it was elusive and assumed the most protean forms; and when he detected it lurking in his self-denial as he had
in his self-indulgence, he broke his fast. A little legitimate income having reached him from Michoacan, he decided to travel. After all, there
were other places for self-improvement than Paris and other forms of
it than self-mortification, and to waste the opportunities which Europe
afforded for a liberal education was the height of improvidence. He
made a walking trip through France and Italy, and the impressions
which he collected were not those with which young men of his class
returned from the grand tour. In Rome he was struck by the universal
mendicity which he saw luxuriating there: "The multitude of beggars
is amazing, the Pope, the bishops, the priests, friars, magistrates, employees, citizens, all beg alms." The lawlessness of the Papal State reminded him of Mexico—the roads were so infested with robbers that
he returned to France by sea. But his observations were those of a casual sightseer, and the principal benefit of his travels was that he returned to Paris sufficiently broadened to be critical of subjects other
than himself.

It was at this time that he met Mora. The reaction was unfavorable
and significant. He found him opinionated and overpowering, he disliked his dogmatism, he suspected his ardor, he doubted his disinterestedness, and he granted him nothing but intellectual discipline and
fluency and eloquence in the expression of his ideas. What he disliked
and what he admired were an index to his development at the time.
His judgment of the reformer revealed how far he was from being, or
wishing to become, one himself. He was too busy reforming himself
not to be impatient of any other ambition, and his aversion to the vocation colored his criticism of the man. He carped, and he respected,
but he was so far from the author of *Mexico and Its Revolutions,* and
from his country and its problems, that he examined his famous compatriot as if he were one more foreign curiosity, and after a single visit
he returned to his own corner of Paris, resolved never to repeat it.
Never was a decision more defensive. Their proximity was dangerous,
for, indeed, they had much in common—discipline, independence, superior character, and a driving conscience—but their affinities served
only to accentuate their differences, because those powers, which Mora
had always directed to the progress of a people, were still devoted by
Ocampo to his own salvation. Conscience he had without a responsibility worthy of it. Although the distance between them was great, it was
one not of nature but of degree and development. The reaction of
the younger man was negative precisely because the older one was so
challenging. Ocampo questioned his authority, suspected his sincerity,
dreaded his ardor, resented his domination, and, after finding every

professional reason for faultfinding, finally asserted his independence by flight.

After an absence of two years abroad Ocampo returned to Michoacan and the life for which he was born and from which he was only half weaned. He was sufficiently chastened, mature, and master of himself to manage what remained of his estates reasonably, on a reduced scale of living, though he was never successful financially; but he valued property as a moral asset, for the independence it provided, and he economized to preserve it. He came home, however, home to his country, to his kind, to himself, and the prodigal returned to his habits. Carefully as he controlled his failings, he could not curb his charity. Though he learned to say no to a certain class of persons—solicitors, as he said, who "regarded as an undeniable right to be served the mere fact of telling me that they were in need"—he would not harden himself to the others, and the others were all about him, and their necessities nearer and more undeniable than his own. Who was he to say which were the leeches? or how to know that he needed the needy no less than they his help? He ran his estates in a feudal tradition of responsibility for his dependents, and took an interest in the welfare of his tenants and neighbors which became a byword throughout the county. Many were the tales told of his bounty by those who benefited by it, and the favors he bestowed became obligations which insensibly undermined his independence. But for this besetting weakness he would have subsided no doubt into the life for which he was born, cultivating his acres, nursing his gardens, botanizing, browsing among his books, and doting on his three growing daughters, for it satisfied him completely, and he needed nothing of the world but a modest competence to meet his unexacting demands.

Much was expected of him, however, by others. As a landlord, he was expected to go into politics; it was the natural obligation of his class, and his modesty was understood neither by his rich nor his poor neighbors, who were only as modest as their incomes. All kinds of people were ambitious for Don Melchor Ocampo, and it was difficult to deny them and to indulge what he called his Spanish indolence with a clear conscience. Social convention and moral responsibility convinced him that superior people were not what they wanted to be, but what others expected of them; and he went into politics. In a succession of offices, as deputy, senator, and governor of his state, he convinced them that he was not wanting in public spirit. Although he held advanced views on some social questions and was absolute in his library, the measures enacted during his administration of the state were acceptable improvements which met with general approval—prison and financial reforms, schools and roads, the founding of an agricultural college—and he won the confidence of the entire community by applying private philanthropy to public life.

As long as he confined himself to public works and measures of relief which gradually ameliorated the general average, he met the necessities of his own class: regeneration from within was an easy way out of their dilemma, pinched as they were by a dwindling economy on the one hand and the approach of reform on the other. But the conditions of the country came home to Ocampo in practical politics, and the conditions of his class when he fell afoul of the clergy, and his own condition by his encounter with the curate of Maravatio. A casual appeal to his charity proved his undoing. Plucking up what he mistook for a mere leech on the poor, he was stung by a nettle with power virulent enough to inflame and infect the whole community against him; and though he indignantly denied that he was a dangerous reformer, he became by stigma and in spite of himself what was expected of him. What Mora failed to accomplish, a country curate achieved. The curate drew blood. But it was not until the wild tale of his youth came true in 1853 and he was mistaken for an enemy or two of Santa Anna, expelled from his country and branded a rebel, that Ocampo actually became one.

The man whom Juarez met in New Orleans influenced him in the only way in which any influence can ever be successful, by quickening his own capacities. Ocampo was a step or two ahead of him in revolutionary development, and he performed something of the same service for Juarez as Mora had once rendered him, calling out latent and unsuspected powers and guiding him toward a destiny of which he was yet unconscious. By general consent Ocampo was accepted as the leader of the little knot of refugees, and on the day after Juarez arrived in New Orleans a meeting was called to consider ways and means of overthrowing Santa Anna. The undertaking was a large one, since none of them had any influence or following in Mexico; but being destitute, with nothing to lose and everything to gain by the attempt, they were not deterred by such considerations. They counted on a brewing rebellion which had broken out in the State of Guerrero under Juan Alvarez, and they hitched their activities to his. Alvarez had a name as a veteran of insurgency and a following of guerrilla fighters as a local cacique, but like most of the heroes of his generation he was a soldier without political experience, and they assumed the ideological direction of the revolt. A political plan was formulated and forwarded to his headquarters in Acapulco by a courier whose fare they pooled their resources to pay. The distance was too great and communication too slow for active contact, but they had a proxy in Ignacio Comonfort, one of their friends who had joined Alvarez as his lieutenant and political mentor, and Comonfort was commissioned to proclaim their plan.

The self-confidence which these steps revealed was the first fruit of exile. Nothing in their situation warranted it, but they maintained it for several months by the sanguine activities to which of necessity political exiles are prone. The Gadsden Treaty was then pending in the Mexican Senate, and as it involved a fresh cession of territory to the United States the position of the Conservative party, which based its claim to power on the preservation of the remains of the country, was extremely vulnerable. Ocampo drafted an appeal to an influential senator in Mexico to hold up the treaty and stated the terms on which the Liberals would take power. He drew up a profession of political faith and claimed the right to intervene "in the name of the majority of Mexicans exiled in New Orleans." He worried the Mexican Consul with officious communications and, when they were ignored, led a delegation to call him to account. Hot from the interview, he repaired to a hotel to record the result and who had said what. The record was clear, it proved that they were not idle, but it proved little else: it was a record of impotence, all the more plain for the gestures of defiance with which they denied it. The Gadsden Treaty was passed, and the American millions which it supplied Santa Anna provided the dictator with a fresh lease on life.

But there were compensations. Their activities were noticed by Santa Anna's government, and they had the satisfaction of seeing themselves denounced in the official press for more than they had actually done—for engaging in treasonable conspiracies, for directing the revolt in the south, for protesting to the United States Government against the Gadsden Treaty, for hiring filibusters to invade the national territory. At the same time their bid for power was recognized in another quarter: Alvarez welcomed their collaboration and Comonfort proclaimed the Plan of Ayutla, which resembled their own. Thus encouraged, Ocampo moved to the border and settled in Brownsville, where he attempted to prod the governors of the adjoining states into a sympathetic reaction to the revolt in the south.

Juarez moved into his rooms in the boarding-house and into the place which he vacated, for Ocampo had immediately distinguished him as a dependable second. But the removal of the leader left a fading glow among his companions in New Orleans, and the correspondence they maintained with him became a record of flat and uneventful days. There were no more visits to the Mexican Consul, no more professions of faith, no more hours of heady talk, no more consultations and plans to lend them an illusion of activity and importance. The revolt in Acapulco made no headway, and they scanned the papers in vain for support from that quarter.

As the months wore away and nothing happened either in Mexico or in Brownsville, the long ordeal of waiting winnowed the group to its original sponsors. The rest scattered to various points with the coming of summer, for the ravages of the climate were acute and they were

aggravated by an epidemic of yellow fever, and the strength of numbers was reduced to that of conviction. The fit survived—and the fit
were four. When the group first gathered, it would have been difficult
to say which of the names on the roll call were destined to figure in
the future and which were to fall by the wayside; but six months later
the summer soldiers had vanished, and four men knew that they could
always count on one another: Ocampo, Juarez, Ponciano Arriaga, and
José-Maria Mata. But on them too the winnowing process was at work.
Juarez was stricken by the fever, and his life was saved by pure
chance, "since we had no funds with which to care for him properly,"
as one of his friends said. He survived, however, without a medical
bill; and his recovery was proof of a physical fitness no less necessary
for the future than moral stamina; and that other indispensable was
repeatedly revealed in the trials which the survivors underwent.

These were many and severe. Homesickness, despondency, doubt—
against these they were proof, being determined to a man to return to
their country on their own terms or not at all. Snares there were, for
Santa Anna offered an amnesty for the weak, but there was only one
case of desertion, and when Juarez caught wind of it he reported it
with a vehemence rare in his writing. "I have not seen the papers," he
wrote to Ocampo, "but those who have tell me that Sandoval, as if the
humiliation of returning by grace of the tyrant were not enough, is
basely abusing his comrades in exile. Poor devil! who has the talent to
exchange his existence as a man for that of a contemptible reptile upon
whom we must all spit!" Constancy cost them no qualms: they were
marked men, and too important not to be braced by their curse. As
time passed, however, the problem of ways and means of overthrowing Santa Anna gave way to the pressing question of ways and means
of keeping alive. They were proof against poverty. Though they were
frequently pinched by it, it was the least of their trials. Ocampo was
steeled to it by a philosophy that stood him in good stead, when his income was cut off by the confiscation of his estates. Juarez was born to
it and returned to it easily. He received remittances from home, where
his wife had opened a shop to provide for the family, but they were
meager and irregular, and at times, like his companions, he was forced
to eke out his means by such employments as were available to
stranded Mexicans in New Orleans. In lean days Juarez kept himself
in a printing-shop or a cigar factory; Mata worked as a waiter;
Ocampo as a potter. Hovering on the edge of penury and the social
pale, they preserved a precarious existence—as men. But as men they
met the test differently. On the most high-strung the strain was naturally the most trying, and on one occasion Ocampo was reduced to the
verge of complaint. Major trials he bore easily, because they could be
met with pride, but the minor ones that mortified it cut him to the
quick. In Brownsville he found a benefactor in a prosperous Mexican

who served as his banker and through whose assistance he would have been free to pursue his political work—but for the womenfolk. The banker had a wife and daughter as sheltered and guarded as Mexican women across the border, and Ocampo was accompanied by a daughter whom he idolized. Finding her in tears one day, he coaxed out of her a confession that she had been berated in the home of his benefactor because of a bonnet, which had led the ladies to remark that Mexican women who affected such fashions were shameless hussies, whereupon he wrote to his banker, renouncing his aid and severing their relations. "You see how futile a reason has led to results as painful to me as they are prejudicial," he confessed, but "the slur could not be stronger, the offense more direct, nor the words more insulting"—and he felt them the more bitterly because he was unmarried. He recalled others that he had suffered in silence—how he had been rebuked in company for some trifling levity, how an "emancipated woman" had been sent him as a companion for his daughter—trifles, trifles, but trifles were crushing in the life of the exile, where philosophy was a futility and a scratch could destroy it, and his susceptibility to trifles was the final humiliation. The affair was patched up, but not the damage to his pride, which he charged to the account of Santa Anna. From the tyranny of little things, more trying than the oppression of despots, he looked to Acapulco not merely for the salvation of Mexico, but for his own moral rescue.

The demoralizing effects of exile—the petty pressure of poverty, the exposure to mean indignities, the privation of any redeeming activity —were an acid test of character; and as time passed and the revolt made no progress, it became more and more difficult for the proscripts to sustain the self-confidence which they derived from their vicarious share in it. Reduced to their own resources, they were mere refugees with nothing in common but a misfortune which they could not dispute; and with the disintegration of the group they became once more what they were before they met, isolated individuals of no importance to anyone but themselves. The triumph of Santa Anna was complete. A pretense of political activity was kept up, but a pretense only, and they subsided slowly and inevitably into such occupations as they could improvise to cheat their impotence. Ponciano Arriaga, who had no patience with pretense, slipped across the border to agitate in the neighboring states; Ocampo, who had no talent for intrigue, cultivated his garden in Brownsville; and Mata, a zealous disciple with nothing to do, acted as a courier for Ocampo and courted his daughter.

Juarez remained in New Orleans, resting from the exertions of his friends. His days were divided between political work—reading the newspapers and calling at the post office—and the study of Constitutional Law. One day he was invited by an American court to sit in on a case involving a land claim in California, a proud day for his friends, one of whom fondly reported that "his opinion was unanimously approved by the members of the court, he was enthusiastically praised and showered with a thousand attentions to which he was justly entitled." Any recognition extended to one of their number was gratefully appreciated by the whole group. But such tributes were rare, and in the drought of attention from which they all suffered his friends were the last to give him his due. A common mediocrity deadened them all, and a dreary monotony of mutual neglect. As the dead level of life sank to a depth, however, that laid bare his submerged abilities, they began to be recognized in the shallows. During the long draining months of flatness and failure his friends dimly discerned the self-sufficiency which sustained him and of which they all stood in need. One of them noticed "his irreproachable habits and his devotion to study, which he interrupted only to visit some institutions of public instruction or welfare, or to visit one or another of his acquaintances." From five in the morning until eight at night he worked over his books; but there was nothing unusual either in his routine or his studies—Constitutional Law—a lawyer without clients keeping in practice and pursuing his professional interests by himself—unless it was his interest in systems of colonization in the American Republic—the scholarly recreation of an expatriate. Nor was there anything uncommon in the mental independence which he preserved by a routine that defeated adversity; nor in the fact that he was never bored by his friends or by himself; nor in his material independence, which he preserved jealously. Repeated offers of financial assistance from Ocampo and compatriots passing through the city were always declined, and though his consistency cost him some privations, they were noticed by no one but a companion who shared them, and who never forgot that for a time they ate for ten cents in the lunchroom of the Hotel St. Charles, until they found a Negress who fed them for eight dollars a month and a rooming-house for eight more; when they received a remittance from Oaxaca for six hundred pesos and they were both flush. In hardship they were all equals, all Juarez—with one difference which his would-be benefactors and close friends both discovered. His irreproachable habits made him unapproachable. Poverty not only stiffened but exasperated his pride. Ocampo once refused a cigar which Juarez offered him and twitted him with an old saying: "No, sir. When an Indian sucks a cigar, the thief is not far." The reply was sharp and short: "The Indian I cannot deny, but the rest—" And Ocampo undid himself in apologies. If Juarez had not been hypersensitive, and Ocampo mortified by one of those slips to which superior people are sometime liable, there would have been nothing remarkable in the anecdote—and they would not have been friends. But they both bruised easily, and in his susceptibility to fancied slurs Juarez was fully the equal of Ocampo.

The small items of that time that lingered in the memory of the exiles, when trifles loomed large for all of them, would have been trivial had they not revealed qualities in Juarez upon which his companions came to rely and which needed only larger times to emerge and impress them. He was dependable, whatever was expected of him, whether to ship plants to Ocampo in Brownsville, or to walk the levees with Mata, or to appreciate the propaganda sent back from the field by Ponciano Arriaga: he had a knack for nursing the talents of his friends; he analyzed the news with a perspicacity which escaped their attention, but they trusted his judgment, and the event constantly confirmed it. There was a terrible moment when the papers announced the death of Alvarez. Juarez assumed, correctly as usual, that the report had been inspired to discourage the spread of the revolt; and throughout all the fluctuations of their prospects he maintained an equanimity, a patience, a confidence equally proof against undue despondency and premature hope—qualities that surpassed their expression and that passed unperceived by the closest observers. A discerning eye was needed to discover their presence, and a microscopic insight to magnify their importance, in the small chores and plodding services which stunted and buried them; and none of his companions had the talent to dramatize dullness. They were dimly aware of a great self-sufficiency but not of its extent, because it was concealed by an equally complete self-effacement.

Exile was a training school for their task, and its discipline a test of their fitness to survive; and of all its hardships the most trying for the great-minded was the grinding test of dullness, which whetted the spirit or broke it. But it was a necessary groundwork for greatness. The serenity of Juarez was a steadying influence on his friends in days of moral drudgery and pedestrian exercises; but a day came when stamina was not enough, when philosophy was too passive, to compensate for political inactivity.

In Mexico the revolt began to make some progress. Alaman died in 1854, but not before he inoculated Santa Anna with that morbid craving for monarchy which he had disavowed because it was premature and unpopular, but which was the dying breath of his brain; and Santa Anna was well fitted to carry the germ and to acclimate the idea in Mexico. His return to power was accepted, like the seasons, as a perennial but transient phenomenon; but this time his return was marked by an abnormal novelty. He assumed the style of a Prince-President and the title of a Serene Highness, created orders of nobility and a Court of exotic splendor, and consummated the covert ambition of his mentor by a domestic imitation of Louis Napoleon. The trial balloon defied levitation, however. The pretensions of Santa Anna were tolerated for a time and then ridiculed until they could no longer be laughed off.

The trappings of royalty only made the realities of the dictatorship more galling and the Napoleonic precedent more glaring; and in anticipation of another collapse, as normal as his regular returns to power, Santa Anna prepared for his supersession by a foreign prince. Though the negotiations were conducted with due secrecy, they leaked out, for his agent was Gutierrez Estrada. The first man to advocate monarchy in Mexico had been driven from the Republic for plucking forbidden fruit, but he gloried in his fall and ran about Europe, a naked Adam, peddling it to anyone who would bite; but no one would. The only result was to discredit Santa Anna, to weaken confidence in the dictator who was merely warming the seat for another, and to hasten his fall. Popular sympathy with the revolt spread, and Alvarez and Comonfort redoubled their exertions to shake off the yoke.

As the prospects of the rebellion brightened and the fall of Santa Anna appeared to be approaching, Juarez became seriously troubled. "Once the tyrant has been destroyed, shall we have accomplished the triumph of principles?" he wrote to Ocampo. "This is what I fail to see, and what saddens me every day, for, say what we will, there is not sufficient patriotism and enlightenment to win liberty without committing excesses that dishonor it, or to secure it, after success, by setting aside all personal ambitions. It may be that these ideas spring from my bad humor at the moment and that the results will belie them. I hope so, I hope so." But his doubts would not down and they raised challenging questions. Was the revolt to triumph without them? Were they to be mere bystanders of an event they proposed to control? And with that question came another. Could the revolution succeed without them? Was it not their duty to indoctrinate it and prevent it from becoming merely one more of those pseudo-revolutions which perpetuated the chronic chaos of Mexico?

By the end of February 1855 his doubts and his promptings moved Juarez to propose that they proceed in a body to Acapulco, or that Ocampo and Arriaga at least should appear in the theater of war, where their presence would be enough to hearten public spirit. "You see the state of the revolution," he wrote. "It seems to me that a unanimous effort by the few men who have the interests of the country at heart would suffice to destroy the tyrant, and I think that the effort will be made when men of ability and irreproachable reputation set the example." In deference to Ocampo, and to his own modesty, Juarez left the initiative to the natural leader, but his days of retirement were counted. Ocampo decided to remain in Brownsville. The fire which he had kindled across the border began to blaze; a governor revolted, a general volunteered, and he invested his remaining funds and energies in fanning the insurrection in the north.

At the same time came a letter from Comonfort, urging Juarez to use his influence to raise his native state; but the next mail brought news of reverses in Acapulco, and Juarez decided that the mission would be a useless expense and remained as modest as his income. When the call was repeated, however, and Comonfort, in desperate straits, short of money, munitions, and men, begged Ocampo to send him Juarez at least and some of the others, Juarez hesitated no longer. His were clearly the qualities of adversity. Ocampo and Mata constituted themselves a Revolutionary Committee, assuming the functions of government and issuing drafts on the customs of the disaffected states, and raised a loan to pay the passage of Juarez to Acapulco. If there was some presumption in assuming the direction of the movement and coming forward at the eleventh hour, no one could do it more modestly than Juarez, and even he recognized that his position in New Orleans, in a boarding-house, in the lee of life, was no longer tenable. After eighteen months of exile, his philosophy was no longer passive, or even pensive: he was pledged to a fresh departure, and conscious of his destination, and crowned with the rings of Saturn. The last to appreciate his abilities and the first to prove them, he set sail, at the end of June 1855, invested with the confidence of his comrades and empowered to use his discretion to deal with whatever situation he might find in Mexico.

I I

LANDING in Acapulco late in July, Juarez went directly to headquarters, where, in the absence of the General, he was received by his son, Colonel Diego Alvarez. The Colonel, according to a story which he told later and which there is no reason to doubt, did not catch the name. "What do you want?" he asked. "Knowing that men are fighting for freedom here, I came to see in what way I could be useful," was the reply. The volunteer was accepted without further question and taken to the camp, where the Colonel presented him to his father as a casual recruit to the cause. Father and son were both embarrassed by his appearance: shabby, bedraggled, and drenched by a tropical downpour, he was in urgent need of repair. "I need hardly say," said the Colonel, "that we did not know what to do to relieve his pressing need, since we had no clothes for the newcomer; we had to use those of our poor troopers, a pair of trousers and a cotton blanket, that is, adding to them a blanket from my father's bed and a pair of his patched boots, all of which, together with a package of good cigarettes, harmonized wonderfully." What to do with the man they had dressed was the next question: "My father, who was glad to accept spontaneous collaborators in the struggle we had started against Santa Anna, was as perplexed as I, and upon his offering to serve as a secretary and repeating that he had come to see how he could serve here, where men were fighting for freedom, he was given some letters of little importance, which he answered and presented for signature with the utmost modesty." It was not until several days later, when a letter addressed to Lic. Don Benito Juarez was delivered in camp and someone took the trouble to ask his name, that his identity was discovered. Then he was questioned again by the Colonel. " 'Here is a letter bearing your name. Does this mean that you are a lawyer?' — 'Yes, sir,' he replied. — 'You mean that you are the same man that was Governor of Oaxaca?' — 'Yes, sir.' — And overcome with confusion, I exclaimed, 'Why did you not tell me?' — 'Why should I?' he replied. 'What does it matter?' "

The story was not only plausible but significant, for the characteristic self-effacement of Juarez revealed something more important than personal modesty—political tact. When he left New Orleans, the revolution was at low ebb; when he arrived in Acapulco, it was flushed with triumph. A fortnight later Santa Anna abdicated and fled the country. The rapid reversal of the situation, which occurred during the six weeks that Juarez spent at sea, restored his mission to its original purpose: it was not with the dangers of defeat that he had to deal, but with the far greater hazards of success. Arriving at the last moment as the emissary of a group that proposed to direct a movement which had managed without them, he was in reality an interloper who could carry out his mission without incurring the charge of presumption only by the most sedulous self-effacement; and the confidence of his friends was not misplaced. He slipped imperceptibly into his place in the revolution and performed his part as a political adviser with the same consummate inconspicuousness that had distinguished him in New Orleans. An occasion soon arose. As soon as the fall of Santa Anna was seen to be inevitable, a sympathetic movement broke out in the capital, his generals deserted, rallied to the plan of the revolution, and proclaimed one of their number "interim" President. The news excited wild jubilation in Acapulco, and Juarez was instructed to write a eulogistic article for the local paper. The unthinking enthusiasm with which this success was celebrated was a measure of the ingenuousness of a purely popular and indigenous movement. Juarez was obliged to point out to the Colonel that the revolt of the generals was merely a maneuver to save their skins and to falsify the revolution, stealing its fruits from under the noses of the revolutionaries and cheating "the patriots who had flung themselves into the fight to free their country from clerical-military tyranny," and that no common cause existed or could be made between them. The Colonel was convinced, and the article was revised to fit the facts. The facts would have been self-evident anywhere else but in Acapulco; in a jungle full of virgin patriots and political illiterates, the services of an interpreter were needed to decipher them. Thereafter the position of Juarez was secure. General Alvarez confirmed his judgment, having come to the same conclusions himself—he was not above taking advice when he agreed with it. They were both Indians, both born to suspicion as their birthright, and they understood each other instinctively. Juarez was given a seat at the council table when the emissaries of the generals came down to negotiate the recognition of their President. Their overtures were rejected, the jungle was full of eyes and ambushes, and they beat their way back, convinced that their man had no chance. The road being cleared, the army advanced to the capital.

"The whole thing has been a farce to continue controlling the country and to baffle the revolution," Juarez wrote to Ocampo. Of his part in exposing the snare he made no mention. He had put in a word at the right moment, but the same decision would undoubtedly have been taken without him, and the real difficulties lay ahead. Alvarez was marching on the capital to establish a government that would put the Plan of Ayutla into effect and develop the program of the revolution; and feeling himself unable to cope with that situation alone, Juarez urged Ocampo to join him without delay. His own position was still obscure. When the army marched through Morelia, one of his friends there came out to meet him and, after searching the lines of nondescript soldiers straggling by and inquiring for him in vain, found him at last far to the rear, alone, and managing a sorry nag. He was, in fact, a camp follower; he had won a footing in the movement, but nothing more, and his place was inevitably with the laggards. He could not compete with Comonfort, who was the political adviser *en titre,* who had borne the brunt of the fighting, and who was entitled to precedence by the services he had rendered the rebellion. Juarez had gained the confidence of Alvarez, but Alvarez had so little confidence in himself after the battle and recognized his political inexperience so clearly that he hesitated to trust himself among the problems, the pitfalls, the intrigues of the capital, and halted his advance at Cuernavaca. Here he was elected President by a council of delegates whom he appointed, and of whom Juarez was one; but he delegated his powers to Comonfort, who formed his cabinet and became the actual arbiter of the situation. Had he been ambitious, Comonfort might easily have monopolized power, but he was generous and welcomed the collaboration of the latecomers from New Orleans. Ocampo arrived at the critical moment, in time to accept two posts in the cabinet for himself and to distribute the rest among his trusted friends. The Ministry of Finance was given to Guillermo Prieto, a poet who had served a term in the Treasury, and the Ministry of Justice and Public Education was handed to Juarez.

To these four men fell the task of completing the revolution. The Plan of Ayutla, which proclaimed its program, was the plan which the refugees in New Orleans had drawn, revised by Comonfort, and revised downward. When he had proclaimed it in the thick of the struggle, Comonfort had been careful to omit everything that might add to his difficulties and had thinned it down to popular generalities— the overthrow of Santa Anna and the restoration of liberty. These generalities were a vacant mold into which, after the battle, specific meaning had yet to be poured, and liberty was defined by Ocampo as the elimination not merely of Santa Anna, but of the clerical-military tyranny of which he was the creature. In Comonfort, however, he encountered a collaborator who was the incarnation of all the dangers of success. Personally he left little to be desired: he was undoubtedly one of those rare Mexicans ready to forego ambition for the public good; he was disinterested, honorable, high-minded, and sincere; but he was a compromiser.

As soon as they set to work, their differences appeared. The first business to come before the cabinet was the preparation of a call for the election of a new Congress. Ocampo insisted on depriving the clergy of the vote; Comonfort balked. He was overruled, but he freely expressed his regret that the delegates who elected Alvarez and from whom he derived his own authority had not been composed one-half of ecclesiastics—a measure which would have obviated all discussion, but which would have made the revolution superfluous. As for the army, Comonfort would not touch it and insisted on retaining and conciliating the generals of the late regime. After a fortnight in office Ocampo resigned in disgust. "As Comonfort explained to me clearly that the revolution would continue to take the way of *transactions*," he wrote to Mata, "and as I am one of those who break but do not bend, I left the Ministry. The housekeeper called for the keys and I handed them over, since I had no right to keep them. But I very much doubt whether by sleight-of-hand, as Comonfort told me he had pacified Mexico and meant to continue governing, he will be able to succeed. I believe that what is wanted is a hard hand. Time will tell who is right."

Prieto and Juarez remained in the cabinet, the former persuaded by Ocampo and the latter by his own conscience, which was of too practical a cast to be satisfied by a self-righteous gesture of renunciation on principle. "What determined me to remain in the Ministry," Juarez wrote, "was the hope of being able to profit by an opportunity to initiate some one of the many reforms which society needed to improve its condition, and of benefiting by the sacrifices which the people had made to destroy the tyranny that oppressed them." If his choice made him an opportunist, it was for high stakes: an historic opportunity had arisen, and might never recur, to transform a military success into a revolution, and it was in imminent danger of being lost in another reshuffle: he for one could not afford to be intransigent. Such an attitude was possible only in exile, in a garden in Brownsville or on the levees of the Mississippi, or in the study, or in the empyrean; in Mexico at that moment it was irresponsible. Ocampo grasped the situation and the man at a glance and, foreseeing the end in the beginning, foreshortened them in a flash. Comonfort belonged to a breed which he recognized with the trained eye of the naturalist, because the characteristics were invariable—the eternal compromiser, which every revolution breeds for its confusion, fatal to himself, his partners, and his cause. To that judgment Juarez eventually subscribed, but at the time he was willing to give the beginner the benefit of a doubt—for a doubt there was, though there was little else on which to build. Convinced of the necessity of drastic reforms but shrinking from the risks of their precipitate application, Comonfort insisted on consolidating his regime before he attempted them. To temporize was not necessarily to compromise; in his own mind, at least, there existed a saving distinction, and though it was a thin one, it provided a narrow margin, which might spell the whole difference between success and failure. Juarez speculated on it. He understood Comonfort as Ocampo could not, with the insight of sympathy as well as of science: the reluctance to dare, the paralyzing prudence of a little success, the stubborn evasion of controversial issues, the temptation and even the necessity of compromise—Comonfort confronted him like his own past, and he had some secret indulgence, perhaps, for his dead self; but he had learned the fallacy of timeserving by hard and bitter experience, and he hoped to guide his alter ego, whom he had outgrown, while he was still amenable to influence.

But the odds were against him. The influences to which Comonfort was amenable were naturally those of his own kind, and he was no sooner in power than he was beset by the enemy. The enemy was not the reaction, routed by the fall of Santa Anna, but the Moderate party, which provided it with cover in days of extremity and whose function as a buffer had often served in the past to ward off revolution and preserve the existing order. The reaction, cowed and discredited but not yet beaten, resorted to its usual tactics and blended with that large and influential third party which held a balance of power that, consciously or unconsciously, was always dipped in their favor. To this party Comonfort belonged by temperament and policy; and pressure was brought to bear to wean him away from Alvarez, who was known to favor a purge of the army and the other radical measures implicit in the Plan of Ayutla. Comonfort resisted; his personal loyalty was at stake, and he was, as one of his friends said, "horribly quixotic." Failing to move him by persuasion, the enemy resorted to threats. Manuel Doblado, the Governor of Guanajuato, and one of the leaders of the Moderates, was rumored to be on the point of revolt, and though the reports were denied, the maneuver alarmed Comonfort. Haunted by the fear of a fresh civil war, he set himself to woo Doblado, and for several weeks the cautious neutrality of the one was pitted against the calculated uncertainty of the other in a prolonged duel of doubt; but in so unsettled a period the threat of revolt was too explosive an expedient not to alarm the Moderates themselves, and they held it in abeyance, biding the effect of another and safer device.

Alvarez, who still lingered in Cuernavaca, was induced to take up his residence in the capital in the confident expectation that he would discover his unfitness for office there; and nothing was left undone to discredit him. With him came the army—an army of *Pintos,* as people called the half-civilized tribes of the south, whose war paint in primitive times had given them a reputation for ferocity that clung to them in the civil war; and their appearance created dismay not only among the respectable, but among the popular, classes and produced a political effect by the most primitive of all political devices—an appeal to the eye no less potent with the cultivated than with the illiterate crowd. Lounging in the Plaza, guarding the Palace, overrunning the city, the *Pintos* were regarded as barbarians by the one and boors by the other, and as a plague by both. They were outlandish, they were vandals, they were invaders, and the dread and disgust they excited were visited on the head of their President. Alvarez was derided and ostracized; at a gala performance given in his honor at the theater, the decent people stayed away in droves, and Comonfort was conspicuous by his absence. Every effort was made to dissociate him from such disreputable company and by the most telling means, for he belonged to a genteel family and had never done anything freakish in his life before; but prudery was a slow political process, and his friends fretted under the occupation of the capital by a swarm of pariahs who possessed it like unclean spirits easy to call up and hard to cast out. "I do not know what cursed constellation pursues us," Doblado was warned by one of his political scouts, "and makes us victims at one time of robbery, pillage, prostitution, and immorality, and at others of immorality, ignorance, barbarism, and brutality! Oh! you would have died of shame, as we all have done, if you had seen the hordes of savages who call themselves the Army of the South, and in whose power the Capital of the Republic lies today! I have found myself wishing that they were the hordes of Attila, for then we should be overwhelmed by fierce but valiant soldiers. These are no less brutal and barbarous, but they are, besides, as imbecile and degraded as the Negro! What is to become of us I do not know. If help does not come from your quarter, here it is completely lost!" The time had come to strike, and Doblado was urged to repeat the threat of revolt.

The crisis rose rapidly, but just before it reached its crest a counteracting influence asserted itself. During those weeks of growing strain and insecurity Juarez had been working steadily against time. Comonfort was clearly slipping, and the only hope of arresting his surrender was to commit him, before it was too late, to an irretrievable step. As the pressure increased, and Comonfort leaned more and more toward the Moderates waiting to board his government, Prieto dropped off and Juarez alone remained at his post. He had prepared the draft of a law reforming the administration of justice, which had been discussed in the cabinet and had met with the approval of his colleagues and Alvarez. Comonfort had not opposed it, though it was highly subversive, for it abolished the judicial *fueros,* or immunities, of the clergy and the army and reduced the members of the privileged classes to the jurisdiction of the civil courts and the common law. But Comonfort was cornered. The measure was a challenge which compelled him to declare himself, and the more he listed toward the Moderates, the more he recoiled from admitting his weakness to himself or his colleagues, for whatever else might be said of Comonfort, he was not without conscience—it was the curse of the compromiser, indeed, and he was bedeviled by it. He lent his sanction to the measure and authorized Juarez to proceed with its preparation, and on the day when the final version was submitted to the cabinet, he absented himself on the plea of pressing business, leaving his colleagues free to force his hand. To this last conscientious evasion Juarez responded by slipping the measure through with the skill of a conjuror, performing a piece of political sleight-of-hand which, light-fingered in effect, was weighty in consequence, and fitted Comonfort's own formula of government. The race against time and intrigue was won by a narrow margin. On November 23, 1855—five days after the arrival of Alvarez in the capital and at the same time that the signal was sent to Doblado to rise—the *ley Juarez* was published by presidential decree.

The effect was immediate and far-reaching. The law emerged suddenly like a dam which caught and clove the swift-flowing current of defeat and sent it swerving and churning in confusion. Even more important than its content was its timing. Comonfort was compromised and braced by it. "Yesterday and today feverish rumors were running in this capital of an imminent revolution," he wrote to Doblado five days later. "The flight last night of General Uraga and the ease with which the enemies of public peace can exploit the recent law on the administration of justice are matters, to my mind, that can encourage the malcontents. To support this law is a duty of the present administration and to pursue Uraga a necessity." The fugitive general was heading toward a region seething with disaffection, where the Indians of the Sierra had been aroused by clerical propaganda. One of their caciques had issued a call to arms to save "the clergy, deprived even of their rights as citizens, the Church whose property is that of the poor, the army destroyed as a class and prostituted by the entrance into the ranks of notorious bandits and jailbirds, the proprietor whose possessions are unprotected by an unbridled government, and the artisan, humiliated by the presence in the capital of the Republic of the filthy, insolent, and immoral horde which the weakness of a few men has vomited upon Mexico out of the mountains of the south, and which threaten the lives and honor of our wives and daughters."

But it was not from that quarter that the revolt came. Four days after the publication of the *ley Juarez,* Doblado raised the banner of rebellion on behalf of *Religion and Fueros.* He missed the psychological moment, however, and his own friends, who had advised him only ten days before that nothing could save the situation but a menacing attitude on his part, now turned on him in protest and alarm and begged him to forbear. For in the meanwhile something had happened. On the same day that Doblado revolted, Alvarez resigned the Presidency in favor of Comonfort, and the Moderates had accomplished their purpose. In ousting Alvarez, however, they were bound by one stipulation: he resigned on the express condition that the legislation initiated under his brief rule would be inviolably preserved, and they themselves reminded Doblado that the reactionary program of *Religion and Fueros* was not, and could not be, a passport to power. They were shocked by a plan which, as they said, "gives the clergy and the army by respecting their privileges a preponderance to which we Liberals have always been opposed, since it subjects the government to an ignominious tutelage, since it makes any kind of progress impossible, and since its constant tendencies to the *status quo,* which are the same as those of the Conservative party, prevent the liberal from taking the true road of improvement. . . ." This was more than a rebuke: it was a revelation. The *ley Juarez,* lying amid the old rubbish of compromises, expedients, and half-measures, made all the old combinations impossible; it acted like a magnet on the elements about it, compelling them to react according to their true nature; it rallied the Moderates themselves to their real bearings, detaching them from their traditional amalgam with the reaction; and though they captured the government, they were forced to adopt its policy. Doblado recognized his error and retrieved it by dropping his ill-timed feint of revolt and becoming thereafter one of the most dependable and progressive members of the Liberal party.

The hand that raised the dam was virtually unknown in national politics. Only a few days before the law appeared the old politician who served Doblado as a political scout measured the lawgiver as follows: "Today I talked with Señor Juarez. He struck me as a rather circumspect man and, to judge by his vague and general conversation, he will not give us many laws, but only those that are strictly necessary and consulting always the general interest, without disclosing in his measures that party spirit which has been the bane of our poor country." Until the law appeared, Juarez could still be mistaken for a safe man, and so colorless that he was given only a few days more of official life; but he held on to give the nation one of those capital reforms the necessity of which was recognized, and the tonic effect felt, even by tepid liberals. That Comonfort countenanced so provocative a measure was both a guarantee and a surprise. A story subsequently appeared that it had been smuggled through the cabinet without his knowledge, a story that Juarez denied, explaining that his chief had sanctioned the measure before he absented himself. But the correction, strictly accurate as a statement of fact, was something less than the whole truth. A strong suggestion of psychological prestidigitation remained and was emphasized by the speed with which the pass was made; and though it was not manual but moral, it conjured up a Comonfort who was not there before.

Produced in haste, the law was imperfect, as its author admitted. Many immunities of the clergy remained intact, and those of the army were merely pared; but a principle had been established and vindicated, and none too soon. A fortnight after the appearance of the law Alvarez resigned, the Moderates came to power, and in the reshuffle Juarez resigned. The Indian President returned to his ranch in the south, not without recalling in a bitter letter to Doblado the services he had rendered the nation in the wars of insurgency; he belonged to the past and shrank into it; but he lasted long enough to cast over the law of November 23, 1855, which initiated the final phase of Independence, and which was forged by another native hand, the protection, the prestige, the long luminous shadow of 1821.

For Juarez also there were compensations; he was too important a person to be dismissed without them. He returned to Oaxaca as Governor, appointed by Comonfort, and settled down to his homecoming with legitimate pride. The lawgiver retired, the law remained, a revolutionary landmark which justified his satisfaction. "Imperfect as this law was," he was able to say when he reviewed his work in perspective, "it was received with great enthusiasm by the Progressive party; it was the spark that kindled the fire of Reform, which later consumed the rotten structure of abuses and privileges. It was, in short, a challenge flung to the privileged classes, and one which General Comonfort and all the others, who for lack of faith in the principles of the revolution or for personal advantage sought to check its course, compromising with the demands of the past, were forced to maintain in spite of themselves, pressed on by the all-powerful arm of public opinion."

The aftereffects had brought forth light. The law was a beacon which called forth the doubters who had not yet declared themselves and brought them crowding to the fore in eager emulation. Seven months later, on June 25, 1856, came the *ley Lerdo* with which the new Minister of Finance, Lerdo de Tejada, disamortized Church property. This law was, in form, a half-measure; it was not confiscatory, but it abolished the immunity of mortmain and forced the sale of ecclesiastical holdings in real estate and investments, releasing and circulating a large fund of hoarded wealth for the benefit of the nation; and it asserted the right of civil jurisdiction no less absolutely than did the *ley Juarez*.

Comonfort had become a lucifer in spite of himself, and his formula of government had developed overnight into a science in which, by feats of legerdemain, the dead hand of the past was being steadily lifted, and the reaction of public opinion was accurately tested by an active demonstration of the repulsions and affinities, the forces that charged and the properties that composed it; it was no longer a compound of conjecture and jugglery. By the summer of 1856 his government, completely manned now by Moderates, had been identified with two measures, which were both major experiments in political physics: one abolishing the legal *fueros* of the privileged classes and the other the economic *fuero* of the dominant caste. Between these two successful tests several minor decrees had been issued to reinforce their tendency: the expulsion of the Jesuits, the abolition of civil coercion in the maintenance of monastic vows, and the regulation of parochial rates. The Reform movement had been resuscitated and was on the march.

12

THE succession of Mora was no longer vacant; but neither was it filled. Hovering over the head of Ocampo for a moment, settling for a longer one on the hand of Juarez, caught up in turn by Lerdo de Tejada, seeking and finding ever fresh recruits, including even a Comonfort and a Doblado, lighting on one eligible after another with a tentative ghostly touch but fastening on none for the furtherance of its ultimate ends, its direction was never in doubt. The succession was a collective enterprise, not an individual adventure, and the impulse given by a single will had yet to be dilated. The dynamic initiative of Juarez was seconded by a few highly placed persons in power, and the rudiments of a movement could be discerned in the response to it of those widely scattered individuals, many and nameless, who had nursed the vision of Reform during the arid years in silence and solitude, in ineffectual reveries, and in the inertia of complete disorganization. "Unfortunately, the Liberal party is essentially anarchic and will not cease to be so for many thousands of years," Ocampo had written a few years before. "The criterion of our enemies is authority. . . . They obey blindly and uniformly, whereas when we are commanded, unless we are told how and why, we murmur and are remiss, when we do not actually disobey and rebel. For every liberal is one in the degree to which he can and will emancipate himself; and our opponents are all equally servile and almost all equally pupils. To be wholly a liberal requires effort and needs the courage of a complete man."

Whether this psychology was the cause or the result of repeated failure, the unruly and invertebrate individualism of the Liberal party had perpetuated the rule of reaction and made progress impossible until one of their faith raised a challenge that massed and marshaled them. Then the lonely believers, so long separated and isolated by an inbred inability to combine, came crowding forward at a call, all the more potent because it was an individual feat of political prowess; all that they needed to fuse their efforts was a focus, a center, a rallying point, and that they found in the Congress called by Comonfort to endow the nation with a new Constitution.

The most important result of the Congress was not the laws but the men it produced—men who discovered themselves and one another in the common task of reconstituting their country and who would have remained obscure and ineffectual casuals of their time but for that dredge. Few of the delegates had figured prominently in public life. The most illustrious was Gomez Farias, but the patriarch of Reform, old, sick, and long since silenced, took no part in the debates. He was a venerable invalid whose presence, in the absence of Mora, was a symbol of a continuous tradition and a living reminder to the deputies of the fresh departure which, to redeem it, they were bound to make; and his seat, which was rarely occupied, was a pedestal about which his heirs assembled piously on ceremonial occasions and from which they caught the speeding touch before taking off on their lap of the race for Reform. They had the advantage of not being so far ahead of their time, and their prospects were better. A fresh start was about to be made with a completely Liberal Congress, from which the clergy and the military had been eliminated, and in which the only division lay between Moderates and radicals, the former malleable and the latter dynamic. The division, it was true, was not clear-cut, for even in the

Progressive wing there was a sliding scale of conviction and courage, and those who could be accounted complete liberals, according to the dictum of Ocampo, were rare; but the indeterminate were dominated by a small knot of complete men who made up in enterprise for what they lacked in numbers. Of these moving spirits the nucleus was formed by the confederates of New Orleans and a number of spirited newcomers who had known moral exile in their own country. Juarez was absent in Oaxaca; Ocampo took his seat late and left it early in dissent; but Mata was an indefatigable champion of every basic reform, and the boldest of all of them was put forth by Ponciano Arriaga. About them gravitated a group of militant tyros—typical representatives of the generation to which the early reformers had looked to carry on their work, the second, the social, levy of insurgents who had been mustering their energies and maturing their talents slowly against the day of delivery and who arrived with the relay of 1856. Some were ephemeral figures who made their mark in Congress and faded after it, while others outlived it and identified themselves with later phases of the movement. Less than a score in all, these men were the leaven of the Assembly; and in the difficult progress of the movement through Congress the dredge brought out the magnetic properties of Prieto, Ramirez, and Zarco.

For the movement passed through Congress under heavy pressure from many quarters. When the delegates assembled in February 1856 the vibrations of the *ley Juarez* were still in the air, transformed into the reverberations of revolt in Puebla, and for six weeks the attention of the Convention was divided between its deliberations and the progress of the campaign against the rebels. For a time the threat of arms and eviction came so close that the Governor of Jalisco, Santos Degollado, offered the Assembly asylum in his state; but Comonfort crushed the revolt with a speed and energy which stimulated Congress. The Progressives were spurred by it and took the aggressive, and during the first six months the creative forces were in the ascendant. Their advance was stubbornly disputed, however. The Moderates, their *vis inertiae* stiffened by the revolt which provided a running accompaniment to the initial sessions, were profoundly jarred by the very purpose for which they sat. The first proposal laid before the Constituent Congress, in fact, was an invitation to desist and return to the Constitution of 1824. "Let us not run the risk of forming a new fundamental law, gentlemen," the orator urged. "Experience has proved that a nation that varies its fundamental law at every step never obtains the benefits of the Constitutional system, but passes, perpetually vacillating, from essay to essay toward anarchy, and from anarchy to complete dissolution. That is why a political authority has said with truth and profound wisdom that a nation constitutes itself only once."

Even more startling than the appeal was its effect: the proposal was rejected, but by a margin of only one vote. The scale was tipped by Mata, who dropped a magnetic weight into it. Before the motion was brought to a vote he attacked it by a diversion, which outflanked it, moving that Congress, as its first duty, should ratify the *ley Juarez,* a touchstone, he said, which embodied "a principle that had been raised to the rank of a dogma by true republicans and without which democracy would be impossible." The debate called forth a full house on the floor and in the galleries, and the government joined in it. The prestige of the law was so powerful that the author of the parliamentary retreat was reduced to fighting a delaying action, lame tactics against the loadstone, for, far from damming, they merely served to accumulate the torrent of votes that drowned him; and the *ley Juarez* was ratified all but unanimously, over a single dissenting vote. Hailed as "one of the bases of the future Constitution," as its cornerstone, in fact, it served to rally Congress, as it had rallied Comonfort and the Moderates before, and to swing the tide of wavering opinion into a long forward sweep that forced the backsliders to abandon any hope of a Constitution that respected the military and ecclesiastical *fueros.*

The margin of victory was so narrow that the radicals were shocked to their feet and roused to a reckless pitch. When the draft of a Constitution drawn on the most advanced model—that of the United States and including its most liberal features—was reported to the Chamber, Ponciano Arriaga, who was the chairman of the Constitutional Committee, himself rose to denounce its shortcomings. Impatient as always of pretense, he saw little else in any constitution which affected abstract rights and liberties, while the basic right, the economic guarantee of democracy, was ignored. "Ideas are proclaimed," he said, "and facts are forgotten. The Constitution should be the law of *the land;* but the condition of *the land* is not constituted or even considered. Are we to practice popular government and have a hungry, naked, and miserable people? . . . Would it not be more logical and more honest to deny our four million poor all participation in public affairs, all choice in public posts, all active or passive voice in elections, to declare them things and not persons, and to found a system of government in which the aristocracy of money, or at most of talent, will serve as the base of our institutions?" For that was exactly what they were doing. Though some social reforms had been accepted by his committee, "all those were rejected which tended to define and determine the right of property, to procure indirectly the division of the immense lands accumulated today in the hands of a few owners, to correct the countless abuses which have passed into daily practice in the name of that sacred and inviolable right, and to set in movement the territorial and agricultural wealth of the country, arrested and reduced to intolerable monopolies, while so many settlements and laborious citizens are condemned to be mere passive tools of production for the exclusive use of the capitalists."

Arriaga disclaimed any suggestion of communism, or promiscuity, or phalansteries, or universal panaceas, or the extravagances of the utopian socialism of the time. "All these systems belong to the future: humanity will decide whether they are chimerical and whether, instead of pursuing reality, their authors are following a phantom. Under present conditions we recognize the right of property and hold it to be inviolable." Here and now, however, the fact remained that societies were constituted not by lawmakers but by landowners. "In the regions of a purely ideal and theoretical policy, while public men think of organizing chambers, dividing powers, assigning functions and attributes, surveying and laying out sovereignties, other and greater men laugh at all that, knowing that they are the masters of society, that the real power lies in their hands, and that they are the ones who exercise the actual sovereignty. The people are right in feeling that constitutions come and go, that governments succeed one another, that codes accumulate and become more complex, that plans and revolts live and die, and that after all these upheavals and changes, after all this unrest and these sacrifices, nothing practical remains for the people, nothing of profit for those unfortunate classes from whom always come those who shed their blood in the civil wars, who give their contingents for the armies, who people the prisons and labor on public works, and for whom, in short, are wrought all the evils of society and none of its benefits."

In this philippic could be heard the click, and the rattle, and the jolt with which Mexico joined the modern world and was coupled to its progress. While earlier reformers had looked to the French Revolution of 1789 for inspiration, Arriaga drew it up to date. "The Sovereign Congress knows that when the French Revolution of 1848 proclaimed the Republic," he continued, "there arose in connection with the right of property the principle of association, the organization of labor, the lot of the poor, and a thousand other subjects of equal significance, questions so grave that they shook society to its foundation." If the coming Constitution was to lift a country whose history had been revolutionary into line with the contemporary world, and a foreign lever was needed, it must be found in that recent movement which raised the question of property—so hastily settled in favor of the middle class —on behalf of the proletariat. The premises were drastic, but his conclusions were mild. He had often heard foreign colonization discussed, he said, as a cure for the poverty of the land, and had often asked himself if *Mexican* colonization might not be possible; if the fertile and uncultivated lands of the Republic could not be distributed among his fellow countrymen; if it would be difficult, by supplying them with seed and tools, and exempting them from taxation for a term of years, and allowing them to work the earth in freedom, without police, or bailiffs, or confraternities, or parochial obventions, or surplice fees, or notarial fees, or legal fees, or prison fees, or poll taxes, or bridge tolls— if it would be difficult to produce from those immense deserts and dark mountains new, prosperous, and happy populations. People believed, or affected to believe, that Mexicans as a whole were lazy, shiftless, and immoral; but were Mexicans the worst in the world? As a compromise, he recommended that the owners of large and idle estates be obliged to cultivate their surplus acres or to sell them to those who would, planting the reform in a system of small land grants; but whatever solution might be adopted, something must be done. "The reform, if it is to be a real one, must be the formula of a new era, the translation of a new phase of labor, a new code of the economic mechanism of the future."

It is not often that a man lives in history by virtue of a single speech: Ponciano Arriaga was one of those unique figures. Though the solution was so much smaller than the issue, his recognition of the real condition of political progress was sufficient to establish him as a far-sighted pioneer, who planted an outpost well in advance of his fellows and towered among them in lonely eminence. For, of course, Congress failed to follow his lead, and the question which he expounded was severely ignored, isolated, and forgotten. His initiative was lost because Congress shrank from the magnitude of the challenge and, paradoxically, because of the support which it received, for it coincided with the appearance of the *ley Lerdo*. Accepted by Congress and incorporated into the Constitutional project, the *ley Lerdo,* which dissolved the largest of land monopolies by liquidating ecclesiastical real estate, satisfied so much of the demand for subdivision and exploitation of idle land, and was so hazardous, as to dispense the Assembly from proceeding further on such treacherous ground and carrying the reform as far as Arriaga proposed. The success of Lerdo de Tajada buried the bid of Ponciano Arriaga—but in an uneasy grave.

The loss of the bid was responsible for the cardinal weakness of the new Constitution, which had no economic foundations and was loaded with top-heavy political ideals that were to prove in practice mortgages instead of assets. Modeled on the American Constitution, it sanctioned existing property rights, as did the original from which it was cast, save in one feature. Reiterating the prohibition of slavery, which every charter after Morelos embodied, it expressly forbade extradition treaties with slave-holding countries and declared that "all slaves who tread the national soil recover their liberty by that very fact." The sole measure of economic relief was an article guaranteeing freedom of labor, or rather—for it had to be read backward—prohibition of forced labor. But the Spanish kings had done as much, only to see their protective decrees flouted by facts. Much was said, on the other hand, of purely political liberties—universal suffrage, the power to impeach, the rights of petition, of assembly, of *habeas corpus,* of trial by jury, and the classic freedom of the press, of opinion, of teaching, of trade, and of conscience, and of these liberties the last carried Congress to the crisis and culmination of its advances.

It was not to be expected that the announcement of an article authorizing religious liberty would pass unchallenged by a Church already invaded in its judicial and economic privileges and unaccustomed to remaining long on the defensive: preliminary protests had been made by the Archbishop of Mexico and the Bishop of Oaxaca, and opinion was tense when the debate opened. The galleries were packed with a dense crowd, hanging over the speakers in a hard white glare of intolerant attention and a focus of murderous appreciation comparable to nothing so much as a Sunday at the bull ring. Nevertheless, as the champions rose and marshaled their arguments, maneuvering with nerve, with skill, and with unfaltering poise and self-possession, the issue obtained a full and fair hearing. "This discussion did honor to the national tribune," the Secretary of the Congress noted on the record. "Good faith, frankness, and civic courage were conspicuous in the addresses of all the speakers, and their sincerity is the best justification of the Congress. The mere discussion of so important a topic is a triumph of good principles. In vain the reactionaries sought out persons to come and insult the representatives of the people. Their intrigues were regarded with contempt. Although from time to time the public seemed excited, and some few tried to mislead it at first, it later gave proof of coolness and preserved perfect order; some jeers were repressed by the dignity of the rest, and the applause which later broke out was entirely spontaneous. It may be said with confidence that many of those who came in a hostile spirit realized that they were not in an assembly of heresiarchs and changed their minds. And to preserve order there were no guards, no police, no precautions. This must be said in honor of a public that has foiled the foolish intrigues of the enemies of liberty."

Under the close siege and support of public opinion, the debate lasted a week and called forth the talents of the Assembly. Their main task was defensive: to place the issue in the proper light and to dissociate the attack on religious exclusiveness from the semblance of an attack on religious faith; and in this the most ardent antagonists united. Prieto, a Christian poet, harped on his piety and harangued the heavens in the hope of being overheard in Mexico; the advocates of freedom of conscience were all apologists, vying with one another in professing their faith and citing Scripture in defense of religious democracy; to a man Congress was composed of devout believers. There was but one exception, and he was by far the most brilliant of its talents.

Ignacio Ramirez was an atheist, the only avowed one perhaps in Mexico. Some twenty years before he had scandalized Prieto and the members of a liberal club, who prided themselves on their freethinking, by denying them a deity. Since then he had gone his way and chosen his own company, browsing among bookstalls, haunting the galleries of Congress, making a name for himself in journalism and pedagogy, teaching but not preaching, suffering persecution and imprisonment for his political heresies, and fascinating and troubling his friends by his religious ones, but always on the margin of public life, in his own eccentric orbit, until he took his seat in the Constituent Congress of 1856. There he occupied a place apart, and a formidable one, because of the devastating intellectual powers which he displayed in defense of every dangerous measure, and on the delicate question of religious liberty his utterance was awaited with dread and dismay. Of what was to come he had already given a hint when the Constitutional project was first broached, and he had arisen, a lean stigmatic figure, and suddenly released his full stature to challenge its preamble. "Gentlemen," he flashed out, "the social pact that has been proposed to us is founded on a fiction. Here is how it begins: 'In the name of God . . .' I well know how much of the fictitious, the symbolic, the poetic, there is in all known legislation . . . but I consider it even more dangerous than absurd to suppose ourselves the interpreters of Divinity. . . . The name of God has everywhere produced Divine Right, and the history of Divine Right has been written by the hands of the oppressors in the blood and sweat of the peoples. And we who think ourselves free and enlightened, are we not combating Divine Right even now? Do we not tremble like children when we are told that, if we discuss religious toleration, a phalanx of old women will attack us, armed everyone of them with Divine Right? If a revolution hurls us from the tribune, it will be Divine Right that will drive us to prison, exile, and execution. . . . Gentlemen, for my part, I declare that I have not come here prepared by ecstasy or revelation. . . . The duty of forming a Constitution is too respectable to begin it by lying."

After that debut Congress was on the alert, but his conduct was more startling than anyone dreamed. To the crucial discussion the firebrand contributed something even more telling than his biting eloquence, his sardonic wit, his towering intransigence, and his scathing common sense—his silence. Save for one brief outburst, he stifled his powers. Lounging in his seat, he tossed no coruscating sarcasms into the ring. Hour after hour, under the most extreme provocation and the most visible strain, he held his fire, his hell fire. One flash, indeed, he could not resist: rising at a critical moment amid clamors of applause and some catcalls, and speaking in "short, sharp phrases that produced a visible sensation," he reminded the House that "in 1824, when the fires of the Inquisition were still smoldering, with one of its ill-quenched brands an article was engraved in the Constitution of the Republic establishing religious intolerance, and that is the article that we have come to cancel in the name of humanity, in the name of the Gospel, and if need be at the cost of our blood." But when, through the tumult of whistles and cheers that broke out in the galleries, there rose the cry of *Death to the sacristans!* he raised his hand to silence it. "Gentlemen," he cried, "Jesus Christ never wished to kill," and brought his speech to an abrupt close. Poised for the thrust and certain of being awarded the ear, he swung on his heel and strode back to his seat. His sense of responsibility was greater than his rage; he refused to prejudice the discussion by his notorious views and incendiary genius and left the trophy to more temperate and conventional men for whom reason was not inseparable from wrath—to Prieto who caressed it with a loose flow of impassioned and popular piety, to Zarco who cornered it with level and relentless logic, to Mata who braved it with bloodless barbs, and to many more who could tame intolerance in that rational spirit which it was so essential, and so difficult, to preserve.

A high sense of responsibility, indeed, dominated the debate, which turned not on the principle—on that all were agreed—but on its expediency in 1856. When it was urged that the adoption of religious tolerance would produce only remote and problematical benefits and was bound, in a country saturated with Catholicism, to lead to civil war and the loss of all the other gains of a democratic constitution, the caution was so obviously sound that it placed a crushing responsibility on those who denied it; and the most tragic hours of the Congress were those in which the contest raged between Opportunists and Inopportunists on the claim of the latter, which became the taunt of the former, and the battle cry of both, that the time for this reform had not yet come. "To those who say that the time is not yet," came the retort —Zarco speaking—"I put the question, when will it come? When the people are enlightened, they reply; when there is prosperity; when there is well-being. But this is to close the question in a vicious circle. . . . If they wish the reform of society to precede religious liberty, we have only to consider what Catholic exclusiveness has produced in three hundred years to abandon all hope. It has produced poverty, abjection, and slavery, it was an element of colonial domination, and it stubbornly opposed Independence."

Zarco holding his temper was more than the equal of Ramirez holding his peace; but Zarco raged no less insatiably, because his hand was raised to indite his Divine Comedy and his tongue was tied by the vision of the vicious circle that forbade his advance. Time! Time! Was it not high time for a reform long overdue, if so backward and feudal a country was to survive, let alone to advance, in the modern world? But he was no match for the Moderates. The timekeepers and the timeservers swayed back and forth, locked in a long, slow, leaden

match, shifting their grips but unable to break them. The dead weight
of wisdom and inertia was a drag against which the vanguard strained
in vain, bound by their opponents in a clinging embrace, which
hugged them where they were weakest and unheeled them on their
own ground. "Make no mistake, gentlemen," they were warned, "the
opinion of parliamentary majorities is not public opinion when it dif-
fers from the opinion of the people. A majority of this Assembly, if it
declares for religious tolerance, will not form a law and much less a
Constitutional law. The country will repudiate it and the law will remain a dead letter, as always happens with those that run counter to
the national will." Heave as they might, they could not cast the hold of
such arguments. The religious wars of the sixteenth century were cited
against them to prove at what cost freedom of worship had been won
in the Old World—were they prepared to pay it? A robust conscience
was needed to face the prospect of Mexico repeating that historical
agony to make up for its secular lag in social development. Young
themselves, they were cramped by the agues, the palsies, the qualms of
time. Worse yet, they were weakened by the very pace of progress.
They were belated pioneers blazing a well-trodden trail, long since
beaten flat, which led nowhere. It was too late, as well as too early, for
freedom of conscience—an issue already obsolete in advanced nations
and a burning one in backward countries only if irresponsible doctrinaires decided to make it one. Was it not wiser then, and more humane, and more farsighted, to mark time with the present?

The lowest note was sounded when intolerance was defended by the
timeservers as an evil, no doubt, but a necessary one in Mexico in 1856.
"Constitutions," they repeated, "are not created or invented; to be good,
to produce the social and political results expected of them, they should
be nothing more than the portrait, so to speak, of the people for whom
they are framed. In the United States, in that pure democracy which is
so highly admired, in that liberal Constitution which is so cried up, do
we not see the most atrocious principle embedded, the most cruel, the
most degrading for mankind—that of slavery? If a people that pro-
claims itself liberal and democratic to the point of hyperbole rivets into
its Constitution an article that dishonors civilization and mankind, will
it be disgraceful for us if, before establishing freedom of worship as a
right, we wait until it exists among us as a fact?" And the most compromising moment was when democratic dogmas were turned against
the Progressives to prove that they exceeded their powers and misrepresented the people. Zarco admitted the charge in a defiant rebuttal.
"You forget," he flung back, "that legislators must be superior to their
period, that from Moses to the first American Congress reformers and
founders of nations have had to overcome resistance."

Between the long and the short view the struggle was highly unequal, and the contemporizers had the advantage. On the short view

there was little to recommend religious tolerance, the only immediate benefit which its advocates could adduce being that it favored foreign immigration and would break the monopoly of the Church in the spiritual sphere which sanctioned its monopolies in the temporal; but in reality they were concerned with an ideal of enlightenment so remote as to be academic in relation to present realities. They were, as their critics insisted, tutors rather than representatives of the people, or, as they themselves claimed, trustees for its eventual development: so far ahead of it that they were highly vulnerable to the charge of irresponsible idealism and were forced to fall back, in self-defense, on their faith in the people, their mystic, unreasoning democratic faith in the right instincts of the masses and their capacity to recognize their own interests and those who represented them. The fanaticism and superstition of the populace might seem to belie that belief; but Mata pointed out that when tolerance had been proposed in 1848, it had provoked thousands of spontaneous protests, whereas today, only eight years later, the people had not moved, and, to secure a semblance of opposition, the clergy had been compelled to mobilize the women, "the simple and artless women who have been forced for the first time to appear on the public scene" and to present a handful of petitions, the signers of which candidly admitted that they had been dictated by the parish priest. There was the rate of progress. Neither faith nor statistics swayed the compact mass of the Moderate majority, however, and the contest, strenuous but stationary, would have dragged on indefinitely had not a halt been called by the umpire. The government intervened, and intervened decisively, to discountenance religious tolerance and to signify its disapproval of any more dangerous measures.

Thereafter the radical bloc was steadily driven back and forced from the floor, protesting. One after another its leaders caught and clung to its supreme appeal. "We are threatened with a revolution, sir," Dr. Gamboa challenged the chair. "What would Don Benito Juarez have done when he issued his law on *fueros* if, foreseeing the revolt in Puebla, he had been intimidated by that idea? . . . Don Benito Juarez, sir, saw that he was going to win a principle with his law; Don Benito Juarez feared nothing; nothing deterred him because Don Benito Juarez is a man of heart, and that same Don Benito Juarez tells us today from Oaxaca—reform, tolerance, everything that makes for progress." But the virtue had fled from that spellbinding name. The *ley Juarez,* a beacon six months before, had dropped far behind and became with the turn of the tide a buoy hastily passed by a Congress hurrying to make port. In the rush of retreat the closing bell alone was heard.

The routed made a last stand at the foot of their first pedestal. "To insult the people," Zarco stood and cried, "to call it fanatic, idolatrous, ignorant, and superstitious, is the only weapon our opponents employ to retard the reform we proclaim. Our people is like all peoples. There is no people without superstitions, there is no people of philosophers, theologians, intellectuals, and lawyers. . . . You wise men, you superior souls who see in Mexico a tribe of savages, must blush to have to represent them. If I thought as you do, I would be ashamed to be a deputy. Gentlemen, the past has been evoked here, and here is a man who is a living monument of that period, Don Valentin Gomez Farias, and I am sure that that venerable survivor of 1824 will vote for freedom of conscience." The decision was dramatic. "The most profound silence reigned, the public repressed its anxiety and voting had something grave and solemn, as all the representatives rose and emitted their votes in clear and firm tones. At first each vote was followed by vague rumors in the galleries and marks of approval and disapproval. The article was declared shelved by sixty-five to forty-four. A few deputies left the hall before voting. The result produced an appalling confusion in the galleries, whistles, applause, cries of 'Long live religion! Death to the heretics! Long live the clergy!' "

This session marked the crisis of the congressional labors and their turning point. Disintegration set in rapidly. The little radical group that had dominated Congress for six months, while it had the support of the government, became, as soon as that support was withdrawn, a discredited minority fighting a stubborn but in general a losing battle to save the remaining articles of their creed. They rallied, they closed ranks, they returned again to the charge with redoubled vigor and sharpened vision. One result of defeat was to reveal more clearly than before the indivisibility of reform and the fallacy of neglecting the economic foundations in a backward and priest-ridden country. Abandoning their crusade for freedom of conscience, they bent their effort to securing the other liberties upon which progress depended, and which would eventually prohibit, as they were at present forbidden by, monopoly of faith. On the day after their defeat, apparently floored but merely driven from the top to the bottom and gaining fresh strength, like the mythical hero, from contact with the ground, they revived the discussion of land reforms. The proposals of Ponciano Arriaga in which, as Zarco said, "there is nothing of robbery or pillage or communist fevers," but which had been protested by a body of large landowners, were reintroduced in a bill recommending a reduction of land monopolies. The author—an obscure Liberal by the name of Olvera, but one of those obscurities who noticed what was invisible to the most brilliant—disavowed any ideas more drastic than those of Arriaga. Agrarian reform, Olvera observed, occurred less and less frequently to lawgivers as culture and acquaintance with the rights of man increased; the French Conventionals and Robespierre in particular never resorted to it, although they professed communism, but "wise and prudent as they were, and working for humanity rather than for the generation to which they belonged, they tried to establish it indirectly by making the rich contribute to improving the condition of the poor through education, labor, philanthropic institutions, and the taxation of articles of prime necessity. And Jesus Christ himself, who was the communist *par excellence,* what did he ordain? Did he command the poor to despoil the rich? No, he confined himself to teaching the rich that it was unlawful to retain their superfluity, because it belonged to the needy. For more than ten years," he went on, "I have been inculcating the idea that the rich themselves, if possible, should direct the drama by sacrificing a small portion of their substance to save the whole, instead of wasting it on foolish revolutions and armed resistance, capable at most of temporarily weakening the movement but never of crushing it; and I firmly believe, sir, that if they had listened to me they would sleep today with a quiet conscience and in secure possession of their estates. If the government stops short, its head will suffer the fate of Louis XVI and succumb to the execration of all the parties that represent the revolution."

In words of evangelical moderation but revolutionary omen, Comonfort and Congress were warned that half-measures were futile in mid-revolution; the enemy would fight the half as implacably as the whole. The promise and threat of Reform had been carried too far to retreat, and the most dangerous of all courses was to temporize. "There may still be time to remedy evils without serious damage to any fraction of society," Olvera concluded; but how much more obscure must his voice become to be heard? "Your sovereignty and the government should reflect seriously on the dangers and the necessity of dispelling them, and the rich also should reflect on their real interests and aid the public powers to save the country by the betterment of the poor classes and by settling definitely a social question that is assuming dimensions as gigantic as they are menacing." Religion *and* revolution, Christianity *and* communism, their coalition was still possible, but the concessions must not be deferred until they were made by force, and the responsibility for that alternative he placed squarely on the timeservers. But an appeal that went unheeded before the defeat of religious tolerance naturally fell flat after it, and the warnings of Olvera followed the proposals of Arriaga into the limbo of unborn reforms.

Religious tolerance was so integral a test of democratic development, indeed, that the victors were demoralized by their retreat from it, and compromise and qualification emasculated even those principles of a democratic society which they were prepared to adopt—so true is it that moral bodies are subject to the same collective distempers as physical ones. The most elementary rights of self-government were mutilated before they were delivered, by restrictions and retractions dictated, as Ramirez complained, by mistrust of the people. Universal suffrage was accepted in form but frustrated in fact by the filtering ma-

chinery of indirect elections. Trial by jury was lost; the power of impeachment was thrown out; an attempt was made to refine away the
rights of peaceful assembly and lawful petition. Freedom of the press,
hedged about with captious limitations, came through thanks to a spirited defense by Zarco. As editor of the leading Liberal paper, the *Siglo
XIX*, Zarco rose to the defense of his profession with militant zeal, but
it was less by trade-righteousness that he carried the day than by the
adventitious aid he derived from a small scandal in which he was then
involved. The French Minister had offended the French colony by
making a niggardly contribution to a relief fund for the victims of a
flood in France, and his compatriots had punished him by a Mexican
cencerrada—a serenade of pots and pans. The incident had been written up in the *Siglo* by the editor himself, and it was upon him that the
nettled diplomat vented his anger, threatening the government with an
international incident if he were not promptly castigated. The government had the weakness, or the address, to call a congressional trial, a
settlement which Zarco accepted with alacrity and exploited to the full.
The case would have been a godsend to the most unskilled publicist,
and he was an expert. He converted the affair into a mock trial, regal-
ing Congress with a solemn account of the *cencerrada* and pillorying
the victim with a humor, a good humor, a moderation and urbanity
that revealed his command of the most admired French qualities, and
exploding the international incident with a single prick. "I can only
repeat," he concluded after a hilarious day in court, "that to receive a
cencerrada may be mortifying, but that it can never be one of the official functions of an ambassador. It would be sad to suppose that the
conquerors of the East should have to come to our shores to the tune
of a frying pan, and that His Majesty the Emperor, and above all the
French people, should have to make a national issue of an event that
at most will set all Paris laughing." Needless to say, he was acquitted.
Under the banter he touched the sore spot of foreign dictation, and
freedom of the press was incorporated into the Constitution in a flush
of patriotic pride.

But it was only thanks to the unflagging energy of the leavening few
that the major principles of democracy came through the thickening
pressure of compromise at all. The stamina of Congress steadily weakened as its work approached completion and the verdict of the country loomed nearer. In October a second revolt broke out in Puebla, this
time against the *ley Lerdo,* and though it was repressed, the effect on
the lawmakers was profoundly troubling. To a few, but a very few, it
was a timely confirmation of their contention that half-measures would
be fought as implacably as whole ones, and a warning, as one speaker
said, "that if you wish to flatter the clergy, it is well to remember that
this class will never compromise with liberty." But they were a minority, fighting to hold what ground they had already won. A motion to

return to the Constitution of 1824 was reintroduced by a considerable majority and was so nearly adopted as to call all that had been accomplished into question and to cast a long mortal shadow over the final months of deliberation.

Time also told on the spirit of the delegates, and the habits of legislative bodies eager to relax after a heavy meal; after sitting over their work for a year they were determined to bring it to a close at all costs. On February 5, 1857, the Constitution was proclaimed. A solemn unanimity marked the closing ceremony. Gomez Farias presided, kneeling before the Bible and swearing his sanction; a hundred deputies stood and raised their hands, repeating the oath in unison; the volume was handed to Comonfort, who pledged himself to preserve it. The finality of the result was crowned by recognition of its fallibility: a philosophical reflection to that effect was made by Comonfort and echoed by Leon Guzman, the vice-president of Congress, in his reply. "The Congress," he said, "is far from flattering itself with the idea that its work is perfect. It well knows, as you have said, that no work of man is so. It believes, nevertheless, that it has achieved principles of vital importance and opened wide a door through which the men who follow us may develop a just liberty to its ultimate consequences."

Such indeed was the achievement of the Constituents of 1856—prospective. The new Constitution was an unfinished effort, a vehicle for progress, and a compromise between the fundamental and the feasible. Primarily a political rather than a social charter, it represented only a relative advance over the Constitution of 1824: like that counterweight against which it was drawn with so much difficulty, it consecrated, tacitly but no less implicitly, the cardinal principle of religious intolerance, which sealed and sanctioned all the other monopolies of colonial society; and the two anticlerical statutes incorporated in it, the ley Juarez and the ley Lerdo, originated outside of the Congress instead of within it. The major taboos were respected. But if the social bases of progress were faulty or fragmentary, political machinery of the most approved modern make had been placed within reach of the people, or the conscious part of it, to improve and complete them. The structural principles of democracy were proclaimed—freedom of thought and teaching and the press, of labor, of petition, and assembly, and a faithful replica of the Rights of Man informed a chronically inorganic nation for the first time of its recognized and inalienable birthright.

The features upon which the mechanics most prided themselves were naturally those which contrasted most sharply with the past. A long list of civil liberties, which by their very nature and length recapitulated and indicted abuses that had flourished freely in the turbulent years of tyranny, guaranteed the right of judicial appeal, of bail, of confrontation with the accuser in criminal cases, of access to the material of defense, of inviolability of domicile and private correspondence;

prohibited previous imprisonment for all crimes except those involving corporal punishment, and unmotivated arrest for more than three days, and more than one trial for the same offense, and unusual or excessive penalties, such as whipping, branding, torture, or confiscation of property, and incarceration for debt, and retroactive laws; and instituted as their consummation and synthesis the abolition of class justice by the *ley Juarez* and by a hundred helpmates in the Assembly, of capital punishment for political crimes. Humanity was not among the shortcomings of the men of '57. It was the redeeming feature of their failings and the carnal defect of the partial reforms of incomplete liberals: the parts were not equal to the whole, but the whole was a mosaic of the collective progress of many minds, varying in individual vision and courage but holding a common inspiration of original generosity, which they labored conscientiously to translate into a working approximation of human justice. And that perpetually unfinished effort produced a few workmen ambitious and fit to develop it further.

The crowning achievement of the Constitution was not the measures but the men it produced, and here too the triumph was prospective. The fighting few who dominated Congress during the first six months distinguished themselves by their constancy during the days of decline, and though their ranks were thinned, the survivors were recognized as the national protagonists of reform. Ramirez, the caustic iconoclast; Prieto, the popular sentimentalist; Zarco, the most persuasive of journalists: Mata, the master-disciple; Guzman, the blandest of zealots; visionary realists like Arriaga and Olvera and sensible ones like Gamboa—all displayed what Arriaga declared was "the first requisite of a public man," character; and each in his own way revealed traits of the national character and talent that contributed essential parts to the making of a popular movement. For it was still in the making, and its momentum and continuity could be counted only by its converts.

One remarkable convert was added to the roster of complete liberals when Congress closed. Santos Degollado, the Governor of Jalisco, was a specimen of what the Constitution could produce in the way of men. He had fought with conspicuous courage in the revolution of Ayutla, but to the Constituent Congress he contributed little, and that little either perfunctory or unfortunate, his idea being to go back to an earlier conservative charter. The Constitution exceeded his convictions, but he underwrote it with a loyalty fully equal to the zeal of those who wrote it, and all the more valuable for that very reason. Association in the great collective adventure of reconstituting a nation worked no conversion so happy as the evolution of Santos Degollado. He outgrew his political timidity and overcame his defective vision by virtue of discipline; discipline was the core of his character, and he showed to what lengths he could carry it in an incident which focused attention upon him at this time. After proclaiming the Constitution, Congress remained in session for an epilogue to its labors, of which he was the subject. He had expelled a British Consul from his state for subsidizing a local revolt; the British Legation had protested to the government, and Comonfort had referred the case to Congress for trial. It was a counterpart to the Zarco trial, but a serious one: the British Legation could not be laughed off as lightly as the French Minister, for the Consul was a partner in an Anglo-American bank and had used his *exequatur* to cover a flourishing trade in contraband, and Comonfort sent a special envoy to London to avert an international incident. But the verdict was the same: the issue of foreign dictation was at stake, and Degollado was acquitted. He conducted his defense by waiving it and offered in his peroration "to continue to play the guilty party, if this will lend another service to my country." The words summed up the man: from anyone else they might have been applauded as a forensic appeal, but he was blind to their histrionic effect; for Degollado was as sincere and as artless as an adolescent. He had the vocation of martyrdom and he proclaimed his calling; and it was that quality, or frailty, of the professional reformer that endeared him to the little band of radicals who knew that they would need it as soon as the Constitution was launched. With him their roll call was almost complete. But the absent were not forgotten. Again and again two names were recalled in congressional battle. When Arriaga challenged the government on a wavering issue, "the party of progress," he said, "has the right to ask the government party: what are its reforms? The *ley Juarez,* the *ley Lerdo.* Needless to say, neither Señor Juarez nor Señor Lerdo belongs to the Moderate party." Whenever the battle was dubious, those standards were brandished; wherever the odds were overwhelming, those names were added to the count to make up for the weight of numbers. And after the battle they were needed more transcendently than ever.

13

FOR the Constituent Congress had demonstrated the radical fallacy of attempting revolutionary reforms by parliamentary methods, and the incompetence of the democratic process, where the force of numbers was decisive and negative, to deal with them. Individual initiative was still indispensable to popular progress. As a mold for men, the Assembly had performed an important function, but a transient one. The inspiration which it kindled, the energy which it released, the solidarity which it created, lost their focus as soon as it dissolved, and the few creative spirits whom it mustered were again dispersed and disorganized.

Ocampo left the Congress long before the end and followed its final stages in critical solitude. When the press cited four names—his own, Arriaga, Lerdo, and Juarez—as successive leaders of the radical fraction within a single year to prove its chronic infirmity, Ocampo bridled. "This shows a lack of intelligence," he wrote to Mata. "I say in turn that we Liberals do not like leaders; that any one of us on any given occasion may be the representative (not the leader) of one or many of our ideas of progress, and that the very text of the paper would prove, if it were true, that we always subordinate persons to ideas." He was the first, however, to succumb to the old anarchy of the Liberal clan. He refused to sign the Constitution and retired to his farm, preferring intellectual solitude to active isolation. Heartsick and weary of half-measures—"We are singularly foolish people," he sighed. "The text is long but the preacher is tired"—he studied the progress of compromise and decay with a deepening disgust and despondency, which he concentrated on one man. For it was the influence of one man, steadily curbing the courage of the minority and moderating the mild temerity of the Moderate majority, that Ocampo blamed for the frailty of a covenant which, by seeking security, provided safeguards against every peril but its own debility. "For more than a year now," he said, "all of us who have been compelled to study the present President—a person whom we knew very superficially hitherto—have been able to appreciate his absolute lack of character, his great dearth of convictions, and his more than ordinary want of education. I am not surprised, therefore, that the present system of government is always afraid of everyone and everything. Whence could it draw inner impulse if it is without conviction, physiological organization, and even the instinct of great things? It is sad nonetheless, and all the more so for being expected, that the fine opportunities incessantly offered to Mexico should be lost to such incapable hands."

Of all the personalities called forth by Congress, Comonfort was the last to reveal himself and the most important because of his controlling position and the infirmity of his character: a pivotal figure who confirmed with every passing hour the horoscope which Ocampo had cast of him as an incorrigible timeserver. If destiny meant to do what was expected of one, and every man after his kind, Comonfort was doomed to compromise, to cater to the clergy, and, given time, to undo the Constitution in deference to a class that would never compromise with liberty. The prognostic was calculated on the nature of the man and the character of the time, and Ocampo was not surprised when, shortly before the Constitution was published, rumors began to circulate of an impending *coup d'état* by the President. Ocampo was merely incredulous and contemptuous. "I do not believe in the *coup d'état*," he told Mata, "because those people seem to me too timid for it. They may have the boldness, nevertheless, for what is bad." He prepared himself, however, for the worst; for with the dissolution of Congress there was no further check on the President, and to counteract his weakness there were only a dozen disorganized and leaderless radicals, none of whom was in a position of power.

Of the original group, the only one who still held public office was Juarez. Returning to Oaxaca in 1856 as governor in the first flush of reform, he was authorized by Comonfort to suppress opposition by force, if necessary, but his familiar methods of moderation and firmness stood him in good stead, and though he was branded as the author of the first anticlerical law, he outfaced the hostility of the local clergy without resorting to force to plant the newly won civil rights which he brought home with him and those that followed. The *ley Lerdo* he supported by personal example, purchasing a small property to encourage those who hesitated to take advantage of the benefits of a law nullified in the capital by the ban of the Archbishop of Mexico. Government by example—his favorite formula—served him well as long as he could collaborate with Comonfort, but friction developed when the President refused to abolish the system of Federal garrisons, a system of long-standing which quartered the capital on the provinces and which had guaranteed every arbitrary regime in the past. Abolition of military, as the corollary to clerical, control, was a reform upon which Juarez insisted. To accommodate him, Comonfort consented to invest him with the authority in dispute; but Juarez was not satisfied or silenced by personal favors and pressed for a statutory reform in Congress, where it was eventually adopted. Thereafter the rift widened, and by the end of the year Juarez had quietly shifted his weight from Comonfort to Congress, adopting its acts and incorporating them in a new charter for his state, under the terms of which he was elected governor. The security of his position was strikingly shown when the Federal Constitution was promulgated. He invited the Bishop of Oaxaca to celebrate it with a solemn *Te Deum,* and the Bishop consented without resistance, save for the polite and private expression of certain perfunctory reservations. Such was the ripe autumnal fruit of his collaboration with the clergy in the past and the fallow years of timeserving, which, almost imperceptibly, he had put behind him; but it was his last triumph of that kind. He had taken leave of conformity forever, and he was accepted by the hierarchy, like the Constitution, with mental reservations and provisionally. Their pent-up ire flared up at his inauguration under the new dispensation. The clergy refused to officiate and the Cathedral was closed, for the avowed purpose of provoking a scandal and forcing him to break the strike; but he avoided the trap by dispensing with the religious ceremonies that consecrated the seating of a new governor. He broke the strike with the tradition. The sensation which he caused merely by failing to appear before the great marble façade where the saints in their niches and the sanctity of the solar orb awaited, in graven agitation, the breaking of the ages, was a spectacular triumph upon which he prided himself; nor was it the only one. "Speaking of bad habits," he noted, "there were others that served only to gratify the vanity and ostentation of the governor, such as the custom of having armed guards in their homes and wearing hats of a special shape at public ceremonies. As soon as I assumed power, I abolished this custom, using the hat and dress of an ordinary citizen and living in my home without a military guard or display of any kind, since I believe that the respectability of a ruler derives from the law and right conduct and not from costumes and martial accessories proper only for stage kings. I am happy to say that the governors of Oaxaca have followed my example."

Republican simplicity broke more than one precedent. The reserve with which he always referred to himself colored for a moment with self-consciousness when he remembered himself as others saw him then, and as a portrait of the period preserves him, a familiar black-coated and easily accessible figure, filling out his loose clothes with solid flesh, the sturdy personification of democracy on the march. The age of Santa Anna was gone forever, and the era of the common man inaugurated. It was not the least of his talents as a ruler that Juarez did not neglect the visible truth of an idea, which he brought home to a people abjectly susceptible to visual impressions and invisibly governed by them from time immemorial. And on that note his memoir ends. Autobiography was abruptly broken off by the onrush of events, which swept the pen from his hand in a formidable draught of national and self-effacing life, leaving the sketch that he had begun to be finished by the controversial judgments and partial truths of other minds.

Thereafter his biography became a political treatise, the fragments were fused in the movement to which he belonged, and the parts lost in the whole. Discretion, patience, pliability, and noiseless determination—his tried and trusted methods of progress—had been carried as far as they could go. The movement was fast approaching the point at which progress depended on what Mora called the law of the excluded middle; and like Ocampo, Juarez braced himself for the crisis. How he prepared for it he recorded in his last calm moment of self-accounting. Although he had taken no part in the framing of the Constitution, he had kept pace in mind and act with the little group of men who had striven to remold the face of a nation and in part succeeded—

on paper—but only on paper. The test was yet to come, and he set his house in order against the reaction that was expected to follow the application of the new code. All the precautions which he took during that critical year—the reconstruction of the state, the acclimating of reforms, the abolition of Federal garrisons, the consolidation of his authority—were inspired by a weatherwise presentiment. "It was my opinion," he wrote, "that the states should constitute themselves without delay, for I feared that, because of certain principles of liberty and progress embodied in the general Constitution, a rebellion might break out in the capital or soon form there, dissolving the supreme powers, and it was well that the states should be organized to oppose and destroy it, and to restore the legitimate authorities established by the Constitution."

The calm before the storm was long and unnerving. The storm, it was clear, was not to be one of the usual local squalls, short, sharp, and clearing quickly, to which the country was accustomed in its many changes of regime. It was a profound and complete convulsion, which gathered slowly, preceded by a long and ominous hush, a general but indefinite uneasiness, a dimming of the sun and a growing haziness and unsettling of the atmosphere. The first flares of reaction, promptly dispelled by the repression of the two revolts in Puebla, were followed by a protracted period of recovery and preparation, during which the enemy reassembled his strength and felt out public opinion, that hypothetical power to which the theorists of democracy appealed so confidently. Public opinion was thrown into confusion and ferment by the unwonted importance attributed to it. To the acute distress of a numerous bureaucracy of devout believers and their dependents, the Archbishop of Mexico forbade the faithful to swear allegiance to the Constitution on pain of excommunication, and the bulk of the clergy re-echoed the ban. But the Church itself was divided: even in the upper ranks of the hierarchy there were exceptions, while among the lower clergy there were not a few courageous, public-spirited, and conscientious priests, as usual, to declare from press and pulpit that no doctrinal issue, no religious question, was involved in the controversy. Nevertheless, and also as usual, it was the institutional spirit that prevailed, the solidarity of a corporation which could not be attacked at any one point without bleeding in all and suffering systematically at its sacred heart. Nor was it merely the members of the Mexican Church who rallied as a body. Rome felt the shock, and contracted, and reacted, with a long ultramontane tremor throughout all the reaches of the ecclesiastical nervous system. The Pope condemned the Constitution in secret consistory and declared it null and void three months before it saw the light. The authors of the *ley Juarez* and the *ley Lerdo* were noticed, anonymously but none the less notoriously, by the Pontiff, who placed their sponsoring laws at the head of a long catalogue of injuries to the Faith, singling out for special censure, as the most obnoxious features of the foetus, the proscription of ecclesiastical privilege and the principle "that no one may enjoy an emolument onerous to society," and sentenced them with all the other works of profanation wrought and contumacious decrees contemplated by the Constituents. Pius IX had long since outlived his liberal beginnings and was moving, hard pressed by the times, toward complete condemnation of the independent spirit of the nineteenth century. The development of the modern world, trembling between liberty and license, had everywhere placed the Church on the defensive; and with resurgent nationalism encroaching on the temporal power in Italy, it was no time to tolerate disaffection in Mexico. Far from settling the sedition there, however, the Papal injunction inflamed it, and a furious polemical effervescence ensued. A rash of pamphlets broke out all over the land, the press carried the discussion into every home where thought and the parish priest could both penetrate, and the controversy raged unresolved for six feverish months.

The effects of a semester of agitation were seen in the new Congress elected in September 1857. Of the incendiaries of the Constituent Assembly only one was returned. Ramirez, Prieto, Zarco, Arriaga, and all the other contrivers of lurid light and flickering freedom but Olvera were cast out, and in their places sat a body of middle-men completely subservient to Comonfort, himself committed to half-light and haze. What had happened was clearer than how. If the electorate could be trusted, there could be no doubt that public opinion had repudiated the *Puros;* but could it be trusted? Did the result represent the real verdict of the country? The machinery of indirect elections allowed full scope for manipulation by the government, for local intrigue and fraud, and for pressure by the disfranchised clergy in parishes of political minors. Whatever the reason, the result was profoundly discouraging to those disciples of pure democracy who had so confidently claimed to interpret the right instincts of the people. It converted them overnight into academic theorists, immature idealists, amateur Prometheans of progress. The real, the heart-searching doubt which their failure raised, however, was whether or not a democratic revolution could be carried through by democratic methods, whether, indeed, any drastic social change could be accomplished without an initial period of dictatorship by an enlightened minority.

As a whole, the *Puros* accepted their defeat philosophically and provisionally as the inevitable consequence of the ignorance of the people, the neutralizing deals and ideals of parliamentary bodies, and the unpopularity of a schismatic experiment; but there were some hotheads among them who could not resign themselves to their rout. One of these was a supernumerary by the name of Baz. He was a minor and fanatical figure—one of those fugitive firebrands thrown up by every social upheaval for a brief effervescent moment—in whom a larger idea than himself had lodged. Generally considered a crank, he was a crank equally capable of speeding the operation, or upsetting the machinery, of forces beyond his responsibility or control. He believed, and made no secret of his conviction, that the Constitution itself was an obstacle to social progress, and that basic reforms could be realized only by a personal dictatorship. But, though he buzzed on his obsession, he would not have acted on his belief had he not quarreled with Comonfort. Elected to Congress, he was obliged by the President to resign the position which he then occupied of Governor of the Federal District, the Constitution prohibiting the occupation of both posts simultaneously. Thereupon he became a declared enemy of the President, who suspected him of plotting trouble, without reason other than his reckless and outspoken radicalism.

Comonfort listened with one ear, and Baz would have buzzed out of the other, had not the other been humming with the same drone, but from a contrary quarter. The conservatives were no less disconcerted by the result of the congressional elections. The worst of the radicals had been routed, it was true, but their nest remained. The Constitution itself was confirmed, despite six months of furious agitation, and so plain an index of their failing hold on public opinion quickened their conviction that dictation by an enlightened minority was essential to their self-preservation. But they lacked leadership. For want of their own they turned to Comonfort, whose personal prestige, conciliatory character, and elastic policy provided exactly the kind of cover they needed. Incorruptible, he was not inaccessible. No bait of vulgar ambition, nothing less than his virtues could betray him, and it was through these that the approaches were made. Pressure was applied to discover his weak spot, and expert fingers, feeling their way through the dense tendrils of his scruples, soon located it. He was intensely vulnerable through a habit, uncommon among Mexican men, of consulting a woman on his problems—a habit that tampered with unbroken custom and rewarded the woman for the silent and submissive life of her sex, lending her an influence warranted by her remoteness from the world and her conservative role in it, and affranchising her at the end of her days; for in this case the woman was his mother. He was a devoted son; she was a devout listener; and she had a confidant of her own in her Father Confessor. Father Miranda was the right-hand man of the Bishop of Puebla, who had been banished by Comonfort for inciting the revolts there, and as he was the moving spirit of a secret society formed to combat the Constitution by every means available to a class without political license, he borrowed the voice of nature to soften the heart and turn the head of their persecutor. For a priest whose calling it was to inculcate scruples, it was not difficult to quicken those of a confirmed prey to them, and to insinuate into that congenial mind the advisability of reforming the Constitution and eliminating its objectionable features, or if that proved impossible, the whole mistaken and impractical charter itself.

Thus beset by the same suggestions, right and left, Comonfort adopted an eclectic mean. "Three courses were open to me," he wrote later in defense of his choice: first, to leave everything as he found it, which would have been "a folly and a crime," and second, to introduce all the reforms demanded, which would have been "no less absurd and iniquitous." "To renovate everything suddenly, without respecting any right, interest, or class, meant that I would be doing what great popular commotions have done in other lands in short periods of violence and vertigo; it meant that I would be embarking on a desperate struggle not only with the classes affected by the revolution but with the whole people, equally concerned in preventing such an upheaval," and "that is what governments entitled to the name never do; that is what men who are regarded as just never do, for whatever the modern world may owe to such cataclysms, created by reckless crowds, and notwithstanding that they may be caused by despair and provoked by oppressive governments, they are nonetheless great wrongs and never to be accepted as political systems. . . . Between these two extremes, one as vicious as the other, there lay a prudent and just middle way. . . . This was the adoption of a careful reformatory policy, which would satisfy the demands of the Liberal revolution insofar as they were just, but would not openly clash with conservative principles or the religious habits and beliefs of the people."

In this honest statement of a humane creed Comonfort revealed, no doubt, what was his real ambition: to be numbered among the just— of all the ambitions of men the most delusive and, in a revolutionary leader for whom justice could not be found in his own generation, the most misleading. The very qualities which honored his character in private life disqualified him for public command. In practice the middle way, the way of least resistance, narrowed down into a purely negative course, which yielded under pressure to whatever stress was strongest; and in the interval between the two Congresses, when he was left to himself, it swerved more and more to the right and was strewn with concessions to the clergy. To steer a middle course successfully required a strong hand, and between Scylla and Charybdis there was only Comonfort. While he resisted the extreme drifts from both sides, he was haunted by darkness at noon, and it became increasingly difficult to lay a true course through the haze or to distinguish between conflicting principles and the common solution that both proposed. It only remained for someone to suggest a personal dictatorship to guarantee the golden mean—and someone did.

When Congress convened in September 1857 Comonfort had come

to the conclusion that it was impossible to govern under the Constitution and was determined to obtain its reform—constitutionally, if possible. He sought and obtained, with difficulty, from an accommodating Congress an extension of his emergency powers. A month later he was elected to the Presidency by a sweeping popular majority, which made his position secure. A month before Congress met, Baz sounded him and found him ready to restore the vote to the clergy; a month after his election, Baz sounded him again and found their differences too deep for repair. Baz came away from their conference convinced that the President was preparing to capitulate to the clergy and that there was only one chance of checking him. "On that day," he said, "I acquired the certainty that he would accept the ministry of Señor Juarez, which gave me some hope of a change of policy."

A Moderate Congress, and the overwhelming majority with which he was returned to the Presidency, confirmed Comonfort in his conviction that he represented the common sense of the country; but the elections had one result which gave him pause. Juarez was elected at the same time to the Presidency of the Supreme Court, a position which carried with it the succession to the Presidency of the Republic in case of any lapse in that office. Or the urns, or his undermind, engendered a doubt of his ability to divine public opinion correctly; or his judgment was clouded, or the oracle that confirmed him had been adulterated. So unmistakable a recognition of a prominent *Puro* compelled Comonfort to placate the radicals who had lost confidence in him and who wished to put Juarez in power, and accordingly he offered him a seat in the cabinet. The seat was the most difficult and compromising of which he disposed at the time, the Ministry of the Interior, which gave the occupant command of the police and official responsibility for public security. Juarez accepted and secured for his secretary, Manuel Ruiz, the portfolio of Justice, to the relief of the *Puros,* who now had two representatives in high office whom they trusted. Juarez, the word went, was "absolutely good," and Ruiz at least "relatively good."

When Juarez came to the capital in the first days of November, rumors of an impending *coup d'état* by the President were circulating so freely that they were openly discussed in the press. For this reason, perhaps, they were generally discounted; they had arisen repeatedly before, and currency had staled them. But the absence of secrecy was no safeguard against danger, as many successful conspiracies had proved in the past; it proved the confidence of the promoters, and in this case it was subsequently cited by one of them in his defense. "A conspiracy in which we wrote freely to officials and other friends of liberty!" he scoffed. "A conspiracy that was practiced every day and at every hour of the day in the Palace! A conspiracy that was known to the police and to the Governor of the District! A conspiracy, in sum, that was confided to writing and communicated by mail to high officials with no safeguard but a smear of glue!" The Minister of the Interior assumed his duties at a critical time, and with every passing day his position became more delicate. A fortnight after his arrival, in a conference with the President, Comonfort spoke of his difficulties— the respect which he felt for the beliefs of his mother—his friendly relations with several heads of the army—their opposition and the necessity of his resigning. To these hints, which he noted in his diary, Juarez made a "satisfactory" reply, without realizing their full import. Though they were intimate friends, Juarez was not in the confidence of Comonfort; but he would hardly have made a "satisfactory" reply, if he had not understood that he was being felt out.

Whatever the reply may have been, it satisfied Juarez without bracing Comonfort. The only real danger at that moment lay in the mind of the President, which he made up like his bed in the morning to be undone at night, and what happened there was what mattered. He was worried, he was weakening, he was wavering, unable to decide what to do or not do, and it was difficult to steady him for more than a day, an hour, or a moment at a time. A ready victim of the most obvious form of propaganda, he was profoundly impressed by the immense amount of mail which he received denouncing the Constitution. The brewing unrest of the country confirmed his worst fears; some incipient revolts had broken out here and there; he suspected plots everywhere, and when, several days later, he was informed that one of his ministers, who had just resigned from the cabinet, was attempting to corrupt one of his generals, he decided to investigate before going to bed. Driving out to Tacubaya, he found the minister, Don Manuel Payno, entertaining Baz in his home there and, his suspicions confirmed, invited them both to confer with him in the Palace of the Archbishop, where two thousand troops of a trusted regiment, under the command of one of his cronies, General Felix Zuloaga, were quartered. Payno, without suspecting the purpose of the interview, gladly accepted so favorable an opportunity to reconcile Baz, who was his personal friend, although they differed in politics, with the President. Payno was a Moderate in politics and a peacemaker by temperament.

The conference was held at night, and the account which Payno wrote of it was both obscure and revealing. Closeted in a little room alone with the President, he was surprised—and not a little flattered— when he was confronted with the accusation. The accuser was nervous, embarrassed, and did not know how to begin or end; the accused was calm, with the calm of innocence, for the accusation was false, and Comonfort, apparently accepting his explanations, settled down to a friendly chat on indifferent matters. Then he rose, opened the doors, and called in Baz and Zuloaga, who were both irritated by the length of time they had been kept waiting outside. "He closed the doors again, and we sat down, and Comonfort, with the help of his cigarette, so useful, so essential in all the compromising accidents of the Spanish race, began the conversation. 'Where are we going? What is this revolution? What are your plans? On what elements can you count?'" The questions were flung at Baz and Payno, who were both dumfounded by them. "We looked at each other in silence, each of us thinking that the other had his plan formed and his elements assembled, and the truth was that none of us had any plan whatsoever; but since the President himself had opened the door so wide for an explanation, we did not wish to appear unprepared or completely useless. For my part, I admit that an impulse of vanity made me spread myself in my chair and speak. 'Plan there is none,' I replied. 'We have merely talked of what everyone says of the difficulties of the government. But here is Señor Zuloaga, who can tell you what is happening among the troops, and Juan José will tell you with his customary frankness what he thinks.' — 'Well, *Señor Presidente,*' said Don Juan José Baz before I had fairly finished speaking, 'I need not tell you that my ideas are absolute and that I have been for years a blind partisan of reforms. To my mind, the monks must not be, because their day is over; the clergy must not hold property but apply themselves to the endowment of their curacies; the nuns must be given back their doweries, and the novitiates of both sexes closed; in a word, we must not tolerate in a Republic *fueros,* or hierarchies, or distinctions, or monopolies, or privileges either. Anyway, I have manifested my ideas in the posts I have occupied, and you and everyone else know them, but it is not a matter of that now, but of talking like statesmen. The prejudices of the ignorant crowd are opposed to many of these reforms, which can only be planted with time, and so, although as a partisan I think as I have said, as a person who might influence events decisively, I would have to dispense with some of my ideas and compromise with the clergy, who, in the confessional, the pulpit, and in every possible way, are waging a war without truce on the government.' General Zuloaga listened in amazement to that sermon spoken with ease, with order, and even with eloquence and enthusiasm, and Comonfort listened attentively, doubting whether what he heard was true or a dream or an hallucination."

Small wonder; for if the motives of Payno were inadmissible, those of Baz were inexplicable. But Baz, speaking as Comonfort thought, continued. "'Now I will say something about the Constitution: the Constitution, as I have not been embarrassed to say publicly, is of such a nature that one cannot govern with it. If we mean to follow the way of progress and reforms, it provides such trammels and disadvantages that it is impossible for the Executive to move, because his hands are tied for everything; if, on the contrary, he must make some conces-

sions to the party that has fought the government of Ayutla for two
years, neither can he do so, since several of the laws against which the
bishops have protested have been raised to the rank of Constitutional
rules; so, whatever way he takes, the Constitution is an impediment,
and there is no help for it; we must set it aside and, as a necessary step,
get rid of the Congress too.' Señor Comonfort, more and more surprised, moved his head, rose, lit another cigarette, and sat down again.
General Zuloaga, with his head bent and one finger in his mouth,
meditated profoundly. As for me, I should have liked to have been a
stenographer to note point by point the peroration of Baz."

He did. The points which Baz was prepared to concede to the clergy
were the three laws which had been raised to the rank of Constitutional rules, the *ley Juarez,* the *ley Lerdo,* and the regulation of parochial obventions. Of these the most difficult was the *ley Lerdo,* since
so much property had been transferred under its terms that it was impossible to repeal it, but Baz was willing nevertheless to make some
transaction with the clergy, "because we have gone as far as we can
go." Comonfort, moving his head stiffly but making no comment,
asked Payno for his opinion. Payno testified that the Treasury, from
which he had just resigned, was bankrupt, that he had always been
opposed to the *ley Lerdo* and had only refrained from canceling it
because of the complications of property title, and that the Constitution
was unworkable. He advised Comonfort to resign. Instead, Comonfort turned to his crony. "And you, *compadre,* what do you think?"
General Zuloaga, drawing his finger out of his mouth, replied that
he had come to Tacubaya to keep close watch over his brigade. "The
soldiers are very unhappy, and to tell the truth, they cannot bear not
being buried in holy ground or given spiritual aid at the hour of
death." For himself and most of his officers he could answer, but not
for the men; he was very much afraid that any night now, when they
were least expecting it, they would be seduced by Miramon and Osollo,
two young officers who had taken part in the rebellions in Puebla and,
pardoned by the President, were very busy close to the Archbishop's
Palace. As for the Constitution, he agreed with the other gentlemen,
it must go.

The conference was now transformed into a council of war. " 'Well,'
said Comonfort, rising as if afflicted and exhausted, but rather with
the weight of his own reflections than with the very trivial ones we had
made, 'I see that we are in for a storm, and that we must take some
course. Let us examine calmly the elements on which we can count;
. . . but let us make no mistakes. Let us see: in the first place, we must
be able to count on Veracruz; this is the most important point in the
Republic, not only because of its resources, but because it is a fortified
town and has very active people. Let us be under no illusions: in Veracruz most of the people are Liberals. In the second place, the interior.

Doblado is more important than you can imagine; besides, he is a bold and active man and has some military footing that is very well organized; he holds the key to the interior, and as Doblado goes, so will Zacatecas, Aguascalientes, and even Jalisco. In the third place, the Federal District. The National Guard is in the hands of the *Puros,* and it will not be easy to make them all agree to a change.'" Baz promised to secure Veracruz and the National Guard, provided the revolution was accomplished without giving an absolute triumph to the clergy. The others promised to sound their friends, and Comonfort surrendered, with one last attempt to preserve his independence and escape. "'Well, said Comonfort, 'my friends speak to me against the Constitution, and I see that in this they agree with the men of all parties, so I shall not insist on sustaining it; but we must explore the opinion of the nation. If it is contrary to the Constitution, we must not impose it by force; but if the men of influence think that it should be maintained, I shall sustain it at all costs or, in the last event, I shall present my resignation to Congress.'"

The meeting broke up at three in the morning, Baz and Comonfort buckling on their revolvers and driving back to town, completely reconciled. On December 1 Comonfort was sworn in as Constitutional President of the Republic, and a week later the conspiracy was an open secret in the states. Veracruz consented to support it, as Baz promised, on condition that the change of policy would favor the Liberal side and that the clergy and the Conservatives would be excluded from the government; and on those terms adhesions came in from several army men in strategic positions. Doblado came to the capital and in three or four interviews with the President attempted to dissuade him; but his attitude was ambiguous. Agreeing that the situation was compromised and that the Reform movement had been carried as far as it could go, he advised Comonfort to reform the Constitution with Congress instead of against it; if this failed, he would then be justified in dissolving the Assembly. As for himself, Doblado hedged. Having just repressed a reactionary movement in his own state, he could not change face so quickly; but he offered to resign from the government of Guanajuato and leave his resources in the hands of the President. As he refused to take part in the plan himself, however, and his name and influence were what Comonfort wanted, this answer was not satisfactory. Doblado returned to Guanajuato after promising to win over another important cog, the Governor of Jalisco, General Parrodi; and as four other states besides Veracruz had signified their assent, Comonfort felt reasonably satisfied of success.

With Baz, who was the center and spokesman of the radical National Guard, the worst of the Reds had been won over; but one remained with whom the President was obliged to reckon. "The only ones who really knew nothing in the first few days," wrote Payno, and he was no longer flippant, "were Don Manuel Ruiz and Don Benito Juarez; but Señor Comonfort did not wish to keep the secret from them very long. One morning, in my presence, he sent for Don Benito Juarez and locked himself up with us in a little room on the mezzanine. Señor Comonfort and Señor Juarez were very good friends and treated each other with much confidence and familiarity. 'I wanted to tell you several days ago,' said Señor Comonfort, 'that I have decided on a change of policy, because the march of the government is becoming more difficult every day, not to say impossible; all the men who amount to anything are leaving the Palace, our resources are exhausted, and I do not know what will become of the country if we do not all try to improve things. Of the physical revolution I am not afraid; I shall face it as I have done so far; but the moral revolution requires measures of another kind, not those of force and arms.' — 'I knew something,' replied Señor Juarez with great calm, 'but since you said nothing to me, I did not wish to say a word to you either.' — 'Very well, then,' replied Señor Comonfort, 'I shall tell you everything now; we must change our policy, and I want you to take part and to join me.' — 'Really,' replied Señor Juarez without losing his calm, and as if he were saying the simplest thing in the world, 'really, I wish you every success and great joy of the course which you are going to take, but I shall not join you.' The conference ended without our being able to obtain anything more than those laconic words from Señor Juarez, and without his making any allusion to me or to anyone else. So, from that moment, it ceased to be a secret even for the only persons from whom it had been concealed a few days before."

The answer of Juarez was even more unsatisfactory than that of Doblado; and he made no attempt to dissuade Comonfort from breaking his oath and his neck, as Doblado had done. Discreetly but definitely, Juarez said good-by to his friend with no further warning than the ironic reflection with which he wished him success. But the warning went no further: Juarez did not inform Congress of the danger, and Congress awoke to it only when a governor denounced the plot and submitted in evidence a letter, written by Zuloaga and Payno, inviting him to join it. The alarm spread. On the following day—it was December 15—the cabinet met with the President to consider the demand of Congress for the immediate arrest and trial of Zuloaga and Payno. Juarez recommended—and he was careful to keep an account of his conduct on that day in his diary—that the summons be obeyed. His opinion was accepted, but it was decided to take no action until the next day. From the cabinet Juarez was called to Congress, where the Assembly interpellated the responsible minister and questioned him on the defense which the government could provide in the event of possible disorders. Juarez reported that as the reactionary movements had not yet been suppressed and the government had only three thousand men of doubtful loyalty in the capital, it was necessary to proceed with great caution and tact and to do nothing to disturb public confidence; that the accused parties would be apprehended, but that the government, being responsible for public tranquillity, would always preserve that first. The answer was considered satisfactory and accepted by Congress. Asked whether he approved a motion to transfer Congress to some other point, in the event of disorders, the Minister advised against any such move, which would merely precipitate panic.

From Congress Juarez was called to the office of Comonfort, and what ensued was noted only by a brief entry in his diary. "On receiving instructions to report, I noted an extraordinary excitement in the Chief, because he believed that he was being attacked. 'Take whatever decision you wish, because I have already taken mine,' I replied. 'I do not believe that we are involved in this, for so far everything has been done on legal ground. In representative governments interpellations by the legislative body are frequent and common, since they are of the essence of the institution and do not imply an attack on the person of the head of State.'" The brief and cryptic note suggests the advice of a criminal lawyer to his client and corroborates the account given by Payno of the previous revelation of the conspiracy, of which Juarez made no mention in his diary.

How much he knew remains hazy, however. His conduct during the six weeks that he occupied the Ministry was the most compromising and equivocal in his political career. How much he knew, or allowed himself to believe, of the brewing Palace revolution was a question which he left unanswered, perhaps because he could not explain it. Whether he was ignorant of a conspiracy that was common talk in the press and the public, or whether he was aware of what was going on and neglected to investigate it, his conduct was equally damaging. For six weeks he did nothing to anticipate or avert the crisis which everyone knew was coming. Why? Was he befogged by the prevailing confusion and uncertainty and drifting helplessly with the flow of events, which he could not control? In any case, he was caught napping at his post. The situation was treacherous, it was true, and called for extreme caution and tact; but was he merely a victim of excessive discretion? Or did he close his eyes to the danger—with one eye half open on Comonfort—and trust him with deliberate blindness? Foreseeing that the man was heading for a fall, did he keep his own counsel and step aside at the last moment? When Comonfort consulted him, he declared himself—but only in private. Two weeks at least elapsed between the confession of the President and the exposure of the plot in Congress, and still Juarez kept silence. Was he shielding his friend at the expense of the country? Or was he biding his time and reserving himself for the supreme moment? Unanswerable questions;

but unavoidable ones under the circumstances. On the most innocent assumption, as on the most disingenuous, he disengaged his responsibility too late to clear it. His position, no doubt, was difficult; politically as well as physically, he was on the mezzanine floor, with the President deserting overhead, and the ground floor giving way under his feet. The governor who gave the alarm did not hesitate, however, and the fact that the responsible minister did, implied a clear neglect of duty. Whatever his motives, they remained his secret, and when the crisis broke he was morally compromised by it.

The next day was recorded in his diary by a blank. The disclosure of the conspiracy precipitated its outbreak, and the accused agents spent the day maturing their plans, unmolested by the police. Payno refused to be arrested and sent word to Congress that he would neither appear nor testify. Zuloaga completed his preparations quietly at Tacubaya, where Baz was busy rewriting a manifesto, which had been altered in his absence, and revising it to fit the original plan. Then that erratic radical buzzed back to Congress to warn his colleagues that they were holding their last session. They sat stunned—"since everyone refused to believe what I said, because of the daily denials made by the government and the assurances which Señor Juarez had given us as a member of the cabinet"—and broke up in confusion. The Plan of Tacubaya was submitted that night to the President for his approval. He read it and sank on a sofa, exclaiming, "I have just exchanged my legal title for that of a wretched revolutionary; but what is done is done, I accept everything, and God will show me the way to take." But he soon brightened and pulled himself to his feet, happy, active, relieved of the weight of indecision at last, and apparently determined to act. At dawn the Zuloaga brigade marched to the Palace, the manifesto was posted on the streets, and the *coup d'état* was accomplished uncontested. The President of Congress and several deputies were imprisoned for effect, and Juarez was arrested as he entered the Palace—an accident that saved his political reputation and transformed him from an apparent accessory to the insurrection into its most conspicuous victim.

He spent three weeks in the Palace, in a little room where he was held incommunicado, in the occasional company of Manuel Payno, who was placed there to guard him against any attempt on his life. Payno thought that possibility improbable. The real victim of the *coup d'état* was Comonfort himself, for instead of consolidating his position, it unsettled and shattered the thin peace which it had been the aim of all his combinations to preserve. The suspension of Constitutional order opened a breach through which the reaction pressed forward, claiming the right of way. They demanded the repeal of the *ley Juarez,* the *ley Lerdo,* and the restoration of parochial obventions. Comonfort resisted, but without support. "Everyone is leaving me," he complained to Payno, and it was true. Seventy ex-members of Congress protested bitterly against his betrayal, and resignations and retractions accumulated on his desk. The states on which he had counted to second the revolution turned against it, and a league of Liberal governors was formed to defend the Constitution. The secession was led by Veracruz, and had Baz been in the capital Comonfort would have shot him, so convinced was he that he had been tricked; but Baz, tipped off by Payno, had skipped. Baffled and confused, Comonfort was completely isolated. All that he had lost—the results of two years of labor, the fruits of the revolution of Ayutla, the blood shed for it—and all that he had gained—the repudiation of all parties, the execration of the radicals, the contempt of the Conservatives, the mistrust even of the Moderates—combined to defeat him, and the end of the middle way was political suicide. He had committed the supreme inconsistency, beyond which lay nothing but collapse, but he floundered on in indecision, doubt, and remorse, blundering and bewildered, without a foothold either of conviction or expediency. He attempted to retrace his steps and retrieve his betrayal. He offered the radicals to restore the Constitutional regime with Juarez at the head of it and to introduce two regiments which they trusted into the Palace as a guarantee of his good faith; but the offer was spurned as a ruse to discover their strength and destroy it. He made advances to Juarez himself, but they were rebuffed with the same independence after the crisis as before it. Of whatever negligence Juarez was guilty before the transgression of Comonfort, he was inexorable now: the issue was declared and the consequences were inevitable—ignominy for the one and glory for the other—and nothing less than greatness could redeem his discretion.

For Comonfort return was impossible; so was advance; and to stand still equally forbidden by the pressure conjured up by his last feat of prestidigitation. Cornered and cramped by the demands of the clericals for his complete capitulation, he managed to keep up a pretense of personal dictatorship for almost a month. For almost a month he inhabited the Palace, a mere wraith of himself. Rising in the morning and retiring at night, rising to the same dilemma every day, he ended his political life competing with his official portrait—a great bust of a man, sitting for posterity in an impasse, but blandly determined to be numbered among the just. "I cannot turn against my own," he told his tormentors. "I cannot banish Juarez and Olvera, I cannot fight Doblado and Parrodi." But he was just Comonfort.

During that month Doblado was the arbiter of the situation. His old friends, the Moderates, urged him to rally to the President and save a situation that was becoming more deeply compromised every day: Santa Anna was reported to be arming in Cuba and the Spanish to be concentrating forces there for an intervention in Mexico. His new friends, the *Puros,* implored him to declare for the League and to save the situation by supporting their program, which was to arm, to accept Juarez as interim President, and to call a Convention, which would elect a Constitutional President as soon as peace was restored. The alternatives were difficult—for Doblado. He was a patriot and a politician. The Moderates, as always, were alarmists, and the terrible consummation of their counsels was Comonfort. The Progressives, as always, were ahead of their time, but for once they were practical; and their best argument was eloquently put forward by Prieto. He hailed Doblado as the coming hero of Reform and made him one. Harping on the weakness of men, the poet derived strength from it. "I have always held and still hold in my heart," he wrote Doblado, "that no one can make a better President than you, but in view of this conflict I believe that legality should be the watchword of the movement, without invoking any name that might arouse jealousy. Power will pass into the hands of Juarez; and Parrodi, Llave, Zamora, and you, and everyone else, will have to follow this moral impulse that is in the popular instinct." The advice was politic, heroic, and compelling; popularity was the prize of abnegation. Doblado hesitated. For a fortnight he held the destiny of Mexico in his hand; for a fortnight he renewed his duel of doubt with Comonfort, waiting to see which way the tide turned, and then, turning with it and turning it himself, he declared for the League.

Holding the key to the interior, Doblado broke the deadlock in the capital. Comonfort consented to take the field against him. But it was too late. Payno, on a tour of the barracks, found a different Zuloaga than the one he had known in Tacubaya. The President's crony no longer sucked his finger; he sulked. "My *compadre* is betraying us," he said; "my *compadre* wants to deliver us to the *Puros,* and we are determined to go our own way." As he went out, Payno noticed a number of familiar faces in the next room. A few days later a second insurrection broke out, this time frankly reactionary. The plan was the same, minus Comonfort. The first had been bloodless, the second was accompanied by some sporadic fighting throughout the city, where Miramon and Osollo stormed and captured several public buildings. A truce was called, and for two days terms were discussed. Zuloaga proposed that Comonfort renounce the Presidency; he would do likewise. No agreement was reached. On January 21 Comonfort left for Veracruz and went into voluntary exile, and the next day Zuloaga moved into the Palace.

In a farewell manifesto, as personal as a private letter, the late President dwelt on his frequent desire to resign the burden of power to the person designated by the Constitution as his successor—and ten days before he shot his last bolt. On the day of the mutiny, he released Juarez.

PART TWO

The Civil War

I

JUAREZ left the Palace on January 11, 1858, with nothing to his name but a liberal education; but that at least was complete. The next day he slipped out of the capital with Manuel Ruiz and made his way across country—walking from farm to farm, sleeping one night in the fields, catching the mail coach to Queretaro—and arriving a week later in Guanajuato. "An Indian by the name of Juarez, who calls himself President of the Republic, has arrived in this city," wrote a local gossip to another in the capital. The words were not merely a sneer; so far as the gossips knew, he had arrived no further than that. Despite his notoriety as Governor of Oaxaca, author of the first Reform Law, President of the Supreme Court, and cabinet minister, a provincial snob could pretend that his name was unknown and his pretension unheard of in national politics. National politics was a collection of unknown quantities at that moment, all of them highly explosive, and all marked "X." No one knew which way the country would turn, anything might happen, and if an Indian turned up in Guanajuato and called himself President of the Republic—well, why not? The head of Hidalgo no longer hung on the Alhondiga.

The gossips were not altogether wrong. One month after the *coup d'état* of Comonfort, Juarez proclaimed his government in Guanajuato against great odds. His legal title rested on an abolished charter, the designation of a deserter, and the good will of a League of Governors sworn to uphold the Constitution that they had agreed to disregard only six weeks before. But his moral title was the burden itself; he came of a race accustomed from time immemorial to bear burdens; and when he composed his first manifesto he remembered his heritage. "Under extremely difficult conditions," he wrote, "the son of Guelatao attained the supreme magistracy." The road from Guelatao had led him far, but by now he knew where he was going, and he arrived in Guanajuato with a liberal education to guide him. He knew that the crisis marked the culmination of a movement that had begun with the birth of the nation and that had repeated for fifty years the abortive throes of a people to constitute themselves freely. Whether they were destined to advance, or to relapse into their insatiable past, was supremely uncertain; but henceforth he stood in lineal succession to Hidalgo and

Morelos, Mora and Farias, insurgents and reformers whose spent lives were invested in his, forbidding him to fail.

The heritage was heavy but bracing; for if the example of his forerunners who furthered the struggle was spurring, even more challenging was that of those who had shirked it. The closest was Comonfort; his weakness, more than a weakness of conviction or character, was a recurring infirmity in all the revolutionary crises of Mexico, the weakness of a man unprepared for his historic task and unequal to it, whose fumbling was responsible, as Mora had once said, "for the innumerable evils of an attempt for which a people are made to suffer and from which they derive none of the benefits expected of success." That infirmity was common to the whole Liberal family, untrained for their mission and forced to gain their experience at the cost of the country. "The speciality of the Liberals," as Prieto now said, "is the talent for prefaces; the works remain incomplete, but the prefaces are divine"— and prefaces were too costly. The time to finish had come. To redeem the failure of Comonfort was a formidable task; but it was one that Juarez was entitled to claim. He had taken the first step to assume it, in fact, when he had stood aside and let Comonfort blunder to his fall; whether he was guilty of willful ignorance or helpless neglect, he had the most compelling of all motives to retrieve the catastrophe. The heritage of his predecessors, the transgression of Comonfort, his own conduct—everything conspired to crown him with the rings of Saturn. The man who carried such a mandate and who was charged with such a sum of life could not be dismissed as a nonentity; and even the gossips knew, when they read his manifesto confidently proclaiming the coming triumph of democracy in Mexico, who Juarez was.

Moral power he had—conviction and character, courage and consistency—but his political strength was still uncertain. His historic role was granted to him by the governors, who were the real powers at that moment, and who accepted him provisionally as a compromise between conviction and confidence, until peace could be restored and a convention called to elect a Constitutional President, when it was generally expected that natural selection would favor Doblado. Thanks to the abnegation of Doblado, Juarez was not obliged to reckon with his host as a contender for power; that problem had been settled, so far as such questions could ever be settled, by the foresight of eight other governors. The triumph of discipline, or discretion, over popularity was the first gain of the Liberal cause in 1858, and a great one; but their choice represented a victory of legality rather than a personal tribute. He was a lay figure of legality, whose principal merit was that his name inspired no jealousy, and an unknown quantity to his sponsors, and even their loyalty to the Constitution was doubtful, as two of their number—Doblado and Parrodi—had been named as sponsors of the late Comonfort's *coup d'état*.

But he had moral power enough, and political magnetism, to attract his own kind. In Guanajuato he was joined by Ocampo and Prieto, who formed, with Manuel Ruiz and Leon Guzman, late of the Constituent Congress, his refugee cabinet; and for this frail skeleton of civil government military support was supplied by the League. General Parrodi, who took credit for initiating it, assumed the supreme command, and with the help of his most active colleagues—Zamora in Veracruz, Doblado in Guanajuato, Degollado in Michoacan, and Arteaga in Colima—succeeded in mustering a force of seven thousand men in seven weeks. The coalition controlled ten of the centrally located states in the Republic—Jalisco, Colima, Aguascalientes, Zacatecas, Queretaro, Veracruz, Oaxaca, Guerrero, Michoacan, and Guanajuato—states so placed that they surrounded the capital and could smother the revolt there by swift and concerted action. The plan of Parrodi was to draw the enemy away from his base by a series of simulated retreats, while his confederates attacked the capital; and in pursuit of it Juarez was persuaded to establish the seat of his government in Guadalajara. When he arrived there in the middle of February, the outcome seemed so sure that he issued a proclamation promising to convoke Congress and call presidential elections, and expressing his confidence in the result by adding that his one desire was to resign power and that he had no wish to retain it one day longer than the brief period of his transient administration required. But Parrodi proposed, and the god of battles disposed otherwise. On March 11 the decisive battle was fought on the field of Salamanca against an army slightly superior in numbers and completely so in generalship. The result was a disastrous rout of the Constitutional forces. Parrodi fell back on Guadalajara with two thousand men and some of his artillery, but Doblado signed a capitulation, which eliminated him, his contingent, and his state from the struggle.

The news was received in Guadalajara two days after the battle. Prieto was impressed by the coolness of the President and the game phrase with which he blunted the shock. "Guillermo," he said, "our cock has lost a plume." But official fortitude would have meant very little if it had not been followed by a proof of physical courage far more apt to catch the imagination of civilians in wartime. Early the next morning a mutiny broke out in the Palace and captured the President and his ministers. This was the first intimation of the gravity of the defeat at Salamanca. The rebels, however, comprised as yet only a single company; the alarm spread, loyal troops occupied the adjacent buildings and laid siege to the Palace, and to swell their numbers the rebels opened the jail and posted the convicts at points of vantage on the roof. One of them, perched in a bull's-eye window commanding the apartment in which the prisoners were penned, trained his rifle on

Juarez and amused himself with a running fire of threats until he was picked off by a stray shot from the besiegers. That particular Conservative produced no impression on the President; nor did those that followed. The rebel commander, who had been suborned by the local clergy, learning that Parrodi was approaching with two thousand men, offered his captives their lives if they would call off the besiegers. Juarez replied that, as a prisoner, he could give no commands and invited him to do as he pleased, but after consulting his comrades, he consented to a truce, and the transient period of his administration was prolonged. The bugles rang out, a parley was called, and intermediaries met in a neighboring convent. While the discussions were in progress a loyal officer, stationed at some distance from the scene and ignorant of the truce, decided to rescue the government and launched a surprise attack on the Palace. The attack was repulsed, but it produced pandemonium in the Palace—and a page of literature.

Prieto was locked up in a little room to which he had retired to write a manifesto for the President. Deprived of light and liberty, "the darkness in which I was immersed," he said, "magnified everything in my mind." His mind was a sensitive plate, and in that *camera oscura* the uproar was registered so indelibly that twenty years later he could still recall the flickering images that flashed through his vision as he applied his eye to the keyhole: crowds rushing by—racing fragments of a shattered kaleidoscope—convicts slipping from the roof with knives in their teeth—shots and shouts urging him to escape—a combustion of sights and sounds that finally lent him strength to break down the door and burst into the bedlam. Approaching the ringleaders, whom he recognized by a huge priest haranguing them, he demanded to share the fate of the President, and was knocked over the head; a few minutes later he came to himself in his presence. "Juarez was profoundly touched, Ocampo scolded me for not having escaped, for he honored me with a tender friendship." Prieto was dimly aware of a great hall with columns and a platform, crowded with eighty other captives for whom time and space had lost their dimensions, for "we had been told that we were to be shot in an hour." On either side of the platform were two little cubicles into which many had managed to retire. "Some, like Ocampo, were writing their wills, Señor Juarez was walking up and down with incredible calm. I went to the door to see what was happening. . . ." And then . . . then . . . Then the breathless pace of his memories, quickening convulsively, rose to a tremendous velocity at which everything blurred but their vertiginous beat. "A tremendous voice, coming from a face that vanished like a vision, cried in the door of the hall, 'They are coming to kill us!' The captives took refuge in the room where Señor Juarez was. Some were leaning against the walls, some seemed to be trying to shield themselves with the doors and the tables. Señor Juarez advanced to the door. I was behind him."

And then everyone knew who Juarez was. "The soldiers entered the hall. . . . The terrible column halted, with loaded guns, opposite the door . . . and without delay, and without knowing who gave the order, we distinctly heard, 'Shoulder arms! Present arms! Ready! Aim!' Señor Juarez, as I said, stood in the doorway. At the word 'Aim!' he grasped the latch of the door, flung back his head, and waited. The fierce faces of the soldiers, their position, the commotion, my affection for Juarez—what it was I know not, but a kind of vertigo seized me, something unaccountable, and swift as thought I seized Juarez by his shirt, put him behind me, covered him with my body, and flinging out my arms and drowning the word 'Fire!' which rang out at that moment, I cried, 'Down with those guns! Brave men are not murderers!' And I talked and talked and talked. What I said I have no idea nor what it was that spoke in me and that made me so strong and so towering, but through the cloud of blood I saw everything fading, and I felt myself subduing the danger, dispelling it, crushing it underfoot. . . . The attitude of the soldiers changed. An old man who stood facing me and whom I apostrophized with the words, 'You want blood? Take mine,' lowered his rifle, and the rest did the same. I gave a cheer for Jalisco. The soldiers wept, swearing they would not kill us, and vanished as if by magic. Juarez embraced me, my comrades surrounded me, calling me their savior and the savior of Reform, and my heart burst in a storm of tears."

The firing squad having been disarmed, parleys were resumed and brought to a successful conclusion. The rebel commander and his company marched out of the city to a point ten leagues distant, and the President and his ministers were transferred to the home of the French Consul. The volubility of the poet rendered an invaluable service to the cause, magnified by the fact that he emerged as the hero of that hysterical hour. In striking contrast, however, to that page of literature, was the laconic note with which Juarez covered the facts in his diary: "On the 13th the Palace Guard rose and I was made prisoner by order of Landa, who headed the mutiny. On the 15th I recovered my liberty." That was all. Of the performance of Prieto he made no mention. No one likes to be rescued, and the President was not impressed by it.

The incident was timely and invigorating in its political value. It met the imperative demand for Constitutional heroes, bestowing on Juarez and his ministers their baptism of fire and the kind of personal prestige badly needed by civilian leaders at that juncture. The steady undemonstrative courage of the President destroyed one disability under which he labored: he was no longer a lay figure of legality; and it was with no vicarious valor that, two days later, he addressed a proclamation to the army congratulating his followers for "popularizing heroism, generalizing the sense of glory, and reliving scenes illuminated by the names of the leaders of 1810." And at the same time, in a manifesto to the nation deprecating the defeat at Salamanca and reaffirming his faith in the eventual triumph of democracy, he renewed his exhortations and his pledge to continue the struggle in the first person. "Whether or not we lose battles, whether we perish by the light of combat or in the darkness of crime, the sacred cause we defend is invincible. The misfortune of Salamanca is but one of the all too common hazards of war. There may be others; we have barely begun the new campaign, and we may see the groping country become once again the pupil of 1821, as its thousand times recognized but inept tutors propose; but democracy is the destiny of humanity in the future, freedom its indestructible weapon, and possible perfection the goal toward which we are going," he declared. "With these beliefs, which are the life of my heart, with this faith, the only title that raises my humble person to the greatness of my task, the incidents of war are contemptible: the idea is above the domain of cannon." These words, which would have been conventional five days before, coming from a man who had just dipped his faith in the great democracy of death, carried an accent of indisputable personal authority.

Power, however, was as remote and problematical as ever. On March 18 Parrodi arrived in Guadalajara, followed at a short distance by the victorious Conservative army, and advised capitulation. The revolt at Guadalajara was symptomatic of the reaction likely to follow the disastrous initial reverse at Salamanca, and as Landa was only ten leagues away, awaiting the arrival of reinforcements, it was decided, on the advice of Parrodi, to remove the government beyond the reach of military operations. With a small escort of ninety men Juarez and his ministers started for Colima the following night. Before the end of the first day's march they were attacked by Landa at the village of Santa Ana Acatlan. The presidential party was hopelessly outnumbered, and though the attack was beaten off until nightfall, it was realized that when the battle was resumed in the morning, though the idea might be above the domain of cannon, its exponents were bound to succumb. Since there was no hope, and no danger, of rescue, Juarez advised his ministers to make their escape during the night, while he remained behind to share the fate of his escort; but the suggestion was indignantly rejected, and under cover of the dark the whole party slipped away across country and succeeded in reaching Colima. There word was received of the surrender of Guadalajara and the capitulation of the Constitutional army, without a battle, by Parrodi. The gravity of the defeat at Salamanca could no longer be minimized: two of the governors of the League were out of the war, their states occupied by the enemy, and the whole plan of campaign was altered accordingly. To repair the collapse, two decisions were taken, both of them destined to have far-reaching consequences. Santos Degollado was appointed Commander-in-Chief and Minister of War with full responsibility for the conduct of operations in the interior, and Veracruz was chosen as the seat of the civil government. The choice of this state offered strategic advantages as well as security: a traditional Liberal stronghold, controlling the revenues of the customs, it commanded the approach to the capital from the sea, whence the attempt to smother the insurrection could be resumed; but the civil and military commands were henceforth separated by a distance that made their co-operation difficult and effectively divided them into distinct spheres, virtually independent of each other.

From Colima the refugees made their way unmolested to Manzanillo, where they were to take ship to Panama on the first leg of a long roundabout journey to Veracruz, and there Prieto enjoyed an experience second only to his great day in Guadalajara. By now the ministers were popularly known as "the sick family," from their habit of driving in closed carriages, with the blinds down, and their desperate political plight; and they presented so forlorn an appearance, in fact, that Prieto compared them to a company of stranded actors. But at least they were a family, and as such they enjoyed privileges denied to happier governments. Prieto was actually sick and profoundly depressed by the atmosphere of Manzanillo, which was a dreary stretch of fever-ridden coast with a single store where two or three Germans gathered to guzzle beer, and he pined for a whiff of salt air. He had never seen the sea before, and with nothing to do but wait for their ship to come in, he was already homesick for Mexico. His humor was honored in a way that he never forgot: since his legs would not carry him, Juarez and Ocampo made a seat of their hands and lugged him along the beach—"I riding proud and triumphant, with my soul singing in my breast, happier than on the first throne of the world"—while the official family brought up the rear. Formality could well be forgotten there—and he was the most informal of men himself—but not that phantastic procession, for he was all fancy and effusion and fellowship. Chancing to look back, he was wonder-struck by the luminous traces which his bearers left in the phosphorescent sand, and "my friends and companions, delighted by my amazement, scooped up the sand and flung it overhead, sparkling like a cloud of fireflies." The sick family was not a funereal one yet, and the world was theirs, there by the sounding Pacific.

And for a few weeks more. At Manzanillo one adventure ended and another began—an adventure in friendship that left luminous traces in the mind of the poet during the six weeks of seafaring that followed.

From Manzanillo to Panama the itinerary carried them, across the Isthmus to Cuba and New Orleans, and the interlude which they spent at sea was the happiest period allotted to the Liberal government— long uneventful days, carefree and irresponsible, out of touch with the world, with only an occasional port of call to break the spell, and nothing to do but to discover one another anew daily, as people did in Mexico, and everywhere else in the world for that matter; and Prieto was the proper medium to preserve the memory of those intimate hours. A poet could contribute something important to the making of a popular movement in Mexico, but though he tossed off songs and ballads profusely, he was an indifferent singer; his real gifts lay elsewhere. Sprung from the people, he expressed the popular spirit by his sociable soul and his prodigal talent for friendship. His whole career was a succession of ardent attachments to the protagonists of his cause, and he put all the imagination of which he was capable into the congenial service of commemorating his heroes. An enthusiast who throve on his own transports, born for sentiment and insatiable of it, he gave affection freely to one after another, performing his chosen part by reflecting their personalities in a responsive mind and communicating to others the spell which they exercised over him with the tireless devotion of a complete hero-worshiper.

His collection of idols was a large one. The first was Ocampo, whom he had approached with some trepidation because of the difference of their social stations, but of whom he made a brother. Artificial differences melted away in their common faith, and so did the real ones of mind and temperament, although the poet frequently fretted at the mental discipline of the philosopher, and whenever he was ruffled by the precision of Ocampo would chatter and scold like an irritated bird robbed of its song. Later he lit on Doblado; then on Degollado; and lastly on Juarez. There he settled. Juarez was the last because he was the most difficult to appropriate; but after Guadalajara, Juarez belonged to his savior body and soul. Thus it was that, on the beach at Manzanillo, borne by his first hero and his last, Prieto touched the seventh heaven of his sentimental career; yet something was still lacking. There were years in the lives of his heroes which he had missed, experiences which he had not shared and without which he could not possess them completely—an impossible satisfaction, yet it was vouchsafed to him too. In New Orleans the whole party repaired to the little hotel where Juarez and Ocampo had spent their days of exile, and there Prieto was able to join them without jealousy in talking over old and new times. Once the continuity of their association was restored, nothing could break it again; for the poet it had neither beginning nor end.

To recover the past and retain and perpetuate it—that was his gift as a friend and his power as a poet, and the faculty for which he was remembered himself. He was a medium for whom time had no meaning and who could always recall its flight and repair its transient ravages. His mind was as porous as a sponge, and the impressions he absorbed were imperishable. Many years later, on another trip to New Orleans, he went straight to the spot; but in vain, it had vanished, or his unerring faculty had failed him at last, but he refused to believe his doubts; to forget was to die. One night, wandering aimlessly along the levees with two friends who had known the sick family in 1858, he happened to turn into a dark and sordid alley, and there, amid heaps of barrels, boxes, and sacks, he stumbled on "the half-obliterated letters of what in other times had spelled the triumphant sign of Barranda House." Was it chance that led him into that back alley? A veritable frenzy seized him, and, calling his companions, he met the challenge. " 'Come here,' I cried, 'come here. . . . Here is the room of Juarez. . . . There is Ocampo's. . . . Leon Guzman, Cendejas, and I down that corridor. . . . There at the end Manuel Ruiz spent his time.' And these memories illumined my soul and my voice rose, demanding homage and love for the eminent men who figured in the front rank of the great epic of Reform." Why had he outlived them if not to recall them to the future to which they belonged? And standing there in that grimy dead end, he officiated in the dark and peopled it once more with its ghostly tenants. One by one, they came out of the murky chambers of his mind, magnified again against the background of ignorant time. "Juarez in all his elevation rose in my memory: his clear and serene brow, his black eyes full of sweetness, his impassive countenance, his body of medium height, but graceful and free, and the limp hair falling in loose strands over his forehead like jet—all this I sought to evoke for others than myself. I conjured up Ocampo with his great mane of hair, and his round face, and his snub nose, and his large but eloquent mouth, and his winning speech and his expressive hands. . . ." The hallucination held, and before it faded he hastened to revive the self-effacing presence of one who was always fading even in life. Everyone knew what Juarez looked like in his official portraits, but not how he behaved with his intimate friends. "Juarez, in familiar intercourse, was very gentle, he cultivated intimate affections, his pleasure was to serve others, and he was careful to efface displeasure even in the lowliest servants. He laughed at the right time, he favored jovial talk and, after kindling it, fell silent and enjoyed the conversation, being the first to admire others. I never heard him depreciate anyone and, as for modesty, I have never known his equal." The vein of memories once set flowing welled up irrepressibly; he talked on and on; and standing his ground stubbornly, he faced and outfaced death with indomitable loquacity and subdued it as he had done at Guadalajara, and caught up the dust and breathed on it and brought it to be again, all as it had been in 1858.

The drift of his mind was indiscriminate, and what lodged in the sponge was casual, but everything obeyed a broad trend, and nothing was too small or insignificant to be lost. From that time—but what was time where past, present, and future fused without beginning or end? —he managed to recollect a trifle or two for the end of the journey. The best was the great adventure at Guadalajara, which had become a mere anecdote by the time they reached Barranda House, but in which he figured by his own right; and not the worst was one which owed its weight to his telling too, but which he told at his own expense. When they had boarded the ship for Veracruz, he hung on the rail, lamenting his lost Muse: some lines he had just dashed off to the fading shore were among his weakest. At that moment a woman appeared on deck, and Ocampo, always alert to the sex, nudged him and murmured "the Muse," while Juarez, turning poet and truant too, chimed in with a jingle recalled from his school days:

> The Lady Muse, *Musa Musae,*
> The Master too, *Dominus Domini,*
> Are off to the *templum templi,*
> To hear a *sermo sermonis* . . .

As a prompter of jocularities, the President had so few opportunities to figure in history that the sally was worth preserving, if only as a relief from the solemnity of his official portrait. But the tyranny of the Seminary had still to be broken, the jingle rattled the harness and reminded them all of the end of a liberal education. The sea wind blew, the gulls dropped away, the holiday was over, and the carefree interlude of six weeks was forgotten when they reached Veracruz.

Six weeks far from the field of action were a long period in the life of an untried government—long enough to be forgotten and to die. In his welcoming address Governor Zamora implied that the presence of the President in Veracruz was not indispensable to the cause, although the eagerness of everyone for the coming contest would be the greater with him to witness it. One word more, and the address would have been a sermon; one word less, and it would have seated Juarez on the side lines; but the band blared, the spectators cheered, and the President was escorted to his quarters. There the last of the little incidents that endeared him to his official family occurred. The house was run by a black woman, who laid eyes on him for the first time the next morning, when he climbed to the roof calling for water. Mistaking him for a *mozo,* she put him promptly in his place and bade him draw for himself. He did as he was bidden, and as he had done so often before becoming a public servant, and not until the midday meal, when she saw him seated at the head of the table, did she discover her mistake. She fled from the room, crossing herself, amid the hilarity of the whole household. Of all the stories told of the President, this was the most popular; it was repeated in many versions, passing from mouth to mouth like a folk tale, and meeting the need for a popular iconography. Anecdotes were few, he did not lend himself to them, and a peculiar value attached, therefore, to those that Prieto took the trouble to collect. Trivial in themselves, they were valuable because of their scarcity, and they bore, moreover, a singular family resemblance, for they had one feature in common in their modesty. Whatever the demands made upon the President—and the range was broad, from the democracy of death at Guadalajara to the democracy of domestic life at Veracruz—he rose to them easily. His companions came to appreciate that power—the only one that he actually possessed as yet—in the long weeks of travel during which they saw him at close quarters and under all conditions, and the time was not wasted that won him the respect and affection of his official family; for the family was the fundamental link in Mexican life and a force more binding than religion or politics; and this was as true of official as of natural families.

With his arrival in Veracruz the demands upon the President grew. In that port of refuge his personal life and that of his official family were fused in the far more formidable adventure of sustaining his government. Prieto had been right in predicting that, with legality as the watchword of the movement, power would pass into his hands and that everyone else would be forced to follow an impulse that was in the popular instinct; the popular instinct was true, stable, and homing, and everything that strayed from it uncertain, tentative, and migratory; and in six weeks that impulse had traveled far and fast. Parrodi and Doblado had dropped out, but the League held fast and extended its territory to the frontier. Santiago Vidaurri, the Governor of Coahuila and Nuevo Leon, was raising an army; fresh contingents were promised by the Governor of Zacatecas, Gonzalez Ortega; and in Colima, Santos Degollado was promptly seconded in his strenuous efforts to reorganize and recover lost ground. Not all that·was lost was bad. Before the battle of Salamanca, it was generally believed that the campaign would be easy and brief; but after the fall of Guadalajara, it was recognized that a prolonged and unequal struggle lay ahead. The first round was lost; the opportunity was lost, that is, of crushing a barracks revolt before it became a civil war; and civil war, long, relentless, and exhausting, was the penalty of that initial reverse; but an illusion had been forfeited, and it was followed by a gain in·morale, in determination, in strength. The popular impulse, spreading and stiffening, gravitated about the government that guaranteed, and the President who polarized, the popular spirit. The turn which the war had taken put an end to the theory, if it had ever been seriously held, that he was merely a formula of transition; he was in power for the duration of the war and indispensable to its triumph; for there was nothing tentative or uncertain in the initiative which he had provided, and it was impossible to regard him any longer as a purely provisional figure. If he was a substitute, it was not for some popular successor but for his popular predecessors, Hidalgo, Morelos, Mora, and Farias. The demand was exacting, but the fictions that had been exploded cleared the air and supplied him with the support to meet it. He was permanent enough to settle down in Veracruz and make a home for himself there; his wife joined him, walking from Oaxaca with his children, and bringing him an accession of strength that he needed, for she knew better than anyone, and long before his official family, who Juarez was.

2

IN THE first week of May the capacity of the Liberal party to sustain the struggle was highly uncertain; and it was already clear that the burden of proof must ultimately rest on the civil government. The enemy possessed two initial advantages, both of which were decisive factors in the balance of forces in 1858.

The Constitution of 1857, which had called forth the best abilities of the Liberals, also had produced the greatest talents of their opponents in the revolt against it. Those talents were primarily and, indeed, exclusively, military. Politically, they were on the defensive. Plan they had none beyond the abolition of the *ley Juarez,* the *ley Lerdo,* and the recovery of parochial obventions. In his first manifesto Zuloaga frankly admitted that the sole title of his party to power was the sacred right of self-preservation and that it was not sufficient, for he invited advice as to what to do next. But without waiting for the answer, and while the clergy were celebrating the wreck of the Constitution and the restoration of their prerogatives, he started a successful military offensive. From the moment that the warring principles were reduced to the arbitrament of arms, the Conservatives had at their command the preponderant asset of a professional army, abundant munitions and supplies, disciplined troops, and trained officers who practiced the science of war with an efficiency unmatched in the camp of their adversaries. The science was simple and the superiority narrow in the primitive conditions of Mexican warfare, but the odds were sufficient for the Constitutionalists to lose the argument on the field of Salamanca. The victor of that day was Luis Osollo, a young officer not long out of school, who determined the course of history by a single battle. Three months later he died of a disease, but the seminary from which he sprang had ample reserves, and his place was taken by a schoolmate who lived to redeem his promise and to write his name large on Mexican history. Miguel Miramon was an even more conspicuous product of professional talent and training, as the Liberals learned before long to their cost. Born of a breed of soldiers, but weak and sickly as a child, he made himself over in military school and proved his vocation early in life. Distinguishing himself first as a cadet in the American war, and later as a disciplinarian in command of a company of convicts, and constantly as a daredevil in many adolescent adventures, he came to the top with Osollo in the clerical rebellions in Puebla in 1856; and two years later, when at the age of twenty-six he succeeded his senior, he was not so much a youthful prodigy as a natural master of his trade, which was much more important. If emergencies produce the men to meet them, Miramon was that man.

The Liberals, on the contrary, labored under the congenital disability of their party. By definition they were civilians and laymen; militarism was the enemy, and they were not adept at a calling they abhorred. Professionals were few among them, and those few unfortunate (Parrodi was one of them), and, being improvised soldiers, they had to learn their trade by slow and costly experience. Degollado was the type. When he took over from Parrodi, the cause found its fitting champion in a commander who was a professed makeshift and who made no secret of his shortcomings. His first manifesto to the army, in which he appealed to the loyalty and fighting spirit of his men on the basis of their common inexperience, was a document that could not conceivably have been signed by a graduate of the Academy. He was the antithesis of Miramon in every respect except, perhaps, in physique and in courage. In appearance Degollado might have passed for a frail and cloistered scholar, with his slight, bespectacled skull, his peering visionary eyes, his faint, waxen, weightless face, and appearances were not wholly deceptive in his case. He had once served as Rector of the University of Morelia. In that capacity he had enforced academic discipline with conspicuous severity, clashing on one occasion with Ocampo, who was Governor at the time, and who was obliged to overrule him to obtain grace for some students for whom he interceded in vain. This rigidity was significant, for Degollado was himself the product of unrelenting self-discipline.

Who or what he was, was known only by the unbending mystery he became. His origin was obscure. The son, or the ward, of a parish priest, he was painted by his clerical enemies as a prodigal whose gaming debts ruined his guardian, and as an ingrate who left the body of his benefactor to be buried by public subscription. If such were the facts, they deserved to be piously preserved, for no more miraculous conversion was to be found in the *Lives of the Saints*. In manhood the name of Santos Degollado came to be invested with a kind of lay sanctity. As soon as he was known at all, he was known for his immaculate character, his selfless spirit, and his driving conscience, and it was that spur that forced him into a profession for which he had no natural aptitude. Fired by the ideals of Reform, he joined the revolution of Ayutla and acquired the rudiments of soldiering in the course of it; and after the overthrow of the Constitution, he was among the first to spring to its defense. He raised money and men with a speed and efficiency that revealed both zeal and resourcefulness and that designated him for high command; and his character and courage supplied the supreme qualifications. What he lacked in science he made up in morale. Embracing an uncongenial vocation in a spirit of abnegation and faith, he instilled his own spirit into his men, sharing their privations and hardships and heartening them by his indifference not merely to danger, which was easy, but to the slow daily death of defeat and fatigue, which was more difficult. With the raw recruits who made up his ranks he was popular. He had all the elementary virtues that appeal to regular troops, and something more: as the commander of a people's army he drilled them in a primer of ideas as well as the manual of arms and taught them to fight by teaching them what they were fighting for. And it was this slight margin of excess value that enabled the civilian soldier to compete with the professional enemy. In Degollado the emergency also found the man.

To feed the wick that nourished the flame was the vital function of the civil government and the first and most pressing duty the President and his ministers faced when they arrived in Veracruz. Degollado was a makeshift general in the same sense that Juarez was a substitute President; but the morale of an army depended on the resources with which it was provided, and the authority of the Commander-in-Chief on an initial success capable of establishing his credit, rallying the confidence of his followers, insuring the teamwork of the League, and checking the contagion of defeat. When he assumed command, he had to contend with a shortage of money, munitions, and men, and with the steadily deteriorating situation in the interior. The fall of Guadalajara was followed by the loss in rapid succession of four other large centers, Morelia, Orizaba, Tampico, and San Luis Potosi. The ring of states that might have overpowered the capital in March had been perforated at five strategic points by May: everywhere the enemy had seized the initiative, and his expanding gains were supported, moreover, by a permanent advantage of position, since he operated close to his base, while the Constitutional forces, thrown on the defensive and struggling to recover lost ground, were thrust farther and farther back from the capital and the seat of their own government at Veracruz. And in addition to his military superiority, the enemy enjoyed a political advantage, which went far to neutralize the value of Veracruz as a port in contact with the outer world and a position capable of isolating the capital: the Zuloaga government had been immediately recognized by the entire diplomatic corps. Possession of the capital was nine-tenths of the law and more than half the battle on the political as well as on the military front, being the reason, or the pretext, for foreign recognition of the *de facto* authority established there. The handicap thus imposed on the Constitutional government was felt in the difficulty of securing arms and munitions and financial and political credit in the United States, which was the nearest and most available market. Sympathy for their cause existed there, they were informed, but it was not negotiable without official sanction. Their first move as a government, therefore, was to send an agent to Washington to bid for recognition.

The agent was José-Maria Mata, who joined his old comrades to run errands for them once more. He was a novice in diplomacy, but he arrived in Washington at a favorable moment. The American Minister to Mexico was on the point of breaking relations with the Zuloaga regime over a question which was the key to American sympathy and which opened the doors of the White House to Mata. He was received by President Buchanan, who gave his bid serious consideration. After jotting down the name of Juarez and satisfying himself of his political life-expectancy and the term to which he was constitutionally entitled, the American President adverted to a matter with which he was more familiar and in which he was more immediately interested and indicated the lines on which a deal might be struck. They began with the Tehuantepec transit. The right-of-way for an interoceanic route across the Isthmus of Tehuantepec, granted to a Mexican subject in 1842, had since passed by sale to an American company and had become a semi-official American interest. The promoters of the company, Emile Le Sueur and Judah Benjamin of Louisiana, were personal and political friends of Buchanan, and the business passed through official channels because the original title, clouded by conflicting claims and legal complications in its passage through many hands, was subject to the protection of the American, and the sanction of the Mexican, Government. A satisfactory settlement had been reached with Comonfort, and confirmation of the contract was taken for granted by Buchanan as a prerequisite for recognition of the Constitutional government—as the test, in fact, of its legitimacy. Buchanan discussed the subject as a diplomatic contractor, confining himself to technical details, and went on to develop these preliminaries by proposing the concession of another transit for a railway running across the northwestern corner of Mexico from Texas to the Gulf of California.

To both these terms Mata was amenable, and he recommended

them to Juarez with one reservation. Besides a loan guaranteed by the American Government, they assured a political connection that would put an end, he believed, to the revolts in his unhappy country. "I may be mistaken," he wrote, "but I am convinced that Mexico is necessarily bound to this country and that, to preserve her independence and nationality, we must adopt a course based on broadly liberal principles, which will satisfy the reciprocal interests of both countries and allow the two peoples to come into contact, so that, knowing each other better, they may come to appreciate each other better and to lose the spirit of aggression on the one hand and of petty mistrust and suspicion on the other." The only question was how broad and how liberal those principles should be. Forsyth, the American Minister, was a stiff customer and a hard matchmaker. "There is a great desire," Mata added, "to acquire a new portion of our territory by purchase. This was the bait by which Forsyth was induced to recognize Zuloaga. Because of this tendency, which borders on mania, I have felt it necessary to make it clear in each of my interviews that, if we are disposed to make fair and profitable concessions for the development and security of American interests, in no case and for no reason would we agree to alienate a single foot of territory."

But that reservation was the crux of the question, and it produced a prolonged deadlock. So far Mata had enjoyed beginner's luck; but now an expert contest began, a long-drawn contest of patience and caution and angling between the two parties. After his first contact with Buchanan, Mata was kept dangling for months, and his government had ample time to give the proposed terms the serious, the very serious, consideration they deserved; for none but a novice could have supposed that the Tehuantepec transit, the projected railway in the north, and the mania for more Mexican territory could be dissociated; they were inseparable parts of a single whole; and the antecedents of the negotiation were sufficient to measure the hazards with which it was fraught.

The mania for more Mexican territory began with the termination of the American war. Together with the loss by the defeated nation of little less than half its original patrimony, the peace treaty celebrated the birth of that policy of expanding empire to which the victor gave the name of Manifest Destiny. Thereafter every American Minister to Mexico had broached the subject of a further acquisition of territory and had been rebuffed; but mania is obstinate, and mania was undoubtedly the word for an obsession which recognized no obstacle to its satisfaction, and which grew with repression. Mata was a novice, but in 1854, with his fellow exiles in New Orleans, he had protested against the Gadsden Treaty, which contained the whole problem in epitome. By that treaty Santa Anna ceded a narrow strip of territory along the northern frontier—the Mesilla—required by American enterprise for the construction of a railway to the Pacific coast; and the sale of the Mesilla was a minimum settlement: the maximum was mania.

Gadsden had come to Mexico instructed to press for outright sale of the frontier states, and he did so with forcible arguments. "No power can prevent in time the whole valley of the Rio Grande from being under the same government," he assured Santa Anna. "All the sympathies of the Mexican states west of that river must and will be with the state or states east of it, and either western Texas must come back to the Mexican Government or the states of Tamaulipas, Nuevo Leon, Coahuila, and Chihuahua will by successive revolutions or purchase become united with Texas. These are solemn political truths, which no one can be blind to." Least of all Santa Anna. Gadsden offered fifty million dollars for a cession embracing the better part of Tamaulipas, Nuevo Leon, Coahuila, Chihuahua, Sonora, and the whole of Lower California; but Santa Anna was not dictator enough to disregard public sentiment, and on the major bid General Gadsden missed. Failing the territorial line, Gadsden was instructed to secure an eligible route for a railway line running from Texas to California, and on this basis the treaty was signed; but even the minimum settlement was sufficient to shake Santa Anna to his fall. The maximum proposals were not abandoned by the American Government, but they were held in abeyance until a more favorable opportunity arose to renew them, and thereafter attention was concentrated primarily on the question of transits.

This question also went back to the American war. The need of knitting the states acquired from Mexico into the American Union made the construction of a transcontinental railroad a national question, which amply warranted the support given to it by the government in the acquisition of the Mesilla. No one appreciated its importance better than Buchanan, who recommended the projected Pacific railway to Congress, but in accordance with American tradition he proposed that government support should be confined to facilitating the free enterprise of private capital. This was where Benjamin and Le Sueur came in. The national question was also a sectional question, since the route favored by nature lay along the southern frontier and served the interests of the Southern states, and Southern capital was invested in its promotion. Because of financial difficulties, the railway was still unbuilt in 1858, but in the meanwhile the promoters had combined the project with other plans and developed short cuts and substitutes extending far beyond the original domestic purpose of a transcontinental trunk line. The ultimate destination of the Southern Pacific Railroad had been proclaimed, in fact, at a railway convention in New Orleans, two years before the Gadsden Treaty, by a local banker by the name of Benjamin. "This straight line of railroad will stop at New

Orleans, but it will not end there as a line of travel," he promised. "That line carries us straight across the Gulf of Mexico to the narrow neck of land that divides the Pacific from the Atlantic. . . . And when we cross this Isthmus—this Isthmus of Tehuantepec—what have we before us? The Eastern World. Its commerce has been the bone of many a bloody contest. Its commerce makes empires of the countries to which it flows, and when they are deprived of it, they are as empty bags, useless, valueless. That commerce belongs to New Orleans!" Mr. Benjamin was then engaged in floating a company to build a road across the Isthmus, and while the Pacific railroad languished, the subsidiary venture prospered. In 1857 he came to Mexico as attorney for the Louisiana Tehuantepec Company, with the backing of Buchanan, and closed a deal with Comonfort, who recognized his title to begin surveys and construction. The parent project had now become subsidiary to its offspring, and the Pacific railroad, still unbuilt, took shape and ramified in the form not only of the Tehuantepec transit, but of yet another branch line projected to run across Mexican territory from Texas to the Gulf of California, in which Buchanan was also interested.

Government patronage was freely granted to both of them. The offshoots offered more advantages, indeed, than did the original trunk; for a while they satisfied the pressing need for transcontinental communication, the shift to Mexican territory of a network of substitutes and short cuts fell in with the whole line of American policy. Imagination traveled rapidly along those lines, and not even a novice could suppose that, in patronizing these private ventures, an American President was not guided by larger aims of national interest. The northern railroad and the Tehuantepec transit were two sides of a surveyor's triangle, the bearing of which could be read on any map; and lest it pass unnoticed, an American congressman had pointed it out from the top of Capitol Hill at the time of the Gadsden Treaty. "I am glad to be at peace with that nation," he declared. "With an American railroad on her northern frontier, and another through her southern territory, acting like magnetic currents upon her social and political organization, American feeling, American energy, and American mind will be brought into contact with hers. Soothed by friendly intercourse, her opposition to us will relax. She will receive in her veins our healthy blood. She will catch our spirit, accept our views, and become assimilated in character with us, and then the whole question of her future relations toward our Republic will be one of friendly calculation between us." And it was that spirit of friendly calculation that Mata encountered in Washington.

The substitution of a policy of peaceful penetration for one of territorial encroachment was an advance, no doubt, but in the same direction. It was a distinction without a difference. Hand in hand with the negotiations for transits the bids for territory were renewed—the one was the shadow of the other. Forsyth came to Mexico with the same mission as Gadsden, modified only slightly by past experience. He was instructed to negotiate two treaties, one for the Tehuantepec transit and the other for the purchase of Lower California, together with a portion of Chihuahua and the larger part of Sonora; but he fared no better than his predecessor. Forsyth was also a disciple of Manifest Destiny, but less aggressive than Gadsden, and he had good reason to be careful, having been promised in Washington that his name would rank among the most illustrious diplomatists of his country if he succeeded. Loath to begin with the provocative bid for territory, and knowing how much depended in diplomacy on the proper order and precedence observed in presenting key questions, he deferred the more difficult at first, and when, under pressure from the State Department, he finally presented it, it produced the expected reaction. Comonfort declared that he would sooner jump out of the window than consider it. Forsyth forbore and, falling back on the easy minimum of the second treaty, rested his reputation on the negotiation of the Tehuantepec transit.

Forsyth was making progress along these lines when the promoters of the Louisiana Tehuantepec Company arrived in Mexico, armed with the blessing of Buchanan, and to his intense annoyance went over his head and concluded a deal with Comonfort satisfactory to their interests, but not to his or to those of their common flag. "I had sounded the government on the Isthmus question and had ascertained that I could, for a consideration, obtain concessions more ample than those contemplated in my instructions," he complained to Washington; "concessions that would have given a virtual protectorate and military occupation of the transit to the United States." The greatest achievements are always those that are missed, and the Louisiana purchase by Benjamin and Le Sueur being an empty bag, useless and valueless so far as he was concerned, he enlarged bitterly on what the irresponsible conduct, unpatriotic initiative, and semiofficial piracy of private capital had cost their country. "I could, too, have obtained a cession of the right-of-way across the northern region of the Republic, almost on the very line marked out for the new boundary designated by my instructions, with such grants of alternative leagues of land from the Rio Grande to Upper California and to Guaymas on the Gulf of Cortés as would not only have contributed a rich fund for the construction of the road, but would have fenced off and concentrated to American use and, ultimately, to American ownership, the very territory that my Government desired to purchase."

After that slip Forsyth was on the alert to recover his footing. By the end of 1857 the favorable opportunity returned. Comonfort was in political and financial straits, and Forsyth asked the State Department for power to make an irresistible offer at the right moment. Before he received the reply, the occasion came, but he was prepared by then to act on his own initiative. The *coup d'état* of Comonfort and the overthrow of the Constitution he reported as passing irrelevances. "I hold that these events in themselves are of little consequence to the country, are only some of the steps in the inevitable march of Mexican destiny. The State is in a condition of rapid disintegration and decay and is tottering to its fall. . . . I may add that, if Comonfort sustains himself, he will have the power, if he chooses, to dispose of public territory." The conjunction of Mexican destiny and Manifest Destiny was now definitely in sight, for Comonfort approached him for a loan of 600,000 dollars to pay his troops, and Forsyth renewed his bid for territory. But it was too late. "He entertained the proposition and considered it for two days, abandoning it finally because the relief it would bring was too tardy for his purposes. I believe I can safely assure you that if I had had it in my power to make an immediate advance in cash of half a million and to have offered a tempting sum for the territories in my July instructions, I could have secured his signature to a treaty of cession." He was not discouraged, however, for "what was true in this instance is likely to be true fifty times over in the exigencies of the next twelve months. The government, whoever may be at the head of it as the result of the revolution now raging in this capital, is sure to be needy, and, watching the opportune moment, the greatest advantage may be realized by the offer of ready money for a negotiation." Comonfort had no sooner fallen, therefore, than Forsyth began to sound his successors. In the kaleidoscopic changes of Mexican politics American policy remained the one permanent and stabilizing factor.

The government of which Zuloaga became the head was, like every Conservative administration, intensely anti-American, but it fell heir to the pecuniary difficulties that made every Mexican government alike in the eyes of the American Minister, and Zuloaga and at least two of his cabinet were sufficiently amenable to his advances to induce him to grant their claims to immediate diplomatic recognition. But he relied, above all, on the clergy, who had the most powerful reasons, as he explained to Washington, to lend him their aid and influence. The government depended on the Church for revenue, since all the coasts and customs houses were controlled by the Constitutional coalition, and the Church had lent its credit to the amount of a million and a half Mexican dollars. This security was difficult to negotiate and was currently discounted at fifty per cent, Mexican capitalists fearing to risk the stability of the government and expecting a Constitutional triumph to be followed by the confiscation of Church property. It was clear, consequently, that the only real security for the Church, certain of being ruined at a single blow by the Liberals or slowly bled by its defenders, lay in filling the public treasury from abroad. "I have had this idea sown in the minds of several of the leading friends and advisers of the clergy," Forsyth informed the Department, "and it has germinated in a way fully equal to my expectations." Both the Archbishop of Mexico, "the purest man in the powerful body of which he is the head," and the Bishop of Michoacan, who managed its finances, entered warmly into the scheme, and within six weeks Zuloaga and his cabinet had reached the point of unanimously recognizing the necessity of a territorial cession. Nevertheless, Forsyth bided his time, for "while the government admits that these measures should and must be adopted, it lacks the courage to do so"—and he at least could afford to wait.

The battle of Salamanca was fought and won, and the bracing effect of that triumph was manifest in the Palace. Forsyth was invited to submit his proposals, and he did so promptly, but after prolonged study they were rejected in what he described as "a paroxysm of political cowardice," for the Liberal government had just landed at Veracruz. The fortunes of war failed to affect the confidence of Forsyth, however, for it was based on the long view of Mexican history and the short term of Mexican governments. "Mexican administrations are short-lived, and the present one already exhibits unmistakable signs of decay. Indeed, I think the rejection of the treaty sealed its fate," he advised Washington. "I already see the visible elements of an early change, and a change of an interesting character for the United States. The time and the occasion are not quite ripe for a communication on this subject. I may only add that, if no untoward event occurs to mar this new development, I have taken measures to master the situation and that the whole must result in making our country the undisputed arbiter of the destinies of Mexico, if our government chooses to accept that office." The measures to which he alluded were no secret in Mexico. A Liberal conspiracy was then afoot in the capital, and one of its leaders, Lerdo de Tejada, had found asylum under his roof.

The conspiracy failed to materialize, however, and so did the collapse of the Clerical government, and the American Minister turned to a short cut. As a last resource there remained but one way of cutting short the vacillations or the existence of any Mexican government, and he recommended it to his own. "You want Sonora? The American blood spilled near its line would justify you in seizing it. You want other territory? Send me the power to make an ultimate demand for the several millions Mexico owes our people for spoliations and personal wrongs. . . . You want the Tehuantepec transit? Say to Mexico, 'Nature has placed the shortest highway between the two oceans, so necessary to the commerce of the world, in your keeping. You will not open it yourself nor allow others to open it to the wants of mankind. You cannot be permitted to act the dog in the manger. . . . Give us what we ask for in return for the manifest benefits which we propose to confer upon you for it, or we will take it.'" Frankly exhausted by two years of fruitless labor, Forsyth reverted to type and the arguments that had failed Gadsden; but it was unnecessary to use them. Zuloaga sent for him again, declared himself insolvent, and promised to eliminate from his cabinet the one member who still opposed a territorial cession. On the following day Forsyth waited for a message announcing the change, and learned, instead, that Zuloaga had changed his mind once more and chosen to cheat fate by another forced loan; and when the forced loan fell on an American citizen, who was banished for resisting it, Forsyth exploded and called for his passports.

It was at this juncture that Mata arrived in Washington. The time was ripe for a shift of recognition to the Constitutional government, but several months passed before Forsyth could bring himself to consummate the break or to abandon the scene of a defeat which he still doubted, and he was in no haste to recommend a new match. "My experience has taught me," he wrote when the alternative was weighed in Washington, "that all parties and all changing governments in Mexico are so much alike, that I do not believe that whatever Mexican policy our government may see proper to adopt should be varied in its essentials, whether Conservatives or Liberals are in power. The only difference should be in the manner of insisting upon it. If the present government should stand, nothing but force would accomplish the purpose. If the Liberal should come in, persuasion might answer the purpose. . . . In either case, determination is indispensable." Such advice naturally cooled any inclination to confer recognition hastily, and after his first welcome at the White House, Mata was allowed to cool his heels in Washington for six months—a highly effective form of persuasion. By the end of that time he was thoroughly convinced that the preliminary question of transits which Buchanan had explored with him was merely the superficial reef, the partial outgrowth of the main, the submerged, the continental mania for land underlying it, and that the imaginary line which he had drawn between the one and the other was indeed the delusion of a novice. Nevertheless, he was ready to risk the negotiation. Mata, no more than Forsyth, was satisfied with the mission of running a fool's errand. He was young, intrepid, and sanguine; during the American war he had distinguished himself by running the blockade and smuggling money and arms into Veracruz; and he believed it possible to repeat the feat in 1858.

For six months the Veracruz government gave the question of transits the serious consideration due to a deal that made the permanence or the transiency of their cause depend on Forsyth, Buchanan, Benjamin, and Le Sueur. The connection of those two questions, one bordering on mania and the other bearing on Mexico, placed the government in a trying position and left them in a deadlock of conflicting claims. The indefinite postponement of recognition prevented them from adequately supplying the army, the revenue derived from the customs was crippled by the immense mortgage of foreign debt secured by those resources and the partiality of the creditor powers to the recognized government in the capital, and the forces in the field had to shift for themselves.

Fortunately the course of the campaign showed a favorable balance in the summer and autumn of 1858. In June Degollado laid siege to Guadalajara, but was forced to raise it by the approach of Miramon, who pursued and attacked him while his men were crossing the bottom of an immense ravine; the battle lasted eight hours and ended in a draw and a retreat on both sides. The drawn battle of the Barranca of Atenquique was followed, however, by a number of uncontested gains for the Liberal flag. In that same month of June San Luis Potosi was recaptured; in July Durango was occupied; in August Tampico was retaken. In September Santiago Vidaurri, leading an army from the frontier into the interior, was defeated and routed by Miramon; but the effect of his fiasco was effaced by Degollado, who returned to the siege of Guadalajara in the first days of October, stormed and captured the city, and scored his first resounding success. But these victories had an obverse side: they were won without the aid of the constituted authorities, by forces that operated independently of them and that lived on the land, improvising and extorting their own resources. Credit and popularity went inevitably to the military command, with a corresponding paling of the civil power that threatened to eclipse even its moral authority, and with the passage of time the demand increased for some major and material contribution to the cause to raise the prestige of the government and prevent it from being relegated to the side lines and the rank of a noncombatant.

Failing American recognition, there remained one alternative, which Prieto urged upon his colleagues. In the cool of a little village to which he had retreated to escape the fever season at Veracruz, he applied his imagination to finance and drafted a program for the end of the war based on the nationalization of Church property. Here was a constructive measure capable of raising the political and financial credit of the party and destroying that of the enemy at a single blow, of supplying the sinews of war, of extinguishing the foreign debt, and of providing something even more important to Prieto than material resources— the reputation of those who initiated it. It was not only as a war measure that he planned it; he was thinking of the future and of the place which its authors would occupy in Mexican history; and what recommended it above all in his eyes was that it would complete what the *ley Lerdo* had begun, and begun badly, in 1856. "The eminent Dr. Mora and Espinosa de los Monteros and Quintana Roo and the whole pleiad of sages, in short, who illumined the future of democracy in our country since the glorious administration of '33, conceived the law of disamortization on the following bases," he wrote to Ocampo. "This whole reform, immense in its consequences, started from the principle that property is national, subordinating the clergy to the government, dispersing the funds in various hands, and abolishing the clerical *clientèle* which gives them the prestige of political power. Lerdo falsified these principles, mutilated the idea like a plagiarist, erected it on a falsehood, set two doubtful proprietors face to face with indefinite titles, and for the sake of the petty collection of internal customs exposed abundant wealth to waste, leaving the clergy their *clientèle* and power; and after so many absurdities all that belongs to him is the glory, enviable no doubt, of having been the first in our country to set his hand to the great work of revindicating the civil power. I think that our conduct today should be confined to restoring to the law the ingenuous expression which it had in the administration of Farias." Partial to his own heroes—and Lerdo was not one of them—he was jealous of their fame. "It is true that we shall not have the merit of originality, but we should not aspire to patents of invention but to the title of good rulers. . . . Look up the works of Mora, read, discuss the matter with our Benito, and give me your opinions," he concluded, "because it will be to our honor to have thought of this even amid our troubles and pains."

Putting his talent for hero-worship at the public service, Prieto accomplished his function in the movement with crowning devotion. The idea was not novel, but it was still nameless and needed a brow to bear it broad enough to merit the succession of Mora. Ocampo was in complete agreement, for it formed part of a comprehensive program which he was preparing with Juarez for the end of the war. But when would that be? Could they afford to wait? And was it not visionary to be so farsighted at that time? These questions were raised when Prieto learned, to his dismay, that his bolt was in danger of being blunted, before it was shot, by the enemy. A group of prominent speculators in the capital, meeting in secret conclave, offered the Zuloaga government three million pesos on the security put up by the clergy. Whence so much courage suddenly? Prieto had the answer. "Father Miranda, who is the soul of this business," he warned Ocampo, "attended the meeting and informed them that he wished to wait merely until December when the United States Congress meets, and that he would find money there, either through the sale of California or through the Tehuantepec transit. He said that Mata was swimming beneath the current, meaning that he knew nothing of the maneuvers of the Padre and that the Yankees were merely looking for the best market. You will see that the padres will nationalize their property. . . ." It was October; the time was short, the danger was pressing; whether the clergy ceded sacred property to the speculators or national territory to the United States, some step should be taken to forestall them; but his warning went unheeded, for besides Ocampo he had to convince Juarez, and Juarez was not to be hurried.

The advantages of confiscating Church property were self-evident; but so were the risks. It was important not to play a trump card prematurely, and there was a distinct risk that such a measure, produced by a government without the strength to support it, would miss fire and recoil on its authors; the challenge would be met by the enemy with every means at his command, and among those means there was one to which the Veracruz government was extremely vulnerable at that time. The unanimous recognition of the Clerical government by the diplomatic corps was a factor that weighed heavily on their councils, for it meant that foreign opinion was officially enlisted in favor of the reaction, and that the great creditor nations whose claims were secured by the customs could at any moment favor the enemy by bringing pressure to bear in the collection of the debt service at Veracruz. As a seat of unrecognized government, Veracruz was a highly exposed position, and a strong hint of such possibilities had been given its guardians that summer by the visit of a British squadron in that very connection. Prieto was panic-stricken when he heard of it. "The business of the English vessels," he wrote to Ocampo, "seems to me extremely serious and no sacrifice too costly to ward off that danger. I do not know why I see in this move a machination of Mexican capitalists, who figure among the bondholders, and whose lives and fortunes are engaged in the present struggle in favor of the clergy. Behind this squadron I see Barron, Iturbide, Jecker, Mier y Teran, and others who will take advantage of the British hand to distract us while they strike us in the back." The British Minister was an avowed partisan of the Clerical government, the British debt was the largest lien on the customs, and the fact that it was held in large part by Mexican bondholders made it necessary to reckon with the British flag as the ready ally of the black flag of reaction. And besides the British Minister there was the French one, whose partisanship was pronounced and aggressive. M. de Gabriac was credited with active complicity in the second *coup d'état,* he was the acknowledged guide of Zuloaga and mentor of his British colleague, and he bore watching in the autumn of 1858 because the expropriation of Church property was a burning topic at that time in France, where the Emperor had announced a decree of nationalization that divided public opinion sharply in Paris. The Orleanist, Republican, and Imperialist press and the peasantry supported the measure ardently, but before the outcry of the Clerical and Legitimist press the Emperor recoiled and suspended its enactment, though it was predicted that, as his popularity was waning, he would not miss the opportunity of refreshing it by issuing the decree eventually. If so seasoned a politician as Louis Napoleon found it necessary to hesitate, Juarez could hardly be blamed for biding his time and observing the effect of the trial balloon abroad. Every move made or contemplated in Veracruz had to be calculated in relation not only to its domestic consequences, but to the position of foreign powers; and before so provocative a measure could be attempted by a weak and unguarded government with its back to the sea, it was necessary to determine to what degree M. de Gabriac represented or misrepresented the bias of the French Government. The value of the measure depended on its timing, and that faculty of which Juarez had given such memorable proof with his pioneer law in 1855 had not forsaken him in 1858.

So the mantle of Mora still went begging: a moth-eaten garment which Prieto tried on for a moment and, finding it too large and too loose for himself or his companions, reluctantly laid away once more on the shelf. "When in doubt, do nothing," was sounder advice than any he could offer his friends, and it was the course which Juarez chose to pursue for six months. But six months were a long stretch in the life of a fighting government, which was on trial before public opinion and which had made no recognizable contribution to the war. It was on the defensive, and the conservative and negative course imposed on it by the dictates of self-preservation did nothing to raise its prestige or to meet the exacting demands and legitimate expectations of the country; and while the problems, the alternatives, the dilemmas that beset the President and his ministers in Veracruz required careful calculation, they met them with a caution indistinguishable from inaction. For six months they made no other mistake. They succeeded in prolonging their period of impeccability to the end of the year; but the situation could not continue indefinitely. Prudence and temporizing were neither popular qualities nor practical securities; when fresh reverses occurred in the field, it became imperative to break the spell of inaction by breaching the diplomatic blockade that created it; and gradually, insensibly, under the strain, every other consideration was subordinated to the value of securing American recognition.

In December the first approaches to a decision were made by the American Government. In his annual message to Congress, Buchanan devoted a significant passage to the situation in Mexico. Abundant cause existed, he declared, for resorting to hostilities against the government holding the capital, because of injuries suffered by American nationals incidental to the civil war, and all hope of a peaceful settlement would expire if that government overcame its opponents. If the latter prevailed, there was some reason to hope that it would be animated by a less unfriendly spirit; and but for that expectation he would have recommended that Congress grant him power to take possession of a sufficient portion of the remote and unsettled territory of Mexico to be held in pledge until the injuries in question had been redressed. The passage exactly paraphrased the prescription of Forsyth. With the Zuloaga government the only possible argument was force; with the

Liberal, persuasion might serve the purpose; and the purpose of combining a threat to the one with a qualified tender to the other was plainly to prepare public opinion in the United States for the application of pressure upon both.

A few days later Forsyth called upon Mata and offered his friendly services to favor a loan and recognition by the cabinet. After spending six months in Washington for no purpose, apparently, but to wear out his patience, Mata accepted the tender with some reserve, but little encouragement was needed to revive his flagging hopes, and he called upon the President, confident that recognition would now be promptly accorded. Buchanan, however, was not to be hurried. It was necessary, he said, to *go slow*. There was a hitch, and, Mata, who had been swimming under the current for six months, was stunned by the pressure he encountered at the last moment. Buchanan was halfhearted, Mata informed his government, because emissaries were on their way from the Clerical government "with proposals very favorable to this country (the sale of the states of Chihuahua and Sonora), and it was proper to wait and see what advantages could be drawn from the indefinite situation in our country. This one trait will suffice to describe the man with whom we have to deal and also to make you understand my position." Mata was weary; he was bored, he was bluffed, he was baffled by Buchanan. Whether the emissaries were a fact or a fiction he was not sure; they might be an invention of the diplomatic corps, which had done everything in Washington, as it had in Mexico, to prevent recognition. He was in Washington, he was in the dark, and he transmitted the facts for whatever they might be worth, together with the despondency which colored his reports and which was worth a great deal at that moment.

If a decision had not yet been reached at the White House, a long step toward it had already been taken. Buchanan himself admitted the meaning of his message, and public opinion in Mexico was prepared for the application of pressure. Two days later a confidential agent of the State Department left for Veracruz to survey the ground for recognition on the spot.

The psychological moment was well chosen. The capture of Guadalajara in October had been a transient triumph; Degollado was not strong enough to sustain it, and by the beginning of December he was forced to abandon the city by a converging offensive led by Miramon from the south and by Leonardo Marquez, his ablest lieutenant, from the north. On the 24th Miramon occupied Colima, and on the 27th he met and defeated Degollado at San Joaquin, capturing three hundred prisoners and all the artillery and munitions. The Constitutional army, broken and demoralized, disbanded and fled in disorder into Michoacan. The political effect of this victory checked, at the same time, the first symptoms of fatigue and discouragement in the Conservative party. Two generals, within a week, revolted against Zuloaga on the grounds of his complete ineptitude and discredit, both declaring for a return to some form of reformed Constitution and both claiming the Presidency for themselves; but both were snuffed out by the success of Miramon, who discountenanced any split and insisted on the solid prosecution of the war to an end that was no longer distant or doubtful. In a proclamation that he issued on New Year's Day in Guadalajara he reviewed the events of the past twelve months and claimed for himself, as the best of the booty, the word on which the Liberals prided themselves, but which rightly belonged henceforth to his flag. The year just ending had raised in Mexico, he said, the banner of progress, "and that word, which is already so hackneyed in revolutionary language and is used to deceive the people, is as stale as it is noxious in democratic parlance, because it produced the Law of dis-immunities, and the spoliatory Law of disamortization, and the Law on parochial obventions, and the ridiculous steal of the Law on Civil Registry; because it led to the discussion of the Agrarian Law, and the Law on religious tolerance, and the Law sanctioning the dissolution of marriage; and lastly, because all classes of society have been abused, and the defenseless population sacked with impunity, by that word." Discussion was down and out. And who was to gainsay his boast? Juarez?

3

WITH the opening of the new year all the elements of action which had remained suspended for twelve months began to develop, and the Liberal government was forced to rise to its responsibilities. Immediately after his proclamation Miramon returned to the capital, ousted Zuloaga from the Presidency, assumed his functions himself, and announced, as the next move, a campaign against Veracruz to bring the civil war to a close. This warning was accompanied by another, which warranted his confidence. The vulnerability of Veracruz was forcibly brought home to its guardians early in January by a joint demonstration of French and British warships, which called to collect arrears in the debt service and to demand satisfaction for forced loans levied on their nationals by commanders in the field. The demands were peremptory and were presented under threat of shelling the town; and the brunt of defending it diplomatically fell upon Ocampo, who occupied the key post of Foreign Affairs.

Like Prieto, Ocampo was convinced that no sacrifice was too costly to avert the danger, but he managed to muzzle the guns with a very small sop. He accepted the allied demands and settled for damages of eight per cent on the customs tolls, with a further raise to ten per cent for the British when the French claims had been fully satisfied. It was his first important negotiation and he was properly elated by the result; for he had scored a point over an adversary who was neither Commodore Dunlop of the British fleet nor Admiral Penaud of the French, but the formidable M. de Gabriac. Writing to a friend, he dilated gaily on "the unfathomable profundities of diplomacy," and invited him "to exclaim like St. Paul, '*O altitudo divinae scientiae sapientiae Dei! Quam incomprehensibilis sunt juditiae ejus et investigabilis viae ejus!*' Our ranchers in Michoacan," he explained, "have made a free, a very free translation of this passage, which runs, 'The high judgment of God not even the Devil can understand!' The text would lend itself to long comment, I believe, if it were applied to M. de Gabriac. M. de —— is so deep in diplomacy that poor M. Penaud, knowing nothing of the facts, tangled himself in such a rigmarole of claims that all I had to do was to yield to his demands. Behold how clever they were! Where they were already entitled to fifteen per cent for a single article, they demanded eight for several." This bungling was the best proof, if any were needed, that the move was purely political; but none was needed: M. de Gabriac was not incomprehensible; the god in the machine, descending too soon, had become entangled in his own wires and remained suspended in mid-air. As a result of the settlement there developed a controversy between the French Minister and the French Admiral which had to be referred to Paris. Already famous, unfortunately, for the *cencerrada* which he had suffered in 1856, M. de Gabriac was destined to be the victim of that indignity again, for his hand was not only recognizable, but exposed, at the most opportune moment for the Constitutional cause.

The fact that the move was made on the eve of the impending siege by Miramon was a matter of concern to all the interested parties, and next to the Liberals themselves, the most interested party at that moment was the American Government. The attempt had long been expected in Washington. Two months before, the American Consul in Mexico City had reported the arrival of a French fleet at Veracruz, at the call of the French Minister, and had predicted that Admiral Penaud would serve certain pecuniary demands on the recognized government in the capital, which it would be unable to meet, that he would then offer to put it in possession of the ports, and that some maneuver would be undertaken for that purpose. The accuracy of the forecast was confirmed by the event, and though the maneuver miscarried, the gravity of the threat was fully appreciated in Washington, where the designs of Gabriac had recently been denounced by Forsyth.

One of the last reports of the retiring American Minister was devoted to a colleague in whom he found a competitor, and of whom he filed an itemized record in the diplomatic rogues' gallery. "This gentleman from the beginning of the revolution of Tacubaya has been the open and active partisan of the Zuloaga party. . . . He spends a large part of his time *daily* in the Palace. . . . He is disliked by all foreigners and intensely hated by the French. . . . He is a schemer, very ambitious and quite unscrupulous. . . . His head is filled with dreams of a European protectorate, to be followed by a Mexican kingdom or empire, and these senseless visions are industriously instilled into the brains of the fanatics and imbeciles who now constitute the government. . . . He is intensely anti-American and has been heard to exclaim with great heat that he was determined to defend Mexico against the Yankees. . . . There is no doubt that he is the regular counselor of the Government. . . ." Nor did Forsyth forget to mention the famous *cencerrada* of 1856, which he emulated. The accumulation of counts testified to the helpless hostility of the American Minister toward an interloper whose influence with the Clerical government he was unable to dispute; and it was one of his main arguments, in fact, for breaking relations, that he expected to succeed to the same favored place with the Liberal government. But the portrait testified to something of far more consequence. Forsyth magnified the importance of the man on whom he focused his professional microscope.

M. de Gabriac was important. Germs are important. The senseless visions of a European protectorate were seriously contemplated by Zuloaga. Six months after his accession he sent for the French Minister and settled his succession with him. He might last for another twelve or eighteen months, he said, before the Liberals triumphed; then Juarez and his friends would come in; but they would be ousted in turn by the Conservatives; the Conservatives would return to power, but would not be able to retain it; and the country would continue to turn "in a circle of anarchy" until the day when the United States took it over. He proposed, therefore, to raise a loan, secured by Church property, to buy four or five warships with it, and to engage a corps of ten thousand French troops under the command of a French general, who would "put everybody in his place"—"beginning with myself," he added—because authority was indispensable, and no one in Mexico was capable of exercising it. The proposal was forwarded by Gabriac to Paris, where it produced no effect. The loan was the least difficulty, Rothschild's offering to float it at a reasonable discount (twenty-eight per cent); but the French Foreign Office was not interested. The Quai d'Orsay was a peculiar institution, a department apart, aloof, independent, self-sufficient, unaffected by changing regimes, and governed by the aristocratic routine of a gentleman's club; and in that stronghold of entrenched tradition bankers were not diplomats, and it was not the

custom to encourage them. French commercial interests in Mexico
were negligible and too insignificant to outweigh a time-honored rule;
politically the idea was also beyond the pale, the accepted attitude toward American affairs being one of complete indifference unless they
related to Europe, which was the only proper sphere for *haute politique* and the development of French influence. The department was
run, moreover, by Walewski, the Emperor's cousin, who was averse to
adventure of any kind and committed to the English entente, which
was the basis of the Napoleonic policy; and the English cabinet, when
it learned of the scheme, frowned on any suggestion of intervention in
Mexico. To have overcome such a combination of obstacles would have
required more influence than M. de Gabriac possessed; for he was not
as big a man in Paris as he was in Mexico. He was not even M. "de,"
but plain Gabriac, who assumed his title from his birthplace in Brit-
tany.

His real importance lay in his insignificance. A restless and irresponsible intriguer, incapable of carrying his government with him, but
able to fire the imagination of foreigners, he provided a conspicuous
example of the latitude that diplomats of his stripe allowed themselves
in out-of-the-way corners of the service like Mexico. He was dangerous because he was dreaded; the fears which he excited were unfounded, but they were sufficient to alarm the American Minister, who
magnified them in the advice that he pressed on the State Department.
"It is not safe for statesmen in the United States," Forsyth insisted, "to
ignore the fact that other nations besides our own have their eager gaze
fixed on this rich and superb country. Whether Mexico maintains her
personality or falls to pieces, we have a deep-seated interest in her future and should secure an influence in her councils. If she cannot stand
without the aid of some friendly power"—and that was self-evident
—"who should occupy the commanding position of benefactor and
friend? If the United States refuse, others must. What if it comes in
the form of a French prince supported by ten thousand French bayonets? Or of British gold effecting a floating mortgage on the territories
which we decline? Believe me, sir, we cannot play the dog in the
manger with our Monroe Doctrine. . . . I can see a multitude of contingencies that will make Mexico the battleground for the maintenance
of American supremacy in America." Fears are facts in politics; and
if M. de Gabriac had not existed, it would have been necessary for Forsyth or any other disciple of Manifest Destiny to invent him. But he
existed; he existed very definitely, independently of the imaginations
he irritated; and for a brief moment he played his part in history. The
demonstration at Veracruz in January 1859 would have been inconse-
quential if his hand had not been seen, or suspected, behind it. As it
was, it was perfectly timed to serve the party it was designed to cripple. The agent sent by Buchanan to survey the prospects of the Lib-

erals arrived in Veracruz just in time to witness it and to include it
among the reasons that he recommended for immediate recognition.

The decision to recognize had been taken in Washington before the
agent left, subject to his judgment on the spot, and his judgment was
formed rapidly. There was little that he could add to the arguments of
Forsyth save some minor matters of detail, such as the composition of
the government, an element with which the Department was still unfamiliar and which, however irrelevant to the consummation of American policy, seemed to him to merit some notice. "It may not be improper or uninteresting that I tell you of the President and his cabinet,"
he wrote after a fortnight of close observation. "President Juarez is a
man of some forty-five years, a full-blooded Indian, well versed in the
laws of his country, a prudent and sound jurisconsult but a distrustful
and timid politician, stern and incorruptible, yet of a mild and benig-
nant disposition; in his intercourse, modest like a child. He has a voice
in the council and is listened to with respect, but he has no influence
over his ministers and is unconsciously, perhaps, under their most absolute and unlimited control." Discounting the nominal head of the
government, therefore, as a mere figurehead, the Constitutional government could be reduced to two ministers. "Ocampo is a gentleman of
great native intellect, and of considerable parts and learning, inflexible
in his resolves, peremptory in his views, rather prompt in discourse and
impatient of contradiction, but high-minded and, like his chief, incorruptible." The other minister was not unknown in Washington,
Forsyth having sheltered him in the Legation in Mexico City, whence
he had recently escaped to Veracruz. "Lerdo de Tejada (who is in
the cabinet at the suggestion of your Agent) has all the brilliant
qualities of the other two, is as pure as they, but possesses more of the
practical habits which constitute a mind turned toward the actualities
of life rather than toward its dreams. He is the most popular man in
his party and is deservedly considered the master spirit of the cabinet.
His tendencies are all American. . . . We should look up to him as the
man most reliable in his preferences for us, frank, open, and always
ready to approach a question and to assume responsibility."

One novelty indeed distinguished the activity of the advance agent
—speed. The celerity with which he formed his judgment was in striking contrast to the dilatory tactics of the Department; but he had good
reasons to jump to conclusions. The situation was satisfactory and the
prospect excellent in every respect but one. The impending siege of
Veracruz he discounted in advance, as did the Liberal government,
which was confident that it would fail and prove the undoing, military
and political, of Miramon, provided the menace of foreign intervention
were removed. But that was the hitch. Once that factor had been eliminated, the balance of forces would automatically right itself and incline

in favor of the Constitutional government, for which public opinion had declared in sixteen out of twenty-two states, and which would already have established itself but for the lack of material resources. It was remarkable, he noted, that troops raised without coercion should have remained in camp for many months without reward of any description, without sufficient clothing or provisions, relying solely on the justice of their cause and their faith in its final triumph, and in this instance it could not be denied that the Mexican people had exhibited a fidelity to the principle of Constitutional government scarcely to be expected from their past history. Something uncommon had certainly occurred in Mexico when an army in which the superior officers received two pesos a day, the subordinates one peso, and the men twenty-five centavos—when they received it—and who were induced to desert before battle by Miramon, who threatened to shoot without fail all those who did not and advertised a schedule of bounties for those who did, and who were repeatedly beaten, flocked back to its banners after every defeat. His respect for such tenacity prompted him to remind the Department that "no obstacle that could be presented either in the mantle of diplomacy, which sometimes covers destruction, or in open discountenance, had been spared the Liberal party, and that powerful foes had recently given aid and comfort to Miramon by crippling their meager resources in the guise of demanding only just compliance with the terms of a former convention." Surely, therefore, the time for protection had come. "The present condition of affairs in Mexico," he concluded, "affords the best, and it may be the last, opportunity that will ever be presented to the United States to form a treaty with this Republic that will secure to them not only sovereignty over a country which recent disclosures and the most authoritative accounts respecting its soil and mineral resources represent as being even more valuable than Upper California"—the long annex, that is, of Lower California —but also the transits. "In my opinion, then, although it may be an experiment, we have no alternative left but the immediate recognition of the Juarez government. The occasion is one which should be improved without the intermission of a single hour of unnecessary delay."

In support of these promises he forwarded a memorandum, approved by Ocampo, covering the points suggested by himself as suitable stipulations for recognition and indicating the willingness of the Foreign Minister to negotiate upon them affirmatively, including the cession of Lower California. This advance was no mean triumph for a minor agent; where Forsyth had failed, a political scout had succeeded; and supposing that his services would be officially recognized in Washington, Juarez favored his nomination as the regular Minister. But the name of William B. Churchwell was not destined, any more than that of John Forsyth, to rank among the most distinguished diplomatists of his country. Forsyth himself had been worsted too often to want the job; a fresh, unspoiled, persuasive talent was needed; and immediately upon receipt of Churchwell's report Buchanan appointed a senator from Maryland, Robert McLane, as his Minister to Mexico. He was still hesitating, however, and accepted Churchwell's advice under pressure from the cabinet, but with misgivings, and at the last moment, alarmed by reports that the siege of Veracruz had begun and that the government he had been hurried into adopting might no longer be in existence by the time his representative arrived, he reconsidered the question with the cabinet. The move, so long weighed and so hastily made, was never more of an experiment than when it was finally settled, and as it was still a step in the dark McLane was granted discretion to confer or withhold recognition, as he saw fit, on his arrival in Veracruz.

The seat of the civil government now became the center of the civil war. All the forces upon which the solution depended—the military ability of Miramon, the menace of foreign intervention, and the support of the United States—were focused there, and the civil government became an active belligerent, forced to defend itself simultaneously against its domestic foes, their diplomatic allies, and the advances of its American friends. Of these forces the least formidable was the first. The city was well fortified by nature and science, and by all the rules of the book in which he was schooled Miramon was bound to fail. The manual of military science offered four possibilities of success, and no more. The first was a siege by starvation, which required control of the seaways, and he lacked it; the second, a siege by pressure and approach, which was impossible because of the sandy terrain and the deadly climate; the third, a siege of nerves and demoralization, which called for a constant and crushing bombardment, and he was short of munitions; the fourth was a siege of assault, which demanded a reckless waste of lives, and his manpower was limited. He tried them all in turn, and the events confirmed the book. Arriving before Veracruz in the first days of March, he spent a month in conducting a field class for six thousand pupils and a masterly demonstration of what not to do with the inadequate resources at his command. The experiment was conclusive, and on March 29 he broke camp and beat his way back to the capital. The foreign fleets remained neutral, biding the outcome of the dispute between M. de Gabriac and Admiral Penaud.

The enemy melted away; the friend remained. On April 1 McLane landed in Veracruz; five days later he accorded recognition; on the sixth he presented his credentials; and on the seventh he sat down with Ocampo to talk business, and the real contest began, and began badly for both parties. McLane perceived immediately that a long diplomatic siege lay ahead of him. Ocampo, he reported, "manifested great uneasiness as to several of the points suggested as proper subjects for adjust-

ment when intercourse should be established between the two governments, especially in relation to Lower California." McLane read him
the Churchwell memorandum, "but I carefully avoided any intimation
that he, the Minister of Foreign Affairs, himself had signed the memorandum," preferring to treat it, not as a written commitment, but as a
gentleman's agreement, since he was dealing with a gentleman whose
embarrassment was visible and vulnerable. Ocampo "continued reluctant to engage himself in any actual cession of territory, but I held him
to his implied obligation to give us Lower California if we desired it,"
an approach against which Ocampo guarded himself with an offer to
negotiate transits and trade favors in the most liberal spirit. McLane
forbore to press the point at their first interview, since he could afford
to wait. "It must be acknowledged, however," he admitted, "that the
depressed and bankrupt state of the National Treasury is the main impulse that will excite him to action."

Contact had been established, but nothing more, and both men were in
an awkward position. To what extent Ocampo had engaged himself by
his understanding with Churchwell was not clear; but Churchwell had
arrived at a favorable moment and had benefited by the discouragement
that preceded him. "I found them rather dispirited on my arrival," he
had noted. "They had been made to believe that the United States would
not take any decided course, but now they seem like new beings and manifest sincere and earnest friendship"; and the tonic effect of his fillip was
labeled Lower California. The dilatory tactics of the Department and the
depressing reports of Mata had done their work, and he was able to touch
on the topic of a territorial cession and to come off not only without
rebuff but with encouragement. What he had gained, however, was a
loose pledge, "a willingness to negotiate affirmatively," which had been
given before the siege and which Ocampo was obviously reluctant to
acknowledge after it. The tonic had worn off and compunction had set
in by the time McLane arrived, but to disavow his lapse was even more
difficult for Ocampo than to commit it. Evasion exposed him to the
charge of having misled the American advance agent by an implied
promise made to obtain recognition and meant to be forgotten after it,
and Ocampo was not enough of a professional diplomat to pride himself on the tricks of the trade. But his embarrassment was due to something more than the odious constructions to which his conduct was
open. The cession of Lower California, far from being a diplomatic
feint, had been so seriously considered in Veracruz that Mata, who had
begun his mission in Washington with an uncompromising refusal to
entertain the idea in June, had accepted it as inevitable by February
and had reached the point of discussing what it was worth—twenty
million dollars in money—with Ocampo, who had been softened up by
then more than he was willing either to admit or to deny.

The American Minister was in a scarcely less awkward position. He

had accorded recognition on the assumption that the Churchwell memorandum had been accepted in good faith and that it represented a
working agreement between the two governments; and the speed with
which he acted now required strong justification. The considerations
which he adduced in explaining his haste to Washington were less
compelling than covering reasons—the very large interests, political
and commercial, already involved in the Tehuantepec transit; the
knowledge that this right-of-way was the subject of decrees by both the
warring factions; and, lastly, "the fact that commercial relations between the United States and Mexico, embarrassed beyond all precedent, seemed to demand imperatively that the representative of the
United States should be heard and his influence respected at a moment
when the fleets of Great Britain and France are at anchor in Veracruz
harbor, exacting the performance of conventions contracted with governments not only not now in existence, but which existed, it would
seem, no longer than was necessary to destroy the independence of the
country and insure the humiliation of all future governments that
might succeed to the direction of public affairs." Of these reasons the
last was certainly the strongest; whatever the war might mean for Mexico, it was a trade war for the foreign powers. The liquidation of the
British Convention bonds was one of the stipulations, in fact, suggested
by Churchwell, who proposed that a portion of the purchase money for
Lower California be applied to their extinction. That point was as important in Washington as Lower California, and the best justification
for its cession by the Veracruz government. But all these reasons were
embarrassing to McLane. Knowing that he was open to criticism for
the promptness with which he had granted recognition, he determined,
after his first interview with Ocampo, to go slow. It was evident, he
wrote, that "extravagant expectations had been excited in regard to negotiations of loans for money, arms, and ammunition in the United
States on the strength of such recognition"; time would cool them.
Ocampo was as impressionable as McLane. "It was not difficult to perceive also," he added, "that he counted somewhat on the brightening
prospects of the Liberal cause as lessening the value of recognition of
the Juarez government by that of the United States"—and the fortunes
of war were fickle.

Within a week the brightening prospects of the Liberal cause were
overcast. The siege of Veracruz had left the capital exposed to attack,
and Degollado had taken advantage of the opening to concentrate all
his available forces against Mexico City. After his disastrous defeat in
December at San Joaquin, he had managed to muster fresh volunteers
in Michoacan, but he suffered from the same shortage of resources that
now prevented Miramon from taking the offensive successfully, and
though he led an army to the gates, his advance died there. Hovering

on the outskirts, he succeeded merely in menacing the city by sudden feints and lunges, shifting concentrations, and swift demonstrations, designed to draw off the investment of Veracruz, but destined to have a deadly outcome. Miramon had left behind him a mate who came up from the rear to strike the feint and to make his name suddenly famous. Speeding from Guadalajara by forced marches to the relief of the capital, Leonardo Marquez fell on the Liberal army and inflicted a crushing defeat on Degollado in the two-day battle of Tacubaya (April 10-11). The result was a rout: the Liberal colors were scattered to the four winds, and the very shirt of Degollado was flown among the trophies over the doors of the National Palace. The disaster was a terrible demonstration of the folly of attempting large-scale operations with the inadequate resources and inflated tactics of guerrilla warfare.

The extent of the disaster was immediately recognized in Veracruz. Ten days later McLane was able to report progress with Ocampo. "The Minister of Foreign Affairs," he wrote on April 21, "avows the readiness of President Juarez to cede Lower California to the United States, but doubts whether the Congress that is to be elected next October could be induced to ratify such a provision in the treaty that is now the subject of our consideration." To meet this objection he recommended to Washington that two treaties be drawn, one for the transits and the other for Lower California, a method that would facilitate the negotiation without impairing its security, since he counted on the consent of Juarez as the best guarantee of success, and the confidence of the President was undashed by the defeat of Degollado. "Should this Constitutional government be established in the City of Mexico before the next Congress is elected, and it certainly will be, for no Congress can be elected to assemble in the capital until that government is inaugurated there," he explained, "a period of some months will elapse during which the Executive branch of the government will be authorized to ratify as well as to negotiate treaties, and in this contingency no difficulty will be experienced in the ratification of the entire treaty." On this assumption he was willing to be accommodating and to separate the easy question of transits from the difficult one of cession.

He was a little too willing, however, to be easy with Ocampo and with himself. The concession was opposed in Washington. "I will tell you," Mata wrote to Ocampo, "what are the two great obstacles to separation. The first is the idea they have of us here as treacherous or astute in diplomacy, and they believe that the proposal to separate the treaties arises from the intention to refuse the one relating to California later. The second is that the President is bent upon distinguishing his term by some piece of big business that will produce great results, to make himself popular and his re-election probable. This is the key." Mata promised to insist on separation, but, knowing Buchanan, with so little hope of success that he proceeded to draft the terms of a contract by which, in return for twelve million dollars in bonds guaranteed by the United States Government, Mexico would mortgage the territory of Lower California for a period of six years, at the conclusion of which, if capital and interest had not been redeemed, title to the territory would be forfeited to the United States.

If the negotiation had been conducted in Washington, Buchanan might have gained more from Mata than McLane did in Veracruz from Ocampo, whose idea it was to divide the treaties; but the fact that it was formulated by two ministers both obliged to retrieve an initial indiscretion affected its development. The separation of the light and heavy matter was a convenient diplomatic device by which each benefited, McLane adopting it to make headway and Ocampo to gain time. For the Mexican a few months of grace were a bright prospect at that moment when there was no other, and McLane was confident that the catch was hooked and that he could afford to play out the line. Time was a coefficient in both their calculations, and a gain for McLane whether he conducted his diplomatic siege by slow starvation, by pressure and approach, by nerves and demoralization, or by direct assault; but time was a partner on which neither could count long, and both were building on loose and shifting ground.

Sinister though it was in its military effects, the battle of Tacubaya was important only because of its aftermath, for it was followed by an atrocity that defeated its political value. Returning from his fiasco at Veracruz, Miramon entered his own capital on the morning of April 11 just in time to witness the triumph of Marquez. He rode out to the field, inspected the results, and returned to the city; a few minutes later an orderly galloped back with an order for Marquez to shoot his prisoners. This had become common practice since the beginning of the war, when a Liberal officer from the frontier had slaughtered his captives on sight and had set a precedent which Miramon adopted by way of reprisal and upon which he improved to induce desertions from the ranks of the enemy. But on this occasion, according to Miramon, the order was limited to deserters from his own ranks and was warranted by military law. As it was executed by Marquez, however, it became an indiscriminate massacre, in the course of which the wounded lying in hospital in Tacubaya were dragged from their beds and butchered together with the physicians and medical students attending them.

It was this feature that gave the day its undying celebrity: Miramon and Marquez sought to escape it by blaming each other for a criminal blunder, the former maintaining that his order had been abused, the latter that it had been obeyed but had miscarried; and by the light of their subsequent records the benefit of the doubt belongs to Miramon, whose career was marked by a fairly consistent respect for those niceties of his profession that constitute its melancholy ethics, while Marquez continued to repeat the same mistakes and the same excuses and to distinguish himself by the ferocity of a born criminal who had never gone through military school. If the massacre was an accident, Marquez was not. "The Tiger of Tacubaya" he was called after that day—a name that clung to him and that was confirmed not only by the flair of the hunted but by the reek of the hunter, who showed his contempt for the technical refinements of war as long as he remained at large. Neither Marquez nor Miramon made any defense of their conduct, however, until they were called to account for it many years later; at the time the massacre was condoned as a normal excess of civil war, and none of those responsible for it was brought to book. In explaining his failure, which by his own standards was a serious one, Miramon pleaded the difficulty of disciplining a successful general in the full flush of triumph; fresh from defeat himself, he was forced to be prudent, but he sacrificed his reputation to his popularity, and the names of Marquez and Miramon were henceforth linked in fame and infamy.

Personal responsibilities were of passing importance, however, for the atrocity was no accident. It was a symptom of the rising fever of civil and religious war. Excesses had been committed on both sides and justified as retaliations for previous license in a futile and unending dispute that merely served to press the responsibility further and further back, where it belonged, resting its accumulated weight on the original warmakers who had kindled the conflict and incurred all its innate and inevitable consequences. Excesses were the salaries of strong convictions and unruly ranks, and the Liberals had their share to extenuate. After the capture of Guadalajara in 1858 fatalities fouled their flag. Two criminals long wanted for the murder of a retired Liberal governor were hanged before the Episcopal Palace by a mob, while Degollado stood by, helpless to preserve his authority. More serious was the assassination of the captured commander of the city, who had surrendered on condition that his life be spared, and in this case Degollado broke the responsible officer, though he subsequently restored him for services rendered to the cause. In both cases authority was the victim; the precedent provoked the reprisal, and the excuse the crime. Nevertheless, the fatalities at Guadalajara were forgotten, while those at Tacubaya were remembered. Why? Why should the one be forgotten and the other remembered, or either singled out for stigma, the whole of human history being written in dried blood, clotting as quickly as shed? Was it not absurd to moralize war, neatly to weigh guilt against guilt, and to regulate the law of nature? But human history is human precisely because of the struggle of mankind to master nature, to moderate aboriginal brutality, and to cheat necessity with choice. Between the massacres at Guadalajara and those at Tacubaya there was at least one saving distinction: the former were not perpetrated against noncombatants nor countenanced by a responsible commander, and though the margin was small, it was enough to make the difference damning. The 11th of April marked a crisis in the mounting tension of civil war beyond which lay the abyss. The breach made in the conventional rules revealed the real nature of a struggle that craved and found its own law, and that broke the feeble restraints under which men like Miramon conducted it as a gentlemen's affair. The bottom emerged, and the inhuman truth came to the top, and Marquez was its man. His rise was equally ominous to his friends and his foes; for where a hundred other outrages were overlooked, the horrors of Tacubaya were noticed and denounced by the world.

The slaughter of the sick and wounded and of physicians hallowed by their calling provided just that jot of excess value necessary to tip the uncertain sympathies and tolerant neutrality of the outer world: a transgression of fair measure that surpassed all precedents and all limits, that was more than custom could stomach, and that revolted public conscience in the tender nineteenth century. It was a detail, and it was a disaster. The outcry was quick, and it was lasting, for it was not allowed to die. The Liberals concealed in the capital exploited their martyrs. Before their blood could cool, an anonymous pamphlet appeared that baffled the police. Arrests were made right and left, and always the wrong ones; copies were smuggled into Veracruz for export abroad; the tale was picked up by McLane and found a platform in the next message of Buchanan to Congress. But no propaganda was needed: the sensation was spontaneous and far-reaching, and many Conservatives, shrinking from the crying shame of publicity and driven beyond the pale by the government that was guilty of it, rallied to the Liberals as the lesser evil. Against this rising reaction the Tacubaya government found no better guarantee than to distract public attention by raising a clamor of its own.

A topic lay at hand, inflammable, blinding, and infallible in effect. In a concerted attack through all the organs of publicity they controlled, the colleagues of Miramon denounced American recognition of the Veracruz government, published the letters of Forsyth, and protested in advance against any treaty involving a cession of national territory. The blast began on April 21, and by May 1 the American Consul in Mexico City felt it necessary to warn McLane that the outcry might well favor the velleities of intervention already manifested by the British and French Ministers. Mr. Otway and M. de Gabriac were dangerous organs of publicity, even though they were mere windbags, for both had long favored foreign intervention and "have always held up to their governments, as an excuse for these acts, 'the dangerous designs of the Colossus of the North.' The publication, therefore, at this time of the correspondence between Mr. Forsyth and the Mexican Minister of Foreign Affairs is particularly indicative of what is to be the burden of the despatches to be sent forward by the English and

French Ministers. . . . However wrong these gentlemen may be in fact, their despatches must have some weight with their respective governments, until such time as they are refuted by events. . . . The French Minister will, of course, move violently to the same purpose. Mr. Otway will unquestionably join his French colleague in forwarding orders for the taking of a hostile position against Veracruz immediately—no matter whether his instructions justify the step or not. I am told that he has declared his determination to avail himself of the first opportunity of crushing the government recognized by the United States. . . . Although I believe that the tone of the instructions from the English and French Governments due by this mail will be pacific and that the game between Gabriac and Penaud will stand drawn, still it is to be feared that the next mail will bring advice and instructions for the French and British Ministers to enforce reparations for the outrages committed upon their subjects; and notwithstanding that those outrages have all been committed by the generals of the clergy faction, the Ministers will be too glad of the opportunity of seizing Veracruz and thus dragging their governments into the first step for bringing about European intervention. I consider the event much to be feared, as I know it to be an important feature in the program of Gabriac. I think, if it is possible, that our government ought to take strong precautionary steps." Specifically, he suggested the occupation of the fortress commanding Veracruz harbor and "the hoisting of the Stars and Stripes there at the earliest possible moment."

Of this advice McLane took the better part. The strongest precautionary step was to change the subject. The blast leveled against the Veracruz government was met by an answering clamor and a joint defense. Ocampo lost his temper in diplomatic language and rejected the protest against the pending treaty in a long and impassioned philippic in which all the resources of rhetoric were employed to paraphrase the old retort of the kettle calling the pot black. McLane joined the war of words with a defense of Forsyth and American policy, remarkable alike for its courage and its reticence and the embarrassment it betrayed by its very verbal ability. He also seconded Ocampo in denouncing the atrocities of Tacubaya and demanding, on the ground that the head of the hospital had once been an American citizen, the death penalty for the responsible parties. The mouthpiece of Miramon, Foreign Minister Bonilla, retorted with a pointed allusion to the practice of lynching in the civilized South from which the American Minister hailed. A sharp cross-fire of mutual recriminations ensued between the three Ministers, the only result of which, when it died down, was that the American Minister had been personally antagonized to the point of becoming an outspoken partisan in the civil war. The strongest precautionary step, after changing the subject so often, was to drop it. The charges raised by the Tacubaya government were still unrefuted, the

letters of Forsyth could be belied only by the event, and the best way
to lay the accusation, obviously, was to let it rest until time answered its
presumption. It was no time, with international complications pending, to discuss Lower California; and that part of the treaty, consequently, remained in abeyance.

What could no longer be held in abeyance, however, was the crying
need for material aid and the crying demand after the disaster at Tacubaya for the Liberal government to raise it. Degollado was undismayed. Rallying his routed forces in Morelia, he set to work with unbroken spirit and unflagging faith to repeat his customary miracle of
recuperation. He had lost a battle, he was confident of winning the
war, but in that battle he had lost a large part of the reputation he had
won in a year of trial and error. Elementary mistakes had been made:
in his haste to reach the capital he had left an army hanging on his
flank and had been surprised and laden with the haunting trophies of
Tacubaya; and in some quarters, close to headquarters, his resignation
was expected to follow. His conscience and his pride forbade him to resign in the hour of defeat, when his peculiar gifts were indispensable,
and he defended his misfortune by insisting that he had risked defeat
to protect Veracruz. But his popularity was impaired, and even that
phoenix of a soldier could not repeat the resurrection that he had
wrought a year before without a helping hand. After vainly attempting
to rise from the ashes, he abandoned the field and made a flying trip
to Veracruz, in the last days of May, to lay his case before the President.

Crippled, discredited, but indomitable, Degollado brought a powerful appeal to bear on his government. His very appearance in Veracruz was a reproach, and it coincided with private advice that the President received from a trusted correspondent in the capital, an elder
statesman who ventured as a patriot, a partisan, and an experienced ex-
minister to act as his political guide. This expert also laid the situation
before Juarez with a pressing force not far from friendly reproach.
Degollado was not to blame; he had done what he could with the elements available, and by blocking the capital he had assured the security of the civil government in Veracruz. To repair the disaster at Tacubaya was, therefore, the undeniable obligation of the government, and
the means of doing so were within reach. Miramon was bankrupt and
making the most ruinous deals, selling the principal properties of the
Schools of Arts and Sciences, Medicine, and Agriculture to the bank-
ing house of Jecker & Co., and these institutions were on the point of
closing. Education was the first concern to be sacrificed to survival; the
next was to be ecclesiastical capital. Miramon demanded a million
pesos to continue operations; he threatened the clergy with nationalization of their property, and a shake-down was impending in the cab-

inet; but such shifts would not be necessary—"they will consume the property in mortmain little by little by little by mortgages and sales in which the principal party will be Jecker." The question arose, therefore: why should a banker be the one to benefit by the pinch? Why Jecker? Why not Juarez? "I believe that it is time for you to decree the complete nationalization of all property held in mortmain. This will prevent waste, and the clergy themselves will not be surprised by a measure which they consider inevitable. I remember that you have already studied plans by Señor Lerdo, and it would be useless, therefore, and foolish, for me to say anything further. What I will say, however, is that the opportunity should not be lost, since there is no further reason to defer a measure that has so long been expected."

Failing the confiscation of ecclesiastical capital, there was only the American treaty, a resource the writer weighed very carefully. "Setting aside the declamations, insults, and slanders of the reactionary press on account of the reception of the American Minister, I cannot deny that the publication of the notes exchanged between Forsyth and Cuevas in reference to a new treaty has produced very serious fears, since it is supposed that our neighbors will entertain the same pretensions as they did then. . . . Unfortunately, all that has been said about our inability to hold our northern deserts to the benefit of the world is quite true, but above these questions of material interest stand those of honor and dignity and the melancholy memories of the Treaty of Guadalupe and the sale of the Mesilla. . . . These reasons lead me ardently to hope that the government will not consent to any cession of territory or to the settlement of claims as proposed by Forsyth." The caution was accompanied, however, by encouragement. "On what bases, then, are we to deal with the United States, it will be said, if we reject these two capital points?" A great opportunity had arisen for Buchanan to initiate a disinterested policy of good neighborship and to make his mark in American history. "If the United States really wish to inaugurate a generous and continental policy in America, if they wish to protect the other republics and to serve universal liberty, they do not need to acquire some few leagues of land for that purpose, at our expense. . . . More glorious advantages, and more practical ones, can be obtained on this continent if they raise their views a little above immediate material interests. I who have seen the world accept as legitimate and even profitable, in the opinion of many, the pact known as the Holy Alliance, which was the compact of the thrones to protect one another at the cost of the peoples and to deprive them of all liberty—I believe it legitimate and advantageous for the peoples to unite to consolidate their institutions and to prevent their destruction by anarchy and despotism. If peace, order, and prosperity prevail in the republics of America, advantages will result not only for them, but for the entire world, and nothing can be said against the government of Mexico should it be fortunate enough to ensure the future of the country. Such an advantage can be obtained only by great concessions," and short of a territorial cession he was prepared to approve of any. The transits and trade favors were a small price to pay for a holy alliance in the democratic interest; "the United States will obtain incalculable advantages that Europe will envy but will not be able to dispute, and we can count on immediate resources and a rich and flourishing treasury in the future." In conclusion, he apologized for proffering officious advice, because of "the interest which, as a Liberal and a personal friend of yours, I feel in your good name. I know only too well your abnegation and patriotism, I know that you will spare no effort for the Republic, and I know also that we have a great guarantee in the intelligence and keen honesty of our friend Mata. All this has encouraged me to speak with perfect frankness and, wishing you the utmost success of your labors, I shall never be the one to censure the concessions that you may have to make to imperative necessity."

Between these alternatives Juarez hesitated no longer: he had hesitated too long, indeed, for his own good, and the frank prompting of his friend left unspoken, though it hinted at, facts too familiar and too painful to bear explicit statement. Discontent and impatience were growing among the fighting Liberals, whether they fought with the sword or the pen, against the passive conduct of their government. What were the President and his ministers doing? Were they doing anything at all? The war was over a year old, desultory and disastrous, succeeding spasmodically, failing consistently, and what had the civil powers, safely entrenched in Veracruz, to show for their share in it? Were they supplying the sinews of war or the fat? Were they doing even their ideological duty and providing the party with revolutionary leadership? These questions were heard with increasing force and frequency and could no longer be muffled or shunned in 1859. Degollado and the elder statesman spoke for Mexico. Even in the United States the press of all shades of opinion was urging material support for the Constitutional government, yet Mata was no further advanced than on the day he arrived in Washington. Churchwell had offered to secure him a loan in Wall Street in anticipation of the pending treaty, but the negotiation had failed for want of security; temporizing was repaid in kind, and the market value of recognition was falling. Buchanan now took the position that no indemnization was due to Mexico for the transits, since this would amount to paying for benefits bestowed on the country by American development, and that whatever price McLane might agree to pay for them would be pure bounty; the deal depended, and his re-election into the bargain, on the big business that remained in abeyance. Mata was resigned to returning Buchanan to the White House from Lower California. But not Juarez. Between the alienation of national territory and the nationalization of Church property the choice was promptly made; and the President met the demand imposed on him by the quick and the dead, recognized the mission for which he had been elected by history, and, rising to his secular responsibility slowly but firmly, like a man laden with years without age, finally promulgated the Reform Laws.

4

THE first of the Reform Laws, and the foundation of all the others, appeared on July 12, 1859, in the form of a presidential decree nationalizing Church property. The rest followed in close succession: the separation of Church and State (July 12); the exclaustration of monks (July 12); the establishment of civil registry for certificates of birth, marriage, and death (July 23); the secularization of cemeteries (July 31) and of public holidays (August 11). Religious liberty, the logical outcome and the crown of the others, was reserved for a later date, but was announced in the program proclaimed on July 12, an epochal date in Mexican history. Conceived as a whole, the Reform Laws were a sweeping proclamation of emancipation of the civil power, which fulfilled the promise and corrected the omissions of the Constitution of 1857 and gave the party of progress a future that revived its fighting faith.

The word "progress" was wrested from the enemy and restored to its original owners; the discussion that Miramon had closed six months before was reopened by Juarez on July 12 with dynamic effect. And on July 12 Miramon issued a proclamation of his own in which, anticipating that effect, he pledged himself anew to destroy the *ley Lerdo,* the *ley Juarez,* and all their corollaries, and to champion "the interests of the Church, vigorously sustaining the prerogatives and independence of that institution"; but at the same he frankly admitted that, despite the incontestable victories which he had won, no advance had been made by his cause and no one knew when or how the war would end; and he appealed to the country to rally to "the fair name of Reaction" in which he glorified—the word "progress" was dropped.

More significant than this admission of weakness was the invigorating effect of that word on the Liberal party. The weary, the fainthearted, the disabled, the defeated, recovered their fighting spirit overnight. Doblado returned to the battle and offered his sword to Degollado and a defense of his previous conduct to his party. In a manifesto to the people of Guanajuato he rehabilitated the perennial summer soldier successfully. He denied that he was a deserter; he had never doubted his duty but only where it lay; if he had hesitated, it was from conscientious and honorable motives, fearing first to precipitate, and then to prolong, a ruinous struggle that would split the country and renew all the horrors of the period of Independence. When he had capitulated, it was to spare the proprietors and proletarians of his state unnecessary suffering; but his discretion had been wasted, and he was now convinced of the ineluctable nature of the struggle, the inexorable necessity of finishing it at all costs, and the right of reprisal which the atrocities of the Reaction had given "the Liberal party, which is the national party, to advance once and for all on the road of reforms, affronting definitely all those that were indicated long ago as the radical cure of the inveterate evils bequeathed us by the Spanish domination." The apology of Doblado, like the declamation of Miramon, was a reflex action that testified accurately to the mercurial virtue of the Emancipation Proclamation.

But bracing though the effect was on the party, Juarez himself benefited very little by it. When he finally rose to his revolutionary mandate, the bolt was belated and the thunder stolen by a combination of circumstances that dampened its thud. Party politics were excited by the first momentous act of his government, and the credit for the Reform Laws, though it was collective, was widely attributed to the initiative of Lerdo de Tejada, who came to Veracruz determined to finish the reform he had begun, if not badly, mildly and tentatively, in 1856. The reasons for this partiality were not far to seek. When Lerdo joined the government he brought with him two assets—a radical program and a commanding personality. The program he showed to Churchwell, in confidence, as his handiwork, and it confirmed his reputation as an enterprising statesman, which the American agent accepted as unquestioningly as he did the assumption that Juarez was a timid and mistrustful politician and Ocampo a difficult idealist. All these conclusions were hasty and founded on hearsay. Placed in the cabinet at the suggestion of Churchwell and on the strength of his pro-American sympathies, Lerdo disappointed his sponsors. McLane found him "very averse to a territorial cession, as he is to any new and enterprising policy connected with the foreign affairs of the country." A new and enterprising policy in domestic affairs, on the contrary, was what he pressed on his colleagues as the only compensation for the American treaty and as the best guarantee against its risks. He pressed against an open door, for their ideas were identical with his. Nevertheless, differences developed between them that more than once threatened the dissolution of the government.

The last of these crises occurred just before the adoption of the program. With sanction assured, Lerdo suddenly resigned and laid the responsibility for his decision squarely on the President. "You and I," he explained, "are making an effort which can be of no benefit to ourselves or to the cause. You are working against your ideas, and hence I lack the confidence necessary to enter fully on the difficult course that, in my opinion, we must adopt. How can anything good come of such a start in so thorny a task as the radical reform of a society like ours? It is a thousandfold better that I retire and that you follow your own inspirations. This is bound to happen in the end and sooner than we think, and it had better be before we compromise the situation by a course that is not in conformity with your ideas." In reply, Juarez discounted the idea of any difference between them, declared himself at a loss to explain it, and, implying very plainly that the misunderstanding was deliberate, induced Lerdo to withdraw his resignation. A week later the program appeared, after a rapid reading in council, with a precipitation as conspicuous as the judgment that awarded it to the influence of Lerdo.

What those differences were was never revealed, but they were thinly veiled and easily guessed. The strain that developed within the government from the day that Lerdo joined it was visible to the naked eye. They were differences not of principle or policy, but of personality and pace. The Reform Laws had been adopted in principle long before Lerdo appeared in Veracruz, but the test of the policy was its timing, and that faculty to which Juarez had proved his title was called into question by his long delay in enacting them. The reasons were deeply rooted in his temperament and training, and Lerdo had neither the time nor the patience, if he had the wish, to appreciate them. What he encountered was the deliberation of a mind that was judicial before it was revolutionary. The expropriation of Church property, prepared by Prieto a year before, had been reserved for a propitious moment, and before Juarez was convinced that it had come, he had to overcome scruples and hesitations and lifelong habits of mind, which, to a practical politician or a professional revolutionary, were merely the subterfuges of political timidity. To the jurist, the measure was a violent spoliation of vested rights; to the statesman, its expediency was doubtful in drawn battle; to the provisional President, his Constitutional right to decree it without congressional sanction was questionable; and to the revolutionary, to postpone it until the end of the war was preferable. His caution was finally overcome by a combination of compelling circumstances—the distress of Degollado, the necessity of raising resources at all costs and of anticipating the enemy's use of the same methods, and the hope of eluding the pressure of American diplomacy. With these considerations the recommendations of Lerdo coincided; but the facts, and not Lerdo, dictated his decision.

Their differences did not end there. When Lerdo joined the government, he did not join the family that composed it. He was a distant relative who arrived on the scene at a trying time to direct public affairs, to mend an administration that had been notoriously neglected and mismanaged, and to patronize its members. Such at least was the impression he produced on his partners. There were times when they felt themselves treated like poor country cousins. His self-confidence made collaboration superfluous, his independence was hampered by it, and in spite of his punctilious courtesy he could not conceal a casual attitude toward his colleagues and even toward the President—particularly toward the President. Juarez had the moral superiority to ignore it, but his friends were profoundly outraged. Ocampo, the closest of them, suffered in silence as long as he could, but when his tongue was finally loosed, he recalled bitterly "the superiority with which Señor Lerdo regarded us, an affectation that led him sometimes into incivilities incredible in a person of his breeding; as, for instance, in failing to attend appointments with the President or the summons that he sent him. So determined was I to preserve our unity that I bore from Señor Lerdo what I would not have suffered from anyone under other circumstances." The antagonism between Lerdo and Ocampo, himself of a peremptory temper and impatient of contradiction, developed into a repressed feud all the more bitter for being buried by discretion and duty. Small mortifications were remembered because they excited a deeper and more impersonal antipathy between the two men. What Ocampo really resented was the intrusion of a personal element, which had hitherto been successfully excluded from the government, and with which neither he nor Juarez could cope. They were not politicians and could not contest the superiority of Lerdo in that respect. He was a master who had the supreme gift of concealing his art. Unconsciously perhaps, and imperceptibly certainly, he contrived to cast his colleagues into the shade by anticipating their intentions, appropriating their ideas, monopolizing their virtues, and attracting attention without appearing to court it. Against that unsettling influence Ocampo was helpless. The philosopher who had always protested against the cult of leaders and insisted, in his innocence, that anyone in turn could be the representative of a ruling idea, now found himself confronted with the fact of a dominating personality that appropriated a program to which no one could claim patent or priority. And as Lerdo did not deny the flattering imputation, and as his colleagues, in the interests of solidarity, did not contradict it, the assumption gained general currency at the time.

And it was a time when personalities were important. The rise of the revolutionary temper aroused by the Reform Laws demanded a figure to personify the idea. In radical circles Lerdo was accepted as that man, and the stature of the President suffered by comparison. The positions of the two men who had started their revolutionary careers together were now completely reversed: the initiative Juarez had given the movement four years before had passed so patently to Lerdo that, in 1859, instead of leading, the President appeared to be led; and among the Lerdistas he was rated a dead weight and a drag on the progress of the revolution. In advanced circles it was common to speak of his irresolution and apathy and to complain—in print—that "to all the blows of fortune he opposes the indifference, the fatalism, the inertia characteristic of his race." And that complaint, under its transparent prejudice and partisanship, raised the real question of whether a member of a subject race, however far he had risen above it, could ever outgrow its bonds and transcend its secular limitations, mounting above the prudence, the patience, the beaten virtues of his people to the commanding position and the enterprising qualities which his responsibility required. At the very time when he issued the laws that answered that challenge and assured his place in history, Juarez himself was the most disparaged member of his party.

His friends suffered in silence and referred the verdict to posterity—the test of the measure was still its timing. By the standards of practical politics the Reform Laws were a war measure, produced to meet an immediate emergency, and as such they were a forced birth. Immediately after their delivery Lerdo left for the United States to raise money in the open market on the security of Church property. The political credit he reaped from the whole program rested, in fact, on the financial credit that the confiscation of ecclesiastical capital promised to provide, and his reputation as a financial expert was unquestioned when he left for the United States. But he reckoned without his host. By the same packet a communication from McLane to the State Department sped him on his way. "Should he succeed in negotiating a loan in the United States with the Church property as a lien or security," the Minister pointed out, "it is not likely that either he or his colleagues will be disposed to cede Lower California in the present condition of the Constitutional government. On the other hand, if he fails in this negotiation, I am satisfied that he will no longer oppose, but rather advocate, its cession." Needless to say, Lerdo failed.

The political strategy of the Emancipation Proclamation was sufficiently self-evident to make that result a foregone conclusion. The value of the Reform Laws as a timely expedient was their least attribute, however, in the eyes of Juarez. "I take great pleasure in sending you the decree I have just signed," he wrote to a friend on the momentous day of July 12. "The most important things that it contains are, as you will see, the absolute independence of the civil power and religious liberty. For me these were the capital points to be won in this revolution, and if we succeed we shall have the satisfaction of having rendered a service to our country and to humanity. I also enclose the program I have published, in which other measures have been voted that are certain to improve the condition of this society." The nationalization of Church property was one of those "other measures," but it was not the cardinal one. For Juarez the initial law, basic as it was in subverting the economic strength and political power of the clergy, and profitable as a source of immediate revenue, was merely the material lever that raised, released, and supported the ideal structure of a secular society; it was a means to an end, and his mind was trained to the long view. But the two aspects were inseparable, and the element of timing affected his timeless fame as well, for most of the capital points of the program had been anticipated by militant leaders in the field, acting on their own authority. Santiago Vidaurri had not waited for sanction to confiscate Church property in his territory; nor had Gonzalez Ortega, who confiscated Church property spontaneously in his state and introduced civil registry there without consulting Veracruz; the dissolution of monastic communities had already begun in Michoacan. Wherever the war spread, it secularized the society it destroyed; so that the action of the Federal government came as an anticlimax and appeared to be merely a belated ratification of an accomplished fact and an automatic response, or even a surrender, to pressure from the ranks. Such was the way in which a sure-footed lawgiver would guide his people, and it was a proof of his political instinct that, before rushing in where the Constitution-makers of '57 had feared to tread, Juarez waited for some popular prompting to force and strengthen his hand; but his sense of pace could be appreciated only in historic perspective, and his chronic caution alone was noticed at the time. To wait for the rising tide was a mark of democratic statesmanship, but before it could float the leader it swamped him. The policy was too slow, too sound, too unspectacular, to have any popular appeal, and the result was that when he produced the measures that consummated the movement, the vanguard of the party had already passed him by and looked on him as its most backward representative. As a measure of popular progress, this was a healthy sign and encouraging to anyone who could observe it disinterestedly, as he did; his philosophy condemned him, however, to be consumed by his political offspring. Conceiving of his function as a medium for popular forces, he identified himself with his office and sank himself in it with the detachment of a genuine public servant. And so literal a practice of the democratic ideal set a lonely example far ahead of his time and impractical in a period of violent transition. Democracy was a distant ideal to a people who had no experience of its discipline, and whose whole history had been controlled by the collective anarchy of personal leaders; and his reserve, his self-effacement, recognized and respected as they were in his private life, were negative virtues in the public man and encouraged the notion of his nonentity.

Now, this was not a negligible matter; his personal prestige was more than a personal disadvantage; the depreciation of the President reacted in turn on the movement, fostering the inherent anarchy of the Liberal party and producing serious disaffection among the leaders in the field. An incipient urge to secede from Federal control began to stir here and there in the summer of 1859. In Guerrero the press complained of the lawless guerrillas that wasted the state and held the President personally responsible for their outrages. "Don Benito Juarez has neither sought nor been able to moralize the revolution; to prevent it from being detested, he lets the good and bad have their way alike, without a thought for the evils caused by his apathy and complete ineptitude," the complaint ran. "It is high time that the legislature of this state sever its relations with a government that produces nothing but harm." The local Red club recommended that the governors of the League be circularized with a petition demanding his retirement. "We acknowledge no other sovereignty than that of the states, which must delegate it to able hands of recognized activity. Don Benito Juarez is able to wait without suffering, but incapable of working and sacrificing himself; he is not the man of the revolution but of the counterrevolution." The severity of the censure was aggravated by the fact that it was signed by Ignacio Altamirano, an ardent revolutionary and a fellow Indian, who vindicated the reputation of his race by the energy with which he belabored Don Benito Juarez.

Democracy was no substitute for personal authority, and the murmurs that ran through the harvest of the summer of 1859 were not long in taking shape. In September Santiago Vidaurrí seceded, in effect, withdrawing his troops from the field and his support from the Juarez government on the ground that what the country needed was a progressive dictatorship; and though further defection was checked by the prompt action of Degollado, who drove the deserter out of the country, the incident indicated to what lengths impatience with the President could lead.

The one quarter, perhaps, where the reputation of the President was safe was in the hands of the enemy. The enemy gave him a tremendous press. The enemy had a long memory and laid the Reform Laws to the original evil of the *ley Juarez,* which in turn was "merely a reworking of the French laws of '93," and since profane history was nothing but a repetition of proven errors, predicted that "the result would be the same, a social ferment exploding in a deadly detonation that caused the downfall of the impious and brought them to death on the gallows that they themselves raised over a mountain of ruins." The enemy gave him no quarter. The enemy exulted in the dissensions of the sick family. The enemy gave him his due and denounced him as the "Constitutional despot." The enemy buried him under a mountain of abuse. The enemy called him a socialist, a traitor, an American, and of all the epithets hurled at him the last was undoubtedly the deadliest,

for the enemy immediately seized the connection between the Reform
Laws and the American treaty and, realizing that American recognition supplied the security for the Emancipation Proclamation, fell back
on patriotism as a last refuge. This line was propagated with a zeal so
persistent that for generations to come devout and unknowing Mexicans were taught that the reformer who despoiled the Church with
one hand sold his country with the other.

The failure of Lerdo to raise a loan in the United States now made
the conclusion of the treaty imperative. Before Lerdo left Veracruz,
McLane had sounded him once more on the cession of Lower California, and in their final conversation the strenuous opposition which
Lerdo had always shown to it—unless at an exorbitant price and at
some future date when, as he said, his direct influence and control over
the government might be greater than it then was—was materially
modified. Warned by McLane that he could not reasonably expect any
pecuniary assistance except for a cession of territory, Lerdo proposed to
his colleagues to reconsider their position and to cede Lower California
for fifteen million dollars. With the departure of Lerdo, however, the
opposition remained, and McLane found himself confronted by a force
in the cabinet which he could not identify and which was so inflexible
that he was reduced to echoing its views. "The cession of territory is
the gravest and most important act of sovereignty that a government
can perform; it is questionable, therefore, whether it should be performed at a moment when it is in conflict with another government
for the possession of empire," he advised Washington, "and this consideration is as important to the party purchasing as to the party ceding
the territory." Without waiving the territorial claim, Washington consented to reserve it while McLane negotiated the subsidiary question
of transits; but from that day the claim was abandoned in fact. The
compliance of Washington, at the very moment when the quarry was
cornered, was remarkable but not inexplicable. Besides the agitation
aroused in Mexico and the risk of precipitating foreign intervention,
two other factors made it impolitic to press the claim at that time. One
was the rise in the United States of sovereign sympathy for the Liberal
cause; one of those forms of popular intervention, springing from disinterested motives, that sometimes upset the plans and force the hands
of statesmen, the pressure of popular sentiment obliged Buchanan to
make an involuntary concession to Veracruz. The other was the Reform Laws. The confiscation of Church property promised to provide
the bankrupt faction with a source of revenue sufficient to dispense
with the American loan and to elude a territorial cession; and of all the
factors that combined to block Buchanan this was the most foiling.
The Reform Laws, appearing at the most favorable moment to produce

their maximum value, demonstrated the political instinct of Juarez and vindicated his uncanny faculty for correct timing.

With the elimination of Lower California from the agenda, the negotiations entered their decisive phase. The reduction of the treaty to transit facilities compelled McLane to compensate for the defeat of the major claim by driving a hard bargain on the lesser; and he was on his mettle. The remaining forms of persuasion were employed for all that they were worth. Financial pressure was still worth a great deal, for the confiscation of Church property was accomplished more quickly by a stroke of the pen than the collection of such tribute could be effected in fact. The most valuable ecclesiastical capital was concentrated in the territory controlled by the Clerical government, and in the outlying provinces the Constitutional authorities had to contend with the moral effects of expropriation. The masses were shocked by the plundering of sacred buildings: paupers themselves, but as pious as proprietors, they were doubly wounded, in their sense of possession and superstition, for the churches were the palaces of the poor, and the poor were deprived of a delusion of splendor and a life of phantasy, which they prized more than the comforts of the flesh. The prosperous classes were reluctant to defy the ban of the Church against the purchase of ecclesiastical spoils and were as poor in spirit as the inheritors of Heaven; and the liquidation of the great asset was slow and insufficient to relieve the insolvency of the government. Pecuniary pressure, diminished but not forfeited by the Reform Laws, still provided a working margin on which McLane was able to operate effectively.

Nevertheless, another six months passed before the treaty was concluded. Even in its reduced scope McLane encountered constant and stubborn impediments. The character of the Minister with whom he had to deal was one of them. With the departure of Lerdo, the master spirit whose practical mentality made him naturally pro-American was eliminated from the cabinet. Ocampo was also pro-American, but for precisely the contrary reason, and whether to emulate Lerdo or to redeem a wrong start, he too was on his mettle. Improving on the pregnant suggestion of the elder statesman, he proposed to convert the treaty into a general alliance between the two Republics for the support of republican institutions in America, an ambition, as McLane dryly observed, "that evinced so little appreciation of the relative condition and power of Mexico and the United States that I have not felt myself encouraged to expect any practical result therefrom." For such a holy alliance to produce mutual advantages more glorious and more practical than a few leagues of land, large compensations had to be made; and those which Ocampo could offer were not sufficient to bribe the American Government to be great. When that delusion had been dispelled and the discussions reduced to their proper scope, the regulations of the transits gave rise to practical difficulties that produced further delays. The most important of these was the right, claimed by McLane, to police the transits with American troops. The demand was warranted by the disturbed state of the country, but it excited national susceptibilities which the most pro-American Mexican could not ignore, and after weeks of fruitless conversation it was clear to McLane that he and that difficult idealist could never learn to speak the same language. Their differences ended in a deadlock; Ocampo resigned, but his successor was equally adamant. McLane paid a flying visit to Washington, and on his return Ocampo was again in the Foreign Office; and McLane used his last argument. An American citizen having been murdered by Marquez in the meanwhile, the American Minister adopted Ocampo's proposal for a general alliance, but in a unilateral sense, and recommended to Washington a punitive expedition by American troops against Miramon, with or without the consent of the Juarez government. The argument convinced Ocampo, the deadlock was broken, and the protection of the transits, under certain express conditions, was granted. "It has been with much difficulty," McLane informed the Department in plain English, "that I induced the Constitutional government to recognize its obligation to seek the aid of the government of the United States when it is unable to perform with effect its proper functions as a government, and it was only when I represented that sooner or later the government of the United States would act without reference to it or to any other government or authority in defense of its treaty rights and to protect its citizens, that I was able to come to any conclusion satisfactory to myself on this point." On December 14, 1859, the negotiations were finally concluded, and Ocampo signed the treaty that was to prove his political and physical death warrant.

Several days previously the *New York Herald* had published a summary of the treaty. The capital points secured to the United States Government perpetual right-of-way across the Isthmus of Tehuantepec and the projected railway bed across the northwestern corner of Mexico, together with the right to police them with its own military forces, with the consent of the Mexican Government or, in cases of emergency, without it. In return the Mexican Government obtained the promise of two million dollars in cash, two on credit for the settlement of American claims, and a bad name. The outcry was immediate and immense. The Miramon government led it with scathing denunciations in the press and a formal protest to Washington against an invalid contract drawn with an irresponsible party. "The Veracruz government," it declared, "in approving the treaty has arrogated to itself titles and powers that it does not possess even by the charter it invokes, and should it be successful, its partisans, in order to establish some regularity in its affairs, would make it expiate by an exemplary punishment so great an offense against the national sovereignty." The charge was true, and the Liberals, galled and angered by their inability to refute it, passed the same sentence on the treaty and condemned their government for transgressing its Constitutional limitations and compromising the national sovereignty. The protests, beginning with attacks in the press, resignations from the militia, and placards posted on the house of the President, swelled into a party scandal, which, far from abating with the passage of time, grew into a standing reproach to the Juarez government. Party lines were effaced in a common patriotic panic; the verdict was unanimous; and the damage was not confined to the domestic effects of the deal. *The Times of London* noticed it as an historic event of mournful significance: "The news of Mexico arriving today from New York is of extraordinary importance for bondholders, for if the treaty that is said to have been concluded in Veracruz should be definitely ratified, Mexico will pass from that day forth virtually under American control. All the northern part of the country will be opened to American colonists, who not only have the privilege of introducing their effects free of duty, but will be able to summon the troops of the United States to their assistance in any difficulties that may arise with the native population. . . . Under such conditions the absorption of the Mexican Republic can be accomplished gradually without provoking the fierce and futile resistance which more direct methods would entail."

In Paris and Madrid, where the dread of American advances was no less acute, political capital also was made of their progress. But the sharpest shock was the behavior of public opinion in the United States. Nearly all the Mexican correspondence in the press was concentrated in the journals of New York and New Orleans, and as no regular correspondents were maintained to cover Mexico, information was supplied by volunteer contributions colored by partisanship and adapted to editorial policy, which made those two poles of propaganda foci of infection for the rest of the country. With one or two exceptions, the press in New York discredited a convention that held no commercial benefits and many political perils for northern interests; but it was in New Orleans, in the home of the Louisiana Tehuantepec Company, that the treaty received its worst press. The *Daily Picayune* appreciated its value in terms that depreciated the loser; the sum of four million dollars, it declared, was "certainly very little to pay for such extensive and valuable concessions. For the right of transit across the Isthmus of Tehuantepec alone, the Polk administration, about twelve years ago, authorized the offer of fifteen million dollars. We bought the valley of the Mesilla a few years ago and gave more for it than is asked of us now, only to secure a route of transit through our own territory and to find that the best trade route remained within the territory of Mexico. We now hold the right-of-way through Tehuante-

pec and a control over two other routes as complete as if we had bought
the territory. In fact, we cannot say whether it is not better to hold the
right-of-way with unlimited power of protection than to have obtained
a territorial cession. We need be in no hurry to acquire territory in
those parts, and it may be assumed that we shall have it as soon as it is
useful or needed." The contempt for Mexican incompetence implied
in those lines was emphasized by an appeal to the Mexicans to "trust
the loyalty and good faith of the United States with respect to the use
which they will make of the powers granted," and an appeal to the
Americans to "abstain from abusing such concessions, avoid all cause
of friction, and reward the liberality of the Progressives in Mexico by
aiding them actively and effectively in their undertaking." The alliance
thus proposed was precisely the kind of trade favor that the organ of
the Catholic diocese in New Orleans had in mind when it wrote with
a contempt that was neither implied nor palliated: "Mexico may be
destined to lose its nationality, but we would have wished that it might
at least lose it nobly. It remained for Juarez to degrade the nation the
more easily to destroy it, and to drown the spirit of independence in
the foulest of slime." The reflection cast on the national colors was the
historic revenge of the party that had lost the last of the Three Guarantees of 1821. The government that was guilty of the treaty was red, it
was green, but it was no longer white; the hue and cry of 1859 called
it yellow.

For the moment the Reform Laws, of recent memory, were forgotten in the clamor that greeted their price—a clamor so universal
and unyielding that it drowned any hope of defense. No dissenting
voice could be raised at the time, and least of all by the Liberal government. A fair judgment of the treaty was impossible without some
knowledge of the concessions refused as well as of those accorded, and
the public remained in ignorance of the demand for a territorial cession, which had been successfully lost in the shuffle, though the presence of the ace in the pack was suspected from old precedent and
scented in the privileges actually granted. Of these the most compromising was the protection of the transits by American troops. On that
delicate point Ocampo and McLane had reached a reasonable agreement, which confined the privilege to its ostensible and legitimate purpose, the security of public thoroughfares running through sparsely
settled and lawless territory, and provided the proper safeguards for
Mexican sovereignty even in cases of special emergency, when it was
stipulated that the right of intervention was limited to the preservation
of order and lapsed with the passing of the crisis, the end of which was
to be determined by the Mexican Government. So far as legal safeguards could secure the future, they had been supplied, but it was
obvious that legal safeguards weighed very little against the laws of
economic progress and imperialist expansion; and when the limited

privilege was applied to rights-of-way acquired in perpetuity, it was inevitable that the inference should be one of indefinite servitude and that the prospect of American troops passing over Mexican territory should suggest a lane of laborious ants traveling eternally, and with unerring instinct, toward their Manifest Destiny. Moreover, a supplementary article extended police privileges to the frontiers of the two countries and made it obligatory upon the government failing to maintain order to seek the aid of the other in the event of any of the stipulations of existing treaties being violated, or the safety of citizens of one country endangered within the domain of the other. The latitude for intervention which such co-operation allowed was limited only by the good faith with which it was defined; but good faith or aggressive designs were in reality irrelevant; war and peace were both phases of the same process, which the best intentions, the most honorable observance of treaties, could not prevent, once they had been concluded. The lines laid across the southernmost and northernmost margins of Mexico traced a magnetic triangle destined, as had long since been announced, to act as a penetrating current on the people they enclosed, permeating, mollifying, Americanizing them; and as the course of history was determined by trade routes and the flag followed the market, the concession of transits was a more dangerous inroad on the integrity of the nation than the outright cession of a remote and unfrequented stretch of territory would have been. The objectionable feature of the treaty, in fact, was not the protection of the transits, but the transits themselves.

The difficulties under which the Liberal government labored might have been urged in defense of the terms under which it closed with the friendliest of its antagonists. Military defeat, financial need, diplomatic pressure, social reform, the fear of foreign intervention—the treaty was the mean resultant of a combination of overpowering forces; but they were equally irrelevant in the final verdict. The treaty was condemned both on its text and context, and the internal evidence of compulsion, which it bore so plainly on its face, aggravated the offense. Fear that the concessions would be abused and mortification that they had been imposed combined to unite Mexicans of all parties in the morbid psychology begotten by the outcome of the American war twelve years before and in raw repudiation of a treaty that published to the world so palpable a proof of their besetting sense of inferiority. There lay the unforgivable sin. The avowal was, by common consent, a deed of servitude and an indelible stigma on the government guilty of it.

In the storm of obloquy that burst about the heads of that government none escaped unscathed, but the brunt was borne, of course, by Ocampo. How much of human flesh goes to the making of public documents was exposed in the strands of himself that he left in that leonine bargain. By a grim incongruity it fell to the intransigent idealist, whose whole political skill was to resign as soon as he disagreed, to conduct a negotiation that he mistrusted profoundly and that compromised him irretrievably; but he performed his inglorious part to the end and sacrificed his reputation to necessity. The treaty was no sooner signed, however, than he retired from office, a marked man, in search of an obscurity which he had forfeited forever. Understanding friends there were, here and there, to assure Ocampo—in private—that he was a prey of partisan criticism. The best of them, perhaps, was a kindred spirit on the staff of the Legation in Paris, who, judging the effect of the treaty from a distance and in broad perspective, hailed it as a piece of practical and farsighted statesmanship. Hot from a dispute with a fellow Liberal, this apologist wrote: "He knows as well as I do that, even were European diplomatic agents to intervene in Mexico, what you least wished to do was to give the United States a hand in our politics. You have fought stoutly to avoid the fatality of the treaty, as he well knows and as do all those who hate democracy, but what they pretend not to know, or really do not know perhaps, is that the treaty, disadvantageous as it seems to be, averts any pretext for the Yankees to take possession of Mexico, in case the theocratic-monarchical faction should triumph, on the grounds of indemnization or incompatability of policy. Even were we to lose our action in the Republic, even were the saints to triumph there, the treaty already settled and accepted, avoids the danger of monarchy on the one hand and that of a *protectorate* and a conquest on the other." But it needed a trained eye to recognize the ultimate purpose of the treaty as a dam, and connoisseurs were few, and their consolations akin to excuses.

Discredit was the first effect of a treaty which inflicted on its authors a diplomatic defeat more disastrous than the military reverses it was designed to relieve. In the chorus of abuse, however, one detail was unanimously overlooked. The deed had not been consummated, and the validity of the treaty depended on two conditions, which were taken for granted in the haste to denounce it. One was the approval of the American Senate, and the other the ratification of Juarez.

5

THE benefits contemplated by the treaty were not pecuniary alone; they were also political. A virtual alliance was implicit in it—not indeed of the visionary kind contemplated by Ocampo, but nonetheless capable of development as a working partnership, and the ground had been laid for it by the right granted to the United States to intervene in support of their treaty rights and the security of their citizens. The use of that right was urged by McLane, even before it was accorded, in a stream of despatches to Washington recommending that the President seek authority of Congress to employ the military forces for domestic duties in Mexico, preferably with the consent of the Constitutional government, but if it were "unreasonably withheld," without it. Consent was a question of diplomatic courtesy rather than of mutual consequence. On this advice Buchanan acted, reproducing the suggestions of McLane to the letter in his annual message to Congress of December 1859. Though the treaty had not yet been received in Washington, the President anticipated its provisions for a political scoop. After rehearsing the events leading up to the constitution of the Juarez government—"General" Juarez, Buchanan called him, not being very familiar himself with those events—he stressed the necessity of sending American troops into the interior for the protection of American citizens. He observed that, since this involved passing through territory controlled by the Constitutional forces, the most acceptable method of securing the object in view would be to act in concert with their government, whose consent and aid might be obtained; but, if not, the duty would be no less imperative. "Such an accession to the forces of the Constitutional government," he added, "would enable it soon to reach the City of Mexico and extend its power over the whole Republic." If this involved intervention, the chronic anarchy prevailing in Mexico warranted an exception, he believed, to the wise and settled policy of the United States Government not to interfere in the domestic concerns of foreign nations. "If we do not, it would not be surprising should some other nation undertake the task and force us to interfere at last, under circumstances of increased difficulty, for the maintenance of our established policy." He asked, therefore, for a law authorizing him to employ a sufficient military force to enter Mexico for the purpose of obtaining indemnity for the past and security for the future. Intervention was warranted by considerations superior to the consent of General Juarez—by the necessity of preventing intervention by other powers and by a general historic warrant for the arrest of General Miramon.

The force of these suggestions was heightened by their context, for they were raised by Buchanan against the background presented by the state of the nation in December 1859. Materially, the American people had never been in better condition, the harvests had been unusually plentiful, the health of the country was excellent, peace and prosperity smiled on the land, and there was every reason to believe, he said, "that we have enjoyed the special protection of Divine Providence ever since our origin as a nation. We have been exposed to many threatening and alarming difficulties in our progress, but on each successive occasion the impending cloud has been dissipated at the moment when it appeared ready to burst upon our head, and the danger to our institutions has passed away." A cloud had arisen, however, with the hanging of John Brown at Harpers Ferry. "I shall not refer in detail to the recent sad and bloody occurrences at Harpers Ferry," he continued. "Still, it is proper to observe that these events, however bad and cruel in themselves, derive their chief importance from the apprehension that they are but symptoms of an incurable disease in the public mind, which may break out in still more dangerous outrages and terminate in an open war by the North to abolish slavery in the South." The state of the nation and the state of the union presented a grim contrast, and the premonition of approaching disaster could not be minimized as lightly as the neck of John Brown. To dispel that cloud something more was needed than the intervention of Divine Providence; intervention in Mexico might prove equally providential. An ounce of prevention below the border was worth a pound of cure above it, and the veiled invitation to relieve domestic tension by a foreign diversion was an inspiration of far-reaching statesmanship —a scoop that brought up the vitals of both nations. The prescription passed unnoticed, however. To the prompting of the President, Congress turned a deaf ear in 1859, as it had done in 1858, and withheld the sanction he solicited for policing Mexico, and the treaty came up for consideration in the Senate only two months later.

Within the limits of the Executive power Buchanan continued, nevertheless, to pursue his own policy. The conclusion of the treaty and the duty of enforcing it created obligations to protect and cooperate with the other party to it, the exact degree of which was determined by his agent in Veracruz, and the opportunities became pressing with the opening of the year 1860. Five weeks after signing the treaty McLane advised Washington that Miramon was preparing to besiege Veracruz again, and among those preparations he included the recent conclusion of a convention negotiated in Paris by the Spanish and Mexican Ministers, Mon and Almonte, by which diplomatic relations between Spain and Mexico, suspended for several years because of a dispute over the debt, were restored, with full recognition of the Spanish claims. The opportunity thus afforded for another raid on the Veracruz government called for corresponding precautions, and McLane sought specific instructions as to the manner in which he was to conduct himself when the city was exposed to siege and assault; and he made suggestions. "When Texas sought admission to our Union, as soon as the Congress of the United States gave its assent to such admission, the President (Mr. Polk) gave directions to the United States naval forces in the Gulf of Mexico to act as if Texas were an integral part of our country and to defend it if assailed— though the Texan Congress had not yet accepted *the act* of admission. With the spirit of these instructions it would harmonize, I think, to direct me to act as if the Treaty and Convention recently concluded by me had been ratified by the Senate of the United States—but this is a view which I did not think it proper to suggest in my official despatch." If this involved intervention—well, the Executive power might well be stretched to protect an investment. "Were the Treaty recently concluded by me with the accompanying Convention duly ratified by the Senate of the United States," he repeated, "it would be the obligation and duty of the authorities of the United States in the port of Veracruz to act in concert and conjunction with the Mexican authorities at that port to protect the lives and properties of citizens of the United States residing there and to enforce existing treaty stipulations"—a course for which there were ample precedents in the conduct of the French, British, and American authorities in Shanghai in 1854, "and each of these governments respectively approved the conduct of their naval officers to the extent of justifying their forcible intervention against the duly recognized authorities of China as well as in concert with them, against the revolutionary movement that then disturbed that part of China." And such was the course adopted when the crisis came.

After the first siege of Veracruz, Mata had been promised that the United States fleet would be ordered to the Gulf to protect his government against the presence of the French and British squadrons stationed there and to insure the negotiation of the American treaty. The unsettled fate of the treaty in February 1859 made it inadvisable to advertise American protection by a large demonstration, but a token force was located in Veracruz to lend assistance to the local authorities or the American Minister in case of danger.

The second siege of Veracruz began exactly a year after the first, lasted just the same length of time, and fared no better, but in one important respect it differed from the earlier attack. Profiting by his previous failure, Miramon made an attempt to complete the siege by sea. Two small transports were purchased and outfitted in Cuba, and four days after the bombardment on land began they were sighted off port, carrying no flag, and making for the roadstead of Anton Lizardo several leagues down the coast, where they unloaded munitions and cast anchor for the night. Their appearance was expected, and in preparation for it the Constitutional government had declared them pirates and requested the American authorities to pursue and arrest them. The invitation was accepted by the senior naval officer—McLane having absented himself in due time. Shortly after dusk an American man-of-war, towed by two small steamers recently leased by the Mexican port authorities, passed the French, British, and Spanish squadrons riding in the roads of Veracruz harbor and, without answering their salute, disappeared down the coast, captured the transports, and brought them into port in the morning. During the night the townspeople had crowded to the roofs, lured by the flash and sound of gunfire to the south. The commander of the Spanish squadron protested against the American right to police the seas, but he was not supported by the French or British, and after several days of imprisonment the piratical captain and crews were sent with their craft to New Orleans and placed at the disposal of an American prize court. The court found against the captors and released the captives after prolonged litigation, which led to a flurry in Congress and an interpellation of the President, who admitted that the American naval officer had acted with his knowledge and consent.

The Conservatives dated the decline of their cause from the incident at Anton Lizardo. They caught at any straw to account for it. The military value of the captured vessels was negligible: they were engaged in arms running and could not have invested or shelled the town without embroiling the foreign squadrons stationed there. Their political value lay in testing the freedom of the seas, and their power of provocation gave them a considerable nuisance value; but whatever the threat, the theory of a siege by sea was thwarted by American intervention, and the breach of international law was acknowledged too late to alter the effect. For another three weeks the bombardment continued by land in a deadly demonstration of impotence. The fury was sufficient to drive foreign residents to their ships and to provoke a protest from the British Commander against the useless slaughter of civilians, but it did no other damage. And promptly at the end of March, when the sickly season set in, Miramon raised the siege and returned to his capital to prepare another campaign in the interior. No one else, perhaps, could have failed twice in the same attempt without a fatal loss of prestige, and his was seriously impaired. His last appearance as a star had been made the previous December, when he returned to the scene of his triumphs in Guadalajara and was welcomed by the clergy with a special liturgy composed in his honor and sung in the Cathedral, likening the sacred name of Miguel Miramon to all the politicians of the Old Testament in turn, hailing him with each swing of the censer as their heaven-sent savior, and hallowing with obsequious eulogies his popular nickname of "the young Maccabee." Thereafter his star waned swiftly. After his return trip to Veracruz his credit fell so low in the capital that Zuloaga reasserted his right to the Presidency and announced his resumption of office. The forgotten man of the civil war was promptly arrested by Miramon, who effaced him without raising more than a finger to his mouth. "I will show him how Presidents are made," he said, and carried him off as a hostage on his campaign. Thereupon the diplomatic corps met and announced that there was no longer an effective government in the capital and that their presence there was required only for the protection of foreign nationals.

American intervention was of doubtful service, on the other hand, to the Constitutional cause. The government, already discredited by the treaty, was further compromised by the one benefit that it produced. The fears excited by the treaty itself were inflamed by an incident that demonstrated to what length one party was prepared to go to protect it, while the readiness of the other to accept such protection added a fresh provocation to the national pride. Designed as a dam against foreign intervention, the treaty was serving, in fact, as a sieve for it, and what it raised was the question of how far the co-operation of one party would carry the other.

That question was of acute concern to the American partner as well. Referring in his first report after the siege to "the rage of the Miramon government against all foreigners, and particularly against Englishmen and Americans, the latter being more bitterly denounced than all the others," McLane observed that fortunately very few of his countrymen remained in the Republic, "otherwise the malignant resentment so constantly manifested against them would involve the two countries in a war of conquest." The working alliance with the Liberal government had broadened the scope of the civil war and brought it to the brink of an international conflict. It was high time to cry halt, and the British Government was already doing so. "The British Government has communicated to both parties its desire to see the country pacified," he continued. "I need only refer in this connection to the opinion heretofore expressed that foreign intervention is the last and only hope of those who desire to establish the reign of law, and that intervention to be effective must, if necessary, be enforced by the presence of the military power of the nation intervening. Such intervention will sooner or later, and I think at no distant day, be offered to the Miramon government, perhaps to both governments, and if so offered, acceptance, if not cordially and promptly manifested, will be enforced by a demonstration of naval forces in the Gulf of Mexico that neither of the governments contending for the possession of power can resist. This intervention may at first assume the character of a demand on both governments for the due execution of existing conventions in virtue of which nearly seventy per cent of the gross revenue from the customs in this country is due to the holders of a certain portion of the public debt known as the Convention debts of Great Britain, France, and Spain, but it will speedily assume larger proportions, and the European element will under its influence recover its ascendancy, extending perhaps to the Central American States." To anticipate these developments it was imperative, therefore, to determine how far the American Government was prepared to go to protect the Monroe Doctrine. "I submit these reflections certainly not for the first time," he concluded, "in the hope that the President will be encouraged to persevere in the policy he has adopted in relation to this country, renewing at the same time the expression of my opinion that if Congress does not confer upon him the necessary power to enforce it, this Legation should be withdrawn and our countrymen in Mexico duly notified that it is not in his power to afford them adequate protection, for the failure of Congress to act is generally regarded here as evidence that the government is not sustained in the exercise of its legitimate and Constitutional discretion, and that either from the intrinsic nature of the opposition it encounters in Congress, or in consequence of some sympathy felt for the Miramon government in the United States, it may rely upon continued forbearance while it pursues a policy marked by atrocious cruelty and inhumanity in war, and by every species of spoliation and exaction."

The protection of the Monroe Doctrine was more important than the protection of the Juarez government, but the complications created by the pending treaty made the one inseparable from the other, and the fears of the American Minister were not unfounded. The war in Mexico had reached the stage at which party principals were identified on both sides with patriotic interests. About the treaty, as a pivot, both factions swung toward their natural spheres: while the Liberal was drawn into the American orbit, the Conservative turned to the European to counteract its effect, and the rotation reopened the momentous question of Mexican independence. To that question the foreigner was no more indifferent than the native. Driven back to the origin of the nation by American pressure, and reverting to their congenital bias, the Conservatives were now clambering up their genealogical tree in search of support; and there, in their extremity, they were reaching for the first principles of national independence proclaimed in the Three Guarantees of the Plan of Iguala—union of Europeans and Americans, a Mexican monarchy, and supremacy of the Church—as their last hope of self-preservation. Correspondence intercepted at Veracruz revealed the desperate efforts that the Clerical faction was making to secure European protection by the offer of a Mexican throne to a French or Spanish prince; and it was high time to cry halt—but to whom? To Miramon? Or to the meddling of France and England? And how? By withdrawing the American Legation and abandoning Juarez to his fate? Or by backing him against a possible coalition of European Powers without the support of Congress and public opinion in the United States? That was the hitch. Buchanan had gone too far to back down, but he could not pursue his personal policy any further because of the opposition it encountered in Congress; and McLane had to reckon not only with the reaction to the treaty in Mexico, but with the equally strenuous reaction to it in the United States.

There the opposition was composed of many factors, all of which excited the national interest and exhibited the national character very crudely. The treaty was a bone of contention between the two parties in office and out of it, and the Republicans seized on it for their own purposes and made political capital of its occult designs. The *New York Tribune* led the attack in an article which called the President's hand without mincing words. "The whole country should understand the question in all its bearings before the government commits itself to the proposed radical change in our relations with that huge, rotten mass of slunk civilization. Whether the consequences in store for us under the proposed new adjustment of our international relations with that country shall be the annexation of its comparatively unpeopled provinces falling to us in disintegrated masses, as fast as we may be able to spread slavery over them, or whether they shall come in the shape of a ready absorption of its area that is already covered by a priest-ridden, mongrel, dwarfed, and semi-savage population, is alike unimportant to us in a national point of view. Either arrangement would be alike mischievous and pregnant in evil consequences. . . . We do not want to get into any Mexican quagmires or Dismal Swamps. If we are after Sonora, let us say Sonora. If it be other provinces, let us name them. If it be all Mexico, let us say so. Let the people understand exactly what the government aims at. We protest against doing things by stealth and under false pretenses. As things now stand, the Free States must fight for their share of new territorial acquisitions. We demand that they shall know when anything of this sort is going on, in order that they may, as Mr. Calhoun used to claim for slavery in California, 'have a chance to get in.' If we are going to take Mexico or any part of it, the people of the North want a chance to get in."

Strenuously as the *Tribune* protested against the stealth of the government and the false pretenses of the treaty, there was some ambiguity in its own motives for undertaking the attack. The leading organ of the Opposition was willing to get in, provided there was anything for the Republican party to get out of the deal. On the day after the attack the treaty was submitted to a preliminary test in a secret session of the Senate, which was fully reported in the columns of the *Tribune* the next morning. The discussion was opened by a Republican senator, Mr. Mason, who was expected, because of his party affiliations, to oppose the prize project of a Democratic administration. But Mr. Mason could not make up his mind. He did oppose it, reluctantly, as a departure from the settled American policy of nonintervention in the domestic affairs of other nations, which he would never consent to sanction; nevertheless, in view of the state of anarchy existing in Mexico, he was willing to make the experiment. "In regard to the objection urged, that Juarez does not represent the regular government, he supposed that he was as much entitled to that recognition as the other faction; and though he now exercised authority over a small district of the country, he believed, though unable to give any positive assurance to the Senate, that the ratification, with the aid which we would render, would establish the liberal cause in power." But none of the speakers behaved as they were expected to do. While Mr. Mason was open to persuasion, Mr. Wigfall, who followed him, was not. His mind was made up and, although a Southern Democrat, he "denounced the whole scheme as utterly unworthy of countenance or toleration. There was no government in Mexico capable of making a treaty, or of carrying out its stipulations if made. We did not want Mexico or her mongrel population. Juarez and his Indian crew could not govern themselves and if brought into contact with our people, would contaminate them." Party positions being thus reversed, the next speaker preferred to overlook the political aspects of the treaty altogether. "Mr. Pugh objected to some of the commercial provisions as favoring certain interests over others, but was willing to make the treaty if amended in those particulars." Mr. Pugh spoke for Republican interests, but another Republican denied them altogether. "Mr. Simmons closed the discussion in one of his strong, conclusive, practical arguments, exposing the sophistries of the alleged commercial advantages. New England has no interest, immediate or remote, in this treaty, but exactly the reverse. It is substantially free trade with Mexico, which would require us, under the clause inserted in every commercial treaty for the last forty years, of admitting each nation on an equal footing with that of the most favored nation, to claim similiar privileges, and would result in destroying our revenue and compelling a resort to direct taxation. This point, and others equally forcible, produced much impression." The discussion was adjourned until the following day, when Mr. Seward promised to take the floor, but the eloquence of the Republican whip was not needed, the treaty being, the *Tribune* reported, "as dead as Julius Caesar." The credit went to

Mr. Simmons, who made it clear that there was nothing in it for the Republican party, and to Mr. Wigfall, who did as much for the Democratic; nor could anyone attribute the verdict to party affiliations, since several Democratic senators, "who yielded to the persuasions of the President and were prepared to conquer prejudices," could now be counted adversely, and the main body of the Republicans, if not all, were pledged to kill the corpse.

The test was by no means final, and the administration was undeterred by a straw vote; but the publicity given to the secret session of February 28, the tirades of the *Tribune,* and the general and open interpretation of the treaty as an option on Mexican territory, made the position of the American Minister extremely delicate. In the face of such feeling in the American Senate, how was he to defend the personal policy of his President and to protect his Mexican partner against the imminent threat of foreign interference? For now, to add to his difficulties, the position of the American Government was directly challenged by the British Government, which assumed the right, as a neutral, to act as arbiter and call a halt all around.

Four days after McLane wrote his warning to Washington, European intervention in Mexico began in the form he had foreseen. Ignoring the opposition in Congress, the European Powers were guided by the general trend of American policy advertised in its discussion in the press and the necessity of checking their predatory tendencies in time. The warning raised by the London *Times* was followed by a move of the British Foreign Office to forestall the pacific absorption of the Republic by an offer, equally peaceful and equally forcible, to terminate the civil war by diplomatic mediation. The support of the Quai d'Orsay was secured, but the lead was taken by British diplomacy, and the offer was communicated simultaneously to the warring factions and the American Minister. The British Minister, Mr. Otway, having been recalled for indiscretion, the note was written by the Chargé d'Affaires, Mr. Mathew, and it gained greater weight from the fact that it came from a minor official who merely transmitted the instructions of Lord Russell. Mr. Mathew notified McLane that Her Majesty's Government would see with satisfaction an armistice of six months' or a year's duration and the election of a National Assembly impartially chosen to determine the future government; though there was no intention of prescribing what that government should be, it should be one that would give some guarantee of stability and order, and hence some advice was in order. "A general amnesty should be proclaimed, religious and civil toleration should be declared, for unless some mercy is shown by opposing parties there can be no hope of internal peace. If this advice intended for the good of Mexico is not accepted," he further explained, "Her Majesty's Government will have no other course than to demand from both parties sufficient reparations for the wrongs British subjects have suffered."

To such terms no reasonable objection could be raised by the American Minister. They were inacceptable to the contending parties and were rejected by both, Miramon ruling out religious liberty and Juarez insisting on unconditional recognition of the Constitution; but their objections were beside the point. The British proposals were addressed to the only party that counted, and they were heavily biased in favor of the Liberal creed as a bid for American support; and as a further inducement, the French plan reproduced the British, differing from it only in omitting any mention of religious toleration. Nevertheless, McLane fully approved and supported the refusal of Juarez to consider any settlement short of his own terms. Four-fifths of the states, he informed Washington, would have refused to acquiesce in a compromise, and the almost unanimous sentiment of the Liberal party would have condemned Juarez for abandoning his functions as a Constitutional President. The working alliance had now reached the point where the preservation of one party was essential to the self-preservation of the American partner, and betrayal would have been a criminal blunder, and McLane insisted sensibly that the only hope of pacifying Mexico lay in the zealous and rigorous prosecution of the personal policy of Buchanan. He deemed the situation serious enough to send a message of his own to Congress. "I submit that before Congress adjourns that body should be fully advised of the present aspect of the Mexican question," he repeated, "that it may appreciate how imminent is the danger of a government based on the ultramontane and monarchical principles of the Plan of Iguala." The British had served notice that they meant business, and having been rebuffed by the Liberals, they were quite capable of courting the Clericals to force a compromise. McLane temporized, and for three months he managed to maintain, without support, an uncertain truce with the British Legation.

Such were the conditions in which the treaty came up for final consideration in the Senate on the last day of May, 1860. They were adverse in every respect, for in the meanwhile it had been subjected to a searching and thorough discussion in the press, which threshed out every aspect of the question save the one in which the American Minister to Mexico was interested. Foreign competition was completely ignored. The Mexican question was debated for its bearing, not on foreign policy, but on the domestic issue that dominated it, and the treaty was involved in the slavery question and grafted to the growing threat of disunion in the United States. Upon one premise all arguments agreed—the underlying assumption that the treaty involved the annexation of Mexican territory. "If a new treaty, of straightforward stipulations, giving us unencumbered commercial advantages and clear grants of land, could be made, we might well hold a complacent attitude in view of its ratification," the *Tribune* conceded, "provided we first had a Homestead bill. The slavery extension party should be met by going ahead rather than by holding back. Let us have the vacant territory south of us and fill it with colonists, and thus overslaugh slavery therein. Mexico is falling to pieces, and we shall soon have an opportunity to obtain the fragments we need on our own terms." Warming to the idea immediately after the defeat of the treaty in the straw vote in February, the *Tribune* appropriated and adapted it to the demands of the Abolitionist party. "If we could run a tier of free states straight across the continent, on the southern line of Texas, we should let in an amazing flood of light on the slavery question in the process. Such a cordon could not be jumped by slavery, and Lower Mexico might fester and putrify at leisure, with comparatively small danger of spreading her contamination upon us. As things now stand, and they would be even worse under this hybrid treaty, we have no security against a peon slavery being established and gradually ligatured on to our southern extremity, to be followed by a weltering process, making our southern limits more vague than the tail of Milton's Satan."

While Horace Greeley's paper was now frankly in favor of an aggressive policy in Mexico, the *Atlantic Monthly,* entering the discussion at the same time, found some strong arguments, however, for holding back. "The people of the United States have to choose between the conquest of Mexico and non-intervention in Mexican affairs. There may be something to be said in favor of conquest, though the President's arguments in that direction—for such they are, disguised though they be—remind us strongly of those which were put forth in justification of the partition of Poland; but the policy of intervention does not bear criticism for one moment. Either it is a conquest veiled, or it is a blunder the chance to commit which is purchased at an enormous price, and blunders are to be had for nothing, and without the expenditure of life and money." But as Buchanan was bent on committing the blunder and was appealing personally to leading Republicans to set aside partisanship and co-operate in perpetrating it, stronger arguments were needed. The divergent objections to the treaty had one common denominator in the intense and outspoken aversion of the American to the Mexican people, and the *Atlantic* proceeded to examine the contaminating consequences, both for the Free and Slave States, of the proposed conquest. "The final cause of the absorption of Mexico by the United States will be the restless appropriating spirit of our people; but this might leave her a generation more of rational life, were it not that her territory presents a splendid field for slave-labor and that, both from pecuniary and political motives, our slaveholders are seeking the increase of the number of Slave States. There is not an

argument used on behalf of the rigid slave codes of several of our
States that would not be applicable to the enslavement of the black
and mixed Mexicans, all of whom would be of darker skins and less
enlightened minds than the slaves that would be taken to the conquered land by the conquerors. How could the slaves thus taken there
be allowed to see even their inferiors in the enjoyment of personal
freedom? If the State of Arkansas can condescend to be afraid of a
few hundred negroes and mulattoes, and can illustrate its fear by turning them out of their homes in mid-winter, what might not be expected from a ruling caste in a new country, with two and a half
millions of colored people to strike terror into the souls of those com-
prising it? Just or humane legislation could not be looked for at the
hands of such men, who would be guilty of that cruelty which is born
of injustice and terror. The white race of Mexico would join with the
intrusive race to oppress the mixed races; and as the latter would be
compelled to submit to the iron pressure that would be brought to
bear upon them, more than two millions of slaves would be added to
the servile population of America, and would become the basis of a
score of Representatives in the National Legislature, and of as many
Presidential Electors; so that the practise of the grossest tyranny would
give to the slaveholding states, *per saltum,* as great an increase of
political power as the Free States could be expected to achieve through
a long term of years illustrated by care and toil and the most liberal
expenditure of capital. The Indians would fare no better than the
mixed races, though the form of degradation might differ. The Indians
of Mexico are a race quite different from the Indians whom we have
exterminated or driven to the remote West. They are a sad, a superstitious, and an inert people, upon whom Spanish tyranny has done its
perfect work. Even if it should not be sought to enslave the Indians of
Mexico, that race would not be the less doomed. There seems to be
no chance for Indians in any country into which the Anglo-Saxons
enter in force. A system of free labor would be as fatal to the Mexican
Indians as a system of forced labor. The whites who would throng to
Mexico, on its conquest by the Americans, and on the supposition that
slavery would not be established there, would regard the Indians with
sentiments of strong aversion. They would hate them not only because
they were Indians—which would be deemed reason enough—but as
competitors in industry who could afford to work for low wages, their
wants being few and the cost of their maintenance small. . . . The
sentiment of the whites toward the Indians is not unlike that which
has been expressed by an American statesman, who says that the cause
of the failure of Mexico to establish for herself a national position is
to be found in her acknowledgment of the political equality of her
Indian population. He would have them degraded, if not absolutely
enslaved, and degradation, situated as they are, implies their extinction.

This is the opinion of one of the ablest men in the Democratic party, who, though a son of Massachusetts, is ready to go as far in behalf of slavery as any son of South Carolina."

The arguments of the *Atlantic* agreed with those of many Southern Democrats who were deserting their leader, convinced that the acquisition of Mexican territory would be unprofitable because of the risks of introducing their peculiar institution there and aggravating the growing race problem of the South. But imperialism would be abandoned only when it proved to be unprofitable; and race prejudice being its badge, it could still be made to repay cultivation. A religious appeal to race prejudice was made by the Honorable Frank Blair, who, speaking at Cooper Union in New York on behalf of American Catholics, represented the Mexican question as a race war in which the whites, menaced by the overwhelming numbers of Indian and colored races, were saved from submersion only by the influence of the Church. "Mr. Buchanan has leagued himself with the Indian Juarez in this war of religion and caste; leagued himself with the chief who has by edict confiscated the property of the Catholic Church and will exterminate its defenders of the white race in order to possess himself of the spoils," he concluded, skillfully confusing the most popular prejudices of his public. "The Dred Scott decision, having already overthrown our free institutions, would carry slavery into this new conquest, and the system of peonage, the hereditary servitude of debt, would still more readily become assimilated to the peculiar institution. Inexorable indeed is the demand for the extension of slavery, when it compels Mr. Buchanan to league himself with an Indian in a war of caste and religion—a war against the proprietory class in Mexico—and to confiscate the estates of that Church whose members in this country elevated him to the Presidency." The translation of the Mexican question into American terms was applauded as heartily in New York as if the speech had been delivered in Dixie or, for that matter, in Mexico City.

Opposition to the treaty came from conflicting sources, but the contradictions of interest combined to create a catholic antipathy to it. Any cross-section of public opinion revealed the knotted motives that militated against its adoption. When the question came up in the Senate in May, they were all summed up in the words of one speaker, who contended that "the ultimate acquisition of Mexico, which the treaty was intended to initiate, would be the forbidden fruit which Mr. Calhoun has described when speaking of Cuba; and while it might tend to the dissolution of the Union, he could not see how the South was to benefit by the addition of that mongrel population. Hence he was opposed to it." Republicans and Democrats were ranged on both sides of the fence, or on it, in a conspiracy of cross-purposes that was perfectly consistent in its seeming confusion, because the forbidden fruit had lost its power to tempt. Falling afoul of the sectional issue which was already dividing the Union, it was rotten fruit for both parties, and rotten fruit matured rapidly. The warmongering maneuvers of Buchanan, annually ignored by Congress, were definitely doomed in 1860, even as a contraceptive to domestic insurrection, for the cloud which was no bigger than a man's hand in December had grown ominously larger by May, and the lengthening shadow of approaching civil war in the United States could no longer be diverted by a dying adventure below the border. The administration mustered its strength, however; the treaty was defeated by nine votes (27 to 18), and the count being close, a motion to reconsider was introduced just as the Senate was about to adjourn and carried in the confusion of the moment. "Thus ends this farce," the *Tribune* reported. "The Mexican treaty was nominally reconsidered and thereby goes over until the next session." Since only three senators, and all of them Republicans, voted to "galvanize the corpse," it could be counted out. "Juarez," the obituary added, "will probably be in exile before the treaty is again considered, if present signs may be trusted."

No one was more bitterly disappointed by the defeat of the treaty than the correspondent of the *New York Times* in Mexico. Though he wrote for Seward's paper, Edward Dunbar was not a politician, nor even a professional journalist, but an American businessman who used the columns of the *Times* to contribute his knowledge of the Mexican question to the discussion, to protest against its manipulation by professional politicians, and to bring about a sympathetic understanding between two liberty-loving peoples—the one interest which had been consistently neglected by Congress and the press in the United States. "Does anyone doubt," he wrote, "that if the administration had, at an early date, marked out an intelligent, decided, and just policy with Mexico, *the result of convictions based on knowledge,* and enforced this policy with that moral power which intelligent and honest convictions always command—does anyone believe, I ask, that this treaty, wrought by an honest and capable public servant, could not have been carried even against the destructive opposition of the Republicans and fire-eating politicians who united to destroy it? And does anyone believe that the Republican party in Washington evinced any *honest convictions based on knowledge* relative to the Mexican question, or any sentiment higher than that of a determination to achieve success in their own thoroughly selfish political purposes, no matter by what means, or at what cost to the country at large?" As a symptom of this spirit, he observed that "There is probably no instance on record where the simple diplomatic efforts of an American envoy to establish friendly and profitable relations with a foreign power have been attacked with such bitter malignity and rude violence as in the case

of Mr. McLane. . . . Had he been a very dolt in diplomacy, as corrupt
as the vilest politician, and a blackhearted traitor to his country, he
could not have been more heartily abused than he has been in his
efforts to sustain the American name and character abroad and the
cause of liberty in Mexico, and to create permanent relations of amity
and commerce between the two countries. Whether such extraordinary
conduct on the part of the American people and Congress, so contrary
to their professions and the spirit of the age, arises from apathy,
ignorance, partisan feeling in politics, or the lack of anything like
real sympathy with freedom in other countries, time alone can determine. At the present moment we are united with despotic agencies
to smother the new-born hopes of freedom in Mexico and cast the
people back into darkness and despair. The United States now occupy
the meanest position toward Mexico that it is possible for a powerful
and free republic to hold toward a weak and despairing neighbor—a
position that will prove a sin and a shame to us in the future."

He was bitter because his country suffered from the reflections that
the Mexican question cast on American character. The failure of the
treaty was due to its manipulation by party politics, but in the final
analysis the ultimate responsibility lay neither with the Democratic
party, which adulterated a liberal policy toward Mexico with predatory
designs, nor with the Republican, which, progressive at home and
reactionary abroad, was equally lacking in moral power, but with the
American people, who had no more moral power than their politicians,
because they had no knowledge of the Mexican question, and hence
no convictions; and their ignorance was due, fundamentally, to their
indifference to the Mexican people. For this apathy he found what
excuses he could. "Much of the indifference, and we may say aversion,
felt toward Mexican affairs generally are doubtless owing to the peculiar character of the correspondence from Mexico that appears in
the public journals," he admitted. No paid correspondents were maintained there, the reports of volunteers were irresponsible and biased,
and his own were an exception to "the manner in which every sound
argument and every statement of fact in favor of the Liberal cause in
Mexico has been opposed throughout those countries called Christian
and enlightened, especially the United States. No sooner has anything
of this nature fallen upon the public eye than perversions, false statements, or flat denials have sprung up in all quarters, and for the time
being truth has been overcome by error." But the press was only
partly responsible for the misrepresentation of the Mexican question.
The prevalent errors of public opinion were fostered by other forces.
In the first place, there was Prescott, who had done so much to
popularize an erroneous conception of the ancient history of Mexico
by faithfully following the exaggerations, inconsistencies, and palpable
errors of the early Spanish historians. "No one has done more to cloud

the perceptions of the present generation, or to throw obstacles in the way of a just comprehension of the Mexican people, their present condition, and the nature of the conflict now raging in that country, than our own favorite historian. Prescott's well-known honesty, industry, and singleness of purpose, combined with his ability as a writer, have given his *Conquest of Mexico*—which is nothing more than a beautiful high-wrought romance—all the weight of truthful matter-of-fact history. Prescott concedes the Christianization of Mexico and his writings are eulogized by Spain. On these premises alone it is safe to conclude that our standard work on the Conquest is unreliable as history." Prescott had never visited Mexico; Prescott had drawn his material from the first Spanish Minister to Mexico; and Prescott, moreover, was temperamentally unfitted for his task: he was "of too gentle a nature, too delicate and feminine in his mental composition, to write the true history of the Spanish Conquest and rule on the American continent." The danger of good writing was never so well demonstrated; for on the basis of Prescott's literary conquest of Mexico there had grown up the flourishing fallacies that still misled public opinion —the common belief that Christianity had ever prevailed in Spanish America because the Church had prevailed there, and the current misinterpretation of the Mexican question due to the almost exclusive possession of the means of manufacturing public opinion abroad by the Church and the retrograde parties in Spanish America. But neither Prescott nor Catholic propaganda were more than minor causes for the callousness of the American public toward the Liberal struggle in Mexico: the primary one was race prejudice.

As propaganda flourishes in proportion to the affinity of a people for it, all these causes were poor excuses for the American people; and it was no better apology for race prejudice to point out, as Dunbar did, that that motive was equally prevalent in Europe. It was the favorite argument of reaction everywhere. In France the groundwork for it had been laid by the Comte de Gobineau, whose voluminous *Essay on the Inequality of Human Races* was known, however, only to a small number of initiates, and a popular application of his thesis to the Mexican question had just been made by the *Revue des Deux Mondes* with material supplied by M. de Gabriac, and by the *London Saturday Review,* which vulgarized the same doctrine across the Channel. According to the English weekly, disturbances in Spanish America in general, and in Mexico in particular, were due to the Indian element. "Many of us have the impression that Juarez, Vidaurri, and Degollado are as actual Spanish gentlemen as Sartorius, Narvaez, and O'Donnell" —the leading Spanish politicians of the time—"yet the truth is that the three persons named, who are all Mexicans, generals, and Constitutionalists, are neither more nor less than full-blooded Indians, and are therefore much nearer relations of the Ojibbeways who were exhibited in London a few seasons ago than of any *hidalgo* in Spain. It need not be said that this circumstance entirely destroys the importance of the Spanish revolutions as precedents." For the benefit of those who had missed the Ojibways, however, the article went into detail. "The difference between a European and an Indian leader is well illustrated by the history of the rival Presidents of the Mexican Republic. Juarez, the so-called Constitutional President who was lately besieged in Veracruz, is, as has been stated, an Indian of unmixed blood. Miramon, who has been styled President of the Church party, is, on the contrary, a Frenchman by the father's side and a Spaniard by the mother's—in other words, a European, descended from two of the finest races in Europe. Of the merits of the contest in which these two leaders are engaged we shall say only that it has been grossly misapprehended in the United States and England. It turns on the confiscation of Church property, and this circumstance has caused some degree of mild favor to be extended here and in America to Juarez, who is the champion of the anti-clerical faction. The Mexican clergy are certainly indolent and ignorant, according to European standards, but with all their defects they alone prevent the Mexican people from relapsing into the beliefs and practices of savage life. The Haytian negro, when the destruction of the whites relieved him from the control of his priests, went straight back to his Obi, which he scarcely deigns to overlay with a thin varnish of Christianity, and the Mexican, whether Indian or mongrel, can scarcely now be kept by all the vigilance of his spiritual pastors from throwing himself into sorcery and fetish worship. The cause of the Roman Catholic Church in Mexico is, therefore, for once the cause of civilization; and if the truth were known, it would probably be found that Juarez, who is panegyrized by the American papers as the liberal and enlightened antagonist of spiritual despotism, is simply the foe of priests because he prefers some private enchantment of his own to the celebration of the Mass."

The virulence of race prejudice abroad could not compare, however, with its vulgarity in America, where it was common to all parties, native to the national character, and indigenous to the arrogant ignorance of the American people. How easily the most vulgar of all the vices of human vanity could be manipulated for political purposes the discussion of the Mexican question in Congress and the press proved. The dense indifference to the Mexican people had been turned into deadly aversion by lumping the Mexican question with the abolition issue in the United States, and for this result Dunbar held the Republican party primarily to blame. "Because the Indians, the aborigines, the *natives* of Mexico, who have for centuries writhed and groaned under the heel of their oppressor, are, according to the best of their ability, endeavoring to achieve freedom, they are abused and denounced from one end of Christendom to the other," he wrote. "And who are foremost in thus denouncing the Indian race of Mexico and doing their best to crush out the aspirations for liberty in this race, because it is *Indian* and has a *dark skin?* Why, they are those who call themselves the leaders of the great Republican party in the United States—leaders who are fairly screaming into the public ear their hatred of oppression, their love for their *black brother* in bondage, their determination to give him freedom at all hazards and to place him on an equality with his white brother at the earliest possible moment! What a fathomless depth of cant and hypocrisy this glaring inconsistency reveals! . . . If ever a great measure of general and vital importance to the whole country came before the United States Senate without the negro in it, we believe it was the McLane–Ocampo treaty, but the negro was lugged in, and of course the ruin of the measure followed."

Dunbar smarted, because for him the first and greatest of the national interests was the national character, and he wrote to defend it. Whether the defeat of the treaty was due to apathy, ignorance, partisan feeling in politics, or the lack of anything like real sympathy with freedom in other countries, the result was profoundly disappointing to his faith in American democracy. The majority was against him, and in democratic theory the majority was right. In practice it had rarely been so wrong; but his efforts to interpret the Mexican question truly and to bring about a just understanding and alliance between two liberty-loving peoples would have passed unnoticed had they not earned him a caustic comment in an American paper. "Mr. Dunbar deems it legitimate in discussing questions of Mexican policy," wrote the *New York Journal of Commerce,* "to arraign and to praise and condemn, giving to his *Mexican Papers* a wide scope and range, and tending, we fear, to involve him quite as deeply in American politics as in the affairs of Mexico." The danger of acting as an interpreter of the Mexican question was that it developed the ability to see it from both sides; and Dunbar was forced to finish what he had begun. "The criticism of the *Journal* is just and to the point," he replied. "Nothing could be more so. I am an American citizen, born and bred, and have the right to vote. I am, according to the theory if not the practise of democratic institutions, one of the people—the masters, who send their servants to Washington to attend to my interests. I find that those national servants in Washington do not attend properly to my interests as a private American citizen, engaged in lawful and legitimate business. Therefore I very naturally claim the right to 'arraign and to praise and condemn' pretty much everybody connected with the government, according as, in my opinion, they deserve, and to investigate the causes that carry individuals so notoriously unfit for their position into power. Not being a disappointed or expectant politician, I feel a glorious independence in being able to apply the knife to *both* of the great political parties, whose politics, as I conceive, are of a destructive character to my own lawful and legitimate interests, and who have brought the whole country to the condition and position so correctly stated by Mr. Seward in his recent Detroit speech: viz., universal dissatisfaction at home and our institutions a hissing and a by-word for all creation abroad. The discussion of the Mexican question *inevitably* involves the discussion of American politics, and of those vital interests in the United States over which the politics of negro politicians have been so long allowed to maintain their destructive ascendancy."

He had the presumption to defend the national character single-handed, because he knew and spoke for the genuine American people, so generous, friendly, fair-minded, and ready to respond to their kind everywhere, but so ingenuous also and easily blindfolded by the theory of their free institutions and the practice of their professional politicians. The Mexican question called up all the devils of American democracy without casting them out—the spirit of liberty perverted by the spirit of imperialism; the unclean spirit of race prejudice; the incubus of plutocratic power and the succubus of popular sanction; the feeble spirit of independent public opinion and the superstitious spirit of majority rule. The majority, if not right, was mighty, and authentic Americans were one in a thousand; and the real damage of the defeat of the treaty was that it drove men like Edward Dunbar first to challenge, then to question, and finally to doubt the virtue of American democracy.

The damage went deeper than that in Mexico. There the only possible defense of the treaty lay in its fruits, and they were bitter. The benefits evaporated, the odium remained. Delusion could hardly go further; but the dregs remained to be drained. The barren bond remained to plague its authors, and Juarez, condemned for the attempt and not the deed, had now to contend with the aftereffects of the ill-fated contract. Though it was not consummated, it was not dead, and the abortion infected the country with fresh complications by its very miscarriage.

The narrow margin by which the treaty was defeated encouraged the friends of Buchanan, and they planned to reintroduce it before the coming presidential election in November; but as the six months provided for ratification had expired, an extension of time had to be secured from Mexico, and after the discussion in the United States had disclosed the real nature of the contract and the close call by which Mexico had escaped foreclosure, consent from that quarter was so improbable that one American paper buried the treaty and both its beneficiaries in the same sneer. "When it was thought that a political object could be promoted by extending aid and comfort to the mongrels and mixed breeds of Mexico, who, under the name of Liberals,

were seeking possession of power but unwilling to fight for it as brave
men should do, the President was prompt enough to recognize the
Indian Juarez, who knows as much about liberty, in its high sense, as
he does about the Koran," wrote the Philadelphia *North American
Independent.* "It turned out like most of his experiments, and the 'Constitutional President of Mexico' has not been able to survive the partiality of his friend in the White House." Though the announcement
was premature, the end of Juarez was imminently expected, and by
no means improbable, since the abandonment of the treaty also begot
beneficiaries who had long been preparing, and who were now free, to
enter the battle.

The shadow of foreign intervention under which the civil war had
been fought for two years thickened in the third year. It was no longer
cast by a pair of officious ministers—the recall of Mr. Otway for indiscretion was followed by that of M. de Gabriac for the same reason—
but by governments directly concerned in extinguishing the civil war
for the security of their national interests. Such was the ultimate result
and actual consummation of the McLane treaty, which, by introducing
into the magnetic field of Mexico a foreign object that excited the
activity of all the others embedded there, virtually reduced the country
to the colonial status which it was struggling to overcome.

The final phase of the civil war began with the British effort to
mediate. A prolonged diplomatic duel ensued between Mathew and
McLane, seconded by Miramon on the one hand and Juarez on the
other, and throughout it the American Minister extended a steady and
decisive support to his partner which foiled all the attempts—and they
were many and persistent—of the British mediator to initiate his
maneuver. Rebuffed in his first approaches, Mathew renewed his peace
offensive in the summer of 1860, but as the failure of the treaty had
relieved international tension and facilitated a more conciliatory approach, he modified his tactics and relied on the force of persuasion
alone. Following the old diplomatic rule that the easiest way to control
a competitor is to side with him, the British Government was negotiating with Washington for joint mediation in Mexico, and Mathew
sought the support and co-operation of McLane on those terms. Searching for some common ground of agreement, he deplored the stubborn
attachment of the American Minister to the Constitution and presented the case on its practical merits. Since the contending parties
were irreconcilable on the question of principles, the sole possibility of
compromise lay in a sacrifice of persons. "Concession of every sort
has been refused by Señor Juarez," he observed. "On the other hand,
the occurrences of the past two years—the utter incapacity of his
leaders, his own want of energy—preclude any expectancy of a party
triumph under his guidance. Indeed, they give consistency to a current

belief that Señor Juarez and his Minister of Foreign Affairs, conscious that the establishment of the Constitutional government in Mexico would reduce them to deserved obscurity, are far from desiring peace. That such is to some extent the feeling on this side—that neither General Miramon nor any member of his government nor any leader of his forces wishes for a termination of the war, unless it be by a conquest that would maintain them in office and command—I feel well assured. Under these circumstances, I feel we have no hope of peace unless by mutual conciliation, arrangements the result of Foreign intervention, or the substitution of a more energetic and capable person as the leader of the Constitutional party in lieu of Señor Juarez." And he produced a candidate: Comonfort. Provided he guaranteed religious liberty, he was the most eligible and, indeed, the only available leader. "I am inclined to think that at the present moment he might unite the suffrages of the Allied European Powers, if the influence of the United States were exerted in his behalf at Veracruz," Mathew continued. "I confess that I cannot but doubt the success of Allied intervention, unless it is supported by some show of force. The United States naturally possess the dominant influence with the government they have recognized, and it might be more easy for them than for any other nation to induce the leaders at Veracruz to acquiesce in a diplomatic settlement and arbitration. Would not, however, the best mode be the adoption by the United States and the Allied Powers, in the exceptional case of Mexico, of a specific form of government—say for eight years—and a demand for its unconditional acceptance by both parties?"

The termination of the civil war by the return of Comonfort would have been a grim judgment upon Juarez and a terrible atonement for supplanting him, had the idea been adopted; but it made no sense in Mexico, and no impression upon McLane. That it was seriously advanced by Mathew would have reflected on his judgment, had the notion originated with him; but he was not the umpire. He merely followed the instructions of Lord Russell, who was himself the proxy for the Prime Minister; to Lord Palmerston there was nothing exceptional in the expedient of compulsory arbitration, nor to his agent in the choice of the arch-compromiser to make it acceptable to Mexico. The solution was eminently British and eminently reasonable in London; and it was the duty of Mathew to produce the evidence to support it. He performed his part industriously, and his findings confirmed, and contributed to spread, the current detraction of the Constitutional President whose elimination was a necessity of British policy. Thus reputations are made and unmade. The weakness of Juarez was indispensable to the success of British policy in Mexico; but knowing that that was the weak point in his argument, Mathew hacked away at his supporters and used a better one to suborn McLane. "Unless I greatly err in judgment," he argued, "the sole object and desire of the United States is to see established in Mexico a government upon the best and firmest basis upon which commerce may thrive and from which foreigners may enjoy perfect religious liberty and due protection and justice. I have imagined, therefore, that the question of a federal or central constitution was wholly unimportant in their eyes." Moreover, he added, he had taken pains to ascertain the sentiments of the Constitutional leaders in the interior, and his investigation gave him good reason to believe that "Señor Juarez greatly errs in supposing that any attachment exists among them to the Constitution of 1857, beyond the broad principle it embodies of civil liberty"; while very little could be said, he suspected, with regard to the claims of *legality,* that word being used on both sides for purely personal ends. Since the Constitution meant nothing to the Mexicans who were fighting for it, what possible importance could it have for foreigners? The tenacity of Juarez in clinging to that bone of contention amply warranted his removal. "He makes no concession for the sake of peace, or in deference to the advice and just demands of foreign Allied Powers," Mathew complained, "but expects a *party triumph* by negotiation, which the most glaring incapacity and want of energy have hitherto precluded his attaining by force of arms, though supported by the most powerful ingredients of success."

The motives of Juarez he could understand, but not those of McLane in supporting him. The just demands of foreign Powers for law and order, stability and trade, religious and civil liberty, met every reasonable demand of democracy. What more did the American Minister want? Surely they could come to an understanding in Mexico; they spoke the same language of capitalist democracy, the British compromise covered their combined interests, Juarez himself meant nothing to his sponsors, and Comonfort was just the man to justify his elimination. So far Mathew was right. What he refused to recognize, however, was the obvious fact that McLane was committed to support the Constitution together with the government he had recognized, the treaty he had negotiated, and the working alliance he had established with the party whose success was essential to the security of American interests; the validity of all his titles was involved in its legality. But George B. Mathew had an uncommon capacity for being baffled by the obvious. It was also obvious that the Constitution could not be discarded without sacrificing the basic right of self-determination, which was indispensable to any kind of democracy; and this point at least he recognized as an obstacle that could be overcome only by foreign intervention, a show of force, compulsory arbitration, and the imposition of a government by the Allied Powers.

But Mathew was no match for McLane. The American and the Englishman spoke the same language, but not the same dialect; and the dialectical difference defeated Mathew. If there was any aspect of the Mexican question which all Americans understood, it was an argument, and undoubtedly the best, that Dunbar advanced in favor of the Liberal cause. "A strict regard for historical truth," he wrote, "compels me to state that British diplomacy in Mexico has from first to last, next to the Church, been one of the chief obstacles to the progress of liberal principles in that country. In this matter the British Government has acted on a false conception of political necessity and commercial interest, namely, opposition to the spread of the institutions and interests of the United States on this continent." Against that national prejudice, which was stronger than all the others and provided the best protection for Mexico, no amount of persuasion could prevail; and all the arguments of Mathew were lost on McLane. He could not do better than Lord Palmerston. Lord Lyons, the British Ambassador in Washington, presented an official invitation for joint intervention, which was declined. More, the American Government asked Paris for explanations of a paragraph in a London paper, announcing joint intervention by England and France, and received satisfactory assurances that the intervention contemplated was purely moral—satisfactory, that is, because a crisis had arisen in the Near East and military intervention by England and France in Syria was imminently expected.

But another Power had now to be reckoned with in Washington. The Mon–Almonte Convention, which McLane recognized as the counterweight to his treaty, became active with the arrival in Mexico in the summer of 1860 of the Spanish Minister. The partiality of Señor Pacheco for the Clerical government to which he was accredited was advertised by the activity, as industrious as it was indiscreet, with which he sought to bolster, singlehanded, its failing fortunes; and within a few weeks of his arrival he was embroiled with its adversary. A Spanish vessel having been embargoed at Veracruz for arms running, the commander of the Spanish squadron, acting on order· from his Minister, threatened to bomb the town and blockade the coast unless the prize were promptly released. The demand was ignored, and tension ran so high that the Juarez government consulted the American Legation on the possibility of securing American aid in the event of a war with Spain. McLane was in Washington at the time, consulting his government, and the incident dramatized the question that he had come to discuss. How far was American protection of the Constitutional government to be carried? Great Britain, France, and Spain, he repeated, were certain to intervene sooner or later, either jointly or severally, and unless it were in the power of the President to anticipate or counteract such intervention, the position of the American Legation would be humiliating. He advised that the Legation be withdrawn in anticipation of such a contingency, unless the naval forces of the United States could be employed to avert it. The President was reluctant to accept either alternative until the fate of the treaty had been finally settled; but the adverse vote in the Senate obliged him to act with circumspection. A repetition of the naval demonstration in March was out of the question in August; and Buchanan, unwilling either to back down or to become embroiled, directed McLane to continue to lend the Constitutional government moral support, but to offer no opposition to bona fide intervention for the redress of legitimate wrongs.

The qualified support with which McLane returned to Veracruz therefore placed the burden of averting intervention on the Constitutional government itself. The only alternative being a military triumph of the Liberals, Mathew renewed his peace proposals, but this time he adopted a different approach. He addressed an appeal, *ad hominem,* to Juarez himself. In a personal note, offering him some friendly advice, he informed him that Miramon was about to take the field with a force of six or seven thousand men and added, "This in no way alters the position of the Constitutional government as to the peace proposals, which, in my opinion, that government should make and publish, but it greatly aggravates—morally—the position of a Republican President who commits the crime of shedding the blood of his fellow countrymen and of the nation that is hostile to him." But he did not moralize unmercifully. "I shall not conceal from you, sir, that the best advice that I can offer you is to accept, *without a single day of delay,* the services of an auxiliary corps from the United States, insisting, however, on keeping their employment secret until a proclamation announces their landing as a Republican legion composed of men of all countries coming to take service under your government, to join your troops, and to fight for Mexican freedom."

The notion of engaging a corps of American volunteers had been debated often and bitterly in the cabinet and the country, and whenever and wherever it appeared Juarez had opposed it. Coming from a diplomat bent on eliminating him as an obstacle to mediation, it received no more consideration, therefore, than was due to a snare that would insure his political suicide. The note was written in French, a language which Juarez understood as well as the ruse of his British friend. The tongue of the tempter would have been recognizable in any language, and Juarez replied in his own, thanking Mathew for his proffered friendship and mentioning in passing, as a matter that merited no further attention, that "as for the forces of the United States, I must tell you that in my opinion there is no need for them. We have sufficient forces in the country."

If Mathew expected Juarez to compromise his cause and discredit himself by accepting intervention in the form of a foreign legion, and to commit the American Government surreptitiously, the advice was uncommonly artful but uncommonly credulous. After failing to dislodge him by way of McLane, the man deserved credit no doubt for so bold an attempt to make him a party to his own undoing. But there was nothing Machiavellic about George B. Mathew. He was simply at his wits' end.

The confidence of Juarez in self-help and the ultimate triumph of his cause remained to be proved, however, and the burden of proof rested on him. With intervention imminent, speed and activity were needed to anticipate it; and at that moment he was faced with a collapse of morale in his camp that marked the crisis of the civil war.

6

THE case for intervention rested on the stalemate into which the war degenerated after two and a half years of strenuous but inconclusive struggle. The fanatical pitch to which the Reform Laws wrought it intensified the bitterness and the obstinacy of the battle, but not its efficiency. In every corner of the country the hum of an implacable hatred could be heard, in harangues, in sermons, in pamphlets, in public rallies and political clubs and private homes, but the maddening drone of the dynamo produced nothing but a monotonous momentum without material issue or moral relief; the driving power vibrated with tireless impotence, finding spasmodic vent in violence without power, in the sputter of persecution, in the polemics of pillage, in the fuming of an interminable feud, in all the by-products of war short of military triumph. Victories and defeats were equally indecisive, and by the summer of 1860 the war had become a conclusive demonstration of the inability of either faction to prevail over the other, which amply warranted foreign intervention to put a merciful end to the convulsions of domestic dissension. More and more Mexicans succumbed to that conviction, and the capacity to resist it became the decisive factor in the final outcome.

When the contest reached that point, the advantage lay with Miramon, who had succeeded in maintaining the morale of his party and his troops by a series of spectacular if fruitless and fugitive triumphs, marred only by his repeated repulses before Veracruz. Degollado, on the other hand, was still "the hero of defeats," and though his powers of recuperation were unimpaired, a long succession of disasters had fostered demoralization among his subordinates. The respect which he commanded was pathetic or perfunctory, and limited to his staff; the malcontents formed their own clique, relieving their feelings in complaints of his incompetence and consoling themselves for their loyalty by professional backbiting. Santos Degollado was still a name to conjure with, but the spell had worn thin, and what it conjured up was faith without hope, loyalty to a cult, and sneers without charity. Lip-service was paid to the cult, but the hero was profaned behind his back. He was "the little saint," "the sacristan," "the Jesuit," "the hypocrite," to those who were surfeited with defeat; his failure to resign was indelicate, indecent, shameless shamming, and to hasten his exit he was discredited by hearsay. He was said to favor hiring American volunteers, and predamned for the one weakness that would confirm all his failures. To the relief of his critics, he left the army for a few months in February to act as Minister of Foreign Affairs in Veracruz—the first real service, they declared, that he had rendered his country—and as he signed the note inviting American intervention there, his days appeared to be counted. However, he returned to the army undaunted, and his detractors resigned themselves sullenly to the cult of incompetence.

In the ranks a thorough reorganization and a strong infusion of professional competence were required to repair the influence of persistent defeat. General Lopez Uraga, a trained soldier who joined the Liberal colors and won a battle for them about this time, described the conditions he encountered in a candid report to the President: "Our troops, accustomed to defeats, are shy of fighting and ready to retire at the first shot. Their leaders and officers, ill chosen, capriciously appointed, and easily promoted, try to drag out the war and to avoid exposing themselves and are the first to quit. No section leader subordinates himself to his commander; if he joins him it is in obedience to some combination which is never carried out and which divides when it should most unite them. Here today and there tomorrow, by dint of isolated efforts, the enemy escapes when he ought to be caught and succeeds when he is weakest. The General of our army, with none to second him, must be everything himself, gunner, mule-driver, quartermaster and division commander; he must fight in the open and direct his columns and attend to his artillery and even to his munitions, for if he does not he will be beaten, and if he does he will be killed, and then, as on the 24th in this city, there will be no one to continue the victory that he had assured, and it will be turned into defeat." Such, in short, was the inside history of two and a half years of Liberal disasters and the condition with which Degollado had contended in vain.

"We are ruining the richest elements, the best personnel, and the justification and idea of our cause by disorder, indiscipline, pillage, and the lack of order and centralization in our operations," the report continued. "I do not believe that an honorable general, who tries to serve the government conscientiously and to do his duty, can miss being killed in the first or second show of arms. I myself should have been killed at Lomas Alta, and I announced my fate to my friends for the second action." Short of a radical change in the constitution, structure, and personnel of the army, he saw no hope of breaking the deadlock. On that condition, however, the elusive chimera of victory and defeat could be tamed, the equation split, and "the campaign will be over, despite all our difficulties. Otherwise, the total destruction of the country is certain, and though the Liberal party will not perish, it will never triumph." That Degollado was able to take the field under such conditions was a remarkable proof of his mettle and the loyalty of his men; but it was no longer enough. He had given them everything of which he was capable: organization and discipline, which had melted away; resources, which had been consumed to no purpose; inspiration, which had drugged and deluded them. The one thing that he could not provide was success, and a tremendous premium had been placed on success by the pressure for foreign intervention in the summer of 1860.

A great reward awaited the man who could break the stalemate. Many had tried and failed, and the season for approximation and experiment had passed; and when a promising figure appeared in the person of Gonzalez Ortega, who won two victories in succession, the first on the field of Penuelas in June and the second at Silao in August—the latter against Miramon himself—it was generally believed that the coming man of the Liberal cause had been discovered at last. A wave of fresh unwonted hope ran through the weary ranks; it seemed as if the balance had been finally tipped; but it had dipped so often that foreign observers discounted these tentative triumphs. The decisive blow had yet to be struck by a co-ordinated campaign and a crushing conclusion. The prospects, however, were favorable; the territory controlled by the enemy had shrunk to three great strongholds— Puebla, Mexico City, and Guadalajara, and Guadalajara was chosen by Degollado as the next point of attack, and Gonzalez Ortega as the man to master it. Trusting to the talent and fortune of his lieutenant, he mustered all his remaining strength to support him; and the strain produced one of the great personal tragedies of the war.

At the outset the campaign was paralyzed by the perennial want of money to move and maintain the troops, and the shortage was so critical in September that Degollado consulted Ortega on a question of conscience. "Our terrible want of money and absolute lack of resources," he wrote, "make me think that, in order to save the country, it is legitimate to appropriate 200,000 pesos from one of the *conductas*

of Zacatecas or Aguascalientes that are leaving for Tampico. Give me
your opinion by return courier and with due secrecy." The risks
were self-evident. The *conductas,* or mule-trains, that carried silver
from the mines to the sea, were entrusted with property for the most
part of British ownership, and it was no time to embarrass the civil
government with foreign complications. Marquez had resorted to such
methods, and his example was enough to condemn them, for he had
been court-martialed by his government, and though he had since been
restored to service, the money had been returned and his conduct
disowned. Nevertheless, necessity was inexorable and the risks had
been carefully weighed by Degollado before he consulted a confessor.

Two weeks later he was relieved of his dilemma, but not by Ortega.
Doblado confiscated a *conducta* on his own responsibility, and without
consulting anyone. "I realize," he reported to Degollado, "all the disadvantages and all the consequences of so grave a decision, but I am
also intimately convinced that if we do not resort to such expedients the revolution will be indefinitely prolonged and the whole
country will sink into poverty and anarchy, losing at last its very
nationality. In the situation of the Liberal party today, we must choose
between two extremes of this terrible dilemma: either to waste three
years of bloody sacrifices, and this when we are approaching the end
of them, or to seize such resources as we can find, whatever their
origin. The alternative is hard but unavoidable: either we authorize the
disbanding of the numerous troops that are now at our command,
or we supply them with the means of subsistence, which, by preserving morality and discipline, will place them in a position to conclude the operations of the war. In the whole extent of the Republic
only three cities are still held by the Reaction. One month of campaign
and they are ours. Are we to lose a situation won by dint of blood
by refusing to appropriate funds, the return of which to their owners
is a matter of a few days? If it were possible to calculate arithmetically
what the country will lose by the continuation of the war, it would be
easy to prove that what we take today is a trifling sum compared to
what the people will have to pay if a war that destroys and annihilates
everything were to last unfortunately one month longer."

The trifling sum was something over a million pesos. But an even
more compelling argument was added by Doblado: he offered to revoke his act and to stand trial for it if it were disapproved. That inducement was irresistible; he addressed himself to the right quarter,
and by exactly the right method, to secure absolution. It was no longer
a temptation with which Degollado was faced, but a challenge, a
challenge to equal and surpass a subordinate, a challenge to his most
susceptible instincts—chivalry, courage, self-immolation—and he rose
to it recklessly. The decision of Doblado altered the whole problem,
and Degollado accepted the accomplished fact and assumed full re-

sponsibility for it—but with a significant difference. The tentative approach to a temptation, which had dismayed and fascinated him two weeks before, was transformed by the cool resolution and robust conscience of Doblado into something which the prompter could not divine and to which the principal was peculiarly liable—the temptation to accept the fact as a personal fatality and the tragic consummation of his unfortunate destiny. The difference was tremendous; and the decision, which had been deliberate and unsentimental with Doblado, cost his superior a moral conflict that had incalculable consequences in his subsequent conduct.

Writing to his government, Degollado repeated the argument of Doblado and added to it an accent all his own. "I have taken on myself the complete responsibility, and I am at the disposal of the government, so that with my head, if need be, it may avoid any international conflict." He would have served his country better, perhaps, had he kept his head, but Doblado had turned it, and beyond the government he appealed to the nation in a manifesto that revealed his state of mind even more clearly. The dedicated spirit spoke the tongue of the doomed. "From the height of that moral scaffold which opinion erects to immolate a man implacably, when he looks back and sees an obscure but stainless life and his consecration to a sacred cause, regardless of his family, or his rest, or his fortune, or his self-esteem, or any of the things that men most cherish, and in a moment, by a fatal vicissitude, faces the loss of everything and finds himself ranked among malefactors, that torment is greater than martyrdom, for in martyrdom the generous hand of glory gives some relief. With my eyes on my cause, with my heart upheld by hope and faith, after every defeat I have risen like a promise of triumph and my cry has been a call to battle and a summons to patriotism. . . . I had given everything to my country; I had preserved, with miserly severity for me and mine, a pure name to leave to my children, some of whom I have left without education and deprived others of my presence in their last moments; yet necessity came knocking at my door and demanding, in the name of my cause, my reputation to deliver over to malediction and contempt, and after a horrible agony I slew my name and closed my future, and plead guilty. In the profound conflict that tortured me in the solitude of my soul, I asked myself: And what of the national name and honor? Cold reason replied then, and repeats now, that the national name suffers far more from the prolongation of the struggle, and that with the loss of independence all will be lost. I conjured up also, as a painful contrast, the conduct of Miramon with Marquez; and it told me that those wrongdoers have made of the wealth which they call God's their treasury, and of His conniving clergy a powerful banker, and that we have no resource but to open the veins of the people and to ask them for their blood. . . . And for this reason I have offered my name and assumed the responsibility that I might have evaded by the generous determination of Señor Doblado to bear it. I have not sought to vindicate myself or to elude my destiny by subterfuges of any kind, or even to win the sympathy of those who are fighting the battle. I am accustomed to having my own devotion to the cause described as a fatal obstinacy and my misfortune as a crime, to the point of not being allowed to die for my cause on the battlefield."

Seldom has a public document been put to such intimate uses. The whole man was exposed, not only exposed but exhibited, his moral anatomy revealed and his motives laid bare: his genius for self-mortification, his infinite capacity for sacrifice, his unflinching courage and disinterestedness—and together with these qualities, his acute appreciation of them. Self-consciousness did not detract from his sincerity—pain is self-conscious and suffering is sincere—but it was the inevitable defect of his qualities, and neither the compensation of self-pity nor the vaunt of self-abnegation lessened the power of his apology. With the complete candor of despair, he appealed to the world without reserve or relief, out of that solitude of spirit in which he was aware of himself alone, because he felt himself severed from the world and morally isolated in it. Henceforth he was a man set apart by his own choice for a foreordained destiny—misfortune, misunderstanding, disgrace, defeat, death—and transfiguration. For every calamity has its compensations. The manifesto was a shroud in which he wrapped himself for a living death and through which shone the transparent stigmata of a spiritual triumph. No soldier could have signed it; it was the effusion of a saint, and the danger of waging war with a saint for a soldier was revealed in the rapture of a man who had found his true vocation at last and who discovered himself to the world exactly as he was, destined for martyrdom and resigned to receive it in its most ignominious form.

How far Degollado was isolated by a fever of soul that magnified himself and his offense in his own eyes he was the first to realize as soon as the inflammation subsided. Writing to Juarez a few days later, and enclosing a copy of the manifesto, he added: "In deference to the truth, and to my great surprise, I must tell you that neither the foreign consuls nor the interested parties have made me any reproach, and that they have spoken to me with the utmost consideration. By what I see and hear, I am led to believe that the necessity of this measure was in the public mind, and all the natives and foreigners who have spoken to me have said that they would consider themselves compensated if the Liberal party triumphs." Emerging from his nightmare into the broad light of day, he was dazed to discover that, instead of a pariah, he was a practical man; but the relief was brief. As his brain cleared, he was appalled by the hazards he had incurred and took steps to check their damage. He restored 400,000 pesos to the British in the belief, he explained, that the next packet would bring British recognition for his government and in the fear that, if he did not, the Gulf ports would be closed by the British fleet. In his haste to protect Juarez, he came to his senses with fresh compunction; his misdeed might be a mere peccadillo in the eyes of the world, but the moral damage to himself could not be undone, and the only effect of his belated caution was to weaken his self-confidence yet further. Of the remaining funds he set aside 600,000 pesos to buy the garrisons of Guadalajara and Mexico City, "and some further pecuniary sacrifices," he added, "may spare us the shedding of blood, put us in possession of munitions, armaments, and supplies of far greater value, and place us in a state of complete peace." Peace! Peace at any price! An intense craving for the end of a struggle to which he had immolated the best of himself, a weariness unreasoning and irresistible, beset him; he was exhausted.

And now came another collapse. The responsibility of success, after the robbery of the *conducta,* was too crushing for a man hounded by misfortune and dogged by defeat, and at the very moment when he had won the means of concluding the war at so cruel a cost to himself, his faith failed him. The moral sacrifice he had made for it was more than a man so constituted could bear; and with the loss of self-respect went the loss of self-confidence. The perversion of heroism violated something too vital to be abused with impunity, and nature—*his* nature—avenged itself for the excessive demand he exacted of it by an inevitable reaction. The urge of self-sacrifice which sustained him was suddenly transformed into the urge of self-destruction; from the dizzy height that he reached in his effort to surpass himself, he slipped downward in a desperate confusion of the suicidal impulse that possessed him; and the first forfeit was followed by a second and far more serious one.

Less than a week after reporting the robbery of the *conducta* Degollado wrote to Juarez, enclosing a copy of a letter he had written to Mathew, the acting head of the British Legation, on his own responsibility, inviting mediation and submitting peace terms, which he proposed at the same time to his own government. To Mathew he advanced them, subject to the approval of the President, but to Juarez he recommended them with finality. "If you approve them," he wrote, "I believe the triumph of the Liberal cause to be infallible; but if you disagree, I hope that you will be good enough to accept the resignation which I presented when I was in Veracruz and which remained pending, inasmuch as this is a pledge of honor that I have contracted. Señor Gonzalez Ortega agrees with the bases I have indicated, and Señor Doblado will do whatever the government decides." The bases indicated by Degollado were to be laid down by the diplomatic corps, together with two representatives of the contending parties, and included religious liberty, supremacy of the civil power, nationalization of Church property, the principles embodied in the Reform Laws, national representation in a freely elected Congress, and the appointment of a provisional President, chosen by the diplomatic corps to serve until Congress assembled and decreed a new Constitution. "The war that I have maintained for these three years has convinced me," he explained, "that pacification cannot be attained by force of arms alone, and I am prepared to sacrifice the form of persons, provided the principles sustained by the Liberal party are preserved and perfectly secured." If both sides rejected his terms, he was resolved to "retire completely from the political scene of my country," but if the enemy alone declined them, he was determined to prosecute the war to the end—a provision that saved his loyalty at the cost of his consistency and raised the question of why the proposal was made at all. The confusion of the scheme was equaled only by its futility. The terms were substantially the same as those that Mathew had repeatedly presented, and that had invariably been rejected by both sides, and the purpose of renewing them at that moment was inexplicable on purely logical grounds.

Upon learning of the robbery of the *conducta,* Juarez had immediately given orders for the return of the money and the trial of the officer responsible for it. He refused to believe that Degollado had countenanced it until the evidence confounded him; and before he had decided how to handle the scandal, he was confronted with a second misstep, which completely nullified the necessity of the first and which created a far more delicate problem. What had induced a man who had just committed a crime for his cause to commit another against it? For such was the verdict at Veracruz: Degollado had deserted. The connection was close, though obscure; but it was not with the psychological problem that the government was concerned. The erratic conduct of Degollado was a political aberration, which could be explained only on the assumption that he was not his own master. The logical deduction was that the return of British funds had appeased Mathew only partially and that to buy him off completely Degollado had consented to promote his peace plan at a highly embarrassing moment for the Liberal government, and some color was lent to this assumption by the admission of Degollado that he was committed to the proposal by a pledge of honor. A pledge of honor, supported by the approval of Ortega and the acquiescence of Doblado, to force the President to accept foreign mediation—this at least was a reasonable explanation of the ransom of a saint by a sensible man who knew exactly what his soul was worth. The result of the robbery was, apparently, a piece of diplomatic blackmail. In any case, the connection between Degollado and Mathew was clear; and so, within a few days, was the real purpose of the plan.

Mathew himself presented the same terms and urged Juarez, if he felt it his duty to reject them again, to retire in order to avoid the dangers that threatened him. The mysterious warning, the liberal conditions, the entire notion of a negotiated peace—Juarez dismissed them all in a reply that accepted nothing but the recognition of his constancy and his consistency. A week later he received another letter from Degollado urging him to resign, and the eloquence of the appeal showed how shrewdly Mathew had chosen his medium. "By sacrificing yourself and saving the country, you will become greater and greater in the eyes of the world," wrote Degollado in words that might have applied equally well to himself. "With your hand on your breast," he adjured Juarez, "place yourself before God, the whole world, and the Mexican nation which is watching you, and let your conscience decide in this difficult matter." Degollado was no longer the accused but the plaintiff, and he appealed to his judge on terms of equality. The mania of sacrifice was upon him; he expected as much of others as he exacted of himself, and in the intoxication and solitude of his own abnegation he felt entitled to dictate. To prove his disinterestedness, he added an article to his peace terms, stipulating that neither he nor Miramon should be eligible for the provisional Presidency, and he challenged Juarez to emulate his generosity and placed him in a position in which it was painful to decline competition. But what he found in Juarez was something more important than generosity: justice. Placed in a position as false as it was embarrassing, the President was forced to emerge from his customary self-effacement and to state the case in its true light; and he did so with an absence of heroics and a cool dignity that reminded Degollado no less solemnly that the issue was not and could never be a personal question.

"I am informed that you felt it necessary to address this letter to Señor Mathew," Juarez wrote after an impressive delay, "because your duty to your country so dictated, and because of circumstances, which you do not describe but which, you tell me, I shall learn later. As your proposal is so firm and decided that you have authorized Señor Mathew to publish it; as you tell me nothing, except that you reserve the powerful motives that have obliged you to adopt a resolution as unexpected as it is perilous to the cause of freedom, the dignity of the nation, and the future of the country; and as until now it is not public opinion, but your own and Señor Mathew's that indicates that I should abandon the Constitutional banner, leaving the settlement of the public administration not to the judgment of the Mexican people, who have shed their blood for almost three years to defend their fundamental law, nor even to the reactionaries who are, after all, Mexicans, but to a foreign body, which, because it helped the rebels of Tacubaya ever since the fatal betrayal of Don Ignacio Comonfort, has been interested in seeing the revolution end by a compromise by which the existing Constitution should be sacrificed"—for all these reasons he repeated what he had already said to Mathew.

To Mathew he had explained, with patience due to a diplomat, the self-evident and elementary reasons that governed his conduct. "If the war had a personal object, that is, if the question were whether I were to remain in power or not," he pointed out, "the decent and dignified course would be for me to retire from the post I occupy; but it is not so. . . . If I were to abandon my post, destroying the legality sustained not only by the city of Veracruz but by the majority of the Republic, I would descend voluntarily to the level of the rebels, deliver my country to the most appalling anarchy, and be as criminal as Don Miguel Miramon, and that at a time when the Constitutional party is fortified by its recent victories and is about to crown its efforts and sacrifices by a definitive triumph that will establish peace. It is not mean personal interests, therefore, that retain me in a power that has no attractions. . . . I remain at my post as a matter of duty and with the noble object of co-operating in the conquest of peace for my country. And I hold the profound conviction that peace will be stable and lasting when the general will, expressed through law, reforms the Constitution and appoints and removes rulers, and not an audacious minority such as that which revolted at Tacubaya in 1857."

To Degollado he repeated himself with equal patience, but in a tone of stern temperance, and concluded: "Since these reasons still exist and circumstances have not changed save in a manner favorable to the Constitutional cause . . . I believe it superfluous to seek to dissuade you from the decision you have taken, and I shall confine myself to replying that I in nowise approve your plan of pacification, and that, on the contrary, in fulfillment of my duty, I shall employ every legal means in my power to oppose it. . . . I trust that you are in good health and repeat that I am your friend."

Forbearance could go no further. In that reply Juarez wrote himself as broad and plain on a sheet of paper as Degollado had done in his manifesto; and he could copy himself indefinitely without weakening his reserve power, for the supply and the demand were unlimited. What Degollado had forgotten, among so many other lapses of judgment, was that the President was the incarnation of a cause; and what the President impressed on him, with such memorable common sense, was that his conduct could not be dictated by motives as irresponsible, as insignificant, and as histrionic as personal heroics. There, for his own part, he let the matter rest, and there it would have ended, had it been a private issue. But Degollado had authorized a public test of his proposals, and forbearance was impossible because of the effect which his defection produced on his fellow troopers.

To a man, the government rallied about Juarez. Within the official family the desertion of Degollado was greeted with consternation, indignation, and dismay. Old friendships were strained or broken, and the moderation of the President was in striking contrast to the bitterness with which Degollado was rebuked by his bosom friends. Ocampo, who idolized him, found not a word to say in his defense, and Prieto, who adored him, found too many to scourge him. "I do not know how to begin," he wrote, "so stunned am I by your decisions both as to the end of the war and the money restored to the British subjects. The former might have ruined us, and it has done you more damage—I say it, baring my soul—than you can imagine. The idea of intervention by the most ignominious of all means, the anomalous representation of foreign ministers to perform acts depriving us of national sovereignty, the evidence that after this infamous request on our part foreign arms will come to realize it, and all this from you, the democratic type *par excellence,* are things that leave me confounded; for I believed that a suicide like that of Comonfort would be unique in our history. On the eve of success to set aside the banner that has led us to it; to repudiate its power when we owe to it the triumph of the idea; and this during a siege, in the midst of enthusiastic leaders; to agree with the enemy to abjure the Constitution on the field of its evolution; to make of the barracks deliberating bodies; to depose Juarez, the benefactor, the friend, the comrade—I cannot explain this, and I am overwhelmed because you have disinherited us of our glory with the atheism of a believer, with the despair of a man of constancy, well nigh with the apostasy of the living incarnation of political society. I cannot, I will not, believe it; I want a denial to dispel this nightmare of shame that makes me weep blood. I told Doblado frankly that I did not understand what had happened, but today I learned it fully; the board met and held the trial and reached the verdict to which you resigned yourself in advance. It is clear that you must withdraw from the scene. I who believed that our greatest misfortune, our most irreparable defeat, would be your absence from the command; I who joined your circle because I felt myself more honored there than anywhere else; I say that you must leave the command; and God grant that you do not leave us weakness, anarchy, and the horrible prolongation of the civil war! As for the money, in refusing to return a single penny, there was a breadth of view; to restore it is to flatter the mighty and to become the hangman of your unhappy countrymen, whose advocate and conscience you were. . . . This substraction by fear, this course which makes the whole crime mean—I do not know what has happened or what I am saying. I offer sympathy to my country for the emasculation of one of its most eminent men and to myself for the death of my purest illusions. Your brother and grateful friend hugs you to his heart and begs you to command him as you will, as always. Your brother, G." The poet,

so sensitive to the spiritual secrets of his friends, was completely blind
to those of Degollado in his downfall because he was then serving as
a liaison agent between the government and the camp, and the factor
that made forbearance impossible was the reaction in the army.

The generals assembled for the siege of Guadalajara met and decided unanimously to condemn the proposal of the Commander-in-
Chief. Though Degollado had resigned himself in advance to the
verdict, coming from that quarter, he regarded it as a betrayal. With
complete candor he wrote to Juarez: "I am sorry to tell you that
Señores Doblado and Ortega assured me in Guanajuato of their absolute approval of the idea which I disclosed to them then and which
they have now opposed with as much heat as little good faith. This
merely proves that I am an impediment to the interested aims of the
men who figure in our political scene." In the conduct of the generals
there were secrets as well, and not spiritual ones—secrets lying so
close to the surface that they were visible to the naked eye, and Degollado was not so nearsighted as to overlook them. Discontent with his
leadership, long brewing in the camp, had been repressed in the interest of union, but his authority was respected by his subordinates only
in form and ignored in fact, and the demand for his removal persisted
in insubordination and intrigue. The power of suggestion was an in-
sidious influence during the period preceding his fall. Only a few
weeks before there had arisen a serious crisis between him and Doblado, smothered by the exertions of peacemakers and settled by the
promise that Doblado should be appointed second in command. The
opportunity to oust the impediment by the capture of the *conducta* and
encouragement of the peace proposals was obvious—so obvious that
one observer imputed the inspiration of both those missteps to Doblado. Degollado did not go so far, but he intimated that he was the
victim of trusted advisers. Whether the offer of Doblado to bear the
responsibility of the robbery was made in good faith or as a shrewd
appeal to his chivalry, Degollado had no doubt that he had been misled both by Doblado and Ortega into believing that they sincerely supported his peace proposals. Disowned by them both, he discovered that
he had walked unaware into a trap, and he found himself tripped and
floored by the very men from whom he had borrowed confidence to
transgress. For him this was but one more drop of gall; but for the
government it cast an ugly and dangerous light on the whole situation. The admission of Degollado that he had concerted his backsliding
with his subordinates, and that he had conceived it before the robbery
of the *conducta* brought on the brain storm which was his best excuse,
made it necessary not only to censure but to punish him.

Therefore the justice of Juarez went further. Degollado was ordered
to Veracruz to stand trial. His friends were later to complain of the
severity of this step. His resignation was indispensable, and he had

offered it; was it necessary also to pillory him? And on what charge? Treason? The construction depended on the intention and the effect. Technically he was guilty of indiscipline in initiating a political proposal without previously consulting his government, but the degree of the offense could be determinted fairly only by the purpose and interpretation of the plan. On the face of it the plan was impractical and could have only one result—the prosecution of the war; and such was the defense, in fact, that Degollado put forward as soon as he came under attack. "My idea, supposing it to be bad, was imposed on no one by force. Its action would have gone no further than a confidential discussion. Approved, it would have been a powerful weapon for the quicker and more complete triumph of our cause. Rejected, it would have been nullified in its effect, to my regret, but it would never have served to favor speculations detrimental to the national cause." The resignation of Juarez was contingent on "the remote event of our enemies admitting" mediation. "What I expect, naturally, is that the Clerical party will stubbornly refuse, but in that case we shall be able to defend the Constitution of 1857 and your government," he assured Juarez, "with full vigor and with the support that the whole diplomatic corps, minus Pacheco, will lend us, and our triumph will be infallible." Consequently, the plea concluded, "we shall continue fighting with better right, since we shall have exhausted the proofs of abnegation of the Constitutional government."

The resignation of Juarez, in other words, was to be a mere gesture, and the purpose of the plan a spectacular play to the gallery; one of his friends, in fact, borrowed a word from the bull ring to describe it— "a new and prodigious *faena* for the Liberal cause within and without the country." But this version of the plan merely reduced it to the puerile level of a flourish and added frivolity to its futility and mock heroics to its manifest folly. A better defense was put forward by the same friend when he explained that it was dictated by fear of forcible foreign intervention at no distant date. "Will it be time then and will it be possible to set conditions? The mediation that may be friendly today, will it not be an armed and violent intervention then?" This was a motive to which the government might be expected to be sympathetic, since it was the same one that governed the conclusion of the McLane treaty, of which the misconduct of Degollado was the final result and the obscure retribution. A standing reproach to the government was involved in all Degollado's apologies. "By reason of that infallible law of compensation, each advance and every crime of our enemies has produced its inevitable reaction," he had declared in his manifesto; "the idea of a treasonable protectorate, that of a continental policy, reprehensible also under the form of protection; the connection of rapacious speculation with a prostituted clergy has begotten the hatred of those powers; the gold of the faith, employed as a blood

value, has justified crimes against property. . . ." The failure of the
government to provide funds had forced him to rob the *conducta;* and
its efforts to do so by "a continental policy reprehensible under the
form of protection" had bred intervention and his peace plan; and
after being neutralized by contending impotences, he was crushed by
them. But the best defense of his plan was not rational; it was the internal evidence that it bore of fatigue and confusion and cross-purposes
that made the whole idea self-defeating, the feeble and pathological
production of a mind profoundly unsettled and divided. The long
strain of the war and the stress of a moral crisis had clearly unbalanced
the judgment of its author, and because of his previous record it could
be claimed that he was entitled to be treated as a sick man and spared
the stigma of public disgrace and indictment. Revolutions, however,
are lost that way.

For there was much more at stake than the fate of Degollado
himself. Rational explanations might minimize, psychological excuses
might extenuate, his offense, but both accepted the incontestable fact
of a surrender of national sovereignty to foreign arbitration, and it
was on that count that he was brought to book. In that state of mind
in which he was obviously not his own master, he had become the
mouthpiece or the dupe of another. The master mind was Mathew's,
about whose aims there hung no shadow of doubt; and behind Mathew
there was Comonfort. The civil war was to end in the return of the
renegade, who was to reap the fruits of his betrayal in the waste of
three years of fratricidal strife and the reward of the prodigal. Nor
was this prospect a hypothetical peril, for Comonfort, after wandering
abroad like a lost soul, had settled on the border and was conspiring
with his friends in the interior to cross it. One of his agents had felt
out Doblado and had pushed audacity so far as to approach Gutierrez
Zamora, the Governor of Veracruz. Incorrigible blindness? By no
means. Comonfort, his agent said, had reformed; he was no longer the
irresolute man of other times; his travels and sufferings had convinced
him of the necessity of "embracing a system with all its consequences";
he had no intention of increasing the conflicts in his country and
would return only if he could bring peace. The best guarantee of a
Liberal triumph was Veracruz; if he could count on Gutierrez Zamora, he would embark immediately; the support of the diplomatic
corps, who would never recognize Juarez, was assured, and intervention was imminent.

To all these arguments Zamora replied with quiet contempt. After
some reflections on the nature of turncoats, whose ideas were as flexible as their characters, he remarked that "we know what peace
Señor Comonfort would make and we prefer war," and he improved
the occasion to explode the great argument that authorized every be-

trayal. "The diplomatic corps will submit to the decision of the country, whether they like it or not," he added. "Neither do I agree that you can be certain that the United States mean to take possession of our territory. . . . As I do your ability and education the justice they deserve, I cannot but believe that the use you make of these vulgarities is the result of the necessity of finding arguments to vindicate your bold undertaking. In the present condition of our country, nothing would be easier for the United States than the conquest you suggest. They will not attempt it," he concluded, "because it is not to their advantage, because it would prejudice the balance of their interests, because it would introduce further complications in the racial question, dangerous enough as it is in the neighboring Republic, and for many other reasons that you know very well."

Comonfort had been judged once and for all in Mexico; the just are judged only once in this world; and justice was done to Juarez at the same time by his guardian angels. But the coincidence of these intrigues with the blunder of Degollado, though both remained abortive, placed Degollado's conduct in too dangerous a context to indulge any tenderness toward his trespass.

Indiscipline, indiscretion, imprudence—however his conduct might be qualified, it could not escape public correction. In lending himself to a maneuver that, whether it failed or succeeded, could breed only disintegration and defeat, he was guilty of demoralizing the movement he had inspired. The focus of infection had to be cut from the living tissue it contaminated; and the penalty was as exemplary as his previous record had been. So long as he had faith and hope, all his failures had been forgiven; when he lost his evangelical virtues, he forfeited the right to charity as well. This was revolutionary justice, and Juarez satisfied even the radicals who belittled his leadership by steering the movement through a treacherous crisis with the unbending will, the basic insight, and the drastic severity of the genuine revolutionary.

But revolutionary justice is rough justice. In strict equity Gonzalez Ortega was equally guilty of debauching the movement, not only because he was privy to the intent, but because he had intended a similar transaction on his own account. Before beginning the siege of Guadalajara he negotiated with the commander of the town for its surrender and proposed a peaceful settlement of the war, without consulting either Juarez or Degollado, on terms which included the resignation of Juarez and the sacrifice of the Constitution, without saving reservations of any kind. The negotiations came to nothing, and the only censure he received came from Degollado, who reprimanded him with an inconsistency which had become inveterate and reminded him that "neither you nor I can depart from our legal faculties, which are the maintenance of the Constitution and the legal government, without appearing to be traitors and disloyal to those from whom we derive our mission."

Copies of the correspondence exchanged in this negotiation were sent to Juarez by Degollado himself, oblivious or indifferent to the light which it cast on his own responsibility. Juarez filed them with the reference, "Degollado and Ortega exhort the President to forsake his post," as further evidence of the contagion undermining the camp. The duplication of disaffection was merely a detail in the dreary routine of recording its spread. The independence of the military power was a danger which had been exorcised for three years by the moral influence of Degollado, and with his collapse the check disappeared. Yet the fault for which he was disgraced was condoned in Ortega. The difference, however, was obvious: Ortega was a success; and, to make the moral more glaring, he succeeded Degollado as Commander-in-Chief. The justice of Juarez was tempered by a sense of expediency no less essential to the triumph of the movement, and the promotion of Ortega was vindicated by victory; Guadalajara was captured within a month, and a swift and unbroken succession of triumphs followed. But the discretion of the President gave his detractors an opportunity, which they did not neglect, to accuse him of catering to the strong and scourging the weak.

Juarez was not insensible to the inconsistency, and though his attitude toward Degollado remained unchanged, it underwent certain subliminal but perceptible modifications with the passage of time. In the heat of the crisis he remained cool. "A government whose duty it is to set the most complete example of morality, and which must in any case obey the laws and enforce them, has merely to judge by those laws any and every delinquent, whoever he may be," he wrote to a friend in defense of his justice. "Hence it is that, in spite of the services lent by Señor Degollado, and although he was one of the persons whom the central government trusted and on whom it conferred a large part of its ample powers, now that that person has departed from the path traced by the spirit of the present revolution and has sought to nullify a law, he has been called to trial as he deserves." The action of justice was automatic, impersonal, and impartial, and the sympathy of Solon perfunctory. A month later, however, reverting to the subject when the crisis had subsided, he wrote: "Like you, I regretted the false step of Señor Degollado, for I shall never be able to forget his previous good services, but he has wronged himself by repudiating a revolution such as Mexico is pursuing and was completely disabused when he discovered that not a single commander seconded his ill-conceived plan. That is why the event has produced no unpleasant consequences, and why our leaders today, stronger and more united than ever, are bearing down on the capital of the Republic with a terrible prospect for the Reaction." And that was why, the danger having passed, it was possible to temper justice not only with discretion, but with mercy. The trial of Degollado was suspended and the case quietly dropped. But though the President contemplated his justice and weighed his triumph without sentimental qualms, the mercy meted out to Degollado was a compromise that satisfied neither the coroner nor the casualty. Degollado suffered from it acutely: suspended sentence condemned him to a living death and embalmed him in the hardening fluid of a clouded reputation without the possibility of clearing it in court; and since some compensation was due him for the indulgence shown to Ortega, the government relented again, permitting him to return to active service on the staff of a subaltern and to redeem his name in the closing weeks of the war.

7

THE Degollado affair was the turning point of the war. The steadying hand of the President during the crisis was heaped with a great reward after it. The removal of the loose gut, the rise of a successful commander, the fall of Guadalajara, restored the flagging morale of the army like the lifting of a curse; and as Ortega bore down on the capital and the Liberal flag surged forward for the final thrust, the pressure for foreign intervention relaxed.

Two weeks after the fall of Guadalajara, Miramon declared a state of siege in the capital and rallied his followers in a manifesto that proclaimed to the most fugitive reader that his days were numbered. But a more patent admission of his desperate straits preceded the manifesto. On the previous night Marquez raided the British Legation, broke the seals of the Convention bonds deposited there, and extracted 660,000 Mexican dollars. The choice of Marquez for this chore was the only feature of the affair that suggested any political sagacity; for while the Constitutional government, rocked by the Degollado scandal, was righted only by the strong hand of Juarez, nothing but the strong arm of Miramon sustained the waning credit of his party, and he forfeited it completely when he counted his days in British bonds. The diplomatic corps protested as a body, led by Señor Pacheco himself; and so glaring an avowal of the extremities to which he was driven dealt the final blow to the confidence of his party, already

war-weary and ready to capitulate. By a reckless use of muscle, and
for the sake of six hundred and sixty thousand pesos, he sacrificed the
initial advantage with which his faction began the war and converted the solid diplomatic support, which had buttressed it for over
two years, into complete isolation at the very moment when the last
hope of his cause lay in foreign intervention.

By that act Mathew was driven into the Liberal camp. He had long
been moving toward it, and the nature of his peace terms made his destination inevitable, but he approached it reluctantly, searching step by
step for a formula of mediation that was not to be found. The plunder
of the British Legation ended his quest. He suspended relations with
the Miramon regime. As he was not authorized to go further, however,
he took up his station at Jalapa, halfway between Mexico and Veracruz, to await the end of the war and the decision of his government
to recognize the victor. This was a purely formal compromise. Actually he had already gone the whole way and favored the winner by
forbearing to press the claims created by the robbery of the *conducta*
and granting a request of the Veracruz government to use the install-
ment then due on the British Convention bonds for the termination of
the war.

The capitulation of Mathew marked the triumph of McLane, whose
unswerving refusal to countenance mediation or compromise had acted
like a magnet on the shifting field of foreign intervention and closed
the forbidden ground to trespassers. The steady support and legitimate
protection which the American Minister lent the Liberal government
during the long diplomatic siege to which it was subjected constituted
the real benefit of his treaty; the treaty, in fact, was the loadstone that
had drawn Mathew into the fold and defeated him, and in the hands of
McLane it had revealed the virtue of the philosopher's stone. Nevertheless, at the very moment when Mathew swung around to the Veracruz government, McLane began to veer away from it. For him the
philosopher's stone had lost all its value. The service which he had
rendered his partner was contingent on the validity of the treaty, and
though he had not abandoned hope of its passage in Washington, the
opposition it encountered in Veracruz was insurmountable—and it
was the opposition of one man. The entire cabinet, with a single exception, was in favor of extending the time for ratification; but the
dissenting member was sustained by the President. The force that had
constantly frustrated the American Minister and that he had refused to recognize was now admitted to be none other than Juarez
himself. "He will adhere to this disposition to avail himself of the
failure of the Senate to ratify the engagements within the time agreed
upon, unless some extraordinary pressure is brought to bear upon
him," McLane notified Washington, "precisely as he resisted originally
the actual conclusion of the same."

Precisely. For two long and lean years McLane had worked on the assumption he inherited from Churchwell and adopted himself, that the President was a timid and mistrustful politician wholly under the influence of his ministers; for four and twenty fruitless months he had attributed the difficulties he encountered to every reason but the real one, to sundry ministers changing places but not policies, to the interference of the frontier states affected by the treaty, to the friends of Comonfort, to systematic opposition within the party, only to realize at last that the one factor with which he had failed to reckon was the responsible statesman who had borrowed proxies and pretexts to prolong and control the negotiation until it had served his purpose, and whose powers of resistance he had seriously underestimated. The President, who had always eluded him, now escaped him completely; and McLane was nettled to discover, and mortified to admit, that the only result of his mission was that he had placed himself and his government in the awkward position of having granted recognition on a memorandum and sustained it for two years on a promissory note, while Juarez quietly eased himself out of his engagements without a claim to hold him, and with incontestable legitimacy. They were both honorable men; but one of them felt abused.

"The final determination of President Juarez will be much influenced by the degree of pressure," he repeated, "that may be brought to bear on him and the actual prospect of his party in the pending civil war"— but what kind of pressure could be applied with the end of the war approaching and the weight of foreign intervention weakening? After standing by the weaker party through a period of extreme stress, McLane frankly regretted the support he had extended to it, now that it was the winning party. "Under these circumstances," he warned Washington, "our relations with this country will be as unsatisfactory as they could well be, and instead of finding any fault with European Powers for supporting with armed forces their respective demands for redress, we will only have to reproach ourselves with failing to provide the same means for pursuing a like policy—and that, too, when a treaty has been concluded that enabled us to enforce our intervention with the consent of the recognized government. . . . I trust, therefore, that the President will not modify in any degree the views he communicated in his last annual message—and it is now more necessary than it was at that time that his recommendations be presented in the double aspect of acting with or without the consent of the Constitutional government, for it is impossible to foresee what difficulties will be encountered in securing that consent, in consequence of the failure of the Senate to ratify the treaty concluded in December 1859." In November 1860, however, it was not easy to outwit Juarez. Duped into playing a purely disinterested part and forced by circumstances to pursue a superior policy in Mexico, the Senator from Maryland was surfeited with superiority and galled by the glorious role he had performed there; and he hastened to retrieve himself at the eleventh hour. He had presented his views, he concluded, from the first day that he had recognized the Constitutional government; and he now presented his resignation.

His resignation was accepted, and so was his advice. Buchanan transcribed it in his message of December 1860, deploring the blindness with which Congress had failed to empower him to send a punitive expedition below the border and harping on the dangers, suspended for the moment but still latent, of European intervention there. But it was too late. The message was his valedictory to Mexico and to his own people as well, for the policy which he had preached so persistently was subject to the results of the presidential election that had been held in November. James Buchanan had begotten Abraham Lincoln, and the end of civil war in Mexico coincided with the crack of secession in the United States.

If the best defense of the treaty was its fruits, this was their final measure, and they were gathered in all their abundance by Juarez in December 1860. As the threat of intervention subsided on all sides, the timing of the long-drawn deal, which redeemed its dangers and reaped its rewards, amply vindicated the dilatory tactics with which he had handled it. Never had his political instinct been exercised to greater effect; never had timeserving been employed more successfully. Merely by temporizing, and on the strength of a prospective bargain, he had managed to secure American recognition, and thereby to break the diplomatic blockade, to facilitate the issue of the Reform Code, and to derive every benefit from an ostensible alliance that neutralized foreign intervention until the independent triumph of his party was assured. For a beginner in international diplomacy, who had baffled both Buchanan and Palmerston and broken the grip of the ruling powers within the country, it was not a bad start. Tortuous, his policy was called by his critics, tactless, and contrary to the popular will, but he had pursued it with an unerring sense of direction, making minor concessions to avoid major forfeits, and brought it to a clear and triumphant conclusion. If the result was due to deliberate strategy, it revealed consummate statesmanship; if it was accidental, the result was no less remarkable, for the risks were as high as the rewards, and he narrowly escaped the penalties of foreclosure and failure; and if, as is likely, it was a compound of both, an expedient imposed by necessity and evaded by determination and delay, a shifting equation daily adapted to changing conditions, a devious improvisation directed by flexible chance and immutable aim, the outcome was equally incontestable: by gaining time the timid politician and incorruptible magistrate of

Mexican destiny had won against overwhelming odds. But he cleared the mark none too soon.

Though the political race had been won by the slow, popular recognition and acclaim went to the speed with which the military campaign was wound up by Gonzalez Ortega. After the fall of Guadalajara he advanced with swift strides, and by the first days of December the capital was isolated and its fall so near that the Veracruz cabinet issued a call for Congress to assemble there and published the long-awaited decree of religious liberty that crowned the Reform Laws. The progress of Ortega guaranteed both steps. With the Constitutional armies closing in for the kill, Miramon had barely life enough for one last lunge. Sallying from the city, he surprised an advance detachment of the investing forces at Toluca and returned with two generals among his captives, one of them Degollado; but this was the death rally. Mustering the mere reminiscences of victory and the ragged regiments that recalled it, he issued once more in force and met Ortega at the village of Calpulalpam where, on December 22, he was finally crushed. On Christmas Day the Constitutional armies entered the capital in undisputed triumph. Contrary to the fears which the dying regime had excited as its last line of defense, the occupation of the capital was accomplished without reprisals or disorders; not a cry nor an act of vengeance marred the occasion on either side; the crowning victory was the triumph of moderation and discipline, which transformed the day of reckoning into a day of reconciliation, and the alarmists were routed by the enthusiastic welcome that the army and its commander received from a city that was both conquered and converted. Many were the spectators, waiting for the vandals against whom they had been warned and watching the troops filing by, who were gratefully surprised by their gallant bearing and who realized gradually that it was given to them to witness the triumph of truth in their time and to recognize the progress of law and order with the return of legitimacy. The magnanimity which the Commander-in-Chief displayed toward a vanquished foe was widely acknowledged and extolled; and so was the chivalry which he showed to a fallen friend. Catching sight of Degollado among the bystanders, he halted the parade, called him out and, handing him the flag, embraced and hailed him as the man who had made that day and that gesture possible. The gesture was greeted by a tremendous ovation from the crowd; the hero of defeats, his disgrace forgotten and his services alone remembered, was swept along by his comrades, and revolutionary justice was submerged by a parade of plain, human, popular justice.

Such triumphs occur, as a rule, only once in a lifetime. The capital was so completely converted, however, and its conquest was so popular, that, by general request, the performance was repeated a week later, and with unabated success.

Word of the battle of Calpulalpam was received in Veracruz while the President and his family were attending a gala performance at the theater. The house was full, for the bill was *Les Huguenots*, and the political value of an opera celebrating the religious wars in France in the sixteenth century was a drawing card by which the impresario profited. Just as the tenor and chorus swung into the heaven-storming air which was the cue for an ovation in Veracruz, the drama was transferred to the President's box. A courier stumbled in, and Gonzalez Ortega stole the show. Juarez rose, the orchestra stopped, and amid a breathless hush he read aloud, in a low voice, a bulletin announcing the victory of Ortega and the end of the war. The house rose as one man to the man who had made that message possible, and then and there the world knew him, as well as his wife had known him always, for what he was. Standing there in the penumbra, silent, self-effacing, retiring, and obscure, his sober mien, his somber skin, his dark eyes shrouded in the shadow of his own spirit like transparent reflections of steel, a statue of a man whose reserve suddenly became obtrusive in the glare of public attention, Juarez triumphed in his turn. The singers swung into the "Marseillaise," bedlam broke loose, the performance ended in an uproar for Ortega and the President, and the audience poured out into the streets on a full-flowing tide of sound that surged through the sleeping city, waking the dead.

But that was in Veracruz. A fortnight later the President left for the capital, and his appearance there, after popular acclaim had twice been tapped by Ortega, threatened to be an anticlimax. The capital had still to be conquered by the civil power. The culminating moment had come, in fact, when the co-operation of the military and civil arms, so severely strained by the war, was essential to secure the peace. The triumph of the movement inevitably dramatized its leadership and excited personal comparisons between the soldier and civilian, which were hardly in favor of Juarez, and a test of their relative popularity then and there was a fair measure of the degree to which the war had actually been won. Who really knew who Juarez was? How many recognized the services which he had rendered his country or knew him better by the end than the beginning of the war? Who could say how the man who had chosen to supplant Comonfort and substitute for Hidalgo, Morelos, Mora, and Farias had made good his promise and won the historic salvation of Mexico and himself? He had redeemed the permanent promise of things to come in things undone; he had kept faith with his forerunners and brought about the indivisible reunion of then and now; he had become the man of destiny who consummated the emancipation of his country, and the result spoke for itself. But who could divine the workman in the work? Two versions of his character and conduct were current, one picturing him as the indomitable champion of a lost cause who had rescued it from Comonfort and carried it with unflagging faith and constancy to a successful conclusion, the other as the merely nominal leader of a movement by which he was himself carried to a triumph that would have been won with or without him. The first was drawn in the broad strokes of a poster, the second in the small digs of partisan design, and it had the advantage of wide circulation in political clubs, military circles, and diplomatic propaganda. Ortega, on the other hand, was the operatic figure of the hour, favored by talent and fortune and a late entrance on the scene, and featured by the spectacular triumph which brought the war to a close. The active and passive agents of victory, as they then appeared to the casual observer, were called forth for public recognition in a critical test not only of their personal stature, but of the capacity of the public to judge their respective services, and few could be sure, when the President left for the capital, whether he would not be welcomed there as he had been welcomed in Veracruz in 1858, as an accessory to the struggle and not as the arbiter, in fact, and indispensable guarantee of its triumph.

But the encounter with the capitaline public dispelled any doubts that the war had indeed been won. Gonzalez Ortega met the President on the outskirts of the city and postponed his entrance for twenty-four hours until the final arrangements for his reception had been completed. Then, on January 11, 1861, Juarez drove into the city that had twice celebrated its conquest with a national solemnity unequaled, as the press said, since the proclamation of Independence in 1821, and for over eight hours he was welcomed with an ovation which, as the press also said, "has just been repeated now with the same spontaneity, the same enthusiasm, the same outpouring of hope and joy, on the arrival in the capital of the Constitutional President of the Republic." The last phenomenal triumph had been accomplished; for Gonzalez Ortega himself had guaranteed that the third and final command performance should be no everyday event.

PART THREE

The Year 1861

I

IN THE lives of nations certain years stand out singly more important than entire periods, because they compress and epitomize them. Such were the years 1821, 1847, and 1861 in Mexican annals, and the last was the most momentous of all. Eighteen sixty-one was the year of the comet. Beginning with a triumph that was rightly hailed as the culmination of four decades of struggle to redeem the False Independence of 1821, it ended in a portentous demonstration that the battle was only half won. The triumph was not permanent; it was merely a pause in the march of the Reform movement and the development of the national destiny. The false start had been corrected, the corporate state had been shattered, but the fact that the victory was won in 1861 instead of 1821 was itself a setback, for the conditions were infinitely more adverse, and the delay was reckoned not in calendar, but in social, time. No revolution could be won locally in 1861: independence meant emancipation not merely from the mother country and the social mold of the colony, but from the whole family of nations of which the misbegotten member had become a vital, vulnerable, and invalid part; and at the very moment when it broke the mold in which it was conceived, it became involved in a far more formidable conflict with the civilization to which it aspired and embroiled with the modern world as the penalty both of its past and its progress. By its origin and its growth alike, it was predestined to produce a foreign as well as a domestic contest between the forces working to reclaim it for feudal exploitation on the one hand, and the powers pressing forward to claim it for capitalist culture on the other. What the victory of 1861 won was merely a brief and breathless respite in the same relentless process. The first phase ended and the second began simultaneously; the transition was swift; and within twelve months the nation, exhausted and divided by three years of civil war, was called to defend its independence again against a coalition of forces and under conditions that canceled the reversal of 1821 and recalled the far more pregnant anniversary of 1847. For four decades the throes had repeated the toils under conditions that became ever more complex and portentous, the periodic return of the years of the comet magnified their fatality, and if 1847 was remembered in Mexico as the *annus terribilis* that first brought the country into foreign conflict and to the brink of collapse,

1861 eclipsed it. Terror was the keynote of those twelve months; and it was struck from the start.

At nine in the morning of January 11, when Juarez drove into the capital, the final ovations of victory were ringing in his ears; at nine that evening he sat down with the cabinet to its realities. A fortnight before, Gonzalez Ortega had proclaimed in an eloquent manifesto the disavowal of vengeance, proscription, or persecution of the enemy, but the first fine raptures were over: the magnanimity of victory, the easy promise of reconciliation or forbearance, the bounty of triumph, and the discipline of the army by no means corresponded to the sentiments of the rank-and-file of the party. The war was not a bad dream from which they awoke overnight; it was a nightmare knotted in the entrails of the nation, a sick and feverish infection that raised implacable passions and imperishable losses, which cried aloud through the press, the political clubs, and all the organs of public opinion for retribution, for primitive justice, for blood. The day of reckoning had long been foreseen and accepted as a necessary purge of civil war by the Conservatives themselves. Expecting no quarter and giving none, they had painted it in apocalyptic colors to prolong their defense, and the very peacemakers who attempted to avert the catastrophe in time evoked it no less violently than the infallible prescience of the vanquished. Two years before, a priest, pleading with his party to compromise before the passions it had excited became the exclusive right of the Liberals, wrote: "Unbridled as they now are, what prestige will be sufficiently powerful, what power will be able to prevent them from running to excesses that will be greater because more general and deliberate? Will the magic names of Juarez and Ocampo and the Constitution of '57 control them and make them vomit the blood from their mouths and spew the venom from their hearts? Wholesale proscriptions and confiscations will be enacted, and the same bandits who rob and kill today will perforce be the leading authorities in the towns, which will become the scenes of the worst crimes, under the protection of barbarous laws befitting a reign of terror." And he predicted the worst because he allowed for the best. "Supposing that Señor Juarez is President then, on what force will he rely to bring the robbers to heel? What balm will soothe those hearts athirst for vengeance? Will they return to work and morality overnight and obey orders which I wish to believe will be issued in a spirit of moderation and justice? He who attempts to stem such a torrent will be declared a traitor." Precisely. The phantom fears that had nourished the defeated for two years were allayed by the conduct and prestige of Gonzalez Ortega, but only for two weeks; after a fortnight of soft peace the public temper turned, soured by an overindulgence in fine sentiments, and the morrow brought up the vindictive dregs, the hard sediment of civil war. Padre Valdovinos had predicted the truth, and the fictitious truce was over when Juarez arrived in the capital to face the exactions, together with the ovations, of victory.

Juarez, no less than Padre Valdovinos, was prepared for the truth. Before leaving Veracruz he had mapped his course with the cabinet and Ocampo, who joined it for a last exacting duty before retiring to private life. The pacification of the country required some degree of appeasement of popular passion; to ignore it was impossible, to cater to it craven, to trifle with it frivolous and foolhardy; and it was decided to prosecute the ringleaders of the Reaction, to banish the bishops who had backed them, to expel their allies in the diplomatic corps, and to couple these examples with a decree of general amnesty. But these measures, taken in the spirit of moderation and justice that the Padre expected of Juarez and Ocampo, were treason to the party in the capital, which had been thwarted for two weeks of the thorough house-cleaning which it demanded. If Juarez had forgotten the circumstances under which he fled from the capital exactly three years before, his party had not, and on the night of his homecoming a test case arose.

The ringleaders of the Reaction had escaped after the battle of Calpulalpam, Marquez and Zuloaga into the interior and Miramon to Veracruz. There the "Maccabee" found refuge on a French warship, where he defied pursuit not by his own countrymen alone, but by the British naval commander, who demanded his surrender to answer for the plunder of the Legation. From his sanctuary he gave out an account of his escape, which was published serially in the press of the capital and which further exasperated popular feeling there. His brother-in-law and principal minister, Isidoro Diaz, was caught, however, and on him the full fury of baffled justice was bent. Word of his capture reached the capital as Juarez was holding his first session with the cabinet, and orders were immediately despatched for his trial under martial law and summary execution of the sentence; but a few days later, on the intercession of his family, the President consented to commute the sentence to banishment, and on the following day the storm broke.

"A grave, an alarming rumor is spreading. If it is true, it will mean the discredit of the government and the ruin of the country. It is said that a pardon has been granted to Don Isidoro Diaz, and that an amnesty will be issued in favor of all the reactionaries." The alarm was raised by the most powerful paper of the party, the *Siglo XIX,* and led by its most eloquent tribune. Zarco, who had spent the civil war in the capital, returned to his post at the head of that forensic organ to wield the scourge with the fury of a baffled civilian. "If this happens, farewell freedom, farewell justice, farewell all public order! There will be no end to the series of mutinies and revolts, and the country, desperate and disappointed, without hope or faith, will recant its exertions, curse its sacrifices, and lose itself in the convulsions of anarchy," he protested.

"The country will not tolerate the amnesty that is announced because it wants justice, because it craves peace, order, morality, and because it cannot consider as political crimes the perjury and betrayal by the authors of the *coup d'état* or the mutiny of Tacubaya or the whole series of robberies, assaults, snares, sacks, assassinations and conflagrations perpetrated by the Reaction. . . . It is true that justice can be administered with mercy, and that our Constitution gives the Executive the right to pardon; but that pardon must not be a scandal or a crime against society as a whole." The scourge was brandished by a good friend, for when the pen of Zarco gave the cue, there were no lengths to which the hue and cry would not run, and the fate of Diaz and the amnesty, blindly confused, became a test of the strength of the government. The real ruler of Mexico at that moment was neither the civil nor the military power, but the press; and the warning was heeded. The government retreated, canceling the pardon of Diaz and holding him for trial in the civil courts; and no more was heard of the amnesty, though its provisions were quietly observed in fact. The cabinet was also recast to appease public opinion, and the three most popular tribunes of the hour were induced to join it. Zarco succeeded Ocampo as Minister of Foreign Affairs, Ignacio Ramirez took over the Ministry of Justice, and Gonzalez Ortega the portfolio of War.

The tension of public feeling ran so high, however, that every concession made by the President was interpreted as a sign of weakness and an admission, not a correction, of error. The press was a jealous and exacting master, the irritation aroused by the amnesty did not subside when the measure was dropped, and even the decrees that met the crying demand were challenged. The banishment of the bishops was approved with one breath and withered with another, and the President was censured for expelling them by decree and permitting them to pose as victims of political persecution instead of holding them for public trial as rebels under the laws of their country. "The banishment of the bishops, for all its appearance of energy, is nothing but a proof of real weakness and a violation of the Constitution," the *Siglo* declared; for though Zarco had been dislodged from his editorial chair and caged in the cabinet, he had left a whole flock of avenging angels behind him, and a chorus of caviling echoed the complaint. The lesser press pursued it and demanded that justice be wrested from the hands of the Chief Magistrate, who administered it feebly and arbitrarily, and restored to the courts and the nation—to the capable and aggressive grasp, that is, of Ignacio Ramirez.

Amid this wrangling the real issue was neglected. The banishment of the bishops was a symbolic sacrifice to the *vindicta publica*. They were convicted on suspicion and sentenced by acclaim, and as the evidence of clerical treason was always elusive, the one certain result of a public trial would have been a domestic scandal and a foreign sensation; and the latter was a consideration to which the government gave more weight than the press. Before leaving Veracruz, Juarez had been advised by McLane to observe all reasonable forbearance in the pacification of the country; and the new French Minister, M. de Saligny, also had urged him to propitiate foreign opinion—officious advice, but well meant in both cases, for the prevailing prejudice abroad against the Liberal party and its Indian leader was only waiting for a case to prove and provoke it. In the case of the prelates the method adopted was the one least apt to prejudice foreign judgment, but for that very reason it was denounced by a press writing to read the world a lesson and to declare the emancipation of Mexico from foreign influence; and the President was allowed no latitude for discretion.

Foreign hazards, however, were a serious consideration in the expulsion of three members of the diplomatic corps—the Papal Nuncio, the Minister of Spain, and the Minister of Guatemala—whom the government singled out as examples on charges of notorious complicity with the Reaction. Here the government and the press were in complete agreement, and the most captious found no fault with the President. Reprisals against the foreign enemy were recognized as a measure of public safety, and there was no dissent as to the necessity, or the justice, of purging the Republic of its avowed opponents. Nevertheless, the step was provocative and the policy questionable. Ocampo, who signed the letters of expulsion—it was his last official act before resigning to Zarco—was careful to state that the censure they conveyed carried no reflection on the governments represented. The Spanish Minister refused to admit any distinction between his public and private character and replied stiffly to that effect, and one member of the cabinet at least thought it impolitic to antagonize him: Gonzalez Ortega, carrying discretion one step further than his colleagues, called on the irate Minister on the night before his departure, deplored their hasty decision, and announced the visit of Zarco to accommodate the affair. Señor Pacheco was perfectly willing to be wooed, for he was loath to believe that he was simply *persona non grata,* and he stayed up all night awaiting the peacemaker; but the night passed without any further approaches, and in the morning the escort appeared promptly at the door, and he drove away unreconciled. He made the journey in company with the prelates, and at Veracruz, where passions ran even higher than in the capital, the party was received with a riot. The carriage of the Nuncio was stoned, the bishops were pelted as they alighted; the Nuncio found refuge in the parlor of the French Consul, the bishops made for the nearest home with lace curtains, and there they were held in protective custody by the police until their ship sailed and they could be safely spirited away. The addled Spaniard was not molested, but his parting impressions of Mexico were highly inflamed; and he was no sooner out of the country than he sent a detailed account of the outrages which the whole party had suffered to his French colleague, to whom he bequeathed the protection of Spanish nationals.

Not until the outcasts were well on their way did the press notice the effects of their expulsion; and then not very seriously. The *Siglo* regaled its readers with a flippant account from its correspondent in Cuba of the appearance of the Spanish Minister and Miramon flocking together in the fashionable promenades of Havana and attending the Opera, where they attracted some attention from the curious but none from the Captain-General, who alone counted. Later references to the affair were relegated to the gossip column. It was difficult to take Señor Pacheco seriously; the only impression he left on Mexico personally was that of a figure grotesquely inflated by gout, obesity, and self-importance, and his political stature was gauged by the parting glimpse of Minister and General parading their misfortunes together amid the indifference of the official and fashionable worlds of Havana. As for the bishops, they were mere ghosts.

The influence of the Church on foreign opinion had already been tested. The efforts which the Clerical party had made to secure foreign intervention had come to nothing, and it was clear that they would come to nothing unless the Church could identify its interests with those of the great Powers; and that danger was a remote contingency in 1861. The victory of the Liberal party and its program were the best guarantees for the interests of the great Powers, which were completely independent of those of the Church, if not diametrically opposed to them.

Abundant evidence of that fact was provided by the experience of Mgr. Labastida. Banished by Comonfort in 1856, the Bishop of Puebla had spent four years abroad in search of support, and although he was an active and energetic churchman, he had traveled the apostolic path to final resignation. His correspondence with Father Miranda told the whole tale. During the last six months of the civil war, from a villa in Viareggio, he followed its development with a detachment remotely resembling that of a disinterested observer. The decline of his cause was accompanied, month by month, by his own moral progress. In July he still saw some grounds for hope. One was Señor Pacheco, another the defeat of the American treaty, and a third the new French Minister, M. de Saligny, who was the likeliest of all, for M. de Gabriac was still working for them in Paris, and "the substitute shows good ideas and intentions and promises to do great things for Mexico, beginning with his passage through New York where he has good connections, particularly with Mr. Benjamin, who has influence." To base his faith, however, on someone who had connections with someone else who had influence, was to rely on second- and third-hand hopes. American capital was still on the wrong side, the European Powers were temporizing, England was weakening, and hence Louis Napoleon as well, and he trusted only in Spain and in Spain only with the help of God. "Spain alone is firmly resolved to favor us. May God give her strength and wisdom, which are needed even to do good!" But Spain could do nothing without England and France; England and France had the strength and the wisdom, but not the need, to do good; and gradually he lost hope in any ground-given god.

By August he was completely despondent. "It is useless to exert ourselves to obtain peace by ourselves," he confessed. "We struggle, but without sufficient strength. The intervention or mediation of Europe alone can afford us some respite, but will it be made? Europe is very much troubled by its own situation." Whatever the prop to which he clung, he fell by it. "I see very clearly," he concluded, "that the sacrifice of ecclesiastical property, its ruin and certain disappearance, are inevitable. But I tremble for the fate of those property-owners who regard it with indifference today or who favor it jealously. Sooner or later their possessions will suffer the same fate. They think to save them, and they destroy the buttress that protects them in that wretched society." Without power enough either to protect or be protected, the Church was doomed. One melancholy reflection leading to another, his mind veered to divine intervention or self-help, which, as the adage would have it, were one and the same thing, and in September he preached that sermon. But he had no faith in it himself. His last hope was Miramon, and that was the faintest of all, for "to sustain it some foreign bayonets would be needed," he added, "and they are not to be had." Hard on that postscript came October and Ortega. In November the British Legation was plundered and everything vanished—intervention, mediation, Miramon, and Miranda; and by December Mgr. Labastida abandoned whatever idea he still entertained of returning to his diocese. So, culling simples all the way, he came to the end of it completely disabused but grateful for four years of exile, which left him exactly where he was, but which cured him of the world, "after having made a trip entirely useless for the Church and the State, though of great mortification for your affectionate Prelate, P.A., Bishop of Puebla." No other P.S. was possible, and the case of the Bishop of Puebla provided a fair enough test to discount in advance the banishment of five more Mexican bishops.

The expulsion of the diplomats was more serious, however, for here the blow struck the professional *esprit de corps* of a caste capable of retaliating and accustomed to an immunity in meddling with the domestic affairs of the country that had never been questioned before; and it was not allowed to pass unchallenged now. The first reaction came from the French Minister, who immediately protested the expulsion of the Nuncio and went so far as to declare, in a heated altercation with Ocampo, that the Emperor of the French would consider it a personal affront. His expostulations were ignored. Before long, however, both the government and the press awoke to the fact that the new French Minister was a man who meant, and who deserved, to be taken seriously. Pacheco and the prelates were phantoms, forgotten as soon as they vanished. But M. de Saligny was the comet.

2

THE successor of M. de Gabriac deserved attention indeed, and soon received it, as an even more portentous specimen of the partisan and irresponsible diplomat that flourished so freely in Mexico, and as a consummate example of the license that the genus had come to enjoy with time and impunity. When he arrived there, he had already been ignored too long for his own good or that of the government to which he was accredited. Neither his antecedents, nor his connections, nor his sympathies, were auspicious. Pierre Elizodor Alphonse Dubois de Saligny was a diplomat *manqué*. After a promising start in the service, he had been placed on the inactive list and had vegetated in semidisgrace, for reasons unknown but that may have had something to do with his peremptory temper, soliciting employment unsuccessfully for ten years until he was suddenly recalled for a mission which linked his professional future with the destinies of Mexico. In May 1860 he was appointed to represent his country in the joint mediation by which France and England proposed to extinguish the civil war. The mission was important because of its bearing on the expansion of American influence in Mexico, but his departure was delayed, and the war was over when he arrived in Veracruz in December 1860. For a man who had been shelved in mid-career and for whom the future had just reopened, this was a setback, but he was prepared for it, for whatever else he may have been, he was not a fatalist, and he set to work with redoubled zeal to attract the attention of the Foreign Office and to win the good graces of the Emperor in what remained of his mission.

When he left Paris the end of the war was foreseen, and he carried contingent instructions covering the protection of French interests and outstanding claims created by the war—debts and indemnities—which he was directed to settle before recognizing the government. Since communication was slow and the normal delay of three months in the exchange of diplomatic despatches hampered efficiency in the discharge of his duties, he had requested and received permission to use his discretion and initiative in these routine transactions; and the latitude and confidence thus invested in him were employed not only to settle public debts, but to pay private ones. He owed his appointment to the recommendation of M. de Gabriac and inherited the friends, the clients, and the obligations of his sponsor, and when he was approached by the Mexican clericals and expatriates for whom M. de Gabriac was working in Paris, he accepted their commissions as a matter of course. He promised to do great things for Mexico, and he kept his word. The confidence of the Bishop of Puebla was not misplaced, for it was precisely through such private commissions that M. de Saligny was able to restore to his mission the importance which it had lost by the untimely end of the war. The confidence of the Quai d'Orsay allowed him ample latitude to operate on margin, and how far he was prepared to stretch it he proved when he protested the expulsion of the Nuncio and honored his obligations to his clerical friends, at some risk to himself, for it was stretching discretion very thin and initiative very far to include the championship of the Church in the protection of French interests and to commit the Emperor to that position. Such was the view that the Mexican Government took when it ignored him, but its security was based on his public character, and it was only on better acquaintance with his private character that it discovered that the distinction between them was as imaginary as in the case of Señor Pacheco.

Several weeks later the government ordered the Convent of the Sisters of Charity to be searched for a deposit of money and valuables concealed there in violation of the law nationalizing Church property. "It was the stormy period," wrote an eyewitness, "when the Liberal party plunged into turbulent agitation, concerning itself incessantly with public affairs, supervising all the acts of the administration in the press and the clubs and attacking those which it considered feeble or deficient and anything that appeared to be a compromise with Reaction." As word of the raid spread, a crowd collected about the convent. Apart from the rioting in Veracruz, no anticlerical demonstrations had disturbed the pacification of the country as yet; the turbulent temper of the capital effervesced in rhetorical agitation, the terror was confined to talk, and the crowd that mounted guard about the convent was curious, watchful, but orderly, no resistance was offered, and the lawbreakers were women. The Sisters chatted amicably with the soldiers, and the investigation would have passed off without scandal if the *Visitadora*, who was a Spaniard, had not protested against the presence of Mexican troops at her skirts and, when they broke down a wall and located the treasure, hurried off to the French Legation to demand protection. M. de Saligny, having taken over the protection of Spanish nationals from Pacheco, espoused her protest and forwarded it to Zarco, who was obliged to choose between Agustina Zuazua and Francisco Zarco. The soldiers were not withdrawn, and on the next day M. de Saligny repeated his remonstrances in his own name and on behalf of his government. As he had not yet presented his credentials, he had no official standing, but technicalities did not prevent him from indulging in personalities and raising his voice and losing his temper. "So!" he ejaculated in a furiously informal note, "your government is determined to drain my patience and break with France? I am forced to think so, when I see it persisting in the incredible outrages of which the establishment of the Sisters of Charity has been the scene for the past six hours. Despite all the recommendations which I addressed to you yesterday, the establishment is still occupied by a coarse and brutal soldiery that indulges in every form of insult to the Superior and the other Sisters. I shall no longer be a witness to such a spectacle, which is a direct and premeditated offense to the government of the Emperor, under whose protection these holy women have been placed in every part of the world. Unless you withdraw your soldiers, whose presence nothing can justify, immediately, I shall send you a protest today, renouncing the renewal of relations with a government for whom, I am forced to say, nothing is sacred."

No government could submit to such an ultimatum without forfeiting national sovereignty, and no responsible minister could retreat from so peremptory a position, but the notice was unofficial, and an informal accommodation of their quarrel was made. The soldiers were withdrawn when they had completed their duty, and the incident was apparently closed, but a few days later, on a new denunciation, they returned to the convent for another search, and the scandal flared up afresh. M. de Saligny mounted his high horse once more and protested, this time with an obscene insinuation, against the orders of the government "to carry out a search and Heaven knows what kind of investigations" and a breach of agreement which he could only explain as a mistake. "Be that as it may, I am sending you this so that you may put a stop to what is happening. Otherwise my orders are so imperative that I cannot but obey them, and I shall be obliged, to my great regret, to break all relations with your government and to leave the capital." Again the soldiers were withdrawn, but the government made its position perfectly clear by publishing a statement in the press that "the establishment of the Sisters of Charity is to continue to lend its service to suffering humanity and needy children under the inspection of the government, and is never to be subject to the protection and refuge of any foreign government."

The press glossed over the incident very lightly, suddenly aware that, however untenable the position in which the French Minister had placed himself, he was a man to be handled with care. The *Siglo,* all amenity and official optimism, nevertheless read him a lesson. "Unfortunately, and we venture to say so because it has passed into a common saying, the generous character and tendencies of the French nation have not been properly personified in Mexico in recent years, and the majesty and prestige of the Empire have served to cover mean and personal connections. The general clamor of the French residents in Mexico proves how its most respectable interests have been sacrificed to the alliance of the French Minister with the Clerical party. . . . The general version of this incident does not agree with the high idea that we hold of the new representative of France." Far franker was the rebuke of the French colony: "The right of the government to control alone and directly the temporal administration of the Mexican Church cannot be denied," it declared. "Is this the end or the continuation of the deplorable conflict between the Cabinet and the Legation of France? We believe that it will be the end."

The end it was not, but it was a halt. Saligny was silenced for the moment, but he had gone too far to draw back, and he referred the dispute to Paris. His position was weak. His formal instructions explicitly forbade any interference in the internal affairs of the country, and had he been requested to produce the imperative orders under which he claimed to be acting, he would have been hard put to attribute them to the French Government. The Order of St. Vincent de Paul, to which the Sisters of Charity belonged, enjoyed the protection of the Emperor, it was true; but the exercise of that pretension had been admitted in only one country in the world, Portugal, and in Mexico it had been consistently denied even by the Zuloaga government. As for Napoleon, who was engaged in supporting the Vatican with one hand and the Italian liberation movement with the other, his clerical policy was equivocal and depended on preserving the balance at home and abroad, and there was no reason to suppose that an attempt to tip the scales in Mexico would succeed. That M. de Saligny was willing to risk a rupture under such circumstances and on so flimsy a pretext revealed so much assurance that the government was obliged to take him seriously, at least until the degree to which he was supported in Paris could be determined. Realizing that the man was serving more than one master, Zarco temporized, but he would have been spared worse difficulties had he accepted the rupture, for the tradition established by M. de Gabriac was unbroken. The persons changed, but not the practices, and the incident acquired a peculiar gravity because it coincided with a negotiation which the French Minister had just initiated with no less nerve, which was equally irregular, and in which there was no doubt that he enjoyed the authority of his government.

This negotiation, of which the public had not yet caught wind, was an affair destined to attain international notoriety under the name of the Jecker bonds. In 1859 the Miramon government issued bonds to the amount of fifteen million pesos and gave the agency to the firm of Jecker, Torre & Co., one of the leading foreign banks in Mexico, in a desperate attempt to reconvert its debts and restore its credit. The market was so low that special inducements were offered to float the issue. The first, and most important, was the privilege of paying twenty per cent of the customs duties with the bonds—a feature designed to interest the foreign merchants, and it was to that public that the appeal was primarily addressed. The Miramon government, it was true, did not control the ports at which the customs were collected, but it had established an inner ring of its own, and the actual value of the reductions was considerable, as the bonds could be picked up at a thirty-five per cent discount. A circular stressing the selling point was sent to all the foreign Legations, and as the principal consideration for Miramon was the political value of interesting the foreign colonies in the triumph of his faction, M. de Gabriac was able to obtain a decree extending the privilege to include all tax payments, by which the French colony benefited to the extent of ten million francs a year.

The second inducement was the signature of the bank, which guaranteed one-half of the interest for five years. This security was not very sound. J. B. Jecker was a Swiss financier who had speculated recklessly for years in many forms of Mexican investment—mines, ironworks, the mint at Guanajuato, public lands in Sonora, claims at Tehuantepec—before he took a flier with the Miramon government. His family and partners abroad considered his scale of operations altogether too American and had repeatedly warned him against overexpansion, and in 1859 the firm was in difficulties. At the time that he underwrote the bonds, however, they were merely a small turnover between a reputable international banker on the one hand, and an insolvent government on the other; but the relative positions of the two parties were soon equalized. In May 1860 the bank failed in Paris. Liquidation was suspended pending a settlement with the creditors. Among the assets were the Mexican bonds, of which only an insignificant fraction had been sold, worth exactly 700,450 pesos, and on these Jecker continued to meet the interest regularly to protect his title to the unsold residue, which amounted to over eighty-six million francs, and to prevent a contract between a government and a bank, both of them bankrupt, from becoming extinct.

As the value of the asset depended on the issue of the civil war, and as the prospects of the Miramon government declined rapidly after May 1860, the relatives of Jecker in Paris and Switzerland began to interest themselves actively in insuring the contract. By October his brother-in-law, Jakob Elsesser, who knew nothing about Mexico, but who was reading a serious German book about it, could see that the future was black, and he busied himself borrowing advice wherever he could. "I must tell you about the bonds," he wrote to a confidant in

Paris from his corner in Ponterrey, Switzerland. "A learned philologist here is busy translating the decrees, the full explanation of which I shall send you later." But even had they been written in a dead language, Elsesser would have understood them without engaging a scholar to decipher their meaning. "Although these acts emanated from a government then recognized by England and France, and the bonds were held in considerable amounts by the merchants of both nations, I have no doubt that once the Liberals come into power, as they soon will, the bonds will be put out of circulation. M. de Saligny has assured me, however," he added, "that the recognizing governments and even the United States would support them, because of the benefits which their nationals derive from them by paying heavy customs duties with paper that they buy cheap."

The services of a Saligny were worth more than those of a philologist, and Elsesser secured them at less cost, merely by unbosoming himself freely to the Minister; but the comfort he derived from consulting him was secondhand, like the encouragement which the Bishop of Puebla drew from his connection with Mr. Benjamin. Valuable though that connection might be for both his clients, what M. de Saligny had to offer were hopes, not guarantees, and gratuitous services were worthless anyway. The assurances of a diplomat who had been so long out of circulation himself, and who had barely been floated again, were valueless without official backing for the bonds, and Elsesser had none. But he set to work and worried what friends he had in Paris, and connections were established there that carried the business into the inner circles of high finance and won a friend at Court in no less a patron than the Comte de Morny, the Emperor's brother, who consented, for a commission of thirty per cent, to promote the affair and to guarantee that the bonds would be honored by the Mexican Government.

Besides the private backing of M. de Morny, the official support of the Quai d'Orsay had also to be secured, however, and this was more difficult because of the guarded attitude toward bankers observed there. The favor of the Foreign Office did not follow automatically from that of M. de Morny, whose indiscretions had embarrassed the Emperor more than once, and as Walewski no longer presided over the department, a different approach was needed to induce the new Foreign Minister, M. de Thouvenel, who was personally incorruptible, to play host to so compromising an affair. The difficulty was adroitly turned, however. The failure of the bank had ruined a number of French depositors, for the most part small investors and charitable institutions whose rights were respectable and whose distress was pathetic, and on their behalf a petition was addressed to the Foreign Office to protect their claims and indemnify their losses with the Mexican assets of the firm. Presented in this light, as a legitimate credit and a national interest, which offered, furthermore, appreciable privileges for French commerce at the customs, the plea was accepted, and the Jecker bonds were included among the public claims which Saligny was instructed to settle with the Juarez government before recognizing it. M. de Thouvenel was an accomplished diplomat and a schooled courtier, and without examining too closely the premises of the amphitryonic affair, he covered himself with a provision that Saligny was to satisfy himself of the legitimacy of the claim before he pressed it. Legitimacy was an ambiguous word in the lexicon of diplomacy, but the services of a philologist were not needed to define it. The interpretation was left to M. de Saligny, and the application to his discretion, and he was empowered to impose recognition of French claims globally, if necessary, by a display of force—one of the usual naval demonstrations employed by creditor nations, of which M. de Gabriac had availed himself in the early days of the civil war—a plain indication that M. de Thouvenel understood the difficulty of negotiating so raw a bit of business.

The deal with M. de Morny was not closed until January 1861, but the affair had taken shape before Saligny left Paris the previous September, and he had contributed to its promotion. M. de Gabriac had made a tidy fortune of his own from his mission to Mexico and lost it in the failure of the bank, and his substitute was in duty bound to help his patron recoup it. *Noblesse oblige* was the more binding upon M. de Saligny that he was a genuine nobleman upon whose title none of the doubts that darkened that of M. de Gabriac could be cast. The Marquis was a man, moreover, of many and enterprising ideas; besides those which he shared with M. de Gabriac, he had his own. In addition to the bonds, the assets of the bank included several other possibilities which opened a large field for French enterprise—the gold mines of Sonora, which caught the fancy of M. de Morny, and the claims at Tehuantepec, which might attract the attention of the Emperor, whose interest in cutting a canal through Central America dated from his youth and was still an unrealized ambition among so many others of Louis Napoleon. By a fortunate coincidence, the Louisiana Tehuantepec Company had fallen into financial difficulties, Mr. Benjamin had come to Europe in 1860 to secure foreign backing for it, and M. de Saligny displayed his political flair in a memorandum that he addressed to the Foreign Office recommending, among other original ideas, that the French Government buy into the American enterprise. With a wealth of combinations at his command, he was in a position to make his connection with Mr. Benjamin serve the interests of France, of the bank, of M. de Morny, of Napoleon III, of the Mexican clericals, and of the Marquis de Saligny all at once; but this embarrassment of riches was purely mental, and his ideas still tentative, when he left France. The bonds were but one among many combinations, but they were the lever to move the others, and the omnibus business on which the success of his mission depended.

The hands of M. de Thouvenel having been washed, and those of M. de Morny greased, the final shaping of the affair rested in Saligny's hands. Between the ways of force and skill, his preference was pronounced, and no small skill was needed to handle a negotiation which not only saddled the debts of the vanquished on the victor, but transformed the agent of the bonds into their owner. For such was the assumption upon which the credit was founded. What began as a conversion of the public debt of a government that had fallen, ended in the conversion of a bank that had failed into the holder of a diplomatic claim against the legitimate government that raised the public debt of Mexico by eighty-six million francs. Baldly stated, those were the facts, and very light fingers indeed were needed to pick the pockets of Mexico publicly. The delicacy of the question was betrayed by the delicacy of M. de Saligny. Promiscuity was his sole asset, and on his passage through Veracruz, he discussed the general claims of his mission with the government; and finding its members, much to his surprise, moderate and reasonable men, he reported to Paris that an understanding could easily be reached with them. Agreeably surprised, he was accommodating in turn and deferred the main question. On his arrival in the capital he received a petition from five hundred bondholders soliciting his support for their claims; he advised them to be patient and to give the government time to settle itself; but he was not allowed to temporize long. In January the deal with Morny was closed in Paris, and in February he received orders from the Quai d'Orsay to act. He broached the question with Zarco, demanding recognition of the bonds in principle and leaving the amount open to discussion and adjustment. The principle that the debts of one government were binding on its successor, regardless of the origin either of the government or the obligation, was sanctioned by international law, both deriving their legitimacy from their recognition; but from the outset he met with a resistance no less firm for being polite and evasive, and snags in what were merely preliminary sparrings tried his skill and his temper severely.

It was amid these initial difficulties that the incident of the Sisters of Charity occurred. Addled by the difficulty of hatching the Jecker affair, and heated by the offense to the Sisters, he exploded. His interference in favor of the nuns was unauthorized and his hectoring sheer bluster, but he was in a huff and, infuriated by opposition on both questions, he applied to the one the arbitrary powers with which he was empowered to handle the other; and the result favored his negotiation with the government. The effrontery with which he browbeat Zarco on behalf of his clerical clients fostered the presumption that he was acting with the same license in championing them as in defending the Jecker bonds, and that in both cases he enjoyed the support of his government. The deduction was deceptive, but one thing was added to another, and though two and two make four in arithmetic, in the science of inference they usually make five. The temper of the public was highly impressionable, and the Legation of France was regarded as the center of all the intrigues and conspiracies against the Constitutional government; and henceforth Saligny was treated not merely with the seriousness due to a suspect, but with the respect due to a diplomat who apparently held two of the controlling forces of his country in his hands, as indeed he did. The interests of the bank and the Church were distinct, but he was able to combine them, and the combination of clerical protection and a financial offensive was a powerful form of pressure to apply to an unsettled government; but suspicion not being an exact science, the sum of the two still made four and their confusion five.

Benefiting by that misconception, the Minister pressed his advantage, but he made small progress in the financial offensive after the alert sounded by the press for his protection of the Sisters of Charity. Suspicion spread, and the attention which he attracted by that scandal shifted to the Jecker transaction, of which the public now became aware. The press was silent but watchful. A discreet warning was raised by the *Siglo,* which changed the subject for the worse and featured the Mirés scandal on its front page. This affair involved the ruin of a Parisian financier cornered by the rival firm of Rothschild, and with him of so many of his highly placed protectors that the Imperial Government was rocked by revelations of corruption close to the Throne and compelled not only to prosecute him, but to appease public opinion by restoring the right of criticism to the Corps Législatif and a measure of free speech to the controlled press. While the *Siglo* spoke in parables, and Zarco in adjournments, it was not easy to crack the Jecker question, and nothing had been settled when, in mid-March, Saligny again became reckless and lost his head in an excess of discretion. He recognized the Juarez government without a guarantee to guard his judgment, much as McLane had done when he took the same step in 1859 led on by the belief that the sale of Lower California would follow, and with no different results. Far from facilitating the negotiation, official recognition deprived the Minister of a normal form of pressure, and one that he was directed to use; and after suffering the same delays and evasions after as before it, he reverted to the only form of coercion that remained and prepared the Quai d'Orsay for extraordinary measures.

The state of the country and the stability of the government were delineated in a succession of pessimistic reports. "In the state of anarchy, or rather of social dissolution, prevailing in this wretched country, it is very difficult to foresee what turn conditions will take," he wrote in April. "Only one thing seems to me certain, the impossibility of remaining *in statu quo*. Everything indicates that we are approaching a new revolution. In these circumstances, it seems to me absolutely necessary that we should have on the coast of Mexico a material force sufficient, whatever happens, to provide protection for our interests." He did not refer to the bonds. For obvious reasons, the subject was too sore to mention. He had just received a reprimand from the Quai d'Orsay for his conduct in the incident of the Sisters of Charity, reminding him that the French Legation in Mexico was established for the protection of French interests and not for those of any religious community whatsoever. Charity beginning at home, however, he was lectured with the indulgence due to a French gentleman who had allowed his chivalry to get the better of his judgment and was scolded considerately. The reprimand was confidential, and, to save his face, it was accompanied by an official letter approving his behavior, which he could show, if necessary, to cover his conduct of the Jecker affair; and at the same time he received peremptory orders to conclude it.

Thus spurred and tamed, he presented Zarco with an ultimatum in May. His language, remarkable alike for its frankness and moderation, made ample amends for the insolence and bluff with which he had threatened to break with him for the sake of the Sisterhood in February. For three months he had been hoping for the settlement of "an important question in which the honor and interests of France are gravely involved," he admitted. "I refer to the question of the Jecker bonds, the only one that can raise serious difficulties between our two countries, and prevent France from giving free rein to her friendly intentions toward Mexico. Unfortunately, this hope has been disappointed. I cannot take it upon myself to postpone any longer the execution of the orders of the Emperor's Government. Nevertheless, before notifying you officially, I have wished to give you another proof of the conciliatory spirit by which I myself am animated; and, accordingly, prompted by a sentiment that I trust you will appreciate, I beg you to inform me without delay of the definite intentions of your government." It was almost an apology, maybe an appeal, and certainly a challenge to Zarco's charity; but the only effect was a tentative understanding, or misunderstanding, which induced Saligny to believe that he had scored a point and allowed him to report progress to Paris. Zarco consented, implicitly admitting the principle, to discuss the amount to which the bank was actually entitled to be reimbursed for the bonds actually sold, the interest paid on them, and the advances made to the Miramon government. This concession represented an insignificant sum and a diplomatic accommodation worth some consideration, but it fell far short of the total credit for the bond issue; and as the resistance of the government to the whole claim remained unbroken, no substantial advance had been made, and it was clear to M. de Saligny that nothing would float the unsold bonds but a naval demonstration. By the beginning of May there was no doubt of it: the legitimate claims of his government had been settled to the satisfaction of his superiors, the only hitch was the Jecker affair, and he was still a diplomat *manqué*. Intimidation had been tried unsuccessfully. The situation was, in a word, serious.

Serious was the word for it for other reasons as well. So far the French Minister had had the field to himself, but in May his British colleague, Sir Charles Lennox Wyke, arrived, and the unbroken tradition of British diplomacy in Mexico made it doubtful whether he would prove a collaborator or a competitor. With Mathew Saligny was on bad terms. In his case there was no doubt. Everything divided them—racial antipathy, religious tolerance, but above all the Jecker bonds, for the recognition of that credit threatened to wipe out the small percentage of customs revenue still available for foreign claims and to deprive the government of the resources necessary to satisfy British indemnities. Mathew was of inferior diplomatic rank, but he still doubled for Russell and Palmerston, and in the protection of preferred claims he had the advantage of having recognized the Liberal government, for which he had developed a pronounced partiality ever since its success, one month before Saligny. His conditions were accepted without question—arrears on the debt service, indemnity for the plunder of the *conducta* by Degollado and of the British Legation by Miramon, although the validity of the last was as questionable as the Jecker bonds, and awkward questions were being asked about it in Paris.

Ocampo, before he left office, had caught an echo of them from his friend in the Legation there, who tipped him off to some trade secrets. "You are not sharp enough to explain *why* that money was kept on deposit in Mexico and in the British Chancery, while *conductas* were leaving for Veracruz and when the remittance of currency to London was advantageous to the rightful owners, our pesos being quoted at that time at a premium as high as ninepence. I will tell you. Mr. Mathew made them sweat and worked them in his own way, when Mexico was so short of currency and loans were so high and speculation so fruitful with individuals and with the Apostolic faction. Familiar as he was with that faction, Mr. Mathew gave them a chance to lay hands on the deposit. This is how the business of indemnization is done, like that of speculation, and if no honor is derived from it, undoubtedly a very high rate of profit is received. I know also that he gave Señor Degollado to understand that he could seize the *conducta,* provided, of course, that he respected English property." Such imputations naturally could not be proved, but they gained currency from many known precedents in the diplomatic game, where nothing was above question but one thing: the business of indemnization was legitimate in English hands, and whether those of Mathew were clean or not could not be judged, since, unlike Saligny, he was not obliged to show them.

English favor offered the government a certain security in dealing with the French Minister. "The touchstone is England," wrote the same friend to Ocampo, "because of her intimate relations with the United States, and because, if she wishes, France will not attack us. In American affairs the reverse of what happens in Europe occurs: over there English influence will predominate, contrary to what takes place in Europe, where Napoleon III is not willing to yield an inch." English favor, however, was contingent upon the financial responsibility of the Mexican Government, and when the new British Minister arrived in Mexico at the beginning of May, the solvency of the government was a matter of urgent doubt, affecting the interests of both the creditor Powers.

3

THE end of the war had by no means relieved the chronic penury in which it was fought and against which the government was called to contend as soon as it was established in the capital. The millions of the *conducta* had carried the last stage of the war to victory, but Gonzalez Ortega was penniless when he won the battle of Calpulalpam, and the burden was laid down barely in time to avert a financial collapse. The days of expedients were over, and the first and most pressing problem of peace was a fundamental financial reorganization indispensable to the consolidation of success. Saligny himself realized it when he advised the Jecker creditors to give the government time to settle itself. So did the press and the public, but in the first flush of triumph attention was distracted from the gravity of the situation by the celebration of victory, the preferred claims of self-congratulation, the pursuit of the guilty, and, above all, by the confidence that, formidable as the problem was after three years of civil war and forty years of hereditary insolvency, the government had ample securities with which to meet it in 1861. The problem was gigantic, but so were the guarantees of confiscated Church property, and so was the financial genius of Lerdo de Tejada. Both these securities were incommensurable, however, and hypothetic.

Lerdo de Tejada was not in the government. He had left it to nurse his health and his prospects as a candidate in the coming presidential elections, which were slated for June and which were a live issue in January. In February he died. The campaign continued posthumously in the apotheosis with which the press lamented his loss. His reputation flared up, towering, immense, incomparable, and with overwhelming unanimity papers of every shade of opinion echoed the void he had left behind him. "The giant of Reform," "the most vigorous and practical mind on which the revolution could count," "the personification of progressive initiative," "the author of the Reform Laws," "the only man who could understand and formulate the idea of our revolution" —a litany of devout voices vying with one another acclaimed, in a chorus of mourning, the memory of a man whose reputation was secure, because it had never been tested. The credit of Lerdo rested on the nationalization of Church property, and great as the value of that measure was in destroying the economic strength of the enemy, its merit as a constructive contribution to national progress lay less in its conception, which was common to many minds, than in its social application and practical administration; and he died just in time to save a reputation which remained mythical.

A gloomy foreboding filled the columns of the obituaries. "In hours of solemn intimacy," wrote one of his friends, "I heard from his lips profound ideas for the work of regeneration. I heard also some of his hopes and his fears for the future of the country. With regret I must say that the latter outweighed the former, for he saw what was happening to the Reform and to the invaluable opportunity definitely to settle the peace of the Republic. He saw that the abundant capital of the clergy would be consumed without benefit to the many and without profit even in producing revenue for the nation and amortizing its enormous debt. He saw that without establishing an adequate system of finance society could not rest on a solid foundation nor peace be the fruit of so much blood shed and so many sacrifices made. What Lerdo foresaw has come to pass, what he conceived and studied for the hour of construction has not been done, because he was deprived of the participation which was his due on the day of triumph; and what the country expected, what the great party of Lerdo imagined when he would come to power, whether by electoral suffrage or the choice of the President, has been lost for ever. . . ." But the opportunity to make political capital of his passing was not lost. "What shall we do now? What direction shall we take? Who is the man to guide us?" the indictment continued. Lerdo was in the grave, and so was the government that had dropped him. "As for the man who will replace Lerdo in the great conceptions which he held for the good of his country, since we have neither the wish nor the ability to indicate him, let events discover him, let them unearth and reveal what we need, for thinking men cannot admit the theory of indispensable men. An inexorable law sends mankind the men whose names it reveres."

The burden was shouldered by Prieto. Returning to the post that he had vacated in Veracruz in favor of the expert, he faced a cruel comparison. An expert alone could penetrate and disentangle, let alone solve, the problems that had accumulated for two generations in the Treasury. Prieto had served two terms in that den of confusion and was familiar with its routine: the perennial deficits could be juggled, the legacy of the civil war could be managed, the makeshifts, the mortgages, the detritus of dead bonds and spurious conversions, the litter of forced loans and chronic default, the long wreckage of a struggle that had drained every resource and reduced both sides to highway robbery, could be repaired while the hope of an issue lay ahead. But what could neither be disguised nor redeemed was the monstrous delusion that led him into the maze and through the toils of the labyrinth to his final confusion. The saving measure to which he looked for relief from ruinous expedients was itself an expedient and the most ruinous of all. The fabulous wealth of the Church was a fable, a mirage luring him on and eluding his reach; the enormous resources of expropriation were an arid waste, guarded by glittering grit. Before he could reach them, he had first to clear away a rank tangle of conflicting claims arising out of past purchases made under Lerdo's original law of disamortization in 1856, their cancellation by the Clerical government, and subsequent adjudications under the final decree of 1859 —an overgrowth so thick and stubborn that his entire tenure of office was spent in coping with it—and then . . . then . . . He went no further, for as he burrowed he unearthed an appalling discovery.

The springs of fresh wealth had shrunk, dried up, disappeared—no one knew how or where. The causes were as elusive as the flight was certain. The wealth of the Church had always been legendary and incommensurable, and it had steadily waned as prospectors approached it. It was a public mystery when Mora valued it at 180 millions in 1838, and ever since the eye of the first reformer menaced it, the mystery had thickened and the millions thinned. In 1858, at the start of the civil war, it was roughly estimated at 120 millions; at the close of the war, it was completely inestimable, concealed by confusion and revealing only an incalculable reduction. Part of it had been dissipated to pay for the war, first by the Clerical and then by the Constitutional government; part of it had been buried by the financial subterfuges of agents of the clergy; part of it had been plundered and consumed by the Liberal forces; part of it had been converted by speculators into paper, which, subject to litigation and continually discounted as it changed hands, depreciated steadily. The whole had perhaps been overrated; but the sum of the parts was a tremendous deception, and none of these reasons accounted for a reduction of fifty to sixty per cent in the resources on which the government counted to establish itself soundly. The fact remained that, with untold wealth at its command, the State was compelled to borrow at the rate of four dollars for one to meet its immediate needs, to resort to the same shifts as during the war, and to dispose of valuable properties piecemeal for a pittance or in batches for a song to cover its running expenses. The realization of its assets resembled a proceedings in bankruptcy rather than the liquidation of national wealth.

Politically, the deterioration was even more disastrous. Depreciation of Church property was due in large measure to differences between the estimated value in normal times and in the adverse season in which nationalization was negotiated, and to the reluctance of the devout to incur excommunication in acquiring it, but principally to the operations of speculators, for the most part foreigners, who rushed in where the native feared to tread, took off the curse and cornered the market, holding their investments for a clear title and a quick turnover, and prolonging the unproductive process; and though these conditions were transient, the results were lasting. The needs of the day devoured those of the morrow. The penury of the government, the need of selling short, the prodigal cheapening of Church property, and the facilities for speculation combined to sterilize the social reform which a redistribution of national wealth was intended to serve; and what actually occurred was a transfer of title from one propertied and unproductive class to another, without relieving the masses or invigorating the national economy, while the government functioned as a broker, squandering its security for a fugitive fee. If the clergy had laid a curse on the sacrilegious hands that violated their treasure—as they had—the result was calculated to satisfy them. And the curse fell not on a financial wizard like Lerdo, who might have exorcised it, but on an amateur who succumbed to it. Prieto floundered manfully for four months, losing ground, losing credit, losing hope, and when he was finally convinced that the great lever of the civil war was a broken wrench, and that the sacrifices, the agonies, the massacres, the concessions, the betrayals it cost had been wasted, he lost heart and announced the imminence of national bankruptcy.

From so crushing a sentence common sense recoiled, refusing to believe and seeking every explanation to evade it, but betraying alarm by its very defenses. The press took a less serious, because a more personal, view of the slump. Prieto was attacked for spreading panic fears, which were counterrevolutionary since they undermined public confidence, and antipatriotic since they affected foreign credit, and which were therefore unfounded. "It is a lie that the country is perishing of inanition," wrote Manuel Zamacona, the new editor of the *Siglo*. "The country is not so much poor as impoverished; the sources of public wealth are not exhausted but choked; as soon as the hand of power

applies itself to releasing them, they will begin to flow immediately.
. . ." The Ministry was at fault—an easy mark—and imputations were
raised, if not of corruption, of incompetence—familiar and reassuring
features of Mexican officialdom. The probity of the Minister was unquestioned, but he was taken to task on every other score. He was
honest, too honest; he was hazed for the innocence with which as a
novice he exposed the veteran vices of his department, and forced to
run the gantlet of the most fearful scourging and the most terrified
tongue-lashing. He was berated for abusing public trust as a poet and
letting his imagination run away with him as a minister. Manuel
Zamacona attacked the secrecy with which he conducted the mysteries
of his department and scoffed at the "Trappist silence" broken only
by the ritual wail of "Brethren, we must all die!" that rose from it.
And when Prieto broke his silence and produced his accounts, the
party whip fell on them and plastered the front pages with triumphant
and itemized evidence of extravagance and mismanagement.

As a poet, Prieto was, by his own admission, a loose, careless, and
incorrect writer, and as a public bookkeeper he was convicted of the
same faults. Preferred claims and obsolete debts settled unsystemati-
cally; back bills for rebellion in 1856 when the government could not
meet its running costs in 1861; senescent senatorial salaries honored at
random; lavish indemnities for minor injuries while war pensions were
unpaid; a cool million a month for the army; exorbitant printers' bills;
press subsidies that the government had sworn to abolish; fat commissions for the denunciation of Church property; thirty-four thousand
pesos for the location of treasure not even concealed; twenty thousand
Mexican dollars for "the precious revelation that the Cathedral contained tapers and reliquaries subsequently sold for a song"; hundreds
of thousands for "various creditors" and unspecified sundries—etcetera
and etcetera to the crack of doom, detail consuming the core, a literary
vice fatally indulged in finance, wrecking the writer and leaving his
critics aghast. Such a picture of prodigality and disorder, incoherence
and favoritism, revealed, if not outright irregularity, a lack of planning
and system that would have been scandalous had it not been customary. But the times were not normal, and though Prieto defended himself in a prolonged controversy with pleas as sound as they were irrelevant—bad debts, Jecker bonds, congenital chaos—he was obliged
to resign. Clearing his integrity by admitting his incompetence, he
escaped with nothing to his name but a reputation shopworn and
damaged, and retired from public service as badly bruised as Ocampo
had been by the McLane treaty or Degollado by trading with the
enemy. The revolution consumed its own with relentless rapacity and
was hungry still for fresh victims; for the specter of national bankruptcy raised by each of its chosen defenders in turn was not laid by
plucking the poet.

The dismissal of Prieto minimized the danger, but not for long. His sucessor was Mata, who risked his name for a few informal weeks in the most treacherous and important post in the government. The antithesis of Prieto—"prosaic as a textbook, positive as an equation, logical as a syllogism," someone said of him—and certainly not prone to nervous panic or imaginative exaggerations, and no less honest, Mata fared no better. And as suspicion spread that conditions, and not man, were the culprit, the alarm revived and the warnings of Prieto were seriously heeded. What more could Lerdo himself have done? Lerdo had done it; he had died. Prieto did more. Before abandoning the maddening struggle, he left his critics four methods of dealing with it— sensible methods of loosening the growing incubus and taming the popular unrest, which, passing from one channel to another, now revived revolutionary bitterness and turned the latent terror against the Treasury.

The prescriptions were all based on reduction of four national liabilities: reduction of the foreign debt service, of dividends on the internal debt, of the army, and of the states to Federal authority. Of these the first offered the easiest relief because it was the heaviest burden on the budget, and the most difficult problem because of the pressure that secured it, and hence it was the one on which despair instinctively fastened. The foreign debt service absorbed almost the entire revenue of the customs, which was mortgaged in its totality in the ports of the Pacific, while at Veracruz the scale had risen from forty-eight per cent in 1856 to eighty-five per cent in 1861, and the remaining fifteen per cent was the subject of competing claims, among them the Jecker bonds. The pressure was throttling, and the critics of Prieto were the first to embrace the most desperate of his proposals. Zamacona led off with a long and eloquent article in the Siglo, feeling out native and foreign opinion. "The public Treasury," he wrote, borrowing the language of the poet, "has become something like the labyrinth of antiquity, guarded by a monster; the monster is the foreign debt that has closed every avenue leading to the land of reconstruction. The Republic was born like those children who bring into the world an organic ailment, the development of which makes it impossible for them to live. The debt that we began to contract in the days when we were born to political life has grown into a parasitical excrescence that chokes us, drains us, and destroys all regularity in the administrative functions of the government. Not a single dollar coming from the maritime customs reaches the general Treasury. It could be said with complete truth, as the Minister of Finance has just explained, that the coffers of the nation are in those vessels that come periodically to collect virtually the total product of our customs, assigned to cover our diplomatic engagements. Why should we suppose our foreign creditors incapable of conceding us a truce indispensable to life and health? We are not afraid that a false scrupulousness on the part of our government, or an inexorable severity on the part of the friendly Powers, will prevent the realization of this idea, which would be the salvation not only of our Republic, but also of all those who have any claim against it." And to make quite clear that it was no sentimental appeal, he remarked casually, "What will they gain by being inexorable and by killing, so to speak, the goose that lays the golden eggs?"

The idea prospered, and before long it figured in political forecasts and was propagated by rumors breathing as freely as the public they fed. Officially it was ignored, and the government gave it no countenance: for Zamacona was not yet a minister, and though the press was a ruling, it was an irresponsible, power. The nemesis that prompted Prieto to compete with Lerdo had produced a dangerous nostrum, as popular as it was prohibited, and as tempting as it was provocative. Zarco was too badly embarrassed by his negotiations with the French Minister to feel him out any further. The broaching of the Jecker bonds had already produced plain symptoms of public gagging to which M. de Saligny remained deaf; and the French Legation naturally ignored those of a general convulsion.

M. de Saligny, however, was the least risk. The British Legation was the gravest. The English debt being the largest, and English influence the heavy weight in determining the reaction of foreign opinion, it was there that the question was explored. In that quarter the possibility of a compromise was considered. The parable of Zamacona and the gospel of Mathew agreed up to a point; the necessity of some degree of accommodation was recognized by Mathew, and he prepared his government for it. "The bondholders might save their capital by submitting to a temporary suspension of interest," he advised London, "and the establishment of a more equitable tariff, which the government are pledged to me to urge upon Congress, may lay down a better basis of revenue." But he qualified his advice. "Mexico," he added, "whatever her distress, should at least commence at home, and the holders of the immense internal debt should be the first to suffer for the ruin their own folly has caused or abetted. I much fear that the Republic has not yet produced men of sufficient energy and honor to adopt this course, unsustained by some foreign interposition. The effort will always be made to make the foreigner the chief sufferer from the undoubtedly bankrupt state of the country." The appeal to his charity satisfied by that compromise, he laid the problem of public mendicancy in more responsible hands. It was his last report and he was relieved of further responsibility by the arrival of the new British Minister.

In London Sir Charles Lennox Wyke was an expert on Latin American affairs, having served in Honduras and other spheres of British influence in Central America. He had lost his health there, and it was during a prolonged convalescence in Europe that he was appointed, at the same time as Saligny, to serve in the proposed mediation of the Powers in Mexico. Of that scheme all that remained was the understanding that the two Ministers should collaborate, and though the situation had changed when Wyke arrived there a year after his appointment, it had changed so much for the worse that it provoked their spontaneous co-operation. With the practiced eye of an expert, Wyke took in the situation at a glance, and three weeks later he wrote a despatch, containing his first and final impressions of Mexico, which reflected the views of Mathew and Saligny alike. From Mathew he borrowed his worst fears of financial collapse, and from Saligny his most sinister prognostics of social dissolution, and the blend was an ominous diagnosis of a country in the last stages of decay, for which he recommended the same prescription as Saligny. In the meanwhile the trial balloon launched by Zamacona rose, wafted from hand to hand, and drifted buoyantly toward the higher spheres of a government beset by internal troubles.

4

THE government was in the last stages of the election campaign and drifting rapidly toward its dissolution at the polls without any visible means of support. One by one its props fell away. The agitation of the financial question profoundly undermined public confidence and cast a pall over the cabinet, and the President himself was taken to task for his provoking serenity. "The President is a rock, nothing moves him, nothing crushes him, he hears nothing, and hence he is good for nothing"—the tone was typical of the restlessly radical wing of the press, where grievances were being accumulated against the day of election. "Once the President stops signing pardons, supporting the employees of the reaction, holding family talks with his ministers, and misguiding his government to the best of his ability, no further reason remains for his being President of the Republic. Ah! how sad to see a whole people groaning under the burden of a Supreme Magistrate, whose sole title to power today is the one he derived from his seat on the Supreme Court! We would gladly give a thousand presidents of the Supreme Court for one man who represented the Revolution!"

The search went on blindly. It was a measure of the panic by which the public was stampeded by the announcement of national bankruptcy that popular feeling turned against the entire cabinet, although the cabinet had been packed with trusted names—Zarco, Mata, Ramirez, Ortega—guarantees, every one of them, of revolutionary energy. They all suffered from the same misfortune. And in that group there was one who could not bear unpopularity. Gonzalez Ortega was a candidate for the Presidency. The death of Lerdo had removed his one serious competitor, for though Juarez was standing for re-election, he was hardly reckoned by Ortega as a rival or even a handicap. Like Lerdo, Ortega had developed the habit of running the affairs of his department independently and of ignoring the President, politely or impolitely; once, on being asked whether he had secured approval for an order, he was heard to reply, "I have ordered his hundred pesos a day to be sent him, and that is all that interests him."

Idolized by the army, revered by the revolutionary clubs, profoundly respected by the press and the public, the hero of the civil war now found himself involved in the rising unpopularity that spread through every branch of the government and that barely stopped short of the War Office; and his heel was touched. The time had clearly come for a test of his political strength. He demanded the dismissal of two of his colleagues, Zarco and Ramirez, because of their popular disrepute, and when Juarez refused to sustain him, resigned himself. His exit was noisy, and a long shadow fell across the front pages of the papers, haunted by the dread of a relapse into the traditional disorders of the past. But the threat was cast by a shadow: the mutiny was purely ministerial, and with a single exception the press rallied to the President. That exception was a paper that demanded that the cabinet be ousted by force, and it merely multiplied the protests of the rest, which closed their ranks to deplore the judgment of a hero who could cheapen the glory of Jesus Gonzalez Ortega by catering "to a few shouts from a group of boys," which he mistook for public opinion. Jesus hastened to agree in an open letter, professing his respect for legality and the sanctity of the civil authority, and Gonzalez Ortega deplored the hasty conclusions of the press and the baseless fear of which he was a victim. His was no vulgar ambition: he prided himself on his principles, he was a civilian at heart, he was sound. The denial was accepted with relief, and the heel was planted firmly once more on the pedestal to which the press hastened to restore him.

Though the alarm subsided as quickly as it arose, it was sharp while it lasted. "We see in this new vicissitude a new reason for foreigners to say 'Mexicans are incorrigible,' a new blow to public confidence, and hence to commerce and every useful enterprise," Zamacona commented—a warning well timed, since M. de Saligny was systematically unsettling foreign credit with predictions of the approach of a new revolution. The air was cleared by the crisis, and in the relief that followed there was a general appreciation of what the revolution had actually gained. Henceforth some things were impossible; the unholy spirit of militarism had been mastered. "The incidents that have occupied the capital for the last three days are perhaps the last manifestation that the military will make in Mexican politics," Zamacona ventured to predict, and he paid homage to the President, who, he declared, "in this affair, as in all the crises through which the revolution passed in its militant phase, has shown the most firm and enlightened faith in the vocation of the civil power and its ability to dominate the policy of the country in the future, despite all the obstacles which the military arm might raise."

The real significance of the incident lay in the reading of public opinion, and the substantial advance that it registered in the rising level and stability of the revolution was ample cause for congratulation. The fact that on the eve of a presidential election, the long-awaited test of the relative popularity of the civil and military powers produced nothing more serious than a ministerial crisis, settled by general agreement in favor of the former, was recognized, even by foreigners familiar with the customs of the country, as a guarantee for the future. The future, to be sure, was foreshortened and focused by the coming elections, but the personal prestige of the candidates was subordinated to the cardinal principles with which they were identified in the public mind. If Lerdo was hallowed as the financial genius of the Reform, and Ortega as its military savior, Juarez was respected as the incarnation of its social stamina—the least visible and most vital of the sinews on which its survival depended—and the recognition of his preeminence was a proof of political maturity that augured well even for an unlimited future.

The cult of heroes, however, was an essential part of any revolution and a stubborn survival of the civil war. Besides the dictation of the successful soldier, Juarez had also to master the appeal of the fallen hero of the war—a far more dangerous rival for popular favor. When Ortega resigned from the War Office, the post which he vacated was offered to Degollado, but as the tender was made confidentially, he refused it. What he wanted was not reconciliation, but a trial and public acquittal or condemnation, and as the postponement of that test had worn his patience raw, he was driven finally to do justice to himself. Attacked in the course of the presidential campaign by a supporter of Juarez, and harassed by what he considered the political exploitation of his case, he wheeled on the pack at his heels and turned on the President himself as a party to his persecution. "How is it possible," he exclaimed in a protest that was carried uncut by the press, "that His Excellency the President can remain a cold spectator of so many insults to one who was his most loyal supporter; who saved him from being forgotten and disowned in the interior; who refused to follow him to safety within the walls of Ulua, although he held no military command; and who never once shielded himself behind shutters during the six days that Veracruz was bombarded? What! Does disgrace deserve no respect? misfortune no consideration? and helplessness no protection?" All the gall which he had swallowed without complaint welled up at last in disgust of a martyrdom of which he was weary. "Well or ill, I have served the national cause and proved, even in my errors, my right intentions and my zeal to be of service to the cause of my country," he declared. "I expect no gratitude, gentlemen, or public appreciation of my services, for I knew when I assumed command of the Constitutional army that in all lands and at all times services to one's country have encountered only envious souls and thankless hearts. The greater the merit, the greater the ingratitude: such is the weakness of humanity. But I believe that I have the right to expect that the verdict of my judges be awaited, that I be allowed to live in peace, that I be forgotten, and that the grace be granted me that Diogenes begged—not to be deprived of the sun."

The biting reproach cast an ugly reflection on the President. Degollado called him coward, he accused him of ingratitude, he taxed him with callous indifference, he shamed him for feeling no duty of generosity, decency, or ordinary humanity and fair dealing—no motive was too mean, no slur too small, to belittle and blacken him. Public sympathy was with Degollado, and he knew it: popular judgment had settled his case out of court; only official sanction was withheld—why? He hinted at the reason in a plaintive aside. "If by any chance my moans find an echo in some generous breast, let him pity me in secret, but never dare to let his voice of sympathy be heard: no, let him not dare, for the men of fortune, strength, and power are against me," he sighed, dropping his defense in a tone to which the public was highly susceptible in the campaign literature of the day. The reproach barely stopped short of arraignment and was all the more crushing for being arrested: no words could have implied more plainly that the President was unwilling to risk a reversal of his verdict on the eve of elections.

The inference was conveyed by the complaint and confirmed by the attack; between the lines of both the public read the familiar charge of machine politics; and the charge, fraught with the full weight and fatal popularity of pain, called the whole justice of Juarez into question. While the Degollado affair remained unsettled, the question it raised could not be begged, and it was never more trying than at that moment. The real question was not why his case had not been brought into court, but why he was to be tried at all. If revolutionary justice required his dismissal, and military discipline his court-martial in a time of stress, what purpose was served, or what motive, when the emergency was over and the war won, in prosecuting a man who was guilty at most of misjudgment, whose error remained abortive, and whose lapse was outweighed by his services? Expediency was justified by its timing; what was necessary yesterday was excessive today; all justice was relative, revolutionary justice was dictated by circumstances, and the circumstances having changed, human justice demanded a higher equity; and it was that justice that was now demanded of Juarez. He had made an example of Degollado—but for what crime? The issue was uncertain, the offense controversial, and the elementary right of self-defense could not be deferred indefinitely without reflecting on his judge. The charge was reversed. Why was Degollado still disgraced? For his own weakness or for that of his case? Was that his real crime? Was he an example of the vindictiveness of the war toward its own champions and the bitterness which it bred among its best sons? Such were the searching questions raised by the delays of the law, and Degollado himself had no doubt of the answer. Persecuted on the presumption of guilt and prosecuted only by the suspension of trial, hounded, without protection but his own pathos, and surfeited with selflessness, he felt himself intolerably wronged and was, in fact, irreconcilable; and when the offer to reinstate him in office was made *sub rosa,* he spurned private satisfaction and held out relentlessly for his public rehabilitation. Although he studiously avoided politics, his case became a political issue, and in one state he was nominated for the Presidency and unanimously elected on a protest vote. His sole title to power was his talent for misfortune, and had he carried more than one state the condition of the country would indeed have been desperate.

For the resuscitation of Degollado was dangerous politically precisely because it produced a sentimental reaction that belittled the President morally. The reasons for the delay of the trial, as Juarez informed the press, were those of legal routine—the transfer of the archives from Veracruz, the assembling of documents, the preparation of the case—but the explanation was unfortunate because it was pedestrian, and the fact that he was satisfied with it produced a painful impression, provoking those who accepted it as a pretext and distressing those who believed it. The worst of it was that it was true. The administration of justice was clogged—the confusion and inefficiency that paralyzed that branch of government defied the most strenuous efforts to reform it and forced Ramirez to resign—but the case of Degollado was not one of ordinary routine. To be slow in circumstances so fatal to the accused was to warrant the belief that it was not the way, but the will, that was wanting to clear him, and the meanest motives were attributed to the President by his detractors. He was accused of aiding and abetting the abuse of a fallen hero, of burying a reputation that menaced his own, and of sealing a case to save an election. The effect of letting the case rest was to convert it into a political trial, and the imputations to which it gave rise were the penalty of its perfunctory conduct. If the failure of Juarez to realize what was expected of him revealed his limitations as a politician, his indifference to such considerations guaranteed his integrity as a magistrate, however, and that was all that mattered to Juarez himself. His justice was impersonal, unaffected by veering moods or changing conditions. If conditions changed, so did persons. Witness Degollado—an unfortunate example of that fact. Would he have ruined himself if men were the same under all circumstances? Was he the man now that he was then? Would the saint have defended himself as the sinner did? He did too much justice to himself not to make the angels weep and the judicious grieve. He weakened his own case by luxuriating in his woes; and the worst of it was that he could not see that he harmed no one but himself by nursing his grievances, that he cheapened his glory by gushing against disgrace, that he cheated compassion by self-pity, that he dishonored by chastening himself like a *meretrix publica,* and that he was turning the fallen hero of the civil war into its heroine. In this phase he was not a serious embarrassment to the President. Men had to be at their best to challenge him. With the same firmness with which he resisted the dictation of Ortega, he ignored the agitation in favor of Degollado, trusting in both cases to the common sense of his public to prove the maturity of their judgment and to hold puerile appeals of hero-worship in place and sentimental impulses in political check.

It was a great deal to expect of any public on the eve of an election. In the course of the campaign the recent past was revived, the civil war was recapitulated, and Juarez himself was faced with heroic comparisons, while the public was torn between conflicting loyalties of principles and persons. Against Ortega he was supported as the personification of the civil power, but it was the principle that triumphed far more than the man, and the prompt submission of Ortega restored the prestige of the soldier with fresh might. Here the rival claims of incorruptible principle and personal glamour appeared to be satisfied in a single man; the rare combination had perhaps been found at last—perhaps, for the proof depended on the process of elimination and the elections were the laboratory—but he might be the blend, and he enjoyed two great advantages over his competitor. Ortega at his best was the hero of a hypothesis and Juarez was a habit. The familiar portrait of the President, everyone knew it, it was a stereotype, unaffected by changing conditions. It neither faded nor gained with familiarity. It was typed for all time, without the subtle modulations of life; it was set once and for all by the war, without graduation or degree by the end of his term in power.

So his war record, reviewed by a paper that followed him from Veracruz to attend the test in the capital, was weighed once more, and the well-known score of his merits and shortcomings rehearsed, before the public went to the polls. "Señor Juarez has much claim to our sympathy," the scorekeeper conceded. "The abnegation of this man in suffering, the faith with which he displayed his image of authority every-where, the good intentions that inspired him, and other virtues that unfortunately are purely personal, had won our favor. This man, nevertheless, did not and does not meet the requirements of the revolution, and we may say that his elevation to the Presidency would be the ruin not merely of the democratic party but of the nation. Señor Juarez, so replete with domestic virtues, is unfortunately very deficient in political understanding and can be accepted only as the representative of society, not its ruler. As a ruler, his actions are unfortunately not open to doubt: his tortuous management, his slight tact, and his obstinacy in sustaining the contrary of what the people want, are very strong reasons for preventing his ascent to the Presidency. Alien to all the events that occurred during the struggle with the Reaction, he performed everywhere, but especially in Veracruz, the role of a mere partisan, receiving good news and bad together with his companions, without doing a thing to secure their success or to repair their defeat. The Liberal troops, losing or winning battles in the interior, maintained themselves practically unaided; inspired by their own enthusiasm and nourished by their own exertions, they saw in the Juarez government a mere principle of legality, not an active, intelligent, and protecting government. The name of Juarez was a banner for the revolution, not a man."

But disqualification added one deed to the undone for his final undoing: "He succeeded merely in producing the McLane treaty without deriving from it the desired resources, and incurring, on the contrary, the ridicule heaped on us by the Reaction for that negotiation. Don Benito Juarez, in sum, exhibits merely something good of which he is not the author, and much evil which owes its origin to his conduct. Such a man not only does not merit the place of first magistrate, but should occupy, on the contrary, the bench of the accused to be tried and punished as he deserves. . . . Señor Ortega," the scorekeeper concluded, "the democratic party, which chooses you today and proposes you for the Presidency, trusts that it will not be disappointed, and that you will not become, like Juarez, the butcher of your own people." The curse of Comonfort had not worked itself out yet, and Ortega gained by it. "You are young and full of noble and generous ambitions." To be Ortega was good; but better yet to be young. To be young amid so many hoary charges of ineptitude, which had hardened with time into the common cant of political controversy, was an inestimable advantage. Age could not stale the confirmed habit of those settled complaints, Juarez was still guilty, arch-guilty, of being Juarez, and as he did nothing even to secure his election, his conviction was confidently predicted by the good bettors. The best of Ortega, however, was still his ambition, and the worst of Juarez that everyone knew who he was. The issue was reduced to simple terms in a cartoon representing Archimedes, on the one hand, declaring, "Give me a point of leverage and I will move the world," and Juarez, on the other, proclaiming, with his hands behind his back, "Give me emergency powers and I will do *nothing!*"

Nevertheless, the onus of nonentity had been borne so long by the President that it weighed very little against the unknown, and by dint of repetition the persistent charge of negation had become itself an ineffectual negative. Something more positive appeared to be needed to annihilate a nobody who would not down, and as he continued to defy the laws of political gravity when the campaign drew to a close, something was done: Congress assembled, and a motion was made to impeach the President for treason. The negotiation of the American treaty was hung on his neck, and in a heated debate his friends came to his rescue. They were not many. Fortune and misfortune made friends easily, but no mean courage was needed, and a rare devotion, to champion mediocrity under a capital charge. That uncommon kind of heroism, however, was displayed by Zarco, who rose to his defense and turned the attack to account by shedding light on much that had remained dark in the vexed controversy.

Zarco had left the government and returned to his trade and was free to talk. Although he had not been one of the official family in 1859, he joined it in spirit and belonged to it by the best of all rights, being a militant civilian himself, and he recalled the conditions that had beset them all in 1859 when, as he said, Liberals had been less plentiful than they were now and the country had lain prostrate, overpowered by the Reaction within and blocked by the diplomatic league without. American recognition had been regarded at that time as a hope and an advantage, "the Liberal party expecting that the moral ascendancy of the neighboring Republic, its mercantile interest, and even its physical support might aid the national cause and hasten the triumph of right principles. Though this aspiration was general among the most patriotic and enlightened Liberals, there was one among them who did not share it, who openly refused to call foreign troops to our aid, whether they were of the regular army of the United States or volunteers who, on touching Mexican soil, would renounce their nationality and receive, at the close of the campaign, public lands on which to settle in recompense for their services to their adopted country. The man who thought this expedient contrary to the national dignity, the man who foresaw dangers to its independence in this extreme resource, who did not despair of the Mexican people, believing that alone and without foreign aid they were certain to reconquer their liberties, was the President of the Republic, and thanks to his stubborn and tenacious resistance then, the idea failed. . . . In like manner he combated every idea of loans if, in contracting them, there were any stipulations that involved large international agreements. . . . Señor Juarez earned from many of his friends then the epithets 'stubborn' and 'pertinacious,' and they were later repeated when with the same firmness he refused to accept conciliation with the reactionaries and the mediation of foreign Powers in the settlement of our internal questions. . . . We have said that the President was almost alone in rejecting ideas that were then held by many Liberals, and in saying this we give every man his due. Many military commanders declared that it was indispensable to engage foreign volunteers; some wanted officers as well as troops. Señor Lerdo de Tejada and Governor Zamora shared these ideas, which, we frankly admit, were ours as well, under those trying circumstances. In vain instances were made to the President, in vain the most studied precautions were proposed, so as not to compromise the independence or the dignity of the Republic, in vain the idea was combined with other projects, intertwining it with the need of colonization, or of realizing religious liberty, or of maintaining the nucleus of an armed force after the triumph for the pacification of the country. Señor Juarez rejected all these ideas; he differed with many even of his close friends; in his correspondence he always opposed the project, and, persevering in the struggle, events have justified him; and it is due to him that the Republic has overcome its oppressors without other aid than its own resources."

This testimony went far to clear the personal responsibility of the President, but it fell short of the mark. By analogy much could be argued; by inference, it was absurd to suppose that the man who was so careful not to compromise the independence of his country was so simple-minded as not to see the treasonable lien in the treaty, or, seeing, so faint-hearted as to submit to it and so foolish as to put his head into the noose. But the defense, adroit yet evasive, left the core of impeachment intact—the derelict danger, the deadly evidence of the treaty itself, the haunting treaty, the nightmare of yesterday, the trial of today, which returned to plague its inventors with all the fury of political persecution and which contained too much meat for the vultures to satisfy them with negative pleas of wrongs undone and extenuating circumstances—and on that score Zarco touched very lightly, admitting its vulnerability by begging the question with feeble apologies. "The text of the treaty, whatever may have been its tenor, is no ground for indicting the President of Mexico," he protested, "since it is well known that the right of introducing amendments and modifications exists until ratification is granted"; and "although great concessions were made to the United States," he pleaded, "not all the advantages which they sought were offered, as is proved by the fact that the convention was not approved by the American Senate." And attacking the author of the indictment and carrying the controversy into impalpable regions where no pursuit was possible, "How does Señor Aguirre know," he challenged, "how can the jury know, what were the intentions of Señor Juarez touching the McLane treaty, what modifications he would have proposed if the negotiation had been renewed, to what articles he would have refused his ratification? This simple question destroys all the charges and hopes so ardently voiced by some organs of the press that this incident would suffice to prevent the present holder of the Executive from ascending to the Constitutional Presidency of the Republic." Obviously it did nothing of the sort; but Zarco could do no more. Not having been one of the official family at Veracruz, his testimony was secondhand, and he left the brunt of defense to those who were in a position to know the whole truth, and above all to the man who, as the closest friend and partner of the President, had most interest in protecting his good name. "We are sure that Señor Don Melchor Ocampo," he concluded, "will not let this occurrence pass unnoticed, and that with the frankness that characterizes him he will clarify all the facts."

Congress gave the President a vote of confidence, but the discussion of the treaty remained on the order of the day. The presence of Ocampo was urgently needed to clear him completely—and Ocampo did not answer the call.

5

ON THE same day the *Siglo* carried a small item stating that "a reactionary band led by a certain Cajiga, acting under orders of Marquez, entered the *hacienda* of Pomoca and seized the person of Don Melchor Ocampo. It appears that this gentleman has already been delivered to Marquez, who will probably demand a high ransom for him or will try to murder one of the men most distinguished in the country for his probity and patriotism." The item was printed under the caption "Reactionary Feats," and mentioned several other cases of the same kind in the vicinity of the capital. Since the close of the civil war Marquez and Zuloaga had taken to the mountains, where they mustered several thousand men who eluded pursuit by the local garrisons and kept up appearances by sporadic hostilities in the back country. Leading the lives of outlaws, foraging far and wide, raiding lonely farms, dashing into Cuernavaca to round up horses, emboldened by the absence of police in the outlying valleys and steered by tips from their partisans in the capital, they resorted to the abduction of prominent persons to nourish the remains of their faction and to keep their phantom cause afoot. The repetition of these feats, multiplying with impunity, had already provoked criticism of the government, and it was primarily to meet a danger that had been underestimated and neglected too long that Congress gave the President a vote of confidence, together with arbitrary powers, to enable him to act energetically—without suspending, however, discussion of the treaty. That was accomplished by the capture of Ocampo. The news reached the capital, by a grim coincidence, at the very moment when Juarez needed the helping hand of his mate, and in the ensuing excitement he was saved by the strong arm of Marquez. Every other discussion was drowned in the clamor of alarm that rose from the press and that rekindled the furies of public vengeance of the first days of triumph. "To restore security and save the captured persons there is no measure that is not warranted and that public opinion will not applaud," the *Siglo* declared. "On the frontier, people snatch their women and children from the Apaches and Comanches and war on them like wild beasts. The soldiers of religion have a more odious character than the savages themselves. The circumstances seem to us to warrant the authorities in using actual reprisals and notifying Marquez that, unless his captives are released, the leading men of the Conservative party here will be shot, and that if he exacts ransom it will be paid by the notables of the same faction. We are sworn friends of legality, but not to the extent of seeing society succumb helplessly to bandits."

Acting in that spirit, the government attempted to save the life of Ocampo by taking hostages; as soon as his capture was reported, orders were issued for the apprehension of the mother of Marquez and the wife of Zuloaga. The former escaped, like mother like son; the latter was released for lack of evidence, but being more valuable as a contact than a hostage, she was induced to write a note to her husband interceding for Ocampo. The good offices of M. de Saligny were secured for the same purpose, and the letter was forwarded with his official advice and under diplomatic seal.

Twenty-four hours later, it was too late. At seven in the morning Juarez was informed by Prieto that a *mozo* had gone to the enemy camp and had returned with a report that orders had already been given for Ocampo to be shot. Ransom would have been forthcoming, had it been wanted. For the past fortnight Juarez had been moving every lever to raise money, begging Congress for a million and begrudged a fraction, begging authority to suspend the foreign debt service and denied a hearing, begging private capital for a voluntary loan to avert a forced levy and delay a bleeding; nothing had been done; but for Ocampo blood money would have been found immediately. It was not ransom that was wanted, however, but vengeance: he had signed his own death warrant with the American treaty. Half an hour later Prieto returned with a letter that left no doubt that their old com-

rade had paid the price. The letter, written by Marquez to a correspondent in the capital, lamented the death of Ocampo and washed his
hands of it.

The day that had begun thus darkly developed into a storm, and
Juarez recorded its significant phases in his diary, as they affected him
personally. What comes to mind first in extreme danger? The fundamental in a man, and he was fully conscious of it. "Considering the
powerful sensation that this lamentable calamity will produce in the
people," he wrote, "I gave orders to double the guards at the prisons
and recommended the utmost vigilance to the Governor of the District,
the military commander, Don Leandro Valle, and the Minister of
War"—precautions that were taken none too soon, for the first thought
of the people was also for reprisals. "In a little while the news spread
through the city, and people of all classes came to us demanding that
the political prisoners be executed on the spot and even insisting that,
if the government did not, they and the people would do justice. I did
everything in my power to dissuade these persons from committing the
slightest offense, since as the legal ruler of society I would do everything possible to have the criminals punished according to law, but
would never tolerate violence against accused persons who were under
the protection of the law and the authorities. That they must bear in
mind that those who sacrificed my loyal friend, Señor Ocampo, were
murderers, and that I was the ruler of an enlightened society. Señores
Don Leandro Valle and Don Aureliano Rivera witnessed this act."
The entry had a testamentary ring, the solemnity of a sworn will duly
witnessed and vouched, the conscientiousness of a creed, and the solitude and self-consciousness of imminent peril. He put himself on record; what was fundamental came uppermost—the sacred trust of society, civilization, law—and the whole man lay there in the legacy of
legality about to be overborne.

The precaution was warranted. The prisons were surrounded by
maddened crowds demanding the surrender of the political prisoners,
and above all of the arch-scapegoat Isidoro Diaz, whose trial had been
pending for five months and whose fate would have been settled on the
spot but for Leandro Valle, who rode through the throngs and bore
witness with an arm and a voice raised wherever they were needed to
the pledge of the President. Authority was delegated to this young officer, who had defended him well on other occasions, at Guadalajara, at
Santa Ana Acatlan when he was attacked by Landa, at the Convent of
the Sisters of Charity when the law was assailed by M. de Saligny, and
who saved the day for him once more on the morning of June 4. It was
not necessary for Juarez himself to descend into the streets, as once he
had done in Oaxaca, to quell a mutiny with nothing but a stick in his
hand and his hand behind his back. Valle was young, intrepid, and
popular; he succeeded in checking the mobs if not in taming them,

and while he held the popular fury at bay, Juarez continued to commit its pressure to paper and to register the salient facts that struck him on that sinister day. The day was only half over, and the popular ferment, unspent, found an outlet in another channel. "The effervescence increased with the assembling of Congress, which decreed various measures, one of them being to empower the government to raise resources by whatever means it saw fit. Señor Degollado appeared before Congress, seeking permission to join the campaign, to which Congress consented on condition that the trial to which he is subject continue." But the bald words of the diary were unequal to what followed.

The dramatic irruption of Degollado was the culminating event of the day, provoking a scene to which the professional pen of the press alone could do justice, and to which it could hardly bear witness, being a mere plume in the wind. In Congress the mob spirit also prevailed. Before the session opened, the lobbies echoed with another riot, anarchic in the streets, antiparliamentary in the Palace. "A triumvirate, a Convention, a reign of terror, and a thousand other such ideas were discussed as political inspirations appropriate to the occasion," the congressional record noted. "The public showed that it shared to the utmost the universal indignation, and although it voiced it at times in a manner not very consonant with the dignity of the Assembly, the rules, which have spoken with much less reason on other occasions, remained mute in the hands of the chairman." The death notice, the authentic thing written by Marquez, the mocking apology which he flipped in their faces, was produced and flung, thick with blood, to a house full of law-baiters, and bedlam broke loose. Up to the last man in the press gallery booing, groaning, gasping, the whole house "broke into a roar of rage as the letter was read in which the monster who makes a profession of predatory killing sheds crocodile tears for his victim and in the name of humanity recommends an end to the savage and barbarous character of the war."

Down from the roof and up from the floor a dense clamor battled back and forth, finally cut short by the Minister of War, who dinned into the ears of the penned audience a reminder that precious time was passing and that, if funds were voted, within twenty-four hours eight thousand men would round up the gangs in the hills. At this point the chair interrupted and read a note from Degollado, begging a few minutes' hearing. In that heavily charged atmosphere the effect was electrical: the debate halted, and what went before was as nothing to the sensation he created merely by sending in his card. Even the pages of the congressional record breathed, and breathed deep, in their tense transcript: "Señor Degollado appears in the hall. The assembly rises to its feet, the galleries burst into prolonged applause and clamorous cheers. Silence being restored, Señor Degollado takes the floor and says

that he has come to ask two kinds of justice: one against the perpe-
trators of the dastardly murder that has just stricken the Liberal party,
the other for himself, so that he be convicted or acquitted in the trial
instituted against him, and allowed to fight the Reaction not as an officer, but as a simple soldier. He swears by the shade of Ocampo that he
will never rise to power, and that his one wish is to go to war, not to
drag defenseless citizens from their homes and murder them, but to
fight the assassins hand to hand; and he wonders that the city is quiet
and is not roused by an impulse of rage and execration against the
monsters who have sacrificed one of the most illustrious citizens of the
Republic. He leaves the hall amid the din of the public that tries to
hold him back."

The ovation continued in Congress, one member moving that the
Assembly constitute itself a Grand Jury forthwith and declare that Citizen Santos Degollado had never forfeited the confidence of the nation,
another challenging the House to decide, once and for all, whether his
fate was to be oblivion or glory, a third moving heaven and earth to
cry aye, and the redundant galleries rising and re-echoing him and calling the roll themselves in the thickening congestion of mounting enthusiasm. When someone objected to overruling the trial, they shouted
him down with cries of "mocho" and "reactionary," while down below roar after roar rose, claiming parliamentary sanctuary for Degollado, acclaiming him, booming him, exonerating him, dilapidating the
law courts, wrecking the prison of the unwritten law, demolishing the
penitentiary of the popular will; and there were no protests when one
orator denounced his persecution by the Palace as hack politics and
republican backsliding to the Bourbon policy of *divide and rule*. Thereupon Degollado returned to the hall. He did not mean to surprise the
Assembly, he said, but merely to rehabilitate himself in order to bear
arms, and he proposed that his acquittal be not declared, but only his
permission to serve. This gallantry completed his triumph, and though
the vote was taken on the terms he proposed and carried by acclamation, there was no doubt in that dense jury that his trial had been definitely killed.

Effervescence—seething in the streets, fermenting in the Assembly—
the word with which Juarez labeled both outbursts of the popular temper was significant of his own. Effervescence, an explosion of volatile
feeling that threatened the fundamentals he was sworn to defend. The
demonstration in Congress he noted in his diary as a statement of fact,
like an item of bookkeeping, but it was none the less eloquent and appropriate. A score had been settled, an account closed. A council of war
was immediately called, and Degollado attended it. As they sat there
side by side, their positions were strangely reversed: both under the
shadow of trial, but one already absolved by popular verdict and the

other still threatened with impeachment, they plunged into the discussion of military plans and tacitly buried the past, brought together by the galvanizing force of the corpse of Ocampo.

But the day of reckoning was not yet over, and that afternoon an incident occurred that Juarez included among his major ordeals because it provoked his temper and betrayed the strain under which he was laboring. The diplomatic corps called on him in a body to intercede for the political prisoners and begged him to suspend the summary execution that they had learned was scheduled for that night. This was too much even for the schooled temper of Juarez. The appeal was not only uncalled for, but offensive in form, the dean declaring that they had decided to make a concerted plea "for the good and honor of the government itself, as they did not wish to see it on the same level as Zuloaga and Marquez, who were bandits." His reply was sharp, and committed to his diary, where he digested it wrathfully. "They were informed with the proper energy"—and when he was stung he had energy to spare—"that the Mexican Government, understanding its duty and dignity, had never thought of proceeding, nor would permit others to act, in a barbarous manner against persons under the shelter and protection of the law and the authorities; that I greatly regretted that they had formed so poor an opinion of the Republic, judging it capable of so base and degrading a deed, and that they had accepted as true a rumor spread by the rabble; and I desired them to withdraw an idea so offensive to the first authority of the country." Whereupon his monitors apologized profusely and withdrew. The diplomats were the last to learn who Juarez was, being a credulous rabble, but they recognized their mistake, and the day ended in a complete vindication of civilization and legality. Then, and then only, was he free to think of Ocampo, and he sent for his body.

In the crowding events and swift succession of crises produced by his fate, Ocampo himself had been all but buried; but in the next few days reports of his passion and death began to drift in, and the tragedy was slowly reconstructed. Living in the seclusion of his estate, busy with his books, his plants, his poor, and his frugal occupations, he had steadily ignored the warnings that reached him more than once that marauding bands were roaming the valley and that he was not as completely forgotten as he supposed. Nevertheless, he was troubled one evening, while the household was at supper, by a sound of scraping on the walls and ordered the women into the cellar while he went out to search the grounds; and though he discovered nothing tangible, he caught the echo of hooves and voices vanishing in the dark. An hour later a neighbor called with news that a reactionary band was heading his way and urged him to flee. "What have I to fear?" he had the simplicity to reply. "I have never harmed anyone." The following morning he refused to accompany his daughters to the neighboring town of Maravatio for the feast of Corpus Christi, and he took leave of them without a fonder farewell than usual. When they were gone, however, his forebodings returned. His housekeeper was worried by the appearance of a stranger who put up with them for a few hours and whom she suspected of being a scout, his horse being branded on the rump with the "R" of religion, and she persuaded her master to leave. He ordered his horse to be saddled, but the man accounted for his mount with a plausible story, and Ocampo sent his own back to the stable, doubly disturbed because he had doubted and because he was not reassured. The next morning it was noticed that he was more than usually melancholy, idle, and silent. Since he had retired from public life, he had indulged his philosophical habits of mind to the full: one was a ready resignation to misfortune, and another a melancholy that verged on misanthropy; but to the latter he had not yet succumbed, and he found comfort in the other. He sat down to the midday meal without appetite, and when his overseer sighted the raiders he went to the window and watched their approach through the shutters, and he was still there when he was captured. He offered the leader the hospitality of his table—a last gesture of dignity, which produced no impression. He was placed on a hack with half a saddle, no reins, and a halter for a bridle, and the party set off at a brisk pace.

At the first halt, a few miles from the *hacienda,* he was hailed by some neighbors on their way to visit him, and he borrowed a pair of chaps from one of them. With his customary consideration he turned their attention into a local jest. "No one will believe that I am from Michoacan, my boy," he said, "for you know very well that the padres wear chaps when they give the Viaticum." The hint went no further, and though his neighbors caught it, they could do nothing. Friends he had all along the way, and all equally helpless. In Maravatio, where every other man was his acquaintance, he spent the night in the inn, under guard, and the best that his friends there could do was to send an appeal to Marquez the next morning—after he was gone. Five months after the close of the civil war there were no police in the region, and the inhabitants took cover when the party appeared and remained at a respectful distance until it moved on. For two days he rode through a land he knew and loved as a naturalist—a land of vast unpeopled spaces, of virgin wildernesses and lawless solitudes, where Marquez was merely a primitive survival and Zuloaga a zoological specimen—and on the third he was brought into their den. Here he was held for another day while they disputed his last one. Marquez proposed to shoot him immediately, but Zuloaga insisted on legal formalities; the primitive insisted that Ocampo was already convicted by the American treaty, but the specimen, who still styled himself President of Mexico, insisted that sentence be passed only after a preliminary trial; and their differences were still unsettled when the troop moved on to the village of Tepeji del Rio the next morning.

Here Ocampo was lodged in the inn, and informed that his journey had ended. He drew up a will, which closed with the words, "I die believing that I have done as much for the service of my country as in my conscience I believed to be good." Even then, and there, he found friends. A Liberal *guerrillero* having been captured that morning and summarily sentenced by Marquez, the local notables interceded for his life and won a reprieve; emboldened by their success, they appealed for Ocampo as well, but they were denied, although they were led by a priest who honored the religion branded on the rump of a horse. The priest was denied the favor of redeeming it even by the victim, who refused the last rites and waived all further formalities. "I am well with God, Father," Ocampo said, "and God is well with me." At two in the afternoon he was ridden out into the open country, and at the appointed place he dismounted and performed the customary rites of such occasions himself, distributing his remaining belongings to his last friends, the firing squad. The relics were few and poor, but the captain drew his borrowed chaps, and he found one last *peso* for a little bugler whom he had overlooked, and no one had been neglected when he took his place and the muzzles were raised level with his silence. There was a discharge, and as the convulsions that were Ocampo lashed the dust, another was fired to silence their indignities. Then the immediate heirs ran a rope under the armpits and hastened to drag the weight of a human life of which they were eager to be rid to a tree, where they hoisted it on a dead limb and left it, by order of Marquez. Through the long summer afternoon the peasants on their way home from market watched it gravitating unably toward the ground, unable to reach and forbidden to touch it; for the limb was withered and not the fruit.

The first to feel its weight was Zuloaga. When the *guerrillero* had been brought in that morning, Zuloaga had agreed to shoot him, and he was working over some papers found on the captive, confident that his orders to hold Ocampo for trial had been obeyed, when an orderly entered and reported that the prisoner had been shot. "What prisoner?" asked Marquez. "Why—Señor Ocampo," the man stammered. Furious that his authority had been flouted, the ex-President sprang to his feet and gave orders that the responsible officer should be court-martialed; but these orders also were disregarded, Marquez insisting that it was all a mistake, and though Zuloaga realized that he had been tricked, he was forced to swallow it to preserve his authority. How much of a mistake they both realized when they received the letters of intercession from Señora Zuloaga and M. de Saligny. Marquez lost no time in repairing it, writing by return courier the letter of exculpation that raised such a storm in the capital; but Zuloaga at least realized that it was irreparable. It was the bitterest day of his life, he said, and his life had known many. He was incapable of killing a chicken, as one of his officers said, but he could not prove it. By then the specimen and the primitive were too busy washing their hands to notice what became of Ocampo. The body was cut down by the villagers and brought in after nightfall, and by daybreak anyone could claim it, Marquez having decamped with his President at his heels.

Four days later the remains were interred in the capital with national honors. The flags flew at half-mast, the government donned mourning for nine days, and the weight that was Melchor Ocampo was distributed in the hearts of the thousands who crowded the cemetery; and there it was transubstantiated into a seething and restless afterlife far more potent than the life he had shed. The fury of the first day, subsiding in the tumult that relieved it, revived at the funeral and was kindled afresh by the obituaries and fanned into flame by the details, the conjectures, the confirmations of the manner in which he died. "Señor Ocampo, who placed his personal dignity above everything, must have suffered much," it was surmised, "from the humiliations to which his assassins subjected him. Perhaps his characteristic pride triumphed at the end and he returned insult for insult and humiliation for humiliation. This would account for the precipitation with which he was killed." The theory was confirmed by powder burns on the face, showing that he had been shot at close range, and pious pens wrote an avenging amen across it and vowed to retaliate in kind. But, above all, it was the tree—a tree, as someone said, twisted and tricked into a cross—and the load hanging from it and yearning in vain for the ground, that haunted the public mind: that last gratuitous indignity could not be borne or buried. The burning columns of the press towered over it night and day, Congress placed a price on the heads of the outlaws, the government proscribed them, but every day their reappearance was reported at some new point, and provocation and impunity goaded the most active agitators in the capital to incite the countryside to a general man hunt. The murder of Ocampo reopened all the unsettled scores of the civil war, the nightmare returned, the terror revived, and the letter of Marquez, deploring its latest victim, recalled so clearly his like evasion of the massacre of Tacubaya that both atrocities were fastened on him by the weight of mass evidence; his mate was forgotten, and the hue and cry of the hurrying man hunt singled out as the one unforgivable felon of the civil war the little man whose instincts ran on four legs and who still reared himself on two.

The inextinguishable invocation of vengeance testified to the veneration in which Ocampo was held far more than to the survival of his spirit among those who partook of his passion and death; but the memory of a man who had lived and died without malice was honored by mercy as well. At the height of the agitation one paper had the temerity to mention the treaty that bore his name, but it was instantly silenced, and Congress, though it did not formally dismiss the controversy, buried it as finally as the trial of Degollado. There the remains of Ocampo rested; the curse was lifted; and the vexed treaty which had been meat for vultures a week before became for all time food for bookworms.

That Ocampo was captured within close range of the capital and encountered no rescue during the four days of his abduction was a striking demonstration of the powerlessness of the government beyond the limits of the city. No effort was spared to repair it, but the measures hastily taken on the morrow of the crime were themselves a humiliating admission of weakness. Every available resource had to be mustered to hunt down a fugitive band of guerrillas, regular troops mobilized, a full-scale campaign planned, and money found to place the government once more on a war-footing; and as the indemnity due to the British Legation had drained the Treasury, the President authorized a forced loan to launch the expedition. These were the humble tributes which he paid to his friend. At the funeral he was silent, leaving eloquence to the orators, who were legion; his homage took the form of bleeding the public of fifty thousand *pesos* to avenge him. It was a week before the expedition could start—an intolerable delay in the feverish pace of public feeling—and without waiting for the main body under Ortega, Degollado dashed ahead with a flying column.

Five days later, while he was being dunned by the Minister of War for another forced loan, Juarez was notified that he had been elected President of the Republic. He noted the fact in his journal as part of the day's work, among miscellaneous memoranda, jotting down the figures with which Congress had cleared his election—five votes—without further comment. That he left to others. Though he had carried the country by an absolute majority, the Opposition attempted to challenge the verdict and to throw the election into Congress, but the maneuver raised an issue—hotly discussed at the time—of how far parliamentary bodies with their cliques, their coalitions, and their intrigues represent the popular will; and Congress ratified the choice of the people, although by so narrow a margin that the question remained unsettled. The result, nevertheless, was a vindication of the elected and the electors alike, and it was all the more remarkable because, as Zarco observed, the President had not lifted a finger to secure a single vote or to defeat the electoral schemes directed against him, and had given the press unlimited liberty, suppressed its subventions, and sued none of his slanderers in court.

So spontaneous a victory was an unprecedented triumph for the democratic process in Mexico, but it was celebrated with a sobriety that led many to believe that the people were disappointed and discouraged—as they were, but not by the sound issue of the electoral urns. The absence of festivities, which also excited comment, was circumstantial evidence of a deeper depression; the public had come of age, a sobering process in itself, and under circumstances of extraordinary gloom. "In the present state of public affairs, a self-respecting people cannot indulge in demonstrations of joy before the bloody shade of Ocampo, cannot celebrate festivities when it knows that society is in danger and that great efforts must be made to save it," Zarco reminded the diehards who compared the drab advent of Juarez with the illuminations and eulogies lavished on Santa Anna, Zuloaga, and Miramon. "Señor Juarez has done well to favor no farces on his assumption of the first magistracy of the country, to make no gifts, no donations, no pledges with the public money; and those who supported his candidacy have shown him a sign of respect in not repeating the flattery and adulation with which other governments have been inaugurated." More unprecedented yet, he had cut his salary. The scrutiny was a trophy that confirmed the qualities of the man— decency, public spirit, and a complete absence of pose—and he met the expectations of his public by continuing to work quietly and steadily, with the electoral campaign out of the way, on the only campaign that mattered, under the pall that hung over the capital. The consensus of opinion was that the country had made a safe choice; and a tremendous premium was placed upon safety in June 1861.

The election returns diverted attention for a few days from the pursuit of Marquez, and the papers were still dilating on its significance when there appeared, amid the large meditations spread formally over the front pages, another of those small items that caught the eye, and the breath, of the reader, like a blood spot. Buried on the back pages, and couched in the cautious and considerate phrases due to the susceptibilities of the public, it reported the disappearance of Degollado. A raw rumor one day, it was a full-grown fact the next: his division had fallen into an ambush, he had been deserted and killed. His body was missing, and so for a few days was the comment of the press. Coming so close on the death of Ocampo, this fresh casualty caused a shock no less profound, but different in effect; the response was slower, dulled by the first blow, stunned by the second, and deadened by a numbing sense of fatality. His fate was felt to be the consummation of a career vowed to disaster, and was accepted with mute relief that a life so incurable had been arrested at last. Misfortune, mortification, disgrace, desertion, death—nothing remained for the complete fulfillment of his destiny but its transfiguration; and that morbid duty was devoutly performed. The rehabilitation hastily begun before his death was amply completed after it, and the response, when it came, rose with the cumulative force of common compunction, discharging a debt long overdue.

The obituaries were both an apology and an apotheosis. "Señor Don Santos Degollado, the immaculate patriot, the purest and noblest incarnation of the ideas of democracy and reform, has ceased to exist"— Zarco led the responses of the press in halting words attuned to the muffled pulse of prostration and dismay. "Merely to know that Degollado no longer exists is to realize that another calamity impends on our country. The soldier of the people, the most distinguished champion of progressive ideas, has ceased to exist. . . ." The desperate repetition dragged on flatly, unable to rise above the crushing fact, rehearsing it over and over in a hypnotic daze, and shifting it to a future free to cherish his death as it deserved. "The name of Degollado will be pronounced by generations to come with veneration and tenderness, as we pronounce those of Hidalgo and Morelos"—and then compunction quickened, and while the hushed tone of the pantheon relayed his apotheosis to a remote posterity peopled with juster men, the dry reiteration of the litany labored to raise the weight of leaden neglect with which his memory was still laden today. "Though fortune was frequently adverse to him on the fields of battle, his spirit was of the antique temper; he never lost hope in the cause of justice and liberty, and his consistency is all the more admirable and heroic because he fought not only against adversity, but also, we are forced to admit, against envy and calumny. But the truth is that without Degollado the leaders who were more fortunate would never have appeared, and but for the defeat of Tacubaya we would never have known the victory of Calpulalpam." The homage was heavy with humiliation and honored the hero whose mortifications it rehearsed by valuing them as he did. The capture of the *conducta* was recalled as a hallowing stigma. "More could not be done by the man who was probity itself than to plead guilty and sacrifice everything for his country. No one has carried patriotism and abnegation so far."

Echoing Degollado to the letter, the mourner made the supreme atonement and offered him the absolute satisfaction of accepting him at his own unqualified estimate. If flaws there were, they were decently veiled and mutely glossed over: there was no frailty in the flesh, no infatuation with misfortune, no fallacy in martyrdom, no pose in self-pity; whatever might mar the transparent truth was effaced by the clean breath of death. His transgressions were forgotten and his errors exonerated in his own spirit, and the devout zeal of the disciple unfleshed the master and made full amends for his worldly mortification. The cloud of his dealings with Mathew was cleared by the dark, for there are no clouds in the dark; and what shone forth in the shadows was his last gallant crusade for Ocampo. "We can still hear the accents of grief and enthusiasm with which he addressed Congress only a few days ago. As Degollado himself said then, let us not offer these victims womanish tears. His shades demand more: they demand energy, they exact justice, and nothing but justice." And on that firmly held note the meditation, moving to its own subdued music, closed. More compensation the most injured could not demand of mortality, more Degollado Degollado himself could not exact from it, and his exit was the *ne plus ultra*. The unerring pursuit of disaster by which Marquez lured him to his ultimate destination secured his transfiguration. All his old friends vied with one another in contrition. "You who trembled at the tears of a child, you who imposed on yourself the privations of a cenobite lest you squander the farthings of the poor, you who were the sanctity of the Revolution"—Prieto apostrophized him, penitent for his own apostasy. Ramirez, the iconoclast, proclaimed him his idol. Exceptions there were none; he was sanctified by common consent; the very surfeit of tribute strained to deny desertion and to forget the fatigue with misfortune which had drained sympathy dry before his death. Congress completed the consecration by discharging his trial with a posthumous decree of national gratitude. The decree was sent to the President, who published it after a noticeable delay, which left the impression of perfunctory acknowledgment of the general verdict. The immortality of Degollado, however, had long since been taken out of his hands, and he paid him the same tribute as to Ocampo, digging down into the pockets of the public for another appropriation, and with results even more melancholy.

The most shocking feature of the disaster was that Degollado had been deserted by his men; some said that one of them shot him in the back. Surrounded, outnumbered, trapped, they were dispersed because they were demoralized, and defeated because they were unpaid. The cult of glory required cash, and the multiplication of heroes regular meals. The engagement occurred in the passes of the Monte de las Cruces, where Hidalgo had flung his untrained hordes against regular troops fifty years before and had won out by sheer weight of spirit— a feat cruelly reversed by the defeat of Degollado on hallowed ground half a century later. What had been gained, what had been lost, in the interval? Another name had been added to the national pantheon: Don Santos had ascended into the empyrean with his peers. A legendary remoteness shrouded his fate, but there was nothing legendary about the rout of his followers or remote in their desertion. Signs of panic appeared in Congress when it was learned that a shipment of arms had been turned back at Veracruz for failure to pay; a delegation waited on the President, who informed them that there were arms enough in the city, but no funds with which to purchase them. Nevertheless, by dint of scraping and extortion, two thousand rifles were procured for the national guard. A new avenger volunteered, and five days after the death of Degollado, Leandro Valle took the same road at the head of eight hundred men.

But the pace of disaster was swifter than the speed with which it was repaired. The following day the back pages began bleeding again, and twenty-four hours later Valle was defeated and dead. The action occurred almost on the same ground, in the treacherous passes of the Monte de las Cruces, but this time the disaster was not due to improvidence or pinched bellies or poor generalship or the obscure curse that dogged the hero of defeat; on the contrary, there were abundant reports of a hard-fought battle and the ability with which Valle made a stand against superior numbers; and he was not deserted by his men. The droves of dead were there to prove it. They were too numerous and too nameless to be mourned in the public prints or mustered into the national pantheon, which was a privileged place with no room for the many and less and less space for the few, and already overcrowded; but for Valle in an especial manner the press raised its black banner, because he comprehended them all in their common pit. The name of Leandro Valle was not, like those of Ocampo and Degollado, one to conjure with; yet it cast a deeper spell on the public. He had the supreme appeal of youth, which supplied its own apotheosis. Cut off in his prime, when the current was flowing full in his veins, he met death with the zest of the green and the vigor of the veteran. When he was told that he was to be shot, he turned his moment to account and, choosing his tree, fell scoffing at his assassins in the style attributed to Ocampo; and by way of retort, they hung him on the trunk where he belonged.

The trunk was severed, and the body of which he had made a banner was left hanging there at half-mast, where the trail of the wilderness crossed the highroad to Mexico; and at half-mast the colors hung in the capital, waiting for the nation at large, and no other avenger, to answer the taunt. Zarco dipped his pen to write a rousing call to the reddening colors. "To kill such a man, and to treat him as a traitor, and a traitor to religion!" he raged, recalling the vigor with which only a few days before Valle had prevented the mobbing of the political prisoners. "Who speaks of religion? The beasts, the tigers of Tacubaya! And the ministers of religion accept such apostles apparently, for their lips hold gall enough to defend their property and their privileges, but they have uttered not one word to repudiate such support or to rebuke abduction, murder, and arson! A bishop cannot be silent when a cleric seeks permission of the civil authorities to legitimize his children, but the entire clergy is mute in the face of these crimes and has no censures for those who raise the cross as the standard of murder and crime or for the priests who fight in the reactionary gangs! But censures they had, and tremendous ones, for the first insurgents who proclaimed our independence from Spain! The Inquisition, the bishops, the chapters, thundered against the patriots and insisted that there were no privileges for them. These are facts to which history is a witness." Witnesses were not wanting either then or now to the timeless and untamed treason of the Church to Christ and its tacit consent to any atrocity that served the Faith and fouled its trust; and the blasphemous silence with which the clergy sanctioned the latest crusade in their favor compelled the popular tribune to wield the scourge on behalf of a cowed people. Never had the Monte de las Cruces been so close to the heart of Mexico since Hidalgo stood there, scanning the promised land, and turned back; the death of the youngest flung the whole nation back to its beginning and telescoped its history in the generation nailed one by one to the tree. "And this party of assassins proposed to form a government and to dominate the people!" Zarco cried. "Marquez has released all those who witnessed the murder of Valle to spread terror and has charged them to tell us in Mexico that this is nothing, that we have no notion as yet of his savagery. This beast promises to shoot, hang, murder, all the notables of the Liberal party, to kill all who have acquired nationalized property, and to put into shackles the insignificant who merely profess democratic beliefs and set them to work rebuilding the dens of the convents! Here is his political and religious program!"

The cup overflowed. More than Ocampo, more than Degollado, the loss of Valle stirred the depths; it reached down into the womb of unborn generations and smothered their existence, and the blight of the future and the waste of the past made the popular temper implacable. The name of Valle conjured up the call of the blood, and the nakedness of the seed, as no other could. His murder was more fanatical than that of Ocampo, his fatality more formidable than that of Degollado, and his tree more forbidding and more far-reaching than theirs. He was all that was never to be, born but for barren death, and now, under the shadow of what was seen to be a systematic campaign of intimidation, terror, naked terror, began to stir in the very vitals of a society stalked and ruled by it, and stifled by its inability to retaliate. "The extermination of the bandits, the action of justice, the salvation of order and liberty"—the exhortations with which Zarco concluded the call were feeble, were tame, with repetition. It was clear that the strength of the enemy had been underestimated and that Marquez was supported by more than audacity.

On the very day after the kill the suburbs of the capital were raided by a flying detachment of the rebels, and they were beaten off not half an hour from the center of the city. The alarm was enough to recall Gonzalez Ortega from the field and to halt the pursuit: he was advised not to risk a clash with the main body. But where was the main body? Within the walls or without? The recurring provocations,

the power that waxed with impunity, the acceleration of pace, the
studied terror, and the taunting threats of worse to follow, proclaimed
unseen support, prospects, accomplices, and the search for them
started. The public, profoundly unnerved, was prodded by a press
sleeplessly ringing the knell and the tocsin, dinning day in and day
out the warning that no one was safe, that henceforth every man was
marked, repeating that there were persons in the capital who openly
threatened the Liberal party as a whole with the fate of the elect, re-
echoing others who derided the debility of the government and compared the justice of Marquez, who needed only a pistol, a rope, and a
tree, with the trammels of the courts strangled in writs and chicaneries,
and harking back to the fact that six months after the capture of the
capital the ministers of Miramon were still unpunished and glorying
in the legal guarantees they enjoyed and the accommodations so freely
provided by the government.

If the smell of massacre was not in the air, it was in the papers, and
Valle was not there to check it. His body was brought in unobtrusively
on a gun carriage, with others collected on the mountain, and would
have passed unnoticed but for an accident. His mother happened to
pass the hearse, and, on learning whose it was, she flung herself on the
coffin, forced open the lid, and embraced the remains, oblivious to the
crowd that collected and the sensation she caused. The contents of the
casket, exposed by chance, were deliberately drawn forth and cherished
by the press. Preserved from putrefaction by the draining of the
veins, the relics were still immune to the seasoning of time, and the
tortures of extinction intact. One eye was closed, the other open, and
the body was riddled by seventeen bullet holes, like pores through
which the vision of his ordeal transpired. The arms, grotesquely
twisted by suspension, had stiffened into the posture of a foetus
reaching for life, and the whole shriveled creature resembled something
between the embryo and the mummy of a man. The lid was lifted
on the image of an abortive generation and closed without comment.
Morbid reflections were lost in the onrush of violent resolutions.

So ended the month of June. Three such casualties in succession
would have shaken any regime, and under the onrush of rising panic
the government was, if not foundering, visibly cracking. A cabinet
could not be formed, the coveted posts went begging, public service
was provisional, and Juarez was goaded to govern by decree and to
meet the emergency with the drastic measures necessary to retain
national confidence. Zarco, as his stoutest champion, headed the demand, insisting that legality could be preserved only by arbitrary
methods and civilization only by exceptional sanctions, and underwriting the prescription with a program—martial law, permanent
councils of war, reprisals, instantaneous justice, mobilization of every

resource, and the raising of money by any means sanctioned by Congress, which had already given him unlimited license. "The task is not long nor arduous; it is a matter of seven million men defending themselves against two thousand assassins," he insisted. "A week of severity will save the situation."

And three weeks later the President met the demand for extreme measures. Roused by the sting of a pygmy, the nation heaved like a giant against its bonds, which were unbreakable because they were foreign bonds. The indispensable condition of energy was control of the national resources; a beginning had been made by suspending payment on the internal debt, but the crushing burden from which there was no release was the foreign debt, and under stress of the crisis the proposal to dump it revived. The idea launched by Zamacona two months before appeared in Congress in the first days of July and was adopted in secret session and passed on to the President. In that atmosphere of brewing panic the buoyance of his trial balloon carried Zamacona to office. Called to the Foreign Ministry to convoy the measure he had so fearlessly sponsored in his sanctum, he shrank from the risks and responsibilities of its passage, however, and it required all the persuasion, the insistence, and the authority of the President to induce him to sign it. But the pilot silenced his misgivings. The risks were common and the responsibilities collective: the heroic remedy originated in a general recognition of its necessity. Passing from mind to mind, begging for adoption, diffused in the public, discussed in the press, debated in Congress, shunned and postponed, developing with the drift to disaster, maturing in the deadly month of June, and coming at last, sanctioned by the dead, into the hands of the President to be applied as a measure of public safety, the mandate was unanimous. Precipitated by an immediate crisis, but prescribed by a permanent infirmity and premeditated as an organic cure, the moratorium was converted, like the Reform Laws, from a passing expedient into an act of incalculable consequence. On July 17 Juarez issued a decree suspending payment on the foreign debt service. It was a second and more dangerous declaration of national independence, and it was made without consulting the creditor powers. A week later the French Minister severed, and the British Minister suspended, relations with Mexico.

6

DEBT suspension placed Mexico beyond the pale of civilized nations. The sentence it provoked was as formidable as the excommunication incurred by the Reform Laws. A canon had been broken as basic to the creed of modern civilization as the ecclesiastical covenant had been to the feudal culture of the past, and henceforth the forces of the world to which Mexico aspired by its progress and those of the society to which it still belonged by its backwardness were leagued against the government guilty of defying them both. Before those forces began to move, however, there was a brief period when their agents were free to guide their direction and to mold the destinies of the country at their discretion; and during that period persons were of capital importance.

Neither the French nor the British Minister was caught unprepared for the shock. The shape of things to come had cast a long shadow ahead, and its deepening density had developed into an inky cloud in their despatches. M. de Saligny, in particular, had primed his government and prepared it for drastic measures of its own by a series of tendentious reports, depicting conditions in Mexico as the ferment of an advanced stage of "social decomposition" that would eventually require intervention. In April, when the only ferment was normal agitation of an electoral campaign, he called for French fleets to patrol the coasts in anticipation of another revolution. In May, when nothing abnormal developed, he fell back on the crime wave and the preference of the assassins for foreigners. In June, when the crime wave carried off Ocampo, and all foreign claims but the British were ignored, he called for another injunction "to support the justice of our claims by force, if necessary." By the first week of July the approaches of panic and financial paralyzation were so close that he could not collect even the legitimate claims acknowledged a few months before, the Jecker business was stalled, the conduct of the government was unconscionable, and he was more than ever convinced, he wrote, "that force alone can compel this government to honor its pledges to ours." A fortnight later the crash came. For month after month he had sent up distress signals and wrought himself to the pitch of outrage that civilized people require before they can conscientiously resort to violence, and when the crisis was reached the groundwork was well laid. With unerring accuracy M. de Saligny had anticipated the collapse, and he acted with unhesitating confidence in breaking relations: he was covered. That he waited a week was due to the lag of his colleague, for the support of the British Minister was essential to his purpose, and their interests were allied but not identical.

His purpose was not clear until it was accomplished. He came to Mexico, he said later, *pour casser des vitres*. His official mission, however, was not to smash windows; that was the consequence of his failure. The systematic incitements he sent to Paris were dictated by the interests he represented and the combinations he served. His mission was important only because of the commissions it carried, his interests were many and various, he was adept at combinations of all kinds, his mind ran naturally to mergers and pools, and he was teeming with ideas when he left Paris. Investment in the Louisiana Tehuantepec Company was a scheme that had much to recommend it on more than one account; he proposed it to the Foreign Office as a feasible means of turning American enterprise to account in a field attractive to French interests by professional alliance with a powerful competitor; but it was a useful connection for other reasons as well. He counted on American as well as British and French support to force recognition of the Jecker bonds, because of the facilities which they offered for cheating the customs; cut rates opened an easy diplomatic channel for the affair, and the pool a pressure which would favor his negotiation. The hopes he held out to Elsesser were based on the prospect of bringing an international financial offensive to bear on the Mexican Government; and the promises he made to his clerical clients to do great things for Mexico were inspired by the same calculations.

All his combinations had one feature in common—an opportunity to exploit the difficulties of the Liberals. Nevertheless, before leaving Paris, he had listened to a friend who attempted to influence him in their favor, and he left France with a mind more or less open—open, that is, to the main chance. A diplomat on the make, M. de Saligny did not allow his partialities to prejudice his prospects or his sympathies to interfere with his success. On his way through Washington he assured the acting head of the Mexican Legation there that the Emperor had no *prévention* against his government, though the McLane treaty led him to think the opposite party the more patriotic; on his arrival in Veracruz he was agreeably surprised to find the Liberals amenable to his advances; and it was not until he met with insurmountable difficulties in Mexico that he began to indulge his itch for window smashing. All his initiatives had come to nothing—the Tehuantepec business was war-logged, the Jecker business was stalled, the protection of his clerical clients was no business of France—but every calamity has its compensations. M. de Saligny was never at a loss for ideas, the difficulties of the Mexican Government were the salvation of his own, and he exploited them relentlessly. Scenting bigger game, he seized the opportunity to turn them to account for his country, his career, and his clerical clients, and set to work to pave the way for a piece of really big business by a series of provocative reports on the "social dissolution" of the country to which he was condemned, the government to which he was accredited, and the party against which he was prejudiced by political bias, personal spleen, and professional flair. The disappointed agent degenerated rapidly into a sociologist, and the nervous alarmist into an *agent provocateur* sedulously instigating aggression against a government that he had wrecked in his reports long before it committed the transgression that guaranteed international sanctions. The debt suspension provided him with a legitimate opportunity to force French intervention and to serve all his combinations at once by a joint offensive of international capital; but he was still one man against Mexico, a person pitted against a people, and until he was sure of carrying his government with him, it was essential to secure the co-operation of the British Minister and to pool their interests.

This merger was not so easy. A French diplomatist has observed that the functions of his profession have broadened with the development of democracy. "The importance of persuading a Prince or his ministers has diminished, that of understanding a nation has increased. . . . The representative of a self-governing nation has been under a more direct obligation to study and interpret the social conditions of the country and has been called upon to assume a greater responsibility in advising his government and shaping its relations with a sovereign people than the minister of an irresponsible ruler." The dictum might serve as a compass pointing to the cardinal quarters and the prevailing forces by which Mexico was controlled in the middle of the nineteenth century. If Saligny belonged to the older school, Wyke represented the newer—negatively, but none the less accurately for that reason. Arriving in Mexico on the eve of a crisis which required some understanding of local conditions for its correct appreciation, he formed his judgment in three weeks and began to forward a series of reports as prejudicial as those of Saligny, not from a deliberate purpose to color or distort, but from a complacent inability or unwillingness to comprehend. He saw the same things, in the same way, for different reasons; but the bias of obtuseness was as mischievous as that of premeditation. His attitude also was determined by the nature of his mission; he came to Mexico to collect bad debts, and his mind had been pre-shrunk for the purpose in London. The Foreign Secretary had been sharply criticized in Parliament and the press for neglecting British interests in Mexico and spurred to protect investments and enforce claims in what was, commercially, an important outpost of the Empire, before the profits of dispossession of the clergy were dissipated. These complaints were more than the buzz of speculators; they had the volume, the persistence, and the hum of an aroused commercial community; and it was in response to this pressure that Wyke was recalled from sick leave on the Continent, where he had spent the better part of a year since his appointment, nursing a liver complaint. The long delay in taking up his duties had given rise to interpellations in Parliament, and though, unlike Saligny, his career was not at stake, he had no less reason to be zealous and to dispel any doubts that he devoted more thought to his liver than to the organic troubles of the Empire. The British debt cramped his mental activity, and to the diagnosis of the organic troubles of Mexico he brought the peremptory judgment of a bailiff, the diplomacy of a commercial traveler, and the impatience of a vigorous invalid.

Under such conditions he could hardly be expected to lose time in studying the conditions of the country, but his interpretation was cursory even under the narrowest construction of his duty. Nothing revealed the mentality of Sir Charles Lennox Wyke better than the contrast between his first report and the last of his predecessor. Mathew had learned to appreciate the difficulties of the government and to estimate correctly its chances of overcoming them. His observations also were governed by the British debt, but they were not subordinated to it. "The hope of Mexico lies in the maintenance of peace," he repeated as his parting injunction. "A wise basis of civil and religious liberty has been laid down, and peace only is needed for the development of Constitutional principles and for the gradual enlightenment of the country. But seeing as I do so many native and foreign elements at work to disturb the existing state of things, I cannot but entertain a conviction that unless the present government or principles of government are in some way upheld by England or the United States—by a protecting alliance or the declaration that no revolutionary movement would be permitted in any of the seaports on either ocean—further deplorable convulsions will afflict this unfortunate country, to the heavy injury of British interests and commerce, and to the disgrace of humanity." The heaviest liability under which the country labored was the moral prejudice created against it by the late regime and the difficulty of recognizing abroad the progress that had actually been made, for "however faulty and weak the present government may be, they who witnessed the murders, the acts of atrocity and plunder, almost of daily occurrence, under the government of General Miramon and his counselors, Señor Diaz and General Marquez, cannot but appreciate the existence of law and justice. Foreigners especially, who suffered so heavily under that arbitrary rule, and by the hatred and intolerance toward them that is a dogma of the Church party in Mexico, cannot but make a broad distinction between the past and the present. President Juarez, though deficient in the energy necessary for the present crisis, is an upright and well-intentioned man, excellent in all the private relations of life, but the mere fact of his being an Indian exposes him to the hostility and sneers of the dregs of Spanish society, and of those of mixed blood, who ludicrously arrogate to themselves the higher social positions in Mexico."

The social benefits resulting from the dissolution of the old order were a material gain for British interests, and their best security. If his judgment was governed by any other consideration, it was by suspicion of Saligny, whose conclusions he contradicted point by point. The threat to peace lay not in the lingering lawlessness, which he recognized as the subsiding ferment of civil war, nor in the recrudescence of the Reaction, but in the very issue that affected the British Government. "The most imminent peril to Mexico, and one that will equally press on any future, as on the present, government," he insisted, "is the deplorable state of its finances. . . . The Mexican Government has been accused, and not without reason, of having frittered away the Church property recently nationalized; but it must be remembered that while forced contributions, plunder, and immense supplies from the Church and its supporters enabled General Zuloaga and General Miramon to sustain the civil war for three years, the Constitutional government abstained from such acts and have the sole robbery of the *conducta* at Lagos, toward the close of the civil war, to answer for. Their reserves, during this lengthened period, were drawn from advances by individuals, on bond for larger sums, payable at the close of the war, and from actual sale of a great part of this property at twenty-five per cent, or even fifteen per cent of its supposed value. . . . From the foregoing details Your Lordship will at once understand the precarious condition of Mexico, and that without some foreign interposition the dismemberment of the Republic and a national bankruptcy appear all but inevitable."

Over the political map drawn by Mathew, with its careful qualifications, Wyke passed the sponge three weeks later. "It will be very difficult, if not impossible, to give Your Lordship a correct idea of the present state of affairs in this unfortunate country," he began afresh, "so utterly incomprehensible is the conduct of the government that at present presides over its destinies. Animated by a blind hatred toward the Church party, the present government have only thought of destroying and dissipating the immense property belonging to the clergy without, however, at the same time taking advantage of the wealth thus placed at their disposal to liquidate the many obligations that at present weigh them down and cripple their resources. The Church property has generally been supposed to be worth between sixty and eighty million Spanish dollars, the whole of which appears to have been frittered away without the government having anything to show for it. A considerable amount was, doubtless, spent in repaying advances at exorbitant rates of interest made to the Liberal party as they were fighting their way to power; but still enough ought to have remained after satisfying their creditors to have left them very well off and in better position as to their pecuniary resources than any previous government." Disgusted by such incomprehensible mismanagement, he gave the government guilty of it short shrift. "The Church party, although beaten, are not yet subdued and several of their chiefs are within six leagues of the capital at the head of forces varying from four thousand to six thousand men. . . . Señor Comonfort, ex-President of the Republic, has arrived at Monterrey in Nuevo Leon, where it is said the Governor has made a pronunciamento in his favor, which will very likely be joined in by the neighboring states, and probably aided by a party in this capital, who are thoroughly disgusted with the weak and tyrannical government of Señor Juarez. . . . Those well acquainted with the country watch this movement with anxiety and say that unless promptly checked it will lead to the downfall of the present government and renew all the horrors of the civil war. In the meanwhile, Congress, instead of enabling the government to put down the frightful disorders that reign throughout the length and breadth of the land, is occupied in disputing about vain theories of so-called government on ultraliberal principles, while the respectable part of the population is delivered defenseless to the attacks of robbers and assassins, who swarm on the highroads and in the streets of the capital. . . . This state of things renders one all but powerless to obtain redress from a government that is solely occupied in maintaining its existence from day to day, and therefore unwilling to attend to other people's misfortunes before their own"—a peculiarity of human nature which completed his disgust. "Patriotism, in the common acceptance of the term, appears to be unknown; no one man of any note is to be found in the ranks of either party. Contending factions struggle for the possession of power only to gratify their cupidity or their revenge; and in the meantime the country sinks lower and lower, while its population becomes brutalized and degraded to an extent frightful to contemplate. Such is the actual state of affairs in Mexico, and Your Lordship will perceive, therefore, that there is little chance of justice or redress from such people, except by the employment of force to exact that which persuasion and menaces have hitherto failed to obtain."

The conclusion was irrefutable. Poverty was a perpetual threat to civilization, and poverty so incurable defied it, and within three weeks Wyke had worked himself to a pitch of outrage at which his views tallied completely with those of Saligny. Between the smug consternation of the one and the calculated pessimism of the other nothing but the main chance was needed to bring about their merger.

After consulting the senior officer of the British squadron, Sir Charles came to the conclusion that only two courses were open to him: not to mention Mathew's, nor to waver between forbearance and foreign interposition, but to choose between withdrawing the Legation and adopting the plan of Captain Aldham; and he preferred the flag officer's. "Captain Aldham, who during the last three years has gained a very clear insight into the Mexican character and the manner of evading their engagements so peculiar to their officials, is of opinion that the time for lenience is past, and that if we mean to protect the lives and properties of British subjects, coercive measures must be employed. He thinks that a blockade is not advisable on account of the large force that would be required for that purpose on so extensive a line of coast, to say nothing of the commercial difficulties to which it would give rise, besides the fact that by so blockading we should be actually robbing ourselves of the percentage of duties levied at Veracruz and Tampico. This plan, then, presenting so many objections, Captain Aldham is of opinion that the next best thing to be done is to take possession of the customs houses of Veracruz, Tampico, and Matamoros on the Atlantic, and of either Acapulco, Mazatlan, or San Blas on the Pacific; to lower the duties on all goods landed at those places; and to pay ourselves by the percentage to which we are entitled but which we now never obtain, owing to the rascality of the Mexican authorities." Whatever objections might be raised to the unilateral action of the British might be safely discounted. "The French have only a small debt of 190,000 dollars to recover, which is being chiefly paid off by twenty-five per cent of the import duties levied at Veracruz on cargoes brought in French ships. The Spanish claim eight per cent on all import duties on some claim of theirs, which is in suspense and therefore the interest thereon is not paid." Both creditors would undoubtedly welcome a control of the customs guaranteeing their efficient administration, and so would the debtors themselves. "From the moment that we show our determination no longer to suffer British subjects to be robbed and murdered with impunity, we shall be respected, and every rational Mexican will approve of a measure, which they themselves are the first to say is necessary, in order to put a stop to the excesses daily and hourly committed under a government as corrupt as it is powerless to maintain order or cause its own laws to be executed."

Provided that any government survived such assistance, and that any rational Mexican could be found among so many national ones, this conclusion was also irrefutable; but patriotism being merely another "ism" in Mexico, such considerations were irrelevant. What was worth some consideration was the point made by Mathew that peace was indispensable to the recovery of the country and the British debt alike. Sir Charles, however, had not yet thought so far. After six weeks in the country his mind was too jaundiced to work either fast or clearly, and, baffled by financial collapse and his inability to deal with it, he saw no further than the punishment of incompetence. Ignoring the risk that coercion might defeat his purpose and by wrecking the government and renewing the civil war prevent the protection of British interests, he recommended the course best calculated to secure that result, and his advice reached Lord John Russell at the same time that the government suspended the debt service.

Wyke was fully prepared for the crisis, therefore, and had done as much to anticipate it as Saligny; yet when it came, his conduct varied inversely to its gravity and differed in a small but significant degree from that of his colleague: where Saligny promptly severed diplomatic relations, Wyke merely suspended them. The difference, slight as it was, corresponded to a fundamental distinction in the aims and interests of the two Ministers: Saligny, pursuing a course of studied provocation for political purposes, required a rupture for their promotion and employed the negligible French debt as a mere lever; while Wyke, exclusively concerned with the economic interests of his flag, had too great a stake to protect to be uncompromising. Caution came late, but it came with the crisis and his recognition of the consequences, and either because of a professional preference for half-measures or a belated compunction, prompted by ignorance of the intentions of his government, he left ajar the door which Saligny slammed. Of this opening Zamacona took advantage to negotiate. The impulsive, confused, and choleric temper of the previous few weeks subsided on both sides; the discussions, acrid at first, strained, defensive, evasive, restored contact and gradually approached an understanding; and Wyke, working with an antagonist eager to propitiate him, proceeded to seek a solution less drastic than the one he had recommended to London. The damage, however, was already done: the problem had passed out of his hands. For a moment, for a brief fateful moment, it had been his to mold and formulate; but the decision taken in London produced complications and set forces in motion which could no longer be controlled.

Mexico had always suffered from the personalities of foreign diplomats, and in the critical summer of 1861 those of Wyke and Saligny loomed large. Together, though from different and even antagonistic motives, they shaped its destiny. The political bias of the one and the economic prejudice of the other were equally misleading; but in any assessment of their joint responsibility the British Minister was undoubtedly entitled to the lion's share, since he represented the preponderant Power.

7

BUT it was abroad that the brood of the nightmare littered. After July 17 the destiny of Mexico was shaped in Europe. Word of the debt suspension was received in London late in August, and though another two months passed before action was taken, the policy adopted by the British Government was determined by the first reports of Wyke and based on the premises he supplied—a derelict country, a government insecure, incompetent, and corrupt, and the necessity of applying disciplinary measures and foreclosing on a mortgage menaced by national bankruptcy in Mexico. His plan was adopted in all its essentials and broadened to meet the objections to it which he ignored or minimized. Russell and Palmerston formulated the problem with more foresight, and molded it even more myopically, at a distance. English interests in Mexico being purely commercial, their primary object was to isolate economic sanctions and prevent them from breeding political complications. Obviously this was impossible. Financial intervention was, *ipso facto,* political intervention: occupation of the seaports and control of the customs were calculated to throttle the government, and what was to follow its collapse? That question could be ignored only by the blind or the British, but they were old hands at evasion, and they met the question by blinking it. The Prime Minister was an expert at taking the first step and avoiding the last, his Foreign Secretary was an accomplished subordinate, and they covered their responsibility and declared their indifference to the consequences by a formula pledging the British Government to nonintervention in the internal affairs of Mexico. But the difficulties did not end there; the formula was sufficient for domestic, but not for foreign, consumption. The collection of the British debt, absorbing the bulk of Mexican revenues, could not be decently executed without consulting the other creditors, and to avoid the appearance of unilateral action it was necessary to collaborate with them. Decency raised the devil, as it always did, in England. As the interests of France and Spain were primarily political, and both were suspected of velleities of intervention, the next step was to extend the formula to include them and to commit their governments to the same pledge of neutrality. This was less simple. Time was required to adjust the English position to that of the other parties and to guarantee the freedom of action of the British Government by limiting theirs. Two months were spent in settling these safeguards, and in the meanwhile the center of political gravity shifted to France, and the primary object became confused with subordinate aims that seconded it there. English initiative was not, and could not be, neutral, since national interests were settled by national characteristics. In England, where the national character was predominantly male, the Mexican question was settled with virile simplicity; but across the Channel it was complicated by an infusion of feminine influence, and in that phase of its development women and women's motives and women's men played an important part in fostering the brood of the nightmare.

In France the effect of the debt suspension was purely political, and there the announcement precipitated a combination far more complex, the elements of which had long lain in solution, waiting to be fused and materialized. Of those elements the most visible and the least forceful, but the one that acted as a catalytic agent on the others, was the ferment of a group of Mexican refugees in Paris. The classic capital of political exiles had become the headquarters of a dozen Mexican reactionaries, dreaming of a restoration of their regime and scheming unsuccessfully to promote it. Feeble in themselves, their potential strength lay in the forces with which they were connected and those with which they had long been seeking to establish contact—the Church and the Court, the Bank and the Throne—influences of the past and the present, whose shifting frontiers met in Paris. There the refugees found protective coloring: clerical, monarchical, speculative, simian, they were nothing in themselves, and not until those forces began to stir did they find patrons; but for a brief period in France as well, persons played a decisive part in manipulating the destinies of Mexico.

Of those futile few the most important were a trio of disappointed intriguers whose names figure in the initial combinations: Gutierrez Estrada, Hidalgo, Almonte. The first was the notorious expatriate who had been expelled from Mexico twenty years before for preaching the gospel of monarchy there, and who had spent his life parading it around Europe. Possessed of a respectable fortune and married to an Austrian countess, he had obtained an entree to most of the courts of the Continent and solicited pretenders from Austria to Spain without success, since he was commonly considered a visionary and a crank. For that reason, perhaps, one court had remained closed to him, and to penetrate the Tuileries he was forced to seek an assistant; and in the person of a prepossessing young diplomat by the name of Hidalgo, who shared his obsession, he found him. The bearer of that illustrious name distinguished it from that of the liberator of his country by conspiring to undo the work of his namesake. The son of an officer who had served Iturbide, he inherited the political faith of the ephemeral emperor and was able to give it the contemporary cachet, which made him so valuable to Gutierrez Estrada. For Pepe Hidalgo—he was known by his familiar diminutive in the highest circles—was a salon diplomat and an accomplished worldling, ingratiating, pliable, presentable, whose social gifts and connections won him access to spheres that were closed to his fanatical friend, and the assistant soon outgrew the master. If Gutierrez Estrada was the sire of the scheme for foreign intervention, Hidalgo was its spark, and Almonte the drudge. Almonte figured in it by virtue of his rank as Minister of the Miramon government in Paris, for though his functions were extinct, he retained their prestige and traded on his position; but he never rose above the role of a diplomatic dummy. His antecedents were glorious: he was the son of Morelos. He was a bastard, and his name was a nickname that recalled his casual birth in the mountains. He began life as a Liberal, but as he learned to know the world better he turned his coat and immortalized his name by attaching it to the treaty that secured the favor of Spain for the ultramontane government in Mexico. The Mon-Almonte Convention was a deed of mutual adoption. His character was colorless. Such was the singular trio of patriots—the namesake of the first liberator of Mexico, the son of the second, and the professional expatriate—for whom the hour had now struck to convert their phantom existence into political life.

Timeservers all, they would have continued to stagnate in their insignificance, however, had it not been for Hidalgo. For in one respect at least he could compare with his homonym. His was the hand that sowed the seed and that reaped the harvest in 1861. How he did so was also a historic story. Five years before, when the revolution of Ayutla had triumphed in Mexico, he lost his berth in the Legation at Madrid, but he met with better luck when he crossed the French frontier on his way to Paris. At Bayonne he bowed to a lady whom he had known years ago as a girl in her mother's salon in Madrid, and who had since become the Empress of the French. She recognized him, and this chance meeting altered the whole course of his career. Old acquaintance was not forgotten; she picked him up and invited him to Biarritz, and there, in long outings together on the water, he entertained her with idle reveries about Mexico and caught her fancy with a topic that made them compatriots, for he was still a Spaniard at heart and she had not ceased to be one by marrying the Emperor of the French.

Eugénie de Montijo had lost many illusions with her maiden name. Unhappy in her domestic life, she longed to play a political role in France and had already asserted herself on the Roman question—a satisfaction that the Emperor owed her for his marital infidelities—and the engaging young lady's man touched a responsive chord, and touched it at the right time. The tribulations of the Mexican Church gave her a fresh lift in life, as he acquainted her with them, and he caught her attention. When she tired of the Church, he changed the subject to a Mexican monarchy, and her sympathy for him grew with her interest in Mexico. She had never heard of any other Hidalgo, and she read the history of his country through his eyes and in them. She allowed him to court her politically. In due time she introduced him to her husband, whom he attended in turn, following him from Biarritz to Paris, Fontainebleau, Saint-Cloud, Chantilly, or wherever the calendar led his seasonal promenades. Hidalgo became a member of the Imperial entourage, on the verge of the Imperial ménage, and found repeated occasions to open his heart to the Emperor. The Mexican question was a topic of remote interest, however, to the husband. The tribulations of the Church left him cold—he had his hands full with them in Rome; the idea of a Mexican monarchy caught his fancy, but without capturing it seriously. He toyed with the notion as a prophylactic to American expansion, which was his pet aversion, but both his aversions and his ambitions were indolent, and though it appealed to his prejudice against an imperialism in democratic dress, it moved his imagination only, not his ambition. His attention was engaged elsewhere. The risks of so distant an adventure, the dearth of suitable candidates, and pressing problems at home made the scheme seem chimerical even to Louis Napoleon, who was something of a dreamer himself.

Hidalgo won a hearing, but nothing more, but a hearing was enough for him. He attached himself to his host in much the same way as Madame Gordon did. When she was asked whether she loved the Emperor she smiled and replied, *"Je l'aime politiquement. A vrai dire, il me fait l'effet d'une femme."* Her mot was cited by a learned physiologist as the clue to the Emperor's character. According to this authority, his temperament was "lymphatico-nervous." "The nerves and the lymph are mingled in him, as often happens in the women of our European West; which explains a well-known mot by Madame Gordon." Perhaps. She was merely a woman; but the authority built a whole theory on her hint. "Where the nerves dominate, the intelligence is facile, comprehensive, fertile in projects, and the imagination inclined to pleasure. If the lymph is uppermost, the mind is slow, the senses obtuse, and, as someone has said, they have to be peeled to be tickled. Suppose these elements united: from their fusion comes a new character, which partakes of both principles and modifies one by the other. Then a man is at once intelligent and dense, bold and calculating, modest and ostentatious, voluptuous and cold, mystic and skeptical, curious and indifferent, mobile and tenacious, indiscreet and secretive, credulous and scoffing, affable and haughty, hesitant and verbose, boastful and careless"—in a word, mutable as a woman and contradictory as a man. "Add to this idea a position, a rank, an elevation . . .

and you have the explanation of his whole reign." The explanation was more mysterious than Napoleon, but it was all that Hidalgo, or Madame Gordon, or the world, had to go on. He was a subject for guess work. Many people were mystified and fascinated by the inconsistencies of his character without contesting his sex. A man with no woman in him would not be a man anyway, but a male; and there was nothing the matter with his manhood. Nor was there any mystery about him more than the normal elusiveness of the great. In his position he kept people guessing, as he was obliged to do by his rank and an elevation that placed him on guard against the world, and Madame Gordon, and Hidalgo. So it was with the Mexican question. His heart was not in it yet; but he was mutable and married to the Empress Eugénie, and that was enough for Hidalgo.

The whole international situation had to change, however, before the second Hidalgo could make any headway. His ideas were premature in 1857 and ahead of their time in 1858; but the outbreak of the civil war in Mexico boosted them, and by the beginning of 1859 they were dangerous enough to catch the attention and excite the alarm of a member of the Legation in Paris, of Liberal sympathies. Andres Oseguerra, the friend, informer, and confident of Ocampo, railed bitterly at the "cicisbeo de la Montijo" and his fatal knack of catering to "feminine sensuality that shrinks from the crack of a whip and swoons, while the scent of blood and butchery thrills it. . . . Why should not our noble énervées give themselves the luxury of emotions," he scoffed, "when there are peoples to pulverize under the wheels of their phaetons for their pleasure?" But he overrated the languid interest of the Empress and the influence of her minion. Gutierrez Estrada, gaining admission to the Tuileries with the help of Hidalgo, annoyed Napoleon and shocked the Empress herself by his fanatical clericalism, his antiquated brand of monarchism, and his anachronistic social ideas; and after defending them at great length he was not invited to do so again. He was de trop at the Tuileries.

Almonte, in turn, tried to gain a foothold for himself in the inner circle, and much more cleverly. He composed a pamphlet in favor of intervention, which he entrusted to Hidalgo to polish and present at the palace. But this bid attracted no attention there, and no notice anywhere, save from Andrés Oseguerra, who noted with satisfaction that Almonte had completely mistaken his man when he trusted his work to Hidalgo and thought "to throw the stone and hide the hand." "I must tell you," he wrote to Mexico, "that by the hand of the Empress the Emperor has received a letter from Hidalgo asking for intervention; it preceded the pamphlet; and hence in the pamphlet there is the I, so much to the taste of the sons of Loyola, with phrases and parentheses of apparent modesty and humility, but the I that says, nevertheless, look at me, I am the author. Almonte thinks that he has been very clever; he thinks that he is a person for Hidalgo, when he is merely a *thing*." Hidalgo was not the man to play second to Almonte, and Almonte came no closer to the Tuileries than he could see from the *impériale* of a public omnibus. The contact man guarded his chosen preserves jealously against poachers; but he himself penetrated no farther than the outskirts of his peculiar domain. Hovering on the verge of the domestic ménage, and familiar with the political household, he was called Pepe here and Pepe there and answered the beck and call of both and the purposes of neither, being without power himself.

So the years of civil war slipped away. In 1859 Napoleon was engaged in the Italian campaign. In 1860 the proposed mediation of France and England in Mexico revived hopes of intervention, but only to disappoint them again, and Hidalgo began to lose heart, as he confessed in an account of his disappointments which he wrote later, for like most of the Creole aristocrats he had less character than conviction and was readily discouraged by adversity. During the years of drought, however, he preserved his position at Court and was allowed to play with ideas that were still unloaded, and the prize of persistence was his in the end.

In the summer of 1861 Hidalgo was at Biarritz again when he was privately informed of the financial crash in Mexico, and he had the honor of being the first to announce it to the Empress and to direct the attention of the Emperor to its possibilities. The scene was preserved by his pen. Dinner was over, the Emperor had retired to his study, the Empress was busy with nothing better than her embroidery, and the friend of the household handed her the letter, which he had just received, containing advance information of the debt suspension. She rose, passed into the study, returned, and invited him to follow her. "Tell the Emperor what you have just told me," she said. The Emperor rose, lit a cigarette, and listened. It was an audience. "Your Majesty, I had long lost hope of seeing those ideas realized of which I had the honor to speak to Your Majesty four years ago, but England, together with Spain, is now irritated by the policy of Juarez, and they will both order warships to our ports. Thus, Your Majesty, we have what we need—English intervention. France will not be acting alone, which was what Your Majesty always wished to avoid. Spain has long been prepared. General Conchal told me not long ago that he had left six thousand men at Havana, ready to land at Veracruz, but that the cabinet at Madrid prefers to act together with France and, if possible, with England as well. French, English, and Spanish squadrons might be despatched to Veracruz and land those six thousand Spaniards. In view of the three combined flags, Mexico would recognize the full strength and superiority of the alliance, and the overwhelming majority of the nation could rely on the support of the intervening powers, destroy the demagogues, and proclaim a monarchy, which is the only salvation of the country. The United States are in the throes of war: they will not move. Besides, they would never oppose the three united powers."

Napoleon was caught off his guard, as he had received no information from the Foreign Office, but the idea was presented with a combined caution and boldness that appealed to him, and he gave it serious consideration. "I have not yet received M. de Thouvenel's despatches," he replied. "If England and Spain act, and the interests of France demand it, I shall join them, but I shall send warships only, no landing troops, and if the country declares that it wishes to organize with the support of the European Powers, I shall lend a hand. Besides, as you say, the state of affairs in the United States is very favorable."

This was sufficient commitment for Hidalgo, and with rare presence of mind he proceeded to go the British one better and to provide for the succession, which they left to chance. "Sire," he continued, "whatever may be the results, we shall have France alone to thank for it. Will Your Majesty permit me to ask whether you have a candidate in view? The Mexicans would accept him from Your Majesty as their own choice." The Emperor turned, lit another cigarette, and answered, "I have none." Before venturing to take the lead, Hidalgo glanced at the Empress. "We cannot think of a Spanish prince," he remarked. "Señor Mon has always assured me that there is no possible choice there." — "It is true," she agreed. "There is no possible choice there, and it is unfortunate, for if there were, he would be the most suitable." The search for an alternative began with two or three German princes, whom the Imperial couple mentioned but discarded because of their religion or the insignificance of their states. Then Hidalgo guided their thoughts toward an Austrian archduke. "But which archduke?" The leading question was put by the Empress and answered by Hidalgo. "I believe the Archduke Reiner was mentioned." — "Yes," said she, "the Archduke Maximilian would not be willing." — "Oh, no, he would not be willing," Hidalgo agreed. — "No, he would not accept," Napoleon concurred. Silence ensued. Then the Empress, tapping her bosom with her fan, exclaimed, "Well, something tells me that he will accept." — "We can but try," said Hidalgo promptly, "and I might write to Gutierrez Estrada to go to Vienna and sound His Imperial Highness." The Emperor assented, and Hidalgo hurried away with permission to use the Imperial telegraph.

It was the crowning moment of his career, and he could hardly be blamed if the *I* of the author dominated his account of it. Neither Almonte nor Gutierrez Estrada could vie with him; not being in Biarritz, they were nowhere. He, and he alone, had won a hearing for his cause—and what more had the other Hidalgo done? Pepe Hidalgo was more fortunate, for he arrived at the right time, and catching the historic moment on the wing, made the most of it. For a fleeting moment he dominated his hosts: the Imperial couple were merely the audience, and he was the impresario pulling crowns from his pocket and princes out of his sleeve. Then the initiative passed from his hand; but that moment was enough to turn the world. Powerless himself, he succeeded nevertheless in anticipating Palmerston, and by playing his cards well and slipping his king into the pack, he trumped the British hand. The morrow proved his accomplishment. Once the winning combination had been played, nothing could stop it, and he benefited by British improvidence, for whatever is left to chance is someone's opportunity, and as sure as anything in this world to be picked up by Pepe. The world was his head, he set it spinning, and his moment made the ephemeral immortal. Hardly believing himself that it was true, he flew to the telegraph office and flashed the name of Maximilian over the wires to Gutierrez Estrada.

Maximilian of Austria . . . Maximilian of Austria. That was a name to conjure with. For anyone who knew the world it was a find. For Hidalgo it was an open sesame. No name in the *Almanach de Gotha* conjured up more pregnant possibilities. Both for political and personal reasons it was a powerful precipitate, as the reaction to it in Biarritz proved. The reaction was as positive as the expression of it was negative, and the unanimity with which the three anglers recoiled from it, the moment it was mentioned, was significant of its fascination for each of them. There were good reasons, in fact, why the Emperor, the Empress, and Hidalgo exclaimed with one voice that Maximilian would not be willing.

Five years before, about the same time that Hidalgo happened in history by his chance meeting with the Empress of the French, the paths of Napoleon and Maximilian crossed for the first time. The younger brother of the Emperor Franz Josef of Austria paid a visit to Paris in 1856, on his first outing from Vienna. The impression that the Napoleons made on him then was described by the young prince in a candid report to his brother, which characterized the writer as well as his hosts. The Emperor of the French, he wrote, "displayed at our first meeting, and during the whole evening, an insuperable embarrassment, which hardly produced a favorable effect upon me. His short unimposing figure, his exterior wholly lacking in nobility"—"vulgar" was the word that first occurred to him, but he crossed it out—"his shuffling gait, his ugly hands, the sly inquiring glance of his lusterless eyes, all these things made up an ensemble that was not calculated to correct my first unfavorable impression. I found the Empress, whom I visited immediately afterward, in a state of great lassitude and weakness; she took uncommon pains to be agreeable, but was at the same time extremely embarrassed. . . . She is quite thoroughbred, but essentially lacking in the august quality of an Empress, and the impression produced on me by her appearance was dimmed by memories of Imperial Vienna." As for the other Bonapartes, they were all very Corsican: old King Jerome reminded him of a senile Italian dentist, and Prince Plon-Plon of a shabby Italian basso; the Princess Matilde was unpleasantly common in appearance. At a state dinner at Saint-Cloud, the Court confirmed his estimate of the master. "The Emperor's incredible lack of ease was particularly obvious; it occurred to me that he still felt uncomfortable in the presence of a prince of more ancient lineage than his own; when he overcomes this constraint, he displays great candor, and the more closely I come to know him the more founded does his confidence in me seem to be. In general, there seems to be a most commendable intention of giving a proper setting to the Court, but the machinery does not work very smoothly as yet, and in spite of the unconstrained manner they try to affect, the parvenu etiquette comes through. . . . I need hardly assure Your Majesty that I take great pains to be agreeable and to let no signs of the unpleasant impressions that strike me here and there appear."

On closer acquaintance the Archduke modified his opinion of his host, albeit with becoming reserve. "Napoleon is one of those men whose personality has nothing winning about it at first sight," he added, "but ends by producing a favorable impression by his great calm and noble simplicity of character. The reckless way in which he speaks in the presence of servants is most remarkable; he often lets fall the most incredible statements in their presence; this seems to me typical of the parvenu, utterly lacking in that *esprit de corps* that makes one careful not to expose oneself in the presence of inferiors." Gradually, however, he warmed to him. "The pleasantest time is at *déjeuner,* when the Emperor can be very attractive in his frankness and amiability. He speaks well and with animation and the effect is heightened by a certain flash in the eyes. On these occasions great candor prevails, in which I join with due moderation." His final impression was almost favorable, and on the eve of his departure he condescended to flatter Napoleon—just to show him how it was done. "Napoleon I had genius," the young Hapsburg remarked. "Napoleon III has cleverness. Genius moves the world, but cleverness rules it." The compliment was a little left-handed, perhaps, but Napoleon accepted it and was extraordinarily friendly and betrayed a certain emotion on parting with his guest— they were like old friends, he said. Once they touched on politics— but only once—and lightly. Maximilian, who was just learning to walk politically, put a candid question to the clever antagonist of his house. "May I assure the Emperor my brother that Your Majesty will proceed in perfect harmony with him in the Italian question, as in all others?" The answer was satisfactory, and the Archduke left Paris highly pleased with himself.

The impression that Maximilian made on Napoleon was unfading. Five years had passed since their meeting, but his first thought, when Hidalgo proposed that name, was that naturally the Archduke would be unwilling to accept a throne from his hand; for however carefully the young prince had concealed his superiority, he was a Hapsburg, and Napoleon would not have been a Bonaparte had he not suffered from condescension. For a long and unforgettable fortnight in 1856 he and his consort had been daily undressed by the appraising eye of their guest, and in 1861 they were still self-conscious at the sound of his name. The Imperial Adam shrank, and his blood turned blue with the chill which the bare mention of it recalled, but the vanity of the Imperial Eve overcame the pride of her partner. The vanity of the female was less modest and more enterprising than that of the male, and an unerring intuition told her that the Hapsburg could be conquered. She tempted, and he consented, and Hidalgo triumphed. None of them suspected that Maximilian might be a Bonaparte too. That discovery remained to be made by a scholarly sleuth, who deduced it from a letter left by L'Aiglon, suggesting that his captivity in Vienna had been consoled by the Archduchess Sophia and that she had borne him two sons, one of whom was the reigning Emperor of Austria and the other his lesser brother; but the proof was as doubtful as it was suggestive, and it was still locked in the secret compartment of an old desk in Vienna. So far as the Napoleons knew, Maximilian was pure Hapsburg. The only family secret of which they were conscious was the family failing of their inferiority in the eyes of the hereditary enemy of their house, and that was an open secret. Had Napoleon been deterred by such considerations, however, he would have been unworthy of his name and would have merited the mot of Madame Gordon on whom he produced the effect of a woman.

There were far better reasons for courting Maximilian politically. The opportunity to patronize the hereditary enemy of his house might be a personal satisfaction, but it was dignified by greater considerations. Many things had changed in Europe since 1856, and the Archduke was a valuable pawn, and the offer of a throne, however remote, a diplomatic gesture liable to relieve tension with Austria over the Italian question, which since the intervention of Napoleon in Lombardy had become so acute as to threaten a general war. Vienna, Venice, Victor Emmanuel—combinations of all kinds were conjured up by the name of Maximilian, and the dream of a Mexican monarchy began to materialize in the mastermind at Biarritz as a febrifuge for old Europe. Nothing was risked by indulging it but a snub, of which Hidalgo would bear the brunt; and vanity, discreetly varnished with politics, involved all three in an adventure which lacked neither the pettiest nor the largest motives for the ruin of Mexico.

The time, the place, and the man had been found by Hidalgo, and out of that tentative conversation a larger and more entangling alliance developed. His mercurial mission ended when he wired Gutierrez Estrada to hold himself ready to leave for Vienna. The old man, who in the course of peddling a Mexican throne for twenty years had kept his head only by riding his hobby, now cleared the ground with one bound. He hurried to the Austrian Embassy, and in the absence of the Ambassador—it was the dead season—submitted the proposal to a secretary, who transmitted it *pro forma* to Vienna. Two months before, he had laid it before the Ambassador, on his own responsibility, and Prince Metternich had humored him to the extent of forwarding it to his Chancellor, whose verdict was what might have been expected: Rechberg declared the idea absurd and unworthy of serious consideration. The telegram from Biarritz, however, turned the steadiest heads. Supported by the tacit sanction of Napoleon, the notion that the Chancellor had described as absurd two months before now commanded serious attention, and he took the train for Miramar to consult Maximilian—a step that conveyed the implicit sanction of the Kaiser. Maximilian had been sounded before and had turned down the idea, but he was accessible to it now on two conditions suggested by his brother and accepted as essential safeguards by himself: that he be assured of the consent of the Mexican people and of the formal support of the great Powers. There was no further need for Gutierrez Estrada to go to Vienna: Vienna came to him. His was the faith that moved mountains, and the conditions imposed were mere hitches. The consent of the Mexican people was not a serious hindrance. The Archduke was famous for his liberal principles. They had won him some popularity in Austria and Italy, and the disfavor of his brother, who was not averse, therefore, to an adventure in America which promised to relieve him of a family problem. The consent of the governed was a concession to the idiosyncracies of the Archduke, covered by the guarantee of the great Powers upon which his guardian insisted as a matter of political dignity and natural affection. This guarantee, however, raised a formal difficulty.

For, in the meanwhile, another factor had come into play—the independence and routine of the French Foreign Office. The first report of the debt suspension in Mexico reached Paris on the same day that the Emperor left for Biarritz, and the first steps to deal with it were taken during his holiday by the Bay of Biscay. M. de Thouvenal, who was also on vacation, came into Paris occasionally to give it perfunctory attention without suspecting the importance it was assuming in the villa by the Bay of Biscay, for Napoleon did not deem it necessary to inform him of an idea that was still nebulous, embryonic, and contingent upon the consent of Maximilian. Following the usual practice in foreign affairs, M. de Thouvenel consulted the British Ambassador and acceded to the British plan for joint intervention. An ultimatum requiring repeal of the moratorium, and the appointment of English and French Commissioners to collect their credits at the customs, was to be presented by both Powers, backed by their fleets; but intervention was to be purely financial and limited, as London insisted, to political neutrality. To this formula M. de Thouvenel made no objection, nor did Napoleon when it was referred to him, since his participation was contingent upon English co-operation, and it was not until the overtures made in his name to Vienna produced a response that the consequences became embarrassing.

In the meanwhile, following another normal precedent, M. de Thouvenel proposed that Spain be included in the expedition. This step was warranted by several considerations. Spain was an acknowledged creditor, with a strong garrison in Cuba waiting to be landed at Veracruz, and a more or less willing protégé of Napoleon. The suggestion was coldly received in London, however, for those very reasons. The aims of Madrid were likely to lead to political complications, which the British Government wished to avoid, and to the resuscitation of a regime in Mexico that was unpopular in England. And had it not been for the growth of the monarchical intrigue, Spain might have been ignored.

But Spain was not to be ignored. There the crisis in Mexico produced an effect that was political only in the narrowest sense of the term, affecting international affairs merely because it excited local politics. National interests were not involved, but national characteristics were. Spain in the middle of the nineteenth century was ruled by the psychology of a decadent nation struggling to recover the position of a major Power in the family of modern nations, and considerations of prestige and national pride, prompted by nostalgic sentiment far more than by material interest, dominated all its governments alike. The government of Marshal O'Donnell then in power was peculiarly susceptible to the question of face, for Marshal O'Donnell had conducted the conquest of Morocco in 1859 and given a fillip to the revival of national sentiment by that enterprise. He had also refused to make an issue of the expulsion of the Spanish Minister to Mexico at the beginning of the year and had discredited him in the Cortes, to the scandal of the Opposition, which, led by Pacheco himself, attacked the government for neglecting the national dignity with a vigor that shook it. The parliamentary feud was at its height in May and had barely subsided when the crisis in Mexico arose, but as it arose in the dead season O'Donnell had time to anticipate its domestic repercussions before the Cortes reconvened.

No sooner was it known that two of the great Powers were consulting than his Foreign Minister took steps to forestall the unfortunate impression at home and abroad of the omission of the third. He telegraphed to his Ambassador in Paris to ascertain the intentions of the French Government and stated his own, which were to act independently, energetically, and without delay. Calderon Collantes compressed into that message the dilemma of a people equally sensitive to neglect of its right to rank as a great Power and condescension toward its claims, and of a government conscious that it could not act without England and France, and he teamed the two horns in a warning that Spain could neither be left out nor left behind. A gesture of independence and a bid for support, the message was so understood by M. de Thouvenel, who invited the Spanish Government to consult and collaborate. As the protection of Spain formed part of the Napoleonic policy in Europe, this step was as automatic as consultation with England, and he did not expect it to be contested in London. Thus encouraged, Calderon Collantes took the lead in two other directions. Without consulting London or Paris, he sent orders to Cuba to occupy Veracruz and Tampico, and, without approaching the English Government, he suggested to the French that the scope of the conversations in Paris be broadened and that the three Powers should combine not merely to exact satisfaction for injuries, but to establish "a regular and stable order in Mexico." Thouvenel replied, after consulting Napoleon, that their views coincided.

Thus the situation stood at the end of September. In the first week of October, when Maximilian accepted the crown conditionally, the principal condition could not be met: a formal offer by the great Powers was, on the face of it, impossible. His candidacy, of which rumors were circulating, excited jealousy in Madrid, where the Bourbons had preferred claims to the hypothetic throne of Mexico; the projected monarchy ran counter to the policy of Palmerston; and Napoleon had been committed to contradictory pledges—to the British definition of intervention on the one hand, and the Spanish version on the other. This involved situation had developed partly, no doubt, because of the slack season, which allowed Thouvenal to shape the preliminaries of French policy in the absence of the Emperor from Paris; but the negligence of the master was no seasonal indolence; it was the habitual state of mind of a dictator who had not received the power of decision from nature and who readily abandoned it to his subordinates. That mongrel psyche of his was to blame. It was during one of those slack periods that he drifted toward the idea that entangled him at Biarritz: impelled by the importunities of Hidalgo and the Empress, he was hurried into a step for which he was unprepared and which carried him further than he contemplated—until he caught up with himself. The prompt if provisional acceptance of Maximilian made it as impossible to withdraw as to square the offer with the conflicting views of

Spain and England, and before the confusion became embarrassing he dispelled it. Thouvenel was instructed to consult the British Ambassador in Paris on the advisability of establishing a stable government in Mexico, and the French Ambassador in London was directed to approach the Foreign Secretary with the same proposal.

Russell welcomed the prospect of a stable government in Mexico, but insisted that it should be brought about by the Mexican people themselves; and at the same time he took a step to break the combined weight of France and Spain and to bring them both under control. On the old and tried principle that the best way of foiling an opponent was to become his ally, and a combination of opponents by joining their company and spoiling it, he consented to include Spain in the expedition, and proposed to keep the combined hands of Paris and Madrid off Mexico by binding them to the English formula of intervention in a written engagement subscribing to its principles. This maneuver compelled Napoleon to declare himself. Duplicity was abhorrent to him—he had no gift for it—and he met the difficulty with candor. In a personal letter to the French Ambassador in London, who was directed to read it to Lord Russell, he set forth his first thoughts and his second and explained his conception of the joint enterprise, not in the ambiguous formulas of professional diplomacy, but in his own direct, forthright, and first-personal style. He spoke English, in short.

What had been a mania with the Mexican monarchists and an idle reverie with Napoleon had developed so rapidly that he was obliged to assemble his ideas hastily to justify it; they were still vague and unformed, but he advanced them boldly. He began by dwelling on the advantage of establishing a stable government in Mexico to check the encroachments of the United States and to open a commercial field equally profitable to the three partners, particularly at a time when Mexican cotton would go far to supply the shortage caused by the American civil war. These considerations had long struck him, he said —but they were addressed to Liverpool rather than to Lord Russell. When Mexicans had appealed to him in the past to rescue their country from anarchy, he had had no pretext to intervene and had been unwilling to risk a rupture with the United States; that hazard was now removed. The outrages of the Mexican Government gave England and France legitimate grounds to act, and though the tripartite pact limited their action to the redress of grievances, he wished to look further and "not to bind his hands benevolently and prevent a solution that would be to the interest of all concerned." And now came the cotton for Lord Russell. Mexicans had assured him that the mere appearance of a naval force would cause the proclamation of a monarchy; they had asked him to name his candidate; he had none, he wished to have none, but the Archduke Maximilian seemed to offer the desired guarantees, and the Mexicans had sounded the cabinet in Vienna and were inclined to believe that the Prince would accept the crown, provided he were formerly invited by the Mexican people and assured of the support of the Powers. He did not press the point; he merely notified Lord Russell. Lastly, there was cotton for himself as well. He would be wanting in sincerity, he concluded, if he pledged himself not to support, at least morally, a political change, which he desired not from selfish motives or unjust antipathies, but from a consciousness that he was working in the interests of civilization as a whole. The final consideration was as sincere as the others and the most compelling of all for Napoleon; a high-minded and unconscionable dreamer, ambitious for humanity and fatal to it, he was incapable of deceiving others without first deceiving himself, and material considerations were always secondary to those large, general, congenial, and cloudy views in which his mind was at home.

Of this notice Lord Russell took no cognizance, since he had no official knowledge of it. He had no desire to embarrass Napoleon, and he did the decent thing. He continued to press for the conclusion of the pact on his own terms, carefully excluding those ulterior aims of which he was privately apprised and which he discouraged by a diplomatic deafness that made them inadmissible. Time was pressing, too; the season for operations on the fever-ridden coast of Mexico was short, and two months had been spent in harnessing the creditors, underwriting the expedition, and adjusting their interests. Under the combined pressure of British consistency, Spanish impatience, and Austrian condescension, Napoleon consented to join the undertaking on terms that converted his false situation into a formal agreement. The London Convention, signed on October 31, represented the triumph of British policy. It provided for consultation among the three Powers in the organization of an expedition to occupy the ports and military points of Mexico; it bound them not to seek any acquisition of territory or private advantage, nor to exercise in the internal affairs of Mexico any influence liable to impair the right of the Mexican people freely to choose and constitute their own form of government; and to complete its international character and guarantee its rectitude, the Government of the United States was to be invited to join it. Nothing apparently could be more explicit; but as a working agreement it rested on the assumption by one party that it meant what it said, and by the others that it was open to interpretation and compatible with mental reservations; so that full intervention was merely a matter, after all, of mutual confidence.

8

TO COMBAT the designs of their creditors during the two critical months when these engagements were forming, the Mexican
Government commanded the diplomatic service of one man.
The foreign service was the first to suffer from the need of drastic economy and was reduced to indispensables: the Legation in Washington
was maintained, and a single minister was appointed to cover Europe
in an omnibus character.

Don Juan Antonio de la Fuente, on whom the choice fell, was
neither poor in spirit nor an untested Christopher. A fellow traveler
who had had joined the government and supported it before, in bad
weather, and been seasoned by adversity, he had sat in the Veracruz
cabinet, where he fought the McLane treaty alone and signed the decree of religious liberty, and had built up a Spartan political record,
which schooled him for the task of representing his country abroad at
a time when the principal qualification of a Mexican diplomat was a
capacity to suffer without complaint. He had also built up a certain
rigidity of character, which was the professional defect of his qualities.
Although he was appointed at the beginning of that stringent year, his
departure was delayed by the difficulty of raising his traveling expenses,
which he supplied himself, and when he arrived in Paris in April he
encountered another delay in presenting his credentials, deliberately
prolonged by the Quai d'Orsay on the pretext that Almonte had not
yet been formally recalled; and after contesting it for four months he
won his first diplomatic victory by forcing his reception at Saint-Cloud
on August 10. Depressed by the unpopularity of his party and his poverty, he was prepared for the worst. He dreaded, he confessed, "a cold
reception, at the very least, if not a harsh and bitter one, but, on the
contrary, the Emperor displayed the most exquisite benevolence."
Gratefully surprised, he was not dazzled, however, by the amenities of
the occasion and accepted them with mental reservations. "I cannot describe the flattering reception accorded me by the Emperor as decidedly
favorable to our interests," he reported, "until I see that the claims of
M. de Saligny are less exacting and bellicose in the extremely serious
negotiation of the Jecker bonds and the new French Convention."

His reception at the Foreign Office ten days before had put him on his guard, and his account of it was uncanceled by the benevolence of the Emperor. "The threats of M. de Saligny," he had written then, "the immoderate expressions employed by M. de Thouvenel; his statement that he approved all that M. de Saligny had done; demands so strong, so unseasonable, and so inconsiderate as those conveyed to the Constitutional government, while every consideration is lavished on the lifeless remains still lingering here of the Reaction, in which I include Almonte, who maintains his good relations with the Emperor, and Miramon, who was invited with his wife to the festivities at Court; the efforts of the bondholders in London to induce the English Government to assume a tone of hostility toward us and their success in many respects; the claim to intervene in the collection of our Federal revenues to take up the dividends of the English debt; the desires of which the correspondent of the London *Times* has made himself the echo, proposing the political intervention of England in our country, also suggested by the *Frankfurter Zeitung;* and above all the union of England and France, admitted by M. de Thouvenel and Lord Russell, and designed to crush the legitimate government of the Republic, which has done them no wrong, while they maintain with the Miramon government, which has offended them, relations of friendship or at least of tolerance . . . all this leads me to conclude that there is some grave design against the Republic on the part of France and England, or that the governments of those two nations may readily carry their demands so far as profoundly to injure the sovereignty of Mexico and make the constitution of the Liberal government impossible."

The telltale catalogue was discouraging, and it was with these signs of a campaign to mobilize public opinion for a coming *coup* in mind that he went to Saint-Cloud and listened with misgiving to the Emperor expressing his sympathy for a country ravaged by civil war and menaced by American invasion, his desire to preserve its independence, and his regret that "so beautiful a country should be so unfortunate." He caught the Emperor in a holiday mood, just before leaving for the seashore, and what he really heard was the hush before Biarritz.

His misgivings were fully confirmed three weeks later, when the first reports of the debt suspension reached Paris. Recognizing the coincidence of the crisis with a premeditated plan of aggression which had developed before it and which would have materialized without that provocation, he realized better than anyone the full fatality of the crash and the futility of opposing the forces that conspired to produce it; but he made a conscientious attempt to avert the consequences. He wrote to Thouvenel, requesting him to waive the rule that limited audiences to one day a week and to grant him an immediate interview, so that he might communicate with his government by the mail boat leaving the next morning. Three days later he was received, and the interview lasted only a few minutes. Thouvenel, who had consulted the

British Ambassador before answering De la Fuente's note, refused to listen to any explanations and, abandoning himself to the utmost excitement, said, "We have fully approved the conduct of M. de Saligny. We have given orders, in agreement with England, for a fleet composed of warships of both nations to exact satisfaction of the Mexican Government, and your government will learn through our Minister and our Admiral what the demands of France are." Then, irritated by his own temper, Thouvenel spoke for Thouvenel. "Personally," he added, "I have nothing against you, and I wish that events permitted me to use more friendly expressions." The Mexican relieved his embarrassment by putting an end to the interview himself and retired with a stiff expostulation. After that there was nothing to do but to suspend relations, and he did so on the same day in a note that needed no answer. He had been recognized for exactly four weeks, and his mission was confined to forcing one door and being shown out by another.

By the same mail that notified him of the debt suspension, De la Fuente received a note from Juarez, directing him to explain the situation to Napoleon in person and to Queen Victoria, and enclosing a draft for five thousand pesos to secure a hearing for the Mexican side of the question in the press. After his experience at the Quai d'Orsay, De la Fuente decided that it would be useless to proceed to London, "since it is practically certain that this step would win us another rebuff such as we have received here. I am further moved to this opinion," he explained, "by the information, sufficiently to be expected by now, that it is in England that the infamous intrigue of European intervention in the politics and government of our country had its origin and is most in vogue." Official doors being closed to him, he could no longer act upon governments or against them except by appealing to public opinion; and that arbiter was also inaccessible. Public opinion meant, if it meant anything, parliamentary opinion—and the parliaments of both countries were in recess—or the press. In France the press was muzzled and not venal enough to be influenced by five thousand pesos. In England the government organs were booming intervention, and the Minister sent some clippings to Mexico with a caveat. "It is quite clear that our British creditors would willingly see us delivered over to any nation in the world, and subjected to the most despotic government that men can imagine, provided the Convention of the English debt in Mexico and the law covering the debt contracted in London were completely observed; and everyone knows that the influence and interests of those creditors make themselves felt only too well in the regions of power." All the channels to public opinion being choked, he chose the only course left to him and remained in Paris in the hope, as he put it, "of penetrating the capital idea of France and England in relation to Mexico." Paris was the listening post of Europe, and if he could not be heard there himself, he could at least overhear the hum of the machinery; and to that post he clung, stranded.

The machinery creaked, creaked loudly enough to give him some hope. "We may be able to profit by the small and doubtful respite granted us by the mutual antipathies of France, England, and Spain," he wrote as the alliance was being forged. But he was too close to the machine to mistake a hitch for a halt in its momentum. If the mutual antipathies of France, England, and Spain had been purely political, there might have been some hope that the combination would break, but they were harnessed to the preponderant Power, whose economic strength and interests gave it the lead and the control of the whole enterprise, and whose initiative determined its nature. The driving power of the capital idea that united those incompatible Allies lay precisely in the competition of capitalist forces from which there could be only a brief respite, but no ultimate escape, for a colonial country. Friction was its fundamental note, and the proof that the machine was functioning; and he dwelt on that note incessantly, urging his government to draw back while there was yet time and to repeal the decree of July 17 at all costs.

His warning was anticipated. The emergency that provoked the moratorium subsided as rapidly as it arose. Early in August Gonzalez Ortega met the forces of Marquez and dispersed them, and though the result was not decisive, the relief was sufficient to allow the government to reconsider the expedient of debt suspension and to take steps to avert the coalition forming abroad: progress in one direction allowed of retreat in another. By forcing the government to such shifts and provoking the crisis, however, Marquez had scored a formidable triumph, which his rout could not efface. The victory of Gonzalez Ortega dispelled the mere wraiths of the nightmare, and it fell to Zamacona to disperse its brood and appease the irritated Powers.

With one of them he found it impossible to treat. M. de Saligny was irreconcilable. Shortly before the moratorium was announced, the government had approached the creditors of the French Convention with an offer of pledges and promissory notes secured by Church property, which they were inclined to accept; but on consulting their Minister, they were advised to refuse any settlement. If there was any doubt that he was acting as an *agent provocateur* before July 17, it was dispelled by his conduct after it.

The return of Ortega to the capital was celebrated by cheering crowds parading through the main streets, and several days later the diplomatic corps called upon Zamacona to protest against an attempt made on the life of the French Minister in the course of the demonstration. Surprised that he had not heard of it before, and that it had not been reported to the police, he ordered an immediate investigation.

The testimony was unanimous that the behavior of the crowds passing
the French Legation was orderly; no one had heard the cries of "Death
to France!" of which the diplomatic corps complained, or noticed any
demonstrations of hostility toward the Minister. There had been some
shouts of "Death to Reaction!" which no one supposed to be directed
against him, and some singing of the "Marseillaise," which no one con-
strued as an offense to his flag. To the attempt on his life there was no
witness but himself. According to his account, he was standing in the
courtyard of his house, at dusk, when he heard a report and noticed that
a column near which he was standing had been nicked by a bullet. The
police studied the story and the premises; the trajectory of the shot that
no one had heard was traced to a point that no one could see; and the
story missed its mark as completely as the bullet that M. de Saligny
produced to prove it. The investigation was dropped at that point, but
it brought out some facts to which the press gave publicity. The French
Legation was known to harbor a reactionary general wanted by the police and to be a notorious center of conspiracy from which communication with the enemy was carried on with diplomatic immunity.
Wisely, no doubt, M. de Saligny was silent, but in his report to Paris
he capitalized the attempt on his life, representing it as the culmination of an inspired system of terror to which the French residents of
the capital could testify, many of them having brought him letters left
in their homes by night, threatening them with fire and death. "Our
nationals have not let themselves be intimidated by these maneuvers,
which everyone attributes to subordinate agents of the government,"
he added. Witnesses to this charge were also wanting; but he was
never at a loss for ideas, nor embarrassed by contradiction. Far from
representing the French colony, which was predominantly Liberal in
its sympathies, he was denounced even by its conservative members as
a menace to their interests, and the leading bankers and merchants
proposed to draw up a representation against his interference and warmongering—testimony which Zamacona hastened to forward to Paris
in the fond belief that his Minister there could still be heard and oblivious to the fact that the correction of calumny, under the best of
conditions, always comes too late.

    Against M. de Saligny there was no defense, and the means which
Zamacona adopted to disarm him were the most deadly: he ignored
him. The French Minister could not be ignored with impunity; he
had already been ignored too long for the good of the country; and he
was now isolated by the negotiations that Zamacona was conducting
with the British Minister. Incensed by the desertion of his colleague,
M. de Saligny retired into the Legation, nursing his spleen against the
day of reckoning and relieving it in inflammatory reports to Havana.
The protection of Spanish nationals, which he owed to Pacheco, provided him with the nearest means of offsetting English influence, and

in his correspondence with the Captain-General of Cuba he harped on the pride of Spain, which had also been ignored too long, and discharged the congested venom he generated into the hospitable mind of Marshal Serrano.

With the British Minister, Zamacona fared better. Wyke was not irreconcilable, he was merely irritated, and though he acted in concert with Saligny up to the rupture with the government, after it the fundamental differences in their interests led to a divergence in their conduct. Wyke was without ulterior aims and not without scruples; and Zamacona, attributing their agreement to the dominant influence of Saligny, set to work to break it on the assumption that Wyke had "innocently seconded" the designs of his colleague and could be weaned away. So, at least, he chose to believe, and not out of charity, for on the slight distinction between a dupe and an accomplice he built his hopes and his diplomacy. The first steps were the most difficult. Wyke was less shocked by the fact of default than by the manner in which he had learned of it, like everyone else, by opening the morning papers, a feature of the case on which he laid great stress in his note of protest. For this lapse Zamacona made ample amends. On the ground of form he was an accomplished apologist, and he lavished all the amenity of which he was a master on his opponent, but with no effect at first except to irritate him further, for Sir Charles had a liver, a legitimate motive to indulge it, and a limited command of language, and he was exasperated by the glib tongues of Mexico that could talk themselves out of anything. It was all that Zamacona could do to induce him to listen; but listen he did rather than to reply indefinitely to Zamacona's insufferable politeness. Wyke had served in the army, had never married, and was inclined to be abusive in his own language, but a foreign tongue was a bit, and from the moment that he was reduced to mere irritation, progress was possible.

Progress was slow, however, for at the outset Wyke insisted on repeal of the decree as the preliminary, instead of the object, of discussion. Discussion was established, nevertheless, by an exchange of communications arguing the ethics at stake. Here the Englishman was at home; the opportunity to moralize was irresistible, and he rose to the bait and was hooked and drawn into a controversy which raged furiously for four weeks. The Mexican took a hard lashing, but he would not let go. Confident of the rectitude of his wrongs, Sir Charles laid down the law with a finality which left nothing to add to it but incessant repetition, and repetition was heaped on the head of his antagonist with indefatigable vigor and crushing weight. "Congress has thought fit to make a free gift of other people's property to the government of the Republic," Wyke ruled. — "Sir Charles Wyke will now allow the Undersigned the liberty of stating," Zamacona demurred, "that the application of the term 'free gift' to what is merely the act of ratifying certain obligations and specifying the mode of fulfilling them amounts to a misnomer." — It amounted to many millions of pesos, Wyke retorted. Whereupon Zamacona condescended to simpler language and, unwinding himself elaborately, went on: "The nation has paid its creditors with the blood of its citizens. . . . It would be sad, indeed, if history were to be obliged to record that this country, after the most trying vicissitudes, came to be governed by men who, without any supernatural ability and inspired solely by their experience and their patriotism, have not shrunk from one final effort—an effort such as never yet has been made—to establish in Mexico the rule of reason and morality, and that this effort was wrecked on the prejudices and skepticism of the most enlightened nation in the world." — "That which is wrong can never come right," came the retort, "for it is a well-known axiom that spoliation as a source of revenue soon exhausts itself." And by way of illustration Sir Charles grounded Zamacona in fundamentals: "A starving man may justify, in his own eyes, the fact of stealing a loaf, on the ground that imperious necessity compelled him thereto, but such an argument cannot, in a moral point of view, justify his violation of the law, which remains as positive, apart from all sentimentality, as if the crime had not had an excuse. If he was actually starving, he should have first asked the baker to assuage his hunger, but doing so of his own free will, without permission, is acting exactly as the Mexican Government has done toward its creditors on this occasion." But he was Old Bailey talking to a schoolboy. "His Excellency has employed a simile, the ineptitude of which is strikingly apparent," Zamacona objected, rehearsing his arguments once more in as homely language as he could manage. But Wyke held his ground against all the circumlocutions in which he was involved and kept the incorrigible casuist at a distance, and the bout continued in a futile discussion of the priority of property over human rights, without practical result other than to maintain the contact, which Zamacona was determined not to relinquish.

Apart from the arguments involved, the honors of the debate undoubtedly went to the Mexican, who maintained the altercation within diplomatic limits and in a tone of indomitable urbanity, which exhausted his adversary; and he had another asset on his side. He conducted the dispute with an eye on posterity—a witness of which Wyke was unaware—and with unflagging confidence continued to add to the record against a day of judgment when, as he reminded Wyke in a pointed aside, "this correspondence will come to light." The warning went unheeded, however; winded but unweakening, Wyke continued to insist on unconditional surrender, and as Zamacona had nothing to offer but appeals and persuasion, no advance would have been made by either side had not help come from another quarter. The deadlock was broken by the American Minister.

A cataclysm had improved the relations of Mexico and the United States. As one nation emerged from its inner convulsions, the other slipped into civil war, and their neighborly relations were so radically altered as to be almost reversed. For the first time in history a Mexican Government found itself courted. The Lincoln administration exercised conspicuous care in the choice of a new Minister to Mexico, and the selection could not have been more considerate. Thomas Corwin was notorious on both sides of the border, like Lincoln himself, as an outspoken champion of Mexico during the American war, and the significance of his appointment was immediately recognized by the Confederate press. "The man who more than any other can attract the sympathies of Mexico" was the warning spread in New Orleans. "He will have great influence in the efforts that are being made to prevent us from being recognized as a nation; and we believe that his appointment has no other purpose. Mr. Corwin has all the talent necessary to occupy a place in the cabinet or to discharge a first-class mission in Europe." The *Mobile Advertiser* took up the cry. "We think that our government should consider seriously how to neutralize the maneuver which the Lincoln administration is putting into play in Mexico. Lincoln has sent to that Republic a man of high capacity, whose presence in Mexico, for various reasons, will be very detrimental to the interests of the South. The Southern States are the ones that principally desired and sustained the war against Mexico. The Mexicans know it and will do everything in their power to avenge themselves on the partisans of our President, Jefferson Davis. They know also that the North was opposed to the war and took none but a very small part in the shedding of Mexican blood."

The appointment of Corwin, like the election of Lincoln, presaged a new deal in American diplomacy. With the rise to power of the Republican party and with control of the Federal government by the Northern and Western states, a pioneer era opened in the relations of the two countries; the sectional split revealed the roots of the past, and it was generally recognized on both sides of the border that the long, wretched history of American imperialism represented sectional rather than national interests and was due to the almost unbroken domination of the American Government by Southern statesmen. Honest Tom Corwin, as he was called in Ohio, did much to honor his name in Mexico. He was the only recruit to the diplomatic corps who presented his credentials unconditionally, and by his accurate and unbiased reports on conditions in Mexico he performed a service to both countries and succeeded in creating mutual confidence and sympathy and effacing many of the bitter memories of the past. His mission prospered; and when an agent of the Confederacy appeared on the scene, all doors were closed to him.

Arriving in Mexico at the same time as Sir Charles Wyke, and making the trip to the capital with him, he continued to act as his traveling companion after the debt suspension; and he put his insight at Wyke's service. In the critical weeks that followed Corwin took steps to exorcise the catastrophe that everyone foresaw by a solution so simple that no one had thought of it: he advised Seward to underwrite the Mexican foreign debt and guarantee the interest on it for five years. With all his sympathy, however, he was as little of a sentimentalist as Wyke himself, and he befriended Mexico in Washington with Hoosier honesty and shrewdness. He was a diplomatic servant, subdued to the element he worked in, and as Seward was an apostle of Manifest Destiny, Corwin adapted his idea to the traditional views of the State Department. "England and France," he pointed out, "are now in possession of the best of the West Indian Islands (for I consider it certain that San Domingo is certain to fall into the hands of Spain before our rebellion is quelled), and Mexico, a colony of England, with the British power on the north of our possessions, would leave on the map of this continent a very insignificant part of the United States, especially should the present unnatural rebellion end in the severance from us of eight or nine, or all, of the slave states. Mexico, I am persuaded, would be willing to pledge all her public lands and mineral rights in Lower California, Chihuahua, Sonora, and Sinaloa, as well as her national faith, for the payment of this guarantee. This would probably end in the cession of sovereignty to us. It would be certain to end thus if the money were not promptly repaid as agreed upon. By such an arrangement two consequences would follow: first, all hope of extending the dominion of a separate Southern republic in this quarter or in Central America would be extinguished; and second, any further attempt in all times to come to establish European Powers in this continent would cease to occupy the minds of either England or Continental Europe. . . . The United States are the only safe guardians of the independence and true civilization of this continent; it is their mission, and they should fulfill it."

The proposal differed from previous liens of the same nature by the sympathy that whetted it. But for the double emergency on both sides of the border and the inability of Mexico and the other republics of South America to defend themselves, he said, "I should not desire either to intermeddle in their concerns or to add any of their territory to ours, except, perhaps, Lower California, which may become indispensable to our Pacific possessions. . . . I cannot find in this Republic any men of any party better qualified, in my judgment, for the task than those in power; if they cannot save her, then I am quite sure that she is to be the prey of some foreign Power, and they, I fear, cannot without *our* aid. I say *our* aid, because she will look in vain for help elsewhere." The aid thus offered was valuable precisely because it was not disinterested. Seward agreed, and Corwin was authorized to open negotiations with the Mexican Government. No more was needed to bring the British Minister to terms, and Wyke began to bargain with Zamacona.

The deadlock was broken. Under the stimulus of American mediation and American competition the British negotiation developed. The American deal, on the other hand, made no progress. No government, and least of all one so recently scorched by the McLane treaty, could be induced, however desperate its extremities, to accept the mortgage proposed by Corwin, but as an equivalent Zamacona proposed a fifty per cent reduction on tariffs for a period of five to ten years. Corwin declined to recommend this offer for fear of antagonizing England and France, and because it offered no real advantage; the most-favored-nation treatment being guaranteed to both those Powers by treaty, he pointed out that their Ministers would undoubtedly demand the same favor. And so it proved. Rejected by Corwin, the idea was adopted by Wyke, to whom it was of more value than to his American colleague, British trade suffering severely from the high Mexican tariffs, and its volume being more than double the American, which was the lowest in the market. Besides eliminating any risk of an American loan, the idea he borrowed from Corwin had other advantages to recommend it: under the high protective tariffs a lucrative contraband trade, which defrauded the government of half its revenues and of which the English held the monopoly, had grown up; and as the British Minister was nothing if not honest, he recognized the necessity of cleaning his own house and was willing, for the sake of a solid moral and material gain, to reconcile ethics and business by a tariff reduction. On that spar his negotiation with Zamacona was brought to a successful conclusion. After three months of hard work, he was satisfied by a concession that made the claims of the bondholders a relatively insignificant matter. "I explained," he reported to Lord Russell, "that so long as Mexico by reducing her tariff really benefited trade, we had no right to insist upon her effectually crippling herself for the sake of being able to square the balance sheet of the bondholders, or fix the exact ticket to be placed on each separate piece of shirting that came into the country."

But an explanation was also due to Lord Russell for the remarkable conversion by which his agent now spoke the language of Zamacona; for such was the result of a trade favor. Association with Corwin had cured Wyke of the diplomacy of a commercial traveler, and borrowing another idea from his American friend, he reflected his sympathetic attitude toward Mexico; sentiment was also a commercial asset. On November 21 a convention covering the most difficult points in dispute and allowing of the resumption of normal diplomatic relations was ready for signature. The *status quo ante* of the 17th of July was restored, plus the tariff amendment, and the rights of the bondholders were insured by a stipulation for the appointment of British inspectors to control the collection of the Mexican customs.

But there were several other factors with which Wyke failed to reckon. One of them was the French Legation. M. de Saligny had followed the progress of the negotiation for three months with growing agitation, and its conclusion provided him with a final argument to embroil Spain with Mexico, for all the others that he found failed to move Marshal Serrano. "But Spain is threatened abroad by other dangers and causes for anxiety," he wrote to the Captain-General of Cuba on November 23. "The English Legation, true to the *frank and loyal policy* which you already know, has concluded, or rather completely closed, an agreement which has aroused public opinion on all sides and which cannot, to my mind, be approved in London. The French Legation is further than ever from any accommodation, however, and aside from the question to which the orders I have received from the Imperial Government refer, and which they refuse to admit here, new incidents have arisen even more serious than those that occurred in the month of August, and they render impossible my stay in this capital, where not only does the press daily and scandalously attack France and her representative, but my life is publicly threatened by the Chief of Police, a consummate criminal, a former highwayman notorious for the many crimes he has committed, and a man who has spent many years of his life in the jails of Chapala and Mexico City. I am preparing, therefore, to leave with the whole Legation, and I hope to see you in Mexico, convinced as I am that you will come in command of the expedition. In Robles' letter you will see the intrigues of England laid bare. The sudden about-face, performed with as much duplicity as stupidity by Wyke (a nigger diplomat), is explained by the reply of my colleague to someone who expressed astonishment at the strange attitude assumed by the British Legation: 'What shall I say? We feel an invincible repugnance against entering into any common action with Spain, no matter what the question may be, and especially when behind Spain we see France.'"

The negotiation of the Wyke–Zamacona convention, which threatened to settle British complaints and to eliminate the necessity of punitive measures, roused M. de Saligny from his state of captive spleen and stung him into furious activity; but his efforts to precipitate intervention from the nearest available quarter were not necessary. The negotiation came to nothing. The stipulation providing for British control of the customs was the last hitch, but an insurmountable one, and for purely sentimental reasons. "The difficulty of getting the President to see the question in its proper point of view," was the apology offered by Zamacona for his failure to overcome it; but Congress was equally stubborn and threw out the convention on that condition, although as an earnest of good will it repealed the decree of July 17 at the same time. But the major concession, which Wyke had demanded four months before, no longer satisfied him; like Saligny, he was bent on bigger business, and he had scented Saligny's running counter to his own. The Mexican objections were more than he could bear, his patience was exhausted, and he called for the passage of the convention or his passports. His ultimatum was accepted; Congress refused to pocket the national pride, and Zamacona resigned.

Great was the satisfaction of M. de Saligny. "Here is more news," he wrote to Serrano the next day. "The famous agreement in which Wyke shamelessly sacrificed all the principles heretofore invoked by England in agreement with France produced a serious revolt yesterday, and I have just learned that at a late hour last night Congress rejected it. Wyke is furious and is preparing to leave. Now more than ever I can say, *nigger diplomacy.*" The failure of the treaty by no means relieved his anxiety, however, and twenty-four hours later he was rattling confidential incitements to Havana at the same breathless pace. "In the enclosed clipping you will find new proof of the duplicity and stupidity of the British Minister, and curious revelations as to a project of alliance between Mexico, England, and the United States against France and Spain. . . . I send you the *Trait d'Union* and two extracts from the *Siglo,* in which you will find curious details about the convention that was rejected the day before yesterday. Every article of this strange document reveals the shrewdness and insincerity of the Mexican Government, no less than the incredible naïveté of perfidious Albion. . . . There is talk of submitting the Wyke treaty to Congress again; I should be greatly surprised if the second attempt fared better than the first. The number of votes against it, seventy to twenty-nine in favor, seems to me to indicate a secret understanding with Doblado to overthrow Juarez. I should not be surprised if he and his ministers had to flee within the next fortnight. . . . I insist that, if you are to act, there is no time to be lost."

But his fears were unfounded. Though the defeat of the treaty did not reconcile him to his British colleague, it restored their collaboration. Wyke was now committed to an uncompromising position. The peremptory judgment of a bailiff which he brought to Mexico was fully justified when he closed the Legation, and he could indulge the impatience of a vigorous invalid with a clear conscience. He had exhausted the possibilities of conciliation. The effort had not been wholly wasted, however, and before leaving the capital he felt it his duty to pay two deserved tributes to his collaborators. "I have only now to express to Your Lordship," he wrote to Russell, "my high sense of Mr. Corwin's conduct through the whole business. He has stood by me in the most honorable manner and, on learning of the rejection of my convention by Congress, refused in the most positive manner to advance the government one dollar of the proposed American loan. Nor can I pass over in silence the service of Señor de Zamacona, the Minister of Foreign Affairs; he at all events has been sincere in trying to second my late endeavors, and his resignation of office proves that there is an exception to every rule, even as regards Mexico."

His late endeavors had been doomed beforehand, in any event, by Russell and by himself. The possibility of a peaceful settlement had been eliminated by Lord Russell as soon as he learned of the negotiations that Wyke was conducting: the proposed terms satisfied the separate requirements of Great Britain, he admitted, but they provided no security that they would be observed any better than previous stipulations and agreements. The conviction so assiduously instilled into his mind that the bankruptcy of Mexico was due to the irresponsibility and dishonesty of its government, that folly was coupled with bad faith and incompetence with corruption, had taken root too firmly for correction and could no longer be retracted after the signature of the London Convention, which had no other writ or ostensible reason for its execution. The late endeavors of Wyke as a peacemaker, indeed, caused his government some embarrassment. When the solution conceived by Corwin was communicated to London, Russell was hard put to refuse the American guarantee and to produce a plausible reason for rejecting the security which it provided, but he was not to be bought off by a trade rival, and the reason he needed was supplied by the American Government itself. The price of the loan destroyed its political value, as the American Minister in London reminded Seward. "You will permit me," Adams wrote, "to make a single remark upon the importance of appearing to divest the United States of any personal or selfish interest in the action it may think proper to adopt. The view customarily taken in Europe is that their Government is disposed to resist all foreign intervention in Mexico, not upon any principle, but simply because it is expecting, in due course of time, to absorb the whole country for its own benefit. Hence any proposal like that which I had the honor to receive, based on the mortgage of portions of Mexican territory as security for engagements entered into by the United States, naturally become the ground for an outcry that this is but the preliminary to any entry for inevitable foreclosure. And then follows the argument that if this process is legitimate in one case, why not equally in all?" But it was Lord Russell who made the most cruel comment on the plan for American mediation when, as a counterproposal, he blandly invited the United States to join the Allied expedition. The invitation was declined, and Seward allowed his plan to lapse. With it vanished the one substantial hope of averting intervention.

9

WHATEVER hope remained was visionary, though not for that reason negligible. The action of foreign opinion—that factor might be expected to make its influence felt in time, but it was of small value as yet, since it was still dormant and uninformed. Inaccessible in August, it had begun to stir, however, in November. The awakening appeared first, where it counted most, in England. Plans for the expedition had been prepared during the parliamentary recess, without consulting the country, and the publication of the London Convention at the end of October confronted the public with an engagement which commanded attention and required explanation. The alliance contracted by the cabinet—or a fraction of it, for not all the members had been consulted—and the rumored ambitions of the foreign partners to the enterprise, raised questions as to its ultimate purpose and original responsibility, which the ministerial press anticipated and met with explanations so inconsistent as to thicken the confusion and quicken the suspicion of those who studied its erratic behavior.

One of the first and most alert of these was the London correspondent of the *New York Tribune,* who came to the rescue of Mexico with an activity that ferreted out the whole affair and a clamor that raised a general alarm, and as his name was Karl Marx he commandeered Mr. Greeley's paper to good purpose. To raise a general alarm by way of the transatlantic press was a circuitous route, but in the tense relations between the war-torn New World and the war-ripe Old Continent his warnings had a wide resonance and were addressed to a quarter vitally concerned with the moves of the British Government and the combinations of the European Powers, because of their bearing on the war of secession in the States. A foreigner in England himself, an international exile, and a citizen of the world, Marx was in a better position than the stranded spokesman in Paris to act as a Christopher for Mexico. "The contemplated intervention in Mexico by England,

France, and Spain," he wrote in the first week of November, "is, in my opinion, one of the most monstrous enterprises ever chronicled in international history. It is a contrivance of the true Palmerstonian make, astounding the uninitiated by an insanity of purpose and imbecility in the means employed, which appear quite incompatible with the known capacity of the old schemer." He said no more than De la Fuente thought; but he spoke and thought more formidably, because he knew whereof he spoke. Reviewing the evident motives of the Allies—the value to Napoleon of a foreign diversion, the ambition of Spain to recover colonial dominion and foreign prestige—and collating them with the professed purpose of the English Government, he came to a conclusion confirmed by the English press itself. "It is, therefore, certain, and has even been expressly admitted by the *Times,* that the joint intervention in its present form is of English—i.e. of Palmerstonian—make. Spain was cowed into adherence by the pressure of France; and France was brought around by concessions made to her in the field of foreign policy." The motives of England were cloudy, but one thing was clear. "There are no people in England who desire an intervention in Mexico, except the Mexican bondholders, who, however, had never to boast the least sway over the public mind. Hence the difficulty of breaking the Palmerstonian scheme to the public. The next best thing was to bewilder the British elephant by contradictory statements proceeding from the same laboratory, compounded of the same materials, but varying in the doses administered to the animal." As an example he cited the first feelers put out by the *Times* and the *Morning Post,* both of them ministerial organs, the latter maintaining that there would be no territorial war, but that, as it would be impossible to deal with Mexico as an organized and established government, the principal ports would be temporarily occupied and their customs revenues sequestered, while the former hoped that "the mere presence of a combined squadron in the Gulf, and the seizure of certain ports, will urge the Mexican Government to new exertions in keeping the peace." Intimidation as a constructive trick was not original with the English, but they reduced it to absurdity. "If then, according to the *Post,* the expedition was to start because there is no government in Mexico, it was, according to the *Times,* only intended to encourage and support the *existing* Mexican Government. To be sure! The oddest means ever hit upon for the consolidation of a government consists in the seizure of its territory and the sequestration of its revenues!" With the conclusion of the tripartite pact these contradictions deepened and multiplied to such a degree that they could no longer be sustained. "The *Times,* which ever since its first announcement on September 27, seemed to have forgotten the very existence of Mexico, now again steps forward. Anyone ignorant of its connection with Palmerston and the original introduction in its columns of his scheme, would be induced to consider today's leader in the *Times* as the most cutting and merciless satire on the whole adventure. It begins by saying that 'the expedition is a very remarkable one' (later it says a curious one). 'Three States are combining to coerce a fourth into good behavior, *not so much by way of war as by authoritative intervention in behalf of order.*' Authoritative interference in behalf of order! This is literally Holy Alliance slang and sounds very remarkable indeed on the part of England, glorying in the nonintervention principle!" So little had times changed in 1861 that the text would have been as true half a century earlier or at any time later.

Out of the mouth of the Thunderer, Marx plucked the teeth of his indictment. "In the progress of its article," he continued, "the *Times* veers around and explains: 'We shall, no doubt, succeed in obtaining at least a recognition of our pecuniary claims; in fact, a single British frigate could have obtained that amount of satisfaction at any moment. We may trust, too, that the more scandalous of the outrages committed will be expiated by more immediate and substantial atonement; but it is clear that, if only this much was to be brought about, we need not have resorted to such extremes as are now proposed.' The *Times,* then, confesses in so many words that the reasons originally given out for the expedition were shallow pretexts. What, then, is its real aim and purpose? . . . *An authoritative interference in behalf of order.* England, France, and Spain, planning a new Holy Alliance, and having formed themselves into an armed Areopagus for the restoration of order all over the world." Was it necessary to labor the point or possible to finish the sentence with a period? " 'Mexico,' says the *Times,* 'must be rescued from anarchy and put in the way of self-government and peace. A strong and stable government must be established' there by the invaders, and that government is to be extracted from 'some Mexican party.' Now, does anyone imagine that Palmerston and his mouthpiece, the *Times,* really consider the joint intervention as a means to the professed end, viz., the extinction of anarchy and the establishment in Mexico of a strong and stable government? So far from cherishing any such chimerical creed . . . Palmerston and the *Times,* then, are fully aware that there 'exists a government in Mexico'; that the Liberal party, 'ostensibly favored by England, is now in power'; that 'the ecclesiastical rule has been overthrown'; that Spanish intervention was the last forlorn hope of the priests and bandits; and finally, that Mexican anarchy was dying away. They know, then, that joint intervention, with no other avowed end than the rescue of Mexico from anarchy, will produce just the opposite effect, weaken the Constitutional government, strengthen the priestly party by a supply of French and Spanish bayonets, rekindle the embers of civil war, and, instead of extinguishing, *restore* anarchy to its full bloom. The inference the *Times* draws from those premises is really remarkable and curious. 'Although,' it says, 'these considerations may lead us to look with some anxiety to the results of the expedition, they do not militate against *the expediency of the expedition itself.*' It does, consequently, not militate against the expediency of the expedition itself, that the expedition militates against the only ostensible purpose. It does not militate against the means that it baffles its own avowed end. The greatest 'curiosity' pointed out by the *Times,* I have, however, still kept *in petto.* 'If,' it says, 'President Lincoln should accept the invitation, which is provided for by the Convention, to participate in the approaching operations, *the character of the work would become more curious still.*' "

And that point Marx felt it necessary to underline. "It would, indeed, be the greatest curiosity of all if the United States, living in amity with Mexico, should associate with the European order-mongers and, by participating in their acts, sanction the interference of a European armed Areopagus with the internal affairs of American States. The first scheme of such a transplantation of the Holy Alliance to the other side of the Atlantic was, at the time of the Restoration, drawn up for the French and Spanish Bourbons by Chateaubriand. The attempt was baffled by an English Minister, Mr. Canning, and an American President, Mr. Monroe. The present convulsion in the United States appeared to Palmerston an opportune moment for taking up the old project in a modified form. Since the United States for the present must allow no foreign complication to interfere with their war for the Union, all they can do is to *protest.* Their best well-wishers in Europe hope that they will protest, and thus, before the eyes of the world, firmly repudiate any complicity in one of the most nefarious schemes."

A protest at that moment might have produced a sharp, and even an arresting, effect on foreign opinion, but in the strained relations between England and the United States it was impossible. Toward the end of the month the *Trent* affair brought the two countries to the verge of hostilities, and when the tension relaxed the correspondent of the *Tribune* returned to the attack with bated breath. The conduct of Palmerston throughout the crisis was highly revealing: bold to the brink of disaster, he retreated at the last moment. And recognizing Palmerston's fondness for "a spirited policy," Marx reduced his recklessness to a professional play for popularity. The frivolity of the motive aggravated the offense, and if Palmerston proposed to apply the same tactics to Mexico, the danger was even greater for Washington. "Many weeks ago he urged Bonaparte to propose a joint armed intervention in the 'internecine struggle,' supported that project in a cabinet council, and failed in carrying it only because of the resistance of his colleagues. He and Bonaparte then resorted to the Mexican intervention as a *pis aller.* That operation served two purposes, by provoking just resentment on the part of the Americans, and by simultaneously furnishing a pretext for the despatch of a squadron ready, as the *Morning Post* has it, 'to perform whatever duty the hostile conduct of the government of Washington may require us to perform in the waters of the North Atlantic.' . . . I may add that the *Nord* of December 3—a Russian paper and consequently initiated into Palmerston's plans—insinuated that the expedition was from the first set on foot, not for its ostensible purpose, but for a war against the United States." That conjecture at least paid Palmerston the compliment of supposing that he had not taken the first step without calculating the last.

Of all the interpretations to which the London Convention was open, that of Marx was the most logical. It was based on conjecture, but the conjecture was shrewd because it was scientific. His analysis was the result of intuition, experience, and *a priori* knowledge of the traditional workings of British policy, which anticipated the palpable proof; and the evidence already confirmed all his deductions. The erratic behavior of the ministerial press was an admission of ulterior aims. The bad news that it was trying so uneasily to break to the British public might be that intervention in Mexico was merely the preliminary for eventual intervention in the American civil war. To that policy the British public was solidly opposed, but its attitude toward Mexican intervention remained to be determined, and by December the expedition was already on the way. A better brake was the impossibility of conquering Mexico, also admitted by an English Government organ, which Marx cited. "If it is desired," wrote the *Economist,* "to thrust upon her a British prince with an English army, then the fiercest wrath of the United States is excited. France's jealousy would make such a conquest impossible, and a motion to this effect would be rejected almost unanimously by an English parliament the moment it was submitted to it. England, for her part, cannot entrust the government of Mexico to France. Of Spain there can be no question whatever." For purely practical reasons, it was not easy to foist a Holy Alliance upon England or smuggle it into Mexico in 1861. But reason had nothing to do with the Mexican question; and the most sensible people in the world became the most erratic when it was necessary to rationalize their interests. If Marx erred, it was in being too logical about the British people; the inconsistencies of their statesmen and their inveterate habit of muddling through the contradictions they created were the greatest danger for Mexico at that moment.

The abortive plans, the secret and still-born aims, and even the conjectural motives of historical events are as material to the record as the facts themselves, and in the inception of a scheme fraught with so much confusion and consequence there was ample matter for the historical critic; and as an historical critic Marx was in a better position to serve Mexico than as a correspondent for the *New York Tribune*. To the practiced eye of the revolutionary the full scope and importance of the enterprise was immediately apparent. Whether it was a deliberate reprise of the Holy Alliance or the casual international foreclosure which it purported to be, it was equally reactionary; consciously or unconsciously, the outcome was the same; but the ambiguity was characteristically English. The confederacy of England, France, and Spain was a politically unnatural alliance of the leading liberal nation of the age with two partners, one of which definitely represented the past and the other an indefinite compromise with it, and the issue was monstrous because the leading liberal was also the leading capitalist power, and the contradiction of economic and political interest produced one of the typical miscarriages of nineteenth-century civilization. The plight of Mexico, emerging from its long struggle for modern civilization only to be overwhelmed by it, was no chance paradox, nor was the course of England in capturing a country both backward and progressive for that civilization fortuitous; the one and the other obeyed the polar attractions of the same axis. And as it was on the revolutions of that axis that the mind of Marx turned, Mexico had a peculiar claim to his scientific interest.

The space which he occupied in the *New York Tribune* was hardly the place to ventilate his professional views, and after the protest which he lodged there in the first white heat of indignation, he gave to the violation of Mexico only the passing and topical attention of a journalist. In his correspondence with Engels he glanced at it occasionally, but as casually as in his letters to America, and Engels ignored it altogether. On Mexico Engels had pronounced himself once and for all after the American war, and his judgment then was wholly scientific and unsentimental. "We have witnessed with due satisfaction the defeat of Mexico by the United States," he wrote in a scholarly review in 1849. "This also represents an advance. For when a country hitherto involved in its own affairs, perpetually torn by civil wars, and without any issue for its development, a country whose best prospect would have been industrial submission to England, when this country is forcibly pushed into historic progress, we have no alternative but to consider it a step forward. In the interest of its own development, it was right that Mexico should fall under the tutelage of the United States. The evolution of the whole American continent will lose nothing if the latter, taking possession of California, faces the Pacific." It was absurd, he maintained, "to place a sentimental value on narrow national prejudices when the existence and free development of great nations" was at stake. Forsyth employed the same argument a few years later. What mattered to the revolutionary was not nationalism, but "facts of world-historical importance" in social development, and he approved the annexation of Mexican territory because "the energetic Yankees" were more capable than "the lazy Mexicans" of developing their resources and of opening the Pacific to civilization.

An equally harsh view of Mexican character was held by Marx at that period. Comparing the conqueror and the conquered in a summary of the soldiership displayed in the American war, he wrote: "We find in the Yankees the sentiments of independence and individual valor in an even greater degree perhaps than in the Anglo-Saxon. The Spanish are degenerate beings. But a degenerate Spaniard, that is the ideal! All the vices of the Spaniard, grandiloquence, bragging, quixotism, appear in them raised to the n-th power, without the solidity of the Spaniard. The guerrilla war in Mexico is a parody of the Spanish, and even the regular troops that flee the field seem to be infinitely surpassed. One must recognize, on the other hand, that the Spanish have never produced a genius the like of Santa Anna!" The summary judgment formed in the days of Santa Anna were subject to revision, however, in the days of Juarez. Since then another breed of Homo mexicanus had developed, and a new generation had pushed their country into historic progress by a social revolution which entitled its protagonists to the respect and support of the leaders of world revolution, and their achievements could be measured by the degree to which they won their championship.

Little as they could do to influence public opinion, Marx and Engels were in a position to serve Mexican progress by the recognition they granted it. The kind of polar power generated by their minds was a fluid intellectual electricity none the less potent for being isolated from the current of events: diffused in the atmosphere of the age, and accumulating energy in polemics and criticism, it flashed forth on occasion with positive and dynamic effect. Such an occasion was the American civil war, to which they rallied public opinion in the English working class, the support of the Second International abroad, and the partisanship of progressive forces wherever their radius of agitation could reach. In the case of Mexico, however, there was only heat lightning. The achievements of the Mexican Liberals were recognized by Marx in the same measure as he noticed every other progressive movement of his time; but no more. The revolution in Mexico, deriving its ideals from the eighteenth century, was a colonial aftermath of the past, a forced growth and a relative advance in a remote province of nineteenth-century civilization. The aspect in which it could claim his attention as a genuine revolution, and a significant part of the forward movement of the world, lay in the transformation of the property relations of society, and the expropriation of Church property was a partial reform which transferred public wealth from one section of the middle class to another, under private title, without affecting the control of production or the exploitation of the masses. As a part of the class struggle, the conflict was confined to the middle class: the proletariat was nonexistent as a conscious or potential political force in a feudal and backward country. It had begun to develop, on the contrary, in the powerful industrial nation to the north, and the passionate interest of Marx and Engels was wholly engrossed by the civil war in the United States, where the destruction of Southern feudalism, the preservation of the Union, and the progress of bourgeois democracy were vital pre-conditions to the growth and progress of the working class; and they agitated its significance strenuously. The fate of Mexico, intertwined though it was with that of its neighbor, fell into second place and was considered only in connection with, and in the intervals of, the decisive stages of the conflict in the States. The sacrifice of the weaker was an outrage, but a side issue, for Marx; his mind was exercised by it, but his heart was not in it.

Finally, the revolution in Mexico suffered from the inactivity in the revolutionary movement in Europe since 1848 and the conviction of Marx that the ascendant curve of capitalism had a long and prosperous course to complete before it could be challenged. "The difficult problem for us is the following," he wrote in a survey of the situation at this period. "On the Continent the revolution reveals, inevitably, an immediately socialistic character. Will it not be crushed in this little corner, given that, in a vastly more extended territory, the movement of bourgeois society still advances in an ascendant line?" If the Continent was a little corner, Mexico was a mere tangent on the chart of social change. The nature of the struggle there, the competition of the American civil war, the lingering influence of former indifference, the scanty information available abroad, the overwhelming odds—everything combined to make the fate of De la Fuente's country a subject of remote and intermittent interest to the seers and surveyors of world revolution.

The isolation of Mexico in the last months of 1861 was bitterly felt by its two representatives abroad. A ghost of a diplomat in France, De la Fuente crossed to London, led by a sense of neglected duty rather than by any hope of being heard, and called on the American Minister—"rather for the purpose of gaining than imparting information," Adams remarked—and through the good offices of Adams was received by Lord Russell, who, caught in the mechanism of an enterprise which nothing but the most rigid consistency could palm off on an awakening public, naturally had nothing to say to him. The interview was a duplicate of the one with Thouvenel, differing only in the frigid indifference with which the English Foreign Minister heard him out before showing him the door. Accustomed by now to that familiar routine, the mortified Mexican returned to Paris, where he invented duties for himself and continued to serve his government with desperate advice.

The expedition had started, and with public opinion beginning to stir, but too feebly to question the venture, the sole hope which he saw of defeating it lay in the expedition itself: in the nature of its composition, the haste of its preparation, the ill-welded divergences, the lines of cleavage which might lead to its disintegration if they were skillfully exploited. Signs of such flaws were not wanting, and he speculated on them. Imprudence in London, uncertainty in Madrid, equivocation in Paris: the common state of mind in the three capitals was one of instability, while the concerted measures taken were materializing with the swiftness of complete confidence. Mastery of the situation clearly belonged to the partner capable of consistency and decision, and it was the confidence of one of them that caused the first crack in the common front. In September, when Calderon Collantes had made his bid to join the expedition, he had sent orders to Cuba to mobilize the garrison, and in December a sharp jolt was caused in London and Paris by a report that a large Spanish force had left for Veracruz without awaiting the arrival of the Allied fleets. Explanations were demanded of Madrid, and though the original orders were promptly canceled, the explanations of Calderon Collantes were accepted by Thouvenel and Russell with conspicuous reserve and mistrust. From the flurry De la Fuente snatched an inspiration. The reaction of the French and English Governments, he pointed out, was vigorous, guarded, and ambiguous. Prompt to check the surreptitious initiative of Spain, they were by no means averse, nevertheless, to profit by the Spanish advance: if it succeeded, they would collect the common spoils; if it failed, they would disavow it as a flagrant breach of treaty. An English paper, in fact, had gone so far as to say that if the Mexicans gave the Spanish a lesson, they would emphasize the absurdity of the recent Spanish conquest of Morocco— "the strange origin and repeated theme of the much-touted restoration of Spain."

"Either I am deceived in what seems to me as true," De la Fuente continued, "or the triumph of our army over the Spanish is certain to be very favorably received in Europe, and the opinion of it formed there will powerfully influence the counsels of the Allied governments; we shall be able to treat with them without difficulty and without great collisions; our name and credit, prostrate at present, will rise, and we shall offer a solemn refutation to those who accuse us of being able to fight only against ourselves. . . . At the point which matters have reached, I think the Spanish invasion, isolated from the Allied forces, is the best thing that can happen to us." It was a case in which a skirmish might save a war, and he urged his government to provoke Spain to take the aggressive and to focus the fighting spirit of the country on the hereditary enemy.

The despatches of De la Fuente passed through Washington, where they were opened, read, and digested by his solitary colleague in the foreign service. The Legation in Washington was in charge of Matias Romero, a junior member of the band of reformers, young enough to add daring and initiative to the zeal with which he defended his country abroad. To the task of winning support from the one people that were inclined to befriend his own he applied himself strenuously; he had to contend with the prevailing apathy or hostility of the American press and an appalling ignorance in public opinion, which culminated in Congress, but he left no stone unturned to present the case of Mexico on its own merits and in its bearing on the United States alike. He went once to the President. Early in that fateful year for both countries, he approached Lincoln while he was still the President-elect, and made a trip to Springfield to meet him on his home ground. The memorable defense of Mexico that Lincoln had made in the Illinois Legislature in 1848 was well worth a pilgrimage to the wilderness in 1861, and Romero, born in Oaxaca and a close friend of Juarez, perceived the importance of establishing personal contact with a man whose origin, whose rise, and whose faith offered so many points of analogy with his own President and so many opportunities for a sympathetic understanding between them.

The interview in Springfield was encouraging. Romero was rewarded with pledges of honest friendship for Mexico, which impressed him as something more than official platitudes, for they were uttered, he noted, "in an explicit and even vehement manner," and were confirmed by the turn the conversation took. Lincoln questioned him particularly on the condition of the Mexican peons, revealing what Romero described, a little sensitively, as "the exaggerated ideas held here of the situation of the Indians who work on the *haciendas*. It is said that they are more abominably treated than the Negroes on the Southern plantations, and it is believed that the abuses which are unfortunately committed in some parts are general throughout the Republic and are sanctioned by law"—an impression he hastened to dispel. "I explained to him in detail how such abuses have been committed, and he showed much satisfaction on learning that such practices were contrary to the laws of the Republic, and that as soon as there was a solidly established government, it would try to correct them. Mr. Lincoln," he went on, "does not seem to be well informed on Mexican affairs, and since the way in which he sees our situation will be the basis of his policy, my first concern was to inform him of the cause of our upheavals, which have become proverbial here and which are regarded by many as incurable, and to show him that they have already been radically cured."

Romero was sanguine, or he would not have gone to Springfield. The liaison with Lincoln was a bond of character, and above all of a class character, which offered a new guarantee for the future of both countries, and Romero was satisfied that "his administration will be guided by the good sentiments which he expressed, since he is a simple and honorable man, and his words bear the stamp of sincerity and not of those pompous and hollow phrases employed by persons trained in the school of false policy, which is accustomed to offer much and perform nothing." The promise of the first interview remained a promise, however, and the contact was no sooner made than lost. In Washington the war-logged President was inaccessible, and his inexperience in foreign affairs left a free hand to his Secretary of State. So far as Romero was concerned, Seward was the President of the United States.

Seward mystified the Mexican from the first day they met, and after studying him for a year Romero still found him "impenetrable." "I find it hard to believe," he wrote, "that a man of his perspicacity and experience should really be ignorant of our internal and external questions; but from the manner in which he speaks and in which he has worked so far, one must infer either that he does not know them in fact, or that he affects to be ignorant of them." He took Seward's antecedents as a politician into account. "Mr. Seward, either because he conducted a systematic opposition to the government of Mr. Buchanan, which favored the Constitutional cause in Mexico, or acting in good faith, was the mainstay of our Reaction in the United States Senate and the most severe and bitter critic of the policy toward Mexico pursued by Mr. Buchanan. Since then he has undoubtedly had to accept facts independent of his will, but which seemingly have in nowise served to enlighten his judgment."

Of the great change in American policy toward Mexico presaged by the triumph of the Republican party there was little evidence in the attitude either of Seward himself or of the Republican press. In an article in the *New York Times* of December 1860, headed "Shall We Have Mexico?" that organ of the incoming Secretary of State had given a fresh twist to the policy of his predecessors and declared frankly that "we are happy to know in view of threatened dissolution of the Union and the consequent disruption of commercial enterprises and other affairs, that prominent members of the Republican party are already beginning to consider the annexation or acquisition of Mexico as a sure means of immediately indemnifying the North for the partial loss of Southern trade and frustrating the projects of propagandizing slavery which constitute a great incentive to disunion."

The policy advocated by the *Times* was developed at great length and with complete candor. "Although we profoundly deplore the disorganization of the Confederation as it now exists, it is a consolation to know that so sad an event will remove the last obstacle to the consummation of the obvious policy of the American Republic. The slavery question will no longer be an impediment, and the people of Mexico can receive from our hands the guarantees of a stable government without incurring the risk of being ruined by slavery. The Mexicans, ignorant and degraded though they are, entertain a healthy prejudice against an institution that would reduce them to the level of slaves. . . . A protectorate, followed by free trade and the right of colonization, would be the beginning. But it is evident that the effect of this intimate contact with the free people of the North would have as its result the *Americanization* of Mexico in its ideas of government and civil liberty; so that after a few years of pupilage the Mexican States would be incorporated into the Union under the same conditions as the original ones. The South would thus be surrounded by states and territories in which the idea of civil liberty, in its broad application, would be the bond of union. . . . This, then, is the policy which ought to have the ardent support of every man in the North, and particularly of those who are engaged in manufacture and commerce. It opens an unlimited field for enterprise and cannot fail to compensate whatever temporary loss we may suffer by the dissolution of the South. If that dreaded event should come to pass, it would undoubtedly harm the commerce and traffic of the North; but we have already shown that, in the Union or out of it, the South cannot do without the manufactures, the ships, the seamen, the tools, and the capital of the North; and when we consider the facilities and attractions which the separation of the South would give the North for the acquisition of Mexico, we can console ourselves with the reflection that, although disunion may be censurable from the point of view of patriotism and national honor, it will not prejudice essentially and permanently the commercial and industrial prosperity of the North."

Although the *Times* of New York was not, like the *Times* of London, an acknowledged ministerial mouthpiece, Seward had identified himself among the prominent leaders of the party as an extravagant disciple of Manifest Destiny, and in a campaign speech in which he gave wings to his historical imagination, he had advocated the inclusion of Canada as well as Mexico in the American Union. The disruption of the Union and his accession to office had undoubtedly sobered him, but, as Romero remarked, independently of his will. And in dealing with the Secretary of State the Mexican was baffled by an insuperable reserve.

That reserve deepened with the approach of intervention. The paralyzing effect of the civil war on American foreign policy and the necessity of neutrality imposed on the Department were recognized by Romero, but there was, he felt, a margin between caution and callousness and a decent difference, which he expected the Lincoln administration to observe. Any other Secretary of State would have been bound to be noncommittal, but the manipulation of prudence by Seward betrayed the hand of the politician in the glove of the statesman. The aid which he proffered, and the support which he reserved, both obeyed his inveterate habits of mind. The lien on Mexican territory in return for a loan to avert intervention was a proposal as unfortunate in its effects on the creditor Powers as on the debtor nation: it reminded the world that American policy was manufactured in the interest of Springfield, Massachusetts, rather than of Springfield, Illinois, and guaranteed the aggression and legitimized the competition of the European Powers in Mexico. If ever there was a time when it would have been politic to be disinterested and statesmanlike to be generous, it was at that moment, when the security of Mexico was a safeguard for the United States and an antiseptic to the league of three governments eager to favor the South and exploit the disintegration of the American Union. And even in the negative aid which Seward extended to Mexico there was a deliberation which discouraged Romero. The invitation extended by the Allies to the United States to join the tripartite intervention was a transparent diplomatic gesture, which no one, and least of all the framers of it, expected the American Government to accept. Nevertheless, when Romero called on him, Seward declined to commit himself immediately as to the reply he would make. "The coldness and reserve of Mr. Seward," he wrote, "have finally confirmed me in the impression that I had already formed, that if, while Mr. Seward is in the State Department, the United States take part in our difficulties, it is only to derive from them what profit they can at our cost, and not because they have the slightest desire to aid us sincerely to maintain our nationality and our liberties."

The reticence of the old Republican on this occasion was a gratuitous offense which inspired Romero with a desperate idea. "After leaving the State Department, I set myself to thinking of the impenetrable designs of Mr. Seward," he continued, "and I should not be surprised if this government approved the plans of the European Powers and joined them, if it found any advantage to be derived from such a step. Reflecting on this subject, it occurred to me that if we cannot prevent intervention, it would be better for us were the United States to take part in it, since in that case, besides increasing the reasons for dissension among the interventors, we should be sure that the Liberal cause would have at least as many votes as the reactionary, for it would not be hard for the United States, with so able an agent as Mr. Corwin, to decide England, which otherwise would be vacillating, wholly in favor of the Constitutional cause. I shall reflect maturely on this matter, and if the result of my reflections is worth the trouble, I shall impart them to Mr. Seward."

Feliciter audax! Meditation convinced him that the most reckless course was the most secure, and as inspiration required speed and there was no time to consult his government, he laid the idea before Seward on his own responsibility and was rewarded with serious consideration. "Apparently impressed by my observations, Mr. Seward said that the matter was sufficiently serious and required time for reflection. Afterward he added in a lively tone, 'It is very hard to have to declare war on a good friend in order to help in saving it'; to which I replied that circumstances and complications made such anomalies necessary, adding that our wish to see the United States appear as our enemy was a proof of the confidence we felt in them." He was not facetious. Paradoxical, extravagant, and supremely precarious as the maneuver was, it was inspired by a boldness of spirit commensurable with the situation, and it succeeded at least in entertaining the seasoned politician for an hour and leading him to declare himself. A few days later Seward definitely rejected the invitation of the Allies, as he had always intended to do, and quite independently, of course, of the exertions of Romero.

Tantalized, mystified, and fascinated by a mentality which he could not master, the Mexican was at his wit's end when he snatched a fresh inspiration from the despatches of his colleague in Paris. The desperate idea of De la Fuente that the best thing that could happen to Mexico was a Spanish invasion was an expedient even more intrepid than his own, and he adopted it and submitted it to Seward for approval, together with evidence he had collected to prove that the anti-American spirit of Spain made such an eventuality a matter of common concern to them both. Although Romero was ostracized by the diplomatic corps in Washington, he had been pursued with attentions by one of its members, and it was from the Spanish Minister that he had obtained his arguments. In a confidential conversation Señor Tessara had pointed out to him, as a friend and racial brother, that the only escape for Mexico lay in submitting to the demands of the Allies; that nothing was further from the mind of Madrid than a reconquest of Mexico, the natural field for Spanish expansion lying in Portugal and Morocco; that, in case of war, Washington would doubtless decide in favor of the European Powers; and that the forces that they would accumulate in the Gulf would be directed not against Mexico, but against the United States. With these disclosures and passages from the reports of his colleague referring to the ambition of Spain to place a Bourbon on the throne of Mexico, Romero attempted to alarm Seward and to ascertain his attitude in the event of a clash with the Spanish contingents at Veracruz. Seward listened "with an incredulous smile" and replied that, for the moment, he could do nothing.

Suspicion of Spain was Seward's weak point. Only a few months before he had attempted and failed to challenge the reoccupation of Santo Domingo by Spanish forces, and that reverse compelled him to depreciate dangers with which he could not cope and to minimize with wary skepticism the alarms with which the Mexican so solicitously fed him. It was a trying moment for them both, for each saw through the other without the possibility of further delusion. "The statement of Mr. Seward that 'the United States have nothing to do with a war between two independent nations' and that 'they cannot impose republican institutions on the people of Mexico,' made under these circumstances and when the memory of events in Santo Domingo is still fresh, are highly significant," Romero informed his government, "and must make us lose all hope, I believe, in this government. No one saw with more pleasure than I the arrival in power of the Republican party in this country, since its antecedents led one to believe that it was animated by really fraternal feelings toward Mexico; no one conceived greater hopes than I of the good results which such an event would produce for my country; and no one has been more bitterly disappointed than I am by the manner in which I see this government proceeding toward my country. . . . All these considerations confirm me in the belief that I have always held," he concluded, "that we must expect nothing from this country in our hour of trial, and that we must rely only on our own elements and internal resources." And he urged his government to engage Spain alone. When the recommendations of Romero and De la Fuente reached Mexico, however, the course of events there had already relegated them to the limbo of lost motion.

IO

A SOLID front against Mexico being the one certain prospect, and self-help the only resource on which the country could rely, the necessity of building a solid front of defense was generally realized there as the hour of trial approached. Concurrently with the diplomatic negotiations, some preparations for military mobilization were made and some precautions taken for the political consolidation of the revolution; but these measures were tentative, because the object of intervention was obscure and beclouded by confused and conflicting reports from abroad. Its primary and ostensible purpose engrossed public attention; rumors of political complications and the attempts made to graft monarchist schemes on financial foreclosure were bruited by the press but discounted by it with sober public spirit. There was a general disposition to minimize alarms and prevent a return of the panic terror which had unsettled the government throughout that trying year. The negotiations with the British Minister inspired a false sense of security, and not until they broke down at the end of November, and the conclusion of the London Convention was confirmed a fortnight later, did the public at large awake to the gravity and the imminence of the danger. Then the convergence of foreign and domestic forces leagued against the nation, the party, and the man that represented it, imposed on all the saving obligation of union; but the fusion was not accomplished automatically.

The nation was identified with a party, and nothing less than foreign intervention could have soldered the schism of the civil war. The remains of the Clerical faction had succeeded in unsettling the country and provoking the crisis, and one of the first steps that the government took to meet it was to issue the general amnesty that the ferment of popular feeling had forbade it to decree at the beginning of the year. The measure was mortifying in the circumstances in which it appeared, and the amnesty was far more liable to embolden than to reconcile the unsubdued remnants of the reactionary party. But a greater guarantee was provided, and a better contribution to closing the breach, by the steps that the Mexican monarchists in Paris took to reopen it. Realizing the responsibility they had assumed in promising Napoleon that an overwhelming majority of the nation would rise on the appearance of the Allied flag, and none too sure of their premises, they took the precaution of appointing an agent to pave the way and guarantee the spontaneous proclamation of a monarchy. Having long lost contact with their country, it was not among their own number that they looked for a missionary. Their choice fell on Father Miranda, who was well qualified to act as their delegate, having a high reputation in Mexico as an agitator. He accepted the commission and moved from New York, where he was wasting in exile, to Havana, where he carried on an active correspondence with his following across the Gulf.

The reports which he received were discouraging. His correspondents were unanimous in painting the party as prostrate and inert, disorganized and demoralized, willing to be saved but unable to lift a finger in self-defense, and confused and alarmed by the prospect of foreign intervention. No one knew what it meant. Some believed that the object was to restore Miramon—"an idea that is intolerable to them"; others supposed it to be instigated by "the few German and English speculators, together with some French socialists, who benefited most from the property of the Church by odious combinations which we all know"—everyone had another inside story to tell. No one knew where intervention would lead, and all looked to Father Miranda for light, guidance, and leadership. For, more than the service of an interpreter, the presence of a reliable leader was indispensable to make proselytes and revive the spirit of a party that was morally cowed and materially crushed. Marquez and Zuloaga had fallen out among themselves and lost every opportunity as it arose; Miramon, after proclaiming in Paris that there was no such thing as a monarchist party in Mexico, was waiting in New York to draw his sword in defense of his native land. Marquez himself warned Miranda that any appearance of coercion would lose them the country and that, unless absolute freedom in the choice of a government were guaranteed beforehand, the remnants of the party would rally to the Liberals as the lesser evil. They were Mexicans after all.

Miranda labored to correct these errors by mail, but correspondence was not enough to dissipate them. There was but one man in Mexico with the moral authority to dispel all doubts, and he was in Havana. He, and he alone, could carry conviction. The confidence which he inspired, as his brother in New York assured his patrons in Paris, was unique: the soldiers would obey blindly whatever word they heard from his own lips, but in his absence they distrusted everyone else. "The first question will always be: Where is the Doctor? If this is what we are told, why is the Doctor not with us? And short of the death of the Doctor, no reply to these questions will satisfy these people. In short, amid so much misery, imbecility, disloyalty, and cowardice as we have seen, the Doctor is the only one who inspires them with unlimited trust. With him everything will be easy; without him all will be difficult." Father Miranda determined to answer the call, but as he was also wanted in Mexico by the police, he decided to remain in Havana until the arrival of the Allied fleets. There was a price on his head in Mexico, and his head was indispensable where it was; but it was also indispensable for an agitator to be on the spot, and as he lacked the first qualification of an advance agent, his influence was indifferent. Instead of preceding the expedition, he followed it; and in the meanwhile his partisans remained passive and patriotic, the boldest hesitating to betray the land of his birth, the most timid clinging to it with tenacious inertia, and the party accepted the amnesty of the government with pathological submission. The unsettled conflict of patriotism and party spirit neutralized the reaction.

If the shadow of intervention was enough to fuse, or confuse, the national feud, not until the expedition actually materialized did the internal dissension of the Liberal party disappear. Success was a severe test of its discipline: the solidarity developed under stress relaxed as soon as the pressure of necessity was removed, and during the first six months of the year the personal rivalries of its leaders and the factional loyalties of their followers were wrought to such a pitch by the presidential campaign that at the close of it Zarco raised a warning against what was fast becoming an incurable and congenial condition. "Shall we always need the needle of danger to make us unite?" he wrote when the catastrophes of the month of June once again closed the ranks. The recrudescence of the Reaction, the difficulties of consolidating the revolution, and the menace of foreign complications combined to revive the agitation of the party and the demand for revolutionary leadership. Death had thinned the ranks of the original protagonists, and of the survivors only two figures of tested capacity and national stature stood out—Juarez and Ortega—as the shadow of intervention took shape. The forging of national unity was the supreme test of the party that was identified with the nation, and of the man who represented them both.

The presidential election had not settled the questions that it raised. In spite of the large plurality with which the country—the quiet, inarticulate country as distinct from the political clubs and partisan press that produced the surface agitation of the capital—had declared for Juarez, the verdict was not accepted without question by the defeated candidate or his followers, who drew a pointed distinction between the choice of the people and the popular choice and counteracted the effect of the election by undermining confidence in its result. Their first move was to secure the succession. Congress appointed Gonzalez Ortega President of the Supreme Court. The elevation of a soldier to the bench and of a defeated presidential candidate to a position that carried with it the Constitutional title to the Presidency in case of emergency was a step the ulterior purpose of which was emphasized by its irregularity, election to the Presidency of the Supreme Court being vested not in Congress, but in the people; but it met with no open opposition. "Señor Juarez has put all his power into play to prevent my appointment," Ortega wrote to his wife, "because he is tottering in the presidential chair and is afraid of falling with my ascent to the Supreme Court. I have offered him no opposition and I despise the meanness of the government, which is discredited to the last degree."

Ortega turned himself inside out in telling the inside story of his appointment, and between man and wife that was proper; but he could not keep it to himself. The appointment was made when he was leaving for the campaign against Marquez, and on his return in August, flushed with victory, his credit was higher than ever; and on assuming his seat in the Supreme Court, he made an address remarkable for its faulty political tact. Readily admitting his lack of professional training for the bench, he repudiated the suspicions to which it might give rise and declared that, if his position there were ever to prove an impediment to the President of the Republic, he would resign. "To foresee such an antagonism is to recognize that it already exists," was the comment of one paper. His followers, however, had no tact at all. Early in September the Opposition in Congress presented a petition to the President of the Republic, signed by fifty-one deputies, requesting him to resign.

The petition was, in effect, a pronunciamento in legal form, a parliamentary mutiny that reversed the verdict of the electorate, and it was made at a time of growing emergency, which heightened its gravity. The method was not less subversive because the lever employed was moral pressure. The petition was designed to discredit the President in public opinion and—more dangerously yet—in his own. His tested capacity was contested by the same charges of inefficiency and inertia that had served to combat his election, and they were pressed home with deadly effect by the approach of an international invasion, which demanded vigorous and undisputed leadership. "The present President of the Republic, to whom we address ourselves," the petition read, "cannot save the situation, and his retirement from the high position that he holds is a necessity as imperative for the salvation of the country as his presence there was important in the first days of the revolution. Throughout it and in the days of trial, he spent the noblest thing he possessed, his prestige and moral power, which he has vainly sought to recover by means of various ministerial combinations that have merely sacrificed other such reputations and sterilized noble and fertile minds. The revolution needs them, Citizen President; it must save the name of Juarez from passing to posterity with the stigma that history will stamp on it if he appears as the man who smothered the seeds of a great revolution."

The Opposition was an amalgam of contradictory elements, dominated on the one hand by the Moderates, the timeserving liberals who had weathered the civil war without suffering it, and on the other by the impatient, battle-worn, radical youth. The latter were the serious dissidents, and they found an eloquent spokesman in Ignacio Altamirano, who had denounced the sloth of the President during the civil war and who returned to the attack as the most ruthless leader of the parliamentary Opposition. "This is a vote of censure," he concluded a scathing review of the work of the ministries, "and not only of the cabinet, but of the President of the Republic, because amid so much confusion he has stood firm, but with the deaf, dumb, immovable firmness given to the god whom the ancients named *Terminus*. This is not what the nation wants; it wants a locomotive, not a milestone. Señor Juarez, whose private virtues I am the first to respect, feels and loves democratic ideas, but I believe that he does not understand them, and I doubt it because he fails to display that vigorous, continuous, energetic action which circumstances such as those through which we are passing demand. . . . What is needed is a new name in power.

The President will render the greatest service to his country by retiring, since he is an obstacle to democracy. . . . To want to remain in a position only to prove a great and continual disappointment in it, is to be willful and to lose the country, carrying the legal principle to the point of sophistry."

Among the radical youth a doctrine was developing, which opposed the free creative spirit of revolution to the deadening legality in which it had set: this was the serious sense of a complaint which paraphrased in ideological terms the personal insurrection against a President whose creed, whose character, whose career, and whose conduct were bound by the book. "The letter of the law kills!" was the text on which one speaker after another rang the changes in Congress; and despite its partisan distortion, it was a genuine cry of distress, incident to any revolution threatened with arrest and defeat from within and without. It was irrelevant and irrational, a maddened revolt against insoluble problems, a confusion of men and things, and a blind search for a personal panacea, prompted by gathering panic, and the rebels called for an autocrat because they felt themselves balked by a bureaucrat.

Public opinion rose to the challenge. The attack failed. In reply to the petition of the Fifty-One, fifty-two deputies drew up a counter-statement in support of the President; but the bare margin was a serious symptom of his insecurity. The response of the press was a solid rally to the principle of legality; but personal defense was subordinate to the principle he represented, and though he was warmly defended, the point of the attack was conceded by some of his most zealous apologists. "Citizen Benito Juarez is not fitted to govern. This has been said for a long time, and we agree. Citizen Benito Juarez is a man of sincerity and firm principles, democratic, staunch in his decisions, honorable, of exquisite sensibility, and he loves his country only too well"—but his qualities were negative. By acceding to the Fifty-One, however, "anarchy would be the fruit of a step as false as it is ill considered," and "the weakness of Citizen Juarez at this moment would be an unpardonable crime." The treachery of the attack lay precisely in its appeal *ad hominem*. "Perhaps the most skillfully contrived part of the document is the appeal to the patriotic sentiments of the Citizen President; but in so presenting the question there is no generosity, no justice, and no political advantage. To expect a man, however strong he may be, to realize that he is the obstacle to the happiness of a whole people for whom he has so often exposed his life, as Señor Juarez has done, is to bewilder and blind him, to expect him to renounce all freedom of choice in the supreme decision imposed on him." He was "the perfect type of what the Constitution requires in the person of the Executive: not men of strenuous initiative, apt for great struggles, but administrators of laws, ready, as Señor Juarez has always been, to receive the inspirations of the Chamber, from which he has drawn his

ministers ever since he was installed." His complete identification with
his office raised the fundamental question of how far revolutionary
progress was compatible with the democratic process: a system was
put to the test in his person, and the fusion of the man and the function was a political fact, an organic growth, which made it impossible
to separate the one from the other. Gradually emerging from the heated
controversy in the capital, where it was obscured by the polemics of
Congress and the press, the issue was clearly visible at a distance, and
it was a writer in the provincial press who stated it in the simplest and
most sensible terms.

"Citizen Juarez is the model man to execute the laws. Give him
those laws, and if he does not execute them, then represent against him,
but do not wound the delicacy of the virtuous citizen without reason.
A profound sensation had been excited in everyone's mind by a phenomenon hitherto unknown in the long catalogue of our aberrations:
the petition of the Fifty-One." And submitting it to analysis point by
point, "supposing," he said, "that the resignation were made and accepted, and that Citizen Ortega as President of the Supreme Court
assumed control of the Supreme Government; supposing, also, that
this citizen surpassed Citizen Juarez in civil and moral virtues; that he
had more abnegation, more energy, more political science, more prestige with the diplomatic corps, more circumspection—would all these
guarantees be of any use to the country during the interregnum? Unquestionably not; for he would be enclosed in a circle of the same
persons and the same difficulties as those that have foiled the great
qualities of Citizen Juarez. . . . It would offend common sense to
suppose that Señor Juarez is not aware of all the evils that afflict the
country, and it would be the greatest injustice to think that he does not
wish to remedy them. If he does not, it is because neither he nor any
man alive can do so in his circumstances. It would be extremely interesting to have a diary of what happens about him, of all that he says
and that is said to him; the world would then know the truth and do
him justice. The time will come when his greatest glory will consist
in what he has neglected to do, and in having done what no one now
wants him to do. More energy of character and more civic courage are
needed, unquestionably, to keep to the legal course than to use extraordinary powers and to defy and scuttle the laws, which is what is
meant by *political tact*. That *political tact* has been shown by Santa
Anna, Comonfort, and all the governments of the Republic, and it has
brought us to our present pass. The greatness of Juarez obviously lies
in his lack of *political tact*." And the last word on the whole controversy was pronounced by the same distant and unbefogged observer:
"Señor Juarez is forced to be the expiatory goat on whom are visited
all our sins without number, sins of which he is entirely innocent, and
the only one innocent."

Prepared for protests, the Fifty-One carried their case directly to the states in a letter to the governors, inviting their support, but the states refused to stir; with three or four exceptions, the governors declared their determination to deny recognition to any power that did not derive from the legal order; and nowhere was this position maintained more firmly than in the native state of Ortega. Throughout the controversy a studied attempt was made to dissociate Ortega himself from it. A public-spirited conspiracy to exonerate the national hero was maintained by silent agreement between his friends and opponents. The latter, indeed, were his best apologists; when they mentioned his name, it was to applaud his probity and to point out how little he would gain by compromising it. "His time will come," as one of them said, "but never by cabinet intrigues. We are certain that he has had no part in whatever has been done on his behalf, which he appreciates, but does not accept." Not all his opponents, however, displayed the same glaring sense of tact. "What heroism! What greatness of soul not to have been a traitor!" one plain speaker interjected. "We are thrilled by such virtue, such abnegation, such fidelity! But do the fifty-one petitioning deputies know why the victorious soldier gave way to the depository of the supreme powers of the nation? Do they know whether this was a spontaneous act of his will or an unavoidable necessity? . . . If for the first time in the history of our country the victorious soldier respected the law and did not place himself in the supreme power, it is because education has taught us that winning a battle is not title enough to govern." Ortega himself maintained an exemplary silence, and the other principal to the affair met it with equal propriety.

The President rejected the petition of the Fifty-One on constitutional grounds and ignored their attacks as a routine incident of political life. It was not even mentioned in the diary, which was supposed to contain so many revelations of intimate truth, as he best knew it. Whether the omission was a sensitive or a sensible one, indicating the degree of importance which he attached to a public discussion of his merits, he gave no sign at the time that he felt the attack. For a man, however, whose acknowledged merits included "an exquisite sensibility," the experience could not but be a severe ordeal. His capacities challenged, his limitations explored, the springs of his being searched out, he was spared no humiliation to undo him, but he was inured to it by habit and heredity.

The psychological vivisection to which he was subjected was fundamentally a blood test. During the election campaign some attempts had been made to drum up race prejudice and to identify his deficiencies with those of an inferior, fatalistic, and apathetic people. These imputations had been indignantly repelled by the press; race prejudice was taboo in Mexico, an alien abuse, and foul blows were promptly challenged. In refuting them a College of Indians published a tribute testifying to the pride, the vanity even, which they felt, that "for the first time since our emancipation from Spain the majority of the inhabitants of Mexico, composed of its real natives, sees that its destinies will be governed by one of their blood brothers, that Mexico will be represented in the eyes of other States as it is, for Juarez is its very incarnation, for Juarez represents its virtues by his modesty, its craving for progress by the progressive laws he has issued, its love for the land by his pre-eminent patriotism." His own people, at least, knew who he was, and to all the other motives, public and private, for retaining his position was added the obligation of redeeming their reputation and vindicating their faith in him. But he was braced by a far greater responsibility. For the President of Mexico his race could not be his people; he was the personification of the nation as a whole and forbidden to fail it by a battle only half won. The damage to his self-confidence, which was the most treacherous effect of the maneuver of the Fifty-One, was blunted by striking the bedrock of a secular trust. Time was for him, but the times were against him, and it was fifty to one that he would fail, for the attack was no routine incident of political life. It was the climax of the terror lurking in the year of the comet. With all due allowance for what was factitious in such agitation, it was demoralizing because it was made at a time when the nation, the party, and the man needed all the self-confidence they could muster to meet a great emergency. The perfunctory support which he received was not sufficient to dispel self-doubt; he alone could do that, and he was the one against fifty who turned the wavering balance. He was baited into being supremely himself, and there was nothing Indian in the way in which he met the test, unless it was the muteness with which he muffled, and the indifference with which he dismissed, the attack. When the crisis was over, the world knew nothing of what it had cost him, but it knew that the inner dissension of the party had been mastered by the man who represented the nation where it mattered most vitally—within himself.

As the agitation subsided, Zarco hastened to depreciate its importance and to congratulate the party on its discipline. "This calm, after so much effort to excite agitation, this publicity and the clash of the most divergent opinions, and the dignity with which the President has acted, and even the polemics carried on by the Opposition, seem to us auspicious symptoms and a clear demonstration that democratic institutions and republican customs are taking root in Mexico." The legality in which the revolution had set had allowed its sinews to knit and braced it against the day of reckoning. When the day came, and intervention materialized, the President and the party were, to all outward appearances, at one. The demonstration of the Fifty-One had produced a sober and unanimous recognition that Juarez was an institution and, as such, inviolable. Whatever the revolution had or had not accomplished, it had achieved the fusion, or confusion, of the parts in the whole, and the result was the best proof of the leadership of the President. His scrupulous selflessness, the collective conscience that consistently governed his conduct, the complete identification with his position, which made him invisible in it and which made a democracy work, were a focal force that compelled his collaborators and competitors alike to conform to a criterion that none could ignore, on pain of losing caste and forfeiting all that, as revolutionaries, they had lived and fought for. The religious inspiration of revolution was safe; and its value was felt when moral power was the only power upon which the nation, faced with an invasion that threatened to sweep away all its other gains, could count.

An English journalist commissioned by the parliamentary Opposition to Palmerston to visit Mexico and report on actual conditions there, arrived in the capital just in time to witness the dissolving scenes of 1861. His first impressions were formed from a seat in the gallery at the closing session of Congress on December 15, when Veracruz was already invaded and emergency powers were conferred upon the President. The setting was a far cry from the House of Parliament: "There was no ornament or gilding, the painting and glazing were of the most ordinary and trumpery description, and the galleries were filled with all kinds of riffraff, both men and women, but there was no interruption or sound except from the members themselves, who made noise enough for all." The performance, nevertheless, was impressive. "At about three the President, Juarez, entered amid an astonishing din of cannon and trumpets. He is a dark, small man, quiet and self-possessed. He is affectionately known in Mexico as the little Indian. Juarez is a very respectable, well-meaning man, and of fair talents . . . and he deserves very great credit for his firmness and tenacity in maintaining the struggle and the cause of legitimacy. . . . All sorts of intrigues and combinations have been formed against him, both in Congress and out of it, thwarting and opposing in order to compel him to resign, but he has stood firm, and they have not yet dared to resort to force, and will not. He has scarcely had fair play in England. On taking his seat, he bowed gracefully on all sides and immediately made the following address in a clear and remarkably pleasant voice. . . ." The address expressed the President's hope that a reasonable settlement might yet be made with the Powers, and the determination of the nation, if that hope were defeated, to defend its revolution and its independence. It was not a speech but a statement, and it received the undivided tribute due to a statement of fact which was at the same time a profession of faith.

When the cheering subsided, the President of Congress replied. Stressing the responsibility placed on the President by the grant of full powers, which made him legally a dictator—"the greatest proof of confidence ever given to the depository of the executive power"—he reminded Juarez that "upon the Executive it now depends (and upon no other) to save the Republic or to plunge it into the abyss," and that when Congress again convened it would exact "an accounting of the power which it delivers into his hands today with such perfect trust." Thereupon the President rose and retired as quietly as he had come in, amid the respectful silence of a House that recognized the stature of the man whom the nation needed in its own hour of humiliation, and who had been hammered into being its man of destiny. That mute tribute was more eloquent than the ovation he had received a year before in the theater at Veracruz or the one that Gonzalez Ortega had given him in the capital.

In the streets the English scout was struck by the martial enthusiasm of the crowds accompanying the volunteers leaving for the front, conscripts whose enthusiasm and confidence, fired by the cry that the Spaniards were in Veracruz, was for once completely unforced. More impressive, perhaps, as a proof of the personal confidence of the President, was the fact that he chose this moment to buy himself a house in the capital of his country.

PART FOUR

Intervention

I

ON DECEMBER 15, when Congress conferred full powers on the President, Veracruz was already submerged. Forewarned for five months, the government was only half armed when intervention actually materialized, and he received the keys when the door was broken. The War Office was in the capable hands of Ignacio Zaragoza, a young veteran of the civil war who began his career on the staff of Santiago Vidaurri, served Gonzalez Ortega as his Quartermaster and succeeded him when he left the Ministry for politics, and who won the confidence of the President and the responsibility of defending the country at the close of that Janus-faced year. But war and peace had been so dubiously balanced in the wavering odds of diplomacy, and war-weariness was so general and delusive, that only the preliminary steps for a general mobilization had been taken and a rapid improvisation was necessary to complete them at the eleventh hour. The burden of national defense reverted, therefore, to the diplomatic arm; and the key post of Foreign Affairs was occupied by a man who was placed there because the Opposition trusted his capabilities more than they did those of the President. The Opposition had rallied to the President conditionally, making a concession to the principle of legality and the necessity of national union for which they expected compensation and exacted a price. For the Fifty-One Juarez was still a little man in a position too large for him, and their opinion, inflated by war-worry and chafing at legal fictions, was impatient of dangerous delusions and deliberate pretense. Whatever might be the Constitutional limitations of his office, there was nothing to prevent him from exercising initiative, resourcefulness, and personal authority, unless it was the constitutional limitations of his nature, and in their propaganda he was represented as a sedentary patriot. Private testimony was adduced from his close associates that he trusted his ministers implicitly and took no active part in their councils, confining himself to occasional recommendations, marking his presence by his silence and making it felt by his attention, relieved only by a mannerism of tapping the knuckles of one hand with the fingers of the other. The Opposition qualified their support, therefore, by demanding that a strong man be placed at the head of the cabinet to make a fresh start in the next phase of the national destiny. The vigorous and commanding partner thus forced on the President was Manuel Doblado.

Doblado enjoyed a peculiar prestige. He was the only leader of the Reform movement whose reputation had not suffered by its progress, and his capabilities, which remained to be proved, lay in the expectations he excited. Repeatedly invited to join the government, he had consistently refused to risk his reputation until the opportunity of crowning it came. The instincts of the politician and the patriot were combined in his conduct, but the call of patriotism finally overcame his caution and in November he had consented to succeed Zamacona. The most striking thing about Doblado was the contradictory sentiments he inspired—trust and mistrust, doubt and devotion—without compromising his integrity or reflecting on his loyalty. He came to the capital preceded by a flock of rumors. He was said to be conspiring with the Moderates, and in league with a general, to overthrow Juarez at the ripe moment; he was known to have contacts in all camps; he was credited with combinations of all kinds; countless were the inside stories told of his tactics, his ideas, his resourcefulness; the one rumor which he did not inspire was that of a cordial devotion to Juarez himself; but these rumors did him small justice, for he was more skillful than any of them. He came to do something more damaging than to supplant the President: he came to save him. He was willing to brace, but it was only by courtesy that he entered the cabinet as a subordinate, and he set his conditions—a free hand in the choice of his colleagues and the determination of policy. His cabinet was accepted, after some bargaining, and the challenge remained in abeyance.

Before long, however, Doblado discovered that the man upon whom Congress conferred unlimited authority was by no means a Constitutional dummy. In the exercise of his discretionary powers, the Prime Minister decided one day to abrogate one of the most valued reforms of the Constitution of 1857, the right of free trial, and he sent a decree restoring judicial costs to the official gazette. The bulletin appeared daily at three in the afternoon, and in the morning of the same day he drove out to Tacubaya, where the President was staying, to report. After listening to Doblado's explanations the President made a single observation—but a final one. "In spite of all that you have said," he remarked, spreading his hands on his knees, "the Constitutional article will not be abrogated." — "But, sir, the decree will be published today in the *Diario*," Doblado expostulated. Juarez consulted his watch. "It is eleven o'clock," he said. "Be so good as to return to Mexico immediately and withdraw the decree from the presses." The Minister drove back to town, the *Diario* appeared without the decree, and no further irregularity disturbed their collaboration. The incident was a minor one, but it saved them both any serious strain. Doblado knew how far he could go and never went further than safety permitted. On major questions he was careful to consult the President in time, and on those there was no room for disagreement.

For the determination of policy was dictated by conditions which left little scope for personal skill. Two years before, when Ocampo had been conducting the diplomatic defense of the Veracruz government against the first rehearsal of foreign intervention, his friend in Paris had written him: "Your conduct and the conduct of all of you answers the question about governments in Mexico yielding to *foreign force* and not feeling themselves honorable men. Political honesty, in fact, has such penetrating properties that it inspires with the genius of government those who lack all the knowledge necessary to form a complete statesman." The words applied with greater force to the full-grown fact of intervention. There was no place for finesse and no latitude for dexterity in dealing with the crisis. Combinations and intrigues were out of scale and proportion to the magnitude of the emergency, and Juarez faced it squarely and set an example of political honesty, recognizing the weakness of the country and the necessity of accommodations and concessions, and adapting his policy to conditions which could not be dissimulated. Doblado had no choice but to follow his lead and rely on the same artless statesmanship. The maneuver of the Fifty-One, which was the last gasp of a propaganda that confounded conditions and men and a modified repetition, this time within strictly legal limits, of the parliamentary mutiny, merely succeeded in placing one more double at the service of the President. Doblado could do no better than to second the plain-dealing policy of Juarez with his own ingenuity. The combination of his incontestable integrity and his reputation for double-dealing served him in good stead, however, in conducting the diplomatic defense of the country, lending him credit for ambidexterity among his adversaries and personal weight against a coalition of incompatible partners. On the same day that he assumed office, Wyke broke with the government, and Doblado made an unsuccessful attempt to persuade him to remain and reconsider; but he did succeed in making an impression, and he maintained contact with the British Minister after he left the capital, and kept his foot in the door which the London Convention had slammed.

Of the scope, the complexity, and the object of the European coalition the government had only an uncertain notion. As late as November 1 Juarez wrote to the governor of one of the states that the demands of England and France were purely pecuniary and might be moderated, while the designs of Spain were patently political and called for military preparations; and one of the first steps he took to mobilize the nation was to issue a proclamation preparing it for the possibility of hostilities with the hereditary enemy. The appeal to atavistic instincts was tactically shrewd, but it missed the mark; the heritage had accrued with the century, and Spain was the least of the Powers leagued against the country in 1861. The government was better inspired in the attempts which it made to appease the English, but it misjudged the central position of France, and while it spared no effort to mollify Sir Charles Wyke, it neglected M. de Saligny.

The scent of M. de Saligny was lost after the run on his life in August. He remained in the capital unnoticed, save for an occasional scandal. Condemned to inactivity, he occupied himself with the accumulation of injuries and outraged reports, the burden of which was invariable—"I can do nothing until the hour of retribution comes"— and he found so little relief for his feelings in official complaints that they overflowed in his private correspondence. Writing to the friend who had pleaded the Liberal cause with him before he left France, he expressed himself on the subject of Mexico with sweeping impartiality. "You know in what spirit I left France. Wishing to remain neutral amid these interminable struggles, I welcomed the triumph of the Liberal party as the beginning of an era of peace and prosperity for this unhappy Republic, but in spite of all my good will, and with all my patience and forbearance, I could not live long on good terms with such people. This so-called Liberal party, which lost no time in confiscating every liberty and substituting for the brutal and stupid despotism of Miramon the dictatorship of M. Juarez—an idiot and a rascal—this so-called Liberal party is nothing but a heap of people without faith or law, intelligence, honor, or patriotism, who have never held any other political opinion than theft. You will understand, then, that a break was inevitable. The parties that have oppressed this wretched nation in turn have abused the patience of Europe too long; the hour of reckoning has struck, and it must be exemplary. What is horrible about this situation is that it offers no means of salvation. Reactionaries, *Puros,* Liberals, are all alike. The former are brigands, the latter are robbers. Everywhere venality, corruption, incompetence. . . . The Republic no longer exists except in name. The other states pay no more attention to what happens in the City of Mexico than if it were China or Japan; they seem determined to let M. Juarez disentangle himself with France, England, Spain, and Germany as best he can, for these scoundrels seem to make it their business to offend, insult, and attack all the civilized nations. What I see here is not merely the most dreadful anarchy, but a real moral decomposition. The decent people (that is the name given to those who still have something to lose, although at bottom they are not more decent than the beggars), the decent people look for their salvation only from abroad. If the cure for which they call in secret does not come soon, we shall see the states split into fragments and war on one another, then will come a race war, and, lastly, the destruction of all social order. Already an insurrection of the Indians is beginning in the Mezquital, where one of their leaders is said to have eight or ten thousand men at his command with whom he commits every kind of atrocity to the cry of 'Down with the whites! Long live religion!' This is but the beginning. We shall see much more. We have been fed far too long in Europe with romances about this rich, this magnificent, but miserable country. You will realize that I cannot remain here forever."

His disgust no longer had any taint of partisanship; it was alien, pure, and unadulterated. In the making of a successful agitator conviction was as essential as in any other vocation, and that letter was the confession of a consummate specimen of his tribe. After nine months of failure he had worked himself into the confirmed and uncompromising conviction of a victim, a state of mind common to people who could not do business with Mexico, and, like them, he could not keep his feelings to himself. He vented them on the slightest provocation, and on one occasion he narrowly escaped corporal punishment for insulting the country in public. The reckless indulgence of his temper, and the habitual state of self-intoxication from which he suffered, were not correctly understood, however, by the Mexicans. They attributed his phobia to another infirmity. It was difficult to treat the war of one man on a people seriously, and one day he awoke to see himself in a lampoon that belittled his besotting obsession. The familiar figure of the French Minister, as others saw him—portly, hirsute, a little Oriental, and bemonocled—was confined by the teasing pen of the caricaturist to the contents of a bottle, and the bottle was labeled "Old Cognac." He challenged the cartoon and attempted to make a diplomatic incident of it, but his protests were ignored as usual, and his lesser self, squat, cramped, and steeped like a toad in alcohol, was preserved for posterity as his indestructible double.

But the solitary inmate of the French Legation was neither helpless nor idle. Unable to do anything himself until the hour of reckoning, and spoiling with the delays in Paris, he had left nothing undone to hasten the coming of the Spanish expedition from Havana. Alarmed by the Wyke-Zamacona negotiation, which threatened to obviate intervention altogether, he had redoubled his efforts to circumvent his British colleague and had called desperately on Marshal Serrano to mobilize without further delay. On the day that the treaty had come up in Congress, he had sent two hectic notes to Cuba in twenty-four hours. In the first he rehearsed the futility of negotiations with the Mexican Government. "Force is henceforth the only argument that should be employed by the Government of the Queen. God grant that we may not have long to wait for it!" he concluded. In the second he mustered every argument to convince the Captain-General of Cuba that the military defenses of the Mexican Government were as weak as its diplomatic ones. "It claims, and there are fools enough to believe it, that it is very calm and has no fear of Spain. Well may we say that those whom the gods mean to destroy they first infatuate! The government, and the scoundrels around it, are trying, as in other times, to excite national feeling against the Spaniards, but they are not succeeding in the least. The mass of people remain unmoved, possibly because they believe the Spanish will not come alone, for it cannot be denied that popular sentiment is far less hostile to other foreigners, and particularly to the French, than to the Spanish. . . . In Guanajuato General Doblado who, though no more honest, has more ability and decency than the rest, has assured the Spaniards that they will find a safe shelter there. Here there is talk of mass expulsions, but I doubt that they will dare to carry them out. On the other hand, the government, which, for all its boasting, now seems to be beginning to tremble, has been trying to control the disorders which it fomented and provoked at first. Desiring to inform you of everything, but not wishing to stain my pen by the recital of unparalleled infamies, I enclose a note that has been sent me, and in which are recounted facts the accuracy of which has been warranted by fifty reliable witnesses. I know the noble and chivalrous Spain very little if she hesitates to rise as one man to avenge such bloody outrages. I pass to another order of ideas. . . ." But there was no other order of ideas for M. de Saligny, and he abandoned only the weak ones with which he began.

Passing to stronger arguments, he stressed the facility with which an expedition could be landed in the disorganized state of the country. "San Juan de Ulua and Veracruz are being disarmed, and the operations must be well advanced by now. Although I am not a soldier, allow me to ask one question: Why confine yourselves to operations against Tampico, instead of taking San Juan de Ulua and Veracruz as well, where no resistance will be offered?" To the mind of a civilian the facility of the operation made it obligatory, and though his information was secondhand and gathered from hearsay, M. de Saligny had contacts in all parties and was able to give Serrano the inside story of the situation in Mexico. "The plan of the government, if it can be said to have one, is to transport the material withdrawn from Veracruz, in part to Puente Nacional and Cerro Gordo on the road to Mexico, by way of Jalapa and the Chiquihuite on the road that passes through Orizaba. In these positions, which are rather easy to defend, the Mexicans propose to meet the Spanish army. . . . General Uraga, who has been appointed Commander-in-Chief of the Eastern Army, is a man of some fifty-odd years, fairly courageous, but inconsistent, presumptuous, false to a degree, and mendacious as a Mexican. But at least he is a soldier (he lost a leg at the siege of Guadalajara), and having traveled and seen Europe, he is in a position to judge and compare. He has no illusions, therefore, as he gave me very clearly to understand when he dined in my house several days ago. The government talks of raising immediately thirty thousand men. . . . But where will they find the men, the horses, the weapons, the money, etc., etc. A foreigner who is a superior officer in the Mexican army, a very intelligent and well-informed man, gave me the enclosed note, numbered 1, in which you will find positive facts as to the true state of the present military situation. From them it appears that there are only four thousand men, and what men! I advise you, moreover, that if the government sends these troops against you, on the next day Marquez will enter the capital. And Marquez is not the only one who threatens Juarez: the latter fears Doblado even more, and not without reason, as you can judge by the enclosed letter, numbered 2, written by General Robles, the only general and perhaps the only man of honor to be found in the country." The next day he added a postscript—the government was in complete confusion, the President could find neither money nor ministers, General Uraga refused to take command unless he received thirty thousand pesos, which no one could raise, and the reasons for speed gained force with every day of delay. "It is still said here that General Prim will command the expedition and also that Gonzalez, the new Minister of Finance and the uncle of the Condesa de Reus, will need only half an hour's talk with his niece to settle the Spanish question. . . . I insist that, if you are to act, there is no time to be lost."

Of all the revelations which these letters contained, the most important was that of the writer. As a picture of conditions in Mexico, they were highly misleading, for they were almost uniformly wrong, although they were flavored with just enough truth to make them credible. The unconscious disclosure of the author, however, was authentic and a self-portrait more damaging than the lampoon that belittled him in a bottle of old brandy. The intoxication of temper, the personal spite, the brain in the belly, the credulity of prejudice, the minimizing of obstacles, the mental monocle, reflected a genius of gigantic proportions fuming for release from its own ferment, and the label would have been a libel if M. de Saligny had not finally burst his bottle.

To what extent Marshal Serrano was influenced by these incitements is uncertain; but the promptings of the French Minister coincided with his own plans. He had completed the preparation of the Spanish expedition in accordance with the original instructions from Madrid, and although he was not ignorant of the provisions for joint action in the London Convention, he had not yet been officially informed of them and was anxious to take the lead in an expedition which he expected to command, for he was one of the political aces of Spain. Saligny toadied at the right time, and on November 29 the Spanish contingent cast off from Havana.

Whatever the reasons for the initiative, there was no doubt of its results. No advantage was gained by the Spanish in the march they stole on their Allies. The orders written by Serrano for his representa-

tive, Admiral Rubicalva, contemplated a brilliant action and a spectacular solo. The Admiral was directed to consult the French and English
if he met their vessels at Veracruz, but "never to lose the initiative,
which belongs to the Spanish Government," to present the Mexican
Government with an ultimatum, to demand its immediate acceptance
or rejection, and to tolerate no negotiations or compromise. If the reply
was such as to require him to take the forts and occupy the town by
force, he was to remind his troops that "the expedition has a highly
special character beyond all ordinary rules. A mishap in Mexico would
be not merely a disgrace and a stain almost impossible to efface, it
would put an end forever to our growing importance in America. . . .
If the Mexican nation, demoralized as it is, in complete anarchy, despised by Europe, and with a small and ill-organized army, were to
make us recede from its forts, ignominy would be the result of our
enterprise." These orders were modified, however, at the last moment,
for just before the transports sailed from Havana, Serrano was officially
notified of the conclusion of the London Convention and obliged, by
fresh instructions from Madrid, to revise his own and to forfeit their
effect. Admiral Rubicalva was directed to occupy Veracruz on behalf
of the three governments, to await the arrival of the Allied fleets there,
and to withhold his demands until then. This operation was completed
without a hitch.

On December 8 the first transports cast anchor in the flat mouth of
Mexico, two days later a second contingent arrived, and on December
14 the town was formally occupied. No resistance was offered, the
Governor surrendering the town, on previous instructions from the
capital, after dismantling the fortifications and retiring to the outskirts
to organize guerrilla bands. The satisfaction of forcing an open town
was enjoyed by the Spanish for three weeks. The occupation of Veracruz accomplished nothing but the landing of a reconnaissance party
six thousand strong, and they landed in a void. The evacuation by the
local authorities was accompanied by an exodus of five thousand of
the inhabitants and followed by a blockade by guerrilla bands effective
enough to cut off all communications with the surrounding country.
No food entered the town, and no information: foragers who went
beyond bounds returned with the crack of rifle fire in their ears or their
bellies, and the embargo was respected on both sides by a tacit truce,
which isolated the Spanish within the city limits. Politically, they were
no further advanced than in Havana. The pledge to hold Veracruz in
the name of the Allies converted the place into an extraterritorial area,
neither Spanish nor Mexican, and the position for which they had
jockeyed was purely provisional. From a military point of view, a base
of operations had been established, but beyond Veracruz lay the *terra
incognita* which was Mexico—a waste zone extending twenty leagues

inland to the mountains—and the strength of the defense established there could not be judged by the forfeit of the port.

After surveying the situation for three weeks, Admiral Rubicalva came to certain conclusions, which differed from those of M. de Saligny. The sanguine prognostics of the French Minister—the internal collapse of the country, the revolts, the betrayals, the overthrow and flight of the President—were promissory notes subject, like everything else in Mexico, to deferred payment. But M. de Saligny had made full allowance for that factor himself. "Nowhere is it so difficult to know what is really happening as in this country," he had written to Serrano. He was not even certain now of arriving in Veracruz alive. Before leaving the capital, he drew up a letter commending his family to the Emperor, in case. He reached sea level in safety, but only to witness the lifeless result of his efforts to coach Serrano. The Spanish flag flew over the town, the Spanish squadron rode in the harbor, but the expedition which he had strained so many arguments to launch had already been boarded by his British colleague. Sir Charles Lennox Wyke, arriving as usual before him, had lost no time in exchanging views with Admiral Rubicalva, and the result of their conferences was a complete agreement that negotiations with the Mexican Government were preferable to an appeal to force.

So much haste to reach that conclusion would have been waste motion had it produced no other result; but some effect was accomplished, after all, by the initiative of Marshal Serrano. The premature and isolated appearance of the Spanish roused the country as nothing else could have done; and when, on the day after the occupation, the President received the country in trust from Congress, he was supported by the motive power of an immense sensation. Though the decision to evacuate Veracruz had been adopted by the government to gain time for the improvisation of a solid defense, there was a sensible difference between a strategic plan and the palpable reality. No spot in Mexican territory was so sore and so certain to produce a national reaction as Veracruz: the country was not, and could not be, prepared for the shock of the accomplished fact. The difference, the incommensurable difference, was felt in the words with which Zarco announced the "incredible fact" in the *Siglo*: "For the past three days heroic Veracruz has been held by the enemy, and the immense distress of its sons will be understood and felt by the Mexicans who recall the glorious history of that city, which has always been the advance post of national independence and which, in succumbing, has always covered itself with a glory which the very invaders respected." Veracruz, the citadel of the civil war, Veracruz the invulnerable, overrun by the Spanish for the first time since 1821, and surrendered without a struggle, was a vision of uncalculated and incalculable value in the sentimental strategy of national defense: the mere announcement was enough to tap unsuspected powers in a prostrate and war-weary people and to lend the nation a second wind, which, short and convulsive at first, daily came deeper, sounder, stronger.

As details drifted in, Zarco displayed them with the pride of a recruiting sergeant: "The occupation of Veracruz, however much it afflicts and saddens Mexican patriotism, is not a triumph for the invaders and can afford them no pride. The evacuation of the town was carried out in complete order: letters of the 15th, which are the latest to arrive, contain details that are painful but that sharpen the sympathies which the Veracruzans have always deserved for their conspicuous patriotism. The National Guard, composed of traders and artisans, left in a body with the commander and, far from suffering a single loss, found numerous recruits. Wealthy people forsook their interests and presented themselves to the government to organize guerrillas to fight the invader. Means of transportation were lacking, many families emigrating on foot, and if these events had not happened so swiftly, it is likely that not a single Mexican would have remained in Veracruz." And with the conventional understatement of a statesman, he concluded: "The event must convince the invader that he meets with no sympathy in this country, and that it has been a fatal error for Spain to expect to find in Mexico any longing for its former and hated dominion. It will soon discover that the Mexicans of 1861 are the same as those of 1810 and 1821." The lines of refugees marching inland were multiplied by the lines of volunteers forming before the recruiting offices in every corner of the country and moving to meet them in a popular outpouring that transformed five thousand vagrants into a nation of homeless patriots. The first call was for fifty-two thousand men, in many of the states the quota was oversubscribed, and the task of the government was to equip and organize, not to inspire, a martial spirit, which, as the bulletins of the *Siglo* said, "appeared in all the states at the first threat of invasion, the people begging for arms and imploring as a favor the right to march against the enemy." Nor were the diplomatic defenses neglected. They were few and meager, being as yet purely moral, but at the head of the government sat a man accustomed to making much of little, and he employed them for more than they were actually worth.

The war of the people that was preparing was preceded by civilian skirmishes in the press, by a war of words, and Zarco, a civilian to the core, was the first to insist that after the invasion of Veracruz the only possible defense was force, but that he expected the government, without compromising the dignity of the nation, to "reserve to itself in its prudence the right moment to open negotiations"; and he recruited the President for that policy and urged him to explain the gravity of the situation to the nation. The President responded with a manifesto designed not only for domestic but for foreign consumption. Communication with the enemy, forbidden on pain of death to the humblest of Mexican citizens, was prohibited by pride to the highest, but there was nothing to prevent the Citizen President from passing over the head of the invaders and addressing the public opinion of the world, unless it was the risk of remaining unheard. Though world opinion had remained deaf or indifferent to the situation until then, the opening of hostilities was a fact which compelled attention, and at the proper moment the President, with that personal reserve and slow saturation of public feeling which marked his rare pronouncements, broke his habitual silence to state the case of his country in a defense that was worthy of it. The arguments mounted by Zarco in the *Siglo* to denounce the Spanish invasion—filibustering, piracy, unprovoked aggression, breach of international law—for such technicalities Juarez had no time and for futilities no feeling: chary of words, he was all matter molded to a mark, and the document he produced was a deed. He engaged the nation to negotiate every legitimate claim, and the pretexts of intervention he paid on the spot, promising that "if the Spanish nation conceals other designs under the financial questions," the policy of his government would be "not to declare war, but to repel force by force insofar as its means of action allow." And with the same plain speaking and plain dealing he denounced the presumption that sanctioned the mobbing of Mexico and improved on the claims of the invader to be leading a civilizing crusade: "Exaggerated and sinister reports by the enemies of Mexico have portrayed us to the world as an uncultivated and degraded people. Let us defend ourselves against the war to which we are provoked by strictly observing the laws and usages established for the benefit of humanity. Let the defenseless enemy, to whom we have given generous hospitality, live tranquil and secure under the protection of our laws. Thus we shall repel the calumnies of our enemies and prove ourselves worthy of the liberty and independence left us by our forefathers."

Zarco was satisfied. "This remarkable document, written with dignity and moderation," he declared, calling the country to attention, "describes truly and accurately the baseless pretexts which Spain may invoke to draw us into war. It will do Mexico much honor in the world that, when our enemies strive to picture us as barbarians, the voice of the President of the Republic, at the very moment when we suffer the affront of an expedition that appears to be piratical, should rise serene and calm to recommend protection and asylum for the Spanish residents of the country, exposed by the imprudence of their government to irreparable evils." Of all the advantages that could be wrung from a victimized people for its defense, the vindication of its good name was the greatest, and its demonstration the most difficult at that moment; but the thing was done. The nationals of Spain, like all other foreigners, continued to enjoy the protection of civilized customs under a government whose moral authority was so manifest that the enemy attributed it to his presence at Veracruz.

With one half of the terror tamed, Juarez turned his attention to the other. Whether his pronouncement would attract any attention abroad was one more of the many uncertainties of the situation; but such was the penetrating property of political honesty that it was answered by a Spaniard who felt its challenge, and who landed in Mexico at that moment.

2

INTERVENTION began formally on January 7, 1862, when the false start of the Spanish was effaced by the arrival of the Allied fleets at Veracruz. As a move for political position, the maneuver of Marshal Serrano miscarried, but it provided a brisk military overture for the appearance of the remarkable man who came in command of the Spanish and who was destined to play a leading part in the psychological direction of the coalition.

The character and contradictions of Spanish policy were epitomized in the choice of the person appointed by Madrid to represent the prestige of his country abroad. General Prim was a national hero. He was not a Spaniard but a Catalan, and though the distinction never affected his loyalty, it contributed to the independence which was the most pronounced feature of his character. Of modest origin, he had made a name for himself in the civil wars that agitated the peninsula in the years that followed the Napoleonic invasion and had crowned his career by brilliant conduct in the conquest of Morocco in 1859, covering himself with glory by spectacular feats of personal prowess that captured the imagination of his countrymen. At the close of the campaign he was raised to the peerage and made a Grandee of Spain, but the titles of the Conde de Reus were never more than pseudonyms for General Prim in the mouth of the people. On his return to Madrid he was received with popular ovations, which, far from being a passing effervescence, were repeated with insatiable enthusiasm in every part of the country through which he passed. His popularity was an historic phenomenon. The Moroccan war marked the close of an era of civil convulsions and the unification of the nation in foreign adventure and colonial expansion; and Prim, who had figured conspicuously in both, was identified in the public mind with the revival of the national spirit. He satisfied its pride and self-confidence more than the government that planned the campaign, or Marshal O'Donnell who commanded it, by the romantic glamour which he gave it. His exploits recalled the heroic traditions of a people still steeped in the past, and their revival in the nineteenth century heightened the nostalgic sentiment that inspired the Spanish bid for a place in the modern sun. Martial glory was their biological urge, and his gallantry appealed to the sex of Spain. His prowess was recognized by the hereditary enemies of the country. The tribesmen of the Riff paid tribute to it, and in the Mountains of the Moon children were hushed with the sound of his name, as they were fired by it in the Pyrenees. In France he was noticed by the military journals and likened to Bayard and Murat, and he gained by the comparison. "He may be a Murat," it was said, "but a Murat without the plume, the polonaise of crimson velvet, and the circus side: his bearing is that of the most severe type of soldier." — "In matters of bravery the French soldiers are a little blasé and nothing can astonish them," wrote one of his admirers, "but the brilliant actions of the Conde de Reus have a peculiar character and an heroic form. His is an epic courage that puts one in mind of the tournaments and of *Jerusalem Delivered*. His *élans* are swift, spontaneous, uncalculated, and yet they seem to be composed for the gallery and are always picturesque: they strike the imagination of the soldier and the people and awake in them a shining and chivalrous side, which is the very genius of Spain." His conversation captured his hearers in the same way that he carried the crests and fastnesses of the Moors; speaking slowly and unimpressively at first, he warmed gradually, his speech becoming quick and curt, his arguments crowding, accumulating, rising to eloquence, brushing aside objections, leaping obstacles, surprising, attacking, pressing, charming and shocking and finally dominating the most critical. One other feature of his character was noted by the same observer. "He is said to love the truth and to be able to understand it, but exceptional qualities and an extremely attractive manner have surrounded him with a great deal of adulation and exaltation."

The laurels which Prim won in the Moroccan campaign were fresh when he was appointed to lead the expedition to Mexico in 1861, and in many respects the choice was inevitable. The government selected the most eligible and seemingly the most suitable candidate for a highly coveted post. His personal prestige entitled him to command an expedition the primary purpose of which was foreign credit, and as a romantic agent he was well qualified to represent the renovation of Spain abroad with éclat. As the representative of an aggressive policy, however, he was no less conspicuously miscast. In the course of his career he had acquired convictions, his horizon had broadened with his rise, he was a Liberal in politics, and he defended his principles with an independence that gave him a unique place in public life. He was famous for a civic courage of which he had given conspicuous proof, and precisely in connection with the Mexican question, when he rose in the Senate in 1858 to protest against an expedition which the government was then planning against Mexico. In view of his position in 1858, it was as remarkable, therefore, that he should accept, and even solicit, command of a punitive expedition against the country which he had championed three years before, as that the government should entrust a man of his well-known sympathies and principles with such a mission.

But what was his mission? The nature of the enterprise was still tentative and unsettled when he was appointed. Involved in local politics, the broad lines of national policy were so blurred that De la Fuente wrote that "no one knows exactly what Spain expects to do, and I believe that even its government does not know." Questioned by the British Minister to Madrid, Calderon Collantes declared that Spain had no intention of imposing a government upon Mexico, but that, like the other Allies, if the appearance of the expedition were to provoke a spontaneous movement and encourage the conservative elements to rise and establish a stable and reliable government, he would welcome the result, whatever form it might take; whether a republic or a monarchy was a matter of complete indifference to him, although in the latter case the Spanish Bourbons would deserve first consideration. He also observed that it should be borne in mind that the convulsions in Mexico were at bottom a race war and that the Spanish elements, which had always been in a minority, were in danger of being eliminated or reduced to the same condition as in the days of Cortés. With foreign critics he hedged, and with domestic ones he trimmed. The Spanish expedition was the product not of a plan but of a state of mind. It was designed primarily for home consumption. The self-confidence of the country, stimulated by the conquest of Morocco, seemed to favor a fresh adventure; the chauvinist press was clamoring for colonial reconquest and a Spanish prince for the Mexican throne; and the government catered to these expectations by the celerity with which it launched the undertaking, without committing itself to any specific object other than domestic popularity and foreign effect. The practiced politicians of Madrid knew very well that its ultimate direction depended upon their partners and waited for circumstances to develop what was, in sum, a prospecting expedition to explore the possibility of restoring Spanish influence in America. Whatever turn it might take, the name of Prim was a form of political insurance, which guaranteed them against every risk. The national idol, the loyal servant of the Crown, the friend of Mexico, the recognized Liberal—each in turn could be trusted to advance the interests and repute of Spain in whatever way he might deem expedient on his arrival in Mexico, and sufficient latitude was given him in his formal instructions, and sufficient discretion in his verbal ones, to allow him to bear full responsibility for the outcome.

The foreign reaction to his appointment was significant. In France the Mexican monarchists were alarmed by the selection of an avowed friend of the Liberals, and Hidalgo and the Empress appealed to the Emperor to prevent the nomination, but without success. Napoleon had made the acquaintance of Prim during the previous summer, when they were both taking the waters at Vichy; there had been an exchange of views, Prim had spoken of his desire of seeing the arms of France and Spain united in some common cause; and as it was a cardinal point in the diplomacy of Napoleon to encourage Spain and to lead it to take an important place in the concert of Europe under his wing, the Emperor recommended to London that the supreme command of the coalition be given to the Conde de Reus. The suggestion found no favor there, and he did not insist, but he did what he could to feature his protégé. The commander of the French contingent was instructed to treat General Prim with all the deference compatible with his own dignity. "You know what excellent relations exist between the Government of the Emperor and the Spanish Government," his orders read, "and it will rest with you to reconcile the requirements of the service and of your own position with the desire for an entente, which will be drawn yet closer by our expedition in Cochin-China, the one at the head of which you are placed, and by interests, in short, of more than one kind."

The favor of Napoleon was guaranteed, in fact, by the necessity of offsetting the weight of England and the English interpretation of intervention. While the English proposed to occupy Veracruz and remain there, a march into the interior was contemplated in both the Spanish and French projects. Prim was instructed "not to wait until the climate and the drawbacks that accompany distant expeditions decimate the troops . . . but to seek out the Mexican Government, wherever it may be, and to impose his conditions upon it." The same directive was laid down in the French plan, with a flexible difference. The instructions given to Admiral Jurien de la Gravière were of three degrees, corresponding, as it were, to the different planes on which the mind of the Emperor moved. The first were official and literal: the terms of the London Convention were to be observed, but only as a starting point; if the "sane part" of the population—a euphemism borrowed from the Mexican monarchists—reacted to the expedition and attempted to institute a power offering some guarantees of strength and stability, the Admiral was not to refuse it his encouragement and moral support. The second set of instructions was confidential and a distinct refinement upon the first. While the Convention was the legal ground of agreement among the three Powers, the idea of the Emperor went much further: the salvation of Mexico lay in the introduction of a monarchy, and the Archduke Maximilian was the most desirable candidate. The co-operation of England could not be expected; for though the English Government did full justice to the idea of the Emperor, it proposed to observe the London Convention literally. Spain was more sympathetic, but not to the Archduke; and the attitude of the Mexicans themselves was doubtful. "If the nation remains inert, then we can do nothing but remain within the terms of the Convention." Some suggestions were added. A proclamation might be issued to the Mexican people, guaranteeing their independence and freedom of choice in the form of a government, but as the guarantee could not be made good by a mere occupation of the coast, a march into the interior would be necessary; the English would not be a party to it, it could only be organized with the support of the Spanish, and as they were unpopular in Mexico, the French troops must be placed at the head of the march.

Besides these written instructions, the Admiral received verbal ones from the Emperor, who repeated their substance to the Austrian Ambassador. Prince Metternich was a skeptic, who regarded the whole scheme with grave misgivings and regretted to see the Hapsburgs involved in a shady adventure; and he desired to know how the free choice of the Mexican people, upon which the Archduke insisted, was to be effected. Such a question, coming from such a quarter, compelled Napoleon to telescope his vision and focus it clearly. The French and Spanish contingents, he explained, would march at once to the capital, and there the Admiral, with the support of the Monarchist party, would convoke a kind of Constituent Assembly, composed of appointed representatives of the various provinces, who would voice the sentiment of the nation in favor of the Archduke. The ultimate development of intervention was thus clearly foreseen by Napoleon when the expedition started, and the distribution of roles as well: England would chaperon the shady adventure to the rendezvous; the next lap, from Veracruz to the capital, would be covered by the Spanish; and in the capital the Admiral and the Mexican monarchists would conclude the affair. General Prim was a form of political insurance for Napoleon as well as for Marshal O'Donnell.

Such were the premises upon which intervention began abroad; and the fidelity with which the Commissioners of the Allied Powers followed their instructions three thousand miles away inevitably developed the latent differences of their governments.

When the Allied Commissioners held their first consultation in Veracruz, on January 9, General Prim enjoyed a privileged position among his colleagues. He united in his person the diplomatic and military functions which, in their case, were divided between two delegates—Sir Charles Wyke and Commodore Dunlop representing the British Crown, and M. de Saligny and Admiral Jurien de la Gravière the French—and his European reputation lent him an authority to which they could not pretend. "I have great satisfaction in informing Your Excellency," he wrote to Marshal O'Donnell, "that ever since the first day the most perfect harmony has reigned among the members of the assembly, and that I have received very marked proofs of deference from my colleagues." Of this initial advantage he made use to commit them to his version of intervention. His first duty was to disarm the hostility caused by the premature arrival of his countrymen, and his first step was to answer the manifesto of Juarez with one of his own. Surrounded though he was by adulation and exaltation, he recognized and honored political truth and met its challenge with all the honesty of which he was capable, and more, indeed, than was compatible with his instructions, and by an adroit blend of discretion and candor produced a document that was a model of political vagueness. General Prim answered Juarez by going over his head. His proclamation was addressed to the Mexican people and only obliquely to their government; it disclaimed any schemes of reconquest or political intervention, but admitted freely that "the three nations we represent, and whose real interest seems to be to obtain satisfaction for the outrages inflicted upon them, have a loftier ambition and pursue a purpose of greater and more general utility." He confined himself to generalities. They came "to extend a friendly hand to a people whom they are grieved to see wasting their strength and consuming their vitality under the fatal action of civil wars and perpetual convulsions. This is the truth, and those whose mission it is to make it known to you wish to add no warlike cries or threats to it; on the contrary, they wish to help you to rebuild the structure of your greatness, which is of concern to all of us. Yours, and yours alone, is the right to establish a Constitution on a durable basis."

If not the whole truth, it was as much of it as Prim could generalize; but as it bound the Allies to an attitude of benevolent neutrality, it irked M. de Saligny, though he held his peace for the time being. The conclusion of the proclamation was one of the General's eloquent codas. He reiterated his pledge to respect the freedom of the Mexican people and exhorted them to trust the good faith of the Allies, "while we shall preside, impassive, over the great spectacle of your regeneration, finally assured by order and freedom! So, we are sure, even the

Mexican Government will understand it, and so will all men of distinction in the country to whom we address ourselves. Those high-minded natures will not fail to understand that they must now forsake arms and act only through reason and public opinion, the two triumphant rulers of the nineteenth century!"

In deference to its distinguished author, the proclamation was unanimously adopted by his colleagues and issued under their joint signature. Its vagueness guaranteed their good faith and committed them to nothing. When it reached the capital the Mexican Government professed to be mystified by it; Doblado declared that no one understood what it meant. If it meant anything, it meant an appeal to the Mexican people, or some part of it, to rise against their government and set up another with which the Allies could deal; but at least that elaborate mass of verbiage confined the conflict to a war of words; and the Mexican Government, and the Mexican people, waited for the action of the Allies to interpret it.

The Allies had no sooner landed than they realized that Veracruz could not be occupied. The climate was Liberal. In the three weeks that the Spanish had held the town, they had run up a sick list of five hundred men, and the arrival of some four thousand fresh troops in a port already congested by the six thousand Spanish who preceded them made it necessary to take up encampments in the neighboring villages. Two days later the movement was made by a detachment of French and Spanish troops, followed by a company of English marines, whom Commodore Dunlop was induced to send along as a token of solidarity, but who returned to town the next day. The distance was short —twelve kilometers—and the march was facilitated by a little leg of railway, of which the troops took advantage to load their supplies on trucks drawn by half-wild mules; but under the torrid sun progress was slow and laborious even for the veterans of Morocco and Algiers. The French, whom General Prim placed at the head of the column, suffered most; in spite of frequent halts, leaden fatigue made the march interminable, and when they reached the village of La Tejeria and pitched camp with sails brought up from Veracruz, the bulk of their equipment being still at sea, the bivouac resembled a shipwreck. The experience of that trial march in the hot country weighed heavily on the councils of the Allied commanders. The desolate plain, the long haul for water, the hostile solitude, the enervating heat, the need of beating the road regularly for provisions, which had to be drawn from the town, the isolation, inactivity, and irritation at the end of it, made them impatient of makeshifts. The French Admiral insisted that the occupation of La Tejeria was a waste of time and that the advance should be pushed at once into the fertile and salubrious highland beyond, and General Prim agreed, but the movement had to be postponed for lack of transports. With a remarkable lack of foresight, no provision had been made for so essential a service; they had expected to improvise it on the spot, but as the Mexican embargo was obeyed by the natives and neither wagons nor animals were to be found in Veracruz, they were obliged to send to Havana for them.

The Mexican authorities had been notified of the advance, and that it was undertaken in no hostile spirit, and no resistance was offered, although some guerrillas hovered ahead and held it under observation. One of them presented himself at the camp and was invited into the presence of the Allied commanders to give him an opportunity of seeing them united. The impression he created enlivened the report of General Prim. "He spent some time with us, and in the course of conversation told me that the Mexicans were highly incensed by the affront offered their flag in not raising it side by side with those of Spain, France, and England. So strange a notion made it difficult for me to maintain my gravity, but I did not think it proper to enter into arguments, which would not have convinced him, and was moved to give him an explanation as laughable as the complaint. 'How could we raise the Mexican banner, when all of you had left and there was no one to mount guard and do it the proper honors?' This ridiculous reason seemed to calm him, and he withdrew."

The harmony which prevailed at the first conference of the Commissioners was seriously troubled at their second, when they met to frame an ultimatum to the Mexican Government and to inform one another of their respective demands. Those of the Spanish and the English were stiff but acceptable. The former called for recognition of the Mon-Almonte Treaty, reparations for injuries to Spanish nationals, and formal apology for the expulsion of the Spanish Minister. The latter embraced all the recognized financial claims, amounting to something over fifty million pesos, security for British nationals, and control over the Mexican customs—virtually the same terms as those upon which Wyke and Zamacona had reached an agreement. The French demands, on the other hand, were exorbitant and provocative. M. de Saligny had prepared a bill for damages, covering accumulated claims, to the amount of twelve million pesos, plus the Jecker bonds, plus undetermined indemnities for miscellaneous injuries, including punishment for the attempt on his life, together with the right for him or his delegates to sit in on all criminal trials involving French residents either as plaintiffs or accused, the right to hold Tampico and Veracruz as security, and the right to collect the customs duties and to lower the tariff by one half, the Mexican Government being forbidden to add any charges of its own to compensate for the loss of its revenues. Clearly intended to be inacceptable to the Mexican Government, these demands were no less so to the Spanish and the English Commissioners. The twelve million pesos and the tariff cut and the humiliating penalties imposed on the Mexican Government they swallowed, but at the Jecker bonds they gagged. With one voice the British representatives exclaimed that the exaction was inadmissible. So scandalous and leonine a contract would never be accepted, Sir Charles Wyke declared, either by the present Mexican Government or any other that might succeed it, and would be enough for the Mexicans to break off all dealing with the Allies and to prefer the consequences of an unequal war to the ignominy of accepting so unjust a pretension. Prim supported him. Admiral Jurien, who had read the French ultimatum in the absence of M. de Saligny, had the grace to say that he was not very well informed and requested his associates to await the explanations of his partner.

On the following day the discussion was resumed. M. de Saligny explained the inflation of the French claims to twelve million pesos as a rough estimate: he had not examined them in detail, it would have taken him at least a year to do so, his government had instructed him to name some particular sum and he had fixed on that amount as an approximation of their value by a million more or less. As to the Jecker credit, he was acting under orders and had no authority to modify them. As he was inflexible, the question arose of whether the Allies were bound to support one another in their joint demands, and since this point had not been foreseen in their instructions, it was decided to refer the dilemma to their governments. This involved a delay, however, of two or three months before the answers could be received, and some action had to be taken immediately; their officers were waiting to carry the demands to the capital with a Mexican escort. As a collective makeshift, they drew up a note to the Mexican Government, reserving their demands and stating that their first duty was to afford the Republic the means of reconstituting itself stably so as to allow it to meet its obligations: a paraphrase, in short, of the proclamation of General Prim, which left its interpretation as doubtful as before.

The consequences of this snag were serious and far-reaching. Instead of presenting an ultimatum and advancing to the capital, the object of the expedition had to be held in abeyance and an indefinite truce granted to the Mexican Government. "I know very well that this decision does not entirely agree with the instructions of Your Excellency," Prim apologized to O'Donnell, "but what could I do? . . . I had no choice but to give my assent, since there was no other way out of the difficulty, and because, like the English Minister, I was convinced that to lend our support to so iniquitous a claim would have been to cast an indelible stain on our government, on our noble nation, and on ourselves."

The Jecker bonds now began to bear interest of an unexpected political kind. Over that stumbling block the Spanish and British Commissioners drew together in combined opposition to French policy. To have supported the French demands, Wyke wrote to Lord Russell, would have meant immediate hostilities with the Mexican Government. "As the Mexicans have determined to abandon their posts and concentrate their forces in the interior, we lose all hold on them unless we follow them there and by force dictate our terms, which, with such a land force as the Allies now have here, would be impossible, owing to the resistance we would meet with from the whole population against the Spanish portion of the expedition. To keep so large an agglomeration of European troops in this small town, with the sickly season rapidly approaching, would be worse than imprudent, and therefore it was determined to be absolutely necessary to move them into the interior as far as the first tablelands, where are situated the towns of Jalapa, Cordoba, and Orizaba. To arrive at these places, however, the troops would have to pass some most formidable passes, which the Mexicans have already fortified and are determined to defend. These considerations convinced both General Prim and myself that we must endeavor to obtain what was required by persuasion, instead of by force. Having agreed to suspend the presentation of our respective demands until we could obtain more explicit instructions relative to them, we then determined to alter the tone of our joint note to the President, and we made it as conciliatory and as pacific as possible." But this was not all. The collective note to the President subordinated the demands of the Allies to the political settlement of the country, and on this problem the English Minister felt it necessary not only to consult, but to advise, his government. "Although the French Commissioners finally adopted the line of conduct I have described, they evidently did so with reluctance, owing to the extreme hostility of M. de Saligny to the Juarez government, which Admiral de la Gravière also seems anxious to get rid of, with the hope of establishing a monarchy in its place. Whether such a change would be beneficial or not remains to be proved; but if it does take place, it should proceed from the will of the nation itself, as any suggestion coming from us on such a subject could be looked on by the Mexicans only as an unwarrantable interference on our part."

Wyke himself was in an awkward position. The largest creditor with the smallest police force at his command—seven hundred marines— and that force forbidden to leave the coast, he was obliged to compensate for this disadvantage by his diplomacy. To support the French ultimatum and provoke hostilities in which the English contingent was not permitted to participate would have aggravated his difficulties, reducing his influence and placing him in the impossible situation of relying on his partners to enforce the British demands. A peaceful solution was imperative, and an accommodating attitude toward the Mexican Government, and the conciliatory note was drawn, accordingly, "with a view to getting the moderate and rational members of the government to accept our intervention in a friendly instead of a

hostile spirit." Convinced that a demonstration of force would be sufficient to bring them to terms and to secure a full recognition of British
claims, and that the actual use of it would serve only to compromise
them, he bent his efforts to preventing any precipitate or provocative
action on the part of his colleagues. The Jecker question provided an
obstruction and secured a truce, by which he gained time and the support of General Prim, whose influence, backed as it was by a preponderance of military force, immobilized the French and obliged them
to submit to the combined weight of their Spanish and English partners.

When this snarl developed, intervention was seven days old. The
proclamation of General Prim, the climate, and the Jecker credit combined to modify its character and to blunt its impact—provisionally but
none the less positively—to substitute negotiations for aggression, and
to give Sir Charles Wyke a diplomatic advantage of which he made
full use to maintain the expedition within the terms of the London
Convention and to make intervention an English enterprise.

The collective note was forwarded to the Mexican Government on
the 14th of January. The bearers were provided with a Mexican escort
by General Uraga, who entertained them at his headquarters and
promised to facilitate the passage of food to the camp at La Tejeria. In
return for these courtesies, Admiral Jurien sent an aide-de-camp to
Uraga's *hacienda* with some gifts of wine and cigars and the compliments of the French and the Spanish, and the French officer returned
with a tip for the Admiral. General Uraga had talked freely. He was
a sworn foe of the Spaniards, he said, but he made an exception in
favor of General Prim, to whom he attributed the peaceful turn which
the invasion had taken. "The conversion of the general appeared to be
recent," the officer reported, "and seemed to be the result of the efforts
of Sir Charles Wyke, who corresponded with him almost daily." General Uraga urged the French to be patient and accommodating. "Although he spoke of Juarez with very little deference, he said that the
President was the representative of the country and that, as a matter
of national self-esteem, they wished him to be respected. 'Secure the
question of form,' he added, 'and all the others will be easily settled.
Juarez is merely a name; we govern behind him; Doblado and Eche-
verria are already at the head of affairs; I myself am destined to take
the portfolio of War as soon as my presence is no longer required in
the State of Veracruz. Tell the Admiral that we shall come to an understanding with the foreign Powers, but that we must go slowly and
cautiously; with time everything can be obtained and, what is more, by
preserving legal forms: Presidency for life, or even monarchy, nothing
is impossible, provided you are willing to wait and let us conduct matters.' " Of the sincerity of these revelations there might be some doubt,

but they appeared to be confirmed by the attitude of Uraga toward the Minister of War, General Zaragoza, who had just resigned to take command of a division under him. "Zaragoza," the report concluded, "belongs to the most advanced Liberal party, and General Uraga regards him as a spy of Juarez. He said in so many words that he is determined to have him shot at the slightest semblance of treason." Of one thing, however, there was no doubt in the mind of the officer who made the report. "I believe that General Uraga is completely won over to the Liberal party of which Doblado is the head. This party obeys the promptings of Sir Charles Wyke, and General Prim himself is merely an instrument whom they flatter, and whom they seek perhaps to seduce by leading him to conceive personal hopes."

The envoys of the Allies spent two weeks on their errand. In the meanwhile, the common stand which the Spanish and English Commissioners had taken on the Jecker question was strengthened by a consultation among the three representatives on the political constitution of the country. This question, which they had carefully avoided in their first conferences, was broached by Sir Charles Wyke, who sounded Prim with some casual remarks, giving him to understand that the British Government would welcome the establishment of a monarchy and assuring him that it had no candidate of its own. Admiral Jurien declared himself, stating that he had positive orders to intervene with all the influence of France in favor of a monarchy and that he meant to put into play all his means of action, public and private, to favor the Archduke Maximilian. Prim pointed out the inconsistency of imposing any given system of government with the professions contained in his proclamation and the joint note which they had sent to Juarez, and the impolicy of antagonizing the majority of the country at the beginning of the enterprise, when the same goal might be reached by patient management, and he persuaded his colleagues to wait "until the march of events shows us the proper moment to exercise, not openly, but with the utmost reserve, our influence in the solution of so important a question." "I need hardly assure Your Excellency," Prim wrote to O'Donnell, "of my firm purpose to profit by every occasion that may arise to neutralize the efforts made by the representatives of France. I shall always bear in mind the secret and verbal instructions of Your Excellency, and rather than submit to the shame that a nation in which we exercised domination for three centuries, which owes us its existence, and in which our language is spoken, should be governed by a foreign prince, I shall work to have the Mexicans preserve their republican institutions, although with the reforms indispensable to the establishment of a strong and lasting power." The political question, like the question of claims, was now indefinitely deferred, and Prim and Wyke, in their common opposition to the French pretensions, drew closer together.

Suddenly, however, their growing rapprochement was threatened by an untoward incident. On January 25 the British Commissioners informed their colleagues that Miramon was about to arrive in Veracruz and notified them that they would not permit a person who had outraged Great Britain by the plunder of the Legation to land. A discussion so violent ensued between the English and French Commissioners that it was deleted from the record. Prim attempted to mediate, but to no avail. The packet came in that same evening, Commodore Dunlop boarded it, took Miramon off, and held him on an English frigate. Thereupon the dispute flared up again. Prim had the utmost difficulty in preventing a schism and in calming the irritation of Saligny and the Admiral, which he shared, and he sided with them so far as to warn his colleagues of England that, if he abstained from solemnly protesting against their conduct, it was only to conceal from the Mexican Government any appearance of discord between them. Miramon was deported, ostensibly as a common criminal, but the intervention of the British Commissioners was admittedly a political commitment: Commodore Dunlop was deterred from arresting thirty of Miramon's partisans traveling on the same ship only by the difficulty of identifying them and his reluctance to aggravate the tension.

Two days later the envoys returned from the capital with an evasive answer to the joint note of the Allies and a crop of rumors with which to interpret it. According to the French envoy, Sir Charles Wyke was negotiating a private settlement with Doblado, the latter was working to overthrow Juarez, and the Spanish were also said to be seeking private advantages. On the next day, January 29, Zamacona arrived with an offer to negotiate, inviting the Allies to meet the Mexican Commissioners at one of the towns on the highland with an escort of two thousand troops and to re-embark the rest immediately. The proposal so shocked the Admiral that he proposed to ignore it and take up the desired encampments on the upper plateaus forthwith, but he was overruled and the offer to negotiate was accepted, though to what purpose none of the Commissioners could say, since their demands could not be formulated until the receipt of fresh instructions from their governments. On the necessity of evacuating the lowlands, however, all were agreed; after spending three weeks in Veracruz they were in a position to appreciate the shrewdness of the Mexican Government in abandoning it.

3

ON JANUARY 25 the Mexican Government issued a decree outlawing the Allies as pirates and pronouncing the death sentence on Mexicans who co-operated with them to subvert the established institutions of the country. The packet which made port on the same day brought in, besides Miramon, a number of passengers to whom the provisions of the decree applied. Among them was Father Miranda. The British allowed him to land. He had no police record.

In Havana Father Miranda and Miramon had approached General Prim, when the Allied fleets had touched there, and had obtained a hearing, but nothing more. Prim had declared that the Allies could not deal with a party represented by scattered groups of guerrillas and that, if they were as strong as they professed to be, they had only to profit by the folly of the government in massing its troops to prevent the passage of the Allies at Veracruz and fall on the capital: the Allies would deal with whatever government they found there. If this reply was not a taunt in Havana, it was mockery in Veracruz. Miranda arrived there to witness the expulsion of Miramon at the very moment when the Allies were preparing to negotiate with the government. From his partisans in the capital he was cut off by the decree, and though he managed to correspond with them, they were too cowed to move. "A document of this sort is a challenge, a declaration of war," one of them wrote him, "and it leaves us no choice but to take up arms to punish such audacity or submit to the scorn and contempt of the entire world if we do not." They waited a week for the Allies to move. His correspondent appealed to him again on behalf of all his friends in the capital. "After the decree of the 25th, what can they expect of such people? How many victims will there be before those gentlemen arrive! For the love of God, urge them to move and straight to this city, or we are lost!" Father Miranda was a man of fine sensibilities who, in the words of one who loved him, "would never wish to appear in the part of an intruder or a mere counselor or officious adviser to persons whom he does not know or whose ideas may not be the same as his own"—not the best qualifications, perhaps, for his mission —and he had no official standing with the Commissioners. The Admiral, who had been advised in Paris to take him as his political guide, shunned him, Prim ignored him, the English blacklisted him. He was as incapable of moving the Allies as of kindling his followers. He carried on an active correspondence with his sympathizers in the capital —conspirators they could hardly be called, for they were inactive—but, as one of them said, they were *"a few poor souls*—one might almost say that the sacred flame has passed to the acolytes. In a word, my friend, there is neither a political nor a military head capable of directing operations." Everything depended on the Allies. "Can they be expected to have confidence or faith enough to risk their social position, their families, and even their lives, when they have no guarantees and no security in Intervention, and when they see it waver in its operations and aims?" Miranda was reminded in a bitter arraignment of the misconduct of the expedition, in which fear was forgotten for the moment in fury, only to return muffled in malediction and self-defense. "If it were not for the assurances which I have received from France," his correspondent continued, "and for some comforting expressions in your letters, I should, like most of the others, be very much disheartened and cursing an Intervention which has done nothing so far but to make our political and individual situation very much worse in every respect. I beg you to say so to Señor Saligny and Señor de la Gravière, not as my opinion, for I implore you never to mention my name, but as that of a noble party that is proud of the principles it sustains and for which it has made many sacrifices and suffers a cruel and brutal persecution, and that in spite of this and the penal prohibitions and abject conditions in which we live here, not even daring to appear on the streets at night, the Reaction is strong and powerful."

Father Miranda joined the waiting list in Veracruz. Beyond the town the plain was scoured by guerrilla bands waiting to arrest him. A brother who had accompanied him to Veracruz pushed on, but at Puebla he was picked up by the police, and he reached the capital only to disappear in one of its vermin-ridden prisons.

The winter of 1862 was freakish; the bracing north winds which prevail at that season failed to blow, and the good months were as bad as the worst in Veracruz. By the beginning of February the French had over three hundred men in hospital, Prim sent eight hundred patients to Havana, and the windless days hung heavy with the stealthy menace of mortality on the councils of the Allied Commissioners. A note was sent to Mexico City announcing their intention to take up encampments in the highlands by the middle of the month with or without the consent of the government, and on February 9, just as they were drawing up a second note to the same effect, a reply was received from Doblado offering to meet them to discuss the terms upon which the government would consent to such an advance. Appointment was taken, and on the 19th Prim and Doblado met at the village of La

Soledad. There, from ten in the morning until four in the afternoon, they felt each other out, and their personal contact contributed not a little to the settlement which they reached.

Doblado came preceded by the usual cloud of rumors, from which only one thing emerged clearly—the fact that he attracted them. Prieto, who admired him, was fond of recalling that Doblado as a poor boy had held his schoolfellows spell-bound by the fantastic tales which he spun for them, and that he had made them pay for the privilege of listening to him. Something of this talent seems to have survived in his sober maturity: if he no longer told tall tales, he inspired them. He was variously reported to be conspiring to overthrow Juarez and to become a dictator, to be maneuvering with the Moderates to call an Assembly of Notables and head a provisional government, to be working with Wyke, who regarded him as the man of the situation, to be dickering with a speculator who had the ear of the French Commissioners, to be collaborating with the notables of the money world to capture the councils of the Allies, to be in relations with the Reaction and ready for any transaction short of a monarchy, provided he emerged in the result: no combination was too improbable for him to figure in it.

Doblado appeared, and the bubbles of rumor burst. He was all candor, and by his bearing, his judgment, and his honesty he won the respect of his opponent. He impressed Prim as a superior and intelligent person, of very good manners, frank and sincere, who had the good taste not to cry up the excellencies of the country or the superiority of the political party to which he belonged. Without pretense or false pride or bluff, Doblado admitted that the Allies had more than enough forces to crumple up the Mexicans and to impose their conditions, and offered a prompt and satisfactory settlement of pending differences, provided the Allies would consent to make a declaration which would dispel the rumors that France intended to implant a monarchy and that Spain meant to restore her ancient domination on the country. Prim gave him the most formal assurances that the integrity of the Republic would be respected, and Doblado then proposed the formal recognition of the government—a bid which Prim eluded politely. With some embarrassment, Doblado observed that his countrymen had taken it very ill that their colors had disappeared from Veracruz and that, "though this might appear a puerile demand, the majority of Mexicans ardently desired that the national flag should float beside those of the Allies"; and this suggestion, which had amused Prim when the guerrilla chief had made it at La Tejeria, was accepted with good grace when it was advanced by Doblado. Thus encouraged, Doblado proposed the return of the customs, and the suggestion was not rejected. Only once was General Prim really jarred. An allusion to the strength of the mountain passes on which the Mexicans relied fired his temper and transported him to Morocco; they represented no obstacle for his troops, he replied sharply, and the vaunted defenses of Mexico would be carried without difficulty or delay. After six hours of discussion, they parted on the best of terms.

The Preliminaries of La Soledad, as the settlement was known, marked a turning point in intervention. The Allies obtained permission to advance to three towns in the highlands on condition that, if negotiations failed, they would return to their original positions on the plain before resorting to hostilities. In return for this capital concession, Doblado obtained a politically valuable equivalent. The first article stated that the Allies entered on the ground of treaties to present their claims, and the second provided for the opening of negotiations in Orizaba, under the pledge of the Allied Commissioners that they proposed nothing contrary to the integrity, sovereignty, or independence of the Republic. The Allies had been led to declare themselves, negotiations had been substituted for military operations, and the government had been recognized in fact, if not in form.

At two o'clock in the morning Prim sent the convention, signed by his colleagues, back to Doblado. M. de Saligny objected strenuously to the raising of the Mexican flag at Veracruz and demanded the repeal of the decree of January 25 by way of compensation, but he was overruled. The return of the customs met with general approval, as trade had fallen off since the occupation and there was almost no intake. The Spanish had spent eight thousand pesos in manning them for two months; the French favored the concession for reasons of economy, if not of politics, and the English for both. Wyke advised his government that nothing would do more to convince the Mexicans of the friendly nature of intervention and to strengthen the hand of Doblado; business would pick up, and "we should thereby benefit our own interests as well as those of our debtor, whose resources we ought to try to augment by every means in our power." Together with the convention, Prim sent Doblado a note inviting him to dine with Sir Charles Wyke and a request for a personal favor: his wife had just landed; she was a Mexican and a niece of the then Minister of Finance in the Juarez government; and he begged Doblado to tell his colleague that the Condesa de Reus and her son were wild with delight at the prospect of seeing him soon in Mexico.

The political question was virtually settled by the Preliminaries of La Soledad so far as the Spanish and British Commissioners were concerned. In explaining to Madrid the concessions which he had made, Prim insisted that "as long as the existing government believes that it has sufficient elements to pacify the country and consolidate the administration and declares itself animated by the liveliest desires to satisfy foreign claims, I have thought, and so have my colleagues, that we had no right to repulse this government by lending moral or material aid to the party opposed to it. Such conduct would be impolitic as well

as unjust, for to us who see things closely here it is evident that the reactionary party is practically annihilated, so much so, indeed, that in
the two months that we have been in the country we have seen no
evidence whatsoever of the existence of such a party. . . . Moreover,
though the French Commissioners had great hopes of easily establishing a monarchy here, for they thought that the monarchical element
was strong in the country, they are gradually being disillusioned and
are recognizing their error; nor can it be otherwise, since by our own
observations and the reports of persons who know the country well,
we cannot doubt that the number of partisans of a monarchical system
of government is insignificant and that they are not men endowed with
the energy and decision which sometimes bring success to minorities."

As for Sir Charles Wyke, he was now fully convinced that a government represented by Juarez and Doblado "affords the best reflection of
public opinion to be found in this unfortunate country." "Juarez," he
wrote to Lord Russell, "is still looked up to as embodying a principle
which the Liberal party fought a three years' war to maintain. If Doblado relied on the moral support which he might derive by accepting
our intervention in a friendly spirit, then he may succeed in re-estab-
lishing order and respect for life and property; and that once done, the
resources of this country are so great that it would soon right itself and
its government be enabled to fulfill all its engagements, thus relieving
us of a task which, under other circumstances, we should find both
hazardous and difficult to perform without the presence of an armed
force here much more considerable than the one we have at our command." Had he come to those conclusions eight months earlier, there
would have been no intervention; but he had finally caught up with
himself, although the world had to be mobilized and an expedition
mounted before he overtook his tail.

Whatever passed between Wyke and Doblado, the result made it
clear that Doblado succeeded in winning over the English and Spanish
Commissioners by telling the true story. Only one formality was required to crown his accomplishment; on February 20 he forwarded
the Preliminaries to Juarez for his approval, "without which requisite,"
he added a trifle gratuitously, "they will have no validity."

On February 25 the French started their march inland without waiting for the formal ratification of the convention, which was received
in Veracruz on the following day. On February 26 Father Miranda
moved. For a month he had been prodded by his correspondents in
the capital; they were desperate, they trusted no one but Napoleon,
they advised him that "our labors should be in Europe and not here,
where for many reasons they are likely to be fruitless." Instead of collaborators, he had to deal with political patients, whose appeals he

could not answer and whose complaints he could not deny, because he thoroughly agreed with them. The flock afflicted the pastor; and from Europe came the same spurring. "Where is the Doctor? What is he doing?" Napoleon himself was asking, as he was informed by Gutierrez Estrada, who forwarded the question with growing anxiety. Father Miranda was missing when he was most wanted, and the searching wind found him out on February 26 and moved him to raise his voice and locate himself with an answering signal of distress. The supreme opportunity was passing, the favorable moment had been missed, and he took up his pen and wrote a long letter to Gutierrez Estrada, explaining the situation and begging him to relay it to Napoleon before it was too late. The time had come to tell the truth. He dwelt on his personal tragedy. He had come to Veracruz "for what purpose? To lend my presence, not without great personal risks, to great mistakes and misfortunes." He rehearsed them. He explained the stalemate into which intervention had developed, incomprehensible in Europe, by the sinister majority which the English and Spanish Commissioners had formed in Mexico. "England has sought to avoid commitments and to extricate herself from the question at all costs, having, moreover, great sympathies for the Mexican reformers; and the Spanish, having entrusted their affairs to Prim, scorn to consider the vital point of intervention. Prim, for his part, has sought to assimilate himself with our democrats, in order to dominate them later and don a crown in Mexico."

But neither Prim nor Wyke drew the depths of his disappointment; the quick of his complaint was the Admiral. "I must frankly confess that I was mistaken in the first judgment I formed of him and that I communicated to you from Havana. At that time I thought that he understood his mission and that he had pre-eminent ability and force of character to realize the idea of the Emperor successfully; but now that I have seen him more closely and dealt with him, I am convinced that he is the greatest nonentity one can imagine. . . . He is the weakest, most changeable, and irresolute man I have ever known. . . . M. Jurien cannot hold to the same idea for two minutes. If he talks to Prim, he accepts his mistakes enthusiastically; if M. de Saligny makes any criticism, he seems to be convinced of its truth; and if he speaks to me, he does me justice; but he never takes the initiative in anything and so far he has let himself be left behind like a little child." Hence Father Miranda himself was still behind the lines. "He has not come to consult me in anything, and he has not accepted one of the suggestions I have made to him. In the presence of M. de Saligny he told me one day that if I were in agreement with Prim I could count on him, but otherwise not. And on another occasion, when M. de Saligny told him that I was unhappy and wished to return to Europe, the Rear Admiral replied, 'If he wishes to leave I will give him passage.' He excuses himself from speaking to me and even refuses to let me continue my journey with the French troops to Tehuacan. . . . Everything that has happened has convinced me that his instructions were not precise and that I have been wretchedly deceived. If I have not already left here, it is because I still hope that the European governments may direct the negotiations, and also because of the encouragement I have found in the firmness and intelligence of M. de Saligny. . . . I forbear to speak of my own person, compromised in a thousand ways and now more than ever since, because of the peaceable agreements and the absence of Mexican authorities in the villages, I am exposed to being captured at any time they choose. My situation, to speak only of persecution—" and he broke off. In reality, he had spoken of nothing else, and he laid down the pen, surfeited with the truth.

Neglected and ignored, a helpless witness to events in which he had no part, unwanted save by the enemy, unheeded save by M. de Saligny, shunned by the Admiral, galled by the offer of passage to Europe and sorely tempted to accept it, Father Miranda drained the dregs of mortification in Veracruz. He was deceived in everyone but himself; and he was on the verge of that disaster as well. He catechized himself, he questioned the world, and he found both wanting. His failure to make an impression on anyone led to but one conclusion, and he barely escaped it by fastening on the Admiral with the vindictive affinity of one nonentity for another. The indictment, drawn from his vitals and written in the thin fluid of his heart's blood, relieved a parasite without a host to nourish his heart; but it missed the truth by a slip of the tongue. His whereabouts no longer mattered; he was in the world but not of it; and when the world ended, doomsday would find Father Miranda among the minnows, floundering in his own depths. His mortal moment had passed.

History, however, has sometimes to notice nonentities when they are placed in decisive positions. A week later he was superseded by Almonte, who arrived from Paris, invested with the confidence of the Emperor, to organize his party. Another nonentity but an official one, Almonte fared no better. He approached the English, who had nothing to say to him. He approached Prim, who told him flatly that he could not count on the arms of the Spanish—nor of the English. "Then I shall rely on those of France," Almonte replied. "I doubt it," Prim remarked, "for I do not believe that the French Commissioners wish to risk such an undertaking without direct orders from the Emperor, and the Emperor is too clever a man to give them." Prim spoke with assurance, having just received a friendly note from Napoleon reminding him that "your dream of Vichy has been realized, the Spanish and French troops are fighting side by side for the same cause." A week later Almonte was as discouraged as Miranda and would have returned to Paris at once if he had not been dissuaded by M. de Saligny.

M. de Saligny worried Sir Charles Wyke. The British Minister attributed French policy, in private, to the personal hatred of his French colleague for Juarez and his determination to overthrow him at all costs. Personally, he considered Saligny a characterless intriguer, "who allowed himself to be swayed by his passions, and also by his pecuniary interests and by aspirations which could almost be described as sickly," but a day came when he could no longer treat him as a pathological case or keep his opinions private. Several days after the conclusion of the Convention of La Soledad, both the British Commissioners complained to General Prim of the conduct of the French Minister. For some time past, they said, M. de Saligny had adopted the system of discrediting in his own circle what he did in conference and what he authorized by his presence and his signature, and he had gone so far as to deny, in the presence of witnesses, that he had signed the proclamation of Prim to the Mexican people. The gravity of the charge made it necessary to investigate it, and after questioning the witnesses, who confirmed it, Prim sent for M. de Saligny and asked him bluntly whether or not he had signed the allocution. To Prim's stupefaction, Saligny replied that he had not. Hardly believing his ears, the Spanish High Commissioner raised his voice and repeated the question. "What! You did not sign the allocution, here, in this very place?" Saligny repeated the denial and added, "Neither did you." Offended but bewildered, and unable to understand a man who could play fast and loose with the truth so insolently, Prim stood on his dignity and remained on the defensive. "On hearing those words," he said in the account which he wrote of the incident, "I admit that I drew back as if I smelled a foul breath and realized that it must be some farce. The English Commissioners, in their severe character, looked astounded and stood off at a great distance. For a long time I was unable to collect myself or to decide what to do, but finally I said, a little more calmly, 'Señor Saligny, be so good as to explain yourself, my head is spinning; tell me, if you please, what all this means!' To which he replied with aplomb, and what aplomb, 'It is true that we agreed in conference to issue an allocution to the country; it is true that we agreed to print and publish it, authorizing it with our signatures; but the material act of signing the draft on the record we did not perform. This is what I meant to say without saying it in so many words.' Then I said to him, livid and convulsed with anger, 'Señor Conde, I shall not answer you, you are in my house and my answer would be too harsh.'" The smell lingered long after Saligny had gone.

But Prim did not let the matter rest there. Having taken the measure of the man, he proceeded to take that of the master. In the light of the scandal with Saligny, he felt it necessary to safeguard the honor of the Allies and to inform Napoleon of the true situation in Mexico himself. Reports had just been received of the imminent arrival of French reinforcements, coming out in consequence of the premature start of Serrano in December, and Prim was uneasy because, as he wrote to O'Donnell, "I think that the Spanish element ought to predominate, both because we have greater ties with this country than the other two nations, and because our government has taken the initiative in this important enterprise." Spanish initiative being responsible for the decision of Napoleon to equalize their forces, there was but one way to counteract it and keep the lead diplomatically. On March 1 Prim wrote to the Spanish Ambassador in Paris, authorizing him to make whatever use he wished of his letter. It was open for Napoleon to read, if Napoleon was still open to advice. He dwelt on the material difficulties that had immobilized the expedition and the harmony that had prevailed among the Commissioners "until in consequence of a certain thoughtlessness on the part of the French Minister, in connection with his language against the policy of the Allies when he approved and signed the agreements, cordiality began to cool."

Having disposed of what could not be said directly to the Emperor, he touched adroitly on what should. He paid tribute to the Admiral as "a worthy and noble comrade, full of good feeling, reason, and loyalty, active and energetic, as skillful in commanding land troops as in sailing a squadron, hence I call him general of land and sea," and to the perfect agreement between them from the first day; and he trusted that the general who was coming to replace him would have the same good qualities, for better could not be found. Then he came to the point, deploring the fallacy of a monarchy in Mexico. "Castles in Spain, my dear Count! How mad and absurd all this is! These *émigrés* never doubt anything since they are ready for everything, provided they can return to their country, recover power, and exterminate their political enemies. . . . My ideas cannot be suspected, since I have always been frankly attached to Constitutional Monarchy, which means that if I saw any possibility of consolidating a Constitutional Monarchy here, I would co-operate with my good wishes and loyal counsels. *Mais, mon cher,* there are no monarchists in Mexico. A few leaders of the fallen party present themselves as such now; they accept the idea; a few other men of financial position, *who will do nothing to translate the idea into reality;* but neither the one nor the other will ever form a thousandth part of the population, and the rest, who will be the immense majority, will combat the monarchy each as he can: some with arms, others with silence and inertia, and the monarchy imposed by foreign bayonets will cause deadly wounds and the throne of the foreign prince will fall to the ground the day that he lacks the support of the soldiers of Europe, as the temporal authority of the Pope will collapse the day that the French soldiers leave Rome. . . . You know how much I venerate, respect, and love the Emperor, as you know my fraternal friendship for the French, and hence you will readily understand how anxiously I await the arrival of the general who is coming to command the troops, in order to know what to expect, for if he brings instructions to support the monarchy against wind and tide, my position will be bitterly painful, since I shall not be able to aid my comrades by seconding the views of the Emperor who has so honored and distinguished me. . . . I believe that my way of seeing and working is in accord with the desires of my government; if not, I shall be relieved and recalled with the satisfaction of having done my duty as a good Spaniard, as a politician, and as a man who will never belie the motto of his arms: *Honor, valor, and loyalty.*"

4

HOW much of a turning point the Preliminaries of La Soledad marked in the development of intervention was fully appreciated by the officers who accompanied the Admiral on his march inland. "At the moment of beginning the march," one of them wrote, "the Admiral had a better understanding of the difficulties over which, undoubtedly, it would have been impossible for him to triumph if, instead of advancing peacefully, he had had to fight." The problem of transports was still unsolved. By repairing two old wagons abandoned on the outskirts of the town, ordering others from Havana, and commandeering wainwrights in Veracruz, the Quartermaster had succeeded in knocking together a small and inadequate convoy, consisting of eleven four-wheelers, thirty two-wheelers, and three ambulances, capable of hauling eight days' provisions for three thousand two hundred men, without including the fodder for one thousand one hundred mules. Local trade was carried in two-wheel carts drawn by four mules, or in four-wheel wagons by eight, ten, sixteen or twenty-four; the wagons, imported from the United States and stoutly built to resist the Mexican roads, could be driven only by teamsters equally tough; a trained man, mounted on the last mule, could manage the long team alone, but the *arriero* was the pin of the convoy, and as the mules were half wild and only nine Mexican *arrieros* had been recruited, the driving, or the dragging, was done by Creole seamen, soft men without energy, and wholly unfit for such duty, whom the Admiral landed for lack of better.

After six weeks in an unhealthy camp, and laden with four days' provisions, the men were hardly able to keep their feet. The march started at six in the morning, and by noon the officers at the head of the column had lost two-thirds of their complement. The Admiral, riding back for water, was shocked to see the crack troops of the Empire lagging, exhausted and breathless, all along the road; the mules, lying down with their packs, marked it like milestones. The missing made camp by nightfall, on two feet or on four, but the ordeal was so severe that at La Soledad a halt of two days was called and a mute tribute paid to the diplomacy of Doblado and Prim. "The history of the Mexican campaign," wrote the same officer, "offers no episode comparable to those first stages. Eighty sick and two hundred unfit remained at La Soledad, and in four days the column had made only eight leagues. What would have happened if the enemy had decided to bar the road, and if the guerrillas had harassed the wretched soldiers, exhausted by fever and fatigue?" Struggling on to reach the limits of the hot country, the column reached the mountains on the sixth day. There their hardships ended. The cumbersome convoy of prairie schooners was abandoned to follow as best it could, and free of their impedimenta, which had served only to afford them some shade in the heat of the day, the men plunged into the passes cool with dense foliage and running waters and advanced rapidly. On the seventh day they reached Cordoba, where they found ample supplies and a bearable temperature; on the ninth, after climbing a gigantic natural shelf leading to the next plateau, they entered Orizaba; and on the fourteenth they marched into Tehuacan in fine order, without any trace of fatigue.

The invigorating effects of a change of climate were immediately visible in the reports of the Admiral to his colleagues. He spoke freely of the futility of the forthcoming negotiations with the Mexican Government and predicted their failure. In Veracruz he had told Miranda that he was forced to follow Prim's policy, since it was materially impossible to do anything else, but no sooner had he reached Tehuacan than he prepared to resume his freedom of action. He collected fresh transports. He picked up twenty-four wagons in Orizaba, and purchased another convoy from Commodore Dunlop, who had collected it at great cost and without authority from his government when he expected to join the march, and who was glad to be relieved of it for three million francs, having just received orders from London to return to his ships.

In the meanwhile, the French reinforcements had arrived in Veracruz, on March 6. The commander, General de Lorencez, carried instructions which redistributed the roles of the French agents in Mexico. He was responsible for military operations, though the Admiral retained a supreme advisory capacity in their conduct and continued

to share the political direction with Saligny. General de Lorencez was
a man of quick decisions and he grasped the situation at a glance.
"Easy as the situation was before, it has now become complicated and
difficult," he wrote to the Minister of War on the day of his arrival. "I
have seen M. de Saligny and Almonte." Basing himself on their information, he reported five days later that Mexico was already in the bag.
"The arrival of the second part of the expeditionary force is providential. General Prim has been obliged to abandon his designs, in
which he had no chance of succeeding, although they would have paralyzed the action of the French who came first and made their situation extremely difficult. General Prim will be recalled before April 15,
the conferences will come to nothing, we shall march ahead and reach
Mexico, and Prince Maximilian will be proclaimed sovereign of Mexico, where his wise and firm government will be easily maintained for
the happiness and regeneration of the most demoralized of all peoples."
The only delay was the Convention of La Soledad, and learning that
the Admiral meant to observe its stipulations and was planning to
withdraw to his positions on the plain, Lorencez hastened to Tehuacan
to intercept his retreat.

A crisis was now clearly approaching. Prim prepared his government
for it. Writing from Orizaba, where he had installed himself with his
troops, he warned O'Donnell that the arrival of Lorencez and the publicity given to the establishment of a monarchy by the French press
presaged fresh difficulties, and assured him that, for his part, he had no
intention of retreating. "I insist on my determination to risk all the influence that I have succeeded in acquiring to counteract those plans,
contrary as they are to the will of the Spanish Government and the political interests of our nation. This does not mean that I shall take an
attitude openly hostile to the dispositions of the Emperor, but I think
I risk nothing in assuring Your Excellency that, united and in perfect
agreement as I am with the British Plenipotentiaries, I am able to oppose a powerful resistance to the aims of France, without permitting
the good relations that exist between Spain and her Imperial neighbor
to cool." Sure of his position, he defended it by reminding O'Donnell,
as he had reminded Napoleon, that "now that the two most considerable of the Allied forces are in the interior of the country, occupying
great centers of population, if there were any monarchical party in this
land, it would already have given some signs of life; it would have
manifested its aspirations in some way and put into play some of its
means of action. If such a party exists, its inertia warrants our belief
that it is powerless, or that the persons who compose it are very inept
and cowardly." The arrival of Almonte had brought the whole issue to
a head. A note had just been received from the Mexican Government,
informing the Allies of their firm determination to pursue, capture,

and punish the enemies of the nation who penetrated into Mexico as proscripts, and he and Wyke had sent a copy to their French colleagues, conveying their approval and requesting permission to reply in that sense, and "I very much fear," he concluded, "that the French Plenipotentiaries will not be of the same opinion, which will cause a serious conflict."

And so it proved. In reply the Admiral demanded a full and unqualified amnesty to allow the Allies to consult the real wishes of the country. He had signed the Convention of La Soledad for no other purpose, he said, "thinking that this truce would give us time to act on the minds of the people without seeming to force them, and would allow us to prepare them for the solution which seemed to me the most favorable." He had assumed that in the mind of Prim, as in that of Doblado, "the Convention of La Soledad was nothing but the adoption, in principle, of the military occupation of Mexico by the Allied forces," and that if there were the least doubt in the mind of the Mexican Government, he thought it only fair to dispel it at once by presenting the demands, which it must accept, and, if they were rejected, by returning to the plain and opening hostilities. But this was not all. "You know, my dear General," he continued, "that with you I am in the habit of speaking without reticence and revealing all that I think. By your prudent and moderate conduct, you have rendered an immense service to your country. You have saved it from the disastrous consequences of an expedition conceived with excessive confidence and which Spain alone could not have sustained without a deplorable disturbance of its finances. You have done more. You have furnished us with the means of reassuring Mexico as to our intentions and making it understand that we have not come to restore a dominion that was no longer desired. To my mind, it was a mistake to give our expedition a color too exclusively Spanish; first, by letting you have the most considerable contingent; then, by providing your personal celebrity and military knowledge with the means of creating so preponderant a role for yourself that the action of the other Plenipotentiaries naturally paled a little before yours. If you had been inspired by sentiments less generous and noble, if you had been merely a soldier instead of a politician, you would inevitably have drawn us into a war in which we would have had against us a national sentiment which your wisdom alone has been able to appease." In conclusion, he assured Prim that the alliance was unweakened by the coming of French reinforcements. "You will merely allow me to be a little more on my guard than I have hitherto been against the habits of a deference that was addressed far more to your personal character than to your superior position. I am determined, in a word, to pursue, at my risk and peril, the aim which I propose to reach. To attain it, I wish to profit by the real sympathy that seems to be felt here for France. Consequently, without renouncing our Allies, without separating our case from theirs in the least, I wish it to be understood by everyone that our expedition is a French expedition, and that it is under the orders of no one."

Delicately, deferentially, but firmly, Prim was informed that he was finished. The insolence of the Admiral was more silken than M. de Saligny's, but even more cynical. The delicacy was stale, the firmness was flat, and with brutal blandness the Plenipotentiary of Napoleon told him to his face that he had been the dupe of the deference shown him until the Spanish had served their purpose as a convoy and a cover for the French. But that was not all. On the following day Lorencez arrived in Cordoba, accompanied by Almonte and Miranda. Against this provocation Prim and Wyke protested with what moderation they could muster. The two nonentities were now placed in a position about which the policies of empire rocked and swayed. To save the alliance Wyke went so far as to give Almonte a character. "No one feels more respect for General Almonte personally than I do," he wrote to the Admiral, "but Your Excellency must surely be aware that he is the recognized head of the party led by the infamous Marquez, Cobos, and others who are now in arms and at open warfare with the Mexican Government. If I have rendered a tribute of personal respect to General Almonte, my impartiality will not be called into question when I inform you that your other protégé, Father Miranda, is a man whose very name recalls some of the worst scenes of a civil war that has proved a disgrace to the civilization of the present century. It appears to me impossible that the government of your august sovereign can wish to extend its all-powerful influence to such a man as this." The character he gave Miranda defied moderation, and about him the flags fell.

Halfway through a letter of remonstrance, Prim was notified that the French would withdraw to the lowlands on the first of April, and he concluded his note with an invitation to the Admiral to meet Sir Charles Wyke and himself to record the rupture of the triple alliance officially. In deference to his last wishes, this formality was accepted, and Prim consoled himself for his failure by wrapping himself in the robes of a prophet. "What a fatality!" he wrote to a friend in Paris. "That the Emperor's Government does not know the true situation in this country is not strange, since it bases its judgment on the estimate of M. de Saligny; but that the latter, who is on the ground, who has lived long in Mexico, and who is by no means a fool, should so compromise the decency, the dignity, and even the honor of French arms, is what I do not and cannot understand, for the forces under the command of General Lorencez are not sufficient even to take Puebla. No, no, no! Mind, I do not deny that the French troops will succeed in taking Puebla and Mexico City as well; but what I emphatically deny is that the battalions which General Lorencez has today will suffice. The

Imperial eagles will roost in the ancient city of Moctezuma when they are supported by twenty thousand more, do you hear? *Twenty thousand more men,* with all the immense material which such a numerous army needs to march through a wasted land; for Mexico is one of those countries of which Napoleon I said, although he was not thinking of Mexico, 'If the army is large, it will die of hunger; if it is small, the earth will devour it.' . . . Do you know what I think, my good friend? I think that the Emperor by no means desires what his agents are doing: these gentlemen are compromising him and will compromise him more and more until, when he wishes to withdraw from this senseless enterprise, he will not be able to do so, because the luster of his eagles and the honor of the Empire will be involved. I do not understand it, and the cold language of Saligny exasperates me. How fatal that man will be to France! I am not a Frenchman, but I shall never forgive him the harm he will do to my brave comrades. . . . The Emperor will be irritated with me, but in his heart of hearts and his high sense of right he will be bound to recognize that I have acted as becomes a Spanish General. . . . The French who follow the crooked policy of M. de Saligny will attack me, but when the facts are known in France, the noble and generous France will deplore what has happened as I deplore it, and will not blame me."

Military judgment was his last card. In 1858, when he had been offered command of the expedition which Madrid was then planning against Mexico, he had refused it both on principle and on practical grounds, estimating that three hundred thousand men and thirty million pesos would be needed to conduct it successfully. In 1861 the combined forces of the Allies amounted to less than ten thousand men, and the French contingent to five thousand. Pitting Spanish sagacity against French folly, he played his trump card and strained every nerve up to the last moment to avert a rupture which he recognized to be inevitable. He went to Tehuacan to argue with Lorencez and the Admiral, only to realize that they were acting under orders from Paris; but still he persisted, hoping to save the situation at the conference with the Mexican delegates, which was scheduled for the 15th of April, and he persuaded them to await it. Although no instructions had yet been received from their governments regarding their joint demands, it was agreed that two should be presented to Doblado, one for the control of the customs and the other for the occupation of the capital, and both unconditionally. The second was the key with which Prim believed that he might yet break the deadlock. Once the Allies were in possession of the capital, he wrote to O'Donnell, the French and their protégés would deploy all their resources to gain partisans, but they would be powerless "against the influence which I have succeeded in gaining by my loyal and disinterested conduct, causing a very favorable modification in the feeling of Mexicans toward Spain and the Spanish. If the French should put nothing but intrigue into play to secure the success of their plans, I would feel no anxiety for the triumph of my policy, for on that ground I have acquired more influence and more means of action than the representatives of France, but everything indicates that it will be a question of force, and that they will shrink from no violence." He reported his plan without confidence, however; the last lap of the race had been run, and he knew it.

On April 9, a week before the scheduled conference with Doblado, the Allies met in Orizaba to record the dissolution of their partnership. Prim made a final halfhearted attempt to preserve it. The rupture would not have been complete, where the agents were so active, without some personal clashes, and the formal proceedings were punctured by flashes that vividly revealed the mentalities of the protagonists at the parting moment. The French Plenipotentiaries entered the conference to force the issue, the Spanish and English to fix responsibilities, and each in turn was possessed by his peculiar power. Prim opened the session with the temperance of a peacemaker, deploring the discord caused by the appearance of Almonte on Olympus, but he was cut short by M. de Saligny, who declared that he had no desire to negotiate with the Juarez government. It was his decided opinion, he said, that they should march on the capital, and when Wyke and Prim remonstrated, he persisted in it, accepting full responsibility for the consequences. His intransigence was covered by his instructions, but he did not miss the opportunity to make it as offensive as possible. He founded his opinion on the growing number of outrages not only to his countrymen, but to the Spanish, from whom he received, he did not know why, a daily swelling number of complaints which should have been addressed to General Prim. The thrust was challenged, but not by Prim. It was parried by Wyke, who expressed his surprise that no word of these abuses had reached his ears; he desired to know of what nature they were and against whom they had been committed. Saligny retorted that naturally French subjects had not gone to the British Legation to make their complaints—an imprudent snap. The British Legation was not to be baited with impunity, and Wyke, who was more than his match in shifting the attack, cornered him with another·question. Was it true, he asked, that M. de Saligny had said that the Preliminaries of La Soledad had no more value for him than the paper on which they were written? Saligny hedged; he had never been able to entertain the least confidence, he said, in anything coming from the Mexican Government, whether in reference to the Preliminaries or any other of its pledges. Then why had he signed them? And why did he not feel himself bound by them? The question was put by Commodore Dunlop. Saligny stiffened. He had no explanations to make to the conference, he replied sharply, as to the reasons which led him to sign the Preliminaries; the Admiral came to Saligny's rescue, protesting that in no country in the world had he seen such a system of terror as that inaugurated by the Mexican Government; Saligny abounded in his opinion, and in the confusion that followed the charge was lost and the discussion diverted.

In the course of the altercation Saligny recovered his aplomb and accused Prim of opposing French policy in order to mount a Mexican throne himself. Prim, who had maintained an attitude of contemptuous reserve, lost his self-possession for a moment and condescended to answer him, but he recovered his composure quickly and preserved to the end a power of dignity which no provocation could betray and which was supported by the decency of his British colleagues. The tension continued in a futile deadlock of friction until the session was raised. Diplomatic to the last and incorrigibly accommodating, the Admiral assumed responsibility for the rupture "before his colleagues, before his government, before the entire world," and the third nonentity, sedulously aping infamy, was allowed to have the last word. Then the minutes were read to the actors and approved, all of them consenting to go down to posterity as that raw hour caught them, save M. de Saligny, who retired before the roll was called.

The hour of truth, as the hour of danger was called in Mexico, set them acting according to their several properties; but its penetrating power went further in the days that followed, and the complete truth transpired in the aftereffects of the conference of Orizaba.

5

JOINT intervention ended on April 9. The last official act of the Allies was to notify the Mexican Government that the French army would withdraw to the lowlands and commence operations as soon as the Spanish forces passed their lines, a movement which they expected to complete by April 20. Thereupon the several protagonists went their own ways.

The way of Sir Charles Wyke led him to Puebla, where in response to an invitation from Doblado to meet him and settle the British claims, he signed a treaty on April 29 which snatched victory from defeat. The settlement secured everything his government required and something more: it was the Zamacona treaty revived, plus the

permission for British consuls to act as interventors in the customs
and minus the control of the Mexican Congress, which had killed
that convention in November, Doblado being invested with full power
to conclude foreign treaties without congressional sanction and the
ratification of the President alone being required. "This is a mere
matter of form, which General Doblado assures me will be gone
through today on his arrival in Mexico," he wrote to Lord Russell,
confident that it would meet with his approval as well. The treaty
was not merely one of those periodical promises by which Mexico put
off the day of judgment; it was guaranteed by a prospective American
loan of eleven million dollars, which was to pass, at stipulated intervals, into British hands; and in the event of the loan failing to materialize, the security on which it was to be advanced—a mortgage to the
United States Government of the waste lands and the residue of
Church property yet available in Mexico—was to be allocated to the
English for the liquidation of their claims. For Wyke the rupture of
the triple alliance was by no means an unmitigated calamity. "Everything I have latterly done," he explained, "has been based, of course,
on the direct violation of the London Convention by the French
Agents, which in the opinion of Commodore Dunlop and myself, has
restored us to a perfect freedom of action in forwarding those important interests which have been entrusted to our charge."

The Minister who was responsible for initiating intervention, and
who had worked so hard and conscientiously to repair the results of
of his shortsightedness, had good reason to congratulate himself on a
narrow escape and an ample reward. But there is such a thing as
succeeding too well and at the wrong time. When the French caught
wind of the convention, they immediately entered a protest with Doblado against any treaty involving a cession or mortgage of Mexican
territory for the benefit of any foreign power. These objections had
been foreseen by Wyke; but what he had not anticipated was that the
prize would be relinquished by Lord Russell himself. The French
protest, however, was a broad hint not to trespass on their territory;
the American loan was a phantom offer; and the British Government
decided to shelve its claims until a more favorable time. Incidentally,
Juarez also refused his assent to the treaty, and Wyke returned to
London empty-handed, as he had left it empty-headed.

For Prim the only way open was the way out, and he pursued
it consistently to the end. Although Doblado extended the same invitation to him as to Wyke to negotiate, he made no attempt to settle
the claims which he had come to enforce; they had never been more
than a pretext, or at most a perfunctory issue, subordinated to "a larger
aim, a purpose of greater and more general utility," which was pitched
too high to abandon it with a bill for damages. Nebulous as that

purpose was, it committed him to the clouds, and having pursued a mirage into an impasse, his sole concern was to extricate himself from a false situation and to beat a dignified retreat. The adventure ended, as it began, in a gesture. But precisely because the Spanish expedition was motivated by national pride, a heavy price had to be paid for pocketing it. The inglorious return of the expedition was bound to produce a shock in Madrid, all the more painful because the discomfiture of the government was amply deserved, motives of vainglory being a frivolous guide to statecraft, and the collapse of the enterprise its logical penalty. Who was to pay for that mistake? Spain or General Prim? He anticipated that question before he made his decision. "What will the Queen and the government say, when they learn of the re-embarkment of the troops?" he wrote to his confidant in Paris. "They will be startled at first; then friends and foes will cry to high Heaven, thinking the time come to sink me; but both will realize before long that I have acted with prudence and abnegation, and inspired by the most ardent patriotism. Besides, with my rank as Senator I shall be able to defend myself against the charges brought against me; and lastly, time will undertake to prove me right." His confidence was well founded. Time did not forsake its own. In the long view, it was not Wyke who struck the better bargain. By his forbearance Prim laid the Mexican people under an obligation of gratitude and performed an historic service to his own country, reversing the secular habits of hostility between the two peoples and opening the way to a new and fraternal understanding—the way out.

This was his personal achievement. What would have happened had a man less intrepid, independent, and equally patriotic occupied his position? The answer was supplied by Marshal Serrano. When the Captain-General of Cuba learned of the decision to withdraw, he attempted to check Prim in a long letter of remonstrance, persuasion, and argument, to which Prim replied item by item. Serrano advised him to temporize and, rather than to break with France, to accompany the march to the capital, sacrificing the Juarez government to the *entente cordiale* with France. "And do you really propose to have the Spanish troops follow so imprudent a course?" Prim replied. "No, my friend and General, this would only cause a sea of conflicts for our country, conflicts which I should never forgive myself for having created, not to mention the strict accounting which the government would demand of me for acting in a manner diametrically opposed to my instructions, because the policy which I began with my colleagues on touching Mexican soil, which I am pursuing with my English colleagues, and which I shall follow to the end, is the policy stipulated by the three Allied nations, the policy of the Queen and her government, the policy, in short, which best serves our independence, because we must be the tool of no one, because it is of greater advantage to

our present and future interests in those remote regions, and because
a course of conduct that is noble, consistent with our offers, and disinterested, will temper and appease inveterate hatreds and create sympathies which later will give us the legitimate and maternal influence
which Spain ought to exercise in these countries." Serrano urged him
to await the instructions of Madrid. And where, Prim replied, was he
to place his troops during the two months that must pass until then?
"That is equally impossible, since by the time we receive the desired
reply we shall have lost a third of our forces and half of the rest will
be in hospital." Lastly, he plunged his pen into an appeal which contained the root of the whole imbroglio—local politics. "Even less do
I understand your thinking that, as a result of the retreat, the O'Donnell cabinet will fall. No, General, it will not fall because, for the
good fortune of Spain, those bitter times are past when at one time
France, and at another England, decreed the life and death of Spanish
cabinets, according to the greater or less docility with which they accepted the observations of those mighty sovereigns."

The controversy did not end there. Serrano carried his resistance
so far as to forbid the return of the troops, to refuse them transports,
and to offer to replace the commander himself. When his injunction reached Veracruz, however, Prim had already embarked two
battalions on British transports, and as for the rest, "if you persist in
not sending ships for them, here they will remain and I with them,"
he shot back. "If they suffer, I shall suffer, and if there is a catastrophe
I shall share it with them, and as I am not going to die, for I feel that
I was not born for so miserable an end, I shall survive it with a clear
conscience." To such arguments, backed by British bottoms and a
heavy bill for them, Serrano yielded, and the final verdict was referred to the home country, where, precisely because Spain had floundered so lamely in her efforts to recover a footing in the contemporary
world, the kind of patriotism represented by Serrano was likely to
find wide popularity, and Prim was in danger of appearing superior
to his countrymen.

The issue was crucial, in fact, to the whole future development of
Spanish policy in the New World. Serrano, who was one of the pivotal
figures in the politics of the peninsula, favored a military enterprise
in Mexico and close co-operation with the French to deal a death blow,
as he said, to the moribund Monroe Doctrine. In support of his ideas,
which he recommended to Madrid, he consulted the Spanish Minister
in Washington; and the latter sent him, in reply, a copy of a memorandum which he had sent to Madrid, assessing the situation and outlining an alternative and equally Spanish policy toward Mexico. "That
the other America and even this one will sooner or later turn to
monarchy, and that Mexico, the country most in need of government
in the world, is probably destined to initiate this great revolution, are

matters that to me have long been beyond doubt," Gabriel Tessara declared; but he doubted whether "working on a numerous population and immense territories, it would be easy to constitute in Mexico one of those diplomatic monarchies, like the one founded in Belgium to maintain the balance of European power, or, in circumstances more similar to those prevailing here, like the one formerly set up in Greece to reconstitute a race and to prepare solutions for the future. It may be said, nevertheless, that the enterprise is well worth the attempt; this may be so for France, which entertains the ambition today of presiding over the solution of the great questions of the century; but it seems less clear in the case of Spain, for the simple reason that Spain has not yet recovered either in America or Europe sufficient influence not to be forced perhaps to surrender the principal role to which it is entitled in this great drama of the restoration of its race. England I leave aside, observing, nevertheless, as well worthy of remark, that this Power plays a lesser part in the question and is condemned to oppose every solution." The candidate to the Mexican throne was the test: Maximilian could be nothing but a French pawn, and the question was whether Spain could compete successfully with France in Mexico. "To secure the triumph of our candidate, I think not. . . . But to defeat any other candidate, I firmly believe that we do have the means and should use them. . . . Thus we shall turn the blow intended for us (for of that there cannot be the least doubt) against the one who deals it, and convert into a great and noble instrument of our influence over the peoples of our race the very question destined to obscure and belittle us once more in their eyes. Great and noble, I say, because the mission of Europe must not be to force the will of these peoples with institutions that offer no guarantee of stability since they are artificial, and in any event the mission of Spain, which has begun to regenerate itself, is to impress those same peoples as at once the most interested and disinterestd champion of their freedom and independence. It is only thus that on the day when monarchy is again born in Mexico, our princes will have a chance of occupying the throne, and only thus that Spain will escape from that kind of diplomatic and political penumbra in which it is hoped to seclude her among the great nations."

Of these alternatives it was the second which Prim had adopted; but less by design than by accident. The kind of crepuscular scheming dear to Gabriel Tessara was as alien to his simple, direct, unambiguous habits of mind as the crude and shortsighted opportunism of Serrano. Though it was later said that he had been sent to Mexico to thwart the candidate of Napoleon, and though he prided himself on his ability to outmaneuver the French, temperamentally he had no gifts for intrigue and no taste for the role of dog in the manger. He followed his instructions to their logical conclusion, and the policy of sour grapes was imposed on him by circumstances. The difficulties of the occupation, the futility of Spanish pretensions, and the competition of the French combined to place him in a situation with which he could not cope; and his liberal principles did the rest. Like any intelligent man in a dilemma, he consulted his deepest convictions and, making a virtue of necessity, redeemed the dignity of his country by a gesture of forced but sincere chivalry. Thus it was that, by a combination of chances—the accident of circumstances, which was adventitious, and the accident of character, which was not—half by necessity and half by choice—he decided to beat that brave and unbargaining retreat which was tò redound to his glory and to prove the most fortunate outcome of the fool's errand on which he had been sent to Mexico. The original responsibility, obviously, lay with the cabinet in Madrid, which might well have foreseen the international complications which carried the adventure beyond its depth. The soldier, placed in a false situation, acted like a statesman, and the politicians who had failed to do so lost the decision to their champion.

Equally consistent was the way which the French Commissioners chose to follow. Immediately after the closing conference in Orizaba, the French troops were concentrated in Cordoba, awaiting the passage of the Spanish, to complete their retirement to the lowlands and begin operations. From Cordoba to Paso Ancho at the foot of the mountains was a short march, which Lorencez expected to cover in two stages, returning immediately; and though ten days were a short delay, he was impatient with the restrictions which the Preliminaries of La Soledad imposed on him. On April 4 the Prussian Minister wrote to M. de Saligny, reminding him that every day of delay was dangerous and warning him of the consequences of a literal observance of the treaty. "Unless your army mounts above Cordoba, and even beyond Orizaba immediately, it will be decimated by the *vomito* and the pernicious fevers that follow the great heats. The first rainfall will bring you all this without fail, and when once the infection reaches the army, it will be too late and impossible perhaps to march. You might easily lose two thousand to three thousand men in a few days. I suppose that you do not wish to ask the Mexicans once more, as a matter of humanity, to allow you to occupy healthy encampments. All other questions and all political proprieties disappear before the danger of sacrificing eight thousand Frenchmen to the epidemics of a murderous climate. . . . The Mexican Government, which knows all these dangers, will do everything in its power to detain you there for some time longer. Moreover, we are on the eve of the rainy season; as soon as the rains set in, the miasmas they produce will cause pernicious fevers, the roads sink and become impassable, and one makes no more progress in a day than in a single hour in the good season." M. de Saligny had nothing to learn from Prussian morality, but the obligations of honor imposed by the treaty were still binding upon the Admiral, who demonstrated his nonentity by his scrupulous respect for them. Lorencez fretted for nine days, as he explained to the War Office, seeking a legitimate escape from his critical situation; and, though men engaged in that occupation usually find what they want, so unsuccessfully that he was finally forced to forge it.

The treaty provided that, in the event of negotiations being broken off and the Allied troops retiring to their original lines, the hospitals which they had established would remain under the protection of the Mexican Government. The French had left three hundred forty-five sick in Orizaba, which was reoccupied by the Mexican forces under General Zaragoza as soon as the Spanish evacuated the town; and on April 18 some patients were transferred from one hospital to another. A few, already convalescent, crossed the town carrying their arms, and Zaragoza, mistaking them for an armed guard, wrote to Lorencez protesting against a precaution as offensive as it was superfluous and requesting that the guard be withdrawn; but upon being informed of the facts by the hospital doctor, he sent a second note to Cordoba on the same day, expressing his regrets and renewing his pledge of protection. On the following day he received a reply offering the same explanation of the misunderstanding which he himself had supplied, and the incident was apparently closed. Unwittingly, however, he supplied the enemy with an idea. The Admiral and M. de Saligny were informed by Lorencez that he had reason to fear for the safety of the sick in Orizaba, imprudently left as hostages in the hands of an unscrupulous enemy, and they were invited to join him in marching to their rescue immediately.

In the afternoon of April 19 the French column left for Orizaba. On the way the advance guard clashed with some Mexican cavalry, who were thus notified of the violation of the treaty and who suffered some losses before they were routed. At midnight of the same day General Prim, who was preparing to leave Orizaba with his wife and child and the last squadron on the following morning, received a note from the French commander, informing him of his approach and the reasons for it, and offering the party his protection. At dawn the Spanish Commander left Orizaba, and half a league from the town he met the French; the bugles rang out, and as he approached he was accosted by Lorencez and the Admiral. "Well, General?" said the Admiral. "Well, Admiral?" Prim replied. And for several minutes they found no words. "What has happened to our hospitals in Orizaba?" Lorencez asked. Prim raised his voice to be heard by the whole staff and the head of the column. "Yesterday," he said, "at five in the afternoon, I had the honor to visit your hospital. I went through the rooms accompanied by the head physician, and nothing indicated the least danger; at seven, at nine, and at eleven I passed in front of the hospital; the same calm; at four o'clock this morning I sent my aide-de-camp to see if anything had occurred during the night, and everything was quiet. Your patients in Orizaba are as safe as they would be in the hospitals of Paris." And with a curt salute he continued on his way.

The violation of the .treaty was the most honest act of intervention, being as it was the logical consequence of the excommunication that placed Mexico beyond the pale of civilized nations.

6

ON APRIL 20, when the French entered Orizaba, the town had been evacuated by Zaragoza, who retired to the mountains above it to fight the delaying action, which had now passed from the diplomatic to the military arm. Up to this point the defense of Mexico had been supplied by the aggressors; the cross-purposes of the Allies had jammed intervention at the gates of the promised land, and when the deadlock was broken something had been gained: time, the dissolution of the coalition, a favoring leaven of foreign conflicts, and the attention of the world.

The fact of intervention accomplished what protests and propaganda could not: foreign opinon was still confused, but its apathy was dispelled. The occupation of Veracruz focused attention on the situation in Mexico and its consequences abroad, and the European press began to investigate the professed purposes of the Allied Powers. In the course of these discussions some enlightening disclosures were made and picked up by the Mexican press for guidance in adapting the defense of the country to the coalition of forces confronting it.

The Spanish initiative, and the increase of French forces which it provoked, raised the stakes and the bidding to a point at which Palmerston was obliged to decide how far he would go, and to play his full hand. He showed it in a remarkable leader in the London *Times,* which sounded public opinion in England. The capacity of the Mexican people for self-government, and the guarantee to respect it proclaimed in the London Convention, were the first cards to fall. "Are these cross-bred, demoralized, bloodthirsty castes, which combine the vices of the white man with the savagery of the Indian, to give lessons of self-government not only to poor Spain, but to France and England as well?" the public was asked. "Decadence in Mexico has been chronic ever since its appearance, and rapid in recent years, and even the solemn and ancient despotism of the Bourbon viceroys was better than the fierce butcheries and proscriptions of rival Presidents." The oracular article then proposed what the confederate Powers had already disposed. After describing the occupation of Veracruz, the panic of the population, the dismantling of the fortresses, and the miserable surrender of the town, the *Times* continued: "Such is the first act of intervention in Mexico. Spain has struck the first blow under the direction of an able and active Minister. As long as his views are just and beneficial for mankind, as long as he seeks to make a name for himself by putting an end to the anarchy that prevails in his former colonies and to convince them by example that peace and good government will soon give the nation a respectable place in human society, he may be sure of the sympathy of all the European Powers, and above all of England." With the blessing to Spain went a corresponding license to France. "The French Government have also determined to act with vigor, in spite of their financial embarrassment and one or two international questions which they have on their hands. A semi-official organ announces that France will send to Mexico an army corps equal to the one she sent some time ago to Syria. A regular campaign is planned, in fact, if that word can be applied to an advance against troops that will undoubtedly flee at the approach of the invaders, contenting themselves with sacking and murdering their wretched countrymen." What remained for England was the last card to be dropped. "It is evident that the French will not permit either England or Spain to take a more active part in these operations than themselves, and it cannot be doubted that France will direct them when once they have begun in earnest, since she alone commands a numerous body of troops in that country. To all this we can make no objection. . . . Mexico City will be occupied for some time, and if the result is as happy as in Syria, the world will have reason to rejoice. In any case, France can count on our complete acquiescence in her efforts to restore tranquillity; certainly, we shall not feel the least envy of any preponderance of French forces . . . and even if the French should extend their occupation for one or two years, there will be no complaint on this side of the Channel. We were never propagandists for the Monroe Doctrine, and we have no desire to assure its principles."

Intervention had no sooner begun than Palmerston prepared to go the whole way, but in a manner that pleased neither Paris nor Madrid. The lead of the London *Times* received a poor press abroad. In Paris the *Journal des Débats* commented caustically on "the attitude of reserve of the English in wishing France and Spain success, without caring to increase the personnel of their expedition, it would seem, and more inclined to desire our triumph than to contribute to its costs. We do not yet know the sentiment in Spain, but two or three papers in Madrid have already spoken. . . ." The permission to act as a cats-paw for England was relished no more in Madrid than in Paris, and jealousy of French preponderance was openly ventilated in the Spanish press. More nettling to the French, however, than the reserve of the English, was that of the Austrians. "But what is more curious," the *Journal des Débats* observed, "is the reaction which the true or erroneous reports of the offer made to the Archduke Maximilian have produced in Vienna. Austria, says today's *Ost-Deutsche Post* in substance, Austria is not yet reduced to the necessity of accepting such favors. Thus, according to the *Ost-Deutsche Post,* Austria would feel herself humiliated to receive for an Austrian prince an empire of eight million subjects, much as an impoverished nobleman might be insulted by an offer of charity. . . . A Belgian newspaper declared yesterday that the most intimate friends of the Archduke are advising him to refuse the throne of Mexico unless France pledges herself to maintain her army of occupation in Mexico and Veracruz for ten years."

In England the announcement that the government was prepared to abandon the conduct of intervention to its Allies would have met with approval but for the sanction extended to their political aims. When the *Morning Post,* improving on the *Times,* came out with an article advocating the candidacy of Maximilian, there was an unanimous outcry in the unofficial press. Intervention was denounced as an international felony. "And what has Great Britain to do with all this?" the government was asked in its turn. "Nothing, absolutely nothing; it serves merely to accompany the housebreakers to the door and to stand there as a lookout, while the crime is committed. And Great Britain accepts this role!" The ministerial press promptly dropped the bid for Maximilian, but the agitation continued, and in some quarters it was freely predicted that the Mexican question and its complications might lead to the fall of the Ministry. In Parliament the Opposition was milder and more manageable; there the Mexican question was employed as a party maneuver and worked for partisan purposes, and the Tories turned it to account. Disraeli reminded the House that England had been the first Power to recognize Mexico and that Canning had done so to counteract the Holy Alliance, and asked how it was that on this occasion England ventured to strike the first blow against Mexican independence.

Disraeli delighted Karl Marx. Himself prone to use the Mexican question as a stick with which to beat Palmerston, Marx relayed the attack on his personal devil to Vienna in his correspondence with the *Freie Presse* and produced proof and copy of his own diagnosis of

intervention out of the mouth of a British Tory. Citing the reply of
Palmerston, who referred his critics to the London Convention and
repeated that all that he required was some form of government in
Mexico with which foreign governments could deal—a reply which
Disraeli himself called suspect—Marx annotated it with his own comment. "He declares the nonexistence of the present Mexican Government. He claims for the alliance of England, France, and Spain the
same prerogative of the Holy Alliance to decide as to the existence or
non-existence of foreign governments, and modestly adds that this is
as much as the Government of Great Britain desires. This, and nothing
more!" Marx and Disraeli speaking the same language would have
been merely a confusion of tongues if they had not been impelled by
like motives. Disraeli made political capital of the Mexican question,
and Marx made a Marxian question of it; the controversy itself was
the question, and not Mexico. But Palmerston was the key to it. The
least systematic of statesmen, he was guilty not of deliberately fostering
a revival of the Holy Alliance, nor of any studied plan at all, but of
laissez-faire; but he laid himself open to such constructions by acquiescing in the combinations of France, Austria, and Spain, and
placed England in the position of a fence for her partners by sheer
improvidence and compromise. English decency revolted, and he was
obliged to beat a retreat. The proposed monarchy provided the easiest
security for British interests, and he continued to abet Napoleon as
long as he could straddle, but his position became more and more
compromising as the complications in Mexico accumulated. The hitch
that developed in consequence of the French ultimatum, the inflation
of the French claims, and the Jecker bonds forced his hand. He
offered to compound the French claims and to support their global
bill of twelve million Mexican dollars in return for the sacrifice of the
Jecker bonds, but Thouvenel hedged, and Palmerston was privately
advised that the Jecker affair would be the subject of interpellations
in Parliament and urged to forestall further questions and explanations on so embarrassing a subject as the Mexican muddle had now
become. Thereupon the French claims were abandoned, and the English as well, and the whole expedition. This decision had been contemplated for some time as a last resource, and when it was finally
taken, the rupture of the alliance had already occurred in Mexico.

The whole homely truth was summed up by the English journalist
whom the Tories had sent as a scout to Mexico. "Very few persons
will feel any disappointment at the result," he wrote when he wound
up the record. "The speculators who were foolish enough to trust to
the promises of half-informed government organs must take the con-
sequencees of their credulity. No honest critic could admit the possibility of the success of the expedition. Earl Russell himself has confessed, plainly enough, that nothing positive was to be obtained from

it. The results he proposed to himself in negotiating the Convention were purely negative. He saw no good to England in such an intervention, but he thought that by participating in it he might hinder the ambitious projects justly attributed to France and Spain. The result has not justified His Lordship's confidence in his own cleverness. . . . It turns out that Spain has no such intentions; but after all our efforts we leave France apparently engaged in a grand scheme for making the Mexicans happy against their will. . . . Now that all fear of disturbing the combination is removed by its dissolution, we hope that the unexampled folly displayed by Lord Russell in this business will be properly stigmatized as it deserves. His own despatches give conclusive proof that he was thoroughly aware of the certain failure of such an expedition and that the desire to signalize himself by a masterpiece of cunning was his motive in involving England in this scrape." So much for the English side of it. "The French, therefore, will be left alone to finish the work. What advantage can France derive from this occupation? What order she does establish will turn to the profit of the two nations that have backed out of the expedition. She cannot make the country pay for it. Is France in a position to bear such burdens? Many members of the Legislative Chamber have protested against the occupation of Rome on account of its cost. This Mexican expedition is not popular. It appeals to no popular passion, it promises no sterling advantage. The organs of independent French opinion go so far as to assert that the encouragement given from England to France to persevere in this expedition is dictated by a desire to see a rival involved in difficulties and disasters, whilst England must reap all the fruits of her labors. . . . Fortunately we have blundered out as we have blundered into the imbroglio." And speaking of blunders brought up Sir Charles Wyke. "People who remember the very decided manner in which Sir Charles Wyke some few months back advocated intervention, and the glee with which he seized the first opportunity for breaking relations, as a means to an end, were naturally surprised at the very conciliatory policy he now seemed inclined to pursue," he wrote when he left Mexico, and he let the words stand in lieu of final judgment. The truth about Sir Charles Wyke was too English, and there was no longer any need to labor the moral.

But the man who made England suffer for want of judgment could not escape it. The diplomacy of the British Minister obeyed the direction of public opinion in England better than did the conduct of the government in London, and the belated support which he lent the excommunicated government of Mexico was appreciated by the Mexicans, who gladly forgot the beginning of his activities in their end; but unfortunately for his reputation they were not overlooked in England, where they were laid bare by the publication of a Blue Book, containing his correspondence with Zamacona. The confidence with which

Zamacona referred their differences to a future day of judgment, when they would come to light, was not disappointed. The publication caught the eye of Karl Marx. "In the matter of brutality on the English side," he wrote to Engels, "the Mexican Blue Book surpasses anything that history has known. Menshikov seems a gentleman compared to Sir C. Wyke. This canaille not only develops the most unbounded *zèle* in carrying out Pam's secret instructions, but seeks to avenge himself by boorishness for the fact that Señor Zamacona, the Mexican Minister of Foreign Affairs (now out of office) and a former journalist, is invariably his superior in the exchange of diplomatic notes. As for the fellow's style, here are a few samples from his notes to Zamacona." He culled them at random. If style was the man, here was the letter, and here was the spirit, of Sir Charles Lennox Wyke. What manner of man was it that could write the homily of the baker and the beggar? Or what sentence could be passed on him worse than the one he himself penned when he wrote: "With regard to the light in which you view the question, as expressed in your above-named note, you will excuse me for stating that it cannot be treated of partially, without also taking into consideration the opinions of those who directly suffer from the practical operation of such ideas as emanating from yourself." What else could emanate from such a man but an imbroglio? In the unwinding of that sentence lay the secret of the snarl that had twisted the temper of the world. There, in that mouthful, was the mind of the man still laboring to finish what he had begun, still chasing the tail of the comet. Marx ferreted out his offenses and dragged them up one by one on the point of his pen, and the grosser they were, the greater his zest. "Zamacona writes to him that the intrigues of foreign diplomats for twenty-five years are chiefly to blame for the troubles of Mexico. Wyke replies that 'the population of Mexico is so degraded as to make them dangerous not only to themselves, but to everybody coming into contact with them.'" *Ipse dixit!* And so on, and so on, to satiety. Wyke was too long-winded and the world too long-suffering, and Marx himself tired. "However, *satis superque!*" he concluded. Enough and more than enough attention had been paid to Pam's puppet, and after singling out a few choice passages remarkable for as clumsy a command of the English language as of Mexican character, he slammed the lid with a snort of disgust. His verdict was, naturally, not the general one, and it was his private opinion; but being the judgment of Marx, it lingered longer.

At the other end of the triple axis interest in the Mexican question waned rapidly when it was realized that the only part reserved for the Spanish in the plans of the Allies was the conclusion of the preliminaries. The third wheel of the expedition worked itself loose by its own momentum, but with the assistance and coaching of the English, and for the same reasons. Jarred into joint action, the weakest and the strongest partners withdrew together, defeated by their own short-sightedness and salvaging from their miscalculations only their unholy alliance; but Prim carried off the fiasco with a saving grace that was not granted to Sir Charles Wyke, and in Spain style could carry off anything.

In France the action of public opinion was still feeble and confused. Here and there a voice was raised in defense of Mexico, but without sufficient authority or information to make an effective protest. The allied antagonisms of the great Powers quickened the misgivings of a public officially informed only of the ostensible object of the expedition, but freely fed with rumors of its ulterior aims, and persuaded of their gravity by the muffled friction of the several parties to intervention. In the Corps Législatif the Opposition, led by Jules Favre, censured intervention on principle and interpellated the government on its true purpose, only to be met with official reserve and caution. The explanations were guarded and noncommittal, the Opposition questioned but could not challenge them, and after four months of uncertainty public opinion was unsettled but still passive.

In reply to the interpellations of the Opposition, however, the government submitted extracts from the correspondence of M. de Saligny in evidence of the conditions prevailing in Mexico and the moral warrant of intervention. Picked up by a Belgian newspaper and reprinted in the Mexican press, this testimony disclosed for the first time the importance of the part he had played, and a remark which he made to a member of the French expedition confirmed it. "My sole merit," he said, "is to have guessed the intentions of the Emperor to intervene in Mexico and to have made that intervention necessary." Ranging from truth and half-truth to exaggeration and fabrication, the reports of the French Minister, which now came to light, could no longer be laid to the credulity of prejudice or the irresponsibility of passion; the bottle leaked, and the contents were seen to be a systematic misrepresentation for a deliberate purpose, which had been crowned with success. The lies were nailed, the exaggerations corrected, the truths explained and the half-truths untangled in the Mexican press, but too late; the distorted interpretation of the country that Saligny had supplied his government for twelve months were repeated word for word, like an echo, in the instructions drawn for the Admiral, which the Mexican press reprinted side by side with their source. The fusion was complete, the trail was lost, it was impossible to say where the agent ended and the government began, and the responsibility of the one was exposed at the very moment when it was covered by the other.

Like M. de Saligny, the Mexican press attempted to read the mind of the Emperor and to divine the ultimate aim of French intervention by political foresight and flair and logical construction. In the course of the search, a writer in the provincial press produced an ingenious and plausible explanation, which had the merit of reconciling the apparent inconsistencies of Napoleonic policy in Europe and revealing, together with their inner coherence, their bearing upon Mexico. "In 1840, when Louis Napoleon was on trial for his abortive revolt against Louis-Philippe," the writer recalled, "he said in his defense: 'I represent, gentlemen, a principle, a cause, and a defeat. The principle is the sovereignty of the people, the cause the Empire, and the defeat Waterloo.'" In the light of that definition a great deal became clear. His subsequent development picked up, one by one, those cardinal points of reference. The principle was vindicated by his election to the Presidency of the Second Republic by an immense popular majority. The cause was redeemed by the proclamation of the Empire. The third promise was still to come, but ever since the resurrection of the Empire his diplomacy had been directed toward paying off old scores and effacing the stain of Waterloo. The account with Russia was settled by the Crimean War; the account with England and Prussia was still pending. Patiently and persistently preparing for it in a shifting game which had perplexed Europe for ten years, Napoleon had quietly built up satellites and alliances against the next reckoning. Hence he had espoused the cause of Italian independence, and by his success in the Italian campaign had carried the frontiers of France to the Alps. Hence he was working, on the side of the Pyrenees, to raise Spain to the rank of a first-class Power and training her to act as his associate. Hence he was maneuvering to divide Catholic and Protestant Germany and to win the alliance of Austria, as a further security for the eventual blow against England and Prussia. Hence, too, compensation had to be found for Franz Josef: the partial dismemberment of Turkey as a trade for the sacrifice of the Veneto was one possibility; the erection of a throne for the Hapsburgs in Mexico was another, and the latter appealed to Napoleon, moreover, as a means of combating in America the spread of republican ideas, which were rapidly gaining ground in France, Italy, and Germany. "From the foregoing," the analysis concluded, "we may deduce that there is a logical connection between the idea that dominated Louis Napoleon since the *coup d'état* and all the acts of his political life, even in their most contradictory manifestations. So we explain his holding an army afoot in Rome with the ostensible purpose of protecting the Pope and the secret motive of preventing Austria from doing so. So we explain that to lull the suspicions of England, he signs treaties of commerce with her and accompanies her on distant expeditions to the China Seas. So we explain that to accustom Spain to be his ally when the time comes for a break with England, he takes her along on the expedition to Cochin-China. And, lastly, so we explain how he now uses England and Spain to carry out his ideas in America, in the same way that he will use Russia and Austria and Italy and Spain to combat England and Prussia, the two great Powers he has still to humiliate to efface Waterloo and win the frontiers of the Rhine, thus fulfilling the great mission of his life." The place of Mexico in the puzzle was, consequently, an integral part of world politics, and it was the force of the Napoleonic obsession, and not M. de Saligny, that made French intervention in Mexico necessary and inevitable.

By the end of April some glimmerings of the truth about Mexico had begun to penetrate the capitals of Europe, and the time spent in winning the attention of the world was worth it. The dilatory tactics of Juarez had not been wasted, but the moral excommunication of his government had still to be broken. An attempt, a stout attempt, to raise it was made by De la Fuente before he left France in the first week of March. Public opinion was accessible and he made an impression in Europe by a parting note of protest which he addressed to M. de Thouvenel. Reprinted in a London newspaper, the note created a sensation in diplomatic circles, where it was agreed that not for a long time had so virile and rigorous a defense of the law of nations reached the French government. His language was scaled to the occasion. "Mexico may be conquered but it cannot be subjected, and it will not be conquered without first giving proof of the valor and the virtues that are denied it," he declared. "Mexico, after having shaken off the secular and deeply rooted power of Spain, Mexico which refused to accept its own liberator as a king, Mexico, in sum, which has just risen victorious from a terrible revolution against the remains of an oligarchy which weighed on its democracy, will not accept a foreign monarchy at any cost. To create it will be very difficult; to maintain it, more so. Ruinous and terrible for us, it will be more so for its promoters. Mexico is weak, no doubt, compared to the powers that invade its territory; but it has the sense of its outraged rights, patriotism to multiply its efforts, and the profound conviction that by sustaining this perilous contest with honor it will be able to preserve the fair continent of Christopher Columbus from the cataclysm that threatens it. I protest, therefore, M. le Ministre, in the name of my Government, that all the evils that result from this unjustified war, and those directly or indirectly caused by the troops and agents of France, will be exclusively of the responsibility of your Government. For the rest, Mexico has nothing to fear if Providence protects the rights of a people that defends them with dignity."

The style, at once sober and florid, seemed Mexican. Lusty by instinct but subdued by civilization, it was the tone of a man innocent of sophistication and familiar with it. It was the original language of nature invaded by knowledge and effacing their frontiers. In that modulation Mexico showed its colors. The words rose like a flurry of wings suddenly escaping the fetters of convention; they were gray but they sang, being male; they followed their native call and they carried the mind in their flight back to the continent from which they came. It was as if the naked Indian were reincarnated in the Mexican Minister to Europe. By some transmigration of souls bygone ages seemed to be talking back to the nineteenth century in its own tongue, and the tongue-tied exotic who had finally found his voice in France defied the secular excommunication of his people at the right time. The attention which he attracted was symptomatic of the importance which Mexico had assumed as a testing ground of the vaunted principle of nonintervention proclaimed by the Powers in concert as the cardinal conquest and creed of the nineteenth century; and in London, where the popularity of Napoleon varied inversely to the favor shown him by Palmerston, his protest was widely applauded.

But De la Fuente told only half the truth to M. de Thouvenel; the other half he reserved for his own government. He left France no longer a Christopher as he had come, to discover the New World to the Old, and before he crossed the ocean again he begged his countrymen to make good his boast. The time had come to redeem their good name and the truth would never be known until they spoke for themselves; that was the way out for Mexico. "Until now they counted on our divisions, on what they call our corruption and nullity; that is why they sent so few soldiers; now that they have seen us move, they think that we have courage only against the Spanish, but that a handful of Frenchmen will suffice to terrify and destroy us. If we defend ourselves well, we shall save ourselves, for the bad season will come and they will not think of sending fresh forces, because they will see once and for all how long and costly is the enterprise of subjugating us, because the peace of Europe forbids it, and because by our public justification we shall have the whole Liberal party of Europe in our favor. The enthusiasm of Mexico and the noble and energetic attitude of our government have won us many sympathies; but if we let ourselves be crushed by a handful of Frenchmen, we shall place ourselves on a lower level than the Chinese or the Moroccans." It would be the story of Cortés all over again.

7

POLITICALLY, therefore, the initial phase of military operations in Mexico was of decisive importance. The press had been forbidden to discuss the defense of the country as long as it lay with the diplomatic arm, but when negotiations broke down the question fell into the public domain. The surrender of Veracruz, valuable as it had been for diplomatic purposes, had produced nevertheless the demoralizing effect of a retreat, and on the eve of the test the government was urged to repair it by every means in its power. A writer in the *Siglo* called for constant proclamations from the Palace, constant articles in the press, mass meetings at every street corner, the tocsin traveling from belfry to belfry, the cry of "To arms, citizens!" repeated every quarter of an hour as a signal for a mass uprising. No civilian himself, he called on the authorities to come out of their offices and show themselves to the crowds, haranguing, spurring, inspiring them, and summoned the Citizen President to mingle democratically with the people, who had so rarely an occasion to see him and to show the affection they felt for him and their confidence in the rectitude of his intentions, the acumen of his decisions, and his tested constancy. A soldier and a strategist, he insisted that on no account should the enemy be allowed to penetrate farther into the heart of the country in the hope of beating him better there, for though defeats might be in store for them, every victory of the invader would cost him losses, which he would be hard put to repair three thousand miles from his base, and for every native that fell, ten would arise in his place. Foreign-born himself but a naturalized Mexican, he knew that guerrilla warfare was the only feasible form of defense for the country and mobility the major advantage of its soldiers, and he adapted his ideas to the demands of the situation. Pitched battles were to be avoided at all costs; the people must raze their fields and burn their villages in the path of the French, harassing them with ambushes, hunting them down over the mountains and through the forests, killing every straggler, cutting their communications, reducing them to their own supplies, and relying on hunger, fever, and the rains to retard their progress. The bad season was beginning, the *vomito* was raging in the rear of the French, the rains would soon make the roads impassable, and their troops were still unaccus-

tomed to the long marches which the Mexicans made so easily, barefoot, barely clothed and fed, eating and even sleeping on the march,
blanketed under the muggy downpours, making their fifteen leagues
a day over roads and trails as primitive as themselves, and always ready
to fight at a disadvantage. These were the demands of a citizen, a soldier, an expert, a cosmopolitan, and a patriot. The system was Mexican, and "the conquest of Mexico of which the French dream will
figure in history beside the disastrous retreat from Moscow," he concluded; "1862 will be the corollary of 1812." A more candid confession
of desperate straits could hardly have been made; and it was not over-
drawn.

Despite the indignation aroused by the occupation of Veracruz, or
because of it, Zaragoza had difficulty in assembling a force of five thousand men to bear the brunt of the offensive. His plans were determined
by the necessity of using these picked volunteers economically, of
adapting his action to the natural advantages of the country and the ap-
titudes of the natives, of protecting them against themselves as well as
the French, and of maintaining their morale and self-confidence at all
costs. The violation of the treaty of La Soledad obliged him to abandon his first and most formidable line of defense at the foot of the
mountains, to evacuate Orizaba, and to fall back on the passes beyond
it, where, in the last days of April, he took up a position commanding
the road to Puebla to intercept a junction between the French and Marquez, who was reported to be approaching with two thousand men.
The French spent a week in Orizaba preparing their march. An adequate convoy had been assembled; the restrictions of the government
having been raised by the treaty, the usual traffic was allowed to descend to the coast, and two hundred and thirty wagons had been added
to the stock collected by the Admiral. The other impediments had been
eliminated: the fever zone lay behind them, the rains had not yet begun, and the Admiral received a reprimand for concluding the treaty
of La Soledad and his formal recall by the mail that reached Orizaba
on April 25. Lorencez was assured by Saligny and Almonte that he
would meet with a merely formal resistance as he advanced, and on
the day after his promotion to the supreme command he transmitted
their conviction to Paris. "We are so superior to the Mexicans in race,
in organization, in discipline, in morality, and in elevation of feeling,"
he wrote to the Minister of War, "that I beg Your Excellency to be so
good as to inform the Emperor that, at the head of six thousand soldiers, I am already master of Mexico."

On April 27 the French left Orizaba, and after a day's march
through formidable but undefended country they reached the Cumbres
de Aculzingo, the mountain barrier that forms the base of the upper
plateau. Of the presence of the enemy they had seen no sign but vanishing scouts, and although a village was burning at the base of the

pass, the people were extinguishing the fire set by the patriots in their passage, and all reports agreed that Zaragoza was falling back on the capital and that the road was clear. After a brief halt for coffee, the column began the ascent. The pass at this point was a narrow valley, running between thick and almost perpendicular walls; the road rose spirally in thirty-seven loops toward the crest, where a ruined jail commanded it. At half-past one the head of the column came within range of the building and was halted by a sharp fusillade, and a moment later the valley echoed with the fire of masked batteries overhead. As the French artillery had been placed at the rear of the column, General Lorencez decided to force the passage by an infantry charge. Shedding their knapsacks with relief, for the heat was intense and the load heavy, the Zouaves advanced *au pas gymnastique,* followed by a detachment of *chasseurs à pied,* who scrambled up the precipitous slopes to the right and left of the ruined prison. The first wave failed to reach it, the second took cover, reinforcements were brought up, but the position was too strong: superiority of race, organization, discipline, morality, and elevation of feeling were lost on the superiority of the mountain. The strenuous ground and the fire of the enemy broke the ranks of the pathfinders groping for a footing on the flanks of the pass, and their spasmodic progress, marked by puffs of smoke in the clear air and the rattle of stones and the gleam of red pants in the underbrush, was followed anxiously from the road, where the long invertebrate column reacted in rapid articulations as more and more reserves were called up. The bugles rang out below and the battle overhead, and for an hour and a half fourteen companies were engaged. By dint of persistence and dash the position was finally carried. At five o'clock Saligny and Almonte saw their faces saved. The battle had lasted three hours, the light was waning, the Mexicans were in full retreat, the French had lost two dead and thirty-six wounded, and they had surmounted the most serious obstacle in their path.

The forcing of the pass of Aculzingo fully confirmed the confidence of Lorencez in the quality of his troops. The vanishing race faded into the Mexican mountains and disappeared overnight. On the next day he crossed a second range without encountering any trace of them and paused in a deserted village to allow the convoy to catch up with the head of the column. The Indians had fled, leaving a population of pigs locked up in their huts; the soldiers broke in, and discipline was relaxed in a lively chase through the lanes, the officers finding it impossible to separate the men from the animals until the following morning, when several cases of dysentery were reported. The process having been completed, the column continued its progress unmolested and rapidly regained its normal elevation of feeling. Of the movements of the enemy it was impossible to gain any information. When an Indian could be caught and questioned, the answer was invariable: *Quien sabe, Señor?* Even when the question was varied and he was asked how many children he had, the answer was the same: *Quien sabe, Señor?* Of their own whereabouts the French were aware only by the certainty that the worst was behind them. Ten days after beginning operations they were on the upper plateau, two thousand feet above sea level, in a healthy and temperate climate, marching through a broad and fertile valley watered by the melting snows of the volcanoes and covered with rich farms that amply rewarded their morality. The treaty of La Soledad was a memory as remote as the trace of the enemy whose line of retreat they followed for four days from one abandoned village to another; and not until they reached Amozoc, fourteen miles from Puebla, was contact established. Here they were informed that Zaragoza had decided to defend Puebla, that he had a strong garrison of four to five thousand men, and that the streets had been barricaded and mounted with cannon. That evening—it was May 4—Lorencez called a council of war and formed a plan of attack based on an abundance of expert advice and his better judgment.

The road which he was following led to the city on the northern side, where it was guarded by the Cerro de Guadalupe, a steep hill crowned by a fortified convent, and the fort of Loreto lodged behind and below it on a spur of the same eminence. Almonte and a Mexican general, who had twice defended and taken Puebla, advised him to attack from the south, where the approach was open and unfortified, and to neglect the fortresses, which were difficult of access and too far removed from the city to use their guns with any effect against an assault from the opposite quarter. Puebla had never been taken from the north. Nevertheless, Lorencez favored that approach. Supported by the commanders of the cavalry and the engineer corps, he preferred to trust to the dashing quality of his troops to carry the forts rather than to fling them recklessly into a network of barricaded streets. In the midst of the discussion a Mexican engineer was announced. Seated and questioned at great length, he supported Lorencez with some very interesting information. "According to him," in the words of a staff officer, "the approaches to Guadalupe offered no obstacles capable of arresting the *élan* of French troops, the moats were partly filled, the fortress had too little solidity to present an effective resistance, and as for the enemy, he did not even do him the honor of admitting that he might offer more than a formal defense. The General was satisfied and, turning toward us, he dismissed us with the words, '*A demain, messieurs, dans Guadalupe!*'"

The next morning, at daybreak, the column left Amozoc, and a little after nine the indistinct mass of roofs and domes that was Puebla de los Angeles swam into sight. The plain was empty, and after practicing a hasty reconnaissance the chief of staff reported that the bulk of the Mexican forces was concentrated on the farther side of the city and that it was clear that no real attack was expected from the north. Nevertheless, when Lorencez laid eyes on the forts, he decided to consult another authority before delivering the attack. He sent a message to M. de Saligny, whom he had left in a carriage, far to the rear, with the baggage. The officer who carried it was instructed to remind him that when they entered Amozoc the whole population had fled and that the attitude of the people hardly seemed friendly, to ask him whether he had any news from Puebla, and to say that his opinion would determine the decision of the Commander-in-Chief and the organization of the attack. "My dear Captain," the Minister replied, "tell General de Lorencez that I have just received this communication from an Indian." And he handed him one of those thin slips of paper which the Indian runners were accustomed to conceal in their hair, their ears, their toes, or other and more privy parts of their bodies, and which the officer accepted with some distaste, not knowing from what part of the body M. de Saligny drew his information. But the Minister was not fastidious, and the message came from Marquez. As nearly as the Captain could make it out, it announced his approach. "You may add," said M. de Saligny, "that as soon as our troops are in sight of the city Marquez will appear, all conventional resistance will cease, and the barricades will fall as if by magic. You will make your entrance under a rain of flowers, to the confusion of Zaragoza and his gang. It would be better, nevertheless," he added, settling back in his carriage, "to enter by the east gate rather than by the one facing you." — "That is impossible," the officer explained. "It would mean abandoning the convoy and your protection and security as well. If the enemy were to take courage and attack and capture the convoy during the involving movement you suggest, it would be a disaster for us. We are compelled by the conditions of our march to remain close to our resources, even at the risk of choosing the point of attack that may not be wholly favorable." — "Very well, but you will see that you have no complications to fear," the Minister replied. "General de Lorencez may approach the city as he pleases, but I should consider it a most serious mistake not to profit by the friendly feeling of which I have been informed, and I shall be obliged to report it."

The Minister was not a military authority, and Lorencez regretted that he had asked his advice. As he waited for it, the fort blazed and cannon balls began to burst over his lines, where the troops were waiting impatiently to attack on the spur of the moment. It was too late to reorganize his plans, and between the Minister and the Mexicans he did not hesitate long. At eleven o'clock he went into action. Two columns of infantry deployed to the right and left of the Cerro de Guadalupe, where they awaited the order to advance, while ten pieces of artillery, sent forward to an emplacement in the center, opened fire about two thousand meters from the mark. For three quarters of an hour the French barrage continued without making any appreciable impression on the massive walls that crowned the hill. The emplacement was shifted to a shorter range, but the closer the approach, the more difficult it became for the gunners to sight the target correctly, the terrain was full of swells, the aim from below was accidental, while the batteries of the convent raked the slopes with deadly accuracy. In the meanwhile, a great deal of movement was observed in the city. The Mexican troops concentrated on the farther side were brought up behind the hill and deployed in a line tipped with cavalry at either end, threatening the columns immobilized by the artillery duel.

After an hour and a quarter the French had spent half their munitions, and Lorencez decided to dispense with the preliminaries and to launch the attack. What gallantry could do was done, but the infantry made no more headway than the guns. Two columns struggled up the hill, attempting to divide the attention of the garrison, only to be mown down in their tracks; some reached the top and rolled into the moat, the depth of the ditch was unexpected, a few managed to prop their ladders and to scale the wall far enough to see the enemy before they fell, but the bugler alone bore a charmed life, blowing it breathlessly into the dead, the dying, the missing. The attempt was repeated again and again with fresh reinforcements and the same result: three waves broke under the triple bank of fire which they drew from an impregnable position; the fourth flanked it and bent. A battalion of Zouaves obliqued to the right and attempted to turn the hill and take it from the rear, but the movement brought them abreast of the fort lying beyond and below it, and the batteries of Loreto went into action, while five battalions of Mexican infantry massed on the hump between the two forts met them with a moving fusillade that drove them back in confusion. At the same time the Mexican cavalry took the field and bore down on two companies awaiting their turn on the plain. They were cut off before their plight was noticed by the Commander-in-Chief, but they formed a square and stood off the charge until they were relieved, winning his commendation for their conduct, for with his attention divided he hardly knew, he said, whether to admire more "those who were marching under the fire of Guadalupe or the *chasseurs* who, undismayed by the numbers of enemies around them, rallied with the utmost calm and killed or scattered the horsemen who flung themselves on them." But he lavished commendation on men condemned to defeat. The flower of the French army was still struggling to grapple with Zaragoza and his gang, and wreaths of smoke overhead were hallowing their failure, when the sky darkened and the usual afternoon storm burst. For five days the approach of the rainy season had been marked by electrical storms of terrific intensity coming up regularly in the late afternoon but vanishing as rapidly as the enemy at Aculzingo, breaking and evaporating in the evening sun;

but on the afternoon of May 5 that defeat was reversed. The wavering field was drenched by a cloudburst of driving rain and hail, and the slopes became so slippery that despite their unflagging efforts the men could hardly keep their footing. It was four o'clock; they had been on their feet since five in the morning and fighting since noon, and Lorencez decided to call it a day. The retreat was sounded.

Unlike the attack, the retreat was executed without precipitation. Harried by the Mexican horsemen, the French fell back with dampened ardor but unbroken discipline and rallied to the mournful bugle at the base of the Cerro, picking up their packs where they had left them in the morning and standing their ground until the wounded were collected and evacuated to the rear, while the ambulance ran the gantlet of the dying cannonade in the dusk. By nine o'clock the survivors were assembled and accounted for in the bivouac. The casualty list reported four hundred sixty-two killed, wounded, and missing. The figure was considerable where no margin could be spared, and as a company of marines was among the missing a searching party trailed them long and stubbornly under cover of the dark. Six men crept over the battlefield, from pocket to pocket, without encountering them. The captain ordered the bugler to play the regimental march. The flourish echoed away without response, and the search continued. Beating their way about the base of the Cerro, and pausing from time to time to repeat the call, they had the field to themselves. As they were within earshot of the fort, the captain was cautioned by his men that they might be overwhelmed at any moment if the enemy chose to investigate, but he refused to abandon the search. For two hours he groped his way blindly about the Cerro. He ordered the bugler to vary the tune. The divisional march was played. As the deliberate bugle sounded off from point to point on the plain, there was an alert in the fort, where it was thought that the French were preparing a night attack, but neither side was inclined to question the issue of the day, and the metallic solo scoured the field unchallenged. At eleven o'clock the party returned to camp, where their calls had caused more alarm than in the fort, and there they found the missing company.

The day that ended in a draw was followed by a morning of truce. When the sun rose, the most profound peace prevailed over the plain, and the only movement observed about the forts was the activity of a detail shoveling the dead underground. The morning that began with a truce ripened rapidly into an afternoon of defeat. General Lorencez had intended to renew the attack on the next day, but the night brought sober counsels, and after consulting his pillow his main concern was to preserve the morale of his army on the morrow of a battle that had been a military debauch. He blamed the disaster on his advisers and vented his temper on Almonte and Saligny; but the commander who was reduced to such shifts was already defeated. For twenty-four hours he lingered before the forts, hoping that the enemy would come out and give battle and that the decision might be reversed in the open field, but he was cheated of that *revanche,* and after waiting for it one day longer he resolved to return to Orizaba. On May 8 the French broke camp and retired to Amozoc, where, at the request of Almonte, two days were spent waiting for Marquez. The retreat was resumed on the 11th. One by one the deserted villages were picked up and passed, the Cumbres de Aculzingo were negotiated in peace, and on the last lap of the descent Lorencez met Marquez and was forced to send back a detachment to rescue his men who had fallen into an ambush in the mountains, and from that engagement the French brought back reinforcements and the credit of having saved their allies from destruction at the Barranca Seca.

On the day after his arrival in Orizaba, Lorencez cast up his account. Writing to Paris, he called for fresh supplies of siege material and reinforcements of fifteen to twenty thousand men. The days of dash and daring were over, and those of sober calculation had begun. He had come to the same conclusions as had Prim as to the number of men required for the conquest of Mexico, and he had formed the same opinion of Saligny: those were his only gains. He spared neither the Minister nor Almonte in his report to the Minister of War. "Such was my situation before Puebla, M. le Maréchal, the city most hostile to Juarez, according to the opinion of those persons whom I was bound to believe, and who *assured me formally,* according to the reports which they had the opportunity to collect, that I would be received with transports of joy and that my soldiers would enter covered with flowers." Nor was it only in addressing Marshal Randon that he hung the weeds on his colleague. He took the whole camp into his confidence in an order of the day addressed to the army. "Soldiers and sailors! Your march upon Mexico has been checked by material obstacles which you must have been far from expecting. You had been told a hundred times that the city of Puebla summoned you with all its heart and that its population would press on your heels to cover you with flowers. It was with the confidence inspired by these deceptive assurances that we presented ourselves before Puebla. . . ." The intelligence service alone was to blame, and he paid tribute to his men. "Soldiers and sailors! You have given proof, on the 5th of May, of heroic courage," he added. They at least had covered themselves with glory, and he had nothing to cover himself with but Saligny. Their relations became strained to the breaking point. The Minister was also a talebearer and had a different story to tell to the War Office, and when he took to the bottle and appeared on the streets in an advanced state of stupefaction, the Commander-in-Chief threatened to have him arrested for behavior unbecoming the dignity of France. The scandal flared up, to the intense satisfaction of the troops and to the embarrassment of the staff, who

attempted in vain to muffle these indecent dissensions. The enemy
caught wind of them and turned them to account in a final humiliation.

The repulse at Puebla was as unexpected by the Mexicans as by the
French. On the night before the battle General Negrete, who was in
command of the forts, called on Zaragoza for his final orders and came
away with scant encouragement. Zaragoza was a man of few words;
with nothing to fall back upon but his faith, he hoarded it; and he
knew when to hold his tongue. "We shall see what you can do tomorrow," he said. Negrete, too, was soldier enough not to promise more
than he could perform. He looked at Zaragoza peering at him crypti-
cally through his spectacles and said nothing, but he left the room
haunted by those owlish words. On his way out he was accosted by an
eavesdropper who caught his ear and warned him that he had been
given command of the forts "to bear the responsibility of the defeat
which they will inflict on us tomorrow." Signs of the same spirit multiplied on his path. Where there are owls there are eavesdroppers, and
his brother officers, crowding around him like night birds flocking together, pressed on his heels to derive what encouragement they could
from his company, one of them wondering where they would be running at that time tomorrow, another swearing that he was no soldier,
a third doubting this, a fourth running down that, and there were reasons enough to support the defeatists. Puebla was, as Lorencez said, the
city most hostile to Juarez in Mexico; the information was correct, and
a double defense had to be sustained—against the enemy within and
without the walls. The forts were the frontiers of Mexico on May 5.

After the battle Negrete turned in a report which differed sharply from
the glowing accounts of his colleagues and was colored by such glaring
denigration of their conduct that it was not accepted by the Minister of
War. Negrete replied cynically that the official version was made up at
headquarters and that he would sign it and send him another from
which the facts of the action were omitted. Backbiting was buried,
however, in the common credit which all the commanders derived
from the action—Negrete for his stout defense of the forts, Berriozabal (the officer who thought himself no soldier) for the stubborn support he lent him on the Cerro, Diaz and Alvarez for the strenuous cavalry charges that disrupted the French lines, and Zaragoza for his
successful control of an attack which caught him by surprise, for he expected it from the south, and his rapid reorganization of the defense.
The result was too unexpected not to be intoxicating, and some of his
officers hailed it hyperbolically. "The French eagles have crossed the
seas to drop the laurels of Sebastopol, Magenta, and Solferino at the
foot of the Mexican flag," Berriozabal declared in an order of the day
congratulating his troops. "You have fought the first soldiers of the

day, and you have been the first to conquer them." Zaragoza was more sober. His report to the Minister of War was a little more than taciturn and a little less than laconic, and his style strictly attuned to the truth. "The French army fought with great bravery; the Commander-in-Chief conducted the attack incompetently. The national arms have been covered with glory. . . . I can state with pride that not once, during the long struggle which it sustained, did the Mexican army turn its back on the enemy." In this tribute the French professed to see as much surprise as pride; but that was to be expected. What really surprised Zaragoza was the blunder of Lorencez; and he was unable to profit by it fully.

During the battle he was obliged to remain on the defensive. Numerically, his effectives hardly surpassed those of the French (4852 as against 4474), and as their capacity to meet European troops in the field had been severely tried at Aculzingo, he was careful not to jeopardize the victory by the counterattack which Lorencez awaited for two days; but he was by no means satisfied with a defensive triumph and he bided his time only long enough to secure resources and reinforcements from the capital and to await the return of the cavalry that he had detached for the pursuit of Marquez before taking the offensive. "As for money, nothing can be done here, because these people are bad and, above all, lazy and selfish," he reported to the government on the day after the French withdrew. "How good it would be to burn Puebla! The city is mourning the event of the 5th. It is sad to say so, but it is a regrettable truth." From the capital he received thirty thousand pesos, enough to cover his expenses for ten days, and in the first week of June, when he was joined by Gonzalez Ortega with six thousand fresh troops from Zacatecas, he left Puebla and descended the Cumbres, fourteen thousand strong, to besiege Orizaba and force the French back to the sea, where the guerrillas and the yellow fever were rapidly decimating the little garrison in Veracruz.

On June 12 General Lorencez received a communication from the enemy which silenced his quarrel with Saligny. "I have sufficient grounds to believe, sir, that you and the officers under your command have sent the Emperor a protest against the conduct of the Minister Saligny," Zaragoza wrote him, "for having misled you into an expedition against a people that was the best friend of the French nation." The note, written from a village ten miles away, offered him an honorable capitulation on the basis of the evacuation of Mexican territory within a specified time. Lorencez replied in a note even more sparing of superfluous words, rejecting the overture but tacitly confirming its tenor. "The Commander-in-Chief of the French forces in Mexico not being invested with political powers by his government, which has conferred them entirely on M. de Saligny, it is impossible to enter on the way of negotiations proposed by General Zaragoza. The Minister of

France alone is empowered to receive overtures of this nature." This was the literal truth, and his style was cramped by it. He smarted in silence, but the breach with Saligny was closed and backbiting buried in the face of the enemy. A similar proposal was addressed by Gonzalez Ortega to the Minister, who, naturally, wasted no words on it at all. The dignity of France demanded his silence. Lorencez himself replied only to gain time. He condescended to notice the diplomatic advances of the enemy because they caught him by surprise in an open and unfortified town in which he was bottled up with a garrison of two thousand four hundred men and the French Minister. Barricades were hastily built and earthworks thrown up, and while he borrowed his defenses from Zaragoza he recalled the contingents which he had sent to fight the guerrillas and to protect his line of communications with Veracruz. The arrival on the night of June 13 of three hundred fresh troops who had just landed from France brought a welcome reinforcement, for on the same night Zaragoza began the investment of Orizaba.

The situation was critical. In his haste Lorencez had neglected to occupy the Cerro Borrego, a mountain overhanging the town. The position was apparently inaccessible, a sheer bluff four hundred feet high, rising vertically from the floor of the valley and clad in impenetrable timber, but at ten o'clock a movement was noticed on the summit, and orders were immediately given to master it before the enemy. At midnight a captain and seventy-five men set out to recover the position. The night was pitch-black and masked the impossible feat from the French as well as the enemy. After climbing hand over hand for an hour and a half, the party paused on the first shelf they found long enough to catch their breath between the abyss below and the bluff overhead. Level with the even layers of the night, they were masters of a horizon bounded by their hearing alone, the darkness and the undergrowth were too dense to see more than a few feet ahead, and they hung there until they heard a noise overhead. Supposing that some natives of Orizaba had sought refuge on the mountain, for the presence of the enemy at that pitch was as improbable as their own, the captain sent his scouts ahead to investigate; but they were met with a blaze of fire, and the attack began perpendicularly. When he caught up with his scouts, he found himself in the thick of an obscure vegetation of human forms struggling to recover a cannon. His three scouts lay wounded and winded, clinging to it with the tenacity of the dizzy, hugging the first solid mass they had mastered and flattening themselves on it. He cleared the ledge before the bulk of his forces succeeded in scaling it and continued the ascent blindly, guided by the invisible retreat of the enemy, who disputed the ground equally stubbornly and equally blindly. An hour later he reached the base of the summit. Here he called a halt and took cover under the thickening fire, fearing to discover his small numbers, and trusting that his trail blazing had been heard in Orizaba. It was impossible either to retreat or advance; either way it was none o'clock for his party; and for an hour more he drew a rain of lead into the bush. At three-thirty he was relieved by the arrival of reinforcements, who had followed the din of distress signals up the mountainside and who doubled his strength. With these he stormed the crest, routed the defenders with a bayonet charge, and fell badly wounded but master of the Borrego.

On the following morning Orizaba awoke to a startling scene. "As the first light of morning stole over the slopes of the Cerro, it revealed a spectacle of striking horror," wrote an officer who visited it. "To the west, about a hundred meters below the first ledge, a rocky platform which the plateau overhangs, we could see a heap of corpses that had been broken in their fall; farther on, lifeless limbs hanging from the notches of the rock and faces that still preserved in death an expression of profound terror; here a wounded wretch vainly trying to lift two corpses before their weight crushed him; there a soldier caught in his fall by a branch that held him suspended over the precipice, turning his eyes on us in terror and appeal"—and Mexicans all of them. More startling yet were the results of that grim night's work when the reckoning was made. One hundred and fifty French had wrested the mountain from two thousand Mexicans with a ratio of losses that had now become customary in such encounters. The picked troops of Ortega who had occupied the Borrego had fled, leaving two hundred dead or wounded, two hundred prisoners, a regimental flag, and three pieces of artillery in the hands of the French, who carried the position at the cost of two killed and twenty-eight wounded. The temerity of the attack amazed the French themselves when they reviewed it by daylight. "If we had had exact information as to the forces which occupied the Cerro Borrego, we would never have attempted to dislodge the enemy with so few people," another officer said. "The success, due to the really exceptional vigor of Captain Détrie, was only possible thanks to the darkness of the night, which prevented the enemy from seeing with how few troops he was dealing, and which concealed the difficulties and dangers of the undertaking from the assailants. Had the Mexicans succeeded in holding this position, which General de Lorencez had not thought it necessary to include in his line of defense, it is doubtful whether the French army would have been able to maintain itself in Orizaba."

Captain Détrie was cited, decorated, and promoted for his spectacular exploit, and the Commander-in-Chief paid full tribute to it in his report. "Unfortunately, M. le Maréchal," he wrote, "the combat on the Borrego cannot be described; but when one has seen the positions and gained an idea of the difficulties overcome in the darkness of the night by climbing them oneself, one cannot but proclaim the heroism of this handful of valiant soldiers." The service which they had rendered him was recognized as the day wore on. It was no casual feat of arms. The battle of Orizaba was fought and won on the Cerro del Borrego. The importance which Zaragoza attached to that position was betrayed when he found its guns trained on his own troops; after shelling the town for twelve hours he raised the siege and beat his way back through the mountains, leaving a long trail of reports borne by deserters that he had great difficulty in preventing his troops from disbanding.

On the next morning a proclamation appeared in Orizaba. "Mexicans! Two great events occurred yesterday in the approaches to this town. The army of Juarez, commanded by the demagogic leaders most famous for their crimes against society, presented itself with threats on its lips and had the impudence to send an arrogant summons to the courageous and chivalrous Commander-in-Chief of the French forces. The most complete defeat inflicted by one hundred and fifty soldiers of the 99th of the Line under the orders of the intrepid and honorable Captain Détrie on four thousand men of the famous division of Zacatecas has been the answer of the army of the Emperor of the French to the hordes of vandals who thought to intimidate it. Profiting by the darkness of the night, Zaragoza has furtively raised his camp, which he dared to pitch in the face of ours with the most arrogant aspect of hostility, and is withdrawing today in disorder and precipitately, closely pursued by the national cavalry, and is going to recross the Cumbres de Aculzingo for the fourth time, and with as much shame as before. Mexicans! The same fate awaits them as often as they dare to face the invincible French army and the enthusiasm of the national army: for these defend the cause of independence and Mexican nationality, and those that of pillage and barbarism. Place your faith, therefore, in the Franco-Mexican army and in your compatriot. . . ." The proclamation was signed by Almonte. Not all the carrion birds were perched on the Borrego, and Captain Détrie deserved better for securing it than the hooting of Almonte. But the son of Morelos was once more on a mountain. The French made no attempt to pursue Zaragoza. Satisfied with the truce which his retreat assured them, and the perch which their eagles had won on the Borrego, they settled down in Orizaba to sit out the rainy season and await the reinforcements required to carry them back to Puebla.

8

POLITICALLY, the repulse at Puebla was a fatal triumph for Mexico. Traveling with the proverbial speed of bad news, the first reports reached Paris in the middle of June and produced a shock that fired public feeling at the expense of public opinion. There was an immediate demand to redeem the national honor, and where vanity and honor were synonymous the way to redeem it was open to no doubt. The Corps Législatif voted reinforcements, financial credits, confidence in the Throne, and despite the strenuous protests of the Opposition and a stiff fight put up by Jules Favre, the session ended in overwhelming acclamations for the flag and cheers for the Emperor. What censure there was—and it was the more severe for being private—was reserved for the Empress, to whom the expedition was generally attributed.

The Emperor moved rapidly to repair the disaster. His first thought was for the morale of the army, and on June 15 he wrote a sympathetic note to Lorencez, congratulating him on the brilliant action at Aculzingo and regretting "the non-success of the attack upon Puebla," which he minimized. "Such are the fortunes of war, and occasional reverses sometimes cloud brilliant successes; but do not lose heart; the honor of the country is involved, and you will be supported by all the reinforcements you need," he assured him. "Express to the troops under your command my complete satisfaction with their courage and perseverance in enduring fatigues and privations. The farther away they are, the more I care for them. I have approved your conduct, although it does not seem to be understood by everyone. You were right to protect General Almonte; since we are at war with the existing government of Mexico, anyone who seeks shelter under our flag will have the same right to our protection, but this must not influence our future policy in any way. It is contrary to my interests, my origin, and my principles to impose a government of any kind on the Mexican people. Let them choose in complete freedom the form they desire; I ask nothing but good faith in foreign relations, and I want but one thing, the happiness and independence of that beautiful country under a stable and regular government."

A fortnight later, however, when the details of the affair of the 5th of May had been revealed to the public, the Minister of War wrote to Lorencez: "I have just received an order from the Emperor which obliges me to send you the following observations. The Emperor admires the courage shown by the troops in the attack upon Puebla, but His Majesty does not feel that the attack was well timed; the artillery should not have gone into action against fortifications at a distance of two thousand five hundred meters. The Emperor recommends that you remain on good terms with M. de Saligny, who is his representative in Mexico, as well as with General Almonte and the other Mexican leaders who are joining us. General Forey will soon assume the supreme command; until then confine yourself to organizing the resistance and your supplies."

General Forey was a veteran of the Crimean and Italian campaigns, but in spite of his experience the Emperor gave him a few pointers of an elementary nature, advising him to attack only in open country and by surprise and to observe extreme prudence whenever the enemy was lodged in fortified places. These professional tips would have had some point had they been addressed to Lorencez, but Forey was prudence itself; dependable, competent, methodical, he always did just what was expected of him and was incapable of surprising anyone. Napoleon left nothing to chance, however. He captured Puebla for him on the map, directing him to avoid the forts of Guadalupe and Loreto and to concentrate on the other side of the city. "An attack on the Carmen has always succeeded in the civil wars," he noted, "and an attack on the barricades will be much less deadly than a siege of the above-mentioned buttresses"; and as the expedition could no longer be treated as a military promenade, he devoted a day in Fontainebleau—July 3, 1862—to going over the whole groundwork again in a long personal letter outlining his ideas as of that date and containing specific political, military, and diplomatic instructions for the new Commander-in-Chief.

There was one precaution, however, which Napoleon failed to take. His confidence in M. de Saligny was unshaken. "As M. de Saligny is the only one who knows the country well," he wrote, "and who is informed of the grievances to be redressed, it is important and even indispensable that the Commander-in-Chief enter into intimate relations with him and profit by his experience and advice. I do not know whether the private character of M. de Saligny leaves something to be desired; I cannot say with what intemperance of language he may be reproached; but what I do know, and what I highly declare, is that ever since the beginning of the expedition to Mexico, his despatches have been earmarked by the good sense, firmness, and dignity of France, and I have no doubt that if his advice had been followed our flag would be floating over Mexico today. People say that he has misled the government as to the state of affairs in Mexico; on the contrary, he has always told me the truth, as I am glad to recognize. He never claimed that the Mexican people were enthusiastic and energetic enough to rid themselves of the government that oppresses them; but he always maintained that, once we had penerated into the interior of the country, we would find friendly inhabitants. The proof that he is right is that, after the check of the 5th of May, as I see by a report of the Prussian Consul in Puebla to his government, the city of Puebla was in dismay on the morrow of our failure; that, silent and sad, it was far from sharing the joy of the Mexican troops. I know, by letters from Puebla, that more than ten persons were shot to cow those who, like them, dared to demonstrate in our favor. I know, by a score of letters from Mexico that have passed under my eyes (among them the reports of the Ministers of Prussia and Belgium), that before the 5th of May the government was stunned, and that the population awaited us impatiently as liberators. Consequently, General de Lorencez was not misled by the reports of M. de Saligny and General Almonte. . . . I do not hold it against General de Lorencez that he failed, anyone can make mistakes, but I do reproach him for casting the blame on those who do not deserve it. . . . In fact, it is by tensions and quarrels of vanity that everything has been compromised at the start in Mexico. I want no more of them; they do too much harm to the success of great projects. The reply of General de Lorencez, which I shall not characterize, to the insolent summons of Zaragoza has produced a deplorable effect, as has the observation by the enemy of the dissensions prevailing between the general staff, M. de Saligny, and General Almonte."

Politically, also, the expedition was recast. For the Emperor the most favorable result of the repulse at Puebla was the inflammation of national feeling in France, but though the public temper had been excited, public opinion was still passive. The expedition was unpopular. The reports of the *procureurs*—a class of officials created to sound public opinion in the provinces—all told the same tale. The *procureur* in Agen, writing in April, reported that "the Mexican expedition preoccupies public opinion rather unpleasantly; it is admitted to be indispensable after the injuries and spoliations that our nationals have suffered, but those injuries and spoliations are not very well known; a single striking fact, and one that would touch the national susceptibilities directly, would excite the country far more than this mass of obscure and anonymous grievances. This expedition is regarded, therefore, as a serious risk from which neither profit nor glory is expected; and as for the romantic side of the question, our wars in China and elsewhere have amply satisfied our fondness for emotions, and as we are concerned with finances today, we are less inclined to be tempted by the extraordinary, which is always very expensive." The commercial and imperial glamour with which the *procureur* of Nancy tried to float the idea in his department met with the same response there. "Whatever may be the future importance of the practical advantages which

the success of our arms in China and Cochin-China has already assured
us, and which the Mexican expedition promises, these attempts at colonization in fertile countries where the moral and commercial strength
of France can obtain a lasting and unlimited expansion excite our
country minds very little," he wrote. "They do not sufficiently understand that the development and future power of modern peoples depend not only on their influence on the Continent, but also on those
vast enterprises that have made England so great a nation in the
world." The concensus of opinion, from province to province, reflected
the same caution, ranging from indifference to incomprehension. In
sum, the French were a homekeeping, unenterprising people, not as
backward as the Mexicans, but not unlike them in their response to intervention in Mexico, blind to its glory, apathetic to its profit, mystified
by its ostensible aims, and anxious only to be left in peace. They needed
prodding, and the repulse at Puebla was the first single striking fact
that touched the national susceptibilities directly. For the moment, all
objections were overborne by the cry of *revanche;* but it was the avenging of the expedition, and not the expedition itself, that was popular in
France. The time had now come, therefore, for the Emperor, as *procureur*-in-chief, to explain the ultimate purpose of the enterprise. The
conquest of Mexico could not be conducted by correspondence nor
even by intelligent subordinates, unless they understood his aims, and
consequently he took Forey into his confidence and initiated him into
his fundamental idea.

"There will be plenty of people who will ask you why we are spending money and men to place an Austrian prince on the throne," he
continued. "In the present state of world civilization, the prosperity of
America is not a matter of indifference to Europe, since it is America
that feeds our industry and offers a livelihood to our trade. It is to our
interest that the Republic of the United States should be powerful and
prosperous, but not that she should gain control of the whole Gulf of
Mexico, dominate the Antilles and South America from there, and be
the sole dispenser of the products of the New World. Mistress of Mexico, and consequently of Central America and the passage between the
two oceans, there would no longer be any other power in America but
that of the United States. If, on the other hand, Mexico gains her independence and maintains the integrity of her territory, if a stable government is set up there by the arms of France, we shall have built an
impassable dam against the encroachments of the United States and
maintained the independence of our colonies in the Antilles and those
of thankless Spain; we shall have extended our beneficent influence in
the center of America, and that influence will spread north and south,
create countless outlets for our commerce, and secure us the raw materials indispensable to our industry. As for the prince who might as-
cend the throne of Mexico, he will always be forced to act in the inter-

est of France, not only as a matter of gratitude, but, above all, because
the interests of his new country will be in accord with ours, and he
will not even be able to maintain himself except by our influence. Thus
it is that today our military honor, which is engaged, the needs of our
politics, the interests of our commerce and industry, all combine to
make it our duty to march upon Mexico, to plant our flag there boldly,
and to establish either a monarchy, if it is not incompatible with the
national sentiment of the country, or a government with some promise
at least of stability."

The diplomatic line which Forey was to follow was also laid down
for him in detail. He was to issue a proclamation, the ideas of which
Napoleon furnished him, to welcome Almonte and all other well-dis-
posed Mexicans, to espouse the quarrel of no party, to declare that
everything was provisional, to display respect for religion but to reassure the holders of nationalized property, to make the Mexican auxiliary troops play the principal part in battle, and to repress vigorously
every word or act offensive to Mexican pride, it being of the utmost
importance to secure the good will of the people and to second them
in the establishment of a government of their own choice. In conclusion, and in words laden with the full weight of the confidence which
he placed in him, the Emperor reminded General Forey that "the farther away an expedition is, the more must it be conducted with a well-
calculated blend of boldness and caution. . . . A cannon shot in Mexico is a hundred times more precious than in France. What I blame
absolutely in the recent affair in Puebla is having spent a thousand
round of cannon shot in a position and at a distance where artillery
could produce no effect."

The most penetrating result of the repulse at Puebla was the development of the Napoleonic idea. The original plan was unchanged, but
the elements were recombined so as to bring out the dominant aim,
giving more prominence to what had remained latent and relegating
to the background what had loomed so large in the first embryonic
version of intervention. The monarchical question was subordinated
to the establishment of a French protectorate in any viable form, and
Maximilian to the modifications imposed by a larger and looser policy,
flexible enough to meet any eventuality; the impractical notion of a political deal in Europe was replaced by the valid idea of a trade war between Europe and America for the division of world markets; and the
visionary trade of the Veneto was discarded in favor of an economic
crusade in the interest of France. The chimerical fancies of the Mexican monarchists faded into an idea which gave fundamental force and
a real *raison d'être* to French intervention, the whole scheme assumed
a broader scope, a basic clarity and substantial design, and a larger
perspective: the Mexican adventure, in a word, was a lever to move the
world. The letter to Forey contained merely the germs of the idea,

however; the full flavor was reserved for the intimates of the Emperor. His ultimate aim, in the words of an initiate, was "to reconstitute the Compagnie des Indes, leaving Mexico her autonomy, consecrated and fortified by a French protectorate." To all the other revenges of time which inspired the political combinations of Napoleon was now added the idea of avenging the loss of the East Indies to England by the re-creation of a colonial realm in the West, of recovering in the nineteenth century the position which France had forfeited in the eighteenth, and of redeeming his historic mission by bringing the Second Empire abreast of the modern world and making it the great colonizing and commercial power which England had become in a hundred years—an idea which Guizot described exactly as Napoleon conceived it as "the greatest work of the century."

And certainly it was no mean undertaking to challenge the established supremacy of England, on the one hand, and the growing competition of America, on the other, at so late a date in the race for world markets. Napoleon had been careful, however, to challenge neither of his competitors overtly and had pursued his object with that blend of boldness and caution which he impressed upon Forey as the indispensable condition of distant expeditions in his first tentative experiments in the reconquest of colonial empire. Training his hand in China and Cochin-China, associating himself with the English in Pekin and with the Spanish in Annam, he had co-operated with his competitors and found the formula which served him so well in launching the Mexican expedition. The tripartite Convention was a combination which protected him against the two partners who had lost their colonies in the New World, and which checked the Americans temporarily, and when the alliance broke down the initial stages of the enterprise had already been covered. With the withdrawal of England and Spain, and the paralysis of the United States, the time had come to move boldly.

But there were other hazards still to be eliminated. The internal liabilities were as serious as the foreign risks. To unite the nation in support of the venture, it was necessary to overcome the apathy, the caution, the conservatism of the French. It was necessary for the Emperor, more farsighted than his people, to become an enlightened promoter and to sell them the salvation to which they were averse and the adventure at which they balked. It was necessary to convince and convert the various sectors of public opinion upon which the Empire was built —the peasantry who were its conservative cornerstone and who supported it on the promise that the Empire meant peace; the petty bourgeois who were impervious to delusions of grandeur; the industrialists satisfied with small enterprise; the militarists who responded readily to the legend of Napoleonic glory, but only on the Continent; the Clericals who were irritated by the equivocal policy in Italy; the Liberals who dreaded its extension to Mexico; the Republicans, the Legitimists, the Orleanists, the parliamentary Opposition—the whole heterogenous mass of critics who constituted the regime. It was necessary, in sum, to unite the nation in an enterprise which represented the synthesis of all the antitheses upon which the Empire was founded and the consummation of all the combinations through which it functioned. But the Emperor was a past master at such combinations, and the moment was propitious. The rupture of the triple alliance had irritated the country against the Allies that had deserted it in the hour of danger: the English were blamed for leaving the French in the lurch, the Spanish for abandoning their natural protectors and abetting the British, and the reverse at Puebla, which fired this resentment and fused the national feeling in a demand for revenge, was a fortunate defeat.

The energy necessary to promote the enterprise had been tapped, but the resources to float it had still to be found. Intervention had now reverted to its original economic basis, and the capacity of France to supply the driving power alone was doubtful. On that basis the triple alliance had broken down under its own weight. Three Powers of a highly unequal degree of industrial development had united for a common and incompatible purpose; the most advanced and the most backward had combined against the middle, and the axis had broken where it was weakest. Midway between both in commercial and industrial development, French economy was ill prepared to sustain a prolonged exertion of national expansion, and the capital to consolidate had to be found, not at the bottom, but at the top, of the economic structure—in the sphere of *la haute finance,* the bank and the stock market and the fevers of speculation on which the Empire was booming, with periodic collapses. The enterprise was a vast speculation by its nature and methods alike, and it was necessary to induce the public to subscribe to the new Compagnie des Indes on the prospect of untold and untapped wealth to be exploited in Mexico. This part of the campaign the Emperor entrusted to professional promoters and specialists, who explored the various phases and expounded the cultural, political, and economic lines of the undertaking. Learned articles on the natural resources of Mexico and the openings for colonization and investment began to burgeon in the press, and budding theories about the French nation as the natural protector of the Latin and Catholic races, and inspired interpretations of the expedition that painted its material and moral returns in terms ever more glowing, far-reaching, and inflated. A French engineer whom the Emperor consulted on the possible output of the Mexican mines was amazed to find that Napoleon knew next to nothing about Mexico. Of the geography of the country he was so ignorant that he believed Puebla, a city of eighty thousand souls, to be a *bourgade sans importance;* of the mentality of the inhabitants he had no notion at all. Perceiving that Napoleon was working in the blind, and supplied

with "data deplorably vague or completely erroneous about a country
that had interested him so long," the engineer attempted to put him
on his guard against dangerous illusions; but in vain. A little knowledge was worse than none at all, Napoleon was on the defensive, and
the only satisfaction which the expert derived from the interview was
the assurance he received from the Foreign Office that the candidacy
of Maximilian had been abandoned.

The dimensions which the idea had assumed in the mind of the
Emperor made it more important than ever, therefore, that he be able
to rely on accurate information from his agents in Mexico. "We have
no one for us here," Lorencez wrote to the Minister of War. "The
moderate party does not exist. The reactionary party, reduced to
nothing, is odious. I have not met a single partisan of monarchy." —
"The Emperor has been shamefully deceived by his minister M. de
Saligny, or others, about the situation of the country," wrote a staff
officer. "We are sustaining a cause which has not and cannot have
partisans; we have with us people like Almonte, Miranda, and others,
who are an object of horror in the country and who make us hated
even by our own nationals. Were we fifty thousand we would enter
everywhere, we would enter Mexico City, but we would not have a
single partisan." But what was an army against a mind reader? Among
all the liabilities of the expedition, not the least was the partiality of
the Emperor for M. de Saligny; and it was inevitable. The colossal
assurance of the Minister whose reports and promises, belied though
they were by experience and refuted by facts, flattered and facilitated
the *idée fixe* of Napoleon was well founded. By feeding his infatuation,
Saligny had made himself indispensable to a man who was bound by
his obsession to believe what he wished to believe, and henceforth his
credit was unassailable. The talebearer whose flair divined, and whose
zeal secured, intervention was supported by the mightiest of all mortal
forces: he had identified himself with a dream. He had nursed it, he
had mastered the mind of the Emperor, and he sucked his marrow.

The expeditionary force left Paris in the last days of July. As
General Forey was about to board the train for Cherbourg, his aide-
de-camp handed him the card of a person who had been persistently
attempting to approach him through the throng of officials gathered
on the platform of the station. The card bore the name of a M. de
Montluc and was covered with scribbled explanations; neither the
one nor the other conveyed anything to the Commander-in-Chief. It
was not that he had no memory for names or that he was unfamiliar
with the history of France. Montluc had been one of the great names
of France in the fifteenth century, but in the nineteenth it was unknown to the Tuileries. Old names that had suffered the ravages of
the ages belonged in the musty salons of the Faubourg Saint-Germain,

which Forey did not frequent. Nevertheless, he advanced to meet his importunate visitor, who identified himself as the Consul-General of Mexico in France and begged the favor of a few minutes' attention. The connection was too curious not to catch it. M. de Montluc took his card from the hand of the Commander-in-Chief and read him its contents. On learning of the repulse at Puebla, he repeated, he felt it his duty to inform the Emperor of the entire truth; he deplored from the bottom of his heart the false and exaggerated reports which had brought the two countries to the present state of hostilities, and he hoped that General Forey would have the good fortune to reopen negotiations. Time was pressing, and he had just enough left to add one word more. He made no reference to M. de Saligny, for he was the friend who had pleaded the Liberal cause with him before he left France, but he did mention the unfortunate interference of Almonte. "But General Almonte is not called to take any part in this expedition," the Commander-in-Chief objected. "He has been much too quick as it is to take an active part in it." — "I am happy to hear you say that, General," M. de Montluc replied. "I am a Frenchman, I want to see my country's flag carried high, but I am in duty bound to observe that M. Almonte is a diplomat who has long been absent from his country, which he does not know, and that he has led His Majesty into error; he is henceforth without credit." Forey thanked him for his information, bowed, and boarded the train.

The whistle blew and the train pulled out, leaving behind it a group of idle officials wondering who the old bird was and where he had been so long. M. de Montluc went home, but not to the Faubourg Saint-Germain, for his name had undergone the adventures of the ages. He had been in trade, and having made a respectable fortune in Mexico many years ago, he felt in honor bound to do what he could for the country that had put him on his feet in France. He summed up what he had done in a conscientious report to Doblado. He had not been idle. He had made repeated attempts to reach the Emperor, but, having no influence at the Tuileries, he had fared no better than if his name had been M. de la Fuente. He had written a letter, rehearsing the familiar fallacies of intervention; but there was no answer. He had written another, recalling the experience of the Americans whose expedition in 1846 cost them five million francs and fifty million men; still there was no answer. He had enlisted the help of a friend, who secured an entree at the Tuileries and who returned with information. The letters had not been received, and the Emperor had been very much surprised to learn of them; he had asked for the name and position of the writer. A summons was expected; but the summons never came. The Emperor left for Vichy, and he followed him there with his friend. They presented their cards at the Imperial villa; they were not received. He returned to Paris and rushed to the home of General Forey at nine in the morning of July 28. The General had just left for the station, and he followed him there just in time to say Almonte and see him off. He still hoped, however, that Mexico would have no cause to complain of the new Commander-in-Chief. "He is a man of decision, brave and intrepid, nothing will stop him and he will be stern on the battlefield," he wrote. "But his bearing is noble and dignified, and he seems incapable of a dishonorable act or of breaking his word, for his physiognomy expresses both a great goodness and a great loyalty. By his respectable and martial physique I well understand the empire he exercises over the soldier, and I am not surprised that he has so often led his troops to victory in our late war against Austria in Italy." And to be perfectly honest himself, he added: "The worst service one can render a government is to leave it in error; it is my strict duty, therefore, to express myself frankly to Your Excellency, and I must add that in my opinion, if you do not influence the determinations of the Commander-in-Chief, Mexico will find in him an enemy to be feared, but an enemy both just and generous."

M. de Montluc represented Mexico very well at that moment. The abrupt termination of his five minutes' talk with Forey left nothing to add to it. He had neither the facilities nor the faculties to divine the scope and purpose of intervention. He had been running industriously after the beginning of the adventure, and in aiming at Almonte and appealing to Forey he was still clinging to the dummies and subordinates. He missed the whole train of events and motives that made its destination inevitable. There was nothing further which he could add to the note which he had written to Juarez ten days before. "I think that I have done my duty. I should not have done it completely, however, if I hesitated to tell Your Excellency that there is but one voice in the whole of the Empire saying that, in the present circumstances, the honor of France demands that the troops reach Mexico City. Like the Americans in 1847, the Imperial Government believes it due to its dignity to sign a peace treaty there and there only. God grant that Your Excellency's Government may succeed in signing a peace so desirable on terms worthy of the two nations!" He was sincerely distressed, but his name was, after all, Montluc.

What M. de Montluc could not add, however, Juarez did. In a note which crossed that of his pedigreed representative in Paris and answered it, he thanked him for his exertions and invited him to desist from them. "We must be under no delusions, my dear sir," he wrote. "There is a deliberate intention on the part of the Imperial Government to humiliate Mexico and impose its will upon us. This is a truth confirmed by facts; there is no help but defense. The Mexican people are resolved upon it, and their government will employ every means permitted by international law in self-defense. The arrival of new and numerous troops has caused no fear or discouragement; on the contrary, it has revived public spirit, and today there is but one sentiment in the whole country, the defense of the liberty and independence of Mexico. The Imperial Government will cause us great damages and great misfortunes; such are the inevitable consequences of war; but I can assure you—I who see and feel with my finger the determination of my countrymen—that whatever elements may be employed against us, the Imperial Government will not obtain the submission of the Mexicans, and that its armies will not have a single day of rest."

The relentlessness of the conflict and the irrelevance of the truth were fully realized in Mexico. In August the press reprinted the speech in which M. Billault, the spokesman for the Throne, replying to the attacks of the Opposition, produced the reports of the Prussian Minister in Mexico as proof of the demand for a monarchy there and the impatience with which the French expedition was awaited in the capital. The systematic misrepresentation of facts had not abated with the departure of M. de Saligny; it had merely passed to a diplomat who acted as his deputy and who improved on his principal. The Prussian Minister, who had assumed charge of French, English, and Spanish nationals when the Allies invaded Mexico, seconded his French colleague so ably that the passing of Saligny seemed to be an optical delusion. The claims which he presented for imaginary injuries and exemption from forced loans tried the patience of the government, but they were borne with equanimity as a routine irritation until it became clear that Baron Wagner had joined the belligerents and was using his position to promote French propaganda.

Though no official notice was taken of the disclosure, there was one man in Mexico who could not curb his indignation; but his name was not Juarez. Ignacio Altamirano, the deputy who had led the opposition of the Fifty-One to the President a year before, rushed into print with a pamphlet attacking the Prussian Minister and demanding his expulsion from the country. The Baron was the straw that broke his back, because he was the surplus of a system, and it was the system that he attacked in the man. The pamphlet was reckless, the times were desperate, and the writer minced no words. Ripping away the proprieties, he plunged his pen into a sore from which the country had suffered too long in silence, and reviewing the abuse of diplomatic privilege, which had become customary and accepted in Mexico, and which had borne such terrible fruit, deplored the type of diplomatic agent whom European governments invariably sent to Spanish America and to Mexico in particular—"their scant diplomatic intelligence, their ruinous passions of the market place, or their total ignorance of our affairs"—as the source of the situation in 1862. The few honorable exceptions—a Prim or a Wyke—only confirmed the rule; the average was "some poor petty consul who has spent his whole life registering

deaths, marriages, and commercial transactions in Algiers or Martinique, or a pen-pusher in some subordinate office, or a noble without
a shirt, escaped from Clichy. With such antecedents it is not easy to
possess that profundity of calculation which makes of a diplomat an
augur, or that probity which proves him a gentleman, or that local
knowledge which makes him familiar with the country to which he is
accredited"; nor was it surprising that the majority, "as soon as they
reach Veracruz, become our tyrants, our spies, and the heads of our
conservative conspiracies," since the ineptitude of the many fitted them
only to ape the few who, more malicious than stupid, "come to our
Republic to foment with their influence our intestinal feuds, to be-
smirch our people industriously, and all to favor their dishonest aims,
or to make themselves interesting to their governments, or even to
others than their own." The category in which the Baron belonged
was not doubtful. "As for the denunciations that he has made to the
French Government of new crimes committed by the Mexican Government," Altamirano concluded, "there is no need to say more to
Mr. Wagner than these words to which, if he is sensitive, he will
listen: enumerate the facts, prove them, or you lie!" And with that
challenge went one to his own government. "To leave him alone, to
contemplate his conduct in silence when it is positively proven, is
tacitly to approve his calumnies and to rate the dignity of the nation
very low. In any event, Mr. Wagner may be sure, in spite of his good
wishes, that far from sighing for intervention and a monarchy, Mexico will defend its independence, and that it is not unlikely that we
may give a yet sterner lesson to the soldiers of the French despot; for
though our troops are not veterans, though they are subject to privations, though they are no match in military antecedents for the French
troops, they are defending the liberty of their country, and when that
happens the peoples perform miracles. As Prussia should know, that
still blushes for Valmy."

The reply was prompt and Prussian. Two members of the Legation called on Altamirano. They were shown into his study, where,
after a few words, one of them pulled on a brass knuckle and swung
at him. As a table stood between them, he missed and was seized by
a servant, who subdued him and allowed Altamirano to escape and
call the police. The police, knowing the meaning of diplomatic immunity, arrested the servant. The pugilist proved to be the nephew
of the Prussian Minister, and the Minister was sensitive enough to
disavow the aggression; but he demanded satisfaction for the pamphlet and threatened the government with blackmail if he failed to receive it. His protest was automatically supported by the entire diplomatic corps. The affair was settled by official routine. The criminal
case was dropped into the lap of the law for prolonged and inconclusive investigation, and the pamphlet was suppressed by the govern-

ment. As for Altamirano, he found some satisfaction in showing his face in public to prove that it had not been bruised by the mailed fist. But Altamirano was as far behind the times, in fact, as Montluc. Baron Wagner and Saligny and Almonte—they belonged to a bygone day. They were part of the prehistoric period of aggression and had survived its antediluvian age; they were merely incidental to the evolution of an idea that had long since dwarfed and outgrown them. Diplomatic squirts no longer mattered. No one mattered but Napoleon. The nephew of the uncle, as the English called him, now wore the brass knuckles, and nothing could arrest him but his own destiny.

That was the one hope for Mexico in the summer of 1862, and a remote one. "Too much has been said, and said officially," Juarez wrote to Montluc, "to prove the good disposition which the Mexican Government had, and still has, to honor all the just claims of France and to terminate the differences between the two countries by just and equitable treaties, but everything has miscarried. They do not want to hear us and they accept as truth only the calumnies and the information that hatred and interest conceive against us." Nevertheless, he still believed that truth would triumph in time, "for you are right in thinking," he added, "that as soon as they are undeceived and have judged us, the unjust war which they are waging against us will cease." He, too, was far behind the growth of events and blind to their fatality, but he was also ahead of the times. Where there was so much hatred, there must be some love of truth as well; time would tell. But he recognized that words were no weapon. The truth about Mexico would never be known without blows. Zaragoza had spoken for Mexico in the only language that the French understood. Words were welcome, words were powerful, when they were the words of fearless friends like Jules Favre or Edgar Quinet, who had stated the case of Mexico in France with ringing eloquence; both were stout haters of sham patriotism and had braved current prejudices with words that were blows. In the echoes of the lone tribune in the Legislature and the tirades of Edgar Quinet that came winging their way across the ocean, the resonance of the repulse at Puebla had never been more sound, but both had been drowned in the din of patriotic hysteria. Hope there was, however, a distant, desperate, but guiding hope, in the words with which Quinet linked the destinies of France, Mexico, and Napoleon. "Under absolutist government," he concluded his arraignment of the Emperor, "to cover the initial error has always been called 'saving the flag.' Here we have another trait of the Bonaparte spirit; it has never stopped short before reaching the brink of the abyss. . . . Because of these senseless enterprises, these theatrical visions, these disloyal attacks, these ambushes on the independence of peoples, this defiance of conscience, this persistence in injustice," he warned the nephew of the uncle, "you have perished once before under the wrath of the world and dragged France down with you in your ruin. Think of that! Learn from your own history! If my words were heard today, many and greater evils might be spared France and the New World; particularly as the power of evil grows with the evil committed; but it would be foolish to expect in our days a cry of conscience to arrest a deliberate scourge. Events will take their course, as the fancy of one man wills them. Who will suffer for the mistakes of that man? The army. Who will expiate them? France." But the time for such words was not yet. Whether they were the warning words of Edgar Quinet or the militant ones of Jules Favre or the mild well-meaning ones of Montluc, they were all irrelevant, redundant, literature. They were the words of the winded, jostled and mauled by the dense multitude, gasping for breath, crying for air, struggling for space. The one way in which the truth could penetrate to France was by the contact of the two peoples—and that was the mission of their armies.

9

THE expedition was popular with the army—in Paris. The colonial expeditions to the Far East and the campaigns on the Continent had whetted the appetite for adventure of the military, who, having sponsored the Second Empire, were a standing claim on the man of the 2nd of December. Eleven years after the *coup d'état* which overthrew the Republic, the man whom the army had crowned in 1851 on the promise that he would revive the martial glories of the Napoleonic era was still temporizing with his destiny. His distant expeditions and episodic wars were known to be mere preparations for the final performance, but the scepter was carried by his globe-trotters, and it was necessary to repeat those exercises periodically to prevent the veterans from staling and to train and inspire the rising generation. Nothing spoiled so quickly as an army without employment, where young and old were thrown together to thrive on thwarted ambition, and when the sword was drawn in 1862 there was a great deal of competition for the supreme command and of intrigue and wire-pulling for places on the staff. As a field for professional promotion, Mexico offered as glowing a promise as Italy or the Crimea, and young officers, and older ones as well, who landed an appointment were the envy of their comrades weary of taking their turn and working their way up on the waiting lists. The War Office was crowded with callers seeking an escape from the dead end in which they were condemned by the caution of the Emperor in Europe and willing to expatriate themselves anywhere for a whiff of fresh air, and Paris was overcrowded with patriots looking for space, *urbe et orbi*. Mexico was merely a means to that end. The expedition was an excursion and a schooling, and what it meant to the average military mind was typified by the experiences of the officers who joined it to make a career for themselves, indifferent to its political purposes and without hostility toward Mexico; and it was through their correspondence with their families in France and the word of mouth which they multiplied among themselves in Mexico that a genuine public opinion was gradually formed here and there.

Captain Blanchot was among the most fortunate. A young cavalryman barely out of Saint-Cyr, he was appointed to the staff of General Bazaine, and for him the future opened on the day that he secured the coveted post, or several days later when he met a schoolfellow on the street and was able to tip him off to a vacancy of which he had inside knowledge. The battle of Paris was the hardest—the battle for official favor first and then with the official bureaucracy to be sent overseas. Although General Bazaine was second-in-command, he was still in Paris three weeks after Forey sailed from Cherbourg, and the impatience of Captain Blanchot to be off made him a bitter critic of the military bureaucracy. Day after day he called at the War Office for sailing orders, and day after day he was turned away, and when they finally came through the clerk informed him that he would be notified in due time, although the orders were lying on the desk at that moment. The irritation of Captain Blanchot with the *ronds-de-cuir* rankled with him for life. Decidedly, he wrote, the saddle bred a better type of soldier than the seat-warmers at the Ministry, and he was still cursing them when he boarded the train for Toulon. Then came the long sea-crossing, six weeks of tedium that would have been intolerable but for the prospect of action ahead; but as the War Office was not responsible for the ocean, he made the best of the unavoidable delay and fought boredom with his pen. He had literary talents, and as the Goncourts and the colonial expeditions to the Far East had brought the exotic into vogue in France, he filled his notebook with descriptions of the picturesque ports of call that broke the monotony of the crossing, and began his military career by writing up his experiences against the day when Captain, or Colonel, or General Blanchot would have the right of rank and years to publish his memoirs.

The first glimpse of Mexico was forbidding. The low-lying coast, flat and desolate, the white cemetery of the city, emerging indistinctly through the spray of a late equinoctial storm, were as gloomy as the news brought aboard by the pilot off Veracruz. Though it was the end of October, the *vomito* was still raging; the roads were impassable, though the rainy season was over; the convoys were regularly attacked and robbed, though the army held the hinterland and the coast; the town was blocked by guerrillas and overcrowded with troops, though the Commander-in-Chief had passed through three weeks before. Forey had gone on to Orizaba, leaving the bulk of his battalions behind, and no arrangements had been made to receive the incoming contingents. Bazaine put off for shore, but the sea was running so high that he was forced to put back, and the night was spent riding out the gale. In the morning the sea had gone down and the landscape was even more bleak under the sun. Captain Blanchot sketched it in a few strokes. "Some old blocks of crumbling walls, some thin and sickly shrubs, alone break the monotony of this soil hardly waved by some wrinkles of sand. To enliven this lugubrious landscape, horrible black birds, heavy and nonchalant in their flight, loathsome vultures covered with crows' feathers, stretching their necks and waiting as it seems for the sea to cast up some shipwrecked carrion to feed their voracity. Farther on, Veracruz extends its long crenellated walls and raises some Oriental-looking belfries into the skies. In the distance enormous sand dunes surround it, to isolate it, no doubt, from the green and smiling world that one sees far away. Really, this city has something that chills one's blood."

To be dumped there indefinitely was a dismal prospect, but the officers who came aboard told the same tale as the pilot. The expedition was stalled, and since the town was already congested, the incoming troops were obliged to remain on the transports. Bazaine went ashore to investigate, and Blanchot to superintend the landing of the horses. The horses mattered more than the men, because of the injuries they had suffered in the stormy sea crossing, and the facilities were as primitive as in the days of Cortés, and the methods the same. The cranes on the mole were useless, the narrow little jetty was unapproachable, and the horses had to be landed by hand, loaded on scows and whipped, rearing with fright, into the water, at the risk of laming themselves in the scramble overboard. Such was the first cavalry charge which Captain Blanchot conducted in Mexico, but he managed it without losses, and the precious freight was somehow coaxed, lashed, hurled, and hauled ashore.

Bazaine had expected to march inland immediately. The ravages of the fever were the one feature of Mexico with which everyone in France was familiar, and the Emperor had given explicit orders to all his commanders to pass through Veracruz without a day of delay, and it was difficult at first sight to explain why Forey had neglected them, but the answer was brought by the convoys that came down from Orizaba for food. Orizaba was blocked by guerrillas, and no more mouths were wanted there; food had to be drawn from the harbor, and with it went the fever. Of twelve hundred men whom Forey had withdrawn from Veracruz to escape it, but who were already infected, hardly fifty had arrived at Orizaba whole. The road was strewn with the corpses of castaways who had fallen out in the line of duty and perished by the wayside, and the guerrillas swarming around Veracruz kept the town harbor-bound. This was a shocking condition, and, more shocking yet, the Commander-in-Chief had been baffled by it. The agglomeration of so many troops in Veracruz confronted Bazaine with a problem which he was obliged to solve before he could land his own men. He took some elementary measures to deal with it, breaking the blockade of the guerrillas and occupying some healthy encampments on the outskirts, but the plain was fever-ridden as well as infected with guerrillas, and the focus of infection was still the town. In La Tejeria, six leagues away, the air stank; in Veracruz, it was fetid. The convent in which the main hospital was established had been cleaned out by the English when they held Veracruz, but no trace remained of their sanitary invasion. The floors were encrusted with filth, the courtyards dank with stagnant waters, and the beds filled with patients resigned to an inglorious grave. Bazaine gave orders to clean up the wards and promised to return every day to see that they were carried out; and so they were, but the patients were carried out with them. The steady traffic to the cemetery, which the French called the *jardin d'acclimatation,* had become a grim joke with the doomed, and everyone was on the waiting list. Bazaine, who had barely missed appointment to the supreme command in Paris, was obliged to take the initiative in Veracruz. He lost no time in communicating with Forey and proposed that a second line of operations be opened on the road running through Jalapa to the upper plateau, where the army could live on a country untouched by the war and above the fever pit. The Commander-in-Chief consented, and a week after his arrival Bazaine set the machine in motion. Six thousand men were sent to Jalapa.

On the next day Bazaine began to land the troops that still remained cooped up on the transports. The operation began briskly and continued rapidly through the morning, the men flinging themselves into the water more quickly than the horses and making the mole on all fours, but by noon it became difficult, and before night it had to be halted—another gale was approaching. It was no ordinary norther. That night Captain Blanchot thanked his lucky stars that he was on shore, even in Veracruz. The blast shook the house, sweeping away sleep, rattling the windows, which he boarded up, and filling the room with an impalpable drift of sand and sound, filtering through the cracks and whirling madly in the dreamless dark; and the day that followed was wilder than the dreams he was denied. When it seemed to be light, he climbed to the roof, blown back by each blast and forcing himself upright, and there on a perch deserted even by the buzzards he stood aghast. The scene begged for description and beggared it. The world was blotted out, leaving him breathless for words. "The earth seemed to have disappeared, the coast could no longer be seen, no more blue mountains, no more green hills. A gigantic yellow veil soaring to the sky, an immense cloud of sand, the dunes shifting and disintegrating under the strain of the hurricane, the sea without surface or horizon, a general vapor of white foam blown by the wind like a fog," defied the topographer. Landmarks were lost in the howling upheaval. The fortress of Ulua and the reefs around it were awash with the sound and fury of the night, and in the offing a French warship had lodged on the rocks; the masts were loosening, and the phantom hulk, pinned on its hocks, seemed about to lurch loose and clear the ledge with each surge, only to settle back and show its sallow underbelly still scraping the bloodless sea. Beside it two schooners were expiring, and beyond, in the mist, he could dimly make out a somber mass of vessels dragging their moorings, heaving heavily with their noses in the wind and a small wisp of smoke evaporating astern, "and that distant vaporous glimpse caught one's heart as one thought that the breaking of one of those cables meant the death of a thousand men."

Who could stand by idly and watch space overtaking men and nature crumpling up his undertakings like toys? Not Captain Blanchot. He hurried to the jetty, but the jetty had disappeared under the pounding cataracts that sent their weight crashing through the grille. The sea flooded the streets that still clung to the shore, and he could only take up his station there and resume his contemplation of the catastrophe at a lower level. Bazaine arrived to organize the rescue. Whaleboats floating in the back streets were loaded on wagons and dragged to the beach, and manned, and launched, and swamped by the first wave. Superhuman efforts were made to fling a cable to the foundering ship, but space swallowed the invaders, and the work of salvage was finally reduced to rigging up shelters for those whom the sea might wash up alive. Bazaine beat his way back to town for coffee. When he returned at noon, the storm was unabated. The beach was littered with casks and provisions unloaded from the laboring transports, and a company of infantry was called out to protect them from pillagers and to collect the corpses that were beginning to come in. Sentinels were posted within call of the deafening surf, and patrols were sent several miles down the coast to hold off the guerrillas who were also collecting; and the day ended, as it had begun, in dogged efforts to organize against the hurricane. When darkness fell, eight ships had foundered and fresh signals of distress were heard in the booming of cannon far to the south. The slow agony haunted the night, but the morning brought relief. The sea had subsided sufficiently to reach the warship with a lifeline and to take off the crew. Five merchant ships were added to the casualties, bringing the total to thirteen wrecks. The transports had weathered the storm, and the landing of the men was speedily resumed in its wake, as more troopships were coming in.

The operation had barely been completed, and the mole was still encumbered with cases of arms and gun carriages, when the wind stiffened and another norther filled another night with the insatiable storming of nature. Once more the morrow was a maelstrom; once more the world faded in a faceless void; once more the webbing of wind and water shrouded the shipping in dense surges of spectral motion; and once more the motions of rescue had to be made. Out of the north a great English brig came running for port; twice she tacked and aimed and missed the passage, and the third time she doubled the breakwater and flew under a strip of sail toward the castle and dodged it and moored in the lee of the mole, and there she broke her cables and cracked up in port within hail of the helpless crowds on shore. Desperate efforts were made to shoot her a lifeline, but the mortar burst and snapped the cable, and the day was spent watching the captain hoisting his wife to the topmast and the men clinging to the shrouds and counting the hours they could keep their heads flapping above their flag. The flag and the skirt flew out the day; then night closed on the welter of waters swelling about them. In the morning the sun soaked up the ravages, and another breathing spell settled over the yellowing surf.

The hurricane passed; the havoc of the fever remained. The gales from the Gulf blew with furious force without purging the atmosphere; the day after a blow the sun healed the storm and the sluggish languor was at work again. The double curse of the mouth of Mexico turned the war into a tremendous malediction: it was as if nature had conspired with the native and sucked up all the speen, the gloom, the ruin, the outrage which the alien had drawn from his soil to spew it back again and overwhelm the invader in an unrelenting blast of retribution. The tail of the hurricane struck a chill into the sun, and the sun cast a blight on the deadly town, where the hearses lumbered day after day to the Botanical Gardens, already glutted with fodder, and the native alone seemed capable of surviving by some special act of creation; and the war turned inward in impotent irritation and complaint.

In such morbid inaction, if the mind was not to succumb to the body, the only cure was criticism, and the conduct of the Commander-in-Chief provoked it. What was he doing in Orizaba? What had he done since he set foot in Mexico? He had deposed one President and threatened the other. He had advertised in the papers that Almonte was not the President of Mexico; he had evicted Juarez in a proclamation promising to respect the independence of the country and to provide it with a government of its own choice; and that was all. There, yellowing on the walls, was his manifesto, six weeks old, inviting the Mexicans to have faith in the French and to move. To move what? Their winds, their climate, their maladies, their mountains? To men keyed to the pitch of the elements, fretting for action and fatigued before they began, buffeted by the blind havoc of nature and staled by the flatness of fever and idleness, taunted one day by the tameness and the next by the terror of that treacherous coast, it was stupefying, as Captain Blanchot said, to be told that the garrison in Orizaba was short of rations and dying of disease, and that there, too, General Forey was crushing the Mexicans with proclamations. After a fortnight in Veracruz the veriest novice had become a veteran critic, and the newcomers joined their jaded comrades in Orizaba in cursing the Commander-in-Chief for neglecting the elementary rules which every beginner learned in school. The waiting list was longer, and the dead end worse, than the ones they had left behind them in Paris. Captain Blanchot caught the infection, complaining bitterly of "the pusillanimity of the High Command" and asking professional questions. "How was it possible to forget the absolute principle that inaction is the loss of the troops, physically and morally? How could the Commander-in-Chief remain inert and confined at the foot of the great range of the Cumbres at the top of which he would find health and abundance, when, in that little hole of Orizaba, buried at the foot of the mountains, lay nothing but famine and insalubrity?" Pusillanimity was a hard word to apply to the conduct of the Commander-in-Chief, but so far as Forey was concerned, the action at Alcanzingo had never been fought and the capture of the Borrego had been forgotten, and Puebla as well.

Amid this distemper his predecessor came out of the mountains. When he left Orizaba, his officers accompanied him for several miles down the road in a demonstration of sympathy, but in Veracruz Latrille de Lorencez was received with perfunctory courtesy and sped on his way with less sympathy than compassion and less compassion than embarrassment. Tall, lean, grave, cold, silent, and a little solemn, as one observer described him, his appearance was not improved by disgrace. He was glum. Although he had been offered command of a division if he wanted it, he declined consolation: he had had his fill of Mexico. It was as much as Bazaine could do to entertain him at the officers' mess. "His presence cast a certain chill," Captain Blanchot noted. "We looked at one another, we found little to say, and we welcomed the end of the meal with relief. General de Lorencez seemed to regard himself too much as a victim of destiny." But the chill went deeper than that. He was, as the Captain also noted, "the second commander to be worn out by Mexico," and the newcomers were beginning to feel the effects of that graveyard of reputations themselves. Lorencez at least was on his way out, and they were not even on their way in.

Captain Loizillon was more fortunate. Temperamentally, he was the type of soldier best fitted to serve in Mexico. Cool, unimpressionable, matter-of-fact, indifferent to everything but his career and completely devoid of the sensibility of Captain Blanchot, he was absolutely immune to the stagnant atmosphere of Veracruz. For him its horrors did not exist. Veracruz was a pretty place. There was no fever. He came in between hurricanes. He was healthy, he was busy, and he had no time to be bored. He was interested in people, he talked politics, and he picked up bits of information to eke out his letters to France. "It seems that Juarez no longer wants to defend himself and is awaiting us in Mexico City, because he is sure of being re-elected," he wrote to his parents. "Everyone agrees, in fact, that if the Mexicans are left free to choose for themselves, it is he whom they will take, since he is honest and belongs to the party of freedom and progress." Relaying the local gossip, he mentioned another topic of common agreement—"As for M. de Saligny, there is but one voice: Frenchmen, foreigners, Mexicans, all complain of him a great deal"—and passed on to more serious matters. These casual observations were mere space fillers; they had no bearing on his future, and he attached no importance to them. They were asides. What really mattered was why he was wasting his time in Veracruz. He had no fault to find with Forey, however, for everyone knew the reason. They were short of transports.

In other ways as well Captain Loizillon was fortunate, for he was one of the first to pull out of Veracruz. On the crossing he had distinguished himself by saving the horses during a storm that was breaking their legs in the hold, and although he was not a cavalryman he was luckier than Captain Blanchot, for this service attracted the attention of General Berthier, who was traveling on the same transport, and through this chance shipboard acquaintance he was appointed his chief of staff ten days before they touched Mexico. A week after landing he led the vanguard of a column to Jalapa, General Berthier having been chosen by Bazaine to clear the road to the upper plateau. He was also the first to see action—if an encounter with some guerrillas could be called action. As it occurred at Cerro Gordo, however, a formidable pass where a great battle had been fought in the American war, he mentioned it *en passant*. Warned that the position was held by four thousand men, he approached it carefully, but all that he saw were some white hats in the underbrush, which were picked off with five or six shots; the enemy fired his cannon three times and fled, and the skirmish lasted exactly ten minutes by his watch. "All these people are pitiable," he wrote from Jalapa, which he reached uneventfully. "They are all highway robbers who murder you in a corner and flee like the cowards they are at the first crack of a rifle. There is no glory in fighting such troops." The cold was intense and the column had two hundred sick, and their orders were to remain in Jalapa.

Now, Jalapa was not a pretty place, and four days later the Captain began to question the High Command and to find fault with General Berthier himself for obeying orders instead of protesting against the obvious error of halting halfway to the upper plateau. Initiative and indifference to responsibility, he remarked, were rare qualities. The population kept apart, fearful of compromising themselves and reluctant to co-operate with the French, keeping to their own side of the street and talking unsociably to themselves, and "with our mild measures we inspire no confidence. We are surrounded by a circle of *guerrilleros* whom we do not try to destroy. From the day that we arrived here, we might not merely have fed on the country, but formed a great center of supplies by spreading out around Jalapa and especially by occupying Perote, the center of the wheat production. Instead . . ." Instead, they had to send wagons down to the plain for victuals from France, a fatigue duty that doubled the sick list. "When we finally decide to extend our radius of action and occupy Perote, it will be too late, all the resources of the country will have been carried off by the guerrillas. I could have no idea," he continued, "of the difficulties and indecision of a war badly begun. General Forey expected to find transports here, and there were none. Hence the uncertainties and the mess in which we have been floundering from the start. We must hope that, once we have assembled our means of action, we shall recover the time lost, but I think that we shall find it difficult to efface the first impression of impotence that we have produced." His pen ran on, in idle, desultory, disconnected reflections. The latest proclamation of Forey was good, "but what effect will it produce? It is addressed to the decent people, and they are such a feeble minority in this land of intrigue, theft, and rapine! Here is where one appreciates France. For the moment, everyone is bored to death. Not a cat will do us the honor of addressing us. . . . I have even forgotten the Spanish I learned on the crossing." He refused to be gloomy, but the best that he could say was that "though I am convinced that we are here for a long time, I hope not to be writing you on the 1st of January, 1864." The date was November 19, 1862.

Three weeks later he was still in Jalapa, still marking time and still repeating himself, like a clock running down; the accent was regular, and it was grating. General Berthier might have had the best role in Mexico if he had occupied Perote a month earlier and informed Forey that he had assembled food for the whole army; far from reprimanding him for exceeding his authority, Forey would have thanked him effusively, "since the cause of our immobility is the lack of supplies, because of the lack of transports." The great native wagons, horribly heavy and terribly difficult to drag over bad mountain roads, were still hauling biscuit, which, known to be rancid when it was shipped from Cherbourg, was sent up from Veracruz under an escort of five hundred men, "who have been hard fagged and who have many sick, and all this to throw away the biscuit which no one can eat." But General Berthier dared undertake nothing himself. "There are times when I think that the stay in the hot country has turned everyone's head and destroyed every intelligence. I say no more, because I do not want to sour my character."

In these conditions, mail from home was a godsend. Three days later a batch came in, "and in good time, for with the dismal weather we have been having for the past week, and this idleness without diversions, and this slowness of the war which seems to have no issue, one's imagination begins to work." Imagination! Against that danger Captain Loizillon was on guard, yet the mischief of idle minds was contagious. He confined himself to facts, as hopefully as he could. Bazaine was expected tomorrow, and as Bazaine was not Berthier, they would probably be moving on to Perote the day after. There they would spend a fortnight before leaving for Puebla, and as the Mexicans were reported to have evacuated Puebla, "pursuing their system of creating a void around us, we shall not have the diversion of a few rifle shots even in Mexico City, for I wager that they will abandon the capital like everything else, and that Juarez and his government will withdraw to the north or the west. Then what will we do?" Exactly. A practical man could not help looking ahead; a captain was bound to. They would have to organize a new government and remain in Mexico to support it and then—then what? "The occupation of Mexico is an impasse, like the occupation of Rome." But he refused to indulge his imagination any further.

Sufficient unto the day—and the day that brought mail from France was bright. But not for long. After six weeks in Jalapa his spleen crept even into his reply to his fiancée. "A letter from you is always a great joy, for here in this country that calls itself civilized and that has only the worst sides of civilization, it is a great good fortune to be able to return in thought to one's own land. It is like an electric spark that restores one for a moment to intelligent life. All that we have seen of Mexico so far is very sad. Materially, a profound poverty, and yet we have crossed a country not yet ravaged by war; morally, organized murder and robbery. Five or six individuals can terrorize a population of two or three thousand souls. The laws are powerless to repress such monstrosities. The timid man, and he is the immense majority of this decrepit and outworn race, tries to appease all parties, which rob his crops and his cattle alike. It is a settled habit to be robbed and to consider it natural in this country. Here is an example. Ahead of us we have a gang of guerrillas who take the field, not to defend their country, for as soon as they see a couple of armed Frenchmen they flee, be they twenty themselves, but to rob travelers. After killing their leader, a dozen of these guerrillas came in and surrendered to us and were incorporated with our allies, the counter-guerrillas. You should see those allies of ours! Where are those poor English whom I hated so much on my return from the Crimea! Well, these deserters stole three horses from a *hacienda,* the owner came to Jalapa one day, recognized them, and informed an officer, who reported to me. On the orders of the General, I went in search of the owner to have him identify the three horses and return them to him. But the affair had long since been settled; he had bought the horses back from the robbers, and when I proposed to have the money restored to him he took to his heels, giving signs of the greatest alarm. Such is the country we are expected to organize!"

If he was not homesick, he was certainly heartsore for France. Marquez had just arrived with his army to accompany them to Perote. That was all that was wanting. "They call this the regular army! When you look at it, you wonder what the word irregular means. This whole scouring of ragged scum is in our pay, moreover; we are not proud of such allies. They have a way with them, though; they arrived at ten and by noon they were all lodged, officers and men. General Bazaine is arriving tomorrow, and it is impossible to find him a home. I am delighted, for I hope that this personal experience, compared to the results obtained by Marquez, will convince him that gentle methods may be all very well but not too much of them; a little energy will show the Mexicans that there is a limit to our patience, that we have been much too good until now, and that we realize at last that they are not worth so much consideration." It was a melancholy letter to write to his fiancée and he apologized for it. "This tendency to see things blackly will be attenuated as soon as we are on the march again, in three days, but unfortunately that distraction will not last very long, for there are only twelve leagues to cover and we shall not have the pleasure of the least little affair on the way."

A little more slowly than Captain Blanchot, but no less bitterly, Captain Loizillon came to curse the conduct of the expedition. "It makes one eat one's heart out to see how little effort is made to get out of the mess in which we have been sinking ever since we came to Mexico," he admitted. "We are made to occupy Jalapa and we wonder why." Jalapa had no strategic or tactical importance, while Perote was a real key to the country, commanding the approach to the upper plateau, dominating the whole slope of the mountains, holding a great grain-growing basin, and defying the guerrillas who cut their communications with the coast. Nothing would have been easier than to occupy Perote, since the Mexicans in their panic terror had decided not to defend it and had attempted to blow up a great fort there and had not even been able to do that. No campaign so easy had ever been made so hard.

With the arrival of Bazaine, the advance was pushed to Perote, but twelve leagues, lengthened by heavy rains, brought no relief to the black mood which had now become habitual with Captain Loizillon. Perote was a sad little village. Strategic considerations no longer mattered. Perote was a sad little village on the road to Puebla. Perote was a sad little village on the way to nowhere. Perote was simply a sad little village. There was nothing worth mention there but the weather. By night the cold was intense, and by day, when the weather was clear —and that was rare in those last days of December—an icy wind blew, chapping the skin and chilling the brain, and clouds of sand followed clouds of rain, "and what is far from comforting is the fact that it is the same everywhere in this Paradise Lost called the plateau of Anahuac."

The reward of reaching Perote was another stretch of indefinite inactivity. Black tedium descended like a pall. For diversion he went to a wake. As this was a custom of the country, he was curious to see a popular pastime. The deceased was the wife of one of Marquez' officers. She had given birth in Jalapa, followed the march in drenching rain, and died in Perote of exposure. Not even the natives could acclimate themselves to so godforsaken a country. The body was laid out in a hut, between four candles that warmed it for the first and last time above ground, and after a glance at it the Captain and his companions made for the fresh air. But no. They were nagged by a woman who brought them cigarettes and who was so distressed when they refused them, that to satisfy her they sat down and smoked in silence with the candles. To entertain them she brought out a bottle from under the body, and a baby, and handed them about. They handed the one to the other and went out, pursued by her pleading. Later they learned that she was the sister of the dead and that she had expected them to wait until a collection was taken to buy a coffin. They chipped in three pesos apiece and resigned themselves to life in Perote. There was an end to everything. By the end of January, no doubt, they would be in Mexico, or in Puebla, or in Perote. Mexico . . . But he refused to brood.

Disgust with the delays of the expedition was general in the army, and it was whetted by the mails from home. In Paris people were wondering also why nothing was happening in Mexico, and the papers were waiting impatiently for word of some important event. It was difficult to believe that the second expedition, like the first, was halted by a shortage of transports. It was incredible, after the experience of the Admiral, that no provision had been made for the elementary mechanics of a speedy campaign. It was preposterous that the same makeshifts had to be repeated, on a larger scale, and with a greater loss of time, for moving the army. Incredible, inadmissible, absurd, it was nonetheless true. It was necessary to send the Admiral, who had returned to the fleet, to Tampico to bring back twelve hundred mules, and, after occupying a port of great strategic value to the enemy, to abandon it immediately to the fever. It was necessary to send to New York and to apply to Washington for fresh stocks of transports, and even to Venezuela, to supply the deficiencies in Veracruz. The failure to foresee and provide would have been disgraceful if it had not been habitual in the War Department. The same thing had happened in the Crimea; but in Mexico it was inexcusable because the fumbling unprofessional conduct of the expedition made it appear an amateur affair at the very moment when the attention of the world was fixed on the vast pretensions of the venture to redeem and organize a people whose congenital inefficiency was precisely the *casus belli*. And to make the situation more embarrassing, a number of Prussian officers were following the army as accredited observers. The time could not have been worse chosen. It was the moment when a pamphlet by Prince Karl Friedrich of Prussia called *The Art of Fighting the French* had caused a sensation in the miltary world. Bismarck was preparing the aggrandizement of Germany, and Moltke was neglecting no opportunity to send his most capable officers abroad. The French Foreign Legion was full of them. They all told the same story; they had all fought a duel with a superior, which forced them to expatriate themselves, but in due time they all obtained their pardon and returned to the Prussian army, and it turned out that they were emissaries of the General Staff sent out to study some special point of French organization. Those who went to Mexico were not obliged to use such subterfuges. Priding themselves on the perfection of their military organization, the French were only too pleased to welcome student observers from Prussia; they were courteous, obliging, sympathetic, sociable, and if they were spies, they were at least frank ones. One day one of them said: "We adopt frankly the theories of the Emperor Napoleon about nationalities, and they authorize us to claim Alsace as German territory." The remark was regarded as being highly original; but the French wished the author of it anywhere but in Mexico when he made it.

To criticize conditions was, of course, to criticize men, and the butt of complaint in the army was not the War Office in Paris but the Commander-in-Chief in Mexico. In the opinion of staff officers, the War Office suffered from overcentralization of the services, the all-powerful *bureaux* of the Department refused to delegate authority, paralyzing the initiative and dulling the good will of their subordinates on active duty, and the traditional rivalry of the War and Navy Departments, each jealous of its independence and reluctant to co-operate with the other, aggravated these administrative difficulties. It was to

such hitches that the General Staff attributed the delays and mismanagement of the expedition, but the army held the Commander-in-Chief,
who was invested with full responsibility in the field, to blame for
them, and he was liable to attack for more than one reason. His record
in the Crimea was poor, perhaps because he had been serving then, as
his apologists said, under a subordinate promoted over his head. In
Italy, on the other hand, where his hands had been free, he had turned
in a brilliant performance. General Forey was by no means inefficient;
on the contrary, he suffered from an excess of professional competence.
Invested with the confidence of the Emperor, initiated into the Napoleonic idea, responsible for the realization of the supreme experiment
of the reign, and studied by Junkers, he could afford no risks. Painstaking and conscientious, and a little phlegmatic by temperament, he followed the instructions of his master literally, determined not to repeat
the errors of Lorencez and preferring to err in the opposite direction,
preparing his advance thoroughly, methodically, patiently, Germani-
cally, repairing shortcomings and omissions, providing for every contingency, and refusing to move until he was absolutely ready. He took
a bond of fate and he paid for it in popularity.

The degree of complaint varied, however, with the rank of his critics.
Colonel du Barail, for instance, was inclined to be lenient. He had long
since won his grade in Africa, and having been delayed himself in
Algiers by the bureaucratic curbs of the War Office, he understood the
difficulties with which the Commander-in-Chief had to contend. Combining the sensibility of a Blanchot and the coolness of a Loizillon with
maturity and experience, Colonel du Barail was blessed with an
equable disposition. Fair-minded and judicious, he always looked on
the best side of things and invariably had a good word for his brother
officers, being friendly to any man unless he maltreated animals. That
tripped his temper. On the crossing he suffered for four hundred
fifty horses, for "I always adored those animals," he confessed, "and
considered them almost as children, children of an inferior race, less
attaching than my men no doubt, but children just the same," and as
they were crowded in the hold in inhuman conditions, packed together
"exactly like anchovies in a barrel or cards in a deck," bruising one
another and barely able to breathe, and Arab horses were "air drinkers,"
he was under a severe nervous strain until they reached Veracruz.
There he collapsed. The crew, irritated by the encumberment of men
and animals that complicated their duties and augmented their fatigue,
unloaded the horses carelessly on the scow, and when a vicious mare
was dropped on them, he lost his temper and fell unconscious on the
deck.

His first glimpse of Mexico was gloomy. Veracruz was like a bit of
the Sahara stuck on the flanks of America, and what with eleven
wrecks piling up on the shore, and the foundering of the British brig

on the day after landing, and the Island of Sacrificios covered like a pincushion with the crosses of French graves, he was glad to be sent by Bazaine a few days later to Puente Nacional, with an ambulance to relieve a fever-ridden battalion that General Berthier had left behind. Being sick himself, however, he was obliged to return to Veracruz, and he remained there until the end of December. Bazaine offered to send him back to France. The offer wounded his self-respect profoundly, and he refused it indignantly, determined to find death or health in Veracruz. Colonel du Barail was the only member of the expeditionary corps, perhaps, who suffered from the consideration of the second-in-command, and Bazaine was the only one of the high-ranking officers of whom he was critical. He studied him closely and wrote him up later. "General Bazaine was one of our most conspicuous and popular commanders. The war in the East and the Italian campaign had attracted attention to him and placed him in the front rank of those whose future seemed to be unlimited. He enjoyed the favors of public opinion and the confidences and graces of the Sovereign. Under the charm of good nature, to which a body a little replete lent itself, and a good coarse face lit by very intelligent eyes, but eyes that were never more than half open, he concealed a knowing and clever mind, too clever perhaps. In his long practice of Arabian affairs, he had learned the secrets not of that great diplomacy which sees things from above and views aims from afar, but of that shrewdness which lies in moving amid intrigues and making use of them, without seeming to take part in them. His courage was universally recognized and imperturbable, he was absolutely impassive in the thick of danger, and affected the coquetry of indifference, which produced a great effect on all his assistants. In these debuts of the expedition, he was already in the full flush of his military fortune and had not yet awakened by his too skillful conduct any suspicion of the loyalty of his character. At bottom, in intelligence and talent, he thought himself a hundred head higher than his Commander-in-Chief. But he seemed to conceal his superiority, he let others proclaim it around him, and loudly enough for the echo to reach Paris, where it was finally heard."

The opinion which he formed of Bazaine predisposed the Colonel in favor of Forey, therefore. When he was fit for active service, he proceeded to Orizaba. Invited to dinner by the Commander-in-Chief, he was agreeably surprised by his bearing under great difficulties. "Instead of the stiff commander enclosed in his dignity whom I expected to meet, I found a kindly man, an interesting talker, a host who wanted everyone to feel at ease at his table. He reserved for the service, and for circumstances when his orders were ill executed, his fits of temper, so terrible but so short, which have given him a persistent but unmerited reputation for violence and brusqueness." But there was someone else who was accountable for the situation, and with whom no one in

Orizaba felt at ease. "General Forey, a slave to the wishes of the Emperor, applied himself to maintaining good relations with M. Dubois de Saligny and insisted that his officers, on their way through Orizaba, should do their duty politely by the Minister of France. He did not conceal his idea from me. The next morning I informed myself exactly when M. de Saligny would not be at home and deposited my card at his door, which he did not return, and we never had any other relations. I shared, I admit, the prejudices and repugnances which this diplomat aroused in the army, and which his entourage helped to augment. That entourage was composed, for the most part, of *déclassés,* of people who had lost by their own fault a reputable position in France and who had come to Mexico in search of a new career, amid the general confusion, either by intriguing for the principal grades in the army which the Conservative party was trying to organize, or by occupying themselves with business. And we all know how elastic that word *business* is! We treated them a little like lepers."

From Orizaba Colonel du Barail continued his journey to the upper plateau to join his regiment under General de Mirandol, who was in command of the cavalry. At the foot of the Cumbres de Aculzingo he was amazed by what Lorencez had accomplished there. "Imagine a vertical wall of prodigious height, stretching as far as the eye can see, without being able to detect where it would be possible to cross it without wings. No road, no crack, nothing! It is only when one rubs one's nose on it, so to speak, that one finds a fissure. . . . Nature has done everything to make this passage insurmountable. It is a succession of formidable positions, where a handful of determined men could stop an army, and we could not understand, as we contemplated them, how our foot soldiers had managed to dislodge the Mexican troops, who made only a show of disputing the passage." It was even more difficult to understand, when he reached his post at San Agustin de Palmar, within easy reach of Puebla, why the front was pushed no farther. Here, on the upper plateau, where life was so easy, for the patrols of the enemy vanished as soon as the binoculars spotted them, Colonel du Barail gained a bird's-eye view of the whole situation and, looking back on the lines from above, he found it less easy to condone the prolonged inaction of Forey in that little hole of Orizaba down below. It was the end of January, the transports from New York, New Orleans, and Venezuela were arriving, the siege material was coming up from Veracruz, and yet the leaves, the sad leaves of his journal, showed no sign of advance. Those leaves, those sad leaves, were sere with the dust of winter. "The moment was coming when we would be able to move, and certainly it was time, for any longer delay would have demoralized the army. The officers no longer understood the tergiversations of the Commander-in-Chief, who remained in Orizaba to give his chief of staff time to recover from a broken leg, and their unruly temper was re-echoed and aggravated by their men. The Mexicans, perfectly informed of the situation, exploited it. Their government flooded us with proclamations asserting their friendliness to France, their admiration for the army. . . . In the regiments that arrived first, there were already some desertions. This rid the army of its worst soldiers and flung out of the ranks men who were not worthy of figuring in them. But this could not continue too long, for after the bad ones, the mediocre would have gone, and we looked forward with joy to the moment when our only relations with the enemy would be by cannon blows." But the tendency was hard to nip because "the absence of the Commander-in-Chief stopped all operations, for General Forey, who kept his lieutenants in check, would have been offended if they had permitted themselves the least little action of war beyond his direction and supervision." The Commander-in-Chief worried him more than the War Office, and the Colonel found it difficult to preserve his equable temper. The Mexicans were concentrating their entire strength unmolested in Puebla, and he gave the enemy his due. It was only fair to recognize that "Juarez turned the time we left him to account very ably and spared no effort to raise himself to the level of circumstances and to give a national character to the struggle which he was sustaining to maintain the independence of his country." To say that much was neither treason nor temper; but there was such a thing as abusing the human animal.

Here were all the makings of a highly compromising situation. As the days, the weeks, the months, wore away, criticism of the conduct of the expedition was varied by criticism of its object. Of its object the troops knew little more than they read in the proclamations of the Commander-in-Chief and the papers from Paris. The redemption of the Mexican people was official cant for the occupation of Mexico; the only mission that meant anything to them was the redemption of the flag, and they were chafing to finish it and return to France. As the days lengthened, they had time to think, to question the official explanations, and to cast about for others of their own; and it was widely repeated and believed that the real reason for the war was the redemption of the Jecker bonds. A friend of the firm, returning from Mexico, reported that the subject was too sore to touch. Everywhere—in camp, at Veracruz, on the steamer—everyone was discussing the bonds; from a by-product they had become the core of the war; efforts had been made to prejudice the officers against them, and so successfully that he met no one in Mexico willing to sustain them except M. de Saligny. The Bear, as the army called Forey, would not hear of them or could not be bothered.

For the bank this was a setback, but only a temporary one. The nephew of Jecker in Paris reassured his family in Switzerland. "As soon as the army, whom the agents of Juarez have persuaded that our firm is the cause of the war, sees the tricolor flag floating on the towers of Mexico," he wrote, "it will no longer abhor us, for the country is rich and beautiful, and the army must have suffered from being confined in Orizaba." Obviously; nothing was so easy as to infect a sore, and Jecker had just naturalized himself a French subject. The French press, he added, was muffling the great projects of the Emperor for fear of giving umbrage to the English, but the plans for colonization, a throne, and a protectorate, which had been mere speculation a year before, were now accepted and would soon be accomplished facts, and before long the secondary interests of the bank in Mexico, mines and holdings in Sonora, Tehuantepec, Tasco, and Matamoros, would be bearing fruit. In the meanwhile, the word was patience. "The character of the Emperor is patience; he has had much trouble with Mexico, and yet has precipitated nothing. In this respect he is said to resemble Jecker." The patience of the Emperor was ample security for the bank. In the meanwhile, however, the army in Mexico continued to believe that the expedition was nothing but a swindle, and no one understood the great quality in which Napoleon resembled M. Jecker.

10

"IF THE Mexicans (*les derniers des hommes*) would but once lick *les crapauds*," Marx wrote to Engels in November, "but the latter dogs themselves—the so-called radical bourgeois— are now talking in Paris of *l'honneur du drapeau!*" The betting at that moment was not in favor of the Mexicans; yet in some respects they were in a better position than the French. If the morale of an army on the offensive was staled by inaction and delay, the ordeal of awaiting the attack was no less trying to the temper of the defenders; but on the other side of the mountains there were no signs of nerves. The condemned could not afford to be bored or peevish or impatient or unprepared; the saving virtue of self-preservation imposed and produced a settled concentration of purpose, and the stamina of the nation rose steadily with the battle array massing against it. The final preparations for the defense of Puebla were completed in the last months of 1862. An army of some twenty thousand men had been assembled there, an auxiliary force of five thousand covered the capital, and fifteen or sixteen thousand more were promised by the states. These resources represented the maximum capacity of the country, but the outcome was awaited with equanimity, for the military superiority of the French was counterbalanced by several moral factors which favored the defense.

The Napoleonic idea was divulged to the world at the same time that the second expeditionary force left France. *L'Esprit Public,* a paper which derived its inspiration from the Foreign Office, interpreted it in a remarkable article that allowed the Mexican press for the first time to read the mind of the Emperor clearly. "The greatness and the scope of the expedition to Mexico are such," the writer declared, "that if the Imperial Government had committed a thousand mistakes it would redeem all its errors by directing this lofty enterprise well. As we have indicated before, the expedition to Mexico is not a political improvisation. It is an idea slowly matured over many years in the mind of the head of the State. The idea of imparting assistance everywhere to the Latin race, threatened by the Greek and the Anglo-Saxon groups, is not one of those spectacles to which political observers should remain indifferent. In the present situation, the mere fact of occupying any point whatsoever on the American continent is in itself an act of supreme timeliness. To set a limit to this occupation would be impossible. Diplomacy can determine when to start a march, but it cannot and should not decide when to return. The important point was to find reasons for going to America. Napoleon has found them and profited by them, and the future will prove that he has done well." With the same candor the exposition continued: "With the expedition to Mexico the Emperor Napoleon continues the development of the political system which he inaugurated in Europe on the day when he asked that Spain be admitted to the rank of the great Powers; he continues what he began in Italy when he flung Austria back into the Quadrilateral, fortune denying him the opportunity to drive her into the Adriatic. The idea emerges, the policy of the reign appears with the genius proper to it. . . . One feels that France, by a stroke of genius, has just recovered the direction of the Latin group, abandoned since the death of Louis XIV. . . . Alone, completely alone, she captures the imagination of the peoples, and she will capture it far more when the peoples realize that France goes to Mexico not only in the name of the Latin group, not only to open perhaps an *American Algiers* for our colonists and our army, devoured by the need of work, but for a greater and loftier idea, which belongs to all races and all peoples without distinction, for an idea beloved by all, for liberty! In taking up a position on Mexican territory, France puts an end to the invasion of the adventurers from the South. The Union, already broken by the present conflict, and which threatened to absorb Cuba, the whole of Mexico, and the Republics of the South, is checked in its advance. And that advance, let us not forget, was that of slavery. In occupying the principal point of Mexico, France says to slavery, 'So far and no farther.' She deprives England of the monopoly of abolitionism, and she takes, moreover, a position in the American conflict as strong as was our position in Rome amid the Italian conflict, without being embarrassed by having to conciliate the interests of the Papacy with those of the natives. . . . We are inaugurating on a vast scale and in proportions which will be revealed before long the counter-action of the Monroe Doctrine." The whole article was a rebuke to the shortsighted and the skeptic. "There is something profoundly discouraging," the writer remarked, "in hearing people say at every step, 'What is the use of this expedition? Why are we spending so much money? What are we going to do under that implacable sky, where the yellow fever reigns and the black ague?' And while some degenerate Frenchmen voice such nonsense behind drawn blinds or under the awnings of our cafés, a handful of heroic soldiers, affronting at once the rigors of the climate and the attacks of an enemy twenty times superior in numbers, give their lives for an idea which perhaps they do not understand, for the honor of the flag is reason enough for them."

Exactly. Zarco devoted no less than seven issues of his paper and all the patience of which his lucid intelligence was capable to the analysis of this remarkable apology, and in the end confessed himself baffled by it. "What does all this intricate *galimatías* mean? What has it to do with the Mexican question?" he asked wearily. "Instead of reasons of advantage and justice, it is necessary to applaud the Imperial policy with rolling drums and to resort to the worn trumpery of historical dates and the question of races and religions, to say nothing in the final analysis, and thus to fill the columns of one of the most famous papers of Paris, the interpreter of the plans of Napoleon III. To interpret the sense of that passage in which are confused Louis XIV, the Graeco-Slavs, the Anglo-Saxons, the Latins, the Spanish Catholics, the Ultramontanes, and to perceive the connection of all this with French policy in Mexico is an enterprise more arduous than to comment the Apocalypse, and we gladly abandon it, trusting that the next packet will bring the solution of these risky charades of *L'Esprit Public,* unless M. Castille has the same pretensions as his Maecenas to be incomprehensible."

Incomprehensible, indeed, was the only word which common sense could apply to the latest version of intervention. The one merit which it possessed was the frank admission that every previous explanation had been a pretext, exploited and discarded to serve the ruling idea of the reign, the creation of an American Algiers. But why involve it then in such an elaborate medley of extraneous motives? Why search for so many reasons when one was enough? Why load it with a multiplicity of irrelevant issues unless the real one was not enough? And why inflate it now with such farfetched, labored, and alien accessories? The conversion of a colonial conquest into a racial crusade was a piece of political claptrap which overreached the mark and, in lending dimensions to the idea, destroyed its depth and solidity. What could be more unfortunate than the pretensions of France to head a hypothetical Latin group? What could be more galling to Spain than the reminder of French patronage and the family prerogative of appropriating her former dominions? What could be more irritating to Italy than to be associated with such a coalition? King Victor Emmanuel had refused an invitation to join the expedition, and the notion of regaining the Veneto at the expense of Mexico had been publicly denounced by the workers and students—a notion which had become the laughing stock of the Continent, including the unsmiling Court of Vienna. Why talk of flinging the Austrians back into the Quadrilateral and driving them into the Adriatic, when Maximilian had been offered a Mexican throne? And what was to be gained by antagonizing the Anglo-Saxon group and challenging the English and the Americans at once? In the Latin half of the New World the extension of French protection had called forth protests of sympathy and solidarity with Mexico. In the northern hemisphere the initiation of the counteraction to the Monroe Doctrine needed no laboring. And why introduce the question of slavery? The choice of Mexico, where slavery had been abolished with the birth of the nation, as the point to check its spread was a gratuitous offense to the party in the American civil war favored by the Emperor and hardly a happy example of timing when Lincoln was enacting the Emancipation Proclamation. A more impolitic omnibus of blunders had rarely been compiled. And if the effect of these assorted apologies was calculated to alienate all quarters of foreign opinion, what impression could they produce at home? The original pretexts of intervention, which had at least been intelligible, were discarded in favor of an inflated fiction designed to dazzle a public skeptical of the practical advantages of the venture and distrustful of its palpable risks, and that public, with whom the adventure was already unpopular, was now informed that no limit could be set to its duration. What was to be made of such a farrago of excuses? If the revelations of *L'Esprit Public* had not been the calculated indiscretions of a government organ, it would have been difficult to believe that they reflected faithfully the workings of the Emperor's mind. The author gave the impression of being both deaf and blind; and unhappily he was not mute.

But it was precisely because these revelations were incomprehensible that they were significant. The evolution of the idea was an enlightening disclosure of the growing distance between the Emperor of the French and the French people, and the latest version of intervention was a valuable revelation of the mentality of Napoleon and the inherent liabilities of the enterprise, thinly glossed over by a megalomania that ignored them. "*L'Esprit Public* admits it," Zarco observed in summing up his diagnosis. "The Napoleonic diplomacy does not know where it is going, it has no determined aim, and so it can go on changing like the phases of the moon." This was an asset for the defense in the long run. "If one is to begin an enterprise in diplomacy without knowing how or when to conclude it, there is nothing surprising in the entanglement which French influence has produced everywhere, in Turkey and in Italy, as in Mexico. By advancing at haphazard and without plan, nothing solid, nothing great, can be accomplished." And through the protean transformations of the idea one feature remained constant and clear, perfectly simple and perfectly comprehensible. "In Mexico, without waiting for the sibyls to explain to us these modern oracles, we understand perfectly well that it is a matter of depriving us of our independence, and this is enough and more than enough for us to frustrate the grandiose project of founding an American Algeria and the comedy of hocus-pocus in which the oppression of Mexico is expected to solve all the questions that Napoleon III has embroiled on the old Continent."

The successive versions of intervention brought forth more and more evidence of its weakness. French propaganda drew a studied distinction between the Mexican nation and the party in power, guaranteeing the people full freedom in the choice of a government, short of the one they had freely elected. This line failing to produce any effect on the defense of the country, the official press in Paris had now reached the point of waging a personal campaign against the President. In the first days of intervention Wyke had laid the responsibility for French policy to the personal hatred which Saligny felt for Juarez; the whole chorus of salaried organs of the French Government was now reduced to the level of Saligny. Faithless, cunning, unscrupulous, sanguinary, savage, despotic—the vocabulary of abuse was ransacked for epithets to discredit him, and obvious as the tactic was, Zarco felt it necessary to devote an article to it; for here it was the obvious that was incomprehensible. "The hatred for Juarez now appears to be a monomania of France and the object and motive of the war. The effect of these studied statements has been null in the whole country, which has striven more and more to identify its cause with that of the government. What does it matter to us, in fact, that the person of the President of the Republic is more or less antipathetic to the Emperor of the French? Since when has this puerile, irrational, and unfounded antipathy been a just cause of war? On what does the hatred of France for President Juarez rest? On nothing, absolutely nothing. For us it is an unquestionable truth that there is no settled aim in the policy of Napoleon in Mexico, and that he is moving at random, without knowing himself how to explain his designs and changing pretexts to continue the war. One of these pretexts, and the most baseless and childish of all, is the hatred for Juarez, a pretext that does not merit a moment's consideration by the

Mexican people, obliged as they are to maintain at the same time their independence, their institutions, and the government that derives from them."

But these blunders bore good fruit. They were not merely duds that fell flat and buried their heads unnoticed in Mexico; they produced a deepening appreciation of the President, a fresh discovery of his familiar virtues. Tributes to his integrity, his tenacity, his firmness and faith, his supreme fitness, his tested trustworthiness, appeared in the press. French propaganda promoted his reputation and compelled his countrymen to recognize what they would otherwise have accepted unawares. Knowledge became conscious. The portrait was always the same, nothing was added to it, nothing subtracted, but the effect was fresh and different because of the context in which it was framed. Untouched by time but heightened by it, the man gained stature with the scale of events; the pressure of world forces was a lever which, leaving him unmoved, raised him to world eminence; the inflation of the Napoleonic idea gave a real elevation to its antagonist, and nothing was more natural than to pit the protagonist of the nation, in a patriotic article, against his personal adversary and to compress the issue into two words—Napoleon and Juarez.

Never before had the President been so completely identified with his people. Now at last he was wholly at one with them. The ranks opened to reveal and closed to rally around him, and as the nation contracted about its chosen representative he became knit to its core and was recognized to be an organic part of it, indivisible, indomitable, indissoluble, a biological necessity of its survival. On him its adverse destiny was concentrated, and in him its undying purpose: he was the incarnation of the moral stamina of his people, and the phenomenon by which a single personality is magnified by its diffusion among many was manifest in the devotion he inspired. Some of his eulogists deplored his modesty, his excessive modesty, but they applauded the practical form in "his exquisite skill in the choice of men," his discernment in delegating authority, and his knowledge of those to whom he entrusted the defense of the country. The men through whom he functioned, himself unseen, were the best proof of his capacity; yet it was on this talent that his detractors fastened to belittle him, for detractors he still had. They were the index of the crisis, the barometer of the popular temper on the eve of battle.

What nervousness there was in the public mind centered naturally on his military appointments. Zaragoza died in September, in consequence of an illness contracted while he was reconnoitering the Cumbres in cold and rainy weather, and the second defense of Puebla was entrusted to Gonzalez Ortega. This appointment was irreproachable and politic. Considered by many to be long overdue, it silenced the muffled friction of the President and the Vice-President. Their relations were of the best. Ortega was embarrassed when he was obliged to forward to the President a communication from Forey flattering to himself but wounding to Juarez, and he did so with profuse apologies. Juarez was obliged to remind him that personal hostilities meant nothing and that there was no reason to blush for them; it was one of the rare occasions when he referred to himself, and when he did so he was reduced to truisms. Ortega seconded him cordially and loyally. He put him on his guard against intrigues carried on in the camp in favor of Comonfort. In the summer of 1861 the ex-President had crossed the border and found refuge in Monterrey, where he was protected by Santiago Vidaurri, who had returned to his fief and who alternately defied and evaded the demands of Congress for his extradition and trial, and Juarez finally extended the benefits of the political amnesty to Comonfort and offered him an opportunity to rehabilitate himself in the defense of the country. He gave him command of the auxiliary army that was to cover the capital and co-operate in the defense of Puebla. This appointment was also politic, but in the eyes of many it was indecent, and it was bitterly criticized in the army, many commanders refusing to serve under him. The unpopularity of Comonfort weighed as little with the President as the popularity of Ortega; but his detractors attributed both appointments to personal and political considerations.

In December Juarez visited Puebla to inspect the preparations for the defense and to distribute medals to the heroes of the 5th of May. No one disputed the honors due to the dead, or even to the survivors of that fortunate day, but their successors were questioned by an officer who was an admirer neither of Ortega nor of Comonfort and who discussed their appointment with the President. General Marquez de Leon distinguished himself as an author by publishing many years later a book which he called *The Truth about Juarez,* in which he recalled that conversation. He began by reviewing the record of Ortega, but was abruptly interrupted by the President, who said, "I know what you are going to say, that he is a coward. I know it only too well, but the nation has agreed to regard him as a great man, and I have placed him here to put him in evidence." Shocked by such candor, the General was equally frank. "So!" he exclaimed. "To rid yourself of a rival you sacrifice the army and perhaps the whole Republic!" To which Juarez replied in a tone of irritation, "And what are you good for yourselves? No one is necessary: ideas are all that matter." — "We are good enough to be killed for that coward," came the retort; "we are soldiers, we have to obey orders," but before he could say more a brother officer intervened and diverted the discussion. The General then took exception to the ex-President. "Be so good as to tell me," he said, "how it is that Comonfort, the author of the *coup d'état* and so bitter an enemy of our institutions, is placed in a position to gain glory and prestige by giving him command of the army of observation?" — "And do you suppose that I have placed him there to exalt him?" Juarez replied. "He too will nullify himself." After that there was no more to be said, and the General withdrew, satisfied that "for that man there was no country and no glory other than his ambition for power." Later he learned that the conversation had been repeated to Ortega and by the President himself.

If this was the truth about Juarez, it remained the secret of General Marquez de Leon. No one else in Mexico saw the reverse of the medal. The truth about Juarez was always incomprehensible for those who denied his honesty, and so were their tales; for the others, it was as simple and transparent as daylight. On his way to Puebla he was met at every stop with outpourings of popular feeling and greeted by delegations expressing their confidence that he had left nothing undone for the defense of the country. In Puebla, obeying the behest to mingle democratically with his people, he was discovered one moonlit night walking with the strollers on the public promenade, who surrounded him and renewed their pledges to give as good an account of the national honor in the second attack as in the first. During his stay there, messages were received from a patriotic organization in Genoa, assuring him of the identity of the struggle in Italy and Mexico, and resolutions of sympathy and support from the students in Florence; the eyes of the world were upon Puebla, and everyone was on his mettle. On his way back to the capital he was accompanied by the same demonstrations of faith, the peasants offering him fruits and flowers with the knowledge and understanding that he was one of them. For everyone who addressed him that man meant one thing and one alone. He was our Mexico. The General did not make sense. What would all those simple folk have said if they had been told that they put their credulous trust in a hypocrite, whose sole patriotism was his lust for power, a fool who confided its defense to cowards and incompetents, and a schemer who defeated himself, and that Juarez was another Napoleon?

I I

IN THE last months of his life Zaragoza had planned to resume the offensive against Orizaba before the French reinforcements arrived. With this strategy Ortega agreed. "If we put all our elements into play, Orizaba will fall into our power, but otherwise we shall probably be repulsed," he wrote to Juarez at that time. "I believe, *Señor Presidente,* that prudence is absolutely necessary, and above all in staking on a single battle all the organized elements on which the Liberal party can count, but I also believe that today the Franco-Mexican question rests wholly on the field of arms, and if our situation is difficult today, it will be more so tomorrow, and that morrow is approaching with giant strides and we shall have to accept battle with greater disadvantages. When necessity marks the way, we must accept it, come what may. The events at Puebla have made the French consider us: the more blows we deal them, the more they will respect us. Only the events to come can wrest the question from the ground of arms." The situation of the French, cramped between the mountains and the sea, a prey to disease, disorganization, and guerrilla raids, was a strong argument for such strategy; but the disastrous defeats at Aculzingo, Barranca Seca, the Borrego, and Orizaba, had proved so consistently the inferiority of the native forces to the French in field fighting that Juarez hesitated to risk a final one, and Ortega agreed again. "I have been much-pleased to see the prudence and aplomb with which you judge the situation," he wrote, and he bowed to his judgment. "You, my friend, have done much and will have to do more, much more, like all of us. I realize that our situation is very grave, much as we may wish to see it in rose colors," he continued. "Nevertheless, it has been entrusted to you, and I have and want to have faith that you will do everything in your power to master it. Though you do not need it, I would like to give you my advice, my friend, not as advice but as an expression of my friendship, my affection, and our mutual interest. Trust the people, the men who support you, and the future, and everything will yield to your will, however stormy the situation may be that awaits us." Gratuitous though the advice was, it was good, and if the confidence of Ortega in the outcome was a little halfhearted, he was at least honest. The offensive against

Orizaba was abandoned by mutual agreement in favor of the defense of Puebla. If all the organized elements of the government were to be staked on a single battle, it was imperative to fight it under the best conditions, and in military judgment at least, Juarez and Napoleon thought along the same lines, the Emperor himself recognizing that wherever his troops met with fortifications it was necessary to act with extreme circumspection. The fortifications of Puebla de Zaragoza, as the city was now called, had been fully completed when Juarez inspected them in December, except in the provision of perishable foodstuffs.

Six weeks later, and five months after the French reinforcements landed in Mexico, Forey was still preparing the attack in Orizaba. The opening of the Chambers in Paris had been postponed to February 15 in the hope that the capture of Puebla might be announced by then, but time meant nothing in Mexico, and slowly but surely the expeditionary force was becoming acclimated to the country, not only physically, but morally. More favored than the rest, Captain Loizillon had put Perote behind him and had reached Quecholac, a little village on the ridge of the upper plateau. Every gain, however, had to be paid for by a fresh delay. "They say that we shall be here for a month and that only then shall we have means of transportation. Presumably Puebla will not hold for more than a fortnight." The date, by the calendar, was January 21, but the complaint was chronic. On February 4: "We are still in Quecholac, harassed by inaction. The prudence of the Commander-in-Chief is becoming imprudence in my eyes; he pays this miserable Mexican army the honor of treating it as if it were a Russian or an Austrian army. . . . Everyone in the army is convinced, and all our combats have proved it, that three battalions, two squadrons of cavalry, and one battery of artillery could cross all of Mexico without the whole of the Mexican army daring to attack them. On this principle, the natural thing to do would be to occupy as much ground as possible in order to acquire the resources of the country, and we do so the more securely that we know that the Mexican generals have shut up their troops in Puebla, for fear they will desert or disband. All this has been said to the Commander-in-Chief, it seems, in every possible way, but he will not listen and merely says that once he starts nothing will stop him. Very likely, but how much time we have lost! . . . For the present, our greatest wish is to advance, to take Puebla, to reach Mexico City, and to return to France as quickly as possible."

The 15th of February came and went, and Forey was still marking time—on paper. From a military point of view the loss of time was immaterial, but politically these delays were damaging since they discouraged "the feeble part of the population that might be for us." For lack of other occupation, Captain Loizillon was forced to interest himself in politics. The sympathetic attitude of the foreigners and the wealthy classes was cooling as they realized the inability of the French army to relieve them in time, and military politics were creating diplomatic difficulties which would prove more serious than the conduct of the war, since there was conspicuous friction at headquarters. "The Commander-in-Chief, who has long known what the yardstick of Saligny is worth," was on bad terms with the Minister; the Minister, forbidden to communicate with the Foreign Office except through the Commander-in-Chief, was muzzled and subdued to the discretion, the deadening discretion, of Forey; and so the mischief grew. The papers in Paris predicted the disgrace and recall of the Minister—unfortunately without foundation. "What a mistake has been made by leaving that man here, the object of general animadversion! And yet, if the first expedition to Mexico had been independent and had not been towed by Almonte and above all by Dubois de Saligny," Captain Loizillon concluded with the logic of lassitude, "it would almost certainly have succeeded."

The strictures of February were corroborated by Colonel du Barail. Transferred to the staff of General Bazaine, he was obliged to leave the front and retrograde to Quecholac. The short march was made in Siberian weather, and he and his regiment arrived bearded with icicles, "like the grumblers on the retreat from Moscow." He spent the month on a cheerless and solitary plantation, busying his men with amateur theatricals by night and professional ones by day. Remembering that on the eve of Austerlitz, when Napoleon I visited his troops, he found them polishing their arms and blowing up their plumes, and believing that those plumes played no small part in the battle, Colonel du Barail insisted on an exemplary *tenue* in his regiment and kept his troops shining their brass until they could see themselves in their cuirasses or even in their horseshoes. At night they put on operettas and playlets. At one of these performances he was introduced to a little man, nervous, dry, alert, of a pronounced Spanish type, whose pitiless eyes reminded him of an Arab chieftain, who turned out to be Leonardo Marquez, and who attended these private theatricals assiduously. By day the men went back to shining their arms, and so the month wore away. Colonel du Barail allowed no laxity. As a colonel he was, he confessed, *pas très commode,* and his inflexible pride in appearances made him unpopular, but it was necessary to keep up the morale of the common soldier, "for General Forey had not appeared yet." Desertions were increasing, even some noncommissioned officers had disappeared, and the Commander-in-Chief was obliged to notice them and to issue several orders of the day, warning the army against the lying proclamations of the Mexican Liberals and the indelible disgrace of forsaking the flag, but "he remained in Orizaba with a persistence which favored a flock of unpleasant comments."

And worse yet, where one looked for Forey, one found Bazaine. Cool, collected, active, resourceful, competent, he emphasized the absence of the Commander-in-Chief by the ability with which he replaced him; but Colonel du Barail liked him no better for that. Finally, on March 10, the Commander-in-Chief left Orizaba and brought himself as far as Aculzingo. There he stopped, at the foot of the pass, and called a council of war, attended by one general of division, the heads of the various services, and his Mexican lieutenants, Almonte and Marquez. "General Bazaine abstained from attending, on the pretext that his presence was needed among his troops, and in reality so as not to take part in the decisions that were to be taken there and to be able to preserve his full freedom of comment. This was another proof of the duplicity which he maintained from the beginning of the campaign until the day when he attained his object, which was to supplant General Forey in the command." As usual, Bazaine did well. The council discussed the best point of attack upon Puebla and narrowed the choice down to the fort of Carmen on the south or the fort of San Xavier and the Penitentiary on the west; the Mexicans insisted that the former was the vulnerable point, and Napoleon himself recommended it; but the council broke up without coming to any decision, Forey preferring to make up his mind when he was on the ground.

Though no decision was reached, the discussion was continued by the heads of the various services in the camp, and in Quecholac Captain Loizillon anticipated the worst. "I very much fear," he predicted, "that with the spirit which has so far presided over the conduct of the war, we shall amuse ourselves with a regular siege that will assure us possession of Puebla step by step, to be sure, but that will cost us a great deal of time and force us to eat our reserve stocks and to spend much of our munitions. Then we shall have to spend at least a month in Puebla to revictual and to make it a new base of operations, and so we shall reach the rainy season, which may well halt our march upon Mexico City." By a brusque attack he believed that the town could be taken in five or six days, but on one condition—that the advice of the engineers, who insisted on a regular attack with parallels and all the rules of the Polytechnique, be disregarded. He trusted that Forey would not fall into that trap, at least, and he pinned his hopes on the fact that, having missed the 15th of February, the Commander-in-Chief had now set the date of March 16, the birthday of the Prince Imperial, as the day for his entrance into Puebla. "It is already very late for that, and I don't believe it possible," he added. But the expedition was in motion, and it was no time to be captious.

All that remained was to warm up the morale of the army. An order to that effect had been issued by Forey three weeks before. "Almost nine months ago," it began, "a small number of you, marching with blind confidence upon Mexico, met in Puebla an obstacle which you lacked the material means to overcome. . . . The time has not been wasted," it went on. "The patience which you have shown in preparing your means of action may have been imputed by the deluded soldiers of the government that still reigns for a few days more in Mexico, in the presumption of their easy triumph of the 5th of May, to the fear that they inspired in you. If they have fallen asleep in that fond fancy," it ended, "let their awakening be a terrible one!" More than the fiat of General Forey was required, however, to rouse the army. The order was dated February 17, and marching orders were not issued until the middle of March. Besides, as Colonel du Barail observed, "The war was carried on without animosity, and the contest was courteous, if one can use that word, or as courteous as possible." The order produced the effect of a draft drawn on the Commissary Department, stocked with every necessary supply but the spirit to move them. But motion was enough to rekindle the spark; if the final preparations were not complete, they were ready, at least, for the finishing touch; and politeness ended at Puebla, where our Mexico began.

The advance columns of the French army, under Generals Douay and Bazaine, sighted Puebla on March 16. Though the thoroughness of his final preparations prevented the Commander-in-Chief from celebrating the day as he proposed, officially it could be said, and it was said, that the investment of Puebla began on the birthday of the Prince Imperial. Actually the operation began on the next morning. The day was made to order. The weather, gray, mean, and damp with frequent downpours and violent storms during the previous weeks, suddenly cleared up; the sun came out, and its rising was saluted by drums, trumpets, and the martial tunes of the French army. "*C'était magnifique!*" said Colonel du Barail. "During that whole day we enjoyed the most grandiose of spectacles. . . . The entire ensemble respired splendor, wealth, and magnificence. The road we were following runs along the crests that form the border of the basin, and, rocked by the elastic trot of our mounts and intoxicated by the spring air, we had before our eyes constantly the domes, the belfries, the terraces, the roofs of the town and the panorama of its environs. From time to time an inoffensive cannon shot from the town, or some yet more inoffensive rifle shots from the mounted sentinels on the plain, flavored our pleasures as tourists by reminding us that we were soldiers. . . . General Bazaine, who was a past master in that kind of operation, had all the roads cut, occupied, and guarded. By nightfall we bivouacked in sight of the ramparts." The operation continued for two days. The entire expeditionary force, twenty-six thousand strong, gradually debouched on the great plain and deployed right and left of the city, swinging around it in a vast involving movement that was superbly performed, even in the opinion of Captain Loizillon, and under great difficulties, as there were no roads and the terrain was full of ravines where the gun carriages, even with quadrupled mules, overpowered the teams, and the men were forced to fall out and put their backs to the wheels, and there were many moments when a sally of the enemy would have thrown the march into confusion. The opportunity to fall on those flanking columns, which were extended so far that the head was ten or twelve hours from the center and exposed to attack before it could be protected, tempted the staff of Ortega, but as this would have meant a field battle, he forbade it. For forty-eight hours the caterpillar movement crawled across the plain unmolested, and although several bodies of Mexican cavalry hovered ahead and held them under restless observation, the twenty-six thousand turned the town and took up positions to the west and south of it without striking a blow. "This first easy success," Captain Loizillon noted, "made everyone's mouth water, and we should have liked to fling ourselves at once on the first outworks called the Penitentiary of San Xavier. We knew for a fact that when we arrived the Mexicans were not expecting us on that side and that San Xavier had no artillery, but it could be crammed with men at any moment. For fear of that eventuality the Commander-in-Chief preferred not to attack it by main force and decided to make a regular siege." The engineers had won the day; but it was an exhilarating day, nonetheless, that canceled six sedentary months, that proved that the expedition was portable, and that placed the army astride the road to Mexico City. Night fell on a brilliant spectacle, the campfires of the French populating the plain, and rockets rising from the beleaguered town in soaring and luminous signals that communication was cut off and that the investment had actually begun.

The event of the next day was the appearance of the Commander-in-Chief. Many of his officers saw him for the first time. Captain Blanchot was one of them. He caught a fleeting glimpse of him, "followed by a swarm of more or less military persons," among whom he recognized General Almonte by his embroidered uniform. General Forey, he noted, looked peevish, but this was said to be his habitual expression, and he was now in full activity, inspecting the town from every direction and making a beeline for one obstacle after another. The spectacle was grandiose. "One might have said an immense pincer, opening to the south of Puebla and closing on the north, behind the city," said Colonel du Barail. With Bazaine on the west and Douay on the south, and Forey everywhere else, "nothing should have escaped from the place. Nevertheless, on the night of the 21st to the 22nd of March, by apathy, by negligence, or perhaps by connivance, the auxiliary troops of General Marquez allowed fifteen hundred horsemen to slip out and rejoin the army of assistance of General Comonfort. The fact was deplorable, for there was certainly no reason to reinforce that army, and this cavalry, useless for the defense of the besieged, would have lessened their resources in victuals." In the theater of war General Marquez was a dead loss, but "after this little mishap, the investment was hermetic, the siege could begin."

After studying the town and the ring of forts surrounding it for forty-eight hours, Forey ordered Bazaine to take the Penitentiary. This decision caused some surprise among the *gens du métier,* who all agreed with Marquez, Almonte, and Napoleon that the Carmen was the surest short cut to a definite success. "To employ a familiar comparison," wrote Colonel du Barail, "to attack Puebla by San Xavier was to seize the adversary by a leg or an arm; to attack Puebla by the fort of Carmen, was to hit him in the belly. General Forey preferred the leg or the arm. The plan seemed to him more appropriate to the artillery of which he disposed. We had fifty-six *bouches à feu,* six of them siege guns. Puebla had ninety-six on its ramparts, of which eight for the fort of San Xavier alone. Fifty-five other pieces in reserve raised the total armament of the place to one hundred fifty-one cannon. And then, was there not M. de Saligny telling us that those cannon, those parapets, those forts, were mere scenery; that behind them a clerical population was fermenting, awaiting their deliverance impatiently, and ready to fall on their knees before their conquerors? General Forey believed him, because one believes what one wants to believe, and he had no idea of the resistance prepared for him. He had said and frequently repeated that he was not seeking new glory in Mexico, that he had had his fill of it in his previous campaigns, but that he wished to conduct a kind of administrative campaign, and to give peace and happiness to a beautiful country and good people who were a prey to pillage and anarchy, and who needed only order and security to fall into step with the most civilized peoples and advance with them on the way of progress. . . . As for General Bazaine, he was what he has been all his life, ambiguous and sly. He saw as little as possible of General Forey. He cultivated M. de Saligny as much as possible and finally convinced him that things would go well only when he, Bazaine, had replaced General Forey. The Minister of France was working for that result, and the army in general, I must admit, shared that conviction."

The Penitentiary with the fortified convent of San Xavier adjoining it formed a single work and a formidable position, commanding access to the city, to which it was attached like an outgrowth, and requiring careful approaches. Trenches were dug, and with Bazaine in command progress was rapid. Captain Loizillon wrote it off in a few words. "The Mexicans probably understood nothing of what we were doing and did not disturb us in the least, and in three days we established our third parallel, losing only two men." His pen, however, raced with his pulse. In point of fact, for facts vary with observers and there were other officers taking notes, the progress of the operation was speeded by a constant pulsing of cannon from the neighboring forts, and the Mexicans understood it well enough to dispute it vigorously. But Bazaine dug in, and nothing could stop Forey once Bazaine had started. As soon as the second parallel was sunk, the artillery went into action and demolished the face of the convent; the third parallel was struck within one hundred thirty-five meters of the breach, and the building was gutted; an attack was now possible. "The fort lent itself to a regular siege," Colonel du Barail observed, "and the hour of its fall could be mathematically calculated." Bazaine, however, determined to carry it by assault, and he took all the proper precautions. A fourth parallel was pushed forward by night and the distance reduced to seventy meters; only the depth of the moat was unknown; and the work was crowned by Captain Loizillon, who led a reconnaissance squad up the last stretch in the dark. He missed the ditch, but he returned with information more valuable, drawing a fire from the convent that left no doubt that the Mexicans were not sleeping on their laurels. For him the hour of truth struck in the small hours of March 29; for the army at five o'clock that afternoon. At two the parallels were packed with picked troops, the survivors of the fiasco of last year in the first, waiting in silence for the signal, and promptly at five, when the slow strokes of a distant churchbell brought them to their feet, Bazaine ordered them over the top. Cheers rose from the trenches, and a long ground swell carried them up the embankment, wave after wave, under a withering fire from the battlements, the terraces, the sandbags and belfries of the gutted building, and from the whole ring of forts that awoke and barked back. But nothing could stop them. The hour had come, and they struck its stride with a giant urge. Smarting with an unforgotten defeat and pressed by a column of newcomers who had never known it, the survivors of the first expeditionary corps swarmed into the building and found it crammed, in fact, with men—men and not mere humankind, but men like themselves, fighting desperately, giving no ground, falling in heaps and dying in droves before the position was carried.

Carried it was, but to a fresh halt. Orders came to go no farther, and they came not from Forey, but from Bazaine. "But even if we had wished to, it would have been impossible," Captain Loizillon admitted, "the enemy having accumulated artillery in all the streets and placed every house in a state of defense." Detached from the town but adjoining it, the position was a target from both sides and a firetrap. Bazaine visited it after nightfall, when the carnage was over. So seasoned, so skilled in his trade, he counted all its victims, nevertheless, his loss; and he moved among them gloomily. Captain Blanchot, who was his adjutant and who had been tied to his heels all day, envied none of those who had known the exhilaration of battle. He had missed the heat of action, and for him the hour of truth struck as they picked their way through the gloom, missing their footing amid heaps of men defending their deathbed with their last throes. The screams of Mexicans trapped in a powder vault which the enemy had fired in their retreat haunted the night with an agony such as he had not heard since the hurricane at Veracruz. Bazaine muttered something trite about the horrors of war, and they continued their rounds.

There were other reasons to be gloomy in the morning. The Commander-in-Chief visited the position and congratulated Bazaine on a success which he had not expected, but which advanced the siege less than he expected. The convent was demolished, but the Penitentiary, which still stood, masked the real obstacle, the town itself, and unfortunately a Mexican engineer had been captured who declared that the town would be defended to the last house. The position was both a salient and a wedge, but behind it every house was fortified, every street barricaded and mounted with batteries, and as the staff scanned the city and compared notes with their prisoner, they recognized the difficulty of taking that dense honeycomb of buildings step by step and block by block. There were one hundred and fifty-eight blocks, of which the Penitentiary was the first, and with his affinity for difficulties Forey was in his element. Even Captain Loizillon was impressed. "In sum, the thing is harder to swallow than we supposed, for these people have a certain power of resistance when they are behind walls," he conceded. "Nevertheless, we hope to finish in eight or ten days, and without too heavy losses, with our system of advancing from house to house." The system was applied with some initial success, but it was slow, and the *élan* of the troops was cramped by it. By blasting their way from house to house, four blocks were wrecked in two days. Alternatives were tried—cannon, mines, night attacks. "Decidedly, we are in for a war of street fighting," Captain Loizillon wrote at the end of the second day. "I think that I was very moderate in saying that we would be finished in ten days. Our night fighting will cost us more in the end than an attack by main force, just as it did at Sebastopol, and when we enter Puebla we shall find little but ruins." And for a moment his mind wandered. "What will these people say to whom we repeat every day that it is not against them that we have come to make war?" Besides, it was bitterly cold; never in his life, not even in the Crimea, had he suffered so cruelly in the small hours of the morning.

In eight days seven blocks were taken, and with every advance the resistance stiffened. The cannon mounted on the Penitentiary were of too small caliber to dent the massive Spanish constructions beneath them. Mines were laid, and night attacks sprung, without doing any appreciable damage to those solid structures which defied the usual methods of dealing with them. The men became discouraged and the officers critical. The inventor of the system was a little old man, who had lost his legs and who lived in a sick chair; but he was the chief of staff. Since he was too crippled to move, the Commander-in-Chief was obliged to visit the ground himself; and there, hemmed in on all sides by tiers of barricades and cornered between convents teeming with marksmen perfectly sheltered, he grasped the obstacles that baffled his best troops and decided to go underground. The sappers sank a subterranean gallery, but as they struck bedrock, and the greater part of the city was known to be built upon stone, the experiment was abandoned. Other expedients were proposed; all of them were accepted, and none adopted. "General Forey is exasperating with his indecision and his lack of firmness in command," Captain Blanchot complained. "He listens to all the tittle-tattle humming in his ears and seems to have no mind of his own: everyone in turn is right and wrong." Bazaine favored an attack on the forts beyond the city, and Forey consented, but without abandoning the system of his crony-in-chief. A council of war was called to reconsider the whole situation. "Règle générale," wrote Colonel du Barail: "when a council of war is called, you may be sure that something has broken down. When all goes well, the Commander-in-Chief appropriates all the glory; when things go wrong, he hastens to share the responsibility with as many others as possible." The conference was an omnibus breakdown. That morning, at the burial of the artillery commander, who had just fallen, Forey had declared, "We will all die, and I the first of all, but we will take Puebla!" In the afternoon he entertained the council of war with his dread of losing his likeliest troops in the streets of Puebla, and wore out his seat trying to do something. In deference to Bazaine, he proposed to attack the fort of Carmen, and in deference to the chief of staff, to continue the house-to-house war at the same time with cannon and mines. But the new artillery commander objected that his field pieces were powerless against the walls of convents and churches, that the eight large siege cannon could not be introduced into the streets, that there were no longer munitions enough to start a second siege, and that there remained only six hundred kilograms of mine powder; and the council discarded that solution. Then Forey proposed a bolder one. The plan which he advanced was not his own, but he sponsored it enthusiastically, for it sprang from the brain of a nameless young officer on the General Staff, and the staff was stupefied by it. It was nothing more nor less than to raise the siege of Puebla, evacuate the sick and wounded to the neighboring village of Cholula, and march upon the capital. An inspiration of genius, according to the Commander-in-Chief, the idea was an incredible piece of political and military insanity, according to Colonel du Barail. "Such a retreat would rally the whole Mexican nation to Juarez," the Colonel commented, "cover us with shame and ridicule, and justify all the attacks of the Opposition in France, and all the galling speeches that were already serving the enemy as gun-wadding. . . . And we were to attempt this folly, leaving behind us the twenty-five thousand brave besieged in Puebla, and with the auxiliary army of Comonfort ahead of us! It spelled certain disaster and assured defeat!" Nevertheless, the council approved it all but unanimously. Bazaine and Douay favored it—their men, they said, were sick of street-fighting. The staff withdrew, depressed and uneasy, and pledged to keep the decision secret; but they reckoned without the ranks. In half an hour the secret was out and the camp seething with indignation. No sooner had the commanders come into contact with their men than they recognized their error and regretted it, and Forey was induced to reverse himself. The breakdown was hastily repaired. It was decided that Bazaine should besiege the forts of Carmen and Totimehuacan to the south, while the other commanders continued plugging the system of the chief of staff as economically as possible; and the Commander-in-Chief, recovering his spirit of the morning, went to bed vowing to get the better of *arrogant Puebla* at all costs. The problem was assigned to each of his generals in turn.

On April 18, one month after the siege began, Captain Loizillon was still in the Penitentiary and at a loss to explain the delay. "The Mexicans are defending themselves with a vigor of which we were far from thinking them capable," he wrote. "Then, too, there has been neither direction nor ensemble in the siege operations. Every twenty-four hours we have had another general in the trenches; usually he adopted neither the way of thinking nor the method of working of his predecessor; furthermore, he had no time to familiarize himself with the terrain in this maze of tunneled walls that we have made to communicate from one house to another, and hence to judge our position properly in order to know what to do. Moreover, the engineers and the artillery worked each in their own way, without a thought for the whole. Such a state of things was bound to bring bad results. That is what has happened." They were all in the Penitentiary. It was a magnificent building built on an American model, with walls two or three meters thick, "only everything in Mexico is ruined or unfinished. The Penitentiary is in the latter state"—and so was the siege. The measure of their predicament was that immense construction, laid out on a large scale, where they were quartered in cells two by two-and-a-half long and broad, penned in but absolutely safe, for the small spherical shells of the Mexicans flattened themselves without effect against those penal walls. Puebla was the Penitentiary multiplied one hundred and fifty-seven fold. A few blocks of cells had been won with comparative facility, but only because the enemy had abandoned them to shorten his lines; a foothold had been gained on the fringe of the town; they were barely abreast of the Convent of Santa Ines, the first bulwark of the inner ring of defenses, and the experts were puzzled to crack it.

It was the turn of General Douay. This commander, who had come out as second to Lorencez, and who was fast spoiling into a confirmed critic of his colleagues, was entrusted with the attack on Santa Ines.

Breaching batteries were mounted on the block facing the convent, and the assault was carefully prepared with all the resources which his own skill plus the ingenuity of his colleagues could suggest, for they put their heads together to help him. Mines were sunk under the street to spring the outer wall, but on the previous evening the enemy had heard the drilling and sunk countermines, and before the meeting of plagiarists could fuse, a storm broke, and in ten minutes the galleries were so wet that it was decided to explode the charge prematurely. "This setback was the cause of our failure the next day," according to Captain Loizillon; but by now he was so accustomed to defeat that he snatched at any excuse to explain it. He had a definite premonition of disaster when he reported for duty the next morning. The semiexplosion of the mine had sapped a part of the outer wall, but beyond it lay a large garden enclosed by an iron grille, which the Mexicans or the concussion had tilted toward them at an impossible angle, and beyond it the Mexicans were entrenched in four tiers of embankments, solidly buttressing the convent. Beginning at six in the morning, the French batteries pounded the target for three hours; thirty of their gunners were killed by the enemy barrage, and by nine o'clock General Douay was informed that munitions were running low and that the artillery could do no more. He gave the order to attack. Two columns crossed the street and broke before they could grapple with the grille. Captain Loizillon would have called off the attack, "but vanity and the will to win drove us to new efforts, which increased our losses. To continue was insane. General Douay decided to halt the attack and ordered the artillery to resume fire." At that moment Loizillon learned that two hundred men had turned the grille and penetrated into the enclosure, and he hastened to warn Douay that they were exposed to death from both sides. This semisuccess, and not the mishap of the mine, was the cause of their failure. Who could be both cool and French then? Not Loizillon. He looked at Douay, and words failed him to describe the expression that came over "the face of that good man. To know his men in the power of the enemy and to forsake them! Or to renew the attack with no chance of success! After biting his lips until he drew blood, he said to me, 'Order the artillery to cease fire.' He was mighty fine in that reverse." As soon as the retreat was sounded, the fire from the convent redoubled, and the daylight was blown out of the block from which the attack was launched. The attempt ended in a general withdrawal.

But the disaster had only begun. Back to the Penitentiary came the casualties—the worst of them General Douay, who, unwounded himself, carried their suffering in his face. He could not conceal his distress. He embraced Bazaine. The staff assembled for another consultation. The meeting was held at the far end of a long corridor, and as the cor-

ridor was vaulted and had excellent acoustic properties, Captain Blanchot, who was stationed within call, heard not a little of what was
said and took notes. The discussion began in an undertone—out of respect for the dying, he supposed—but it soon became heated, voices
were raised, and sharp words were exchanged. Both Bazaine and
Douay blamed the system of street fighting, the inventor defended it
stubbornly, and Douay finally lost patience and declared bluntly that
Colonel Auvergne was incapable of judging the question, being unable to see its effects for himself. Brutal as the words were, and fully
deserved, Captain Blanchot could not but admire the pluck with which
the cripple replied, creaking nervously in his chair, that if need be he
would have himself carried to the breach. His system was doomed,
however, at Santa Ines. Bazaine and Douay recommended taking the
outer forts one by one and waiting for the town to starve or surrender.
After all, someone said, from a military point of view the town was
already captured, since they were masters of the salient where they were
sitting, and if the madmen who commanded Puebla insisted on waging a war of savages, destroying a town to build barricades, that was
no reason to continue a contest which was no longer one of professional
arms, but of revolutionary hordes. Others favored abandoning the
siege and making for the capital, where they would be welcomed with
open arms. But the boldest suggestion of all was made by Forey, who
was heard to say, *"Ma foi, messieurs,* before leaving France I asked for
equipment, which was refused me. Well, I decline my responsibility,
and so can you, if you wish." Captain Blanchot hardly believed his ears
as he jotted down those incredible words, which would have been
damning in a military court. The Commander-in-Chief declining his
responsibility! Forey blaming the seat warmers in Paris! There were
some words which should never be spoken. There were some slips
which could not be made in decent society. Merely to be within earshot
of them was a disaster. The debate dragged on inconclusively, interrupted for a moment by a captain of Zouaves, who arrived from Santa
Ines with a list of casualties, which he handed to Forey. Forey read it
without comment. There was not a sound from him then. The Zouave,
speaking in a cold, stern, and nervous undertone, said that two hundred
soldiers and their officers were still resisting in a corner of the convent
. . . that they were fighting . . . that they could be heard . . . that
. . . that . . . He waited; he could say no more. Finally Forey broke
the silence. "Too bad!" he said. "Too bad! Unfortunate effects of war!"
The discussion subsided, and nothing had been settled when the Commander-in-Chief rose to his feet an hour later and walked out, saying,
"My word, talk it over among yourselves and come to some understanding." The staff followed. Passing through the ranks of wounded
lying on the floor, Forey was followed by looks of disaffection, which

fortunately he did not see, but which others did—Captain Blanchot, and the staff, and the limping troopers returning from Santa Ines, glum, silent, demoralized, but marching at least in pairs.

No, there were some things which one could not do to a Frenchman. There was a woman, for instance, in Puebla, who came to her window and flaunted her buttocks in the face of the Frenchies crammed fifty-men deep in their dens across the street, until someone took a pot shot at her. And there was Forey.

At the very moment when the retreat was sounded from Santa Ines, Forey received a letter from the Emperor informing him that he knew from a reliable source—the United States Minister in Paris—that the army would meet with no serious resistance either in Puebla or in Mexico City. The contents of the letter, which Forey could not keep to himself, excited the most bitter reflections in the camp. Colonel du Barail subscribed to them. "We said to ourselves, in Paris they will not understand what we are doing here. They will never be able to explain why we cannot get the better of these Mexicans . . . and yet we were doing what we could, we were not sparing ourselves; but besides our previous slowness, which allowed Juarez to prepare himself, we knew, vaguely at least, other moral causes for this extraordinary tenacity. In the first place, Puebla had always passed for the reactionary and Cleri-cal capital of Mexico; it was called Puebla de los Angeles, and until then it merited its name. Hence the Liberal government had a double interest in prolonging the resistance: it proved that the dissident party was obliged to fight with it against the invader, and at the same time it completely ruined the citadel of its political adversaries to pun-ish it for a long opposition. Then, too, from all corners of the world adventurers had flown to Puebla, attracted, some by a sickly love of crises, others by cupidity and the chance of gain, and others yet by their hatred of the Empire and of France. All these aliens were careful to keep out of range of rifle fire, but by their presence and their speeches they overexcited the determination of the Mexican officers to surrender only at the last extremity. Finally, our own political discords served to prolong the siege. I have already mentioned the opposition of the famous Five of the Chamber of Deputies to the expedition of Mexico. The speech made by Jules Favre on that occasion, translated into all languages, had been shipped in bales to Puebla. The besieged showered us with copies, and it is a curious example of human complications that that bile, poured out on the floor of the Legislative Chamber, should have been molded, on the other side of the earth, into bullets of lead that may have struck the sons of those who elected Jules Favre." Otherwise the world would not have been round. And the worst of it was that the political infection of defeat traveled, with the Emperor's letter, all along the line.

Captain Loizillon made a stubborn attempt to minimize the disaster.

"After this wretched affair there was some discouragement," he admitted; but the attempt was not very successful, and the depth of his discouragement was betrayed by his determination to master it. "We are bound to get the better of this city of Puebla de los Angeles," he insisted; and no doubt, had it been Puebla de los Angeles, he would not have been wrong. But it was Puebla de Zaragoza. "Only it may be long," he continued, "for the Mexicans who are in there are not the Mexicans we know. The defense of Puebla, in short, has been perfectly organized and conducted. We cannot put up the least little earthwork but it is laid low on the same day from the city. What will the Emperor say when he receives this news? he who assured us by the last mail that he knew in the most positive manner that we would meet with no resistance either at Puebla or Mexico City? What miserable war we are fighting here, and what damage it will do to France!" His mind veered away and returned to it, searching for some more plausible explanation of the stalemate than the incompetence of the Commander-in-Chief or the technical confusion and shortcomings of the siege: politics were an inseparable part of the picture. "We have come to attack the most vital and progressive part of the country, the one that is strongest and most numerous. We are relying on the party that is rotten and finished. We have come, in short, to combat the Liberal principle on which we pride ourselves at home." They had come to Mexico, in short, because they had been fed on rancid biscuit in France and had not tasted Jules Favre in time. "Add to that the influence of Saligny, the man who is responsible for our being so wretchedly engaged in this war and who has so hampered the military command. To hear him, he would have gone from Orizaba to Mexico City with a single battalion of Zouaves!" And, speaking of the devil, he had just appeared before Puebla.

Lingering in Orizaba even longer than Forey, Saligny arrived at the front lines just in time to witness the disaster at Santa Ines and to add to the general irritation in the camp. Captain Blanchot was detailed to find him quarters. The assignment was difficult. Headquarters were overcrowded, and no one could or would make room "even for a clerk of the Quai d'Orsay"; but he acquitted himself creditably of an irksome commission. He found an accommodating general willing to share a mill with the Minister, and as the Minister arrived in five carriages, one of them loaded with women, no one could have done better than Blanchot. He was curious to see a celebrity whom he knew only by hearsay, and as usual he made notes. His first impression was favorable. He was pleasantly surprised to find, after a few words with him, that M. de Saligny was a man of "extremely agreeable culture." His taste in women was good, too, and the Captain was highly impressionable. His first impression was canceled, however, by his second. With the Minister came another *gros bonnet,* M. Budin, an Inspector of Finances fresh from France; and as M. Budin came unannounced and no arrangements had been made for him, the Captain naturally expected Saligny to offer him a quarter of his half of the mill. But there were some things which neither as man to man nor as one Frenchman for another M. de Saligny would do. M. Budin was forced to sleep in a tent. As he began his career in the army, however, he did not complain.

To Captain Loizillon, as to everyone else in the camp, the Minister was a thorn in the flesh. He was incorrigible. After the fiasco at Santa Ines, it was true, he had had the grace to go to Forey and make an *amende honorable*—but how many other windbags had been punctured by that disaster! M. de Saligny admitted that he was mistaken and said that he would never have believed the Mexicans capable of such energy, trying, as the Captain put it, "to repatriate himself with the Commander-in-Chief, for this time the facts spoke louder than all his assertions." But he had not mended his ways. A few days later, in Cholula, where the refugees from the siege, the clerical population of Puebla, and the French were quartered, he let his tongue run and declared that the army was wrong to attack the town and that, even now, he would undertake to capture the capital himself with a single platoon of cavalry. "And this is the man to whom the policy of a country is entrusted! Poor France, she might play such a fine role at this moment in Europe and she is paralyzed by this stupid war! If I tell you all this," the Captain explained to his parents, "it is because I know that public opinion in France agrees with us. When I left you, I knew more or less to what sort of a war I was going; but not being charged, after all, with the political direction of my country, I regarded this war merely as a good opening to make a campaign and work at my career." So had Saligny—but the comparison was too odious—the less said about Saligny the better. "Now that I reread this letter, I am tempted to tear it up. I have let my pen run, and it has run faster than I wished. Yet I tell you nothing that the whole of France does not know. We still bear in mind the honor of France and of the flag for which we are responsible, and which is our religion. I will no longer set a date for the capture of Puebla. It may last long, it may be over in a week. All that we need is a successful attack. Let our soldiers once meet the Mexicans nose to nose, and for all the energy of those who command them, we shall follow them from house to house, from street to street, and master the town." Having gotten the better of himself, he broke off and mailed the letter. It was April 30.

The responsibility for the disaster was bandied back and forth between the Minister and the Commander-in-Chief. "What were you doing since you have been here," said Forey, "not to know that the Mexicans would defend themselves like the Spaniards in Saragossa?" — "It is your own fault," Saligny retorted. "You soldiers think of nothing but wounds and scars, crosses and grades. You should have left Puebla and marched on the capital, where we would have settled the Mexican question." Completely disconcerted, Forey multiplied councils of war and succeeded in producing nothing but fresh recriminations among his principal officers; for it now appeared that the nameless genius on the general staff who had proposed to abandon Puebla derived his inspiration from M. de Saligny, and that, after ruining Lorencez, the Minister was now performing the same service for Forey and making room for Bazaine.

The attack on Santa Ines on April 25 cost the army, in casualties, three hundred thirty-five losses, killed or wounded, plus seventy-six captured, without counting the two hundred who penetrated the convent and who were officially listed as missing. Everyone was asking, and no one knew, what to do. The 5th of May came and went, and the stalemate was unbroken. The anniversary was marked, nevertheless, by a ray of fresh hope. On that night the forces of Comonfort felt out the French positions in an attempt to introduce a convoy into the town. The attempt was repulsed; it was repeated the next night; the persistence of the effort left no doubt that hunger was draining the defense, and confidence returned to headquarters. Thereupon Bazaine proposed, and after long argument persuaded Forey to allow him, to lead a night attack on the army of Comonfort ten miles away. On the night of May 7 he fell on the enemy at the village of San Lorenzo, surprising and routing them and returning with twelve hundred prisoners, three flags, and eight large cannon. With the permission of Forey and three squadrons and three battalions more than he had, he would have pursued the fugitive remnants of the army of Comonfort to the gates of the capital, if need be; but that was asking too much of the old man.

From that day Bazaine became the great favorite of the army. "The soldier," as Colonel du Barail said, "happy and proud to feel himself commanded by a real warrior, lavished on him the proof of blind and unlimited confidence. But, as always happens, his popularity was carved at the expense of that which the Commander-in-Chief might have obtained. They were compared with one another, and that comparison was not in favor of General Forey." Sluggish with age, physically inactive, showing himself rarely to the soldiers, he was rough, irascible, and discouraging when he did, and returned to headquarters as he came, flat on his feet. "What a difference from General Bazaine! Day and night, in the trenches, in the bivouac, he was seen moving about without pomp or embarrassment or escort, on foot, his cane in his hand, good-natured, talking familiarly to everyone, joking with the soldiers, listening to them, explaining to them what they had to do and how to do it, and walking, in short, very skillfully toward his goal." But he had not reached it yet. Forey ordered him back to the forts. The siege was resumed with fresh vigor. Assured that the garrison was starving and alarmed by the approach of an inglorious triumph, Forey pressed the attack on the forts of Carmen and Totimehuacan. Confidential overtures for a capitulation were received and rejected; but the appearance at headquarters of the Mexican general who brought them tipped off the army. On the 17th, at one o'clock in the morning, a series of explosions rocked the town, and at five o'clock Forey received a note from Ortega, informing him that he had disbanded his army and destroyed his armament, and that the town was at his disposal. An hour later the liquidation of the defense began, and the truth leaked out.

Captain Loizillon was deluged with duties that morning. The disbanding soldiers came pouring out of the town in confusion. "These unfortunates," he wrote, "arrived in our camp to the number of twelve hundred, dying of hunger, naked, and crying like wild animals. We made two depots for them. I was in charge of one. After trying to make some order, I chose some of their men to go to the commissary and fetch food for the others. As soon as they caught sight of the biscuit, they fell on it, and it was impossible to prevent them from stifling their hunger, but this scene was nothing compared to what happened when I had the food brought to the prisoners' camp. Those unfortunates fell on the ones carrying the victuals with such violence and fury that I could not think of stopping them. It was a veritable pillage, but happily a partial one, for after a while we were able to take from those who had too much enough to give to those who had nothing. These wretches, half of whom had nothing but a pair of pants, had spent the night under a downpour of rain, for we have been having storms every night for the past week, forerunners of the wet season."

The prisoners included 20 generals, 303 higher officers, 1179 subalterns, and over 11,000 noncommissioned officers and soldiers. As the officers had surrendered unconditionally and were protected by no written agreement, Saligny proposed to deport them to Martinique or to the French penal colony at Cayenne, while Almonte wished to shoot them on the spot. "There is no written convention, it is true," Forey replied, "but in place of my signature on paper there are laws of honor which are even more binding. There are traditions in the military fraternity which I shall not fail. By the obstinacy of its defense and the courage of its commanders, this army may have excited the anger of politicians, but as for us soldiers, it has compelled our esteem and consideration, and I shall never allow these good people to be treated as malefactors." The officers were sent to France as prisoners of war. Of the soldiers, five thousand were incorporated, by their own consent, in the forces of Marquez; the rest were sent to Veracruz to work on the railroad. To prevent the prisoners from escaping, the buttons of their pants were cut, so that generals and privates were obliged to hold them with both hands, and the battalions which escorted them could distinguish the decent people from the rest if they tried to slip away.

INTERVENTION 509

On May 19 the French army finally entered Puebla to the sound of bugles, drums, trumpets, and regimental bands, and with flags flying, as it had greeted the sun two months before. General Forey, riding at the head of the column, was surprised and disconcerted to see not a single authority to receive him at the gates, not a spectator in the streets, not a woman in a window to smile on his men. It was a dead city. The column advanced through the ruins, the blare of martial music barely dispelling the lugubrious silence, to the Cathedral, where the clergy sang a solemn *Te Deum* in honor of Forey and the French army. But the bells were silent. The fall of Puebla was fittingly celebrated five miles away in Cholula, where the clergy had fled the siege. There Colonel du Barail was amused by an enthusiasm which, as he said, was equally divided between the invader and the Good Lord. "For three days the churches vomited into the streets a flood of relics and statues of saints, confessors, and martyrs, escorted by a swarm of cherubim in costumes of Opera dancers. It was almost a Carnival, for everyone wore costumes of the sixteenth or seventeenth century. . . . The clergy directed all this with an air of compunction and indescribable beatitude, and the Indians prostrated themselves in the dust, beating their breasts. It was touching, but a trifle comic. And the music! Clarinets, cornets, trombones, chimes, bass drums, cymbals, whined, brayed, roared, lowed, thundered waltzes, polkas, schottisches, which the musicians performed from memory and without notes, not too badly but too often." But General de Mirandol, who was quartered in Cholula, was not amused. If there was anything calculated to breed enemies of Mexico, it was Mexican music; and after enduring the din for three days and nights, he called out a picket of cavalry and dispersed the devils.

It was in no spirit of triumph that Captain Loizillon wrote the epilogue to the siege. Puebla had been captured somehow—but how? In his official reports to Paris the Commander-in-Chief stated that he had found substantial stocks of food and munitions in the town, and he attributed its fall to the vigor with which the attack on the forts had been conducted; these versions might pass muster in France, but not in Mexico, and the Captain tipped off his parents to the truth. One of the first things which Forey had done was to found a paper in Puebla, which was "trying to gull public opinion and make people believe that the town had surrendered not to starvation, but to our attacks." The triumph of May 17 was almost as humiliating as the defeat of May 5, and the army was praying in the Cathedral for marching orders, "so as to give the Mexicans no time to make another defense like that of Puebla in the capital."

Having gotten Forey into Puebla, however, it was hard to get him out. He lingered for two weeks—long enough for Captain Loizillon to digest his memories of the siege and to reflect coolly on its results. He had lost some of his best friends, he had seen them in their agony, he had missed them bitterly, and he was surprised and pained to realize how quickly he had forgotten them. He wondered why—self-preservation, no doubt: to feel their sufferings so sharply was a form of self-pity. But if he hardened himself to their pain, he could not reconcile himself to its purposelessness. What had they died for, in fact? The plain and the approaches to the camp were strewn with the speeches of Jules Favre—a preposterous state of things, he protested; had one ever heard the like of it? But even worse was the antidote to that poisonous propaganda. The French replied in kind and reprinted for the benefit of the enemy the speech of M. Billault, the spokesman for the Throne, guaranteeing the Mexicans complete freedom to choose their own government, even if this meant the re-election of Juarez. What were they fighting for then? To overthrow Juarez or to reinstate him? To wage a war of pure form, a professional exercise, at so cruel a cost, for an empty gesture of patronage? The effect of such propaganda was double-edged. If the pledges of Billault meant what they said, they reduced the whole expedition to absurdity; if they did not, the result was the same. The Emperor had backed the wrong party from the beginning, and the proof of it was that in Puebla, the levitical city *par excellence,* they had been received as coldly as everywhere else, while in Veracruz, which they had held from the start, the shops closed and the women donned mourning when they went to church. Worse yet, Ortega and seven of his generals had escaped in Orizaba, and three prominent Frenchmen there had been arrested on suspicion of facilitating their flight—"such are the people we are fighting for!" M. de Saligny would certainly make the most of this scandal, as well as of the delay in advancing on the capital, "especially if we meet with resistance in Mexico City, for after the capture of Puebla the Mexicans were so demoralized that they had already made their preparations for departure, but they have gradually recovered confidence and are awaiting us."

M. de Saligny did make the most of it. Colonel du Barail, watching his feud with the Commander-in-Chief, saw the crisis of his intrigues approaching; for the Minister was cornered and on the defensive. When the Mexican prisoners reached Veracruz, only 13 out of 20 generals, 110 superior officers out of 303, and 407 out of 1179 subalterns answered the roll call. "M. Dubois de Saligny profited by this mass flight to blab against our generals, whom he could not forgive for the siege of Puebla, which had given the lie so strikingly to his optimistic prognostics, and which he persisted in representing as a useless act of war, due to the desire of the heads of the army to draw up resounding bulletins. General Bazaine alone found favor in his eyes, because his cunning crony abstained from all criticism and had succeeded in making the Minister of France believe that he abounded in his views." Forey was delighted by the escape of Ortega, so great was his admiration for him as a soldier; and if he could have laid his hands on him, he would gladly have put him into the provisional government which Saligny was organizing for the capital.

On June 2 four foreign consuls arrived with word that Juarez had abandoned the capital. Marching orders were immediately issued, and Captain Loizillon was sent ahead to find quarters for the army in the capital. At the moment of departure he was smitten with fresh misgivings. "Until now we had believed that Mexico City was probably the knot of the war, but now we begin to have grave doubts. It seems certain that Juarez will withdraw with his whole government to Morelia, which lies twenty-four hours to the west, and it follows that we shall be masters as usual only of the points we occupy. After eighteen months of war, we shall have conquered the road from Veracruz to Mexico City: that will be the result." M. Budin had come out of his tent and was hiring customs inspectors and other employees en masse, and a mining engineer had just arrived at headquarters. "From these indications," he concluded, "we suppose that the Emperor means to make a conquest of Mexico. I do not believe that it will be a conquest very popular in France, any more than with the army here."

12

BUT Juarez had yet to be heard from. After the fall of Puebla he issued a proclamation exhorting the population to defend the capital to the last extremity and to merit the attention of the world by emulating the example of Ortega; and for a few days feverish preparations were made for a last stand there. For a few days the President almost forfeited the freedom of the country to its glory; but Juarez knew better. However spectacular such a stand might be, and impressive to foreign opinion, the destinies of the nation had not been entrusted to him to say die, and having staked all the organized resources of the government on a single battle, he recognized that the defense of the capital was untenable and abandoned it for the defense of the country. Congress, in its closing session on May 31, gave him a fresh vote of confidence, and he pledged himself once more to honor the bequest with which the Assembly expired in his hands. "Adversity, Citizen Deputies," he said, "discourages none but contemptible peoples; ours has been ennobled by great feats and we are far from being shorn of the immense obstacles, material and moral, which the country will oppose to unjust invaders. The vote of confidence with which you have again honored me engages my gratitude to the Assembly of the nation in the highest degree, though it is impossible for me to engage my honor and duty in defense of our country more than I already have."

Superfluous words; the struggle had not ceased, and his farewell was only as fugitive as the flight of time. At three in the afternoon the booming of cannon announced the dissolution of the Assembly. An immense crowd collected in front of the Palace. The departure of the government was set for the same day; but the decision, though it was taken in haste, was unhurried in effect. With that deliberation which lent gravity to the most common, and regularity to the most momentous, of his acts, the President waited until sundown to order the lowering of the flag at the normal hour. The crowd saw the colors hauled down as usual. The men raised their hats and the women their children for the last time; and save for the ranks of troops presenting arms, the playing of the national anthem, the rolling of drums, and the presence of the head of the nation with his ministers and military staff on a balcony of the Palace, the final formality was performed as simply on the evening of May 31 as on any other day. The flag was handed to Juarez, who raised it to his lips and cried in a clear high voice, *Viva Mexico!* The crowd responded in unison, with that rising inflection which lends buoyancy and suspense to every utterance of the native voice, and the solemnity was over. The last stand in the capital was a spectacular display of common sense. In the morning the government was gone, and the foreign consuls hurried to Puebla to inform Forey that the city was his.

On June 10 Forey made his triumphal entrance into the capital, riding between Almonte on his right and Saligny on his left, amid the flowers, cheers, and ovations which they had promised to Lorencez— lavish tribute to the truth of the adage that everything comes to him who waits for it. In a telegram to the Minister of War, which he forwarded without an hour's delay, Forey wrote history as it should be written, everyone speaking for himself. "I have just entered Mexico City at the head of the army. With a heart still thrilled I address this despatch to Your Excellency to announce that the entire population of this capital welcomed the army with an enthusiasm verging on delirium. The soldiers of France were literally crushed under the garlands and nosegays of which nothing can give any idea but the entrance of the army returning from Italy on August 14, 1859. I attended a *Te Deum* with all the officers in the magnificent cathedral of this capital, which was filled with an immense crowd. Then the army, in wonderful form, paraded before me amid cries of *Vive l'Empereur! Vive l'Impératrice!* After the parade I received the authorities, who harangued me in the Government Palace. These people are avid of order, justice, and real liberty. In my replies to their representatives I promised them all this in the name of the Emperor. At the first opportunity, I shall have the honor of giving you full details of this reception, unparalleled in history, which has the scope of a political event whose reverberations will be immense."

Forey spoke for himself and to himself and, unfortunately, to no one else. The author of that telegram, like the author of any form of literature, had his critics; but happily on June 10 he was unaware of them. In the army marching so smartly behind him, however, one of the most persistent and unsparing was treading close on his heels. Captain Loizillon was the first French officer to enter the capital, and having made the rounds for a week he knew the city as well, he said, as if he had lived there for ten years. In his search for quarters he met with the tail end of a resistance none the less stubborn for being passive, and was not surprised by it, since it was the same welcome which the army met everywhere else. "But I was surprised," he wrote to his parents, "by the display that took place at the official entrance of the Commander-in-Chief. The balconies were draped with hangings; the windows were crowded with women, one prettier than the other. The picture was satisfying, in short, thanks to the orders of the commander of the city, who had unlimited credit for this reception. The people were attracted by curiosity rather than enthusiasm. The places where we were applauded or showered with flowers were rare, and those few demonstrations had been organized by the police and the commander of the city. Nevertheless, the Commander-in-Chief has taken all this for true coin, his vanity preventing him from judging things at their true value."

The telegram of June 10 cost the paymaster exactly eighty thousand francs. But Forey was satisfied. In a proclamation issued two days later he announced the completion of the first part of his mission. The ignominious flight of the late government, he declared, "must destroy all their illusions and make them feel their impotence to retain the ruins of a power of which they have made so deplorable a use. The military question, therefore, is settled. There remains the political question." And as the claque was waiting for the opening of that question, he went on talking.

PART FIVE

The Empire

I

FOREY went on talking as usual. The military question was not closed. The army knew better. "The ignominious flight of the late government" was merely Forey full of manifesto. As a matter of fact, it was a tactical retreat which, far from closing the military question, merely extended it into territory which decentralized the war and prolonged it indefinitely. Puebla was the key to the capital, but the back country was the key to the conquest of Mexico.

Nine days after leaving the capital Juarez unfurled the flag, ninety miles to the north in San Luis Potosi, and issued a proclamation which exactly defined the position of the French in what was left of our Mexico. "By reconcentrating in one point the enemy will be weak in all others and, dispersed, will be weak everywhere. He will be obliged to recognize that the Republic is not confined to Mexico City or Puebla— for life and spirit, the sense of right and strength, the love of independence and democracy, and the noble pride aroused by the iniquitous invader of our soil are sentiments disseminated among the whole of the Mexican people." To those synonyms for common sense he trusted to convince the French that "the subject and silent majority on whose rising Napoleon based the success and justification of the greatest crime of the nineteenth century is a chimera invented by a handful of traitors. The French were deceived when they supposed that they could subdue the country merely by the sound of their arms, and when they thought to consummate their insolent project by violating the laws of honor, and when they declared themselves masters of Puebla by occupying the fort of San Xavier. They are miserably deluded now by the belief that they dominate the country, when they have barely begun to feel the difficulties of their ill-judged expedition; for if they have spent so much time, invested such resources, and sacrificed so many lives to obtain some few advantages, what can they expect when we oppose them with a whole people as an army and our dilated country as a battlefield?"

But if the military question was not closed, its character had changed, and changed for the worse. Manifestoes favor their authors. The backbone of organized resistance had been broken at Puebla; what remained was the symbolic resistance of the scattered members, and though several divisions were still in the field and reinforcements were promised by the states, the hope of opposing the French with a whole people as an army and an entire country as a battlefield was manifestly inflated by patriotism and dilated by defiance. The manifestoes of the President were written for him; and Juarez knew better than to boast. In field fighting the native forces had been consistently worsted and their fighting qualities exactly defined by the enemy. It was impossible to deny the verdict which the French had passed on the flower of the Mexican army at Puebla as a body of unseasoned soldiers, incapable of resisting a vigorous attack in open country, fleeing before a bayonet charge or a hand-to-hand combat, but tenacious enough under long-range fire and redoubtable as soon as they were behind walls, for experience had repeatedly proved its truth. During the siege several cavalry encounters had occurred on the outskirts, in which the French had invariably routed forces that outnumbered them, the army of Comonfort had been rushed from the field in half an hour, and, worse yet, the prisoners had gone over to the winning side and turned their guns against their late comrades with a facility which shocked the French themselves as the most deadly of the national habits and the most damning proof of patriotic weakness. The whole strategy of defense had to be recast accordingly, and the author of the manifesto knew that the best way to strengthen a weak story was to displace the interest. By reverting to the natural form of warfare of the country and employing guerrilla tactics over a vast stretch of territory it was possible to dispute the progress of the French, cutting their communications, menacing their movements, compelling them to extend and thin their lines, and presenting an effective because a fatiguing resistance merely by keeping the military question open; and a campaign was planned along those lines. It was impossible, however, to do more. Since there was not sufficient material to garrison the large towns, hostilities were confined to a systematic feint. If ever faith was needed, it was needed then—but not by Juarez. He was his manifesto in person, and he compressed it into three words—three of the commonest words in the language: *no tenga cuidado*. Was there a more overworked phrase in Mexico? Yet when the fainthearted brought him their fears and heard him say, "Do not worry," it was as if those words had never been spoken before, or by anyone else. It was impossible to doubt, for there was no doubt in him. How vulnerable his position was in San Luis Potosi he revealed later, but at the time he merely repeated his daily "Do not worry, we shall win," and people discovered how much meaning the most hackneyed words had when they were spoken by him; and nothing else.

He could not honestly say more; but his faith was neither blind nor unreasoning. Before the siege of Puebla Ortega had written to him: "If we place Puebla at the height that I want, and I will do it, we shall remove the question from the ground where it now rests and force a crisis on the moral terrain; and if we do this, Mexico will rise to a height at which it has never been before and is not now. And we will do it, because it is not in the sphere of the impossible." With those words he handed the key to the situation to Juarez, and in the new phase of the struggle, which was now a test of endurance, Juarez had the saving qualities of tenacity, courage, insight and faith, the staying power, the native strength, needed to force a moral crisis in the camp of the enemy. That was his task, after Ortega's. The military question was only half the battle; it was inseparable from the political question, and with the occupation of the capital the French fell heir to the problems which had wrecked his government and upon the solution of which the consolidation of their triumph depended. From the moment that the contest shifted to that ground, victor and vanquished were on an equal footing, and Juarez settled down to observe the experiments of the French with the confidence of experience. His plan was simple: to fight a delaying action in the field and to gain time for the political difficulties of intervention to develop. For him, even more than for Forey, it was true that all things come to him who waits for them, and he could afford to wait, while Forey was in a hurry to finish.

The difficulties of an easy triumph were clear to Captain Loizillon from the day that the army occupied the capital. "We had no sooner arrived," he wrote several days later, "than the clergy began to ring all the bells to make up for the constraint they had suffered under the Juarez government, which had fixed the hours when the bells might be heard. Since then we have been deafened. Under Juarez, processions were forbidden as they are in France. Last Thursday the clergy asked permission to hold the procession of the *Fête-Dieu*. The Commander-in-Chief not only consented, but attended the procession with all his officers. The Mexicans looked for all the world as if they were mocking us. All that we lacked were tapers in our hands." It was not merely months that had been lost in reaching the capital, it was centuries of progress. "The reactionaries think themselves masters of the situation and have no doubt that we shall restore all their property and retrograde influence to the clergy. With all our good will, it is impossible to do anything so exorbitant, and the result will be that we shall have the reactionary party against us, and that we shall maintain ourselves here only by force."

In that din of bells Juarez was heard from far more clearly than in his proclamation in San Luis Potosi.

Although Colonel du Barail studiously avoided politics, believing like most of his brother officers that they were none of his business, he also noticed the first palpable effects of the occupation. The welcome which the army received on June 10 dazzled him, and he accepted it at face value, for "at every step the enthusiasm increased with the contact of two Latin peoples, of lively imagination and vibrant nerves, soaring to the sound of their acclamations and the spectacle of their joy. It was a moment of profound and fraternal delirium, the memory of which will be ineffaceable in the souls of the actors and the spectators. When the head of the parade emerged in the great square surrounded by porticos, where the Cathedral stands, and the open doors disclosed the gilded interior, and on the threshold a glittering clergy, in gala array, it was as if the souls of two peoples had been wedded in a *féerie*." Those for whom history is a pageant had their fill of it that day. But, he added, "that lovely fete was followed by the day after. The 10th of June marked the triumph of the French army, the 11th marked the triumph of the Clerical party, which had summoned it and which it came to sustain. . . . A monster procession was organized for that day, and nothing was neglected to give it an incomparable effect. The triumphal arches of the day before served for this new parade, which was escorted by three squadrons of cavalry and three regiments of French infantry, and which was hailed with the same enthusiasm, the same flowers, the same acclamations, and the same smiling women. The politicians of the army and the French mission thought that we were going too far and throwing ourselves too much in the arms of the Clerical party. It is certain that all the acts of the Commander-in-Chief were designed to render ostensible the protection we gave to that party." Thus, as one example out of many, every Sunday a military Mass was celebrated in the Cathedral, attended by an entire division. One regiment was ranged in the church, while the rest of the division, with its regiment of cavalry and its batteries of artillery, was massed on the square and executed, under the orders of a general, the movements and maneuvers of arms prescribed by the ritual at each phrase of the divine service. The Commander-in-Chief, with his staff, was always present at the Mass and reviewed the troops after it. "This parade produced an excellent effect in that it showed the capital splendid troops, but it was pointed out that it offended the feelings of the Liberal party, which it might have been wiser to woo by some concessions, instead of deepening every day the gulf that separated us from it."

But, being a mere bystander, Colonel du Barail indulgently watched the Commander-in-Chief walking into that booby-trap. "I admit that it was practically impossible to keep the balance straight between two parties as uncompromising as the Clericals and the Liberals. The Clericals were not far from demanding the restoration of the Inquisition, and the Liberals the expulsion of everything that wore a cassock. General Forey lost his Latin amid all these intrigues and contradictions. His intentions were of the best, he had been very much touched by the welcome extended to the French army and himself, and he wanted to work sincerely for the happiness of Mexico. But the task was above his strength, especially as he lacked that continuous energy without which nothing great can be done; a caricature, a newspaper article, was enough to infuriate him and make him contradict the measures which he himself had decreed the day before. . . . On the next day, the 12th, we had a pompous and sonorous proclamation from General Forey, followed by a decree officially delegating the direction of affairs to a triumvirate entrusted with power until the establishment of a definite government."

The proclamation of June 12 set forth the French program and opened the political question. After a lengthy preamble appealing to all moderate Mexicans to forget their differences and form a single party, the party of order, forswearing the names of liberals and reactionaries, which bred hatred and vengeance, Forey specified the principal points of a free and united nation. Religion would be respected, but so would the holders of Church property, who would not be disturbed in the possession of their titles, fraudulent claims alone being subject to revision. The press would be free but controlled, as in France: two warnings would be followed by suppression. The Mexican army would be reformed by a law of moderate recruitment, which would put an end to "the odious habit of taking by force and tearing from their families the Indians and the laborers, that appealing class of the population who are thrown into the ranks with a rope around their necks, and who provide the sad spectacle of soldiers without patriotism or the religion of the flag, always ready to desert one leader for another; this being sufficient to explain why there is no national army in Mexico but only bands of ambitious leaders quarreling for a power which they employ to wreck the resources of the country and to seize the wealth of other people." Forced loans, as well as forced levies, would be abolished, and the persons and properties of citizens protected by law. Taxes would be scaled in proportion to income, and the possibility of eliminating them altogether on articles of common consumption, taxes which weighed so heavily on an impoverished peasantry, studied. The financial agents of the administration would be suitably remunerated and corruption severely punished. Vigorous measures would be taken for the suppression of brigandage, and the administration of justice would no longer be venal. The Catholic religion would be protected and the bishops recalled to their dioceses. "I believe," Forey added, however, "that the Emperor would be pleased if the government found it possible to proclaim freedom of faith, that great principle of modern society." Never, perhaps, was so unsparing a prescription mentioned so casually; but it was not pressed. It was the only point, however, that was optional. "Such are the essential principles upon which the government to be established will be based," the peroration repeated; "they are those which the new government of Mexico must endeavor to follow, if it wishes to take its place among civilized nations." In conclusion, a general amnesty was proclaimed for all who rallied to the new order in good faith; those who remained deaf to the voice of conciliation would be declared enemies of the nation and pursued wherever they might find refuge.

The French program, sanctioning the expropriation of Church property and recommending religious liberty, was a formidable foil to the fugitive government in San Luis Potosi; but it was no less so to the promoters of intervention. It could not be dismissed as another manifesto full of Forey: the Commander-in-Chief spoke for his sovereign, on instructions from Paris, and he opened the political question only to close it. The hopes of the clergy, dilated by the arrival of their protectors, shrank rapidly when they realized that they could expect nothing but ceremonial concessions and military Masses, and the reactionary papers revealed their irritation by filling their columns with eulogies of Marquez, to whom they attributed the success of the campaign, without so much as mentioning the French—an impertinence for which they were promptly suspended. Thus cautioned, the Clerical organs subsided and awaited the constitution of the new government to reassert their claims to attention.

Within a fortnight of the proclamation Forey produced a provisional government. Captain Loizillon was struck by such speed—"you see that if we worked slowly in war, we are advancing rapidly in political affairs," he remarked—but the explanation was simple. Forey had finally found a problem in which he met with no opposition; and the thing was done by M. de Saligny. The result was nonetheless remarkable, since a singularly elaborate mechanism had been devised for so simple a purpose. Thirty-five notables, individually selected by the French Minister and individually approved by Forey, drafted three of their number to form a provisional government, and two hundred and fifty others to determine the permanent form of government most suited to Mexico. Colonel du Barail, who attended the opening of the Assembly, was embarrassed by its appearance. The notables seemed to have been simply picked up off the streets—"poor devils whose physiognomy, manners, and costumes by no means corresponded to what we then thought the representatives of a people should be like"; and even admitting their fictitious character, he felt that "it would have been franker and more becoming on our part not to resort to such methods, which deceived no one, and which made the most indulgent laugh." The original thirty-five were allotted, like larvae, an ephemeral life of five or six days, and there the natural features of the process ended for Captain Loizillon. "As I write these lines, the cannon of rejoicing are being fired to celebrate the installation of the Assembly. It is completely free to choose, provided it decrees a monarchy. Consequently we expect to receive Prince Maximilian at the end of October or the beginning of November. Amid all this, the Mexicans are of an exasperating indifference. They manifest no feeling for us, we are no further advanced than on the first day, and we have not been able to form the slightest relation with any native family. The population understands that all our fine proclamations of universal suffrage are a poor joke, since we are masters as usual only of the points we occupy. In the whole of Mexico we hold only Veracruz, Orizaba, Puebla, and Mexico City. With that equipment how can we consult the popular vote? To be sure, all our military operations in this campaign have been unpardonably slow. If the Commander-in-Chief had wished, after the surrender of Puebla on May 17, we might have profited by the fine weather we still had then to occupy Queretaro, Guadalajara, Guanajuato, and San Luis Potosi. By occupying these large centers of population, we should have had indisputable power and influence, and we would have thrust brigandage far back and reassured the inhabitants as to their lives and property. Instead, we are shut up in Mexico City, and the stagecoach is stopped and plundered at one league from the city without the robbers being disturbed in the least."

The Assembly labored and brought forth two foregone conclusions. The first was the provisional government, composed of three men: General Almonte, who presided over it; General Salas, whose name, as Colonel du Barail said, would not encumber the pages of history; and the Bishop of Mexico, acting as substitute for the Archbishop, who was still absent in Europe. The Assembly was picked up off the streets; the government was picked by M. de Saligny. Of the three caciques, as they were popularly called, Almonte was, according to Captain Loizillon, "a reactionary of little value," Salas "a mummy unearthed for the occasion," and the Bishop "a vigorous man who immediately set foot on the others and who directs everything." Hence it was not surprising that the triumvirate attempted to attenuate the force of Forey's proclamation by a manifesto of its own, stating that the Church no longer had an enemy in the State and that all pending questions would be settled between them; nor that the clergy, thus encouraged, took heart, and that priests appeared in the houses that had once been Church property, warning the tenants not to pay rent to their landlords, since the sales effected under the inspiration of Satan would soon be revised and those who disregarded the warning would be obliged to pay a second time to the rightful proprietors. To Forey it came as a surprise, nevertheless, to find that the provisional government considered his proclamation a provisional statement. In a statement to the press he declared that it was final. "The French army," he repeated, "has come to Mexico to serve as a safeguard for all legitimate interests. It will fulfill its mission, and while I am at the head of it, my manifesto will be a truth." The truth was brought home to the Bishop by Almonte and Saligny, who roused him out of bed one morning to deliver a personal admonition from the Commander-in-Chief; whereupon he subsided, biding the arrival of the Archbishop.

If the docility of the puppet government was doubtful, that of the

Assembly was not. On July 10 the notables completed their mandate and proclaimed the monarchy. "To celebrate this vote, the Mexican army has fired a hundred round of cannon in the square, amid the complete indifference of the population," Captain Loizillon noted. "All these comic votes, which we are trying to pass off as the will of the nation, are nevertheless unavoidable; there is nothing else that we can do." To secure a semblance of consulting the country at large meant to extend the occupation beyond the capital; the rainy season made this operation too difficult for Forey, and though Bazaine was preparing an expedition, the Commander-in-Chief refused to be hurried or to realize that the political and military questions were inseparable. He was guarding his rear. The indifference of the civil population distressed him. To break the ice, he gave two balls, the first at his own expense, the second on behalf of his officers, who were obliged to contribute to the cost, pro-rata according to their rank. Though the subscription cut heavily into the pay of lieutenants and captains, the second ball was a success, so true is it that people enjoy only the pleasures for which they are made to pay. From the peristyle to the top gallery the principal theater was lavishly decorated by the artillery with military trophies and emblems, clusters of flags and bayonets gleaming amid bowers of tropical flowers and Bengal lights, and the boxes were occupied by five hundred Mexican ladies displaying their family jewels and their latest Parisian gowns. There were beauties galore. "Supple, graceful, small, mignonne, sprightly and quick-witted, with her flat complexion, her eyes like black diamonds shadowed by long lashes, her fleshy red lips disclosing teeth as white as pearls, her abundant ebony hair, the upkeep of which is one of her great cares, her opulent and delicate shape, and her arched foot, the Mexican woman might pass for one of the wonders of creation," wrote Colonel du Barail. "She is alluring and languid, and if one were to judge her by her appearance and even by her love letters and her beguiling glances, one would swear that she keeps in her blood all the ardors of the sun under which she blooms. Those of my comrades, however, who had the time and the temperament to devote themselves to that kind of comparative study told me, and I took them at their word, that her passions were entirely on the surface and that everything was sacrificed to the façade. It is nonetheless true that, on that night, the French officers, in their number one uniforms, appeared to be perfectly enchanted." Mexican society was perfectly willing to be entertained at the expense of the foreigner and even to reciprocate the advances when a match could be made, and when the couples retired at dawn "they parted delighted with each other and convinced that by sparking all night they had accomplished an act at once very agreeable and very politic. There relations were formed and romances sketched, several of which ended in the most honorable denouement—marriage." The thaw was worth what it cost. The contact of two peoples, so difficult with the men, was finally brought about by the women, whose natural superiority to national prejudices made the young bloods of the French army indifferent to politics.

Colonel du Barail, not being a young blood, left the ball early and returned to his quarters in the fashionable suburb of Tacubaya. Like the average officer, he was indifferent to politics unless they affected him personally—and in Tacubaya they did. On his arrival he had been assigned a splendid villa belonging to the Escandon family, who had emigrated and were living in Paris, where they were at the head of the Mexican conservative colony and had done more than anyone else to bring about the expedition. "They expected considerable advantages from our expedition," he wrote, "and frankly they would have contributed very lightly to the success of the campaign by putting their uninhabited house at the disposal of one of the officers who were risking their lives in an expedition undertaken for their benefit and to serve their interests with a good grace"; but on presenting his billeting card, he found the house closed and was informed by the caretaker that, on orders from M. Escandon, it was reserved for the use of a superior officer who might some day wish to transfer his headquarters to Tacubaya. He withdrew, "admiring the patriotism of these people who ask France for her blood and her gold, without even wishing to offer hospitality to one of her sons," and took up other quarters; but the Escandon villa, which remained unoccupied and which he passed every day, did more than anything else to disillusion him with the expedition. Like the young bloods who expected more than they received from the Mexican women, that whited sepulcher became for Colonel du Barail a symbol.

With some it was one thing and with others another, but always small things and revealing irritations, that built up public opinion bit by bit in the army. With Captain Loizillon it was everything at once. After a month in the capital he was as indifferent to the French program as the average Mexican; what mattered was not the prescription which Forey had written but its enforcement; anyone could write a manifesto. "As I think I have said before," he wrote to his parents, "what Mexico needs for its regeneration is a strong and honest government, which will be pitiless with the thieves and rascals. To establish such a government, however, there are difficulties which seem to me insurmountable, judging by the way we are working. To do anything would require an occupation of ten years, a numerous army, and a heavy investment of funds before the country could bear, and that will not be until brigandage is extinguished. The Mexicans know this very well and understand that France alone can do it, while Austria cannot. In fact, they wished to make Prince Napoleon Emperor and had to be formally ordered to name Maximilian. Maximilian being chosen, something must be organized for him, a government, an army, etc. This is the difficulty. The basis on which everything must rest is the army." In itself this difficulty was not insurmountable. His prescription was simple and drastic. By disbanding the army of Marquez and trying, hanging, or deporting the former highwaymen who were his generals, by organizing a nucleus with those Mexican officers against whom there was the least to be said, and by placing French officers over them to instill the rudiments of French discipline and administration, it would be possible to produce a good native army in time. "But instead of all this, instead of posing the principle of probity and regeneration, we are coddling all these people because Marquez is the man of the reaction, and the reactionaries are already sore with us, since they are convinced that we do not mean to restore the old order of things. M. de Saligny, who is himself a reactionary, flatters this party by every kind of concession; he has just had the commander of the city dismissed because he permitted himself to arrest a priest who is a thief and an assassin. An investigation into malversation of funds has been quashed. You know that it is we who still pay the Mexican army; naturally, these people carry over the same habits with us as with their government; that is to say, they steal as much as possible. With us it is more difficult. They manage it, nevertheless. . . . You see that in such conditions it is not enough to replaster, everything must be demolished and rebuilt. If we do not, as I very much fear we will not, we shall make a sorry gift to poor Maximilian."

In the meanwhile the burden rested on the French army, and it became more irksome every day. "In whatever direction one turns," he concluded, "one is obliged to recognize that we shall occupy Mexico for a long time, and that it is impossible to foresee the moment when the troops can be sent home, for if we wish to pacify the country and make it safe, which is very difficult, the twenty-five thousand men whom we have here are far from being too many; they are not even enough." Where there was a will, there was a way, no doubt—but the will? "In the whole army there is but one desire, to return to France, and that desire is mine more than any other," he admitted frankly. It was raining incessantly, he could not even ride for exercise, he was bored to death, and for him, as for Forey and everyone else in the army, the only form of recreation was to talk politics.

When Forey drove through the city it was always in great state, in a carriage with four horses, preceded and followed by mounted hussars, and with a large tricolor flag floating behind him; but he was at his best when he appeared on foot on the fashionable promenade of the Alameda. Then the children would flock to him, crying, "Here comes Don Forey! Here comes Don Forey!" and hug his knees and claim him for one of their own. He was fond of children and made friends with them easily, and as the curious collected and watched the Commander-in-Chief sitting there with the little creatures crawling comfortably all over him, like Nilus with his river gods, they wondered whether he had not mistaken his vocation in life. He enjoyed, and the children enjoyed, and so did the spectators, the paternal, or rather the grandfatherly, feeling, which he wasted on their elders. But Captain Loizillon had no other diversion from his profession but politics.

After six weeks of boredom and irritation he made politics his business, for they affected his personal future, his pride as a Frenchman, and the welfare and fortune of the army; and tired of talking, he acted. He decided to pass up a promotion, which he had been promised in six months, and to sacrifice his career to his public spirit, and wrote a long letter to a lady in Paris who had access to the Emperor, explaining "the situation as it is, setting aside all personal considerations." The letter was outspoken, it was indiscreet, but "I think that it is the duty of a decent man," he explained to his parents, "to inform public opinion in France of all the indignities and stupidities of which we are impotent witnesses. And I have told the truth and the whole truth." Now, when he was exercised, Captain Loizillon could wield a scathing pen, and for eighteen closely written pages he let it run in an unsparing review of the fruits of intervention. Six weeks were a short time, perhaps, in which to form a fair or final judgment, but the verdict was the culmination of nine months of close observation and bitter experience, and it reflected the common feeling in the army, where opinion was as solid as the uniform; it was not necessary to drain the wine to know that it was sour. As a text, he clipped two police ordinances from the local papers, one prohibiting work on Sundays, the other compelling people to kneel on the passage of the Sacrament through the streets and to remain in that position until it disappeared. "When the Liberals came to power," he explained, "they suppressed this stupid and ridiculous custom, which we have restored, and which consists in carrying the Sacrament to sick persons with an escort of soldiers and a deafening din of bells capable of killing the patient before he has time to swallow his Savior. These two ordinances need no comment. They prove sufficiently the pretensions of the clergy and the way they are taking to recover their influence." The intimidation of tenants in anticipation of the return of Church property was another symptom that needed no comment. "As you see, we are in full reaction, and no one is surprised by it, since it could not be otherwise with the constitution of the provisional government"; but what was astounding was that "we stand by and watch as if it did not concern us. The reactionaries, nevertheless, mistrust us, for they feel that when the direction we are taking is known in France, things will change. As for the Liberals, they blame us for everything—they reproach us for not putting this government, which we have created and for which we are responsible, in tutelage,

and they do not forgive us for restoring here what we have abolished
in France. They believe that these are not the intentions of France and
the Emperor, but they judge things by what they see."

Things—and persons. "They blame all the mistakes made on M. de
Saligny, against whom there is a heat of which you can have no idea.
Since the mail came in, it is said that M. de Saligny has been recalled
but that the Commander-in-Chief has retained him on his own authority and has written to the Emperor to leave M. de Saligny in Mexico,
as he is the only man who understands the situation and the only one
capable of constructing the empire. Assuming that it is true that the
Emperor has had the happy idea of recalling M. de Saligny, it may
seem strange that the Commander-in-Chief should give him so great a
proof of devotion, since everyone knows that they are not on good
terms. But there is an explanation. It is very easy to decree an empire,
as we have done, but to organize an empire is another matter. What
have we organized since we have been here? Nothing. The Commander-in-Chief knows it better than anyone; he should busy himself
about everything, and he concerns himself about nothing. He knows
perfectly well the mess in which we are floundering, but as his part is
done he aspires only to his Marshal's baton and a chance to return to
France and gather his laurels. Maximilian and M. de Saligny will work
things out as best they can; it is none of his business. He is continuing
the same line of conduct which he has pursued ever since we came to
Mexico—not to compromise himself and to pass the responsibility to
others."

Caustic, reckless, relentless, slashing right and left, Captain Loizillon
reserved his severest strictures, however, for the Commander-in-Chief.
All the bitterness that had accumulated in the army under the shiftless
conduct of the siege of Puebla welled up as he recalled the disgraceful
scene at the end of the whispering gallery when Forey broke up the
council of war with the ineffable words, *"Mon Dieu,* try to come to
some agreement!" If the town had not run out of food, they would be
there yet. "The Commander-in-Chief and his entourage may say as
much as they please that the siege of Puebla was the greatest feat of
arms of modern times; we do not agree. We regard the sixty days we
spent before Puebla as a defeat all the greater in that the Mexican officers told us afterward that they did not believe that they could hold out
for more than five or six days. They admitted that after the capture of
the Penitentiary on March 29 they were so sure that the town was lost
that they saddled their horses themselves in preparation for flight, and
it was only after they were quite certain that we would not pursue our
success that they occupied the positions and the houses that stopped us."

On his military record Forey was a dud, and his political record was
a muddle. "By our improvidence and the internal political line we are
following we are setting everyone more and more against us. If we con-

tinue, what a sorry task we shall give poor Maximilian, and what a disillusionment we are preparing for him! When he lands at Veracruz
and sees that his whole empire consists of the road to Mexico City, a
road on which he will have to be heavily escorted not to be carried off,
and when he finds in his capital neither finances, nor justice, nor army,
but organized pillage and the parties squabbling and tearing one another apart, to what saint will he turn? As the ideas of his country are
not very advanced, naturally he will fling himself into the arms of M.
de Saligny, Marquez, and the reaction, and then everything will be irreparably lost, and France will exhaust her army and her treasure without succeeding in seating Maximilian on his throne."

But if the diagnosis was gloomy, it was not hopeless. An unrelieved
diatribe would have marked the writer as a sourbelly, and Captain Loizillon was careful to add that the remedy lay with Napoleon. If the Emperor realized how his policy had been denatured and his ideas misinter-
preted; if he recalled M. de Saligny and replaced him with an honest man
who would attend to the affairs of the country before his own; if he recalled General Forey and gave the army Bazaine, who was a man of
great intelligence and the best guide for Maximilian; and if Maximilian,
whom Bazaine could steer in a liberal direction, were made to understand his position; then, then it would be possible to make of Mexico in
less than ten years a rich country, capable of repaying the expenses of
the war, dispensing with French support, and realizing the promises
expected of it. With roads and railroads so easy to build on the upper
plateau, farming and industry would flourish, and it would no longer
be necessary to import from abroad the raw materials that were more
valuable than gold and so abundant underfoot—iron, of which there
were large deposits to the west of Morelia; timber, of which the virgin
forests provided a prodigal supply; and all the untold resources, which
would efface these transient difficulties. "This is what Mexico might
become if we had two intelligent and disinterested men at our head,
but unfortunately the task has not even been begun and perhaps it will
never be, to the great misfortune of France and her government. This
is what saddens us, and this is why I have told you frankly what I
think, what we all think. Now that I have opened my heart to you," he
concluded, "I feel relieved."

The letter had a curious fate. The lady to whom it was addressed laid
it before Napoleon, who was so much impressed by it that he sent a
copy to Bazaine. Pierre Loizillon wrote the kind of loveless letter that
Louis Napoleon liked to read. For some time past he had been convinced by the difficulties and delays of the expedition that he had been
misled by his agents, and as he had no official information service in
Mexico, he had taken to consulting the private correspondence of his
officers overseas in search of the truth. The truth, the whole truth, bare
and unbiased, was difficult to find; the correspondence of the superior

officers, colored by ambition, jealousy, or apology, was suspect, but the letter of an unknown captain who had nothing to gain and much to lose by his denunciations, and who jeopardized his career to satisfy his public spirit, seemed to be *la vérité vraie*. Seemed—for who could be certain in a world where all was seeming and the ruler regally removed from reality? But the critic who laid the blame on men and not on things was always credible. To check the findings of Captain Loizillon, Napoleon sent them to Bazaine, omitting the name of the writer, and Bazaine attributed the letter to a highly placed malcontent on the staff. Who but Douay would have dared? Who but Douay had a tongue as rough as a cat's? The soul of discretion himself, Bazaine filed the letter with a single dissenting comment: the reflections on Forey were not altogether fair, he thought; they were dictated, no doubt, by the resentment which the officer who wrote them felt for the failure of the attack on Santa Ines during the siege of Puebla. Thus unbeknown to him, promotion came to Captain Loizillon.

The letter confirmed, though it did not affect, the decisions of the Emperor. Two days after it was posted, Forey and Saligny received their letters of recall. In the case of Forey, the Emperor softened the blow by conferring on him the coveted dignity of a Marshal of France, and he couched the letter of recall in the most considerate terms. "A Marshal of France is too great a personage to be allowed to struggle with the intrigues and details of administration," wrote Napoleon, and he authorized Forey accordingly to delegate all his powers to Bazaine, whenever he saw fit, and to return to France to enjoy his success and the legitimate glory which he had gained. By an unfortunate slip of the pen, however, the Emperor also referred to Bazaine as a Marshal. Forey was profoundly shocked, for he expected to complete his work, as he called it, and to consolidate the throne he had erected for Maximilian, and though he knew that he was to be honored with the Marshal's baton, he did not expect to receive it where he did. No amount of congratulation could console him.

But it was one thing for the Emperor to recall his agents, and another to uproot them. Both deferred their departure on every possible pretext. For Forey this was not difficult, since the date was left to his discretion and he took what was a phrase of courtesy, as he took all his instructions, literally. Consequently Captain Loizillon found a great deal more to say before he felt really relieved. "The Marshal," he began again, "in spite of his vanity, has not wholly digested the eulogistic letter which the Emperor wrote him, and what surprises me is that he has recognized that his recall is really a disgrace. He cannot swallow it, and instead of resigning the command to General Bazaine, as it is his duty to do, he preserves it, covering himself with a phrase in the Emperor's letter allowing him to judge the time." There was nothing surprising about Forey after all.

His title cost him his dignity. Together with the letter of the Emperor, he received another, and not a polite one, from the Minister of War, directing him to hand over the command to Bazaine; but he put it in his pocket without mentioning it to a soul. He was a walking dead-letter office of such dodges. He was prodded, he was teased, he was twitted, but the Bear, as the baiters called him, refused to budge. The junior officers rallied him pitilessly and in public. The Marshal, they said, recognizing that there was nothing to be done with the Mexicans, was eager to be gone and was only awaiting the arrival of Maximilian because, after occupying the first place in Mexico, he could not remain in the second. "I trust that it is strong enough," said Captain Loizillon, and he could say no more, "this dose of vanity that prevents M. Forey from playing second to an Emperor!" And since Forey suffered from such an acute case of mistaken identity, someone had to tell him the truth. A paper published an open letter congratulating him on his honors and expressing the hope that they would spur him to emerge from his *apathy* and send out his armies, in a radiation of glory, to pacify the country. The letter was signed by someone calling himself "the principal inhabitants of Mexico," whom everyone supposed to be M. de Saligny—for the letter was witty, malicious, and insolent—and but for one word Forey would have swallowed it. The word apathy nettled him, however, and he took exception to it in a reply which left the wits speechless. The Commander-in-Chief informed the principal inhabitants of Mexico that, "though not a Mexican himself, he was obliged to remind the Mexicans that their roads were impractical for a regular army, laden with cannon and munitions, at this season, and that he did not propose to yield to their impatience—he who had resisted so successfully the impatience of the French for the siege of Puebla!" No one could cap that. A patter-song made the rounds of the barracks— *Partira-t-il? Partira-t-il pas?*—and the couplets grew, week by week, month by month, like the bids of an auctioneer. Recalled in August, he was going in September; September came and went and still he was not gone. Ridicule groaned—and Forey, but not for the same reasons. He had his fill of Mexico, it was all that he could do to manage Almonte, and he had to watch the government he had appointed as if it were the enemy party. "I assure you," he wrote to the Emperor, "that I should prefer to attempt another siege of Puebla than to be here as a moderator of these people who do not want to be moderated." But he was wedded to his difficulties, and there was something about Mexico that made it impossible for him either to take or to leave it.

To uproot M. de Saligny was even more difficult, for he was attached to Mexico by ties that left him bleeding at the roots like a mandrake when they broke. He was deep in debts and deals. Since the return of the Minister to the capital the French Legation, which had long passed for an office of *tripotage,* had resumed operations on an unprecedented scale. A flourishing trade in fraudulent claims was in full swing, the business was booming, and the Minister had collected a considerable advance on his commissions when he received his letter of recall, and his credit collapsed. His creditors reclaimed their advances, and the business and the scandal broke together. He exploited his misfortune. Assembling his creditors, he convinced them that their only security lay in preventing his recall and induced them to mount a cabal in the press. A paper subsidized by his associates lamented the loss of a man who had made himself indispensable to Mexico by his intelligence, his integrity, and his skill in steering intervention to port, and petitions were addressed to the Emperor on his behalf by the provisional government and the municipalities of the neighboring *pueblos*. He let it be known that he had devoured his patrimony in representing France in Mexico and could not leave the country, having contracted fifty thousand francs' worth of debts, which he was waiting to pay by the sale of his last remaining lands in Normandy. He applied to the provisional government which he had created for a bounty, and Almonte persuaded the Assembly to grant him a substantial relief; but still he lingered on, to the disgust of Captain Loizillon, whose gorge rose again at the spectacle of such cynical mendicity. "If only the Marshal were gone," he raged, "General Bazaine might prevent this new indelicacy of Saligny, who begs charity like the wretch that he is. What opinion can people have of France when they see her represented in this way?" Everything that could be said about Saligny had been said to satiety, yet he found something to add to it. To free the flag from further disgrace he was forced to bring up fresh charges and to go far back to find them. It was high time for the Emperor to change his agents, he wrote, "and above all, let him not send us any more of his former spies. Saligny should be a lesson to him. When you pay a person to deceive his master in your favor, you may be sure that he will deceive you later. Saligny is the convincing proof of it." Like a flash in the dark, the allusion to the past activities of Saligny was obscure but illuminating; it was the psychological key to his whole career. "He has deceived the country and the Emperor as to the resistance we would meet in pursuing the course he has imposed on us; that is to say, by attaching us to people like Marquez and Almonte, who are thieves, immoral, and incompetent. If we had come here alone, in our own name as Frenchmen, all parties would have welcomed us. Aside from the stupid reactionaries and the rabid Liberals, we should have had the whole laborious mass of the nation for us—a nation that at bottom is far more liberal than we are. With their help we would easily have extinguished brigandage and given the country whatever government we wished. Whatever the form, the country would have accepted no matter what, no matter whom, as soon as it saw us trying to establish here the same principles as in France. It is because the Emperor, relying on M. de Saligny, has followed the opposite course that we are in this muddle, and Saligny plunges us deeper and deeper into it, because his interests are all linked with the reactionaries."

The fury of Pierre Loizillon was evenly divided between Saligny and Forey. The false start which the Minister had given to the expedition could be corrected only at an incalculable cost of time and toil. The Liberals, profiting by delay, and masters of the greater part of the country, were recruiting fresh troops, and though a single column of artillery would always be sure, he believed, of traversing the whole of Mexico without encountering any serious resistance, yet "we are so few for this immense surface that we shall never be able to occupy it all at once. We shall be forced to run after an elusive enemy, who will tire our soldiers by marches and countermarches and kill more of us by fatigue than by fire." It was September, and Forey was still stalling. "In refusing to hand over his command to General Bazaine, Marshal Forey shows himself to the end what he has always been, a vain nonentity. He thus impedes future operations, since General Bazaine needs material time to prepare the expedition and to begin a new liberal policy. M. Forey, in fact, has attained the apogee of his reputation by retarding operations even by his departure."

Forey was no longer a laughing matter nor Saligny an object of contempt. The personal, the political, the military questions were all indissoluble, for in the meanwhile the Mexicans could not decide on which foot to dance attendance. Fearing that the recall of the Minister and the Commander-in-Chief would be followed by the recall of the army, and alarmed by rumors that Maximilian, informed of the true state of affairs, had refused the crown, they foresaw with terror the return of the Liberals, who were mustering their forces in San Luis Potosi. Every day of delay compromised more and more foully the success of the expedition and, what mattered far more, the good name of France. Fortunately for the honor of the army, it was not true, as some people said, that the procrastination of the Commander-in-Chief was due to the same motives as the tenacity of M. de Saligny—the Marshal at least was not mercenary—but in the hour of liquidation their two figures melted and ran together like tallow in a single shapeless mass.

Pierre Loizillon kept his comments for his family now, for they were no longer fit for general circulation, and in his baffled fury he flung out the boldest of his barbs, not at the underlings, but at Louis Napoleon himself. "This is what the Emperor has come to with his favoritism and his mania of investing with the highest dignities the faithless men whom he used to accomplish his *coup d'état.*" Saligny, the ex-spy, and Forey, who had been an accomplice of the 2nd of December, were a fit pair and had served Napoleon as he deserved. Immanent justice was on the march in Mexico.

So Pierre Loizillon; but not the army. He had been warmly congratulated by more than one of his fellow officers for the courage with which he said what they all thought in his leavening letter to the Emperor; but they were not prepared to think further than Forey and Saligny, and the ferment subsided as soon as the pressure was removed. Politics began and ended with a commission and a promotion, and the Emperor, who had not slept for a week before learning of the capture of Puebla, had been liberal with recompenses. Forey, even more lavish than his master, managed to offend the army yet further by conferring the *Légion d'Honneur* on a number of Mexicans; but the ranks merely sang and grumbled. The French soldier was *bon enfant* and went on singing his patter-song:

> Like lightning everywhere
> A rumor runs the town,
> And joy is in the air,
> The word goes up and down.
> Soldiers and civilians,
> Like partners in cotillions,
> Shake hands and shout and dance,
> And you repeat with me,
> Forey and Saligny
> Have been recalled to France!

But with every passing week the sing-song grew and the couplets kept pace with the calendar. Colonel du Barail, who was on the list of promotions and who became a General, was still indulgent with Forey, but he was forced to admit that "his situation was becoming false and bizarre. He no longer commanded. He no longer received anything from Paris." All orders were addressed to the General Commander-in-Chief, and when he claimed them the postmaster ignored him. The truth, penetrating slowly, overcame him at last, and in the first week of October Forey finally left for France. There was a brief ceremony at headquarters; the infatuated old man bade a fond farewell to his officers and took some time to laud Bazaine at great length; then he mounted and rode away, the third commander to be worn out by Mexico. The younger officers listened to his effusions with stolid coldness, but the older ones were moved. Sentiment was a matter of seniority, prompted perhaps by a presentiment of the insecurity that accompanied every promotion. Forey was the living example of it, and General du Barail was one of those who pitied him, for he had foreseen his destiny from the day he had landed in Veracruz, and he now beheld its inevitable conclusion in the triumph of Bazaine. "With his great bulk of a drum-major, his strong jaw, index of energy and also of obstinacy, and his violent and gruff bearing, which concealed a good will of which he gave proof by lavishing on his subordinates all the recompenses that he could grant them during the campaign, General Forey was bound to succumb in the struggle between a lion and a fox, himself endowed with the courage of a lion," he wrote in retrospect. But for Saligny he had no pity. Saligny was the army-killer, "the author of all the mistakes made, the executioner of Admiral Jurien de la Gravière and General de Lorencez, the promoter of the reactionary and Clerical policy, opposed to the taste of the Mexicans and even to the political institutions of France, and, in a word, the principal obstacle to the pacification we desired."

Saligny lingered longer, despite formal orders from France that he was to leave with Forey, if he had not already gone. The Assembly of Notables voted him a bounty of five hundred and seventy thousand francs, but as it could be cashed only out of the French loan Bazaine objected. Eventually, however, on the advice of M. Budin, the Commissioner of Finances, he consented to pay the debts of the Minister to be rid of him. But still M. de Saligny stalled, and it now fell to the fox to hunt down the—but to what animal could Saligny be compared? The toad in the bottle had lost his legs and now crawled on his belly. "If General Bazaine has a little vigor and keeps his promises," wrote Captain Loizillon, "he will ship M. de Saligny home by force, and he will do well, for if he were to leave that viper here, he would have cause to regret it." But Bazaine was not the man to set his heel on the head of his protector. He delegated that duty to his subordinates when he left for the campaign in the north early in November; and they shrank from it too. For a month longer Saligny managed to elude the process-servers, pleading a marriage that he had in view and his decision to resign from the service and settle in Mexico, and not until peremptory orders came from France to ship him home without further delay did he yield. In the first days of December Bazaine was relieved to learn that the blow had been dealt by M. Budin. "What you tell me of M. de Saligny does not surprise me," he wrote to Budin. "I expected some violent scene when the order of departure, a little severe no doubt, was delivered to him; but why did he put himself in this position? He has no one but himself to blame for the disappointments that afflict him and the rigorous measures prescribed for him."

Before leaving Mexico, however, Saligny snatched one consolation from it. It would have been strange had he found something to love in that land which he had spent himself in abusing; but nothing was impossible in the mutations which men underwent there; and in the bosom of an ultraclerical family he found a woman willing to bear the honor of his name. He was married on Christmas Day, and the next morning he slipped out of Mexico. His forced repatriation satisfied his countrymen; retribution overtook him, ironically, not for the ruin of

Mexico, but for the damage he had done to France; the sentence passed on him by the Emperor merely confirmed the verdict of the army. The officers were relieved; the men were mollified. The French soldier was a good trooper and so far as he was concerned, whether in Mexico or in France, *tout finit par des chansons*. His patter-song ran with repetition to eleven couplets; the first were tripping, the last were lame, but the incantation had worked; and the closing chorus coupled Forey and Saligny in a single jingle and sped them on their way with the best wishes of the army:

> The author can but say
> That if man proposes,
> Haply it is today
> The Emperor who disposes.
> And so be off, my friends:
> Be it long, be it short,
> We wish you a good trip,
> And when you quit the ship,
> May you be wrecked in port!

2

SO JUAREZ was heard from once more, vicariously and unrecognized by those who spoke for him. Merely by abandoning the capital he forced a moral crisis in the French army; but much more remained to be done before an army of soldiers could become an army of civilians. Nevertheless, the war was now being fought on another front. When Bazaine took command, intervention was two years old and public opinion in France was rapidly approaching the saturation point.

The flare of patriotic feeling that followed the repulse at Puebla in 1862 flickered out quickly, and in the fruitless year that elapsed before Puebla was captured in 1863 the fundamental sentiment of the country came to the surface. Napoleon needed no information in Mexico to know what the army felt, the temper of the home front reflected the mood of the soldiers overseas, and the reports of his *procureurs* told him the truth, as they were paid to do, faithfully. "Ignorance of the aim in view," as one of them said, "the sacrifices of men and money imposed on the country, our soldiers exposed to the perils of an inhospitable country more than to the bullets of the enemy, the doubtful or disproportionate compensations for these sacrifices, and the very slowness of the results, influence people unfavorably. They realize, no doubt, that the government has been carried further than its first projects, but they regret the expedition and desire above all that it may not be prolonged by a permanent occupation, and the most ardent wishes are made that victory may soon crown the glorious efforts of our troops. Whenever our people do not understand either the significance or the scope of a political measure, whenever a direct and palpable interest does not touch them from the start, they remain, if not hostile, at least cold and indifferent, and it would be desirable that by the time of the coming elections they should have nothing to remember but difficulties overcome and the triumph of our arms." The *procureurs* told the truth without flattering their employer, but they tempered it with a tact that told more than they did; and it was no wonder that Napoleon, knowing their fidelity to the soft pedal, was unable to sleep for a week before learning of the fall of Puebla. The parliamentary elections, which were held in May, increased the Opposition by over a million votes, and far from counteracting their effect, the fall of Puebla redoubled the demand for an early withdrawal of the expeditionary force. The value of the victory lay in the opportunity to retire with credit from Mexico, and the occupation of the capital was dreaded by the *procureurs* as a fresh source of public worry even before it was accomplished. "Some people say," another continued, "that our soldiers meet with enemies who are not very brave, it is true, but obstinate, that no fortunate solution is possible, that after losses and battles we shall arrive in Mexico City to raise a shadow of government that will fall immediately after our retreat. In all classes a single idea seems to prevail, and that is that once our honor has been avenged by a fine victory we should withdraw from so distant and costly a war."

To convince the French people to the contrary was difficult; it was necessary to discard all previous versions of intervention, to sweep away misconceptions and half-truths, and to tell them the whole truth. The press publicized and expounded the idea of the Emperor; the *procureurs* propagated and explained it; but they could not popularize it. In whatever way it was presented, the idea would not take. Military glory in Mexico meant nothing. "No one has ever seen the people of France excited for a distant war; those remote peoples, who have no fame for power or strength, do not seem rivals worthy of France; to move France the battlefield must be in Europe," the moving finger wrote. The economic motive was equally unappealing—"The project of a large and flourishing colony exploiting the mines is not even understood." The peasantry were suspicious of the Jecker bonds, and all the more scandalized by them in that they were covetous as a class and *âpre au gain* themselves. In the industrial world it was feared that the occupation would lead sooner or later to a war with the United States, and "the vigorous impulsion given to the industrial movement by the government of the Emperor and the economic reforms due to his initiative have developed in the country, as their consequence, peaceful needs and aims." In one province alone was there any appreciation of the possibilities which Mexico offered as an outlet for French trade: in Normandy a few industrialists, deprived of their American market for two years, were preparing to follow the flag, but not until the field was thoroughly pacified; and in every other department the *procureurs* reported thumbs down. The political aims of the Emperor were one more motive for caution, because their bearing on the War of Secession in the United States had been bruited too soon: "It is said that our occupation is connected with the preconceived idea of recognizing the South and, consequently, of its separation. But the division of the great Republic is still a pure hypothesis." The more ambitious the idea, the lower was the reaction to it—and the more fundamental. Honesty was undoubtedly the best policy, for the French people responded to it, but they responded without confidence because they were more honest with the Emperor than he was with himself. The better the meaning and scope of the undertaking were understood, the more profoundly did it antagonize the national instinct of self-preservation, and the more clearly did the irritation of popular prudence, skepticism, common sense, and intelligence admonish the Emperor where the national interest really lay. Hence the Emperor persisted. He was on his mettle. The concensus of public opinion insisted that Mexico was no business of France; it was his business to prove that it was.

The war of one man against a people, which had ruined Saligny, was now undertaken by Napoleon himself, and under far heavier odds, since he had to contend with the common sense both of the French and Mexican peoples and to overcome their combined resistance. The betting brought Karl Marx once more into the war. "To my mind," he told Engels, "there is no doubt that he will break his neck in Mexico, if he is not hanged beforehand." But Marx favored the loud pedal; his confidence was not borne out by the facts in the summer of 1863. The truth lay somewhere between the professional overstatement of the revolutionary and the professional understatement of the *procureurs*. The resistance of the French people was passive, and between active opposition and reluctant consent there was room for Napoleon to operate. Although he professed to attach no importance to public opinion, except for its effect abroad, he was guided by its promptings, and the pressure was strong enough to force him to anticipate the growth of the Opposition before it reached the saturation point. The correct solution of any question could be found by defining it correctly. The Mexican question had been defined for him both by the French and the Mexican peoples; and since the solution on both sides was to withdraw, it was essential to complete and consolidate the conquest of Mexico quickly. This was the task which he delegated to Bazaine. The instructions which he sent him were a duplicate of those which he had written for Forey and differed from them only in their urgency. They were definite and driving, but they betrayed no impatience. Whatever mistakes he made, Napoleon never nagged, and no nervousness transpired except in an occasional hint. Among other directions, Bazaine was urged to discover evidence, if possible, that Jules Favre was in the pay of Juarez. Had Bazaine been obtuse, he would hardly have realized that it was his duty to avert a domestic crisis in France, but he was anything but obtuse, and his conduct and his reports answered the unspoken dictates of the Emperor and provided the best evidence that he understood the true situation there, if not as clearly as Karl Marx, at least as well as the French *procureurs*.

"M. le maréchal Forey will already be far from Mexico when you receive this letter," the Minister of War wrote to Bazaine as soon as he was appointed to the supreme command. "You must have been struck by the mistakes which have been made since the entrance of the army into Mexico City. I have no doubt that you have already set to work to repair the unfortunate measures decreed by your predecessor." What those mistakes were the Emperor specified in a series of notes to the new Commander-in-Chief. The principal one was the erection of the Assembly of Notables and the premature proclamation of the monarchy before the country at large could be consulted; it was imperative that "the election of the Archduke Maximilian be ratified by the greatest possible number of Mexicans, since the hasty nomination that has been made has had the great disadvantage of not seeming, in Europe, the legitimate expression of the will of the country." Maximilian was hesitating and had made his acceptance of the crown conditional upon two guarantees—the full and free confirmation by the whole nation of the vote taken in the capital, and the complete occupation of the country to protect its independence and integrity against external dangers—and consequently it was imperative to extend the occupation to the provinces without delay. Napoleon was also afraid that the provisional government was too reactionary and that it had enjoyed too much latitude under Forey. "Although there is a provisional government, an indispensable measure in order to dispel the impression that I mean to keep Mexico," he wrote, "it is the duty of the French general to decide everything by his influence," and he expected Bazaine to direct it in a more conciliatory course. Above all, he was not to foster reaction. He was to organize the Mexican army in preparation for the eventual withdrawal of the French garrison and to provide the security necessary to enable the provisional government to obtain a loan in Europe immediately.

For the rest, he was to apply the French program, as set forth in the proclamation of Forey of June 10. Napoleon himself had defined French policy correctly, and all that was necessary was to correct its initial mismanagement by Forey and Saligny. His confidence was unimpaired, because he still blamed men and not things for the difficulties which the expedition had encountered; and having broken Forey and Saligny, there was no reason why a competent and dependable commander should not right the errors committed and vindicate the validity of the idea.

The work cut out for Bazaine suited his capacities exactly. Temperate, tactful, energetic, resourceful, always able to turn an obstacle when he could not surmount it, and never defeated by difficulties, no one was better qualified to combine conquest and conciliation successfully; yet such was the settled skepticism bred by the bad beginning of French policy in Mexico that even his most devoted admirers doubted whether he could undo what Forey and Saligny had done. The Regency, as the provisional government now styled itself, had taken the bit in its teeth and was openly defying the High Command to reverse its gains. A decree had been published confiscating the property of the patriots and another was in preparation canceling the *ley Juarez* and placing the priesthood once more beyond the pale of the common law. "Such obstinacy and blindness are inconceivable," wrote Captain Loizillon. "General Bazaine does not know what to do. The only thing would be to declare a state of siege and to oust the Regency; but this is an extreme measure, and I understand that he dares not employ it. Radical measures, moreover, do not recommend themselves to his character, which is marked, perhaps, by weakness. *Il ménage trop la chèvre et le chou.*" With the goat within reach of the cabbage, it was impossible to part them, however: the craving of the animal for the vegetable kingdom had been indulged too long by Saligny; and despite Bazaine's desire to humor his charges, he was compelled by the nature of things to adopt radical measures. The decree confiscating enemy property was highly impolitic, as he pointed out, since it provoked reprisals in kind by the patriots, who appropriated estates in the interior, broke them up among the peons, and used them to interest the Indians in the social question, but it was not until his objections were sustained by Napoleon, who disapproved the decree as an elementary blunder, that he succeeded in reducing two of the three members of the Regency to reason. Confronted with the Imperial proscript, Almonte and Salas yielded and repealed the punitive measure. But the contest with the three caciques had only begun. The circulation of the promissory notes issued by the Juarez government against nationalized property was paralyzed by the opposition of the clergy, the intimidation of tenants of former Church holdings was sustained by the courts, and once again *natura rerum* obliged Bazaine to put an end to an intolerable state of things. At his

bidding, Almonte and Salas issued another decree reassuring the holders of nationalized property. But a new antagonist had appeared on the
scene in the person of the Archbishop of Mexico, who returned to join
the Regency in October, just when Bazaine assumed active command,
and who succeeded in delaying his departure on the campaign in the
north for a fortnight. Armed with the authority of Rome, the Archbishop protested against the guarantees given to the holders of secularized property, produced the instructions he brought from the Pope,
and guaranteed, for his part, that the measure would alienate the only
friends of intervention; and as the Archbishop was the once seditious
Bishop of Puebla, Mgr. Labastida, Bazaine was obliged to break him
in before he could begin military operations.

"It is correct to say that our worst enemies were the people whose
triumph we had come to assure," wrote General du Barail. "Mgr. Labastida was the most unpopular, and the most justly unpopular, man
there. I am an admirer of the French clergy, a convinced Catholic, and
an unyielding adversary of people who call themselves anticlerical, but
I owe it to the truth to admit that the Mexican clergy, when I knew it,
was so demoralized, and ignorant, and compromised in every possible
fashion, as to justify, to some extent, the anticlerical passions of the
Liberals. . . . The Archbishop was the important man, the head and
arm, of the triumvirate. Still youthful, fat, with a blooming pink face
trimmed by a triple chin and a little belly that was just begging to grow,
Mgr. Labastida was the type of the papistical churchman, unctuous, saccharine, and false. To hear him speak, one would have thought him a
Liberal and believed him resigned to every concession. But at bottom
he harbored the oldest ideas, he was headstrong as a mule in his immobility, he regretted the Holy Office and the autos-da-fé, and he was
the great stumbling block to the success of our intervention and an
invincible obstacle to the conciliation of parties."

Bazaine came to the same conclusion very quickly. On first acquaintance he found the Archbishop "an enlightened man and perfectly informed of the intentions and the will of the Emperor"—which explained his apparent liberalism. But a few days later he reported to
Paris that "unfortunately his ideas are those of the Roman clergy,
almost those of the Spanish clergy of the time of Philip IV, minus the
Inquisition; we cannot count on his intervention to reach a solution
by conciliation, for his only reply to every combination is *non possumus*.
If we let him have his way, we would soon have another Rome in the
New World. He is a man of conviction, who seems to be loyal but who
lacks the necessary *sang-froid* when the interests of the Church are at
stake; we will keep him in the *juste milieu*." He overruled the protests
of the Archbishop, isolated him from his colleagues, circumvented him
by the Mexican military system of "creating a void around him," and
neutralized him sufficiently to let him rest, when he took the field in

the first week of November. But he won only a truce. At a farewell dinner that he gave a few days before his departure, General du Barail noted that "official civilities were exchanged between the triumvirate and the High Command; but they looked at each other a little like cats and dogs, making velvet paws, nevertheless, and it was not without uneasiness that General Bazaine left behind people whose acts and behavior he mistrusted profoundly, people whom he considered as both a little dense and very dangerous."

The military campaign was of minor importance. "You want to know the real condition of the country," he wrote to the Minister of War. "I will define it for you in a few words. In all the places which we occupy peace prevails and the populations declare for intervention and the monarchy; everywhere else it is war and the most disheartening mutism. This state of things will last as long as the Juarez government is in San Luis, with governors in the capitals of the states of the interior and great resources in the ports of the Pacific and the frontiers of the north, and still in possession of the appearances and certain forms of legal power. It is indispensable, therefore, to force him back or to let him wear himself out where he is, which would undoubtedly happen were the government of the capital more patient and tolerant in its acts and more conciliatory toward the moderate Liberal party, for there is such a party, and its leading men are ready to rally to the monarchical intervention, but they are held back by the line of conduct pursued by the Regency. The best and quickest solution would be the arrival at an early date of the Sovereign, and I am convinced that the great majority, without distinction of party, would gather about his throne."

The enemy had mustered about twelve thousand regular troops, and there were guerrillas more or less everywhere, "but these flies are not to be feared, all their boldness being confined to armed robbery." The Juarez government was disintegrating, and his principal generals, Uraga, Doblado, and Comonfort, had given out through their friends in the capital that they were ready for negotiation, but as the Emperor had forbidden any dealing with the enemy and, above all, with Doblado, who was reputed to be the most cunning and unscrupulous man of his party, Bazaine gave them no encouragement. In the case of Doblado he was sufficiently intrigued, however, to discover how much truth there was in his feelers, and through a confidant he received an offer of terms: to restore the Reform Laws, to annul the Regency, to create a provisional government headed by Bazaine himself, and to declare a truce and suspend all armed movement while the country was consulted on the form of government it desired through universal suffrage. Bazaine replied that there could be no question of bargaining but only of unconditional adherence; and his comment to the Minister of War echoed his judgment of the Archbishop. "Your Excellency will judge by this exposé of the ideas of the most adroit man in the Liberal party, but also, we are told, the most dishonest, the political line that this party proposes to pursue, and will be convinced, as I am today, that there is no hope of organizing this country solidly by conciliation." Between the Archbishop on the right and the Liberal party on the left, the one as irreconcilable as the other, a middle course was possible, however, by studied moderation, patience, and perseverance. As for Juarez himself, the mere announcement of the campaign was enough to dislodge him; he was at bay and reported to be preparing to retire, with his few remaining adherents, to the deserts of Durango or even to emigrate to Texas. "I have good hopes, therefore, that the campaign which I am about to undertake will produce definite results about the end of the year."

The reports of Bazaine made good reading in Paris. Accurate, level-headed, sensible, temperate, and optimistic, they convinced the Emperor that he had found an alter ego in his new Commander-in-Chief; and Bazaine's conduct bore out his reports. He had the gift; he adopted the maxim of his master and reminded him of it—patience and deliberation in political affairs, lightning speed in war—and he worked on it as effectively as he had promised. The campaign was concluded within two months. One after another the key cities of the country— Queretaro, Morelia, Guanajuato, Leon, Aguascalientes, Guadalajara, and San Luis Potosi—were occupied without opposition. Three Liberal divisions concentrated in the north fell back before the advance of the French, refusing to give battle. Bazaine was prepared for these tactics. "The enemy Generals," he reported before leaving the capital, "are said to intend to make a void before our columns and to maneuver on our flanks and our rear; I will take care of them." And believing that a crushing blow in the field would have a decisive political effect, he led a column against Doblado, who had renewed his diplomatic advances through an unexpected channel—Mgr. Labastida. "I have done all that I could within the limits of the possible," he wrote to Napoleon, "to lead General Doblado to our cause, but he wanted to hold an interview of the same sort as that of La Soledad, and I preferred to give chase." But although he narrowly missed contact with him more than once, he was obliged to abandon the pursuit of a vanishing foe. Another division under General Uraga, after an unsuccessful attempt to recapture Morelia, beat a swift retreat before General Douay, who was also unable to establish contact. A third contingent under General Negrete covered San Luis Potosi until the approach of the French forced the Liberal government to abandon that capital in the last days of December. Guadalajara was occupied in the first days of January, and there the pursuit of an elusive enemy rested. The principal aim of the expedition had been accomplished. The occupied zone comprised the richest and most populous provinces of the heart of Mexico, and the consolidation of the French conquest was henceforth secure. "For some time yet the country will certainly be overrun by the fractions of the Juarist army, but I shall treat them as bandits," Bazaine reported to the Emperor. "All the populations are delighted to be delivered of the Juarist yoke and bless Your Majesty." The new French Minister was less sanguine. "In some places, particularly in Guadalajara," he informed Paris, "the people were very chary of demonstrations." But in France, naturally, it was the reports of the Commander-in-Chief that were preferred and accepted without question.

In each of the occupied cities adhesions to the Empire were secured from a number of notables, in some cases willingly, in others by threats of arrest and expulsion, and by adding to these a census of the entire populations it was possible to pass off the result as the full and free vote of a substantial majority of the nation required by Maximilian and the Emperor. The total figure was impressive: six and a half million votes in favor of the Empire out of a population of eight million people. The validity of the vote could not be reckoned literally, Bazaine was careful to explain. "The number of these adhesions is not the result of universal suffrage. . . . But it is nonetheless the expression of the great majority of the liberated states, for the Indian element that inhabits the countryside always follows the Mexican element that lives in the large centers. The Indian masses have never been sincerely consulted by any party, and the pretext is simple: they are regarded as creatures without reason. To make them *gente de razón* one would have to change the whole social organization of the country by a wave of the wand. How could we set up electoral lists when there is no civil registry here? Though I am convinced that the acts of adhesion represent the opinion of the reasonable people of Mexico, and that the Archduke can rely on this manifestation without remorse, I have had a plebiscite prepared and I have no doubt of the vote." Bazaine had no pretensions to be a magician; he had done as much as could reasonably be expected of him, and by the end of the year, as he had promised, he produced definite results. Qualitatively, if not quantitatively, both the political and the military questions could be said to be settled.

As for Juarez, no one knew where he was after his precipitate flight from San Luis, and his whereabouts no longer mattered. During the campaign, an agent of Bazaine had made contact with the principal minister of Juarez, Sebastian Lerdo de Tejada, and obtained from him a letter signifying his personal willingness to consider an honorable settlement with the French, provided Bazaine guaranteed the independence of the country and respected its freedom to choose its own form of government. This was all that Bazaine needed to prove that the Juarez government no longer existed; and he pursued the subject no further. Through his chief of staff he replied, as he had to Doblado, demanding unconditional capitulation, but coupling it in a magical formula with his promise to respect the freedom of Mexico; and there, being rational people, the matter was dropped by both parties. The immoderate Liberals troubled Bazaine less than did Mgr. Labastida. A crisis had arisen during Bazaine's absence from the capital, the goat was after the cabbage again, and on his arrival in Guadalajara Bazaine found his army menaced with excommunication by the Archbishop. Between a broken foe retreating ahead and the little belly of Mgr. Labastida growing behind him, there was no doubt in his mind which was the more dangerous, and he returned to the capital.

3

IN BAZAINE, Juarez found a redoubtable antagonist. Intervention had now entered upon a rational phase, which defeated him on all fronts, and before he left San Luis he was forced to realize that he had met his match in the new Commander-in-Chief, who weaned away his political and military support, called his bluff, ripped open his manifesto, and exposed his boast of combating the French with a whole people as an army and an entire country as a battlefield. The loyalty of his military leaders was so doubtful that Zarco despaired of the outcome. Writing to a friend in the capital who supplied him with paper and a printing-press, he promised that "with this weapon, rather than with guns and cannon, we shall wage a stiff war on the French and their allies. Things are going badly, though, very badly here," he admitted. "Our leaders are deserting every day. . . . There is no people in our country; it is in vain that we address ourselves to the Mexicans. The peace promised them by the so-called Empire flatters their hopes. As for us, we shall be obliged to take refuge in Durango or on the northern frontier. For my part, I intend to leave for the United States and await the outcome of the situation there. Our Don Benito Juarez is spoiling everything with his fancies. He has a new idea in his head and is courting Doblado, the hypocrite, the rascal, and Uraga, the perfidious. The former, who is a double-dealer in every respect, will betray whenever he judges it to his interest. As for the latter, if he is given four men and a corporal, he will take them over to the Imperialists, provided they leave him his rank of a general of division and the houses which he has adjudged to himself."

Heartening as the political difficulties of the French were to Juarez, recapitulating his own and confirming his achievements, his position was seriously weakened by the swift and irresistible advance of Bazaine. When he abandoned San Luis Potosi, he was obliged to relinquish the vital center of the country and to retreat into regions which were not only remote, but backward politically, where the pulse of national life was passive and sluggish. Of the temper of that territory he was fore-warned by his son-in-law, Don Pedro Santacilia, whom he sent ahead with his family as far as Saltillo, and who served him at the same time as a political scout. Santacilia, who was a Cuban exile and revolutionist and new to the back country of Mexico, was impressed by "the fine nature of the inhabitants," but he was also struck by "their deplorable backwardness and subjection to the customs and prejudices of past ages," and his reflections drew a little homily from his father-in-law. "It is because their immediate rulers do not have a profound belief in the principles of liberty and have no faith, therefore, in the progress of humanity," Juarez explained, "and do not strive to improve the condition of the people, removing the obstacles which prevent them from seeing their nakedness and misery. Nevertheless, we must not lose heart; being as there is in those people a right inclination toward what is good and a natural instinct for liberty, all they need is to have at their head a decided partisan of liberal ideas to issue from their abject condition, and that day will not be long in coming, given the irresistible impulse of the age. In the meanwhile we must continue our propaganda, trying by our writing and even in our conversation to educate these people, inculcating ideas of freedom and dignity, with which we shall do them practical good." Whether it was his son-in-law, or his children, or his ministers, or his commanders, or his chance ac-quaintances, whoever doubted heard his magical formula, and *do not worry* became a byword that won him, willingly or unwillingly, the devotion of all who depended on him.

When his wife proposed to move on to Monterrey, however, even he hesitated, for this was distinctly treacherous territory. Monterrey was the capital of Santiago Vidaurri, who had ruled the states of Coahuila and Nuevo Leon for ten years as a virtually independent domain. Vidaurri was the type of the local cacique and the arbiter of the fron-tier, and his loyalty was doubtful. Attached to his territory with the tenacity of an autocrat, popular with his people and jealous of his independence, he had repeatedly proved refractory to the authority of the central government. During the civil war he had played fast and loose with it, in 1861 he had harbored Comonfort in defiance of the demands of Congress for his extradition, and together with evasive pro-fessions of friendship for the President he had manifested his insub-ordination and hostility to him on more than one occasion, and on a number of pretexts, which made it imprudent to trust his hospitality. For once Juarez was worried, and he advised Santacilia to reconnoiter the ground beforehand; and it was with undisguised relief that he learned that his wife had received a letter from Viduarri welcoming her to Monterrey with the most chivalrous cordiality. Touched where he was most tender, he conveyed his thanks to Vidaurri "for kindnesses which I shall never forget in my gratitude," and he improved the occasion for a political understanding. How deeply he was moved he revealed by his uncommon expansiveness. He charged his son-in-law to go to Monterrey himself and explain to Vidaurri that his personal enemies had never been deliberately employed or protected by the central government. "If they have been employed, it is only for the good of the public service, and I have never lent myself to being the instrument of their vengeances against him," he condescended to say; and to prove it he carried candor to the most intimate lengths. "He cannot be surprised that I have employed them when their services were considered useful, when for the same reason I have employed even those who have most injured me in my honor and reputation," and he cited examples: the deputy of Coahuila who moved his impeachment for the McLane treaty and "who accused me gratuitously of being a traitor to the country"; a minister who abused him personally in a public session of Congress; the leaders of the Fifty-One who petitioned him to resign and undermined his reputation as a public functionary by their votes and their writings; "and, nevertheless, I have called each of these men to important posts because their services were thought useful, and many of them have lent and are lending them now. In short, you know how I treat my enemies and can paint my character to Señor Vidaurri." He answered his complaints with the indulgence of an adult. The question of Comonfort, which had strained their relations to the breaking point, was dead, definitely dead, for Comonfort had just fallen in a skirmish with the enemy; and if the notice of his death published by Zarco seemed too cold to Vidaurri, no doubt it was. "I have felt and blamed it also; but I could not oblige that gentleman to write otherwise, since Zarco does not exercise any influence over me, as some people mistakenly believe or affect to believe, nor I over him, and I have no wish to offer any suggestions to him or to any other public writer concerning their writings, and I do not want to contract obligations which may deprive me of the freedom to act against them when they make mistakes in their profession. I think that if Señor Vidaurri listens calmly to these reflections and weighs them in cool blood, he will be convinced that he has no cause to complain of me."

The portrait was part of the defense of Mexico. Such expansions were rare and only a serious emergency could provoke them. Vulnerable, intensely vulnerable where his family was concerned, he repaid a favor to them by abandoning his habitual reserve; but his personal feelings were not permitted to cloud his political judgment and he passed without transition from the one to the other. "I agree with you," he con-

548 JUAREZ AND HIS MEXICO

cluded his instructions to his son-in-law, "that Vidaurri must be attracted or eliminated. I favor the former extreme. Only if this is not sufficient to utilize him for the good of the nation should we resort to the second. Work, therefore, for the former."

The result was doubtful when he left San Luis Potosi, and as he made his way northward he met with pronounced signs of disaffection from other quarters. In Saltillo, where he rejoined his family, he was approached by emissaries from Doblado and Ortega, requesting him to resign. They appealed to his patriotism, his public spirit, his abnegation, exactly as the Fifty-One had done, and with the added argument of Bazaine. Repeated reports that Maximilian was wavering, repeated assertions that Napoleon would never treat with Juarez, and the increasing political difficulties of the French led them to believe, they said, that some form of composition with the enemy was possible, and that the Republic might yet be saved in the uncertain period of transition, provided the person to whom the Emperor of the French objected were eliminated in time. To such forms of political backwardness, coming from enlightened leaders and not from the benighted mass of the people, the President replied with the same patience. He explained that, after pondering the proposal long and giving it all the consideration it deserved, however much he pressed his poor understanding, he could not find a reason sufficiently compelling to convince him of its advantage; on the contrary, he considered it an extremely perilous experiment, which would place them in a ridiculous position, provoke anarchy and bewilderment, and cover him with ignominy, since he would be betraying his honor and duty by abandoning voluntarily, in the bitterest days of the country, the post with which the nation had entrusted him. There was no assurance, he added, that the enemy would treat with Ortega or any other Mexican who refused to accept intervention, and he repeated the self-evident fact, which the French were daily demonstrating, that the invader was pursuing the destruction not of individuals, but of the government which the nation had given itself, and that, no matter who headed it, the result would be the same. It was true that the situation was, for the moment, unfavorable, and he was under no illusions, but he knew that it was their duty to fight in defense of the country, and between the defense and the betrayal of a mother he saw no honorable mean: it was his error, perhaps, but an error well founded and one which he cherished gladly and which deserved indulgence; and he begged them not to take amiss his decision to decline the invitation, which they had been so good as to make him, to resign. The letter was a little manifesto, and the style, adapted to the intelligence of his counselors, complimented it. If not educated, Ortega and Doblado were sufficiently edified to drop the subject, and Doblado accompanied him to Monterrey.

Something more than reason was required to deal with Vidaurri.

Secure in the quasi-independence of his states, he was determined to preserve their neutrality and to avoid being drawn into the war by the presence of the central government on his territory or the trespassing of the President on his private domain. As such he treated a demand addressed to him from Saltillo to relinquish the customs revenue to the general government, and after a fruitless correspondence the controversy reached a point at which it became necessary to persuade or to eliminate him. Thereupon the President moved to Monterrey with a small escort of troops. Within sight of the city he wrote to his wife in Saltillo to reassure her. "At ten o'clock today I make my entrance into the city. I did not do so yesterday because this Señor Governor, who is very fond of talebearers, believed that we were coming to attack him and had made preparations for defense, taking possession of the artillery in the citadel and spreading word that no help was to be given to the government. As all this is nothing but bluster and clowning, I do not let on that I understand and am continuing my march. I might have entered last night, but contrary to my custom and character, I wish to make a solemn entry. As there is plenty of good sense in the population, the people are already preparing curtains for the reception. We shall see what trick this gentleman will try next. Wait until I write you to prepare your trip. Pick up the clothes brushes which I left on my shaving table. Regards to our friends and many hugs for the children. Your husband who loves you, Juarez."

Although he minimized the situation a little for her sake, he always paid his wife the compliment of telling her the exact truth and sharing his sure judgment with her. Doblado occupied the city, but the artillery which he drew up on the public square to salute the solemn entry of the President was snatched by Vidaurri and confiscated for the defense of his citadel, and a tense situation ensued. After spending three days of uncertain truce in Monterrey, during which the entrenched cacique dickered and parleyed, unable to decide between bluster and bloodshed but refusing to capitulate, Juarez returned to Saltillo, where he summoned him to trial and declared the disputed territory in a state of siege. Vidaurri retorted with a remarkable maneuver. Combining defiance and evasion with a practiced hand, he proclaimed himself in open revolt against a government that had forfeited its authority by failing to defend the nation, and at the same time he published a letter from Bazaine inviting him to rally to intervention and resorted to the extraordinary trick of proposing to submit the decision to a popular referendum. A clash could no longer be averted, and Juarez put an end to Vidaurri's tragic clowning. To the perversion of the democratic process he replied by forbidding it, and to the proclamation of insubordination by returning to Monterrey in force. Before Juarez sighted the city again, Vidaurri escaped and slipped across the border into Texas, and this time the President made his solemn entry amid the enthusiastic acclamations of a population that needed only the presence of a decided believer in liberal ideas to display its common sense and declare for the national cause.

In reclaiming this far corner of Mexico Juarez found himself fighting Bazaine on familiar ground. Vidaurri, and to a lesser degree Doblado and Ortega, were still imbued with the mental habits of the past and steeped in a persistent tradition of personal politics. The kind of accepted convention by which personal amenities were combined, normally and naturally, with political hostilities; the habit of conducting public affairs by personal favors; the cult of cant, which Mora had diagnosed long ago as the cause of what he called the charlatanism of the national character and the result of clerical education; the manipulation of democratic ideas and public spirit for personal ends —all this was old Mexico, new Mexico, perennial Mexico. On this ground Juarez was well ahead of the French, but he was hard-pressed by them, for not only Vidaurri, but Doblado and Ortega, had been approached by Bazaine, and though they resisted, the tradition was indigenous and died hard. The occupation of Monterrey had one palpable result, however: Bazaine abandoned the plebiscite which he had proposed to hold in the occupied provinces.

4

THE crisis which recalled Bazaine to the capital was sufficiently threatening to interrupt the pacification of the provinces. The Clerical party was seething with revolt, and no sooner was his back turned than the Archbishop reiterated his protests against the liberal articles of the French program with all the strength which he could muster. His strength consisted of two bishops, two archbishops, and his own character.

Mgr. Labastida had lost none of his intransigence during the seven lean years he had spent in exile. Neither had his companions, though their banishment had begun later and their ordeal had been shorter. They were a compact group of men, whose common mentality was formed by their profession and the habits of the past, and who were impermeable to change, although intensely sensitive to experience, and experience had not been spared them. They had known dark days during their exile, days of dejection so deep that they had believed their cause to be irrevocably lost and had almost resigned themselves to their destiny. Even Mgr. Labastida, who was of a nature more unbending than his brethren, had been reduced at times, as he confessed to Father Miranda, to longing for half an hour's talk with his faithful coadjutor to brace his spirit, which was completely broken by unrelenting adversity. He recalled as the happiest period of his life a few weeks that he had spent with the Sisters of St. Mary in New York. Since then he had felt at home nowhere. In Paris he had been politely ignored; no one consulted him, no one told him anything, and as he observed the progress of intervention he had been forced to recognize that it was a purely secular crusade. The failure of the reactionaries to react to it at the beginning had hurt him profoundly; his own hopes died, as he said, when he saw that those *corpses* took no part in it. Prostrated by their apathy, he was not permitted, however, to rest in despair. Worse ensued when the promoters of intervention turned against it and cursed it, and he had had the galling experience of being congratulated on not returning to Mexico and urged not to do so while a foreign flag flew there. Few mortifications—and he had known many—were so bitter as those felicitations; for though he was a member of a supernational body, he was not a supernatural being, but a Mexican born and bred and attached to his country by ties which differed from those of the laity only because he was bound by his vows to regard Mexico as a Franciscan foundation. In Rome, in Viareggio, in France, wherever he went, he had been merely a visitor, without the consolations of the gray nuns of Manhattan or the company of Father Miranda, and when the call had come to join the Regency he had drained the dregs of deception and lost no time in seizing the opportunity to play more than a passive and vicarious part in intervention.

His fellow prelates had suffered the same experience and had been even more brutally exhausted by it. When they were recalled to their dioceses, they hesitated long before answering the call and weighed carefully the penalties of exile against the advantages of homecoming. The Archbishop of Guadalajara was an infirm old man of seventy, who had barely strength to crawl home and none to be turned back again, and he postponed his departure until the French could guarantee his diocese. The correspondence which he conducted with his parish was marked by the patience, the prudence, and the plaintiveness of an exmartyr. He was happy to learn, he wrote to his flock, that Citizen Benito was giving ground and that the day was not far distant when he would discover that *dominatur Excelsus super regnum hominorum,* but as long as *deserving citizens* like Comonfort, Doblado, Uraga, and Vidaurri were still at large, and particularly "my excellent subjects Gonzalez Ortega and Ogazon (whom I give you or anyone who wants them)," he preferred to wait. The other bishops banished in 1861 were of a like mind. Before casting off from Europe, they met in Barcelona to decide the cardinal points to be settled on their return to Mexico; but so unsettled were they by the prolonged uncertainty of their position there that they could come to no agreement either on the election of bishops, canons, and curates, which was a matter of primary interest, or on the question of ecclesiastical property, which would be, of course, the first point to be touched. They were displaced persons who had lost their bearings with their occupation. The best that the Archbishop of Guadalajara could promise his flock was that in all probability they would begin with the question of patronage, "that is to say, the servitude and slavery of the Church, by which we lose the little liberty which our immediate predecessors conquered at the cost of so many sacrifices, and like the Spanish clergy we shall have to kiss the hand of His Majesty and collect a revenue or a salary more wretched than an actor's or a coachman's. How much better it would be for us," he concluded, "to live on the alms of the faithful than for our clerics to have to frequent the antechambers of the palace!" Personally, he was prepared for the worst, but collectively they were uncowed. Time could not temper the claims of the Temporal Power, nor experience the trials which they had endured in defending it; and Mgr. Labastida was armed with the authority of Rome.

Their misgivings vanished as soon as they touched their native land. In Veracruz they were welcomed with honors, which atoned for the stoning with which they had been greeted there two years before. On their passage to the capital the Indians turned out with pinwheels and turrets of flowers, clinging to the wheels of their carriages to kiss their hands. Mgr. Labastida was touched to tears. The people were good, he said, the people were long-suffering, and they needed only the presence of their pastors to declare themselves. Years of expatriation and persecution were forgotten in the demonstrations of undying loyalty which accompanied their progress, and they arrived in the capital prepared to resume their ancient prerogatives only to find themselves wrecked in port.

An alien hand had intervened, and the position to which they returned was worse, as Mgr. Labastida declared in his protest against the French program, than the one they had left. Then the government had manifested its principles frankly and the Church had defended itself gloriously: now the government consummated the ruin of the Church and dealt it a blow equivalent to the death of all human hopes. "Then," he made bold to say, "the Church had only one enemy, the government that persecuted it; now it has two: that same government which still lives in the land, which has its own resources and an army that disputes the ground inch by inch, and which counts on the support of its principles in the camp of its enemy, and the government of the capital, whose favorite occupation is to carry into effect the destructive designs of the other in the moral and religious order."

In one of his first interviews with Bazaine he warned him that he would need fifteen thousand more men if he meant to impose the French program, and no sooner had Bazaine started his campaign in the north than the Archbishop began to agitate actively in the capital. Ousted from the Regency by his colleagues, he retaliated with a collective protest by a synod of seven bishops excommunicating any government that sanctioned the spoliation of Church property and requiring restitution and reparation as an essential condition of absolution, aye, *in articulo mortis*. The pronouncement, abetted by the Supreme Court, which refused to act on cases involving Church property, created a sensation, and the Regency retaliated by dismissing the members of the bench in a body. Thereupon the protests redoubled. Incendiary leaflets were slipped under doors, calling for a general insurrection against the French. General Neigre, the commander of the city, notified the Archbishop that, reluctant though he was to use force, he would do so if necessary; the Archbishop disavowed the leaflets, but found blood enough in the bottom of his inkwell to deny the authority of the Regency and to pen a sharp note to General Neigre. "The Church suffers the same attacks today as during the government of Juarez," he repeated. "Never has it been persecuted so cruelly, and we are in a worse situation than at any other period." As Bazaine had left only a skeleton garrison in the capital, the crisis seemed sufficiently threatening to require his presence; but it subsided with his arrival, for it was founded on bluster. The Archbishop went so far as to threaten to close the Cathedral to the French army, and Bazaine to say that he would open the doors with his cannon; but neither went any further. The excommunication was not recalled, but it was held in abeyance; and the din of the regimental Mass—the Mass of the deaf, it was called—continued to be heard in the city every Sunday.

The crisis had, in fact, a salutary effect: public confidence in the French program was braced by it, for it was clear that Bazaine meant exactly what Forey had said. At the same time, the revival of clerical insubordination and the vigorous action of the authorities provided a test case that fathomed the fanaticism of the public and brought to the surface a profound and confirmed indifference to the bids of the Archbishop. Seven long years had elapsed since he had fomented revolts in Puebla, and the day had passed, and passed irrevocably, when the lifting of an episcopal finger could make and unmake Mexican governments. The agitation was a posthumous fiction, promoted by men who did not know that they were dead. The comatose condition in which they had existed so long had numbed their perceptions and made it difficult for them to realize that time had finally prevailed, but the truth penetrated at last. Some of them weakened. The Archbishop of Guadalajara came to terms with Bazaine, who was preparing a budget for the Church under the dreaded dispensation of State patronage; the lower clergy were perfectly willing to be supported by the State, and at the age of seventy he reached the age of reason. If the Church had been a democratic organization and the issue submitted to a popular referendum, the hierarchy might have yielded; but the Archbishop of Mexico refused compensation or compromise, although for the sake of peace he allowed Bazaine to repair his villa in Tacubaya for him. The concessions of Mgr. Labastida did not compromise the Archbishop, however. Deserted, he was adamant. Defeat was all that he would accept from the French, and defeat he accepted provisionally, temporizing in a trance that still passed for life. The brain still beat, and beat fast, under the stealthy approaches of extinction; and in his extreme hour he laid the flattering unction to his soul that, though everything else failed, there was still Maximilian.

Of all the hopes that buoyed him, this was undoubtedly the most desperate. The Archbishop had visited Maximilian in Europe and had come away enchanted and singing the praises of the sovereign-to-be. But the turn which intervention had taken was prescribed by its purpose, and the French program was imposed by necessity and adapted to the nature of things. After a false start Napoleon had been forced to realize the fallacy of basing intervention on a moribund reactionary minority and obliged to shift it to the living and progressive forces of the nation; no other course was possible. If an invisible protectorate was to be established, the autonomy of the country respected, and the result to be self-sustaining, it was essential to induce the majority to accept it. If an American Algiers was to be created and a flourishing market opened for colonization and commerce, it was necessary to nourish the productive forces of the nation, to preserve internal peace and property relations, to protect accomplished facts and established reforms. If a dam was to be built against Anglo-Saxon expansion, it was imperative to adapt it to the pressure, to fortify the native economy, and to introduce a congenial civilization capable of mollifying the animosity of the American neighbor to the experiment. If the acquiescence of foreign Powers was to be secured and domestic opposition appeased in France, it was important that that culture should be at least as advanced as in Europe. If a backward and bankrupt country was to be modernized, if a disorganized and demoralized people was to be regenerated, it was indispensable, in a word, to appropriate, develop, and crown the work of Juarez. These conditions were axiomatic; the premises produced the conclusion. The liberal line adopted by Napoleon was dictated by the inherent logic of the situation and indispensable to the consolidation of his conquest; and whether the proconsul who carried it out was called Forey, or Bazaine, or Maximilian, the policy was the lifeline of his Mexican Empire.

The clerical question was, in reality, the easiest to regulate, having been definitely and irrevocably settled by the Reform movement. The insistence of the Archbishop, and of the Vatican, on the restitution of Church property was not merely incompatible with French policy; it was materially impossible to cancel a *fait accompli* without upsetting the feeble economy of the country or to revoke a reform which had transferred property to so many productive sources and economic roots; and as the sole compensation that the French could offer was the support of the Church by the State, and as this solution, which meant the surrender of the independence and political power of the Church, was inacceptable, the Clerical faction was doomed to defeat all along the line.

The other articles of the French program presented greater difficulties. The reorganization of the Mexican army was the most pressing and the most baffling. The Regency abolished the forced levy, but to replace it by a law of moderate recruitment, as in France, was to raise the racial problem in Mexico. "This is a work that can be successfully developed only in times of peace," Bazaine wrote to Napoleon. "In this country ideas are still so backward that a former Minister of War, General Blanco, told me recently in a conference on recruitment that he did not believe it possible to subject the white race to recruitment like the Indian; no son of a colonial family would consent to mingle with men of color in camp, unless he served as an officer. And it is quite evident that the Indian race is inferior at present; but this is because ever since the Conquest no regime has done anything for it, and it is only exceptionally that some few have succeeded in being accepted in the caste of the *gente de razón.* The denomination sufficiently indicates that this race, so deserving of interest, has always been treated as an inferior to be held in tutelage; hence it has remained completely indifferent to what happens in its country, of which the masses have not the smallest parcel."

The creation of an honest and efficient civil service was equally indispensable and equally difficult. Consulting native advisers again, Bazaine forwarded a report that traced all the revolutions of Mexico to the immorality of the army, *empleomanía,* and the criminal leniency of its governments. The army, instead of being composed of the most select elements of society, was made up of its scum: criminals were commonly condemned to the ranks. *"Empleomanía,"* the report continued, "that is to say, the monomania and craving to live at the expense of the government, is a malady inherent in Mexican character and education; for a people that considers itself dishonored by work and is always inclined to dissipation and idleness can find no incentive in any honest occupation," and official employment was merely a means of satisfying its pride and filling its pockets. None of these difficulties was insuperable, although the support of the Mexican clergy, the Mexican army, and the Mexican civil service was a costly solution, and the financial burden was the main objection to the expedition in France.

The Commander-in-Chief was encouraging. During the campaign in the north he had begun the training of the Mexican army, with the backing of French troops, and he pronounced himself satisfied with the conduct of Tomas Mejia, an Indian commander who had led a column against San Luis Potosi, and of Marquez, who had given a good account of himself in repelling the attacks of the Liberals on Morelia. The civil service was reliable as long as it was supervised by the French. The essential reforms could be effected in time; but time was the *sine qua non*. The results obtained by Bazaine in six months were sufficient, however, to win the confidence of the Emperor, who trusted his judgment and competence unquestioningly and gave him carte blanche to continue. Though much remained to be done, the initial blunders had been corrected and a fresh start had been initiated with effects sufficiently promising to prove that the enterprise was feasible. Force had been reduced to a minimum, and although French courts-martial functioned throughout the occupied territory, deportations and executions were few, the amnesty had been extended, and ample time given to the wavering to reflect and rally to the new order. The combination of conciliation and authority, and the benefits of law and order, peace and protection, had begun to make an impression on the reserve of the general public; and though the situation was by no means settled, it was stabilized and controlled, and Bazaine had made it acceptable to Maximilian, whose advent, repeatedly doubted and deferred, was finally announced in Mexico on May 15, 1864.

5

THE proconsulship of Bazaine marked the apogee of intervention. The Opposition in France, boasting almost two million votes, had made an impressive stand on the Mexican question in the sessions of the Legislature that opened in November 1863. In anticipation of it, the Financial Commission, reporting on the supplementary expenses of the budget, had seen fit to say: "The government hopes that the end of 1864 will see the close of the expedition. We are unanimous in advising it to put an end to the Mexican expedition, not at any price, God forbid! but as promptly as the honor and interest of France permit. The expression of this wish corresponds to the general sentiment of the country." The Financial Commission spoke without partisanship and with indisputable authority, and its recommendations carried great weight. The majority, which had shouted down the invectives of Jules Favre twelve months before, now listened to them with sensible attention and silent assent. In a message to the Senate the Emperor appealed for the confidence of the country, rebuking the shortsighted and the fainthearted and promising that the expedition "begun for the redress of our grievances would end in the triumph of our interests." Jules Favre demanded that the government treat with Juarez and withdraw, and he was supported by Adolphe Thiers, who emerged from a long retirement to put his reputation and talent at the service of the famous Five of the Opposition. Their election, he told them frankly, meant little or nothing, while his was an event of European importance, and French politics would henceforth be a dialogue between the Emperor and himself. He devoted a part of that dialogue to the Mexican question. "Treat with Juarez and withdraw," he repeated. "Above all, do not engage in an attempt of monarchical restoration, for even without taking a formal engagement, you would be morally bound to the man you placed on the throne. And you, my colleagues, after encouraging the government in its designs, you will be in a poor position to refuse him later the troops, the sailors, the millions which he will demand to complete the mad operation that you have undertaken. So far you have not engaged your honor, but the day that the prince leaves with your support and your guarantee, you will have to sustain him, no matter what happens. The probity of France will be engaged. We have been told that to abandon General Almonte would be a shame; how would it be a shame to abandon Almonte and his friends, to whom we owe nothing and who have compromised us? And when a prince is there in Mexico, led on by you, when your soldiers have overrun Mexico to enable the country, as we are told, to vote for him, when you have done all this, do you dare to tell us that we will not be engaged toward that prince? Well, I tell you that it is an engagement. Let those who will, take it. For my part, I reject such a responsibility."

The tepid common sense of Thiers was decried as either simple-minded or inspired by systematic opposition. "The government cannot treat with Juarez, the man who has shed the blood of our nationals and outraged our flag," the spokesman for the Throne replied; "nor with Almonte, who does not represent a regularly constituted authority; it can negotiate only with a government issuing from universal suffrage. And if Maximilian is elected by the Mexican nation, by treating with this sovereign, the French Government will not contract a permanent and indefinite solidarity for the maintenance of an Empire in Mexico." M. Rouher, the spokesman for the Throne, was an honest man, and his speech was one of those about which he was accustomed to say, when he was complimented on it, that it meant nothing. "You do not want the truth," Thiers retorted; but M. Rouher told the truth. When the count was taken, the Opposition rallied only forty-seven votes out of three hundred; but those forty-seven included several members of the majority whose loyalty to the Emperor was above suspicion, and the famous Five flattered themselves that three-quarters of the Assembly were tacitly on their side. As the Assembly was merely a consultative body, however, it could only register public opinion without imposing it on the irresponsible sovereign.

The triumphs of Bazaine tipped the wavering balance of public opinion. The sounding taken by the *procureurs* in January were still uncertain. "People wonder," as one of them said, "whether it is possible to rely on the stability of the institutions which we are striving to organize amid that mobile and undisciplined people. The hesitations of the Archduke to accept the crown, and the campaign just opened to expel Juarez definitely from the provinces where he maintains himself, have brought about a reversal of feeling less favorable to the supreme strivings of our enterprise." But in the next three months the uncontested occupation of the central provinces in Mexico mollified public aversion to the adventure in France; there was a perceptible softening of popular gumption, and here and there the reports of the *procureurs* indicated that the idea of the Emperor was beginning to take. In Rouen the margin was rising, and the very reasons that previously discouraged confidence in the industrial world were now acting in reverse. "People think, on the contrary, that our colonial power and commercial relations are not in proportion either to the development of our navy or the progress of our industry, and they regard with favor the formation by our arms and under the protection of France of a new empire offering large outlets for French production. This war will become completely popular if the government can assure the reimbursement of the expenses made by France. This is the only point that preoccupies public opinion."

In Angers the barometer rose many degrees higher. "The Mexican expedition, better known in its cause and commercial and political consequences, will soon take the place due to it in everyone's mind as one of the most fertile and glorious events of the Second Empire." In Corsica "the end of this Mexican expedition, which has been represented, in some ways, under such false colors, and which will be one of the brightest pages of a reign that will have lacked no glory," was hailed as pure Bonaparte. In Bordeaux "the glorious conclusion of a difficult enterprise" was already taken for granted and compared to "the brilliant marvels of the expedition to Egypt," and other Napoleonic associations were recalled in honor of the nephew of the uncle. "The national pride has applauded the spectacle of a prince of the House of Hapsburg receiving a crown from the hands of the Emperor," the reporter asserted, although he added that opinion was divided on this point. Some provincials regretted that "our sacrifices do not serve to assure the throne at least to a French prince, and that we are offering it to a prince of that House of Hapsburg, which is accustomed to astonish the world by its ingratitude. Others, on the contrary, consider the obligations and, consequently, the dangers, less great for our country by the choice of a foreign prince. The public is divided between these two opinions, but the majority seem to incline toward the former." In March there was a flurry of alarm when it was learned that the United States Congress had passed a bellicose resolution against the monarchy in Mexico, but their State Department put the soft pedal on the threat of hostilities, and the nervousness in France abated sufficiently to abet the entanglement. The buoyant confusion of public feeling that prevailed at that moment was the most favorable phase of intervention for Napoleon; the common denominator of its conflicts was Maximilian, and to swing the wavering tide all that was needed was to seat him promptly on his throne. A loan was floated in Paris to launch him, and the public responded: for Maximilian was the best guarantee that the troops would be withdrawn without further delay.

Immediately after the proclamation of the Empire by the Assembly of Notables in the summer of 1863, a Mexican delegation left for Europe to offer the crown to the Archduke. Headed by Gutierrez Estrada, Hidalgo, and Father Miranda, they were received at his castle of Miramar on the shores of the Adriatic in October. The accounts of their reception which they sent to their friends in Mexico were unanimous in their enthusiasm. For once Father Miranda knew felicity. "For my part, my friend, I feel myself very feeble and without words to portray the emotions which I felt," he wrote on his return to Paris. "Perhaps it is because I have not lived among princes nor in palaces that my imagination was so profoundly stirred by the palace of Miramar and, more yet, by the princes whom I met and conversed with there, appreciating their most noble characters, full of kindness and gentleness, the glories of their lineage, the magnificence in which they live, and all the grandeurs and attentions that surround them. Perhaps because ever since I was born I have seen nothing but tears in the eyes and pains in the heart and have been witness to great miseries and lawless passions in those who have undertaken to rule us; perhaps for this reason I have been captivated by the great and heroic sentiments of the Archduke and Duchess, who have accepted our country as their own, exchanging their present fortune for a future that cannot be exempt from vicissitudes and afflictions and that, though it were only to go to rebuild ruins and calm rancors, would be enough to dismay the best-tempered soul; and perhaps because coming from Mexico with my memory charged with pictures of horror and desolation, crimes and scandals, which necessarily carry with them feelings of humiliation, I have been enthralled by the generous desires of those who, to regenerate us by placing themselves at the head of our society, must sacrifice their repose, their high position in Europe, their rooted affections, and even their family. This can only be the work of the Almighty." The common miracle of happiness brought out the best in Father Miranda. "I know very well," he added, "that if this letter were to fall into the hands of one of our demagogues, he would laugh at us because we let ourselves be impressed by grandeur; we in our turn will laugh at them, who preach equality as long as they are not superior to others, who declaim against the grandeurs of the world as long as they cannot build palaces, and who ridicule decorations as long as they are not adorned with them. I am moved to say this, because I have been delighted to see that some of our heroes of Puebla who fell prisoners are going around here looking for crosses. Such is the world."

On October 3, 1863, the Archduke accepted the crown conditionally, biding the ratification of the vote of the Assembly by a popular referendum. The whole deputation regretted the delay, but so understanding was Father Miranda that he found it perfectly reasonable. "We shall have to wait a few days longer," he concluded. "But you will understand, as the whole press of Europe has understood, including the English, that the question of Mexico is settled; that the conditions imposed by the Archduke were those naturally to be expected, and that the substance is that for our unfortunate country a new era of glory and felicity has already opened. Miramar and the 3rd of October, 1863, will henceforth be indelible in our history."

Six months later, the ratification having been obtained by Bazaine, the delegation returned to Miramar, and there, on April 10, 1864, the Archduke formally accepted the crown. After the ceremony he countersigned a Convention with the Emperor of the French, subscribing to the conditions under which he accepted it actually. The Convention stipulated that the French troops of occupation should be reduced to twenty-five thousand by the end of 1864 and gradually withdrawn, at stated intervals, during the next two years, as the development of the Mexican army permitted their replacement. The Archduke then retired to his rooms, prostrated by doubt and regret, and at the dinner given that night to the delegation and the visiting dignitaries assembled for the occasion, the Archduchess presided in his place. There were many reasons for the indisposition of the Archduke, and not the least of them was the Archduchess.

The limited guarantees under which Maximilian accepted the crown were liabilities which placed extraordinary stress on his capacities as a ruler. His political gifts were taken for granted—it was another of the necessities of intervention—for they were unknown. In Lombardy, where he had served his brother as governor in 1858-59, he had picked up some experience of administration; but the experience had not been happy. He had pursued a liberal policy, which won him some popularity with the Italians, but which alarmed the cabinet in Vienna and led to his recall just before the intervention of Napoleon in Italy. The unrest in Lombardy was blamed on his leniency. Stung by the reproach of "false mildness and saccharine softness," he protested against it with significant sensitiveness; strong measures combined with beneficent laws, he insisted, were not foreign to his nature; he himself had recommended the strong measures which Vienna adopted at the last moment, but he had done so when things were still quiet, and they could be represented as part of a systematic plan. A hint of the harsher Hapsburg streak flashed forth in his defense, but this was unusual; by nature he was mild, easygoing, and benevolent. After the abrupt interruption of his political career, he retired from public life. Transferred to the command of the Adriatic fleet, he spent some years in foreign travel and eventually settled down at Miramar. Miramar was a place and a man. The place was a picturesque nook of the Adriatic coast, just beyond Trieste, where he bought a fisherman's hut and converted it into a castle surrounded by romantic gardens; and there the man busied himself in mildly intellectual pursuits and would have been perfectly happy, for there and there alone he felt himself completely independent of the world, had he not been a young man willing to dally with the world, which beckoned to him beyond his idyllic retreat. When the crown of Mexico was offered to him in 1861, he welcomed the opportunity to renew his inconclusive experience in Lombardy and make a fair test of his talents in America; for he had been married for four years to an able, intelligent, and pertinacious princess who had his best interests at heart.

The Archduchess Charlotte was the daughter of King Leopold of the Belgians. She had inherited her share of the enterprising qualities of the House of Coburg, which had placed its members on half a dozen thrones in Europe; her marriage was not only brilliant but a love match; and she was by no means satisfied to while away their lives in Miramar. "What a position!" King Leopold exclaimed when he heard of the offer, and the Archduchess Charlotte took after her father. Nevertheless, Maximilian hesitated for three years. He was not too proud to accept a throne from Napoleon. Many years had passed since he had amused himself at the expense of the *parvenu* of the Tuileries, he had outgrown the callow condescension of youth, his pride had matured, and he admired Napoleon as a statesman. But officious advisers of all kinds—seasoned Austrian diplomats, Sir Charles Wyke, an emissary of Juarez—reasoned with him and pointed out the risks of the adventure. His mother put her finger on its weak spot; she described it as an act of *lèse-nationalité;* and the progress of intervention confirmed her dictum. But life was slipping away, and after hesitating for three years he was ripe for adventure. He was going on thirty-two; his wife was as charming as ever, but she was childless. He was under no illusions as to the validity of the vote collected by Bazaine, and he admitted to a confidant that the venture might fail, but he insisted that it was worth the attempt.

If his political experience was small, it was promising, however. He met the essential conditions of French policy in Mexico. He was a liberal, and though his liberalism was of a kind not uncommon in royal families—the liberalism of the younger branches, a French wit called it —it sprang from something better than junior ambition. Liberalism, as a form of political opposition and personal advancement, offered little prospect of a future in Austria for the younger brother of Franz Josef and just enough to segregate him indefinitely in Miramar. His faith sprang from the heart. After his unfortunate experiences in Lombardy, a weaker prince might have recanted his convictions: Maximilian did not. In Mexico, on the other hand, liberalism was indispensable to the success of the French program, and he was eager to vindicate his conviction there. In a secret article of the Convention of Miramar he underwrote the French program and pledged himself to issue a manifesto to that effect on his arrival in Mexico; and his political gifts, after all, were immaterial; they were supplied by the demand.

While his political philosophy recommended him to Napoleon, it hardly squared, however, with the tenets of the party that summoned him to Mexico. But his clients were not deterred by it. They owed their success to Napoleon, and if they were duped it was by their own choice. They came to Miramar not to question but to kneel, and they were too dazzled by their catch to examine it closely. With a reserve as regal as it was politic, Maximilian indicated the direction he intended to take very lightly. He pledged himself to defend the independence and integrity of the country, and he alluded to the importance of constitutionalizing his government at the earliest possible opportunity. One member of the deputation had been drafted, in fact, to sketch a Constitution on the prescriptions of the Archduke, including religious liberty, freedom of the press, equality before the law, and other features which differed imperceptibly from the Constitution of '57; and the text had been submitted to Napoleon, who approved it but advised its adjournment. It was not by parliamentary liberty that one regenerated a nation in the throes of anarchy; what Mexico needed, he declared, was a liberal dictatorship, liberty would follow by itself. The project was deferred, accordingly, and even Gutierrez Estrada, a declared opponent of Constitutional monarchy and a fanatical Clerical, felt no misgivings. Flushed with triumph, he agreed to everything. He had reached his goal, and the most diehard of reactionaries was the most grateful.

One gift Maximilian possessed in a superlative degree, and it was his greatest asset as a ruler. He had a winning personality. Everyone who came into contact with him fell under the spell of his Viennese charm, and with a single exception the Mexican delegation succumbed to it. Gutierrez Estrada led the chorus of praise. All that he could say—and he said a great deal—fell short of the truth: his loyalty, his nobility, his energy, his exquisite distinction, his singular benevolence, his pure and spacious brow, his lively blue eyes full of goodness and gentleness, his superior intelligence—on these he dilated with untarrying loquacity, and yet words failed him. Maximilian, to his mind, was *perfect;* and as a last perfect tribute he stopped talking. Gutierrez Estrada was as pathetic in his joy as Father Miranda. To a man, the delegation was fascinated and agreed that they had made a providential choice: the single exception was Father Miranda. In his painful peregrination through life he was destined to take exception to all his successes, and on his second visit to Miramar he felt that they had made a mistake. Maximilian, to his mind, was a man of light character.

If the character had been as commanding as the personality was winning, little would have been left to be desired. High-minded, well-meaning, conscientious, earnest, and generous, Maximilian had many superior qualities, but they were the product of superior circumstances. His facile affability, his unforced benevolence, flourished readily in the thin atmosphere of royalty; they had never been exposed to common experience. His virtues were crown-bred, and there was no escape from the superiority of his birth and breeding. In his exalted station in life men were obliged to show him their best sides, and his benevolence was necessarily a form of familiar condescension. The misfortune of Miramar was that everyone was on his best behavior there, and the Prince above all. He was, alas, a godsend. Good will he had in abundance; but will? Familiar observers found him wanting in stamina. On closer acquaintance, one member of the delegation, who developed into a historian later, described him as a man who was highly impressionable and unstable, light to the point of frivolity, volatile to the verge of caprice, incapable of sequence in conduct or thought, prone to passing attachments, averse to hardship, fond of effect, at once irresolute and obstinate, and apt to take refuge in trifling occupations to escape serious problems. At the time, however, the Mexican delegates were not familiar observers. Triflers with destiny themselves, they accepted him at face value and were satisfied with the play of appearances that rules the world. Maximilian himself was aware of his weaknesses and labored to overcome them. He grew a beard to harbor his chin and parted it just below his shortcoming.

The guarantees which Maximilian offered were equal, in short, to those which he received. Here, in the high noon of intervention, all equations were even. Of all the available royalties, he was the most qualified, and he engaged himself deliberately and by no means blindly. But at the last moment his determination was subjected to a severe test. His brother had consented to part with him on condition that he renounce his rights of succession to the throne of the Hapsburgs, and he had agreed to abandon them as long as he or his dynasty ruled in Mexico. The agreement was not reduced to writing, however, until he paid his farewell visit to Vienna, when he discovered that the renunciation which he was expected to sign was absolute and unconditional. Outraged by what he regarded as a trick to force his hand, he stormed, he protested, he refused to deed away his rights, but his brother was inflexible, and two weeks of extreme tension ensued. His father approved him, his mother interceded for him, in vain; he returned to Miramar. Both brothers appealed to Napoleon to intervene. The Archduchess wrote to the Empress Eugénie, informing her that they had decided to renounce the throne of Mexico. There was consternation in Paris. Napoleon wired to the Archduke that it was too late to refuse, that his honor was engaged to himself, to Mexico, to the subscribers of the Mexican loan, and he sent an envoy to Vienna. The Chancellor explained that the renunciation was indispensable, "not so much for the Archduke personally as in view of the sons he might have under the influence of the climate of Mexico, which is said to work wonders. . . . You talk to me of a conditional renunciation, but how can you expect Austria to consent to be ruled by a prince who had just been chased from a foreign throne?" The Emperor Franz Josef admitted that it was a little his fault for letting matters slip until the last moment; but that was all. The envoy went to Miramar. Maximilan insisted that his honor as an Archduke, and a husband, made it his duty to act as he did, and when he was reminded that his honor was engaged to the Emperor, to France, and to the world, "I know it," he replied; "the Archduchess knows it also, but I cannot but be concerned for the future of my wife and of the children whom I hope to have in Mexico." — "We know very well," the Archduchess added, "that we are doing a service to Napoleon III by going to Mexico!" — "Your Highness," the envoy replied, "will recognize that the services are at least reciprocal."

"These hesitations," he wrote to Napoleon, "prove that with a distinguished intelligence and a cultivated mind, the Archduke has not enough firmness of spirit and, above all, not enough confidence in the great enterprise which he is going to attempt." Obviously a great deal was expected of the sexual potency of the Mexican sun. Finally, after a week of furious indecision, Maximilian yielded. Franz Josef came to Miramar, and on April 9, after a long and pathetic discussion between the two brothers, in the presence of all the archdukes and high officials of the Court, the Family Pact was signed. On the next day Maximilian accepted the crown of Mexico. For the next three days he was inaccessible. He confessed to a friend that if someone were to tell him that the whole thing had been called off, he would shut the door and dance for joy, but Charlotte— He said no more; there was no more to be said. In her arms it was impossible to be halfhearted. He had recovered his confidence when he boarded the frigate which was to bear them to Mexico, and he looked his last on Miramar with only a passing regret. The place was mortgaged as well as the man; he was deep in debt, his creditors were dunning him, and a substantial sum had been set aside from the Franco–Mexican loan to save that romantic retreat from the world.

Politically inexperienced, socially sheltered, morally privileged, and mentally immature, Maximilian gave his measure on the sea crossing. He devoted days to the annotation of a manual of Court etiquette, with meticulous personal instructions for the benefit of the Mexican Chamberlain; and he wrote a letter to Juarez inviting him to meet him at the capital to discuss their differences and seek an amicable understanding acceptable to the nation.

6

THE letter was received by Juarez in Monterrey. He answered it as a matter of courtesy although, he explained, "in great haste and without a meditated editing, because you must realize that the delicate and important duties of President of the Republic absorb all my time, without permitting me to rest at night." As he answered the Archduke after hours, he went directly to the point. "It is a question of endangering our nationality, and I who, by my principles and my sworn pledges, am the one called to maintain the integrity, sovereignty, and independence of the nation, have to work actively, multiplying my efforts, to meet the sacred trust which the nation, in the exercise of its powers, has confided to me. I propose, nevertheless, to reply to the principal points of your letter." Lightly, but laboriously, he met Maximilian on his own level. "You tell me that, abandoning the succession to a throne in Europe, forsaking your family, your friends, your fortune, and what is most dear to a man, your country, you have come with your wife, Doña Carlota, to distant and unknown lands to satisfy the summons spontaneously made by a people that rest their felicity and their future in you. I am amazed, on the one hand, by your generosity, and on the other, my surprise has been great to read in your letter the words *spontaneous summons,* for I had already perceived that when the traitors of my country appeared at Miramar as a self-constituted commission to offer you the crown of Mexico, with several letters from nine or ten towns of the nation, you saw in all this merely a ridiculous farce, unworthy of serious consideration by an honorable and self-respecting man. To all this you replied by requiring the will of the nation to be freely manifested through universal suffrage; this was to demand an impossibility, but it was the demand of an honorable man. How can I not wonder then, when I see you come to Mexico without any advance having been made in the conditions you imposed; how can I not wonder when I see you accept the offers of the forsworn and their language, and decorate and employ men like Marquez and Herran, and surround yourself with all that condemned part of Mexican society? Frankly, I have suffered a disappointment: I thought you one of those pure beings whom ambition could not corrupt.

"You invite me to go to Mexico, the city to which you are bound, to hold a conference there in which other Mexican leaders in arms will participate, promising us all the necessary forces to escort us on the way and pledging, as security, your public faith and your word of honor. It is impossible for me to accept your summons, sir; my occupations do not allow it; but if in the exercise of my public functions I were to accept such an intervention, there would not be sufficient guarantee in the public faith and the word of honor of an agent of Napoleon and a man who is supported by the Frenchified part of the Mexican nation, and who represents today the cause of one of the contracting parties of the Treaty of La Soledad. You tell me that you have no doubt that the peace and felicity of the Mexican people would come of our conference, were I to accept it, and that the empire would rely on the service of my lights and the support of my patriotism by placing me in some distinguished position. It is true, sir, that contemporary history records the names of great traitors who have broken their oaths and their promises and failed their own party, their antecedents, and all that is most sacred to a man of honor, and that in these betrayals the traitor has been guided by an obscure ambition to rule and a base desire to satisfy his own passions and even his own vices; but the present incumbent of the Presidency of the Republic, who has sprung from the obscure masses of the people, will succumb—if in the designs of Providence it is ordained that he succumb—fulfilling his oath, warranting the hopes of the nation over which he presides, and satisfying the promptings of his own conscience. I am forced to conclude for lack of time, and I shall merely add one more remark. It is given to men, sir, to attack the rights of others, to take their property, to attempt the lives of those who defend their liberty, and to make of their virtues a crime and of their own vices a virtue; but there is one thing which is beyond the reach of perversity, and that is the tremendous verdict of history. History will judge us. I am your obedient servant, Benito Juarez."

Juarez was not accustomed to waste words, and that statement, if it answered no other purpose, served at least to define the different levels of life upon which they lived. It was the only service which he could render Maximilian.

General du Barail finally succumbed to Mexico in the first days of March. He had spent twenty-five years in the service, twenty-three on active duty, the fever which he had contracted at Veracruz had wrecked his health, and when Bazaine offered once more to send him back to France he accepted the favor no longer as an insult but gratefully. On the crossing he was leaning on the rail one afternoon, when he noticed in the distance "two little trails of smoke, ever so light, like that which slips from the end of a cigarette, between two inhalations," which the captain identified as the frigate *Novara* and its escort bearing Maximilian to Mexico, and which soon disappeared in the dusk. "Poor Maximilian! I thought. What are you going to do in that atrocious country which I leave without regret; amid those people who have been tearing one another apart for more than forty years; in the thick of those intrigues fed by fanaticism and greed; in that country where men huddle together in the towns like sheep to escape the bandits that make the countryside uninhabitable; in this Mexico without trade or industry; in this Mexico which has been killed by its mining wealth, leaving civil war the only possible branch of human activity, as formerly in Spain? The very defenders of your throne, those Mexicans who have called you, will abandon you, because you cannot go through with their retrograde plans. And this French army which has shed its blood to give you a throne will necessarily play the same role with you as it did at the beginning of this century with the crowned brothers of our great Emperor, for whom our marshals became rivals and adversaries. If you succeed in bringing order out of this chaos, prosperity out of this poverty, and union into these hearts, you will be the greatest sovereign of modern times. But I very much fear that the task you have undertaken is above human strength. Poor fool! You will regret your fine castle of Miramar!"

On his arrival the homebound invalid was summoned to the Tuileries. In the waiting-room he met General Auvergne, Forey's chief of staff, also disabled, who was delighted to find support for the interview; for they both supposed that they had been summoned to give the Emperor a firsthand, sincere, and disinterested account of conditions in Mexico. "We entered the Imperial study, where the Emperor received us as he knew how to receive. One of his most attaching qualities was a blend of exquisite goodness and perfect simplicity. Un-

doubtedly Napoleon III had in the highest degree the pride of the
great name which he bore and the sense of the great duties which that
name imposed. But in private life he was profoundly friendly and
simple, without superciliousness, without pose, and even familiar,
though that familiarity, served by a supreme tact, never went so far
as to allow his interlocutors to forget their rank and his. From the very
first words, Auvergne and I felt completely at our ease—completely at
our ease, and completely lost. The Emperor did not ask our opinion
about the expedition, nor about the future of the new Mexican Empire,
nor about the real attitude of the population, nor about the Liberal government of Juarez, nor about the best means of attaching Mexico to
Maximilian, nor about the campaign which we had just made in the
north and which, meaningless from a military point of view, was important politically, nor, in a word, about anything important; he posed
none of the questions for which we had laboriously prepared our replies.
He confined himself to asking us about the installation of the troops in
the newly occupied regions and the sanitary condition of the army
outside of the Hot Country, where the *vomito* was endemic during
six months of the year. 'What is done,' he said, 'to preserve the men
from the rays of the sun that are so dangerous?' — 'Sire, we have headcovers.' — 'Ah!' And we had to explain what headcovers were by
resting our handkerchiefs on our hats. Visibly the Emperor knew more
about Mexico than we did, or did not want to risk having his ideas de-
ranged by ours. When he rose to dismiss us, however, he said, 'When
you left Veracruz, had the Emperor Maximilian arrived?' — 'No,
sire, but he was not far from it, for we passed his ship off the Antilles.'
The Emperor merely said, 'It is his business now to impose himself on
Mexico.' And he added some words of which the text escapes me but
which meant that he was disposed to recall his troops and impatient to
finish with Mexico. One felt that his idea might have been put this
way: 'Let Maximilian work it out by himself. I wash my hands of it.' "

Napoleon had no time to waste; his attention was engaged elsewhere. He had resumed the writing of a life of Caesar, which had
been interrupted for a year, and of which he had just completed the
preface.

With the arrival of Maximilian at Veracruz on May 28, 1864, the invasion of Mexico by Viennese charm began. The welcome which he
received there was so cold that it brought tears of chagrin to the eyes
of the Empress, but he passed through the town rapidly, leaving behind him a manifesto that began with the words, "Mexicans, you have
desired me," and the hospitality of the people improved as they advanced. The carriage broke down, a stagecoach was borrowed to continue the journey, and though Carlota admitted that it needed all their
youth and good humor to resist the lurching and jolting, they made

light of hardships; they were determined to please and be pleased, and save for the roads, which were unspeakable, they found everything better than report. In Cordoba, in Orizaba, in Puebla, they were welcomed with flowers, odes, addresses, and chimes, and when they entered the capital the demonstrations left nothing to be desired. The best families turned out on the outskirts to meet them, the second-best in the suburbs, and everyone who could beg, borrow, or hire suitable attire and a hack lined the road to cheer them as they passed and to follow them in a solid procession through the decorated streets to the Cathedral, where the clergy advanced to bestow their blessing amid the booming of bells and the din of a multitude delirious with enthusiasm. In the round of festivities that followed—balls, receptions, military parades, religious and theatrical performances—Maximilian was at his best. Blond, august, graceful, elegant, he represented well, and what he represented was a dazzling novelty in Mexico. Eager to make the acquaintance of his subjects, he invited the most notable to his table, and one day a week was set aside for a public audience open to all comers on application for a card of admission at the door. On these occasions the palace was crowded with enthusiasts. The glamour of authentic royalty combined with easy accessibility attracted the curious, and once they came within reach of his personality they were won; not only his partisans, but his adversaries, and even the indifferent, recognized its spell, and within a fortnight he had conquered the town by his charm. He was ably seconded by his wife, and as the Imperial couple received their guests with exactly the right word for each one, the personal touch worked wonders. The response was, if anything, too cordial. The Empress was amused but taken aback by the familiarity of her Mexican friends; the Emperor, with all his approachability, drew the line at promiscuity, and it was one of the necessary but unfortunate effects of his first acquaintance with his people that he spent ten days in adding the finishing touches to the manual of etiquette: the precedence which he gave to such matters was noticed as an indication of the distance which he had yet to travel to arrive in Mexico.

On the day of Maximilian's arrival the Archbishop published a pastoral letter exhorting the laity to allegiance to the sovereign and expressing his confidence in the solution of the "extremely serious clerical question." It was the first anniversary of the proclamation of Forey, and after twelve months of French administration the clergy were uneasy and their collective conscience was troubled by the sin of omission to settle their complaints. For serious questions, however, there was also a table of precedence. A multitude of other pending problems demanded the attention of the sovereign, and it soon appeared that the suspense in which they had remained under the provisional government was to be prolonged indefinitely. The *Official*

Bulletin published an abundance of Imperial decrees, the importance of which varied inversely with their number, but there was no indication that even the preliminaries had been considered for the decisive measures required for the reconstruction of the country, and as the weeks passed public impatience grew. A hint was dropped by a local French paper. The Emperor Maximilian, it was said, seemed to have been profoundly imbued, during his stay in Lombardy, with the wisdom of the Italian proverb *"Chi va piano, va lontano,"* and he was well advised, no doubt, in not proceeding by spectacular effects, as the former rulers of the country had, but he was in danger of going to the opposite extreme and encouraging by too long a delay the suspicion that he lacked a fixed plan or the power of decision.

The judgment was hasty, but impatience was understandable in a people that had been living for a year in suspense and uncertainty. Forey had set up a purely provisional regime; Bazaine had strengthened and lengthened it, but still provisionally, as a steward for the sovereign. The Emperor was extremely conscientious. Daily he was at work in his study; and even in his carriage, on his way to Chapultepec, where he had established his residence, he was seen compiling voluminous dossiers and transacting official business. But he labored under the difficulty of being an alien, a novice, a newcomer. He was determined to acquaint himself with the conditions of the country at first hand, thoroughly, patiently, responsibly, and if in the process of Mexicanizing himself he lost time—well, he acquired one of the national habits; and if he lost the confidence of his subjects the more closely he came to resemble them—well, that was inevitable. Precipitation, he said, was the principal error of the preceding government, and planning was his strong point. He examined every pending question personally and carefully, drawing up a chart, with appropriate subdivisions of the main headings and detailed specifications for study, complete in every point that could occur to the most painstaking mind, save for a date line. There was a Commission on Finances, headed by a new French expert, M. Budin having done nothing but advance money for a year. There was another for the reorganization of the Mexican army, headed by Bazaine, whom he appointed not only for his obvious qualifications, but because he seemed to be too much inclined to rest on his laurels and to need spurring. There was yet another for the reform of the judiciary, of which he himself assumed charge, but as the best magistrates were partisans of the Clerical faction, this measure was held in abeyance until the others had been settled. And so the reports accumulated, and the weeks passed, and the dust raised by the arrival of the sovereign settled on the dampened enthusiasm of a public surfeited with bureaucratic routine; and unreasonably but relentlessly the first faint traces of rust appeared on the crown.

Then, when impatience began to quicken, the Emperor left the capital for a tour of the provinces. From August to October he inspected the outlying points of the occupied zone—Queretaro, Guanajuato, Leon, Morelia, Toluca—to acquaint himself with conditions and to acclimate himself to the people. The purpose of the trip warranted the time spent on it. It was imperative, he wrote to his father-in-law, to know the people themselves before taking any decision; it was necessary to demonstrate on the financial markets of Europe that the country was quiet and that the sovereign could cross it freely; it was indispensable to prod the activity of the military command and to force Juarez, whose government was in extremities, out of the country. Such was the plan; and the results equaled his expectations. Lightly escorted, he crossed the country freely, the French having taken extraordinary precautions to clear the roads and explore the surrounding country all along his itinerary. Everywhere his reception was cordial. Crowds of Indians came from distant *pueblos* to acclaim him as the patron of their people, and he lost no opportunity to identify himself with the masses. He wore the native costume, he flattered the national pride. In Dolores he celebrated the anniversary of national independence in the house of Hidalgo and made a speech in which he grafted the empire onto the work of the democratic insurgents. He inspected hospitals, poorhouses, prisons, the work of the miners in the mines, the industrious poverty of the countryside. He studied the clerical question in the parishes through which he passed. In one, where the population had never been baptized, he called out the priest and ordered him to work—if need be, with a hose. He dissociated himself ostentatiously from the Clerical faction, refusing to attend any *Te Deum* or to enter any convent, and performing his devotions privately at low Mass, without official pomp. In Morelia he snubbed Marquez and reviewed his soldiery reluctantly. The time was not wasted; he returned to the capital thoroughly conversant with conditions. "I was able to realize during this excursion," he wrote to Napoleon, "that the inhabitants of the provinces have more intelligence and nobility and are more patriotically devoted to me than those of the capital, who unfortunately have suffered the bad influence of the foreign element too long accustomed to profit by disorders and revolutions to make their fortune. I believe in the devotion of the majority of the Mexican people, and I think that with the devoted co-operation of the Marshal I shall be able to wait calmly for the realization of the loan which M. Fould promises me for next spring and which will assure the future." The loan was the most important object of his trip. Within the charmed circle drawn around him by the French, the devotion of the people was secured by his Viennese nature; but beyond it, the pacification of the country was so little advanced that he was convinced of his duty to protect his people with an iron hand and he directed his Minister of the Interior to consider all armed guerrillas as groups of bandits and to treat them with inflexible severity under the martial law created by Forey in June 1863, establishing courts-martial to deal with troops of armed malefactors.

To French garrisons in the occupied zone his advent was a blessing. Major de Tucé, who had come out with Colonel du Barail, was stranded in Guadalajara that summer. Belonging to a family of radical Republicans, he was the last to talk politics, but he did warn them not to trust the papers. "What a frightful country! or rather what frightful inhabitants!" he wrote to his sister in April. "Maximilian will be a great man if he manages to make anything out of it. . . . Maximilian would render us a great service by coming; but will he come? I can hardly believe it, unless he is blinded by ambition, and if he has taken any information about the country. I have just received your letter and the papers you sent me. I read: 'The campaign in Mexico may be considered finished. The enthusiasm of the towns that have fallen into the power of the expeditionary force, the adhesion of the Juarist generals, the arrival of Maximilian, the organization of the resources of the country by French employees,' all that belongs to the kind of *bonnes blagues* that are told to Parisians." A month later, he was more blunt. "No one sees any escape from our situation. We cannot find any pretext to leave; we have not advanced a step. The Mexican armies are not very redoubtable, it is true, but they are still intact and preserve their unity. They use a very good system, always keeping clear of us and never engaging battle; they retreat as we advance, and when we withdraw, since we are not numerous enough to occupy every position, they return quietly and settle down again in the places they occupied. The territory is so vast that they can go on playing that little game as long as they like." Life in Guadalajara was tedious. The only diversion was churchgoing, and "as the French are not very demonstrative, the inhabitants say that we are Jews." Outside of the cities it was worse. The French troops were demoralized by fatigue, boredom, and the exasperation of pursuing bandits, and their only diversion was to take to pillage by way of reprisal. The situation was summed up in a stanza by Victor Hugo:

> On vient, on pille, on tue, on passe et, sans effroi,
> On laisse des pays brûlés derrière soi.
> Et les choses qu'on fait dans le sang et les flammes
> Sont illustres, si non, elles seraient infâmes.[1]

It was only by quoting poetry that he could talk politics. The coming of Maximilian was a great relief, therefore, and of all the gains of the trip

---

[1] We come, we kill, we loot, we pass and, unblenching,
Leave behind us a land scorched and stenching.
And the things that we do in blood and flame
Are glorious, or they would be our shame.

into the interior the greatest was the good will of the disgusted French garrisons.

On his return to the capital he was welcomed with enthusiastic demonstrations. During his absence the Empress had acted as Regent, and he was pleased to find that she displayed a marked aptitude for her duties; her tact and ability were universally recognized, and her popularity was second only to his own. As the questions left to her discretion, however, were necessarily minor ones, and even these had to be referred to the Emperor wherever he might be before a decision could be taken, his return was awaited impatiently. Bazaine described it as a triumph, and it was.

Napoleon was becoming impatient. For five months Maximilian had done nothing very thoroughly. It was time to show more resolution, he wrote him; it was essential to begin with big things, to lay the foundations, and to build; in founding an empire perfection could not be attained at once; perfection was neither possible nor important; anything was better than protracted uncertainty. Maximilian agreed, and in November 1864, after a reasonably brief interregnum, he announced that he would now begin to govern.

7

THE five months that followed the advent of the Emperor were a trying period for the patriots: a period when persistent adversity had not yet hardened into habit, when heroism was still tentative and fruitless, when failure was tame and inglorious and defeat friendly and sensible, and amnesty offered an easy retreat to reason and security. The French program sapped the defenses, thwarted the strategy, and drained away the dwindling area of moral, military, and political resistance upon which the President depended to worst, fatigue, and foil the invader. Fatigue and discouragement began to thin the ranks of what appeared to be a lost cause. Liberals of the first hour foresaw the last, and intellectuals, whose loyalty was fed by no popular sap, were peculiarly liable to such weakening and weathered the small hours with extreme difficulty. Manuel Zamacona was one of them. In the summer of 1864 he wrote to Juarez in a strain so desperate that he lapsed into scriptural imagery. "I have more reason than the apostle, I believe, to turn to you and to cry like him, *Save us, O Lord!* for I

feel the waves mounting higher and higher to engulf us; the very surface of the ground we tread is giving, and I cannot look for salvation in
a supernatural prodigy but in the union of human forces. The waves of
intervention are advancing, sir, and meeting no dam, no resistance.
This remote corner, which they have not yet reached, is crumbling
under our feet and becoming dangerous and enemy ground." A man
who could write like that in real pain was already lost; everything deserted him but his style, and his style betrayed him. Manuel Zamacona had been reared in a Seminary, and he slipped into its language
as readily as men in mortal extremity revert to their original training.
His rational convictions were acquired, and the frail securities of reason failed him so completely in a funk that the very avowal of genuine
alarm was couched in the fluent, unreal, reminiscent idiom of his
cradle. He had more reason, indeed, than the disciple to despair,
having lost his faith in supernatural succor without finding it in human
forces, and reason being merely a motive for incredulity and destruction. It was impossible, he confessed, not to be impressed by the prodigious progress that intervention had made in realizing hopes and
plans which, a year ago, had excited their derision and which they
had not hesitated to call chimerical; in a year they had fallen from
the glorious pedestal to which they had been raised by the heroes of
Puebla, all the great centers of the interior were lost, and, worse yet,
the easy military triumphs of the French were followed by a moral
conquest of equal facility. His convictions were staggered. It was a
time that tried the tenacity, the vision, the faith, of the firmest; it was
no time for the timid to think. His convictions, being purely intellectual, were tender; his faith was a mental attainment; and the sensible
disciple could only fidget, unable to walk on the waters of Galilee without wetting his feet. Happily for Juarez, he was not obliged to answer
Zamacona's appeal. The letter miscarried and fell into the hands of the
French, where it found its proper destination, for it served their propaganda admirably. Bazaine filed it with much other material of the same
kind, which warranted him in writing to Napoleon that the Juarez
government was *in extremis* and that no one mentioned it any longer.

Bazaine was patient, and he was sanguine. In that season of decidu-
ous patriots he had only to wait for desertions to ripen. General Uraga
had abandoned the unequal struggle and gone over to the empire—but
without his army. Doblado, leading six thousand men to battle in
May, had been defeated at Matehuala, and after dickering for a safe
conduct to the capital, changed his mind and emigrated to the United
States in July. In losing the battle he lost none of his fame as the most
adroit of Mexican politicians. "They say," Bazaine reported to Paris,
"that Doblado told his friends that he had only to get himself beaten
to extricate himself honorably in the eyes of the country. One way is
as good as another, and this one paints the man. As for Juarez, I do

not believe that he will be able to maintain himself in Monterrey after the discomfiture of Doblado, and Vidaurri is said to be returning to the campaign to drive him out if he does not leave." Doblado and Uraga, however, had never gone through the fire at Puebla; those who had, found security in peril, and Ortega, Diaz, and Berriozabal were still in the field with two to three thousand men each; and though Bazaine was reluctant to extend his lines, he sent three columns against Monterrey to satisfy Maximilian and to drive Juarez out of the country, or, at least, into the Desert of Mapimi, where he could not recruit troops or find supplies.

Monterrey was abandoned by the republican government in the middle of August. The evacuation was completed under fire of a troop of Mexican turncoats. Juarez was at table when the attack penetrated the neighboring streets, and a messenger was sent by his escort to urge him to hurry, but no one had ever seen him run in his life and least of all for it, and he finished the meal with the messenger and drove away under a spatter of bullets. A few miles from the city he was joined by a battalion, which covered his retreat, and he was well on his way when the French entered Monterrey four days later. On the later stages of a long journey, which carried him slowly northward and which lasted two months, there were stretches when he traveled without escort, protected only by the country and the people—ample protection as the distance increased between him and the contagious line of desertions. The country was vast and sparsely settled, and the enemy faded into a phantom, an almost forgotten memory. One day, however, the presidential party was halted by a dust cloud scouring the plain and bearing down on them, and as they had lost contact with their small escort and there was no cover in sight, Juarez alighted and proposed that they meet the fate which had finally overtaken them. He led them toward it; but they had not gone very far before the wind shifted and the cloud lifted, revealing a flock of sheep grazing peacefully on the plain, and the ministers returned to their carriages, relieved and amused, but not a little bewildered by the behavior of Don Benito. Shepherd-wise, had he known all along? No one ever discovered the answer, for no one dared to put the question. Prieto, however, who was one of the party, treasured the anecdote and added it to his small store of wayside tales of the President; they were fewer than ever, and he was down to his last hero.

Of the loyalty of the people there was no doubt. In one village, as the President was about to enter his lodgings, a blind drummer approached and addressed him with a natural eloquence, which was noted, not without envy, by one of the ministers. "What he said went like this. 'Never have I so much wanted my sight as now to see the most eminent man of my country. Those who see say that the sun is more beautiful at its setting than at the beginning or in the middle of its course; and so the President of the Republic seems greater to me in this remote state than in Mexico, commanding those who command. His eminent virtues are well known to me, for there are some things so clear that even the blind can see them.' Then that good Mexican played reveille on his drum with spirit and skill." Sometimes the demonstrations of the people embarrassed the President. In the *pueblo* of Hidalgo del Parral the inhabitants unhitched the horses and would have drawn his carriage themselves if he had not forbidden it as a tribute unworthy of free men; but not until he alighted and let them embrace him did they desist. When he entered the capital of the State of Chihuahua, the crowds invaded his lodging and forced him to accompany them to the site where Hidalgo met his death and to make a speech at the base of the monument; and not satisfied with the hero on the pedestal, they hailed him as a second Hidalgo before they released him.

During the long migration of the government Ortega attacked the French and was defeated at Majoma in the State of Durango, and simultaneously the port of Matamoros, valuable for its revenues, was lost to the enemy. In Chihuahua the government was removed by a vast stretch of trackless territory from the enemy, but also from its partisans, and reduced perforce to the role of a distant observer of events over which it could exercise little or no control. Following from afar the spreading progress of the French and the repeated defeat of their own forces, receiving belated reports of recent reverses, repairing them with meager and dwindling resources and relaying encouragement by a slow and irregular correspondence to the remaining centers of resistance with which they maintained a remote and uncertain contact, the President and his ministers were obliged to draw heavily on their inner resources to maintain their own confidence. But wherever he was, everyone knew who he was. The house which he occupied stood open day and night, and his friends warned him more than once to keep the doors closed; until one day he answered them once and for all. "The good cause is not pursued," he said. "What can they do to me?" — "But you should be careful." — "Of whom?" — "Of the enemy." — "Why? If we are going to win? You will see." And they did. The blindest could see the morrow made man in those dark days. His were the fruitful virtues of the sun, breeding faith in the desert. Devotion sprang up around him, seeking how to serve him, and seeking in vain. The wife of a deputy who followed him from San Luis would gladly have looked after his wants, but he had none. His habits were frugal, his self-sufficiency was forbidding. His house was furnished with bare necessities borrowed from the republican families of the town; and having where to lay his head, he needed nothing else. He sat up late at night, reading and writing, slept little, rose at dawn, went out to take the cool of the air in the public garden, retired to his room and remained working there all day. What could one do for such a man? She could only sigh and say that the Señor Presidente was certainly a very sweet man, a very sweet man.

Wants he had; but they were those of the desert. The official family of 1864 was as scanty as the sick family of 1858. Of the comrades of that day only Prieto was still in the struggle. Ocampo, Degollado, Miguel Lerdo de Tejada, Zamora, were dead; the rest were dispersed and inactive. Manuel Zamacona was—where? Manuel Ruiz had found a corner of his own, neither here nor there. The waters of Galilee were everywhere, and the old crew wading in them one by one. Ignacio Ramirez was in a port of the Pacific, sneering at the everlasting President. Ignacio Altamirano was in Acapulco, reading Tasso. Zarco was in the United States. Doblado had crossed the border; the rest were not far from it. Moral resistance was concentrated in the little knot of incorruptibles who formed the official family of 1864, and two of them at least compensated for the missing. In Sebastian Lerdo de Tejada, a younger brother of the reformer, and José-Maria Iglesias, Juarez found loyal collaborators and kindred spirits. In them, too, the flame fed its own sightless substance, and no less steadily than his; they were equal to the trust which he placed in them, but they were not the fellow travelers of earlier days. Though the official family of 1864 was as sound as the sick one of 1858, it was an official circle, not a family, and for the daily renewal and nourishment of faith Juarez was forced to rely on himself alone.

His personal life assumed an importance, therefore, or rather a prominence, which was of public interest. His personal life was concentrated in his family, and as he had sent them to the United States, it was from this want that he suffered most acutely in the desert. A brood of nine boys and girls, ranging in age from a married daughter to an infant granddaughter, being too numerous and delicate to accompany his peregrinations, he banished them with his wife and son-in-law before leaving Monterrey; and as he was out of touch with them during the two months that he spent on the road, he was, he wrote, in an "unending torment, knowing nothing of your fate." It was his very being that he had banished. In Chihuahua another two months passed before he heard from them, and when he finally learned late in December that they had arrived safely in New York, he escaped, as he said, "from a state almost of desperation." It was not relief, it was liberation, that the mail brought, and he recovered his customary spirit immediately.

Writing to his son-in-law, he gave him the latest news of Mexico, muffling the bad, making much of the good; for the absent merited the best. "This Chihuahua is a calaboose where we are in rigorous incommunication; but it will not be long before our bayonets open a way into the interior. Since the defeat which the French inflicted on our forces on September 21 at Majoma near Durango, they have been so poorly supplied that they could not conduct their expedition against this state and have given us time to recover. We lost the action when we had all the advantages for success and all the probabilities on our side, because Señor Gonzalez Ortega did not engage all his forces but only a small part, which fought heroically, and the other, which was the larger, remained drawn up and retired in order without firing a shot; and the worst was that when that force, of fifteen hundred men at least, was already ten leagues from the enemy, without being pursued, the commanding general let them disband, because of neglect or disgust. These facts have not been published nor should be, with the enemy facing us, and I inform you of them only so that you may know one of the causes of our disasters. Ortega is here now, living in retirement in his house. He has been prompt enough, nevertheless, to ask me to hand over the command to him, on the ground that my period is over. He did not read the Constitution and has placed himself in a ridiculous position. In spite of the poverty of our Treasury, we are working actively to repair our losses. All our leaders operating in various parts of the Republic are encouraged and full of enthusiasm, and I hope that in the coming year our situation may improve, either because our forces may advance in their operations, or because Napoleon may withdraw all or a part of his, or because Maximilian may lack resources, for he is not the one to perform the miracles that we have wrought to sustain a prolonged struggle."

But the miracle was possible only because his family was safe. "I am very sorry that you lost your baggage," he added, "but as long as you saved yourselves, nothing else matters, the loss can be repaired." The news of Mexico merely paraphrased the news from New York. The family was the living cell, the unit of the nation, and the welfare of the one was indispensable to the defense of the other. The line between his public and private life was so thin as to be imaginary, and he crossed and recrossed it constantly. "I have suffered no less than you from your absence," he wrote a week later; "but fortune has not forsaken us completely as yet, since so far no evil has befallen any of our numerous family, and I count on you to take care of them. That is my greatest comfort." When things went badly on his side of the border, he expected instinctively a corresponding disaster on the other, which would break the balance and his power of resistance. And in the first days of the new year to which he looked forward so hopefully, it came.

Indirectly he learned that his favorite son was sick. His heart leapt, his mind leapt, with a terrible presentiment, to the unerring conclusion, and he wrote to Santacilia that he understood that it was only to break the blow that the information said no more; "but really my

Pepito no longer exists, no longer exists, is it not true? You will understand all that I suffer by this irreparable loss of a son who was my delight, my pride, my hope"—and he begged him to forgive the blots, because his head was lost. But in his next letter, three days later, he wrote as if nothing had happened. Refusing to believe his forebodings, he banished them from his mind and, protecting himself with a salutary pretense that his boys were going to school, he begged their guardian "not to place them under the direction of any Jesuit or any sectary of any religion; let them learn to philosophize, that is to say, to investigate the why and the wherefore of things, so that in their transit through this world they may be guided by truth and not by the errors and prejudices that make men miserable and degraded." His defense was drawn from his deepest experience. He, too, had passed through the Seminary, but his faith in reason supported him in his mortal extremity.

Three weeks passed before he wrote again—three weeks of silent suspense. He braced himself for the worst, he awaited it resolutely; but his ignorance, his certainty, and his presentiment gave him no rest and, for all his determination to bear the blow philosophically, he was "sunk in the most profound sadness," and he could only hope against hope that the next mail would calm his grief or increase it by a confirmation to which he was not yet schooled. When the confirmation came, he had no philosophy left. "It is too much that my spirit suffers and I have hardly strength enough to surmount this disaster, which drains me and hardly lets me breathe. My adored son is dead and with him died my fairest hopes. This is horrible, but there is no remedy"—and since disasters never came singly, his mind turned to his wife. "Now I am afflicted by the health of Margarita, who is not well. I am writing to her to console her, but in the matter of natural feelings advice serves very little. Do all that you can to fortify her spirit and incline her to submission," was all that he could say. He enclosed a newspaper with the latest news of Mexico; there was nothing important to communicate.

Though his power of resistance was not broken, it was taxed to the utmost by a trial under which his patience almost passed away. His official family surrounded him sympathetically, but they suffered from the intolerable merit of being sound. For weeks, for months, his stifled lamentations seeped through the even tone of his letters, and the name of his "unforgettable Pepe" cut his breath and the connection of his thoughts. Once, by an unprecedented lapse, a pause of the laboring mind, in an official communication to the Legation in Washington, he alluded to his personal loss side by side with a public issue and on the same level with it. The balance was broken, but he controlled the better part with a will not only unshaken but braced by his ordeal. The wound was still raw when, at a banquet given him by the people of Chihuahua on his birthday, he rose to his feet for the obligatory speech. He got through the opening phrases haltingly. "I drink to the independence of the nation, Citizens. That on invoking that sacred name everything may yield to the Fatherland. That we may make it triumph or perish. That the sentiment of Independence may be the bond of all Mexicans, excluding none but the enemies of the Fatherland." When the applause subsided, he continued more freely: "Gentlemen, to give one's life for Independence is a great good; to give it when a man is bound by the example of so many worthy Mexicans would barely be doing one's duty. Without any affectation of modesty, without any hypocritic sentiment in the bottom of my glass, I repeat that as men we are nothing, that principles are everything. That, greater than all despots and their power and their armies, our cause will soon triumph; and that Mexico will renew the splendid testimony which it gave to the world on the 16th of September, 1810, proving itself worthy of the triumph of its sacred autonomy." The ceremonial words were greeted with cheers and shouts of *Viva Juarez,* but his friends were still unsatisfied. One of them proposed the health of his family, and, rising once more, he said hoarsely, "I see the country here and I say to it solemnly that my sacrifice is nothing, that the sacrifice of my family would be much, would be infinite for me; but if need be, so be it." And unable to control his feelings, he sat down, amid stentorian *Viva's!*

8

ON THE first day of the new year the President issued a manifesto reminding the Mexican people—lest they forget—that after three years of a bloody and unequal struggle they were still afoot and determined, as on the first day, to defend their freedom. Maximilian also opened the year with high resolutions. He was Mexicanizing himself rapidly; and so was Carlota. "We dress *à la Mexicaine,*" she wrote to Eugénie. "I wear a sombrero when riding. We eat *à la Mexicaine,* we have a carriage with many mules and bells, we are always wrapped in *sarapes,* I go to Mass in a mantilla; in short, if we have any *arrière-pensées* of emigrating, they do not appear. It is not reform that changes men, it is the way it is done, and in everything external and childish we conform to Mexican customs and amaze the Mexicans themselves." The *arrière-pensées* had not wholly disappeared, however, and no little resolution was needed to face the new year firmly.

Anticipating the desires of Napoleon, Bazaine had informed him on the day that Maximilian entered his capital that the pacification of the country was sufficiently advanced to reduce the expeditionary force to twenty-five thousand men, a figure sufficient to support the Mexican army. These assurances were repeated regularly for the next four months, and in the first days of January 1865 eight thousand French troops were repatriated. The optimism of Bazaine was not shared by his protégés. Though the reduction was stipulated in the Treaty of Miramar, Maximilian objected that to enforce the contract at that time was impossible; no one knew better than Bazaine that the basis of the Empire was the French army, that not a man could be spared, and that the original forty-seven thousand whom he had under his command were too few, as it was, to occupy and hold the vast territory over which they were extended. Bazaine was obeying orders from Paris; the Minister of War urged him to hasten the repatriation of the troops in order to lighten the budget and appease the criticisms of the Chamber, but the Minister was guided by the sanguine reports of the Commander-in-Chief, and the Commander-in-Chief was not an irresponsible lieutenant. He was the trusted adviser of two sovereigns and was expected to temper instructions with advice, and his judgment was generally blamed both by the Court and the army as an unscrupulous willingness to cater to the wishes of his master in Paris prematurely. His critics fancied that they had finally discovered his weak point. The Commander-in-Chief, in a word, was a courtier. He stood higher than ever, however, in the favor of Napoleon, who had just raised him to the rank of a Marshal of France—prematurely, in the opinion of Maximilian—and to lodge their objections the Imperial couple were obliged to go over his head or behind his back. Maximilian wrote to Napoleon and Carlota to Eugénie. Though the eventual recall of the troops was inevitable, she admitted, the later the better; the people, despite their friendly disposition, being so apathetic, partly by nature and partly by reason of their misfortunes, that a sudden reduction of the French effectives would produce serious discouragement and insecurity. Not to mention Juarez, who still held three rich provinces in the north. "There is unfortunately one idea," she reminded her friend in Paris, "which has not yet been developed in our good Mexicans, the sense of self-defense; between ourselves, it must be said that they let themselves be robbed and plundered without any resistance, and as it will need time to inculcate such notions, the troops of Your Majesty are our sole refuge." Carlota was a valuable asset to her husband: the appeal of a woman to the chivalry of the French was a security which her father had suggested for just such an emergency. Maximilian applied the same argument to the Emperor, and between them they made it perfectly plain that the French protectorate was a pyramid without a base. The troops remained in Mexico, although a few battalions were sent home to satisfy public opinion in France, but these were immediately replaced by fresh contingents. The arrival of an Austrian and a Belgian Legion failed to satisfy Carlota. "We need troops," she repeated. "The Austrians and the Belgians are very good in times of calm, but when the storm comes, there is nothing like the red pants."

The position of Bazaine was not easy: obliged to serve two masters, he naturally inclined to the real one, but the instructions which he received from Napoleon frequently contradicted those which he received from the Minister of War. With the nominal sovereign of Mexico his relations were correct but occasionally strained. He was annoyed to find that the functions of the courts-martial were frequently impeded by reviews of sentence and the pacification of the country retarded by the clemency of the Emperor. He felt that Maximilian was currying favor at his expense and too willing to assume the *beau rôle,* leaving the harsh and ungrateful one to his partner. The Emperor, in a word, was a courtier, and what he was courting was a facile popularity that reflected unfairly on the French. Conquest and conciliation could be successfully combined only by a single hand. By way of concession, Maximilian authorized the shooting of prisoners taken in battle. Sometimes he trespassed on military questions. For reasons known only to himself, he insisted on raising the blockade which the French fleet had laid to the Pacific coast, destroying the fruits of eight months of work by the Admiral and lending Juarez a new lease of life, and on this point he maintained his judgment despite the remonstrances which Bazaine addressed both to him and to Paris. The regulation of their respective positions was a delicate matter, and no little tact and forbearance were required to oil the bearings; but both men were by nature accommodating and their collaboration was rarely marred by visible friction. Within his own sphere the Commander-in-Chief remained supreme, and as he respected the independence of the sovereign in political affairs, before Maximilian knew it he found himself governing alone.

Of all the problems that demanded the attention of the sovereign on his arrival the most pressing, if not the most important, was the clerical question. On his way from Miramar he had paid a visit of courtesy to the Pope, but instead of discussing the position of the Church at headquarters, he had preferred to postpone it until his arrival in Mexico, and the only understanding which he reached in Rome was that a Nuncio should be sent to settle it there. Nothing was gained but time, and far from facilitating the solution, the delay aggravated its difficulties, dilatory tactics being to the advantage of the Vatican. Bazaine advised him to settle it himself, before the arrival of the Nuncio, "accomplished facts excluding all discussion," as he said. The advice was good for a beginner, Bazaine having guaranteed his success; and all the better that the Nuncio was known in Paris to.be difficult. "His character is not very conciliatory," Eugénie warned Carlota, "and I think that his long stay in Paris has done little to modify his ideas in a more liberal sense." She promised her help and the support of her consort; but she added that they were not on the best of terms with the Pope, and that Cardinal Antonelli, the Papal Secretary of State, said frankly that the worst of all recommendations was that of the Emperor of the French. Maximilian was free, therefore, to deal with the question alone.

On the suggestion of Eugénie, Carlota, with the technical assistance of the Almoner-General of the French army, drafted the project of a Concordat modeled on the one by which Napoleon I had liquidated a similar situation in France in 1814. This project embodied all the principles that were anathema to the Mexican clergy: religious toleration, modified by recognition of the Roman Catholic cult as the religion of State; the support of the Church by the State, with the corresponding obligation for the clergy to exercise their ministry gratuitously and to cede all their revenues to the State; the explicit recognition of the right of patronage inherent in the monarchy, and the implicit recognition of the expropriation of ecclesiastical property by the Republic. This left for discussion only the determination of some minor points of ecclesiastical jurisdiction such as civil registry and the re-establishment and regulation of certain conventual orders. Between them the ladies prepared a neat surprise for the Nuncio. Carlota was pleased with it. The project, as she explained to her helpmate in Paris, appeared inoffensive at first sight and was nonetheless liberal. Not that it was flawless. She regretted the recognition of a religion of State and apologized for that concession to local conditions. Contrary to the assertions of Gutierrez Estrada and his friends, she had found that Mexico was very moderately Catholic: a contradiction in terms which she attributed to the fact that "the pseudo-Catholicism formed by combination with the Indian religion under the Conquest died with the property of the clergy, its principal basis." But as a people needed a religion, and Protestantism, being less costly, was making many converts and presaging the coming of Anglo-Saxon influence, a purified and modernized cult was indispensable for the preservation of the Spanish race and culture, and the Concordat was on the whole a satisfactory compromise. Eugénie was convinced and undertook, for her part, to mollify the Apostolic Delegate in Paris. She discussed with him the intransigent character of the Nuncio, and he went so far as to say that his colleague wished to appear very black in order to pale little by little, and that with time and patience everything could be settled with Mgr. Meglia.

Besides the character of the Nuncio, however, the time was not propitious. The relations of Rome and Paris were extremely strained. On September 15, 1864, Napoleon had concluded a Convention with the Kingdom of United Italy, committing him to withdraw the French troops of occupation from Rome within two years, in return for a pledge that the Italian nationalists would not attack the Papal capital by arms, agitation, or intrigue. Despite these safeguards, the Vatican was alarmed: Cardinal Antonelli declared that the Holy See could have no confidence in them, cited the broken pledges of Piedmont in the past, the loss of four-fifths of the Pontifical States, and notified the French Government that the limits of usurpation had been reached and that the Convention would not be recognized by the· Pope, who had not been consulted. The Pope wished to protest immediately. "I have the conscience of the Catholic world on my side, the Catholic world is with me," he said. In private he complained that he was treated like a minor and a man under interdict. Cardinal Antonelli persuaded him, however, to wait until the cardinals, the bishops, and the Catholic Powers had been consulted. Three months later the Holy Father issued an encyclical granting a Jubilee to the faithful and accompanied it with a *Syllabus Errorum,* denouncing the pernicious doctrines of his time, which was sent to all the bishops of the Catholic world. The list was long and comprehensive, covering all the accepted political principles of the nineteenth century. Erroneous was the right of freedom of conscience and religious tolerance; erroneous the right of the civil power to define and limit the rights of the Church; erroneous the denial of the right of the Church to acquire and possess and to defend its possession by force; erroneous the denial of the Temporal Power; erroneous the separation of Church and State; erroneous the principles of nonintervention and freedom of opinion; erroneous the necessity for the Roman Pontiff to "compromise with progress, liberalism, and modern civilization."

The pronouncement created a sensation in France. The government, regarding it as an anathema directed against the Emperor, demand explanations. Cardinal Antonelli replied that any resemblance was purely coincidental. The *Syllabus,* he said, had a purely spiritual character, without temporal bearing, and the anathema was directed against socialism and the evil passions of the age. He gave his word of honor to the French Ambassador that it contained not the least political *sous-entendu,* that the Congregations had been working over it for years, touching and retouching it twenty times over to remove any semblance of an appeal to one nation rather than to another, and that the situation created for the Pontifical Government by the Convention of September 15 had not influenced in any way the form, the spirit, or the time of· its publication. Despite these denials, the French Government prohibited its promulgation on the ground that it challenged all the structural principles upon which the constitution of the Empire was founded. The Bishops obeyed more or less willingly, some of them reading, interpreting, commenting, and explaining away the provocative features of the Papal pronouncement by the customary *distingos* between doctrinal absolutism and practical tolerance, which the Vatican invariably invoked whenever it was cornered; but the controversy agitated and divided the conscience of the Catholic world, and though so categorical and anachronistic an anathema was doomed to defeat in France, it backfired in Mexico. The fanatical piety of the Mexican people was well known in Rome, and the resuscitation of the clerical question provided Cardinal Antonelli with an excellent opportunity to demonstrate that there, at least, the Papal pronouncement was law. The protest was in preparation when the Nuncio was appointed, and the character of the instructions which he carried was enough to make him, in the words of one observer, the *Syllabus* in person.

The choice of Mgr. Meglia was no accident and his mission no coincidence. He landed in Veracruz late in November 1864, and arrived in the capital, where he was welcomed with conspicuous honors, in time to officiate at the celebration of the great religious holiday of the year, the feast day of the Virgin of Guadalupe. Several days later, after a collation in the Palace, the Emperor broached the question lightly. He outlined the main points of the Concordat, and as Mgr. Meglia made only some minor objections, Maximilian was convinced that the draft had been swallowed and sent him an emissary the next morning to open formal negotiations. But the encouraging signs of political pallor vanished overnight. The Nuncio now declared that he could accept none of the points proposed and produced the ultimatum of the Vatican. His instructions were limited to accepting the abolition of the Reform Laws and the restitution of Church property with full indemnization for what had been lost, the exclusive recognition of the Catholic cult, the unrestricted freedom of the bishops in the exercise of their pastoral ministry, the re-establishment of religious orders, the supervision of education by the ecclesiastical authorities, the prohibition for anyone to teach or publish false and subversive doctrines, and the complete emancipation of the Church from its bondage to the civil power. The consternation of everyone concerned was extreme, and none was more concerned than Carlota. She admitted that her political tact was faulty, she was nettled, she was flippant, and she amused Bazaine by saying that there was nothing to do with the Nuncio but to toss him out of the window. Maximilian was of the same mind. After two weeks of fruitless negotiations, he notified Bazaine that he would proceed to ratify the Reform Laws on his own responsibility, unless the Nuncio capitulated. Bazaine made no objections. But before taking so drastic a step, the Emperor took others to avert it. He sent intermediaries to the Nuncio to mollify him; his choice of peacemakers was not happy, however. The first was the one extreme Clerical in his cabinet, the next was Mgr. Labastida, and both returned convinced that the Legate was adamant. As a last resort Carlota was allowed to try her hand on him. The appeal of a woman, so persuasive with the gallantry of the French, was wasted, however, on a man in skirts. She talked and he listened for two hours by her watch. "Nothing has given me a truer idea of Hell than that conversation," she wrote to Eugénie, "for Hell is nothing but an impasse without issue. To try to convince someone and to know that it is sheer waste, that it is like talking Greek to him because he sees black and you see white, is a task fit for a reprobate. Everything slipped over the Nuncio like polished marble." At one point he observed that the clergy had made the empire, and she bridled. "One moment," she said, checking him sharply, "it was not the clergy, it was the Emperor, on the day that he arrived." The Nuncio let it pass, like all her remarks. She tried every possible approach and every conceivable tone, serious, playful, grave, and even prophetic, but nothing took. "He brushed aside my arguments like so much dust, offering nothing in their place, and seemed to delight in the void he left around him and the universal negation of light." Finally she raised the session and referred him to the Emperor.

As a final respite, the Emperor deferred the ultimatum until the first day of the new year. January 1, 1865, passed without weakening on either side. A week later, the Emperor went a step further and issued a decree subjecting the bulls, despatches, and rescripts of the Court of Rome to the *exequator*. Though this was a minor question, it contained the whole issue of authority in little and contravened one of the capital proscriptions of the *Syllabus,* and the Nuncio replied with a protest in which he asserted the absolute authority of the Church "as a perfect, independent, and sovereign society" and developed the thesis in unmeasured terms. "All the Faithful who compose it are subject in conscience to the decisions of their Pontiff," he continued, "whether they concern dogma or have morality and discipline as their object. What would become of this right of the Pontiff, in fact, what would be left of it, if an act by one of his subjects, be he emperor or king, sufficed to prevent the promulgation of his decrees and to arrest its effects?" The issue was joined, and the note of the Nuncio was returned to him with a sharp comment from the Minister of Cults. "I cannot accept this idea, which may have escaped Your Excellency, in exalting the sovereignty of the Roman Pontiff, that the Emperor must obey him as his *subject*. You will allow me to remark that this word is highly improper. Those who, borne away by an unmeasured zeal, push the Papacy beyond its bounds and strip it of its character, forget the severe lessons of history, forfeit the benefit of a prudence more powerful than any presumption, aggrandize in appearance and weaken in reality the supremacy of the Holy See, and far from making its real authority respected, render it odious. I repeat the opinion of the great Bossuet." The reflex action of the *Syllabus* was now in full swing. Neither the Nuncio nor the Emperor could relent, and a month later Maximilian took the last step. He published two decrees establishing the religion of State, declaring religious tolerance, and confirming the nationalization of Church property except in cases of fraudulent transactions.

The clergy protested, the Nuncio protested, but Maximilian maintained the high resolution with which he opened the new year, undismayed, and waited for the storm to blow over. *Tout passe, tout casse, tout lasse,* was as true for one side as the other. But Carlota was worried. The situation was as strained as it could be, she wrote to Eugénie, and the country charged with all the tension it could bear, and though she believed it better that the storm should break once and for all, it was a *mauvais quart d'heure* to pass and she wished it were over. The reunion of Church and State had produced such a wrench that the era of revolts, far from being over, had only begun perhaps. They were pestered with notes from the Nuncio and petitions from the bishops, respectful in form, but in form only. Mgr. Meglia was merely a mannequin manipulated by Mgr. Labastida, whose bad Italian she recognized in every line of his secondhand communications; they were ridiculed by the Liberals, who rejoiced in their discomfiture; they were censured by the Conservatives, who still fancied themselves temporal subjects of the Pope; and such was the bitterness of all parties that one might suppose that the Empire had never come between them. The role of the mediator was ungrateful, and they could not miss being bruised; but they did not flinch. Old professionals in statecraft like King Leopold questioned the wisdom of jostling the clergy; but Napoleon approved. He congratulated Maximilian on his energy, regretting only that he had not spared himself unnecessary animosity by treating the question as already settled and closed by Bazaine; but now that the thing was done, he urged him to persevere.

Mgr. Meglia remained in Mexico for five months, encouraging the ferment of the local clergy by his presence, and opposing every accommodation by a steady *non possumus.* In defense of his rigidity he pleaded that he lacked sufficient instructions and authority; the Holy See had not foreseen, and could not suppose, that the Imperial Government would consummate the work of Juarez; and he could only refer the whole question to Rome. Months passed before fresh instructions came, and when they did, they approved his conduct. Balked in France, the Holy See was unbending in Mexico. An adept at temporizing, the Pope understood that the question could not be settled there as long as the French remained in Mexico; and, biding a better day, he relied on time and procrastination to solve it. The Nuncio, accordingly, remained at his post in protest, and both sides settled down to a protracted siege in which neither succeeded in wearing out the other. "I do not know," Carlota wrote wearily to the happier woman who wore the crown of France, "whether Your Majesty knows that the Holy Father, who has a playful character, says of himself that he has the evil eye. Well, it is a fact that ever since his envoy set foot on our soil, we have had nothing but troubles, and we expect no lessening of them in the near future. We lack neither perseverance nor energy, I think, but I wonder whether, if difficulties continue to accumulate at this rate, there will be any possibility of overcoming them. . . . The task of subduing a corrupt clergy is a thankless one, and, for my part, I should have preferred that the preceding government had undertaken it." Juarez was where he was because he had; but her mind did not wander so far. Maximilian turned his attention to more important problems—the army, the finances, colonization schemes, a philanthropic project for the relief of the peons—and sent a commission to Rome to circumvent the Nuncio, who would neither give in nor go away nor yet be ignored. Then, one day, the importunate presence disappeared. The Nuncio left Mexico without notifying them, and though he passed through Orizaba, where they were staying at the time, without taking leave. The Church never said good-by.

They succeeded; but not with impunity. The conspicuous share which the Empress had taken in the conduct of this question had not escaped notice and she paid the penalty of public attention in her private life. Her activity reflected on the independence of the Emperor, and he was sensitive to his sovereign prerogative. He prided himself on his independence and apologized for it in turn. "My character is not of the happiest," he confessed to a friend, "and among other defects I have a sense of absolute independence such that even the Empress, with all her tact, never comes to my study to interrupt my work unless I send for her. She knows my weak point and adapts herself to it, and harmony has never been disturbed." Harmony was never disturbed for the man, but she suffered from his seclusion and showed the mortification which it cost her at times. Identified as they were in their public life, his independence was only apparent, and it appeared to be a refuge from her devotion and intelligence. Intellectual companionship was her sole solace for a childless marriage, and she prided herself on their close collaboration and craved her rightful place as his helpmate; and though she adapted herself to his weak point, the *ver solitaire* wormed its way into her confidence and betrayed it. She was subject to moody spells, and her attendants noticed her brooding reserve more than once and were startled by flashes of a haughty and forbidding temper unlike her normal behavior.

In their public life the consequences were also unsettling. The Clerical faction was definitely antagonized, and though the presence of French bayonets prevented it from reviving the era of revolts, it carried on a relentless underground campaign, which required the close attention of the secret police and which eluded them with a muffled maneuvering tenacity that made the intangible menace of clerical disaffection haunting and ghostly. Bazaine was not alarmed, having been through the whole thing before and satisfied by his experience that the influence of the clergy and the fanaticism of the people were much overrated; but there was no doubt that the testing of the *Syllabus* had seriously damaged the position of Maximilian in Mexico. Even the moderate Conservatives, stampeded by their spiritual directors, complained that the Empire was merely Juarism without Juarez and called the Emperor a crowned demagogue. By reopening a closed question Maximilian borrowed trouble, which the pioneering of Bazaine might have spared him; but no one can benefit by another's experience and least of all a prince who was obliged to acquire his own by the disabilities of his royal birth. What would have become of his independence as a sovereign if he had not invented difficulties for himself? Or, for that matter, what would have become of the independence of the Pope if he had not done the same? The Nuncio was right: it was a common liability of all rulers.

The conflict with Rome ended in a draw. The sovereignty of Maximilian was successfully asserted, but his independence was modified by it. At Miramar he had conceived of his role as a mediator and an arbiter above party and faction and had expected to govern by a coalition of parties; but this theory was abandoned after the agitation aroused by the Concordat. Having alienated the reactionaries, he accepted the alternative and surrounded himself with Liberals; but when he appointed a notorious radical to his cabinet, Bazaine objected. Maximilian insisted that he was merely following the Marshal's own policy, but Bazaine replied that he was the Baptist, not the Messiah, and persuaded him to adopt his own brand of liberals—the Moderates. The others were as irreconcilable as the Clericals, and both united in combating the Emperor as an interloper and calling him "the Foreigner." The insecurity of his position, even with the steadying hand of Bazaine to guide him, quickened many an *arrière-pensée,* and his own among others. His brother having reported the Family Pact to the Reichstag, Maximilian drew up a formal protest and despatched it to Vienna. The effects of this indiscretion were what might have been expected. In Vienna the Mexican Minister was threatened with his passports if he presented the protest; the Courts of Europe that were notified of it were indifferent; in Mexico the repercussions of the *démarche* reminded the public that the Empire was still tentative and undermined what confidence the Emperor had won by his resolute conduct of the clerical question. The word was passed around, and idlers remarked on the extensive improvements which he was making in his castle of Chapultepec—as if he meant to stay.

The word was passed around in Chihuahua as well, where Juarez summed up the position of Maximilian at the height of the conflict with Rome. "By half adopting the Reform Laws," he wrote to Santacilia, "Maximilian has betrayed the clergy and the Conservatives without attracting the national party. He has delivered himself over to the Moderate faction, which has lost all governments and all notable men who have submitted to its direction, and which in moments of serious conflict will forsake him to receive the conqueror on their knees." What the Moderates were worth as a basis of government the alien had yet to learn; in the meanwhile, however, he had alienated the reactionaries, and "though they remain quiet because they are cowardly, at least they no longer lend the *Desired* the effective co-operation which they offered him at first. In the isolation in which the Austrian has placed himself, money alone can postpone his defeat, but in this respect his situation is even more desperate. His budget is calculated economically at thirty million pesos, and the national revenues, which in prosperous times have never passed fourteen, will not reach four now in the domains of the Empire; and as he must cover his enormous deficit in order to maintain, increase, and equip the armed forces to continue his conquest, he will have to resort to violent measures against the people and against the rich, alienating their sympathies, provoking their resistance, and even propelling them into our ranks. This is bound to come, infallibly and before very long, unless the Archduke performs, as he certainly will not, many miracles like those of the five loaves." The conqueror, secure in Chihuahua, could afford to wait.

Ten days later, writing to one of his commanders, he reported some desertions to his ranks instead of from them and raised his voice to the full tone of conquering conviction. If the capital error of Maximilian was the original sin of invading the national sovereignty, his attempt to correct it by betraying his Mexican backers crowned all the errors of the *Syllabus*. The drift of desertions and the disaffection of the clergy were significant symptoms, since Maximilian "believed that we real Liberals were so simple-minded as to become his partisans merely because he adopted some of our Reform Laws, without realizing that even were he to adopt them all, he would never obtain our submission, because what we defend above all is the independence and dignity of our country; and while a foreigner interferes in our affairs with his bayonets and tries to impose his despotic will upon us, as Maximilian is doing, we will never accept his domination; we will make war on him to the death and we will reject all his offers, even though he work miracles. We need no foreigner to come and establish reforms in our country; we have established them all without help from anyone. Only the so-called Moderate Liberals, the cowards and the men without dignity or shame, now surround Maximilian and applaud his measures;

but those wretches are worth nothing, and when fortune begins to forsake their master they will forsake him also and come out on their knees to meet the new conqueror; but then their repentance will be barren, because the nation will call them to account for the blood they have shed." Never had his faith been less visionary; nor was it belied by the competition of Maximilian in questions of far more consequence than the clerical affair.

9

IN THE clerical affair—for a question so often concluded and so shopworn with repetition could no longer be described as anything more than an affair—Maximilian had figured at his best. Though he had borrowed trouble, he had braved and tamed it, and his conduct, firm, consistent, clear-cut, a little too square to satisfy old politicians, had been decisive enough to compare favorably with his forerunner's. His task was, however, a labor of supererogation, his triumph was guaranteed by the French, and in that prearranged problem he enjoyed their full support. It was not until he attempted to emancipate himself from his protectors that he struck the real difficulties of his position—difficulties which involved major affairs—difficulties which turned on *les affaires tout court*.

The Convention of Miramar provided military but not financial support; on the contrary, it provided for prompt reimbursement of the expenses of the French expedition, and the French Legation immediately attempted to collect; but as this stipulation was impracticable, the running expenses of the Empire continued to be borne abroad. Financial support was supplied by Napoleon unofficially. The loan floated in April 1864 was a dowry to cover the initial expenses of a regime whose only resources were the customs and its credit; and the Bourse, not the French Government, was responsible for the bond issue. Upon this basis Maximilian was expected to build, but the ingenuity of financiers condemned his government to insolvency from the start. To create confidence in the nascent Empire, an English bank was induced to combine with French firms in floating the bonds, in return for an allotment to satisfy the claims of English creditors of the Mexican foreign debt. Shrewd as the arrangement was politically, financially it proved disappointing. Few shares were sold in England, and the result of the operation was that the English bondholders were paid off with French subscriptions. The loan was expected to produce 190 million francs, the public subscribed 102,600,000, and commissions and discounts reduced the net to 96 millions. From this fund Maximilian drew 8 millions for his public and private expenses; 27 millions passed into the hands of the English creditors; the remainder was deposited in Paris to the credit of the Mexican Government and reserved for payment of interest on the debt, the reimbursement of the French Government, and the indemnization of French nationals in which intervention originated. Under the terms of the Convention of Miramar, repayment of these charges was to begin in the summer of 1864, one month after Maximilian arrived in Mexico. The balance with which he landed was barely enough to start him, and as it was necessary to dazzle the Mexicans into devotion and to take them by their weak side of ostentation and display, the dowry was soon dissipated in ceremonial costs, in the upkeep of a diplomatic corps accredited to all the Courts of Europe, in the running expenses of the administration, and in the personal stipend of the Emperor and the pin-money of the Empress. By the end of 1864, when Maximilian returned from his tour of the provinces, he informed Napoleon that, despite the devotion of the Mexican people, he dared not test it as yet by raising a voluntary contribution, and as the deficit amounted to a million and a half a month, if he was not to meet it by inflation, another foreign loan was urgently needed.

In April 1865 a second loan was floated in Paris. This one was more successful than the first, producing 170 million francs, but the liabilities were correspondingly larger. An international consortium was formed, including French, English, Dutch, Swiss, and German firms, and to the thirty-five charter members two hundred subsidiary banks associated themselves in a dazzling financial constellation. The scale of the operation required broad securities, the bankers demanded a quasi-guarantee that the French Government would not withdraw its military support until the Empire was well consolidated, and it was necessary, therefore, to manipulate public opinion, which, adverse as it was to any extension of the occupation, was loath to support a new loan or to accept indefinitely the expenses of an expedition that had already added 93 million francs to the floating debt of France. There could be no question, therefore, of an official guarantee; but the condition was met without it. The ingenuity of financiers was matched by their imagination. M. Corta, the second financial expert sent to Mexico, returned with glowing tales to tell and was made to tell them to the Chamber at the critical moment. M. Corta was a spellbinder. He vouched for the popularity of Maximilian in Mexico and related the legend of a lost Aztec deity whom the Indians had awaited for ages as their redeemer and whom they recognized reincarnated in the blond prince with the blue eyes: a legend that had its foundation in the counting-house. He dilated on the openings which Mexico offered for investment, immigration, colonization, labor markets, railway and steamship lines, and mining enterprises; when he sat down, the Minister of State rose and took up the tale of gold, silver, iron, and coal mines and newly discovered oil wells, and, turning to the benches of the Opposition, assured them that they had nothing to fear, that the loan was being signed at that very moment, and that the government was not responsible for it; and amid a storm of bravos the objections of the Opposition were overwhelmed and a vote of confidence was carried. The Assembly, swept off its feet, countersigned, without knowing it, the pending contract, which was actually signed only nine days later. The loan was oversubscribed in three days, the rush of small investors recalled the bright days of unquestioning confidence in Napoleon, the subsidiary banks were swamped with clients untying their stockings, and the syndicate pocketed seventeen millions in commissions in seventy-two hours.

The fresh lease of life lent Maximilian was won, however, on margin, and Napoleon was well aware that the weak side of the enterprise lay *du côté de la Bourse*. The reports of the *procureurs* told a truer tale than those of the stockbrokers. The approaching end of the civil war and the dread of difficulties with Washington, as one of them said, whetted "the desire for the termination of an expedition which weighs heavily on our finances and which, though it flatters the national honor by the blaze of glory that attaches to it, has always offended the public. It would be wrong to see a denial of these findings in the facility with which the Mexican loan has been concluded. Capital has no opinion. The success of the operation is due entirely to the credit of the financial firms that patronized it, and also to the growing vogue of such combinations, more ingenious than moral, that renew the excitement of the former lotteries and their risks. Who can resist the lure of an interest of fourteen per cent and the prospect of a gain of five hundred thousand francs?", The boom could not be repeated indefinitely, and by April 1865 it was clear that since Maximilian could be sustained neither by speculation nor by his own revenues, the only solid basis for the economic consolidation of the Empire was to develop the resources of the country rapidly; but this required a prolonged occupation, and between the pressure for a speedy recall of the troops and the necessity for a quick turnover the contradiction created a deepening dilemma, which the second loan merely deferred.

The only solution was Sonora. The mineral wealth of Sonora—gold, silver, mercury, platinum, and precious stones—offered a lucrative field for the kind of enterprise upon which Napoleon was obliged to depend for the construction of a colonial empire, and the exploitation of this virgin territory had figured among the projects of Morny and Jecker in the inception of intervention. Jecker had offered the French Government the cession of the rights which he had acquired many years ago from a Mexican Government to survey and delimit all public lands there, together with the holdings which accrued to him with that privilege and which amounted to a third part of the property in prospect, for ten and a half million francs. Napoleon took the idea, but not the offer, and in 1863 he had instructed Bazaine to secure from Almonte the concession of all the available mines of Sonora for a term of ten years against the refunding of war costs. These claims had been included in the secret articles of the Convention of Miramar, but Maximilian had refused to recognize them on the ground that they constituted an alienation of national territory, and the article had been deleted. Shortly after his arrival in Mexico, the proposal had been revived in a modified form, but it was even more inacceptable in Mexico than in Miramar, and Maximilian had turned a deaf ear to it. In invoking his coronation oath, he was on firm ground, and though Napoleon waived any claim to the territory and confined his rights to the exploitation of the mines, his partner persisted in regarding the concession as a disguised annexation of national territory, and so did his subjects. Five papers protested. Their directors were arrested by Bazaine and disciplined by French courts-martial, but the proposal was not pressed. Besides its obvious impolicy, there were now foreign complications. American fortune-hunters were filtering into the region, and the imminent end of the American civil war imposed caution on a plan which had been workable in 1863 but which was belated in 1864. Lorencez had been too quick, Forey too slow, and Bazaine too busy to develop the idea in time. Urged by Napoleon to occupy Sonora at the earliest opportunity, the Commander-in-Chief postponed action until the center was secure, and in 1865 the risk of a clash with the United States revived the nervousness of the French people and prompted the *procureurs* to warn Napoleon that "the cession of two large and beautiful provinces like Sonora and Chihuahua would not have consoled them for a war, the duration and results of which frighten the stoutest minds." The affair, therefore, was allowed to languish.

The Franco–Mexican Empire continued to operate, therefore, on margin. Since constructive measures for the economic exploitation of the country were prohibited, economy in its administration was imperative, but matters were not improved by the measures which Maximilian adopted to relieve his financial straits. After squandering his first loan, he economized on the second, and where he could least afford it. Early in 1865 he disbanded his Mexican army, which had become a useless drain on the French war chest, from which it drew twenty-five to thirty-five million francs a year. Though this measure was adopted on the advice of M. Corta, it found small favor in France, since three hundred thousand Mexicans, thrown off the payroll, were free to swell the bands of guerrillas and bandits, and though Carlota insisted that it was better than to provide for an army of potential rebels, the reform was abandoned. Bazaine, who was busy shifting the burden of occupation to the Mexican troops, objected, Maximilian reconsidered, and what had been undone was restored. Plans were studied for the reorganization of an indigenous army with a nucleus of French volunteers, for a Foreign Legion, for rural guards to be paid by the localities which they protected, and for other makeshifts and substitutes; but these projects also languished.

Other problems claimed the attention of Maximilian. Every month brought more and more to do, to undo, and to redo; the burden of work which he assumed fatigued the French and wearied the Mexicans as they stood and watched him diligently attending to his prolific and fruitless duties. He was too busy to accomplish anything. But Maximilian himself was undismayed. Napoleon, Bazaine, the Church, the Conservatives, the Moderates, the Liberals, the American Government, the patriots, and even Juarez himself—everyone was patient with him.

10

THE abortive designs of Napoleon on Sonora were not wholly lost. A good deal of publicity was given them by a Mr. Gwynn of California, who carried on for some time a negotiation with the Emperor of the French for the creation of Franco–American colonies there and a co-operative exploitation of the country, which would have eliminated any danger of friction with the American Government; but the American Government objected, and this project also was abandoned. The reverberations of the affair were far-reaching, however. Like the sonority of a sea shell, the idea was an echoing cornucopia, and though Maximilian would not hear of it, other ears were cupped to the phantom contents and it set other minds humming with fantastic notions.

Ideas are never lost, and this one begot a curious by-product. Doblado had not abandoned the defense of his country by crossing the border, and he busied himself actively in serving it in the United States. In the autumn of 1864 he was alarmed by a rumor that the American Government was about to recognize Maximilian, and though the report was a notorious canard in New York, he rose to it like a hunted bird from cover and hit on a remarkable dodge to discover and avert the danger. He hurried to Washington and consulted Romero, who was at tne head of the Legation, and between them the two diplomats hatched a scheme to ascertain the intentions of Seward, which Romero reported to Chihuahua. "Discussing with General Doblado what it would be well for us to do in view of the present circumstances, we agreed that he should say, as a private person expressing his own opinion alone, that he believed that the supreme government would do well to sell Lower California and a part of Sonora to the United States; that he was ready to recommend this measure to the President; and that he thought it easy of realization. By acting thus we thought that we would be able better to interest this government in not recognizing Maximilian, and even in learning what it would do if such a settlement were proposed, without compromising ourselves, since, of course, I was not to appear officially or unofficially in the affair." But even that safeguard was dropped as he developed the idea. "For the purpose of learning whether, after the re-election of Mr. Lincoln," he explained in his next note, "Mr. Seward would be willing to express himself a little more explicitly in connection with the affairs of Mexico, and seeing the impression which the idea emanating from General Doblado had made on him, I decided to have a conference with him to treat that affair. General Doblado thought that by informing Mr. Seward of his way of regarding the alienation of national territory, the idea would occur to him that if Maximilian were to cede Lower California and Sonora to France, and we would be willing to cede them in that case to the United States, they might wish to make a settlement immediately for that purpose in order subsequently to allege their right of ownership." The idea was one of those diplomatic devices at which Doblado was an adept, and, having no official capacity himself, it had no binding effect in the mind of its author. It was merely a feint to discover, a combination to unlock, the guarded counsels of Seward; and Romero, whose judgment was not always equal to his zeal, saw no danger in their acting together as a pair of patriotic decoys.

The offer was communicated to an intermediary, who promised to reveal it confidentially to a close friend of Seward, who would relay it in turn to the Secretary of State *sub rosa;* but the connection had not been made when Romero called at the State Department to judge its effect, and he was obliged both to explain and disavow it in the same breath. Seward had not heard of it and would not hear of it when he understood what Romero was trying to say. He explained, in turn, what should have been obvious to Romero from the start, that the policy of the American Government was dictated by its major interests and that the recognition of Maximilian was diametrically opposed to them; and he assured him that not only would no consideration induce him to recognize any other than the republican government in Mexico, but that he and Lincoln were determined to uphold it without the

alienation of a single acre of Mexican territory; adding that at the conclusion of the civil war his country would be too much occupied with
the question of slavery and the reconstruction of the Union to entertain
any such design. Romero doubted no longer—for until then he had
been unable to make up his mind whether Seward was the falsest man
on the face of the earth or an honest friend of his country. Something,
therefore, had been gained by his indiscretion. The designs upon Mexican territory which Seward had entertained in 1861 had finally been
dispelled; it had taken a war to do it, but it was done; and the American Secretary of State was not only indifferent to Sonora, but completely disinterested in his support of the independence of Mexico.

If the elaborate farce so solemnly performed by two experienced Mexican diplomats had resulted merely in their discomfiture and produced
nothing more humiliating than an elementary political homily, it would
have been harmless. But the mere fact that the offer was made and
known was damaging to the government which Romero represented,
and when Juarez heard of it, he was seriously alarmed. Although Romero shared the responsibility, there was no doubt in his mind with
whom the idea originated. "I already knew of the labors of Doblado,"
he wrote to Santacilia, "and I always feared the fatal influence of that
man on the Legation, and to prevent it I wrote at great length to
Romero, telling him to be careful and to reject the suggestions made
to him to the detriment of the integrity and independence of Mexico."
That the offer was a mere stratagem was immaterial; once it was made,
he was obliged to treat it as a bona fide offer and to rebuke the imprudence of Romero, and he did so in a few earnest words, reminding
him with great forbearance that the proposal was prohibited, that it
would raise the country against the government, and that it would give
the French a powerful weapon with which to consummate their conquest. "Let the enemy conquer and rob us, if such be our destiny; but
we must never legalize a crime by delivering voluntarily what is demanded of us by force. It would be bad to let ourselves be disarmed by
superior strength; but it would be worse to disarm our sons, depriving
them of a good right, which, more valiant, more patriotic, and more
constant than we are, they would make weigh and be able to redeem
some day." But the caution came too late. Juarez was attacked in the
enemy press for attempting to buy American aid by a cession of national territory. M. Corta carried the tale back to France and named the
figure—seventy-five million dollars—for which the President offered
to betray his trust. Such attacks, systematic and persistent, had pursued
Juarez ever since the McLane treaty, and the indiscretion of Doblado
revived them. That the tender was compromising apparently had occurred to neither of the confederates, or at least not to Romero: the
antecedents of Doblado made his ingenuousness doubtful. His reputation for duplicity was perhaps undeserved, but it was persistent, and his

conduct on this occasion went far to confirm it. The idea could hardly have occurred to a candid mind, and however honest the purpose, the artful patriot betrayed the native bent of the most *rusé* of Mexican politicians in the trickiness of his methods. It was one of those moments which reveal a man in a flash and give his full measure: the best and the worst of Doblado were combined in this affair, and the elusive truth was entirely consistent with the ambiguity of his fame. One real service, however, Doblado rendered the President: the affair arose at the same time that Juarez learned of the death of his son, and it diverted his mind from himself; the curse of too clever an assistant was an unconscious antidote, and, having thrust Doblado back into the shadow where he belonged, he recovered himself in the necessity of conducting the defense of the country, without officious meddlers, on his own simple system of plain dealing and unequivocal diplomacy.

With the approaching end of the civil war in the United States, American aid became available to the republican cause in Mexico. The two struggles, north and south of the border, had been interdependent from the start, and Juarez, identifying his cause with that of Lincoln, had favored it materially by permitting the passage of Federal troops across Mexican territory, by refusing to receive Confederate agents, and by maintaining a sanitary belt in the rear of the rebels. When his government was pushed back toward the border, the solidarity of the two struggles increased with their proximity, and in April 1865 Juarez breathed freely for the first time since the death of his son. "I celebrate and applaud the inflexibility of Mr. Lincoln," he wrote to his family, "for his triumph, even though belated, will be of more benefit to us than a quick peace with a sacrifice of humanity; the final result being, as my unforgettable Pepe used to say, that with time and our tenacious resistance we shall wear out the French and compel them to abandon their iniquitous enterprise of subjugating us, without foreign assistance, and that is the greatest glory I desire for my country. It is enough for us that the North destroy slavery and do not recognize Maximilian." Moral aid was all that he expected or needed. "Perhaps," he added, "in view of the recent triumphs of Lincoln and the explicit refusal to recognize Maximilian, Napoleon may be meditating a new twist to his interventionist policy, but even if he is not, the attitude which the North has taken by that statement and its successes will spread great discouragement, if they have not already done so, among the invaders and traitors of Mexico, since they must realize that even were they to subdue the entire Republic, which is very difficult if not impossible, they will have gained little or nothing, facing a colossus which because of its great resources and the principles of liberty which it sustains will not lack motives to take part in the defense of the oppressed, scattering the invaders and traitors with a single breath. This the enemy knows very well, and the majority of the Republic, and this kills the enthusiasm with which they worked in the first years of intervention; hence I judge that they are already reaching the period of their decline and that the reaction of the peoples against their oppressors is beginning."

But to accelerate the process he was prepared to accept material aid under certain conditions. "Nevertheless, if that Republic succeeds in ending its civil war soon, and that government, as a friend and not a master, should wish to lend us some assistance in soldiers or money, without exacting humiliating conditions or the sacrifice of a single inch of our territory or any decrease of the national dignity, we would accept it, and secret instructions to that effect have been sent to our Minister. As for any other aid than that of the government, I consider it extremely difficult because of our lack of resources, for I am convinced by experience that a foreign and collective force, unaccustomed to the poverty to which our soldiers are subject, would have to be well paid and supplied to be useful; otherwise it would become a plague by its insubordination and errors, and in that case the cure would be worse than the disease. Hence those persons who have applied for permission to bring volunteers from that Republic for the national defense have been met with the condition that they provide their own resources; but as I said before, it is extremely difficult to obtain those resources and people. We have no choice, evidently, but to continue the struggle with what we have, as best we can, and as long as we can. This is our duty; time and constancy will help us. Forward, and no fear!"

Duty was not the word; it was too tame. The driving power that sustained him was passion. As a duty, the defense of the country was tiring; as a passion, it was imperishable. As best we can and as long as we can—the words were none too sanguine—but if they betrayed fatigue, they defied it. The military situation was not as favorable on his side of the border as on the other. He referred his family to the map to follow it. Negrete was facing twelve hundred French in Durango, in the desert of Mapimi. A small force was marching to reoccupy Saltillo, which was weakly defended. A new and promising commander, Escobedo, was expeditioning toward Monclova and Piedras Negras, and "thus the traitors of Monterrey are in conflicts and in a worse situation than we were in August of last year." In the northern theater of war, the situation in April 1865 was what it had been for a year, a shifting contest of maneuver and position, without lasting gains or losses on either side and a shiftless succession of desultory actions and desert marches fatiguing and fruitless for both. The activity of the French was concentrated in the far south. Rumors of the fall of Oaxaca, defended by Porfirio Diaz, were confirmed in the middle of the month, ten weeks after the event. The port of Guaymas on the Pacific fell to the French on March 29, and this loss, being closer, was learned at the same time and brought the enemy much nearer. The local commander, lacking artillery to resist the four transports carrying the enemy, abandoned the town to spare the population the ravages of a futile resistance. "Nevertheless, General de Castagny, the assassin of Ghilardi and of the governor of Aguascalientes, Don José-Maria Chavez, without previous intimation or any of the customary formalities of war among civilized peoples, began to bombard the defenseless population, causing some casualties among innocent women and children." But his passion was imperturbable. The fourteen hundred French landed by Castagny in Guaymas "remained shut up in the town, like those at Mazatlan, because our guerrillas have immediately began to battle them, and Generals Pesqueira, Garcia, Morales, and Patoni are ready to fight the columns that try to leave the town to penetrate into the interior of the state." On the same day Saltillo was stormed and captured, the booty including one hundred and fifty prisoners, three pieces of artillery, and all the armament and material of war of the enemy. To assure this triumph and recover completely the states of Coahuila and Nuevo Leon, Negrete was marching with his division in that direction and would probably soon occupy Monterrey, his forces being superior in quality to those of the traitors. By the end of the month Juarez was awaiting word of that success by every mail. A respectable lady had read a letter from the capital announcing an imminent offensive by Bazaine against Sonora and Chihuahua, but as Bazaine relied on the pacification of Nuevo Leon and Coahuila to cover his flanks and insurrection was brewing there, the situation was promising. Passion throve on promises, and the passion of Juarez supplied the performance with its persistence. In the first days of May Negrete occupied Nuevo Leon and Coahuila and moved rapidly against Matamoros, and as the fall of Richmond and the end of the civil war in the United States was learned at the same time, Juarez predicted confidently that these events would reanimate the people of the interior. "Soon the fire will assume colossal forms, and we shall see whether Maximilian is capable of smothering it."

The value of American aid, if not indispensable, would have been decisive at that moment in realizing these promises, and before the fall of Richmond Romero went to the front to interest Grant and several of his generals in securing it. He returned to Washington with promises which raised the hopes of his government; but American aid depended on many factors beside the good will of the winner. While these negotiations were pending, Lincoln was shot. The report rang out in the deserts of Chihuahua with disastrous effect, for, as Juarez wrote to his family, "the latest courier from El Paso made us all happy; and had we not received at the same time the fatal news of the infamous assassination of President Lincoln, our satisfaction would have been complete. I have felt this disaster profoundly, for Lincoln, who was working with such constancy for the full freedom of his fellow men, merited a better fate than the knife of a cowardly assassin. I am awaiting the next courier with the utmost anxiety to learn what turn matters will take in that Republic after the definite triumph of the army and the unfortunate death of Lincoln. I do not know the antecedents of Mr. Johnson or his opinion on the question of Mexico, although I assume that it will be favorable to our cause, since, springing from the people as he has said, he is bound to share the opinion of a people that wants no European monarchy in Mexico. We shall see, and in the meanwhile we shall continue our struggle undismayed."

Though the loss of Lincoln was a severe blow to Juarez, the succession was secure: Johnson justified his confidence, and Seward remained in the State Department, and his Mexican policy was unswerving. Variations it had undergone throughout the vicissitudes of the civil war, fluctuating with the fortunes of the North and modified by the progress or impediments of the French, but its fundamental direction had never been in doubt. The index finger pointed steadily to the eventual evacuation of Mexico, but the voice was never raised above a whisper. In 1864, when the tide was turning in favor of the North and Congress passed a bellicose resolution against the monarchy in Mexico, he muffled it and informed Napoleon that foreign policy was the exclusive province of the Executive and that his conduct of it was unaffected by the temper of Congress. He was hard-pressed by the temper of public opinion. In the elections of 1864 a rising demand for a more aggressive attitude figured in the platform of every party, and in the closing months of the civil war there was widespread agitation to employ the troops against the French in Mexico, but he continued to ignore it. When the time came, and the colossus which had the will and the power to scatter the invader with a single breath was free to move, Seward promised to puff but insisted on treading warily and speaking softly. The Mexican Legation was crowded with volunteers offering to enlist, Grant was sympathetic, Sherman was interested, Schofield was willing to lead the expedition and his negotiations with Romero were progressing when Seward intervened and sent the General on a mission to Paris to get his legs, as he put it, under Napoleon's mahogany and tell him to get out of Mexico diplomatically. The soldiers argued like statesmen. Sherman insisted that a clash was inevitable, Grant reasoned that the survival of the Empire would oblige the American Republic to remain on a permanent war-footing and would corrupt American democratic institutions by introducing the habits and mentality of militarism for their protection; but the statesman went his own way. Diplomatic and moral aid Seward was willing to provide; military assistance he refused to countenance, except in the surreptitious form of arms-smuggling. Actual hostilities he was determined to avoid at all costs, confident that he could obtain the same result by carefully calculated, persistent, and increasing diplomatic pressure, backed by the bellicose popular temper, which he muzzled, curbed, and displayed— in a word, by a war of nerves. Juarez understood his policy, accepted it, and suffered by it.

In the summer of 1865 this factor began to tell. Napoleon was weary, uneasy, and on the defensive. The initial miscalculation which had led him to synchronize intervention with the war of secession in the United States and to speculate on the dissolution of the Union and the triumph of the South could no longer be corrected, because it was linked to another original error. The power of Mexican resistance, which he had underestimated, had prevented him from consummating his conquest during the first two years when the fortunes of the Confederacy were in the ascendant, and had maintained the instability of the Empire until the triumph of the Union was assured. Historically correct as the timing of the venture was, the delays in its execution had turned the clock against him. Faced with the growing hostility of the American people and the nervousness of the French public, he was forced to wind up the adventure as quickly as possible, and his diplomacy and his arms were directed in a double drive to clearing the way for a face-saving retreat.

In July a general offensive against the forces of resistance in the north jeopardized the security of Chihuahua and obliged Juarez to retreat to El Paso in the first days of August. "This squall will pass and does not mean a definite triumph of the enemy," he informed his family before leaving Chihuahua. The Governor of the state, less confident, urged him to cross the frontier, and the advice, coming from one who should have known better, provoked him to an unusually long and uncommonly curt reply. "Don Luis," he said, "no one knows this state better than you. Show me the highest, most inaccessible, and dryest mountain, and I will go to the top of it and die there of hunger and thirst, wrapped in the flag of the Republic, but without leaving the national territory. That never!" The French were forty leagues away when he left Chihuahua, and the pursuit was close enough to force him to talk and even to sing. When loyal Mexicans urged him to play into the hands of the enemy, it was necessary to repeat and spread the denial, and on his way to El Paso he wrote to a friend: "Wherever I may be, on the summit of a mountain or in the bottom of a ravine, abandoned by everyone perhaps, I shall not cease to uphold the banner of the Republic until the day of triumph." The frontier being the dividing line between triumph and failure, he was compelled to brand the pernicious idea that he had crossed it; that was the only real danger then, and his retreat to El Paso proved it.

In El Paso his American friends had an opportunity to meet him; nothing prevented them from crossing the border, and one of them did. Mr. Bartlett combined the duties of a customs collector and a press correspondent on the other side of the river, and life being what it was then and there, he welcomed any diversion from the one and any copy for the other. On the morning of August 15 he happened to be on the Mexican side and was struck by an unusual commotion. The placid peace of El Paso—"the droning buzz of insects, the gentle rustle of foliage, the incomparable sunshine, the little goat herds scrambling over the naked hillsides of the town, an occasional *vaquero* or muleteer sauntering through the great streets"—was disturbed by two couriers dashing about and shouting, "Juarez is coming, Juarez is here!" The announcement penetrated the drowsy little town in time to draw a crowd when the President and his escort drove in several hours later, and before the hubbub died down the stray American managed to make his acquaintance. He was struck, first, by his unheralded points. "His expression of countenance was winning. His manner was that of a cultivated gentleman and scholar, easy and dignified. His conversation lacked the fluency and vehemence characteristic of the Spanish. His voice was low and pleasant and he frequently paused, as if weighing the import of his words. His dress was that of a Citizen President, and, from an American point of view, faultless"—black broadcloth coat, white linen vest, white gloves, and highly polished boots. "His dress fitted his sturdy compact figure to a nicety and was worn with the grace of a finished cosmopolitan." So this was Juarez. Bartlett made the most of the opportunity "to study the Zapotec Indian" whose celebrity had crossed the border long before he arrived in El Paso, and he observed him, as he said, "with the curious eyes of a young American who had personally known Lincoln, Grant, and other great heroes and statesmen of the American conflict," without being disappointed. Subsequently he saw more of him, and "the longer I knew and the more I studied him, the more was I impressed with the greatness and goodness of his character." Mr. Bartlett did not keep his opinion to himself, and neighborly relations were soon knit with the American bank. Juarez was repeatedly invited to cross the river to receive the homage of his American sympathizers, and though he was obliged to decline these tributes, he went as far as he could and accompanied his official family to the shore when they accepted an invitation to a ball given in their honor at Fort Bliss.

His fame had traveled further in South America. In Lima and in Santiago de Chile his name was cheered in public demonstrations of solidarity with his cause; in Montevideo a medal struck in honor of Zaragoza was dedicated to him; and on May 1 the Congress of Colombia declared him *Benemérito de América* and placed his portrait in the National Library as a homage to his merits and an example to the youth of Colombia. He learned of these tributes with embarrassment. "I have seen the decree consecrated to me by the Congress of Colombia," he wrote to his family immediately after his arrival in El Paso.

"I am grateful for this favor, but it does not go to my head because I know that I do not deserve so much eulogy: I have simply tried to do my duty and nothing else." Nor did the tributes of his American friends turn his head. In July an emissary of Maximilian brought a bid for recognition to Washington but was unable to deliver it: Seward refused to receive it, and Juarez recognized that the American Government had gone as far as it could. He warned his family not to expect anything more. "According to telegraphic despatches published in the Denver paper, which we have here up to the 30th of July, Mr. Seward is still in the cabinet of that Republic, and I am very much afraid that even were that personage to leave the Ministry that government can do nothing in our favor, because it has too much to do to reorganize its administration and extirpate the germs of revolution which still lie concealed and which will begin to develop, once the first moments of surprise at their recent victory have passed, not only in the fields of battle, but in those of the government. Naturally it foresees them and hence it must be very careful not to compromise itself in a war with France or with any other powerful nation. A prompt collision with France would be possible only if Maximilian or Louis Napoleon provoked the United States by some act, and that is what they are least likely to do, since they will have to deal with a colossus before whom they will humble themselves to placate it in every possible way, dropping without a blush the insolence and pride with which they treat the weak. There is little to hope, therefore, of the mighty, for they fear and respect one another, and the feeble are the only ones sacrificed, unless they try to shake off their oppressors themselves. Nothing of all this surprises me, for I have long held the conviction that whatever Mexico does not do to liberate itself, it cannot expect or decently wish other governments or nations to do for it. Negative aid is all that that nation can give us, such as not recognizing Maximilian and not shooting us in the back, as Negrete says the Confederates tried to do to him at Matamoros. It is always a help not to have a neighboring people as an enemy, and that is enough for me."

With his back to the frontier and the French in Chihuahua, his position was more dangerous than he was willing to admit. Between the prudence of his friends and his foes the margin of safety was narrow. American aid was a dubious asset at best; military assistance being forbidden, moral favor and diplomatic protection were liabilities which quickened the pursuit and cornered him. But redoubled pursuit was the best sign of the straits of the French, and he had abundant evidence that the tide was turning in his favor. Deserters were looking back, he noted without surprise, for he knew his countrymen better than the French. "This is the world, and the Mexican world is capable of astounding Louis Napoleon himself, if he were to spend a few days here. These people of Mexico are strange! For anyone who does not know them and who is foolish, their ovations and flatteries are intoxicating, they sweep him off his feet and destroy him; and if he is weak, their curses also drag him down and destroy him." Nor was it only the deserters who were doubting. The skeptics, the scoffers, the detractors of the past were returning to the fold and recognizing their errors. Altamirano, who had once railed at his stationary progress and named him the god Terminus, now made handsome amends. "It matters nothing," he wrote him, "that those birds of prey who abandon our sacred cause, because it does not serve their well-being, which was always their motive, are deserting in droves. Better that the great party of the nation should be purged and better that we be alone than in bad company, as Riva Palacio says. No good can be expected, anyhow, of disheartened men. This is a question of justice and faith, and what guarantees our triumph is the great flame that burns inextinguishably in the heart of the father of our country. Certainly, those who falter have only to look to you to be calmed and comforted. So, when false rumors published abroad said that you had left, or were thinking of leaving, the territory, and some credulous souls were doubtful, I told them with a smile of anger and scorn: it is easier for the earth to leave its axis than for that man to leave the Republic. That man is not a man, he is duty incarnate. But where is he? they objected. I do not know the name of the line of land that he occupies at this moment, I replied, but he is in the Republic, he works for the Republic, and he will die in the Republic, and if only one corner of the country is left, there you will be sure to find the President. In saying this I have done you no more than justice, and I should be ashamed if I had doubted your virtue and your faith for a single instant."

The god Terminus reaped the tribute of time, and the deity was duly grateful. Moral support, when it came from his own countrymen, was not spurned, however tardy it might be. Among other returns of time, he was happy to learn that the deputy who had moved his impeachment for the McLane treaty had recently died, recanting his error—or so he was told, he could not be sure—but "be that as it may, the truth is that my enemies have no reason to be so," he wrote to Santacilia. "If I have done any wrong to the traitors, it has been by an error of understanding and not by deliberate intention. Vengeance is not my forte." The flux and reflux of fortune, which brought the drifters to his feet, also carried off some old and tried comrades. He was distressed to hear that Zarco had been approached with some timeserving proposal, which he supposed was spurned, "since that would be to break fast a few minutes before midday." In that dark hour before dawn, which for him was already the meridian, he had no patience with those who lacked his own vision. Zarco did not disappoint him, but others did. Gonzalez

Ortega had crossed the border, six months before, ostensibly to skirt the occupied territory and re-enter the country to resume operations— but he did not return.

Only one defection mattered, however, to the French—his own. The aim of the offensive against Chihuahua was to force him out of the country; in the instructions which Bazaine received from Paris great stress was placed on this thrust for its political effect in Europe and the United States. At the same time, however, Napoleon warned Bazaine that, although the attitude of Washington was not yet menacing, it might soon become so, and the dynamic indecision which he communicated to his commander neutralized the desired effect. The column which held Chihuahua was forbidden by Bazaine to advance farther, because of the difficulties of a long march across the desert and the danger of flaunting the French flag too close to the border, which was teeming with American troops and troublemakers. To attain the desired effect a short cut was taken. Late in September the French commander in Chihuahua reported to Bazaine a rumor that Juarez would soon pass the frontier. The tense was changed in transit, the rumor reached the capital as a fact, and Maximilian acted on it.

On October 3 Maximilian issued a statement and a decree which revealed the pernicious effect of that error. "The cause sustained with so much courage and constancy by Don Benito Juarez has already succumbed not only under the national will, but under the very laws invoked by that leader in support of his titles," the statement read. "Today that cause has degenerated into faction and has been abandoned by the fact that the leader has left the country." Hence the decree. The decree outlawed all the remaining forces of resistance and, assimilating both regulars and guerrillas to the robber bands, made the death penalty mandatory, within twenty-four hours and without appeal, for anyone caught with arms or belonging to a group bearing arms under no matter what political pretext. Ostensibly directed against the swarms of brigands operating between the lines, the decree was actually a dragnet deliberately confounding criminals and partisans in its meshes and placing them all indiscriminately beyond the pale of law and the rules of legitimate warfare; and at the suggestion of Bazaine, an article was added imposing penalties of fine and imprisonment automatically on any person or community harboring such bands, aiding or abetting them in any way, or failing to denounce and combat them. That it was barbarous Bazaine himself admitted. In a confidential circular sent to his officers he cited a list of atrocities committed by the patriots and instructed his commanders to retaliate in kind, to take no prisoners, and to educate their men to their mission in Mexico. "Reprisals become a necessity and a duty," he wrote. "All these bandits, including their leaders, have been outlawed by the Imperial decree of October 3, 1865. . . . Our soldiers must understand that they are not to return their arms to such adversaries: this is a war to the death, a war without quarter between barbarism and civilization. On both sides it is necessary to kill or be killed." But it was not only barbarous, it was a blunder that betrayed the desperate extremities of the French and paid the most terrible and transparent tribute to the indomitable defense of the country by Juarez.

The decree was the first fruit of the war of nerves. Its resonance was tremendous, as it was meant to be, and more so, indeed, than was intended. The courts-martial had long been practicing its rigor quietly and inconspicuously, but, as one apologist said, why write it? It merely confirmed and proclaimed what had become common practice ever since the occupation of the capital by Forey. To put an end to the numerous robberies committed by night, the military police rounded up the suspects every morning and brought them before the General Staff, where they were publicly flogged; the capital soon became livable, but not the countryside. There, at the same period, the courts-martial were created by order of Forey to try the bandits, and sentence was executed within twenty-four hours and without appeal. In this branch of warfare Bazaine simply finished what Forey began. After two years the country was still uninhabitable even in the occupied zone, and with the extension of the lines the scope of martial law spread. It became increasingly difficult to distinguish between bandits and guerrillas: the bandits became patriots as soon as they were caught, and the guerrillas wasted the land as long as they were at large; and the French garrisons found it convenient to confuse them and necessary to apply the same summary system to both for their own preservation. "One of the sad consequences of guerrilla warfare," wrote a French officer, "is that it drives both adversaries to use reprisals against one another. In the conditions in which we were fighting in Mexico, alone in a country in full insurrection, every attempt against our persons or our interests had to be pitilessly repressed. The conduct of our adversaries would have sufficed, if necessary, to legitimize the methods of repression which we employed. Hence we see light columns scouring the country, burning hostile villages, and carrying out raids to punish the inhabitants for their complicity with the enemy. Sometimes inoffensive people whose conduct excites our suspicions are victims of a situation imposed on us by circumstances. When we find French arms in isolated habitations, the owner is shot and the huts are burned; the arms probably come from soldiers killed in an ambush. Moreover, the mere fact of an inhabitant being caught with arms in his possession, whatever they may be, makes him liable to the death penalty. This is the only way in which we can impose respect on a country of ten million inhabitants with a force of occupation relatively very feeble."

The cruelty of the weak was carried as far as the length of their lines and their extremities required. At first the resistance of the patriots was respected by the regular troops. "The Mexicans have given proof of tenacity and intelligence in the inch-by-inch defense of their territory," the same officer acknowledged. "These qualities honor the dissident troops all the more that they are recruited most of the time by main force among the inhabitants of the villages and ranches which they cross, and frequently entire bands mutiny and abandon their leaders to return to their villages. Needless to say, these bands, armed with bad guns and cannon badly mounted and managed, were not much to be feared; the permanent chase which we gave them inspired a salutary terror and usually they retreated at our approach"; but they were not the only ones. "Besides these elements of inferior grade, we met guerrillas composed of energetic, vigorous, well-seasoned men, knowing the country admirably and making the most of all its resources. Those *guerrilleros* are the ones that sack the *haciendas,* waylay our convoys, and fall on our small detachments and destroy them; as a general rule, they fall back before us and attack only by surprise and when they are ten to one." The regular troops were easily thrown into confusion and routed by their own methods. "The Mexicans often make the mistake of attacking without waiting for the arrival of all their troops and get themselves beaten in detail by an adversary much less numerous. Bayonet charges by the Mexican infantry take place in the greatest confusion. Now they all run in disorder without shooting; now some fire while running; others stop to take cover; then the whole confused mass rushes forward with shouts and wild ululations, accompanied by insults and coarse abuse."

But as pitched battles were rare, the brunt of the war was borne by the guerrillas. To combat them a counterguerrilla force was formed in 1863 under the command of a daredevil by the name of Dupin, who made his name a synonym for savagery wherever he operated. After cleaning up the state of Veracruz he was transferred to Tamaulipas, which he terrorized no less efficiently. The inhabitants took to the trees. "No one would ever believe," one of his men said, "how easily a man was hooked to a tree. Anyone suspected of having had relations with the enemy was put to death by us; the guerrillas did the same thing on their side, so that the poor devils who lived there had only one prospect in life: the noose." There was nothing new, therefore, in the decree. "Dupin had done nothing else," as someone said and everyone knew. The character of the war gradually effaced the distinction between regular and irregular warfare, and the decree merely sanctioned and generalized the drive for wholesale extermination of the enemy in a paroxysm of martial law and the adoption of the law of the jungle. But why write it? Why write the Empire in the red for all the world to read? The pernicious effect of that error was not confined to Mexico: foreign opinion was incensed, and Washington protested to the French Government. The French Foreign Minister washed his hands of the responsibility and referred the American Minister to the government which Washington refused to recognize in Mexico. "What is this Juarez government in which you are interested?" he replied coolly. "It has neither army, nor finances, nor administration, nor a capital. Who knows the names of its officials and officers? Its power is a mere fiction." And he turned the protest by a renewed bid for recognition of Maximilian.

The responsibility was a joint one. Bazaine acknowledged his share of it. "The Emperor, whose character seems to be essentially patient, wished to wait until Juarez had left Mexican territory before promulgating this law," he explained to Paris. "His Majesty had finally decided, on my advice, to give a proof of firmness, which has produced a good effect on the Conservatives." Maximilian had contemplated the measure for over a year. For over a year he had been complaining to Napoleon of the inactivity of Bazaine, of the premature repatriation of the troops, the insufficiency of the French forces, the failure to organize a Mexican army, the cost and the difficulty of pacifying the country, and, his complaints being fruitless, he was forced to make constant concessions to the Marshal. On his return from the provinces in 1864 he had proscribed all armed guerrillas and sanctioned their summary execution by the courts-martial; subsequently he countenanced the shooting of prisoners taken in battle; later he notified Bazaine that sentences were no longer to be communicated to him; and when American hostility became alarming, he took the last step and surrendered to the implacable necessity of crushing resistance with ruthless celerity. The situation dictated the decree. He was too nigh to the tree to be squeamish. Nevertheless, there was an essential distinction between Maximilian and Bazaine. For the soldier the measure was a professional expedient, justified by an emergency, and he enforced it efficiently; for the sovereign it was a menace, and he attenuated its effect by an offer of amnesty, which he extended for one month and renewed for another. Between the theory of the threat and the practice of the fact he continued to compromise desperately, the helpless victim of a measure tragically compounded of qualms and expediency. Bazaine had no qualms, but Maximilian was haunted by them. He murdered with mental reservations, he hedged, he quailed, he qualified, but he killed; and the conflict compromised him irretrievably. Though his patience wore thin under pressure, he consented to the sanguinary edict reluctantly and evaded its consequences stubbornly. He gave private instructions that it was not to apply to his honorable adversaries and that if Juarez and his ministers were captured, sentence was to be suspended and he was to be notified immediately. For even then he had not abandoned the hope of a compromise, and it recurred as the insecurity of his position developed during the next two months.

In November the French Foreign Minister made formal overtures to

Washington for the recognition of the Empire and offered, in return for it, to withdraw the French troops from Mexico within a reasonable length of time. Seward retained the offer and rejected the condition and concluded an accomplished diplomatic note with soft but significant words: "Until the last four years," he said, "whenever an American statesman or citizen was asked what country of Europe was least likely to alienate the affections of the United States, the answer was always—France." Seward said next to nothing, but enough, in a war of nerves, to produce the effect of a powerful understatement, and Napoleon began to negotiate actively for a diplomatic settlement of the Mexican question. When Maximilian learned of these overtures he became seriously alarmed. "The European press suggests," he wrote to Napoleon, "that Your Majesty intends to announce publicly the withdrawal of your troops, within a very short time, according to an arrangement similar to the Convention of the 15th of September. I must tell Your Majesty that such a declaration would undo in a day the work created by three years of painful toil, and that the announcement of any such measure, coupled with the refusal of the United States to recognize my government, would be enough to make all the hopes of the right people crumble and to destroy public confidence irretrievably. What is more, the honor of the French army would suffer regrettably in the opinion of all of America, for people would not fail to attribute its precipitate retreat to a very different motive." Maximilian found himself suddenly in the same position as the Pope. Like him, he was not consulted; like him, he was treated like a minor and a man under interdict; like him, he was about to be dumped and abandoned; and like him, he protested. At the same time he received a letter from Baron du Pont, his former secretary in Europe, transmitting a message from Don Jesus Teran, a friend of Juarez living in Switzerland, who had attempted to dissuade him from accepting the crown before he left Miramar. Teran advised him to conclude an armistice with the Constitutional government, to send the French army home, and to withdraw before it was too late, and he offered his good offices to come to an honorable arrangement with Juarez.

Of this advice Maximilian retained only the idea of an armistice, and he answered in a manner that excluded the hypothesis of hypocrisy— one inconsistency of which he was incapable—and which sinned, on the contrary, by a simplicity of which no one else would have been capable. Teran, he wrote to the Baron, was a true patriot; "like his master, he has the best intentions for the country; if he is correctly informed, he must know that in every discussion I defend his master and that I always recognize how useful he has been to Mexico in many ways; but the same thing has happened to him as to our good old friend Gutierrez, it happens to everyone, he exaggerates and he forgets facts. . . . I believed what Teran told me before I left Europe; I knew that the ideas of the poor exiles and of the embarrassed Regency were mere phantasmagoria, I never nursed any illusions; but I found that the situation was not as bad as Teran painted it then, and as he still wants to make it appear now; this country is better than its reputation, and better, precisely, in the sense contrary to the exiles. All that Gutierrez and his friends have said is false and founded on irreparable errors of more than twenty-five years of involuntary absence. The country is neither ultra-Catholic nor reactionary, the influence of the clergy is virtually nil; that of the old Spanish ideas is practically effaced; but, on the other hand, the country is not yet liberal in the good sense of the word. I am trying to avoid the only mistake of my predecessor, who in the brief period of his Presidency tried to undo and reform everything." With Juarez, therefore, he was prepared to be patient. "I am very anxious to come to an understanding with Juarez," he continued, "but first of all he must recognize the decision of the effective majority of the nation, which desires tranquillity, peace, and prosperity, and he must decide to collaborate with his unshakable energy and intelligence in the difficult task I have undertaken. . . . Let him come and aid me sincerely and loyally and he will be received with open arms, like any other good Mexican. There can be no question of an armistice, since there are now no loyal enemies but mere gangs of savage bandits, the natural consequence of so many years of civil war; gangs like those that have done so much harm in Italy and Hungary." The Hapsburg might compromise, but could not capitulate, and he concluded with bland condescension: "You may say that I am ready to receive Juarez in my Council and among my friends." Specifically he proposed to offer him his old position as President—of the Supreme Court.

At the time that Maximilian indulged in these amenities fifty sentences had been executed under the decree of October 3.

I I

AT THE same time that Juarez provoked a moral convulsion in the camp of the enemy by his indomitable defense of the country, he was threatened with a split in his own. The position of President of the Supreme Court, which had promoted his own destiny so imperishably, was a source of hereditary trouble. By virtue of it Gonzalez Ortega had claimed the succession to the Presidency of the

Republic, to which he was legally entitled, in December 1864. This was a miscalculation for more than one reason—arithmetically, in the first place, the legal term of the President expiring only a year later, and morally in the next—and Juarez paid no serious attention to him at the time. His mind was burdened with more serious troubles at that time: his son was dying. Several months later, when Ortega left the country on official leave and failed to return, he gave the matter no further thought. "It is clear that he wants to rest, and only when it is cooked and fried will he again claim the Presidency," he wrote to his son-in-law, and he refused to notice the rumors that Ortega had joined his detractors abroad, "for it would be degrading to descend to the slime in which such filthy reptiles move." But though he ignored, he could not forget him, for, like Doblado, Ortega was busy with the defense of his country abroad. Learning that he was enlisting volunteers in New York, Juarez notified the Legation that these activities were unauthorized, and he alluded to his irresponsibility in another matter in a note to Santacilia. "I must tell you also that Ortega has said that I have great interest in recommending him as the future President of the Republic, which I doubt, although Ortega may have said it, because of his natural lightness; but it is not true." He continued to treat him as a light weight as long as he could. He even managed to wring a little amusement from his ambition, and a little pity: "He is tired and discouraged, as he told me once, and needs to be far from the enemy to revive his stricken spirit. I will tell you a spill that that good man took when he was in Parral, while I was in this city of Chihuahua, at the end of October last year. He went to a dance given by the people of that place, and at the hour of toasts Artega raised his glass and drank to the prompt disappearance of Benito Juarez, who had caused so many ills to the Republic, from the command; but before he had uttered his last words Doctor Manuel Robles, an inhabitant of Parral, rose to his feet, full of indignation, and with courage and spirit proposed that Ortega withdraw those words injurious to the first Magistrate of the Republic, whom the nation judged very differently than Ortega, and said that if Señor Juarez had not been able to do all that he wished it was because those who coveted the supreme command were an impediment to him and hampered him by a systematic opposition. Ortega did not expect this discharge, which disconcerted him, and he suffered the humiliation of withdrawing his toast and offering a thousand apologies to Señor Robles. What worse punishment for so high a personage as Ortega? Although the incident has been notorious in this state, we must keep it to ourselves."

His next reference to his rival was still tolerant of a nuisance. "I have been informed of the speculation of G. Ortega and I am not surprised, since he has long been known for his fondness for money and his unscrupulousness in the means of obtaining it. This is one of the reasons that make him so feverish for the Presidency of the Republic, which he regards as a means of enriching himself and satisfying all his vices. In this respect Ortega belongs to the school of Don Antonio Lopez de Santa Anna. Hence I have not only entrusted him with no commission, but have hastened to tell you and Romero that he carries no authorization for anything." By September 1865, however, with the expiration of his legal term only three months away, Juarez was compelled to think seriously of what the challenge of a lightweight champion might mean for Mexico. "Here, too, people are worrying about what will happen after November," he wrote to his son-in-law. "I am on the rack, for everyone makes the future fate of the country depend on my decision. You can imagine what my head is like." His occasional comments on Ortega, cutting, contemptuous, incredulous, were silenced by the dilemma which the contender raised. The situation was delicate, and the man was not.

The Constitution prescribed that if for any reason an election had not been held before the expiration of his term, the President was to retire and the Executive power to be exercised provisionally by the President of the Supreme Court; and since no election had been or could be held, the pretensions of Ortega were legally indisputable. But it was no time to change horses in midstream, and least of all for a tired hero who had dismounted and abandoned the battle for over a year. Strict construction of the Constitution at that time was suicidal. It was the season of tired patriots. Doblado had just died in New York. "He would have left a grateful memory if he had died in defense of his country," was all that Juarez allowed himself to say. Negrete was resting, and for him Juarez had a word or two more. Negrete, disobeying his orders to remain in Coahuila to distract the attention of the enemy and protect the insurrection in the surrounding states, had fallen back on Chihuahua and forced Juarez to retreat to the frontier; and after upsetting the whole plan of campaign, he had resigned from the government, disgruntled because he had not been received with arches of triumph, and retired to private life, notwithstanding his rank as a general of division. That was the trouble, as Juarez observed bitterly. "Only Escobedo has succeeded in starting for San Luis with a thousand men, and I expect that he will do something profitable, because neither he nor Naranjo nor Treviño, who are going with him, are yet generals of division. These, with very rare and honorable exceptions, can no longer stand the punishment of the campaign, and so we see some submitting to the foreign yoke, others going to foreign lands to rest, while their country struggles against its oppressors, and others doing little and that little unwillingly. Fortunately, there is no lack of men of heart and burning patriotism who fear nothing, and with them we shall win. For them will be the glory and gratitude of the nation." Negrete had ruined his plan of campaign, and Ortega threatened to wreck public confidence completely to gratify his ambition. On the other hand, the risk of ignoring Ortega and disregarding the Constitution was grave, although that was obviously the sensible course to follow. Before leaving the capital in 1863, Congress had bestowed on him emergency powers ample to warrant that solution; but he hesitated to stretch them. "As for prolonging my functions as President of the Republic," he wrote to Santacilia, "a measure that many people advise me to adopt for the good of the country, I have decided nothing, because the matter is too serious. Although by the broad powers given me by Congress I believe that I can make such a statement, some are bound to question the legality of the measure, and Ortega, or any governor or commander, has only to disown my authority to rekindle civil war, and that would be the ruin of this wretched society. I have made no such statement as yet, and mark you, Guillermo Prieto and Manuel Ruiz are already preparing to protest the prorogation." The dilemma, pitting his political instincts against his legal principles, split his own convictions, and the danger of disrupting the defense of the country at the most crucial period of the war paralyzed his will power. He hesitated as long as he could, promising his family that he would be guided by circumstances, the law, and public opinion when the time came, but procrastination brought no relief from a responsibility which in the end he was obliged to meet alone.

Amid these incertitudes a counterweight was dropped into the balance. While he was debating his duty, he learned that another of his sons had died in New York. "My dear son Santa: I am full of profound grief because of the death of my beloved son Antonio. My brain is clouded and I can hardly trace these lines," he began a letter to his son-in-law and broke off, unable to say more. A week later he tried again. "After closing my letter of the 15th Señor Lerdo gave me yours of the 15th of August with the news and details of the sickness and death of my beloved Antoñito. I had already learned by the papers and other letters of this new disaster to our family, and you can suppose what I suffered and suffer without the consolation even of being with you to share your grief and console ourselves mutually. The only thing that calms me a little is that you and our trusted friends there are trying to counsel and strengthen poor Margarita, for whose health I fear so much." Then he changed the subject. He refused to brood, and the shock was salutary. The balance was almost broken by this fresh blow; but he reverted, in self-defense, to his responsibility to Mexico and turned his attention again to Ortega. The scale was tipped by a feather; the very levity of his antagonist lifted his burden, the clouded brain cleared, and he saw his duty with the vital lucidity that comes of suffering a life-and-death ordeal in inaccessible solitude. His sons died for his country. He made up his mind subconsciously; consciously, he continued to doubt; but he scoffed at the doubters. "Prieto and Ruiz are still very cautious and very much exercised for pure love of . . . the country. The question of the Presidency robs them of sleep. It is pitiful to see those little Angels suffer." And with significant scorn he brushed them aside.

Psychologically his decision was already taken, and six weeks after his bereavement he made it public. In the first week of November he issued a decree proroguing his tenure of power until elections could be called, and at the same time he indicted Ortega for trial as a military deserter. The indictment was as amply warranted as the decree, but the complication of the two questions made the charge highly explosive. The challenge to the prestige and popularity of a military hero, whose appetite for power had been whetted by four years of abstinence and submission, was a crucial test of his own. He scored a double triumph. The first and most difficult was over himself: in the case of Juarez *vs.* Juarez he liberated himself finally from those legal fictions which limited his real leadership. The force of circumstances had made him, in fact, an autocrat, but he was unwilling to acknowledge it until the crisis compelled him, in spite of himself, to recognize the truth. The other triumph was easy. In the middle of November he returned to Chihuahua, which the French had evacuated, and where he proposed to remain only a few days, as he informed his family, "if, as is likely, the French return, for it is not credible that, determined as they are to eliminate the government of the Republic, they will regard my residence here with indifference. Do not worry. I shall locate myself somewhere where they cannot easily deal me a blow." In that exposed position the loyalty of the population was a fair test of the effect of his decree. His reception was excellent, and "I believe," he added, "that the part that defends the national independence will receive these resolutions well and approve them." The first of December came and went without protest and proved the correctness of his judgment. "What I expected has happened, to wit, that even though General G. Ortega were capable of assuming command, he would not come, as he has not come. The advantage, therefore, of dictating the prolongation of my functions is more justified than ever today, since it has prevented the headlessness of the country and the definite triumph of intervention. Prieto and little uncle Ruiz are still in the opposition; but no one pays any attention to them." And he turned his attention to more important matters. "I am happy to hear that you are the same as usual, although you must be suffering severely from the cold now. Fireplaces are a help, but you had better not hug them too closely so as not to contract more sicknesses. I believe that cold, like heat, mortifying though it is, is a necessity, which the laws of nature have established to fortify and preserve man, plants, and animals, and we must not disobey those laws if we do not want to incur the penalty of our sin." A week later he was fully convinced of his accomplishment. "If, consulting my personal interest and selfishness, I had retired on the first as I could have done, today anarchy and discord would reign, and the American Government would have withdrawn recognition from Romero, saying that we were incapable of governing ourselves and fit to be slaves. I believe that I have saved Mexico from that stain, and I am satisfied." Pledges of support and approval poured in, and Ortega contented himself with protests across the border, which awoke no response in Mexico or in Washington.

The triumph cost Juarez some old friends, however. Ruiz, Prieto, and Negrete declared for Ortega, but he had foreseen their defection, and when they fell away they were not missed. Negrete was no loss. Ruiz, who had been his helpmate for fifteen years, went over to the Empire, and for him Juarez wrote a rough epitaph: "So ends the political career of a man of whom I tried to make a good citizen, but he was bent on being the contrary. Let him eat his bread." Prieto attempted to retrace his step at the last moment, and to straddle, but too late. There was a painful scene, of which Juarez kept a cruel record. "He told me that he loved me dearly, that he was my bard and biographer, and that he would continue to write whatever I wished, if I wished, and—hello, how was I? I thanked him, pitying so much debility and paying no attention to his untruths. The poor devil, in short, is out of the fight, like Ruiz and Negrete. They amounted to something because the government made them count. We shall see what they can do now by themselves." Of all the trials of life the most tiring was the company of weightless little people, and the fact that they gravitated to Ortega was a relief. It gave him a sense of his own weight. As for Ortega, his comment was curt. He supposed that he had seen the light. "If he has any shreds of judgment and sense left, the best he can do is to keep his mouth shut." The withering of old patriots left Juarez intact. There were fresh ones to take their place, the young and the green were coming up to meet him, "but even if I were to remain alone, it would not be bad," he repeated. "Better alone than in bad company."

12

BEFORE the end of December the return of the French to Chihuahua drove Juarez back to the border. "Probably Maximilian will be saying again with the assurance of genius that I have crossed to the United States and who knows what else, but do not mind him, you know that that is how he is—self-crediting," he wrote on his return to El Paso. His family were worried for his safety, having heard of a plot to abduct him. He reassured them. He was on his guard, he was expecting the arrival of a trusted battalion, and the author of the plot had revealed it to Romero. Besides, he was in El Paso, where there were no traitors. Besides, Bazaine was shy of the border. Besides, the date was December 21, 1865, and finally, "if, as we expect, Mr. Johnson has said something important in his message to Congress, Maximilian will be completely desperate and the French thinking seriously of withdrawing from the country."

President Johnson did say something important for Mexico in December 1865. His message to Congress contained a thinly veiled threat to the French, which fully satisfied Juarez. "He said what he had to say, and what he said does us no harm," he wrote a month later. "On the contrary, I was agreeably surprised, since I expected little or nothing. I have never had any illusions as to the open aid which that nation can give us. I know that the rich and powerful neither feel nor, far less, try to cure the calamities of the poor. They fear and respect one another and are incapable of breaking a lance for the quarrels of the weak or the wrongs done them. This is, and has always been, the world. Those who will not recognize it merely deceive themselves." Hence the importance of the message for Mexico. "Instead of complaining, the Mexicans must redouble their exertions to rid themselves of their tyrants," their President repeated. "Thus they will be worthy of being free and respectable, for thus they will owe their glory to their own exertions and will not be miserable slaves for whom others must think, talk, and work. The mighty may sometimes consent to raise a hand for a people that is poor and oppressed, but they will do so for their own interest and advantage. This will be an eventuality that must never serve as a sure hope for the feeble. That may happen in our present conflict, and only for that reason will Napoleon withdraw his forces, and then it will matter nothing that he has sent and is still sending more troops, which he will have to recall, if he is so advised by his dread of the United States or his interest or both, as is most likely. We shall see. And we shall continue our defense as if we were sufficient unto ourselves."

He repeated himself, but with a firmer accent than ever before. He repeated himself with the regularity of a rifle loading and unloading, gaining speed and precision with experience and training his mind by the repetition of the same exercise to a degree of skill that transformed the faith of passion into the confidence of science. His self-sufficiency was such that he felt himself fully a match for Napoleon and measured himself against him familiarly. Nine months before he had begun to tease him and to refer to "the approaching defeat of the new historian of Julius Caesar." To the trained eye the liberation of the country was near enough for such liberties. "By some letters, which we received the day before yesterday from San Francisco, dated the 20th and 21st of April," he wrote then, "we are told that said historian has died; but clearly the news is mere talk, and it is better that the tyrant should live to witness his final defeat, which seems to me indefectible." He sent to New York for a copy of the first volume of the *History of Caesar* by the Emperor of the French and received it three months later in El Paso. In Paris people read it as an apologia of the Empire and searched it for political parallels and personal allusions; but of these there were few. The book was a sober, objective, scholarly study of its subject, which disappointed the public. The curious dropped it as soon as they discovered that it was not entertaining. Nor was it amusing in Mexico. The self-revelation of the author was implicit in the interpretation of his hero, and the point of view of the Emperor was expressed in the closing lines of the volume: "Let us not look for small passions in great souls. The success of superior men, and this is a consoling thought, comes of the elevation of their sentiments rather than from the speculations of selfishness and cunning: that success depends on their skill in profiting by circumstances far more than on the blind presumption of believing themselves capable of causing the birth of events, which are in the hand of God alone."

That was, no doubt, how Napoleon saw himself; but under the circumstances it was not very amusing in Mexico. If Juarez hoped to read the mind of the Emperor in his *History of Caesar,* there was little to learn from it, unless it was the fact that he had taken the time to write it. One passage, however, had some bearing on his position at that time, when he was preparing to prolong his tenure of power. In defense of his *coup d'état* Napoleon wrote: "Legality may be legitimately violated when, society running to its ruin, a heroic remedy is indispensable to save it, and the government, sustained by the mass of the nation, makes itself the representative of its interests and desires." But the analogy was painful, and he was not near enough yet to his triumph to agree with Napoleon. His confidence in the coming end was founded on legible facts: the growing discouragement of Maximilian, "the entrance into power of the plebeian Johnson," the fatigue of the French, and his own untiring energy, "despite our poverty and the defection, fatigue, or ineptitude of most of our generals," in kindling and rekindling inextinguishably one candle after another for the wake of the moribund Mexican Empire. Nine months later, he was in a position to write a history of Caesar himself.

The new year opened so favorably, in fact, that he celebrated it by reviewing the successive retreats and narrow escapes which he had made for two and a half years and casting up an account of what scientific resistance had actually accomplished. The truth could be told now. Had the French sent a thousand men after him in 1863, when they captured San Luis Potosi, "it is certain that they would have scattered us as far as Monterrey," he admitted. "When I left the State of Durango after our defeat at Majoma, if they had sent a mere five hundred men, they would have taken Chihuahua and driven me to this place, and when they reached Chihuahua last August, if they had continued their march here, when I had no more than twenty unarmed men, they would have put me in peril. Finally, when they had money in abundance two years ago, and a flourishing and well-equipped army, and the prestige of novelty, and the good will and collaboration of the Clerical party and all the traitors, if they had known how to make use of those assets, they might have gained possession, although only for a short time, of the whole extent of the country. But now we can say to them what the *gachupin* said to the fowl when he wrung its neck: Too late, my feathered friend! Now things are different, not only because they lost their best opportunities and their physical and moral power, but because of the attitude which that Republic has taken toward them and our obstinacy in not letting ourselves be subjugated. They are fighting without a future, without hope of winning, and you know how the saying goes: he who has no hope of conquering is already conquered. We keep on going, and time will soon confirm this truth." Though the complete emancipation of Mexico was a matter of time, the most important phase was won—the independence of illusion, the illusion of defeat, the illusion of doubt, the illusion of aid—while the French were still fighting the truth. That was the measure of his accomplishment; and he did not omit to mention one other testimony to it. "Our good Don Chucho Ortega has given no signs of life yet. If he were so blind as to make some scandal, we will shut his mouth."

13

BY THE end of 1865, in fact, intervention was virtually over. In November Napoleon, abandoning the next volume of the life of Caesar and worried by the soft words of Seward, began to jog the elbow of Bazaine and to urge him to hasten the reorganization of the Mexican army in view of an evacuation within a given period. "I hope that the Americans, in spite of their bragging, will not want to go to war with us," he wrote, "but with that danger averted, we must know in what condition we shall leave the country after our departure. The Emperor Maximilian must realize that we cannot remain in Mexico indefinitely and that, instead of building palaces and theaters, it is essential to establish order in the finances and on the highroads. He must be

made to understand that it will be easier to abandon a government that
has done nothing to provide its own means of subsistence than to sustain it in spite of itself." His irritation with Maximilian reflected his
mistrust of Washington. Rebuffed in his bid for recognition of the Empire, the French Foreign Minister, Drouyn de Lhuys, fell back on tacit
toleration and, denied again, settled for strict neutrality. But even to
this formula Seward declined to commit himself; he replied with an
invitation to set a definite date for the French evacuation, and without
waiting for the reply Napoleon anticipated it. In January 1865 he repeated his injunction more urgently: the longest delay which he could
grant for the recall of the troops, in relays, was one year or eighteen
months, and Washington was notified at the same time of this decision.
Napoleon was on the run, but the orders were to walk. Seward had initiated the beginning of the end: intervention was bankrupt, but the
liquidation required time, time to disengage the honor of France, time
to withdraw with dignity, time to preserve appearances and to prolong
the agony; and it was the duty of Bazaine to make haste slowly.

The dominant question of the coming year, therefore, was the succession. Two solutions were considered in Paris, and of these the one
that was manifestly impossible was the one, naturally, that Napoleon
favored. "Circumstances stronger than my will oblige me to evacuate
Mexico," he explained in his instructions to Bazaine, "but I do not wish
to do so without leaving behind me every chance for the Emperor Maximilian to sustain himself with his own forces and the Foreign Legion.
You must devote all your zeal and intelligence to organizing something
durable in that country, so that our efforts will not have been sheer loss.
To accomplish this difficult task you have a year or eighteen months.
If, perchance, the Emperor Maximilian were to lack the energy necessary to remain in Mexico after the departure of our troops, it would be
necessary to call an assembly and organize a government, and to bring
about by your influence the election of a President of the Republic
whose powers would last for six to ten years. That government, naturally, should pledge to pay the greater part of our creditors in Mexico.
It is clear that we must not resort to this combination except as a last
extremity. My liveliest desire is that the Emperor Maximilian maintain
himself." To persist in a proven delusion would have been inexplicable
had that solution been a rational choice; as a face-saving evasion, it was
psychologically logical and tragically intelligible, but it was none the
less a criminal inconsistency, which involved Maximilian in the same
guilty toils and enmeshed him in the same penultimate makeshift. The
solution was the measure of the man, and by refusing to face defeat
squarely and make a clean break Napoleon merited his name of "the
Little."

Maximilian, in turn, abetted his destruction. He was a willing dupe
of the subtlest form of betrayal; for Napoleon was frank, he concealed

nothing, he promised nothing, he laid all the cards on the table for his partner to play, he left the decision to his choice and shifted the responsibility imperceptibly to his shoulders by appealing to his pride and his independence, and Maximilian rose to the challenge. To the kind of treachery of which the motive alone was misleading and the means loyal, he was intensely susceptible. No less than Napoleon, he flinched from admitting his defeat and, at the very moment when he was free to emancipate himself from his protector, he could not bring himself to acknowledge by a simultaneous retreat that he was merely his creation and his creature. His dignity also demanded a decent delay; he had a year or eighteen months to demonstrate his independence; and he resolved to remain.

Between the beginning of the end and its consummation the phase of transition was a period fraught with extraordinary peril for everyone concerned. The liquidation of intervention was dangerous because it prolonged the ordeal unconscionably, because it was barren, abnormal, and absurd, because sanity and obsession were still inseparable, because the dying adventure bred morbid delusions and the brood of the nightmare could not die with the dream, and because the deadly indecision of lingering and desperate life favored the most unforeseen fatalities.

One brief flare of indignation Maximilian did indulge when he was formally notified in the middle of February of the decision to withdraw. He replied by a stinging note to Napoleon. "Your Majesty feels obliged by a sudden pressure to disregard the solemn treaties which you signed with me less than two years ago, and you inform me of it with a frankness that cannot but do you honor. I am too much your friend to wish to be, directly or indirectly, the cause of any danger to Your Majesty or your dynasty. I propose, therefore, with a cordiality equal to your own, that you withdraw your troops from the American continent immediately. For my part, guided by my honor, I shall try to come to some arrangement with my compatriots in a loyal manner, worthy of a Hapsburg. . . ." But he recovered from the first shock rapidly and made the best of a bad situation, which he blamed on Bazaine. Bazaine reciprocated by regretting the inertia and inefficiency of the civil administration. The explanations of Maximilian contradicted those of the Marshal; and those of the Marshal contradicted each other. His military reports were optimistic, his political reports discouraging, and the discrepancy was so marked as to move the Minister of War to ask whether they had been composed by the same person. Bazaine admitted the contradiction and contended that both reports were true, as they were, but so were those of Maximilian.

These mutual recriminations were an old story, which the emergency aggravated, but which had been repeated persistently and impotently for over a year. Maximilian contended that his government was para-

lyzed by the difficulties of pacifying the country and could not be fairly
judged until it was able to function. Six months before he had stated his
case cogently and correctly. "I painted the situation very frankly to
Douay and Dano," he wrote then to Napoleon. "I told them, and I
proved, that the administrative and political questions were going well;
I could not say as much for the military and financial affairs. They had
to agree with me that too many troops had been sent home and the
war had devoured too much money. In these two points lies the plague
of Mexico; all the other questions can be settled with time and patience.
How often have I preached to the Marshal not to precipitate the repatriation of the troops and to keep to the figures fixed by your treaty, but
alas, in vain! Feverish to satisfy public opinion, Bazaine forgets everything and prepares for a near future." In December 1865, alarmed by
the *pourparlers* in Washington, he repeated the argument desperately:
"To develop resources and facilitate their recovery, to prevent those resources themselves from being partly absorbed, the Empire must be
pacified. It is urgent to find a solution of this problem, because the war
is causing the ruin of the Mexican treasury by spending sixty millions a
year. . . . I have insisted on the necessity of a prompt pacification to
balance the budget. In this connection, how to explain the precipitate
shipment of troops to Europe, contrary to the will of the Emperor of
the French and the treaties we have signed? And at a time when there
were dissidents two hours from the capital! How explain the system of
sending troops to important points and withdrawing them a week later,
sacrificing all the persons who had declared for the Empire, a fatal combination which occurred three times in succession at Monterrey, on the
frontier facing the Yankees, and which stifled the germs of good government that General Brincourt planted at Chihuahua in an occupation
of a few days? . . . With these military and financial methods the great
idea of the regeneration of Mexico will be lost. Without order and economy in my finances, with an ever-growing deficit, I cannot govern.
With a population whose confidence is constantly shaken by an ephemeral protection, I can accomplish nothing stable. For everyone knows
that on the return of the *guerrilleros* anyone who has declared for the
Empire will be hanged or shot without mercy, and no one manifests
any good will, therefore, for a government incapable of defending its
subjects."

By February 1866 the near future had become an impending foreclosure and an inexorable fatality. Cast on his own resources, Maximilian was mortgaged to ruin. His resources were all hypothetical or
hypothecated. He was promised a Mexican army still to be organized
and a Foreign Legion yet to be constituted. Financially he was bankrupt. The second loan was exhausted; he was obliged to appeal to Bazaine to meet the bills of the civil administration, and to oblige him
Bazaine had already dipped twice in the coffers of the army to the

amount of two millions, incurring a censure after the first advance and a peremptory order, after the second, not to repeat it. Politically he was played out. The great social reforms were no further advanced than when Forey had announced them. Financial reform had baffled a succession of French experts: the first had paid out, the second had cashed in, the third had just died, the fourth was losing his mind, and the customs were impounded to cover the money advanced by Bazaine. The clerical question had been recapitulated, the resuscitation of the army suspended, and judicial reform was what it had always been, a dead letter. The extinction of brigandage, to which the French attached more importance than to all the other reforms combined, produced the edict of October 3. The record revealed, in every branch, an incontestable deficit; yet Maximilian, ignoring his own diagnosis, insisted that he could govern while the French were going, and after they were gone. He put his head deliberately on the auction block. That his position was untenable without French support he was fully aware, but he persuaded himself that the evacuation was a false alarm to expedite the organization of a Mexican army, traced it to the influence of the Commander-in-Chief, and, minimizing the ultimatum as an idle menace or, at most, a remote contingency, attributed all his troubles to the fatigue, the servility, or the satisfaction of the Marshal. He pressed for his recall in Paris and contended confidently that with another commander the country could still be pacified and the Empire saved.

To organize the retreat in such conditions was an ungrateful duty, and Bazaine bore the brunt of it. He was notified by the French Government that the limit of sacrifices had been reached and that not another penny could be advanced to the Mexican treasury. The reorganization of the Mexican army was a mockery. The Marshal might as well have been asked to reassemble the sands of the sea. Maximilian himself regarded his Mexican army as a necessary evil, the nursing of which was indispensable to prevent it from deserting to the enemy. "One can have no idea in Belgium of the Mexican army," wrote the commander of the Belgian Legion to his government; "that is to say, of the five or six thousand bandits that compose it, mule-drivers and bakers' boys suddenly turned colonels. Mendez himself, one of the best, was a tailor's apprentice a dozen years ago, wanted in Mexico for stealing handkerchiefs. To obtain men, they were taken by force and brought to the barracks between two rows of bayonets. As soon as they were led through a field of sugar cane where they could hide, they deserted. The day that the French army sails, the Empire will collapse with a bang."

Bazaine put it a little differently: "As for the Mexican army, the enclosed chart will show Your Majesty that its effectives have a certain importance, but it needs to be moralized, to attach itself to the cause that it serves, and that is not the work of one year. Its units must also be fed by all races and classes of Mexican society . . . but it is to be feared that sons of good family will still fight shy of the ranks, which are accessible therefore to the intrigues of people of low origin. As for the soldier, represented generally by the pure Indian, he obeys without devotion because he still believes that he is serving foreigners hostile to his race, and he seems indifferent to military enterprise of any kind. That is the bad side of this character which is of an extreme docility, but which will serve a bad cause as well as a good, since it always serves the most enterprising. We must achieve, by good laws and with time, national homogeneity and the development of a communal organization, to have Mexican soldiers with a sense of solidarity to one another; unfortunately, we are far from that yet." But Bazaine, knowing how necessary the Mexican army was to Napoleon, tempered the truth tactfully and told only so much of it as he judged advisable and acceptable to the shorn visionary in Paris. Napoleon needed subterfuges, and he supplied them loyally, too loyally; it was not his way to wound a deluded invalid with the whole brutal truth. Others did that. Dano, the French Minister, felt it his duty to strip away pretenses and to warn his government that any hope of consolidating Maximilian was chimerical and the complicity of the prince in his own undoing mere feeding the wind and folly. He proposed to cut the knot at once, to prove to Maximilian that his position was impossible and persuade him to come to some arrangement with Juarez, and if he refused, to capture him, ship him back to Europe, and save him in spite of himself. Abdication was the only clean and honest solution; it was a consummation devoutly desired by the army, by the Mexicans themselves, by everyone but the Court, and Bazaine himself suggested it discreetly to Napoleon. "I believe that we must act without the consent of the Court of Maximilian, whose ill will, based on mutual recriminations, is not far from ingratitude. . . . The longer we remain, the less will the Mexican Government try to consolidate itself, and it is perfectly willing to use the resources which Your Majesty will leave at its disposal, as an obligatory debt contracted by France toward Mexico, as long as possible. Now that the American question is eliminated, there is no longer any reason to hesitate, since gratitude, the more we prolong our situation here, will no longer be commensurate with the benefits bestowed by Your Majesty."

The best means of forcing Maximilian to abdicate was to speed the evacuation; but Bazaine, knowing how mortifying that solution was to Napoleon, refrained from pressing it. On the contrary, he noted, with mental reservations no doubt, but without comment, that "the Emperor Maximilian seems to believe that after the departure of the French troops the entire Mexican nation will assemble more compactly about his throne, the presence of a foreign army no longer serving as a pretext for the true patriots to avoid him." When the American menace loomed large, he made hasty preparations to meet it, fortifying the capital and concentrating his far-flung troops, but as soon as it subsided, he relaxed and planned to extend the evacuation beyond the time limit set by Napoleon. "The instructions of Your Majesty will be executed," he reported, "since the situation is as prosperous as possible, now that the United States seem resolved to observe neutrality. . . . The news from the northern frontier as well as from the interior is good, and by profiting by this year I have every reason to believe that armed resistance will not have the least importance in 1867. The Mexican Government will have to do the rest, and it will be solely responsible for its faults, Your Majesty having done everything in its interest that it was possible to do." He proposed, therefore, to repatriate the Expeditionary Corps in three shifts, the first in November 1866, the second in March 1867, and the third in December 1867. The first would arrive in France before the opening of the Corps Législatif; thereafter the responsibility would be shifted to Maximilian. "From a military point of view the country is as pacified as it has ever been," he observed truthfully. "The government, therefore, will have to complete the work." The constant accommodations of the Commander-in-Chief made the line between truth and misrepresentation ever fainter and his advice more and more obviously unreliable and double-minded.

Confronted with the incongruous reports of Maximilian and the Marshal, and the tactfully inconsistent advice of his alter ego, Napoleon, whose own mind, naturally frank and loyal, was now deeply and inadmissibly divided, indulged a small habit sanctioned by a great emergency and delved into the private correspondence of his officers in search of the truth. And there he found it. The truth welled up like a drain suddenly released. The habit of tapping irregular channels of information had already ruined Lorencez and Forey, and it undermined Bazaine in turn. The reputation which he had built up laboriously in the early stages of intervention was badly damaged by the last miles of the home journey. His efficiency as a commander was derided; his duplicity as an adviser was denounced. "The Marshal lives by expedients to dazzle the eyes of the Emperor and the governments, which have shown, it must be admitted, a *credulity* equal to every test," wrote General Douay. "While the Marshal enjoys his season of credit, there is nothing to do. We must wait until the crisis breaks, then the coffers will be empty; that will not be long, for the second loan will soon be exhausted. They say that in February there will be nothing in the bottom of the box. . . . The only thing that might get us out of this muddle and this rigmarole in which we are floundering and will flounder *indefinitely* would be a good hard collision with America. . . . I don't know how much reason I would have to rejoice in that eventuality personally, for I cannot delude myself: I have to do with a great hypocrite, and I have had time enough to penetrate his profound military ineptitude, which is masked by superficial appearances and the bluff that has made any number of dupes until now." That his judgment might be discounted Douay was well aware, for he had been designated to succeed Bazaine in case of his recall; but he disclaimed any personal bias, and for the best of reasons: "You may be sure that if I were given the succession of the Marshal, as things are now, I would refuse it. Conditions will be no better, certainly, in a year or in two years. Yet I remain in Mexico; not with the ambition of reaching the command, but simply because I do not wish to seem to myself to be yielding to disgust or obeying a feeling of bad humor. I continue to wait with a great deal of calm and resignation until our resources and patience are exhausted in France; . . . 1866 wears the same aspect as 1865 or 1864. The fallacious promises of Marshal Bazaine will vanish in as many disappointments as before. It must be admitted that he meets with insuperable credulity, since the same lies still have the same success. You can have no idea of our hilarity when we read the stereotyped phrase in the bulletin of *Le Moniteur:* 'The bands have been destroyed, etc.' If history has always been written this way, it must contain plenty of impostures."

His opinion was borne out by so many of his fellow officers that he could write, without fear of contradiction, "I believe that the time is coming when Marshal Bazaine will reap what he has sown. The opinion of the army is by no means favorable to him, and yet we all sang his praises at the beginning of his command. Today we are playing variations on that tune. . . . What still protects him against a revolt of opinion is the general dispersion of all our elements over an immense surface that prevents the condensation of ideas." The Intendant-General of the army, with no ax to grind but that of the army, was no less unsparing of the Commander-in-Chief. He condensed his opinion of the Marshal in a few merciless words: "Vulgar in his sentiments and even in his education, skeptical, sly, selfish, partial, and unscrupulous, he esteemed no one, no doubt because he judged others by himself. It cost him nothing to lie." His moral callousness was the most striking feature of his character to a foreign observer: "Bazaine was very ignorant, certainly very intelligent, and very brave. He rarely told the truth; when he did, he never told it entirely. He deceived habitually, unconsciously, everyone who served under his orders, everyone addicted to him as well as those who were indifferent to him. He attached no importance to this fact: men meant nothing to him." Devoid alike of moral sense and professional and personal dignity, according to another officer, he had only an uncertain conception of the national honor and his own.

The correspondence of the officers brought up something more important, however, than the discredit of the Commander-in-Chief: a bald exposure of conditions in Mexico. What Bazaine reaped was not what he had sown—it was the ruin of intervention. The harvest bred the humbug. He was as false as his position and as honest as his master: he humored, he hedged, he trimmed; and if he was a fraud in the eyes of the army, it was because the army had penetrated and exploded the enormous fallacy of intervention. His reticences provoked the ire and the revelations of his subordinates, and the truth welled up in endless regurgitations of disgust, anger, alarm, and despondency. Mexico was a military purgatory, as one of them said, from which no one saw any way of escape. Douay, hankering halfheartedly for a clash with America, but knowing that way out to be impossible, groaned under the necessity of "preserving the sad position of a good peaceful civilian, who has decided to keep his temper and sing the psalm of recantation to save his precious skin." He was up to his mouth in the Slough of Despond. "The situation is such that we are sinking deeper into the impasse, and I should be embarrassed to give any advice, either to advance or withdraw," he admitted. "To advance, we should have to make new and enormous sacrifices, make a *coup d'état* in the government of Maximilian, etc. To withdraw is so heartbreaking that I prefer not to think of it." So heartbreaking, in fact, that General Brincourt, when he was ordered to evacuate Chihuahua, obeyed under protest and tendered his resignation, preferring to break his sword, as he said, than to abandon the population under his protection to the reprisals of the patriots. The humiliation of retreating before the American menace was galling, and all the greater that everyone knew the American menace to be mere bluff. A border clash on the first day of the new year was promptly disavowed by Washington; but the war of nerves went on, driving the French back from the frontier and deeper and deeper into their internal difficulties. The capture of Hermosillo by the patriots, and the killing of some French civilians there, created a panic in the capital, where the French colony anticipated wholesale reprisals at the end of the occupation. The foreign banks were closing, the French firms were seeking to liquidate their affairs, but there were no buyers; commercial life was at a standstill, the stalemate paralyzed all activity, and the knowledge that everything was purely provisional killed all confidence in the future of the Empire.

Lieutenant Colonel Brissonet was not an alarmist, but he had been breaking the bad news for a long time to France. "Everyone is frightened by the task that France has undertaken; everyone is worried by the difficulties into which she plunges, the moral engagements she contracts every day and that enclose her more and more," he wrote while there was still time to be farsighted. "Is this not known in France? Or do people not want to know it? We have put a fetter on our feet, which will lame us for a long time, and we have satisfied no one in Mexico! Liberals and Clericals detest us alike; we have answered the expectations of no party. All have come to regard us as foreign invaders, who have imposed a government on them that they did not want. Success alone could have saved us in their eyes, and our intervention has rekindled questions that would have been settled today: it has revived party hatreds, renewed civil war, and given a pretext to the bands that pillage and ravage the country. This is what is being said loudly, and it is true. So the Mexicans add that, having done all the harm, we cannot leave before a little good has resulted from our presence here; until the government is solidly established; until its army is organized; until its finances are sufficient to sustain it. But this is to expect the impossible; this is to ask France to lend Mexico two hundred millions every year and to keep up an army of thirty thousand men for ten years or more; this is to ask that Mexico be peopled by other men, for there is nothing to hope of the present race, and we should have to wait until some millions of Europeans were pleased to come and settle here. But immigrants have come and are still coming from Europe, and all who have money return very soon, for there is not an inch of ground to give them. . . . The great landowners are opposed to immigration, knowing that they would soon cease to be great feudal lords, and they will not part with a parcel of their lands."

Forced by their experience to think of the purposes and results of intervention, the officers felled its pretensions, one by one, in self-defense. With commerce scuttled, colonization eliminated, America antagonized, Mexico ruined, what remained of the chimerical scheme of invading, violating, exploiting, and regenerating Mexico? Hypocrisy? By no means. Napoleon was honest, and in his mind these were necessary stages in the redemption of a people and the development of a benevolent idea. That was the root of the disaster, and it was there that the ax was laid. Maximilian, sedulously imitating his sponsor, was the disciple and the victim of his dying delusion. "He hates to be harsh, but his goodness is weakness in the present situation," Brissonet complained with those who were begging the question in 1866. "Everyone recognizes that he works a great deal, but it is to be feared that he is far more a theoretical than a practical man, and so far nothing has been founded on the numerous laws that he has promulgated. . . . A great uneasiness reigns, therefore, in the whole of Mexico; everyone sees that the situation is strained and that it cannot remain so. Since we can find no favorable solution, we worry, we torment ourselves; we are even discouraged. Do not believe that I exaggerate; I see things very coolly, I think, and I paint them in softened colors. Besides, light must be beginning to dawn in France on this Mexican question, and the truth will appear with all its consequences. God grant that that knowledge may lead us out of so false a situation as quickly as possible."

"For me, the great plague of Mexico is that there are Mexicans," wrote another officer. "The Indian is good, easy to train, and of a proverbial mildness; it is a race as much under the lash as the Negroes. The Indian does not belong to himself, he belongs to such and such a landowner whom he obeys blindly. When you ask one of those men where he comes from, he says, I belong to such and such a *hacienda*. All these people are good, they even make excellent soldiers, hardy and sober beyond belief. But what is bad is the *ranchero,* that is to say, a gentleman who owns four or five square leagues of land with two or three Indian villages on it; a bastard race, boastful, immoral, and un-principled; born in disorder, used to living in it, and preferring a slightly adventurous life, some pronunciamentos from time to time, and even some shooting against any stable government that might come and disturb a life almost of medieval *grands seigneurs* by making them pay a tax, dividing lands of which they have stolen a part, or building roads that would unite the whole country but would deprive it of all its adventurous life. It is that race that puts up with us only through fear and is merely waiting for our departure to resume habits with which we interfere. Fortunately they are not very numerous. If, by some cataclysm, they were to disappear and their place to be taken by a layer of those hardy colonists of the United States, I wager that Mexico would gain enormously. As for the Mexicans of the cities, who wear gold-embroidered jackets and hats with braid, they are yet worse. They have a certain veneer of education and sentiments all the lower. They are the ones that generally fill the government berths, and never has robbery been organized on so vast a scale: it is admitted that the State is a milch cow and that everyone is entitled to suck, according to his position." The great mistake of Maximilian, he concluded, was that he had not treated Mexico as a conquered country, appropriated part of the territory to the State, decreed a vast stage of siege, and crushed all resistance with an iron hand. "Like all slightly savage peoples, the Mexicans have a great respect for force and submit to it easily. Instead of that, the Emperor has made himself a Mexican, which no one asked him to do, has flaunted liberal ideas that have no relation to the needs of a country so little advanced, and has surrounded himself with men who have flung themselves at his head and who have served all gov-ernments."

Though the complaints varied, the tone was always the same: it was the chorus of the conqueror conquered by conscience and circumstance, baffled by both, and seeking relief in cynical disgust. The army had ac-complished its mission in Mexico: the friction of two peoples infected them both, and the compression of defeat sprang the expression of the truth. By February 1866 the farsighted, the nearsighted, the hindsighted, had all come to the conclusion that the great plague of Mexico for its benefactors was that there were Mexicans; and the breakdown of in-tervention was inventoried by the officers with a brutal clarity that contradicted the bland equivocations of the Commander-in-Chief and called for a clean quick end to the pernicious error of the Emperor. If anything was worse than defeat, it was to deny it, and the most shame-ful solution of all was to prolong the sham.

The double exposure of Mexico and the Marshal had been current for many months, and Napoleon met both complaints in swift succession. Shortly after Bazaine received his orders to organize the retreat, he received permission to delegate the evacuation to Douay and to return to France. Like the recall of Forey, his removal was couched in optional terms, but they had the same hollow ring, and, like Forey, he chose to ignore it. His dignity also demanded a decent homecoming, and he determined to do his duty to the bitter end. And bitter it was. Maximilian distrusted him, the army suspected him, and the proof that he had lost the confidence of Napoleon added the last jarring touch to the fatal indecision of the situation. The closest advisers of Maximilian were all anti-French, and the task of the Commander-in-Chief was hampered by a solid phalanx of officials reluctant to co-operate and determined to keep him at a distance. His counsels were questioned, resented, deferred, and adopted only when they became indispensable. His patience was equal to all the demands made upon it, but as his influence was systematically neutralized, he confined his activities to a minimum and accomplished only halting results; results which lent credit to the charge of his incapacity by the very conscientiousness with which he discharged his thankless task. To consolidate Maximilian and liquidate intervention at the same time was an impossible assignment; and so *festine lente,* he temporized industriously, indifferently, and fruitlessly.

It was a time for bold resolutions, and one was suggested to Bazaine by a voice in the dark. An obscure observer, living beyond the American border, followed the unfolding of the Mexican tragedy with a penetrating and passionate insight that moved him to try conclusions with untoward destiny and wrest triumph from defeat. The margin was narrow, the advice desperate, the solution revolutionary. "If you want an army, a government, and a people in Mexico, you must suppress peonage," he insisted. "If the Emperor Maximilian wishes to remain in Mexico, he *must* suppress peonage. This is the condition *sine qua non.* Mind you, I do not say that on this condition he will remain; but I do say that it is the obligatory condition to have a chance of staying, and that if, having done this, he is compelled to leave, he will leave at least with honor and will have carved himself a great name in history." Here lay the hope of eclipsing Juarez. "Juarez is an Indian, and it would be absurd to deny that he has proved himself an energetic representative of modern ideas and laws in Mexico. But has he achieved this Reform, which of all Reforms seemed to belong to him above all men? That he favored it, *in petto,* I have no doubt. I infer, therefore, that neither he nor the other men of really advanced and honorable sentiments *dared* to proclaim and accomplish it. That the men of the Liberal party dared not slay the beast proved, with the evidence of an axiom, the economic ignorance, the routine egoism, and the general rottenness of the party. It is nonetheless true that Juarez committed his capital error by compromising with the crime of his party. When all the living forces of the nation were aroused against intervention, if he had proclaimed the abolition of peonage as the indispensable complement of Reform and accompanied the measure of emancipation with a law granting land to all peons who bore arms and served honorably, our illustrious Forey would probably not have been forced to prepare himself Pueblas to obtain the baton. Be that as it may, the men of conviction in the Liberal party, by failing in their first duty, have also missed their main chance. They have deserved—historically—to be vanquished, just as the Polish aristocracy of 1830, national though it was and formidable as much of its revolution was, also deserved defeat for failing to affranchise the serfs." Where Juarez had missed, therefore, it was for Maximilian to dare. To have soldiers, you must make citizens, the prompter dinned into the ears of the Marshal; by emancipating the peons Maximilian would liberate himself, muster the masses, and, whether he succeeded or failed in maintaining himself, achieve his moral independence at least and perhaps his political salvation, surpass Juarez, emulate Lincoln, and not merely Mexicanize but Americanize himself, "saving at the same time the honor (the so-called honor) of this poor intervention and, what matters far more, the lofty interests of France, of Mexico, of America, and of the world—for we have reached a period when the field of revolutions, wars, and all events of importance is no longer this or that nation or even this or that continent; now, as the Apostle said, 'The field is the world.' "

These promptings purported to be addressed to Bazaine; but what could they mean to that prudent, timeserving, baffled bystander, whose own counsels were consistently ignored, and who was engaged in beating a safe retreat from reality? The author attached enough importance to his gospel to give it to the world; two years later he published in Brussels his letters to Bazaine, shrouding his identity in an anonymity that added to the weight of his counsels the portentousness of an unknown oracle. The name of Victor Considérant was little known; the idea deserved to be well known. Portentous it was, as a potential reserve of human power; but nothing more. What could it mean to Maximilian, who was already discredited in Mexico as an impractical theorist? Maximilian himself provided the answer. He professed, and felt, a veritable Indiomania; Carlota recognized the plight and the importance of the Indians, the only class, as she said, that labored and made the State live; and the emancipation of the peons was a project which they had both caressed. In April 1865 a mixed commission, composed half of Europeans and half of Mexicans, was set up to study measures for the amelioration of their conditions. After investigating conditions on the great estates, a French engineer, who had been sent out to organize the agricultural exploitation of the country, recommended a humanitarian reform, despite the political risks which he recognized. "This project concerns me greatly," he reported, "but without the assent of Your Majesty I dare not frame a decree which is a complete revolution, but a revolution that is useful, necessary, and urgent. I have seen the Indians very closely during the year that I spent on the *haciendas*. I have lived their life and wept for their lot. I have been shocked by the barbarity of their masters and the exactions of all kinds exercised by them. I have seen men beaten until they bleed, I have literally put my finger into their wounds; I have fed families dying of hunger and driven to work by the lash of the overseer; I have seen men dying of exhaustion, laden with chains, dragging themselves into the sun to end their lives under the eye of God and then flung into a hole like dead dogs. All this is nothing. The landowner speculates even on the feed of these poor people and on the rags that half clothe them. He makes them buy all their food from him, and at a higher price than in the market in town; he sells them usuriously the poor cloth that they need; so that, in the final reckoning, the Indian receives no more than one *real* for a workday of fourteen hours. The Indian is driven deeper and deeper into debt, and in this his master is powerfully aided by the priests, who make the peon pay for the formulas of religion at an exorbitant price and exploit his superstitious credulity to the limit. The liquidation of Holy Week is always a loss for the peon, and his condition is constantly growing worse. As a result of this system, there is not an Indian family that owes less than one hundred piasters. The general debt of the Indians on a *hacienda* is at least twenty thousand piasters."

Bazaine approved the reform, but as it threatened to subvert the authority of the landowners, the commission studied it academically and came to no conclusion. During an absence of the Emperor from the capital, Carlota attacked the problem herself and carried it through the Council with a single dissenting vote, and, as she wrote to Maximilian, "amid a thrill of enthusiasm." "Strengthened by this success," she added, "I developed social theories on the cause of revolutions in Mexico, which have come from turbulent minorities resting on a great inert mass, and on the necessity of restoring to humanity millions of men, instead of calling colonists from afar, and of putting an end to a plague to which Independence had brought only an ineffectual cure, since the Indians, citizens in fact, remained nevertheless in a state of disastrous abjection. All this took, to my great amazement, and I am beginning to believe that it is an historic event." It was. What she won was a decree abolishing corporal punishment, limiting working hours, guaranteeing salaries, and reducing the mortgage of debt slavery fastened on the peon by the proprietor and transmitted from father to son to perpetuate his legal bondage; but the decree was a philanthropic half-measure that fell short of full social reform by the distance that separated it from a revolutionary proclamation of emancipation and an endowment of land, and that missed delivery.

A cry of alarm was immediately raised, and by a liberal minister of the Crown. "The natives remain quiet only because of their social prostration," he objected in a memorandum to the Emperor, "but by character and spirit of race, as soon as they are excited and given means to face the whites, they will think the time come for insurrection and vengeance, and then woe to Mexico!" Fear and guilt fastened the fetters on the master in Mexico as tenaciously as in the United States, and Maximilian was an amateur Lincoln. Nevertheless, he persisted and published the decree in November 1865, a month after the draconian edict of October 3, doubling the odds against him. The philanthropic half-measure suffered the same fate as the benevolent edicts by which the Spanish kings had attempted to protect the native proletariat against the established abuses created by the Conquest. Maximilian was three hundred years too late. The idea was born, it was baptized, and it was buried in a litter of papers bearing the Crown, the Eagle, and the Serpent, where it expired under a mound of legislation destined never to be enacted. Like the other reforms, this one remained a hypothetical resource, and it was late in the day to steal the revolution from Juarez.

14

THE catharsis of the Mexican question was a slow, unnerving, subliminal disaster. Seward did nothing to hasten it. Satisfied by the assurances of the French Government that the evacuation would be completed in a year or eighteen months, he rested his accomplishment on that long-term note, and Juarez, who was hardened to temporizing, having practiced it so long and successfully himself, accepted another year of delay in like spirit. "The replies of Mr. Seward to the French Government," he wrote to his family in February, "are worth a battle won and confirm my calculations that if we do not triumph completely this year, at least our cause will improve one hundred per cent." The winning of that battle was celebrated in Washington. His wife went there in March to nurse the mother of Romero through an illness and found herself suddenly, and much to her surprise, the center of public attention. Cards were left at the Legation to welcome her to the American capital, and a reception was given in her honor at the White House, the first social function to be held there since Johnson assumed the Presidency. Seward followed suit with an unofficial dinner, at which he said everything that could be expected of him; he toasted the success of temporizing and repeated more than once his conviction that before the end of the year the French would be out of Mexico. Two days later he conducted her through the State Department, showed her its historic documents, and presented her with his portrait. Not to be outdone, General Grant entertained her with a ball, attended, unexpectedly, by the President, who broke his seclusion once more to manifest his sympathy for her country, and, more surprisingly yet, by the French Minister and Madame de Montholon. Although she was hampered by an alien language, Doña Margarita managed to place her word with timely political effect, aided by the Spanish Minister, who served as her interpreter. The pointed attentions shown her raised her visit to the rank of a diplomatic event, and the comments in the Mexican press recognized it as such.

While the limelight was turned on his wife in Washington, Juarez was measuring shadows in El Paso. There the penumbra of the Empire was known by premonition rather than by report; reports were remote and unreliable, and he groped in the dark, guided by instinct more than by knowledge. By the middle of April the brief hours allotted to Maximilian for the great luxury of doing good seemed to have run out. "It seems unquestionable that he has changed his political plan," he wrote, "surrendering by order of Napoleon to the exclusive influence of the retrograde party, and that he will establish in consequence a regime of intolerance and terror, and I should not be surprised if the Camarilla decreed not only my own extermination, but that of every Liberal who does not submit to the Empire. But as public opinion now stands, this new tactic will merely precipitate his fall. Do not fear; I am careful and among people whom I trust entirely."

Not until the good was drained out of him could Maximilian really succumb to his destiny, and he was not so desperate yet. The report was untrue, or rather it was premature; truth traveled more quickly than facts, and Juarez, usually so careful to advance nothing which he did not know for a fact, merely anticipated the inevitable turn which Maximilian would be forced to take sooner or later. The creeping shadow touched Juarez, as it touched everyone else in those days of somber suspense, on the uneasy borderline between reality and fiction. It was a period when every possibility had to be considered—even that the promise of Napoleon to withdraw might be a mere feint, though that was unlikely. "I do not believe that he means to gain time by entertaining the United States with a false promise. That is done only with the weak; but not with those who, like the United States, *can* oppose and punish such perfidy." That was his nearest approach to doubt; his confidence would not have been complete had he not known what it was to doubt, if only to deny it, and he steeped his faith in the shadow to make it whole. Good news reached him as slowly as bad in El Paso; it was not until the middle of May that he learned of his wife's visit to Washington, and he gave it no more importance then than it deserved. "I am very glad to hear that you are all well and that the old lady, who wrote me also, had a good time in Washington," he wrote to his son-in-law. "Now to other things." It was not to Washington that he looked for assistance. He allowed for last-minute slips in his favor, however, as well against him. "Like you, I believe that given the circumstances of intervention and judging by the natural order of events, the French will finally leave the country at the end of this year and that this is the best we can expect of the pride and caprice of Louis Napoleon; but since in political questions, as well as in war, nothing is fixed and certain, and any incident, even the most insignificant, may upset the best-laid plans and give matters an unexpected turn, it would not be surprising were the retreat of the invaders to be precipitated or the so-called Empire to crumble. The reported rupture between Austria and Prussia, a reaction of the Liberal and Oppositionist party in France, and the exhaustion of Maximilian's resources are causes which may soon influence the catastrophe of the Imperial drama, before the time Maximilian is said to have set for the creation of an army to sustain him." So, re-creating incessantly the balance between shadow and substance with his customary equanimity, he continued to watch the lengthening shadow of Maximilian warily and to wait patiently for the impending purge. It was not by adventitious aid or foreign contingencies, however, but by its own inherent and organic logic that the Mexican tragedy worked itself out. Anything else would have been a mutilated triumph, which he neither expected nor desired, and even as he wrote the bubble was bursting and the illusions that sustained Maximilian were evaporating, one by one.

In May Maximilian demanded a subsidy for a few months more and threatened, if he were denied, to cede the Isthmus of Tehuantepec to the Americans. Although Bazaine was neither alarmed nor angered by this tempestuous language, as he called it, he consented to relieve him as cheaply as possible and advanced two and a half million francs a month for May and June, awaiting the decision of the French Government. The decision of the French Government was made at the same time. Almonte, who had been sent to Paris to negotiate a revision of the Convention of Miramar and an extension of financial and military support, was met with an ultimatum. The Foreign Office denounced the Convention and insisted on taking up the lien laid on the Mexican customs by Bazaine, on pain of withdrawing the troops at once instead of at the end of the year. The small investors who had subscribed the second loan were awaking to their own delusions and demanding guarantees of their government. Guarantees the government would not give, but it took them to cover its own deficit and appropriated half the customs revenue to secure the liquidation of French credits. The news was received in Mexico at the end of June. The financial ultimatum was more crushing than the military; as the customs provided the Empire, like the Republic, with its sole substantial revenue, and they were mortgaged up to seventy-six per cent to meet the foreign debt service and the running expenses of the administration, the foreclosure of the French mortgage meant the immediate collapse of the Mexican government. The delusion of doubt was dispelled, and the illusion of aid would have been completely dissipated but for Carlota. The first impulse of Maximilian was to abdicate, but she dissuaded him and determined, defying the saving disillusionment of defeat, to go to Paris herself and appeal to Napoleon in person. Buoyed by her indomitable spirit, Maximilian recovered his own. The instructions which he wrote for her were an indictment of Bazaine, a requisition on Napoleon, and an ultimatum couched in imperative terms. "The Emperor must engage to pay twenty thousand mixed troops until the end of the year 1867, to subsidize the Mexican Government with a stipend of five hundred thousand pesos a month, to remove Bazaine immediately, to replace him by General Douay, to organize a Mexican army before withdrawing the troops, and to sign a secret convention embodying these stipulations." Otherwise—but there was no question of anything else. *Ce que femme veut* . . . The bubble had burst, but the bandying of ultimatums to and fro kept the wraith afloat in a feverish contest between fallacy and infatuation.

Carlota left Mexico in a disturbed state of mind, which was betrayed by her erratic behavior on the way to the coast. In Puebla she rose in the dead of night and insisted on visiting the local prefect, who was absent; the house was closed, but she went through the empty rooms before she was satisfied and consented to retire. In Veracruz, as she was about to embark, she refused to enter the launch until the French flag had been removed and replaced with the Mexican colors, and retired to the waiting-room until she was humored. On board the ship she sent for the captain and complained of the drumming of the engines; every thud shook her brain and echoed in her head, she said; the machines were driving her mad. Upon his objection that this inconvenience was unavoidable, she had her cabin padded with mattresses to deaden the sound, but the implacable drive of the engines continued to haunt her during the crossing. She was inaccessible, silent, and morose, and complained of muffled pains in her head.

She arrived in France at the worst possible moment for her mission. The impending war between Prussia and Austria broke out while she was at sea and was over when she landed at Saint-Nazaire. The unexpected defeat of Austria in ten days jarred the delicate balance of power in Europe, and the battle of Sadowa added a fresh plume to the syncopated pinions of the Prussian eagle. In two preparatory wars—

the first fought with Austria for the dismemberment of the Duchies of Schleswig–Holstein and the second against her for a test of power— Bismarck had advanced the position of Prussia to a point which alarmed Paris. In both conflicts Napoleon had remained neutral, and the French felt themselves losing caste as the arbiters of Europe. The rising shadow of Prussian militarism was a fresh motive for expediting the recall of the troops from Mexico, and on the day that Carlota landed in France, Fould, the Minister of Finance, addressed a memorandum to Napoleon, urging him to force the abdication of Maximilian without further delay. "If I am well informed," he wrote, "he will not resign himself until he is thoroughly convinced that he can expect no succor from France. He is beginning to feel it, the voyage of the Empress Carlota proves it. If Your Majesty tells her frankly that, whatever may be your personal feelings, you can give her no assistance without convoking the Corps Législatif, whose opinion is not doubtful, the Empress Carlota will lead the Emperor to the determination which I consider the only one possible." Napoleon telegraphed to Saint-Nazaire, pleading illness and begging her to defer her arrival in Paris until she had visited Brussels, but with the driving power within her unabated, she proceeded to Paris.

By an inexplicable slip, Almonte, Hidalgo, Gutierrez Estrada, and the dignitaries sent to receive her went to the wrong station, and she drove to a hotel in a hired cab. There she was visited on the next day by the Empress Eugénie, who attempted to fend her off, but Carlota insisted on an interview with Napoleon, and threatened half banteringly, half bitterly, but obstinately, to break in if she were denied. The meeting took place at Saint-Cloud, behind closed doors, and a highly colored account of it was later given out by her lady-in-waiting, who sat in the anteroom. Listening to the rising murmur of voices, she heard the discussion culminate in a violent outburst by Carlota crying, beside herself, that she should never have abased herself before a Bonaparte; whereupon the door opened, and the Emperor invited her to attend her mistress, who lay on a couch in a dead swoon. What actually occurred, however, Carlota informed her husband in a series of hopelessly rational missives. However overwrought she may have been, she never lost control of herself. Closeted with Napoleon and Eugénie, she closed with him at once. "I controlled myself and said, 'Sire, I have come to save a cause which is your own,' and I spoke to him for two hours with a great deal of conviction. At one moment I saw him weep. He is in a sickly state and gives the impression of a man who feels himself lost, and who no longer knows what to do nor how to act, for I think that his attitude is natural and implies no feint or dissimulation. For the past two months he has been in a state of complete prostration. This is the explanation of the great power of the ministers, who forget that France cannot be governed without a head.

Unity or anarchy. He imagines that nothing is done or said now as he wishes and that his authority is unrecognized." It fell to her, therefore, to hearten him as she had heartened Maximilian, to revive his confidence and flatter his will; she stressed his immense power, she reminded him that France had twenty millions of people, important capital, unlimited credit, and that a nation with so many victories to its credit could not afford to forget its supremacy in Europe and evade its engagements in Mexico. She deluded herself, as she was forced to do to perform her mission; and she left him, foiled but unfaltering. She had two more interviews, which came to nothing. Napoleon, she noted, had been in his decline, physically, for two years; the Empress was incapable of conducting affairs or curbing the ministers. "They have become old, they have become children again; often they both cry. I do not know whether this makes matters any better." She tried every possible approach, every correct form of coercion, short of personal reproach. She read the ultimatum, she presented him with an album of his promises, she shamed, she challenged, she cheered, she reasoned, she cajoled, she pleaded, and, above all, she persisted as only a woman could in the teeth of defeat, but she merely sank deeper into the lap of denial. The sick man of Europe spoke of Mexico as if he had given no attention to the question for a long time, and he wept more copiously the second time than the first.

In despair she fell back on the ministers and went over the head of the sovereign to the underlings. In a conference with the Ministers of War and Finance, she drove home the desperate financial situation to which they had condemned Maximilian, and which neither he nor any other government could master: a budget of 34 million francs cut in half by the foreclosure on the customs, an expense account of 64 million for the Mexican army alone. She heaped figures on their heads. Of the two loans, amounting nominally to 516 millions, the Mexican Government had actually received only 126,500,000 francs to cover 150 millions in war costs; and when she demanded to know what had become of the difference, the Minister of War and the Empress, who hovered within hearing, were dumfounded, and their consternation increased with the explanations made by M. Fould. The first loan had been undersubscribed, the second had been offered at a discount of sixty-three per cent to offset the discredit of Mexico; 17 millions had been deducted for commissions, 20 millions forfeited to the bankers, 800,000 paid in hush-money to the press, and the dazzling international combination, turned inside out, was exposed for exactly what it was worth. Nor was this all. The Minister covered himself with countercharges of peculation in Mexico; she retorted that he had condemned them to dishonor and bankruptcy and that the result was blamed on the incompetence, the inexperience, and the hesitations of her husband. Moreover, the French indemnities remained at the same figure set by Saligny in 1862 to wreck the Republic, the Jecker credit had been liquidated to oblige Napoleon, and the fraudulent claims upon which intervention had been floated, plus the millions it had since cost, had all come out or were still to be collected from the pocket of the French taxpayer. M. Fould paid tribute to her eloquence and begged leave to retire before she converted him; the Minister of War proposed to examine the military question; and the Empress Eugénie, burying her face in her handkerchief, sank sobbing on a sofa. Carlota was too disgusted to continue. "It is all slime," she wrote to her husband, "from beginning to end." She had waded too deep in the dregs of adventure, the slime was unredeemed by a single iridescent trace of the bubble, and she went back, over the heads of the ministers, to the master. In a final interview with Napoleon her demands were softly but flatly rejected. "Then we shall abdicate," she retorted. The invalid mustered courage to pronounce the last word. "Abdicate," he said.

Of one satisfaction he could not fleece her, however. She won a moral triumph, as she wrote to Maximilian, "for here every word is a lie, but you must not believe that I begged of these people. I told them just what I thought and I stripped them of their masks, but with no lack of courtesy. Certainly nothing so painful has ever happened to them in their lives." Napoleon she judged without indulgence. He was not an invalid, not a victim of circumstances, not a political captive, no; denial was dictated "not by fear of the Opposition, nor far less because of the attitude of the United States; no, he has done a bad deed, which had long been prepared. . . . He is as amiable as Mephistopheles, he even kissed my hand when I took my leave today, but it is all playacting." She left for Miramar, but not without winding the web of illusion once more about her beloved. She urged him to dismiss Bazaine immediately and replace him with Douay. There might still be some hope then, and that bubble rose in her mind like a drowning breath. Her last word of advice blurred all that she had written before. "That they want you to abdicate I can see very clearly here," she wrote, "but I think that you should resist as long as possible. . . ."

After spending a fortnight in Miramar in a vain attempt to rest—to rest, to be faithless, was the final impossibility of her mission—she resumed her maddening duty once more. A cable from Maximilian informed her that he had formed a Conservative cabinet and suggested the possibility of propitiating the Pope, securing the Concordat, and inducing him to intervene with Napoleon. Her mind hit on that idea and missed in the supreme anguish of devotion. She left for Rome, turned back, continued her journey, and ended it. Never had she been more lucid than in Paris, where her intelligence flamed up to a tapering point in the grip of Napoleon, but the wick was consumed, and the light was quenched in Rome.

In Rome she was received with becoming honors. Cardinal Antonelli visited her in her hotel, and an audience was arranged without undue delay. The Holy Father accepted her plea benevolently and adjourned it gently and indefinitely. Giovanni Maria Mastai-Feretti was seventy-four years of age, and he had determined to procrastinate. Two projects of a Concordat had already been drawn and discarded, a third was under consideration, but nothing could be done until it had been submitted to the Mexican clergy; as for interceding with Napoleon, he promised to see what he could do, though he admitted that it was difficult. He sent her away apparently satisfied. To an old man who thought in terms of eternity it was easy to temporize for two or three months longer; but to his importunate daughter the delay was deadly. Three days later she returned to the Vatican alone and unannounced and, flinging herself at the feet of the Holy Father, implored him to save her from the spies and assassins of Napoleon. Her agitation was so alarming that her physician was summoned. He pronounced her insane. She refused to abandon her sanctuary and was permitted to spend the night in the Vatican, and there her mission ended in stark staring mania. In the morning the Papal officials found her where they had left her, sitting bolt upright in a chair, rigid, silent, and unsleeping, the willful moody mouth opening and the hollow eyes closing only to consult her spies in Heaven. She was induced to return to her hotel, where she spent the next few days in suspicious seclusion, sleeping surreptitiously on her feet, refusing food unless it was prepared in her presence, going out alone to draw water from the fountains of Rome, poisoned by protection, fleeing persecution, dreading her own shadow. Her brother, the Count of Flanders, was sent for, and he brought her back to Miramar; and there the wandering mind, driven from pillar to post, baffled in Paris and benighted in Rome, rested at last in haunted obscurity.

15

MAXIMILIAN, in the meanwhile, had capitulated to Paris and surrendered the customs. With his independence he surrendered his simplicity, and a strain of mild disingenuousness, of dissimulation, of disloyalty even, warranted by the conduct of his protectors and prompted by it, was observed by Bazaine. The Marshal was a man of few words, but he knew exactly when and where to place them, and after the departure of the Empress he dropped into his reports exactly the right ones to relieve the troubled consciences and ease the embarrassed councils in Paris. Mentioning the general belief that she cared more for her crown than did her consort, he added, "Certain officers close to the sovereign are trying to convince him that his interests lie in Austria rather than in Mexico, and two or three secret missions have just been created, perhaps to sound the situation." In that case they were quits all around.

Now, too, another phase of his nature, by no means unfamiliar but never before so pronounced, became noticeable because of his plight. Buoyed in the absence of Carlota by the volatility of his disposition, he sought solace and support in a saving frivolity, which was his best means of maintaining himself in Mexico. Abandoned to himself, he followed the bent of his nature and, reverting to the congenial habits of royalty in distress, found refuge from the world in carefree solitude, idle occupations, and truant recreations of one kind or another. A French officer, counting the days of the Empire in September, noticed his nonchalance in the face of disaster. "You must not suppose that the Emperor is so much affected as all that, for his great occupation is to go to Cuernavaca to visit a young Mexican who has just borne him a son, which delights him beyond words; he is very proud to have proved his aptitude for paternity, a point which had been much contested. In the meanwhile, the country is without direction, without confidence, without a penny, and all the more opposed to the Emperor (whom it does not know) that everyone feels that we are leaving for good. There even seems to be a sort of tacit understanding between us and the principal dissident leaders to respect one another and make our retreat easier. In all the places which we have abandoned and which have been occupied by the dissidents, there has been no violence against our nationals, and the Liberal leaders are preceded by proclamations stating that they have nothing against the French. This is very clever of them and very lucky for us, but it bodes no good for the future of the Empire." For the Emperor, however, fatherhood was no mere pastime. He benefited by the Mexican sun at the most perishable season of his reign. His infidelity to Carlota was the sole fruitful result of their sterile adventure together, and the borrowed love that bore him a son in Mexico brought him some relief from their blighted ambition. By birth, by breeding, by nature, he was essentially a solitary. Bored by society, he had long since abandoned its burdens to Carlota, who, not very worldly herself, had relieved him of the duties of representation; and once she was gone he retired completely into the congenial solitude of Chapultepec. There he led an idyllic life, which reminded him nostalgically of Miramar, cultivating his leisure with trifling avocations, taking his ease in the happy humdrum of daily life, following the drift of events indolently, and foiling adversity with fatalistic frivolity, and as the knot tightened, he loosened his end of the slack. His vital instincts did not desert him; nature protected him against the coming blow; and he needed all the resilience of his temperament to bear it when he learned, early in October, of the collapse of Carlota. The shock felled him for a few days. He shut himself up, refusing to see anyone, and when he reappeared he took the first steps to abdicate.

Without notifying anyone but Bazaine, he left for Orizaba. His sudden departure created a sensation in the capital, where it was interpreted as a flight. The Conservative cabinet which he had just formed resigned in a body, but Bazaine compelled the ministers to remain at their posts, and the flurry subsided and was followed by general relief that the inevitable solution had been reached at last. Bazaine was informed of it by a letter from the Emperor, promising to send him on the morrow "the documents necessary to put an end to the violent situation in which I find myself, and not only I, but all of Mexico," and conveying his testamentary instructions. "Among many others," Maximilian wrote, "there are three things which trouble me, and I wish to discharge whatever responsibility belongs to me: (1) that all courts-martial cease to intervene in political crimes; (2) that the law of October 3 be revoked in effect; (3) that for no reason whatsoever shall there be any political persecution, and that all kinds of hostilities cease." Nothing could have indicated more clearly his intention to abdicate. Nevertheless, the days passed and the promised documents were not forthcoming. Maximilian remained in Orizaba, and the days grew into weeks, and the weeks into months, of suspense and uncertainty. All his personal belongings and the valuables of the palace were packed and prepared for transportation to Veracruz, where an Austrian frigate was waiting to take the sea. The stricken sovereign had taken the penultimate step, but before he could take the last, other influences intervened.

The ministers followed him to Orizaba and pleaded with him not to abandon them. A deputation from the Conservative party offered him two millions on demand and men in abundance. He hesitated, he reconsidered, he doubted, he brooded. Napoleon himself now urged him to abdicate, and counsel from that quarter was galling. His mother wrote him, reminding him that he could not decently leave with the baggage of the French army and that it was his duty, however doubtful his prospects, to stand by his subjects and to perish in the ruins of his capital, if necessary. No less compelling was the advice of his former *chef-de-cabinet,* a Belgian busybody by the name of Eloin, who had returned to Europe some months before to reconnoiter the prospects there, and who urged him to defer his abdication until the departure of the French and to consult the country as soon as the pressure of foreign intervention was removed. If the country refused to support him, Eloin wrote, "then and then only, having accomplished his noble mission to the end, His Majesty would return to Europe with all the prestige that accompanied his departure and would be able to play the part to which he is fully entitled." On his way through Austria he had noticed the general discontent prevailing there since the defeat at Sadowa. "The Emperor is discouraged, the people are impatient and demanding his abdication, and the sympathies for Your Majesty are visibly spreading throughout the entire territory of the Empire. In Venice they are clamoring for their ex-Governor." Eloin knew very well that in knocking together the heads of three Emperors, the weakest was not the least wooden, and he touched the obstinate bitterness of the Family Pact at the right time. The French knew it also, for his letter, addressed to the Mexican Consul in New York, fell into the hands of the republican representative and was published in the American press. The advice of Eloin was plausible and well calculated to appeal to Maximilian at that moment. To outwit Napoleon, to abandon Mexico voluntarily, to return to Europe independently and not without compensation, to recover the rights he had forfeited in Austria—the combinations suggested by his scout were worth consideration at least, and thought, and afterthought, and waiting for the opportune moment to exchange his abdication for that of his brother. Finally, there was his present *chef-de-cabinet,* Father Fischer. The successor of Eloin was a German adventurer who had entered the Church in Mexico after failing to make his fortune in California. His private life was disreputable, but he won the confidence of Maximilian and succeeded in rendering the Church a service that amply redeemed his peccadilloes. He prepared the way for a transaction with the clergy, drafted a new Concordat, went to Rome to negotiate it, and, returning from that mission a month before Carlota failed in hers, arrived in time to reclaim the wavering sovereign. Intervening at the crucial moment, he offered him the means of emancipating himself from the French by a deal with his cloth. Money and men were promised. When the responsible minister was asked where the money was to be found, he replied that that was a state secret; but men were cheap. Miramon and Marquez had just been recalled from Europe, where they had been diplomatically banished by Maximilian— Miramon to study military tactics in Berlin, Marquez to inspect shrines in the Holy Land—and they placed their swords at his service. Father Miranda was past recall, having died two years before in Puebla, but his mission was accomplished by Father Fischer. The crows flocked back to roost, everyone found his perch, and the Empire reverted to its original bias. The trunk was rotten, the branches were topheavy, the roots decayed, but the props were stubborn. Smarting from the long deception of intervention, cheated of its promises and crushed by its penalties, the brood of the nightmare clung to the Crown with the tenacity of self-preservation and settled their scores with Napoleon by bribing Maximilian to pay his debt to them.

He temporized for six weeks. He was sick—not malingering, as the French supposed, but nursing a bad case of dysentery—and suffering both in body and mind. His indecision retarded his recovery and increased with his convalescence. He killed time laboriously, botanizing, herborizing, roaming the fields inquisitively with a net, collecting ideas from Creation, and fleeing misanthropy in communion with nature—innocent simulations of activity which were noticed impatiently by the French. "Not satisfied with a clear sky, Maximilian spends his time chasing butterflies," one observer reported; but he added that the sovereign was literally secluded by his Conservative keepers. The gatekeeper was Father Fischer, who guarded him sedulously against the influence of the French. Beset by conflicting influences and contradictory impulses, Maximilian made up his mind slowly every morning and unmade it again every night. But this "agony in the impossible," as Bazaine called it, could not continue indefinitely, and the captive finally compromised provisionally. The decisive influence, according to Father Fischer, was the hand that rocked the cradle. The letter of his mother, warning him that his return with the French was impossible, that his brother forbade it, that his position in Austria would be ridiculous, and that his honor as a Hapsburg bound him to Mexico, tipped the balance. Determined to abdicate, the Emperor capitulated, nevertheless, to the Conservatives—conditionally. The alliance was wrought with mental reservations on both sides. The Hapsburg was distrusted by his allies of the last hour as cordially as by his avowed enemies—a distinction, indeed, without a difference—and though they retained him as a buffer against the return of the Liberals, they suspected him as an adulterer who had deceived them royally and despised him as a failure whom they were forced to defend for their own preservation. Maximilian, on his side, accepted the alliance as a temporary and tentative expedient. His principles were also reduced to self-preservation, and it cost him nothing to close with the Conservatives; his backsliding was redeemed by the saving grace of insincerity. So, buoyed by his levity and his burden alike, he braved the raw breath of defeat and, under the combined influence of Father Fischer, the foreclosure of the French, the tenacity of the reaction, his foreign prospects, his honor, his isolation, the promptings of his mother, and the memory of Carlota, he obeyed the last injunction of her failing mind and resolved to resist as long as possible.

16

FACILIS *descensus* . . . and the descent continued all along the line. The succession sapped the subordinates with the sovereign, and in the process of disintegration Bazaine met disaster in turn, although on a smaller scale and a lower level—the plane reserved for a proxy who carried out his instructions consistently and performed his futile duty to the end. The mean end of intervention was his to drain and the dregs were discharged on his head. Harassed by critics of all kinds, covert, carping, covetous of a back against which to rub their several sores, he was surrounded from the sovereign down by a hierarchy of hecklers itching to make him the scapegoat of their common misadventure. Accused by Maximilian of deliberate shirking and subversive inactivity, by his brother officers of bluffing and sycophancy, by the army of rusting and routine, he was belittled by lieutenants homesick for leave, depreciated by generals jockeying for position, discredited and undermined high and low. He stood off the swarm with stolid taciturnity, but not with indifference—disgust sometimes lifted the closed lip. When he was accused of making his fortune out of the wreck and lining his pockets with the liquidation of the Jecker credits, he noticed the libel and stooped to deny it; but besides such gross charges, there were others, which reflected on his loyalty to Napoleon and which were not so easy to deny, because they were subtle, elusive, psychological, shadowy. They hung about him like a haze, impalpable and unproven, but they emanated from a conviction that was held unquestioningly by a great number of familiar observers; and their persistence finally decided Napoleon to send his personal aide-de-camp, General de Castelnau, to Mexico to investigate the situation and supervise the evacuation, with full powers to remove the Marshal if necessary.

General de Castelnau arrived in Mexico early in October, when Maximilian left the capital, and as it was his duty to induce him to abdicate, it was to this phase of his mission that he devoted his first attention. Although he passed Maximilian on his way to Orizaba and lodged in the same inn, he was not received by him; and on his side the envoy of Napoleon avoided a meeting for fear of aggravating the strained relations between the sovereign and his protectors and receiving a rebuff. He was further alarmed by rumors that Maximilian meant to make the French as much trouble as possible before he abdicated and that he proposed to issue a manifesto full of recriminations against his allies and to hand over his powers to Juarez at the last moment. He reported these rumors without vouching for them. "Has he really had such an intention and does he still have it? Did he conceive it himself or has someone inspired him? . . . I do not know, but I do know that everything may be feared from a man like the Emperor Maximilian when, reduced to extremities and with his heart ulcerated, he thinks that he has found an expedient likely both to save and avenge him," he wrote a fortnight after his arrival in the capital. As these fears were still bodiless, he was unable to combat them; but the abdication of Maximilian was imminently expected, and he devoted his attention to securing the succession in such a manner as to safeguard the dignity of Napoleon.

Among his best advisers was Lieutenant Colonel Brissonet, who gave him the benefit of his experience of Mexico. In anticipation of the crisis, Brissonet had already presented his suggestions to Paris. "I do not have the presumption to indicate a solution for so complicated and difficult a situation," he wrote, "but I see general opinion taking shape every day in favor of Juarez and I have no doubt that after our departure he will again be placed at the head of the government of this country. It is he, therefore, whom we must interest, in the last analysis, in our nationals and in the Mexicans who have rallied to the Empire. . . . Remembering the past, however, I know and feel that the French Government cannot enter into open relations with Juarez. Since he is the only one who can give us the guarantees that we must demand, we shall have to have recourse to him in the end; but instead of doing so directly, we can work in a roundabout way. Juarez is not the man who has been so decried in France; he is a Mexican and has many of the defects of his race undoubtedly, but few of his countrymen have so many qualities. He is disinterested, he is ready to efface himself if the interests of his country so demand, he is anything but bloodthirsty. . . . Because of the appreciable advantage in his eyes of hastening our departure, it might not be impossible to induce him, after the abdication of the Emperor Maximilian, to resign his power, his legal term having expired, and to present himself anew to the suffrages of his countrymen. A provisional government would then have to be set up, which we would recognize, and which would be headed by an influential man of the party of Juarez, having all his confidence and being almost avowed by him. We would deal with that government, and as soon as the treaty was concluded, the evacuation would follow. Once we were gone, Juarez would be re-elected, of course, but we would not have belied our past toward him and our guarantees would be assured."

This idea was adopted by Castelnau as the best of all face-saving schemes, and he recommended it to Napoleon with some added refinements of his own. "We have already abandoned the whole northern part of the country, and we shall soon hold only the two roads that connect the city of Mexico with Veracruz and with Queretaro," he explained. "All the rest of Mexico, that is to say, practically the whole of the country, is or will soon be in the hands of Juarez, whose power and prestige are growing daily with what we lose. I must add—forgive me, Sire, for insisting on these sad facts—that for the past six months the progress of the Juaristas and the failures of the Imperial troops have been continuous, so that the audacity of our enemies knows no bounds, and we can no longer dissimulate: Juarez will be the master and the sole master of the position as soon as Your Majesty withdraws. In these conditions can one expect Juarez, who has been fighting us for five years without despairing of success and who is on the eve of attaining it, to renounce the benefit of his laborious triumph and to consent to the conditions of an enemy whom he no longer fears? What am I saying? We cannot even count on his consent to present our conditions, although he alone can guarantee their execution: he would have to efface himself and sacrifice his own person, and a secondary personage of the Liberal party, whom we would choose and he would accept, would have to be his secret mandatory, his figurehead (since we refuse to pronounce his own name), and pledge himself to us by a treaty which Juarez would tacitly approve and which would bind him as well. And all this for what? To accelerate the victory of his party, a victory which cannot fail him, a victory which will be complete if he is willing to wait a few days longer; and he a man patient and persevering beyond all others, and who knows so well how to wait!" Although he appeared to be arguing against the plan, the General supported it: like a skillful advocate, he loaded the objections to give greater weight to the solution. "However omnipotent he has become, I think that Juarez will not resist our demands too obstinately," he continued, provided the influence of Washington were brought to bear on him to force his resignation. "Juarez is painted to me as a kind of antique Roman, animated by the purest and most ardent patriotism, and perfectly willing to sacrifice his personal ambition to his country. If this portrait is true, it may be less difficult than I fear to induce him to remain in the shadow when the Emperor Maximilian abdicates and to accept, without protest or struggle, if not the dictatorship of Marshal Bazaine, at least the provisional government which would follow immediately. It might not be so hard to lead him to this conduct if, as I said before, he is advised by the United States to adopt it for the public good, and this may be expected if the provisional government is given to a man who enjoys his full confidence and who is, so to speak, his second self, which I believe possible if we pledge ourselves to Juarez not to combat his candidacy to the Presidency and to accept his election frankly and cordially if he is chosen by the Mexican people, as seems inevitable." The influence of

Washington could be secured, he believed, because of the eagerness of Seward to speed the evacuation, and as Juarez, omnipotent though he was, was in no position to resist it, the General proceeded to select his successor. There were three possible candidates. The first was Ortega, whom he discarded in a few cursory words, although Napoleon favored him. "Disconsidered in the eyes of all parties because of his political ineptitude and his immorality, he is, apparently, a prostitute of low grade, a Lovelace of the sidewalks, a man lost in vices and lacking all the qualities required by the part proposed for him." The next was Manuel Ruiz, whom he eliminated also, although Bazaine favored him, because he was a deserter whom Juarez would never accept. The third was his own choice and Brissonet's. "He is the most notable man of the Liberal party after Juarez, he is the soul of his counsels, he is his other self whom I mentioned a moment ago, Señor Lerdo de Tejada. Endowed with uncommon intelligence, a fine character, and an energy that excludes neither gentle ways nor a flexible and conciliatory spirit, he is the only man whom Juarez might accept as the head of the provisional government, if we can draw the President of the Republic to our plans. Later we shall have to manage, if possible, to have the elections to the Presidency maintain Lerdo in power, to the exclusion of Juarez." Thus refined, the plan passed muster, and General de Castelnau endorsed it confidently.

These tributes to Juarez were the first and most important result of the mission to Mexico of Napoleon's emissary. To cheat Juarez of his personal triumph was the least difficulty of the scheme; the greatest was the irresolution of Maximilian. The plan was predicated on his abdication, and he continued to defer it indefinitely, to the intense irritation of Castelnau, the French Minister, the French colony, and the French army. The army, fatigued and humiliated by defeat, blamed its commanders for the failure of the expedition; the officers, even more discouraged than the soldiers, longed for a quick finish but a clean one for the French flag, and the hitch not only held up the evacuation but prevented an honorable settlement with the enemy for the protection of French nationals. The French colony, fearful of reprisals, was impatient for the abdication of the Emperor and exasperated by his procrastination. His indecision created an extremely trying situation; and Bazaine was accused of prolonging it deliberately for his own benefit. When Castelnau first heard this accusation, he refused to believe it, and though it came from the French Minister, he attributed it to the overcharged atmosphere which he found in Mexico. "Among foreigners and Mexicans alike, impatience and anxiety are at their climax," he explained to Napoleon. "Our nationals are agitated by an anxiety which Your Majesty must understand. Some have thought of naturalizing themselves Americans to claim the protection of the United States, if ours fails them. Others are liquidating their affairs to be able to leave with our troops. Countless conjectures and plans are made everywhere and in every sense: it is a general fever. M. Dano himself, usually so cool, suffered the contagion for a moment and, in an access which troubled his good judgment, he said to me a few days ago: 'It is impossible that the Marshal is not deceiving us. He is betraying us, he is conniving with Maximilian, without our knowledge and on his own account.' I must add that I had no difficulty in bringing him around to a saner opinion and his usual *sang-froid*. Your Majesty will see in this fact the measure of the agitation, the uneasiness, the fear and mistrust, that torment everyone here, even the best minds. Such a situation cannot be prolonged without great danger." The seed of suspicion was sown, however, and in his next report Castelnau confessed that he was less refractory to the repeated warnings of the French Minister. "Be on your guard," Dano insisted, "be on your guard against the Marshal. I am certain that he is trying to make all your efforts fail. . . . Any means will serve him to prolong his stay in Mexico. He is retained here by many private interests, and I am convinced that he would console himself for a military disaster if that disaster were to prevent the departure of the army at the end of this winter."

Suspicion ripened with familiarity with it, and a number of small incidents gradually confirmed the misgivings of Castelnau. By the end of December he was morally certain of the duplicity of the Marshal, and though he lacked material, palpable, irrefutable proof, he expected to obtain it soon. "I know," he wrote to Napoleon, "without the least possibility of doubt, that Marshal Bazaine is betraying the interests of Your Majesty to serve his own, which bind him to Mexico, and now that I know it, my constant concern is to foil his underground maneuvers and remove the obstacles which they create for me. I hope to do so without violence, without noise, without scandal. I even hope and wish to do so without breaking with the Marshal. . . . Besides, what matters is not to unmask him but to paralyze his ill will and oblige him to serve the interests which Your Majesty has entrusted to him in his public and ostensible acts. In this respect I have not a single complaint to formulate against him: I shall see to it that his secret acts are no longer in contradiction to his official conduct. Otherwise, and if I catch him in flagrant crime of treason, I shall make use of that advantage to control him so completely that I shall have nothing more to fear from him, and I hope not to be forced to employ the eventual powers which Your Majesty has given me to break his resistance."

Familiarity with the Marshal gave him the psychological proof which he needed to pronounce the word treason. Studying the suspect closely, and remembering that Bazaine had served for many years in Africa, he traced his behavior to the habits of craft which he had acquired from the natives. "Marshal Bazaine has natural talent," he wrote. "He is of an equable and genial character. He exercises over those who surround him a certain attraction by his agreeable manners and a good nature by which one is readily taken in, but when one knows him a little better, one notices that he has no perseverance in his ideas and no frankness. The Emperor Maximilian says of him repeatedly that he says yes and does no. He has never been known to prepare a plan of operations and follow it. He tries to get out of his straits day by day, never attacking a difficulty squarely but contenting himself with circumventing it or deferring the solution. From his passage through the Arabian offices he has preserved a habit of dissimulation, of intrigue, of deceit, and thinks that he has obtained a great advantage when he succeeds in deceiving a great many people about the same thing at the same time." Improvisation, inconsistency, evasion—these habits would not have been sinister had Bazaine not been a slave to one other, which contradicted and confirmed them: he was ruined, paradoxically, by his fidelity. His professional failings would have passed unnoticed and he would have been the most dependable of soldiers, had he been a bachelor; but the root of his double dealing was that he was not single. "His marriage is the result of a conspiracy between the Empress Carlota, Señora Almonte, and Madame de Montholon," the General added. "That marriage is the cause of everything."

This was one explanation of his conduct, but not the best, though it presented some excuse for it. During his service in Africa Bazaine had saved a young girl from a brothel, educated her in a convent, made her his wife, and was deceived by her during his service in Mexico. She committed suicide in Paris to prevent a scandal, but the gossip was concealed from him, and, the most faithful of husbands himself, he was so profoundly affected by her death that only a dogged sense of duty prevented him from resigning his command and returning to France. Marriage was a habit with him, however, and several months later he began to court a young Mexican girl of good family. The match was encouraged by Maximilian and Carlota as a means of attaching him to Mexico, and when the wedding took place in June 1865 they bestowed the palace which he occupied on his bride as a marriage settlement, with the provision that it was to revert to the nation if for any reason the Marshal and his bride left Mexico. They succeeded only too well, and the second marriage of the Marshal, if not the cause of everything, was one of the many interests which retained him in Mexico. His bride not only attached him to her native land, she put him to sleep. The slackening of his energies was noticed and deplored; his intelligence was extinguished, his physical and moral activity declined, he fattened, and his eyes, sunk in flesh like a pair of peering dimples, gave him the look, as someone said, of a man "who is always tired and trying to see." After a year of marriage his domestic life became a matter of public concern. "The Marshal suffers without suspecting it the absolute influence of his wife, who is or seems to be very astute," wrote one observer. "She would be delighted to remain for some time as Madame Dictator." Socially ambitious and surer of herself in Mexico than in France, for her social education left something to be desired, she was said to dictate the inactivity of the Marshal and the indecision of Maximilian in order to put off as long as possible the dreaded day of departure for Paris. She was believed to be beguiling the doting old man with dreams of succeeding Maximilian as dictator, president, viceroy, or even as emperor. Fantastic as these notions were, they found credit because the infatuation of the Marshal was as notorious as the ambition of his wife and her family. Nothing was too extravagant to be believed, and the gossip was repeated in Paris. The mildest of these insinuations was the charge that the Marshal was stalling in order to dispose of his palace, which, although it reverted to the nation by the terms of the marriage settlement, he was trying to sell and for which there were no bidders. Such were the unfortunate results of a marriage upon which the fate of Empire depended in 1865 and with which it was even more deeply involved in 1866. Bazaine was unreliable because he was twain. He was Achille François Bazaine, and he was Pepita de la Peña; and in the opinion of the army the temporizing of the Marshal and the procrastination of Maximilian were due to a bad case of marital fidelity.

That there was a connection between the one and the other there was no doubt. On December 1 Maximilian announced that he had reconsidered his decision to abdicate and had determined to retain the Crown until a Congress could be called to decide the destinies of the nation. The announcement created consternation in the capital, and when the members of the Council which he called in Orizaba, themselves deeply divided, returned to the city, they were so impressed by the general dismay that several of them proposed to reconsider. At this moment Castelnau obtained the material proof which he needed to substantiate the duplicity of the Marshal. Three reliable witnesses—the aide-de-camp of Maximilian, a member of his Council, and Archbishop Labastida—testified in writing that Bazaine had not only encouraged Maximilian to adopt this decision, but that he promised him that the troops would remain in Mexico until the end of the year 1867. Highly incensed by these revelations, Castelnau was more embarrassed by them, nevertheless, than Bazaine. "The Marshal knows as well as I do that the abdication of the Emperor Maximilian is our only spar of salvation in the wreck that threatens us," he wrote to Napoleon. "Like us and with us, he expressed bitterly and impatiently the sentiments which the delays and vacillations of the Emperor caused him; he longed for his abdication, and when the decision of Maximilian to preserve the Crown and return to the city of Mexico was announced, he exclaimed in our presence, 'Well, they will hang him!'"

But the information was dynamite; he dared not use it. What was he to do? To dismiss Bazaine and hand over the command to Douay?

The scandal appalled him, and after due consideration he decided to deal with the delinquent discreetly. He went to see him, intending to confront him with the evidence and to steer him straight with the threat of exposure; but he found it difficult to corner the Marshal. "At my first remarks, and before I supported them with the evidence which I had in hand, he broke out in denials that would have hoodwinked me had I been less well informed. And when I put him between the sword and the wall he tried to escape my conclusions with tortuous justifications, miserable subtleties, and protests that pained me profoundly. I tried, nevertheless, to convince him of the futility of his excuses, and, without resorting to useless threats, I left him a prey to feverish emotion and to reflections which will inspire him no doubt with salutary resolutions. Be that as it may, I shall redouble my vigilance, and if, after having exhausted all means of conciliation, I have no possible recourse but rigorous measures, I shall not hesitate to use them." Those were the words of a man defeated by his own discretion and apologizing for it.

One step, however, Castelnau took to make the Marshal toe the line. He forced him to draw up and sign, with himself and the French Minister, a petition to Maximilian to reconsider his decision and to spare himself, his allies, and his subjects the penalties of a futile and fatal resistance by his prompt abdication. With this document Castelnau and Dano went out to meet Maximilian, who was returning by slow stages to the capital and who received them at a *hacienda* near Puebla. He was all amiability and he agreed with all their arguments, but having made his decision public, he was obliged to abide by it. Personally, he said, he had no desire to retain power and proposed to do so only until a Congress could be called—an expedient that Napoleon himself had suggested to him—and he had no illusions as to the verdict; the election of Juarez was bound to follow, and that was, after all, the best solution for a people to whom monarchical institutions were profoundly antipathetic, and he would be the first to congratulate the elect of the people and to wish him a happier fate than his own; after which, as a simple Mexican citizen, with his heart unburdened and his head high, he would take the road to Veracruz and Europe. Castelnau and Dano pointed out that when Napoleon had suggested the calling of a Congress, that expedient was still feasible, but that it was no longer practicable: the Conservatives would refuse to take part in a Congress in which they would be outnumbered, and the Liberals to countenance any discussion of their triumph; abdication was the only real solution, and they presented their petition. He glanced at it nonchalantly and handed them a telegram that he drew from his desk. "Here is something fresher," he said to Dano. "Read it." It was a message from Bazaine, assuring him that the Empire was still feasible and promising to do everything in his power to sustain it. "As we bent our heads before this monument of duplicity," Castelnau wrote, "the Emperor said, after enjoying our confusion for a moment, 'You do not seem to be accustomed yet to the way in which the Marshal works. As for me, I have been used to it for a long time, and I have long known what confidence to place in him. I deplore his lack of frankness, of which I, more than anyone, have been a victim. But today, without trusting him any longer, I use him as an instrument to execute my own designs. The Marshal has been ruined by his alliance and the influence which he has allowed his wife and her family to gain over him. He seeks to deceive everyone and imagines that he is deceiving everyone, when no one is any longer his dupe.' "

After this fresh about-face by Bazaine, Dano advised Castelnau to dismiss him at once, but the General preferred to follow the advice of an officer whom he was in the habit of consulting and who pointed out that as his command had only a few more months to run, it was best to muffle the conduct of the Marshal until he returned to France. But it was impossible to muffle the scandal. "All this is now in the public domain," General Douay wrote to his brother, "and you can have no idea of the discredit into which the Marshal has fallen. The things that are said aloud in the Expeditionary Corps are enough to make your hair stand on end. It is no longer the usual *cancans* and tittle-tattle, but the greatest accusations which come from the most official and authorized lips. One must go back to Cardinal Dubois to find such a scoundrel, abusing of his trust to betray his country and his master. He must have completely lost all moral sense to have risked retracting himself in so solemn an engagement as the negotiation of Dano and Castelnau. After those gentlemen left Mexico City, it seems that there were domestic scenes in the Palace of Buenavista. The whole tribe of the Peñas attacked him. The young Maréchale, who is with child, made the big fountains and the great levers play, and they wrung the famous retraction which was sent to Maximilian from the wretched numbskull. And this is how the interests of the State and of our country are sacrificed to the events of the bedroom!"

The bitterest enemy of Bazaine, Douay was nevertheless indulgent, or blind, in blaming his behavior on his bedfellow. With a little more perspicacity and a little less prejudice, he might have realized that the derelictions of the Marshal were due to more sinister causes than his uxoriousness. They were dictated by his duty. Napoleon had charged him to wind up the Mexican question before it involved him in insoluble difficulties, as best he could and as quickly as possible, and Bazaine, reading between the lines of that injunction the inadmissible irresponsibility of his master, used and abused of his license because he was baffled himself by the problem. Though he prided himself on possessing the patience of an Arab, his patience was worn out by the contradictory orders and shifting counsels which he received from Paris, and he obeyed them as best he could by daily makeshifts, improvisation, temporizing, and procrastination; and when the impatience of Paris became pressing, he followed the line of least resistance and chose the easy way out. Fatigued and irritated by the vacillations and tergiversations of Maximilian, he humored him, but what was mere indecision in the sovereign became criminal complicity in the Commander-in-Chief, and by giving Maximilian his head at the risk of breaking his neck, Bazaine laid himself open to the charge of deliberately misleading him and abetting his downfall. The influence of his wife coincided with the counsels of expediency, but while his marriage may have been responsible for his minor failings, the real cause of his ambiguous conduct was his fidelity to Napoleon. Douay, like everyone else, preferred to believe that it was Napoleon who had been victimized. "The Emperor must have been badly deceived about the situation," he wrote, "and the Marshal who sees it turning to his confusion continues with imperturbable audacity to assert that he has merely executed the orders of the Emperor; and declining all responsibility, he casts on our sovereign the weight and odium of all the measures which have made our expedition fail." Bazaine collected his papers, in fact, to prove that all the faults imputed to him had been properly authorized; and so they were; but he suffered the penalty, nonetheless, of not being Napoleon.

Whatever the reasons, the results were disastrous. The reputation which he had laboriously built up was ruined. "The Commander of the Expeditionary Force will leave much of his prestige here," wrote Castelnau in the most damning of his findings, "and I have not found a single corps or service commander who does not say that hereafter he will do everything possible not to be under his orders." His disgrace was all the more ignominious for being muffled, and the Marshal's baton barely served him to beat an orderly retreat and to mark time during the dissonances of the last hundred days. Shadowed and controlled by Castelnau, he was obliged to walk a straight and narrow path with a gun at his back. Paroled by his keeper and placed on his good behavior, he was given an opportunity to redeem himself when Maximilian returned to the capital. In a final conscientious effort to save him, Castelnau sent the Marshal to plead for his abdication, and Bazaine expounded the dangers of his situation frankly but without effect. Maximilian was shaken; he admitted that his situation was desperate; he recognized the weakness of the Conservative party; he realized that a Congress could not be called; he knew that he was being betrayed by the very men who induced him to remain; but he could not run away —yet. The obstinate folly of keeping up appearances to the bitter end baffled Castelnau, and his irritation with the Marshal turned against Maximilian. He wrote his epitaph in a few exasperated lines: "He is a Utopist who remains incessantly shut up within himself, taking no part in the life of his people, whom he does not know, having no relations with the men who might enlighten him, and spending his life in drawing up decrees which have no effect and which are not even published by the prefects charged with enforcing them. He is accused of frivolity and absolute lack of frankness. He is charmed whenever he has a chance to be disagreeable to us or to uncover us in the eyes of his own set. Never ask him to do anything because it might please France or the Emperor; that is enough to make him do the contrary. If anyone hates us more than he, it is the Empress, who once before dissuaded him from abdicating when he wanted to do so, with atrocious scenes." Once before! By a singular lapse of memory, Castelnau referred to Carlota as if she still belonged to the land of the living; but she was entitled to her place in the epitaph. The mindless woman in Miramar, the barren wife who had brought forth nothing but mania, was avenged by the end of the adventure.

But for the necessity of protecting the French colony, Castelnau would gladly have abandoned the German dreamer, as Bazaine called him, to his doom. In the beginning of January he received the reply of Napoleon to his proposal to treat with the Liberals, minus Juarez. Napoleon accepted it promptly. "It is important to settle the question as quickly as possible," he wrote, "but I do not wish to treat with Juarez at any price, since any understanding with him would look too much like a defeat. If later the force of things brings him to power, that is a matter of complete indifference to me, but we cannot treat with him today." He directed Castelnau, accordingly, to secure the abdication of Maximilian immediately, to obtain the necessary guarantees from a provisional government headed by Lerdo de Tejada or anybody else, and to embark the troops by the end of February or the beginning of March at the latest. The only part of these instructions which could be carried out was the last. The obstinacy of Maximilian created an inextricable imbroglio, which could only be cut, and it was necessary to use the knife. In a supreme attempt to save him in spite of himself, Bazaine and Castelnau decided on a drastic operation: all the cannon, munitions, and military stocks which the Army could not carry off were destroyed to deprive the Conservatives of the means of prolonging a suicidal resistance. Besides this measure of merciful surgery, Bazaine planned to hand over the city before his departure to one of the republican commanders who were waiting to attack it, on his guarantee to maintain order and protect the inhabitants, and he so informed Maximilian, who made no objections. When he discussed the plan with Castelnau, Castelnau was taken aback by it. And what about Miramon? he asked. Bazaine gave him a week to be defeated, his men were already deserting, and they would melt away as soon as they met the enemy. He also proposed to carry off Marquez and Maximilian by force, if they made any difficulties. Without going so far, Castelnau approved the plan and the choice of Porfirio Diaz as the commander to occupy the city. "Diaz, the friend and compatriot of Juarez, the most distinguished general and powerful leader of his party and a man of order, honorable and energetic, would be, in fact, the man best fitted for this role, if he wants to accept it," he wrote to Napoleon. "This is the opinion of the Marshal, and mine, and of everyone else. The great influence of Diaz over the republicans and over Juarez would allow us to treat with him more surely than with anyone else to secure through him the conditions indispensable for our dignity and desirable for our financial interests. This, then, is the plan which I shall endeavor to follow, as best I can." He could do no better, after all, than Bazaine. But the last makeshift fell through, like all the others. The American Consul established contact with Diaz and offered, on behalf of Bazaine, to put him in possession of the capital, provided he agreed to supplant Juarez; but Diaz refused to treat with the enemy, and the Mexican question drifted impotently to its fatal conclusion.

On February 5, 1867, the last of the French army left the capital, filing through the streets with drums beating and banners flying. A mute multitude watched them depart without demonstrations of any kind, and behind the drawn shutters of his palace Maximilian also watched them until the muffled shuffle died away; then he turned to his secretary and said that at last he was free. At Orizaba Bazaine paused, halted by news that Miramon had been defeated in the north, and sent word to Dano that he could still extend a helping hand to the Emperor and offer him accommodations on the transports. But there was no reply; Maximilian had already left for the front, and the march continued to the sea. The movement was completed with perfect punctuality and discipline, although there were some small hitches: the Maréchale, pregnant and balky, repeatedly deferred her departure, and there was some doubt whether the evacuation would be terminated on schedule, but the Marshal, himself irritated by his domestic difficulties, overcame them with a success that restored his reputation as a soldier. "Despite his mistakes," wrote one of his critics, "the Marshal is still usable, and in the best of conditions. At the first war, if the Emperor makes his wife remain in France, you will again find the great soldier."

A month was spent in loading the troops on the transports, and on March 12 Bazaine boarded the last one, the fourth commander to be worn out by Mexico. Before sailing, he issued a proclamation congratulating the troops on their professional conduct and the glory they had won in Mexico. Such was not the general sentiment in the army. General Douay, dogging his heels to the end, congratulated himself on having escaped the supreme command. "The Mexican affair will be a veritable catastrophe," he wrote to his brother. "I have foreseen it, as you know, for a long time. The government will do well to leave it, if possible, in the shadow and in silence. Marshal Bazaine may escape, for this reason, the punishment which he deserves for his culpable intrigues; but he will not escape the infamy to which he is vowed by all the decent people in the army. . . . Besides, matters have come to such a point that Castelnau will have to reveal all his acts. Yes, my dear friend, seeing the tragic end of the Commander-in-Chief, how wise I was when I said that I might not be able to assume the succession of Marshal Bazaine! I knew the extent of the evil and I saw no remedy for it but a radical amputation. What authority would I have had to secure it? . . . Nothing less than the arrival of a Grand Inquisitor was needed to clear up the situation." The subsequent record of Marshal Bazaine was the logical result of giving a dog a bad name.

One of the last to leave was Captain, or rather Colonel, Loizillon. He had won his stripes and advanced his career, but his promotion mattered little to him in 1867. He was heartsick. Since he had written his famous diatribe exposing Forey and Saligny, which Bazaine attributed to Douay, Pierre Loizillon had developed, and on the eve of his departure he wrote a letter to his parents in France in which he raised his eyes from the personalities through which the expedition miscarried to the purposes and results of the expedition itself. "In beginning this war, there is no doubt that the Emperor had a great idea: to build a barrier against the invasion of the United States, and to establish a strong government in Mexico which would depend upon us politically and economically and of which we would have claimed as a guarantee for our credits the occupation of Tehuantepec. We would have profited by that opportunity to cut the Isthmus, as we have cut the Isthmus of Suez; we would have spread little by little, like a drop of oil, absorbing Guatemala and reaching Panama without being noticed and confronting our rivals with a *fait accompli.* We would then have had the finest colony in the world, since the trade of India and China is carried by that route and the English would have lost the profit and influence which we would have gained. Unfortunately the South was crushed when we least expected it, and, on the other hand, we placed an emperor here contrary to the tendencies and wishes of the country, which certainly did not want a German." Such mistakes could not be made with impunity. Napoleon had been blinded by looking too long on the unsetting sun of the British dominions; and by overreaching himself he had opened the eyes of France to the *folie des grandeurs.* The army had paid by a humiliating defeat for his visionary ambition, and the Colonel spoke for colonel and private alike when he said that no one was proud of the part they had been made to play in Mexico. They were burning for revenge against a real enemy. "We are impatient to be in a squarer position, facing the Prussians, for example"—and he owed them that satisfaction, but would they find it? Now was the time for Napoleon to tear up the treaties of 1815, to take his historic *revanche,* and to redeem his mistakes in Mexico on the Rhine. But would he learn? Or would he miss once more the ripe moment for his ruling idea? Of one thing, however, Pierre Loizillon was sure. "Let the Emperor beware," he concluded. "He has deceived everyone, he will deceive no one any longer, and he may well be deceived in turn; if he lets time pass, he will risk not only having no ally, but raising a coalition of all the Powers against us." Such was the result of the coalition of 1861 and the fatal exposure of the weakness of France, and with that valedictory he turned his back on Mexico. His sentiments were shared by many of the 1100 officers, 22,234 soldiers, 4500 Austrians, and 800 Belgians who boarded the transports with some thousands of leagues of Mexico on the soles of their feet and the sweat of homecoming on their brows. Like his shipmates, Loizillon was homesick; but among them there was one other who was also heartsick; and no one was surprised when, on their arrival in Toulon, no military honors were rendered to Marshal Bazaine.

17

THE long, slow, time-laden chronicle of intervention was formally closed by the sailing of the French army, but it was not finished. Something essential was lacking to close the account. Desire had sickened of a surfeit of failure, despair had stiffened into an ailing and tireless tale, but the lame and impotent conclusion of so ambitious a venture could not be tame, and the liquidation was brief, swift, and purging.

The wreck left the succession not only unsettled and disputed between Maximilian and Juarez, but claimed by lesser contenders as well. Besides the principals there were secondary candidates for the imminent vacancy—interlopers who were sucked into the vortex, spinning in the wreck, and who had to be eliminated before the protagonists could face each other, the succession be cleared, and the issue resolved. And in the last six months of 1866 two of them challenged the inevitable solution.

In the vast dissolution of Empire, no element of the human comedy was lacking, and the sediment of miscellaneous tragedy contained a litter of crude farce. One of the pretenders was Santa Anna. Since his banishment in 1855 he had been living on the island of St. Thomas, biding his time for another return. Rallying to the Empire, he landed at Veracruz and was expelled by Bazaine; shipped back to his Virgin Island, he reverted to the Republic and offered his sword to his countrymen in periodic proclamations; time passed, but he grew no older. The world went its way without him; the perennial weathervane waited indefatigably for a passing wind to flap his banner, but there were no bidders until, in the summer of 1865, Mr. Seward paid him a visit. What happened was unimportant. Seward bade him good-day and good-by and went his way; but what matters in human affairs is not so much what actually occurs as what men think has happened to them—the history of their progress is nothing else—and what happened in the mind of Santa Anna was important to him. Though the talk turned on every topic but politics, he believed that it had an ulterior purpose, and here and there, in Mexico and elsewhere, a story went the rounds that the visit of the American Secretary of State to St. Thomas was connected with the succession. Seward, who was cruising in the Caribbean, had no object but to visit one of its curiosities, but he was not unwilling to foster the impression that it was a political call, since what happened in the minds of the French was important to him at that time. At all events, he did nothing to contradict it, and the assumption that Seward was considering Santa Anna as a possible substitute for Juarez gained ground. Acting on it, Santa Anna sent an agent to Washington to sound his chances, but the reply was discouraging—he was advised to join Juarez. Galling as the suggestion was, he swallowed it and offered to take service under his old antagonist, but he reckoned without his host. The best service which Santa Anna could render his country, Juarez wrote to Romero, was to live far from it, and it was the only service he would accept. Nevertheless, Santa Anna went to market. In the summer of 1866 he started for Washington. On his arrival in New York he was interviewed by the reporters, who remembered very well who he was and who found him remarkably hale and hearty for his age. He was too well preserved to notice anything else and he went no farther. Settling on Staten Island, he sent an agent to Washington to lodge a bid for recognition and an offer to sell another strip of Mexican territory to secure it. Both bids were ignored; but his exertions were not wholly wasted: they completed his record. The purposes which men serve are not always those which they know, and those which they serve unwittingly are sometimes the best. Before abandoning Staten Island for St. Thomas, he issued a manifesto to his countrymen in which he insisted that, whether they liked it or not, he was the history of Mexico—which was true; but it was also true that he was an anachronism. Though he had grown no older, his compatriots had long since reached the age of reason, and the resurgence of that superannuated opportunist marked the end of a period and served a purpose, pointing the course of the times like a buoy amid the racing currents and the progress actually made. Some things were henceforth impossible, and Santa Anna was one of them.

Santa Anna was, as Juarez said, a political cadaver which nothing could resuscitate, and he eliminated himself. What happened to him was the natural result of an empty body spinning in the vortex and drawn by the force of gravity toward the vacancy that attracted it, and he spun himself out on the outer rim; but another pretender reached the inner circle and narrowly missed the center itself. The antics of Santa Anna were crude farce; the activities of Gonzalez Ortega were a tragic comedy.

In the autumn of 1866 Ortega decided to assert his claims to the Presidency. As long as he had confined himself to manifestoes and protests, Juarez had ignored him. After the first of these attacks he wrote to his son-in-law, "I shall decide what reply to make, a decorous reply, of course, for it is repugnant to the dignity of a government to descend to the forbidden ground on which the silly criminal Gonzalez Ortega basks. Fortunately, he addresses himself to the Mexican people, to whom he and I are equally well known, and hence the government pursues its course imperturbably, being obeyed and respected without question by the authorities and the people." But when, in October, Ortega finally decided to brave the common sense of his compatriots and cross the frontier, he commanded serious attention. The American authorities arrested him before he reached the border and imprisoned him with six of his followers—long enough to prevent him from joining his partisans in Matamoros, which was held by a Republican Colonel who had declared for him and who was besieged by a force loyal to Juarez. American intervention went further. On the orders of General Sheridan, American troops crossed the river, occupied Matamoros, hoisted the Stars and Stripes, and summoned the commander to capitulate; the commander preferred to surrender to his own countrymen, and the American troops were withdrawn, leaving the Federal forces in control of the town. Both Mexican commanders protested against American trespassing, but the apparent collusion was exploited by Ortega in his protests, and he succeeded at least in causing a highly compromising international incident. Henceforth it was impossible to regard him as a mere nuisance, and when he was released and allowed to enter Mexico, he was arrested by his own government and held for trial.

Blandly denying the charge of desertion on which he was indicted, Ortega continued to insist on his right to the Presidency and to regard himself as a martyr to Constitutional principles and a victim of political persecution. If his claims were weak in 1865, they were worse in 1866, when, after he had waited a year to advance them, the country had accepted and sanctioned the decision adopted by Juarez; but Gonzalez Ortega had a weak head for politics. In prison he was reduced to his own mental orbit, and the confinement was closer than his cell, for the range was narrow and there was no possible escape from it; and with the infatuation of perfect good faith he fancied that what had happened to him was the work of a man named—Juarez.

If the comedy lies in the lures of the ego and belongs in a world of its own making, the self-deception of Ortega offered a fair example of its origin, for he was far removed from reality; but at that point comedy and tragedy are closely akin. The substance is the same, and in his case the issue was equally apt for either. Comedy, it has also been said, lies in the incongruity of the vital and the automatic, the conflict of the free play of initiative and the rut of inflexible habit; and by insisting on the automatic application of the Constitution, regardless of conditions, common sense, or popular consent, to gratify his famished ambition at all costs, Ortega exposed his mental limitations with comic solemnity and deserved well of the Muse. His bid for power came to nothing, but it begot serious consequences both for himself and Juarez; and only the common sense of their countrymen saved the situation from turning to tragedy.

The tragicomedian eliminated himself, but not by his own levity alone. His specific gravity was sufficient to lend some weight to his claims and to require the application of force to reduce him to reason. The current carried him close to the center before it swept him back to the circumference of the succession; and it was only after prolonged incarceration and incontrovertible familiarity with the world and himself that he resigned himself finally to the fate of an eccentric pretender.

The center was, as it had always been, Juarez. And the center was quiet. About him the vortex revolved in voracious momentum; within him it accumulated power, security, self-possession. Unmoved himself and unmoving, he awaited the inevitable solution of a situation in which everything worked for him and everything converged toward him. He was the political pivot, the moral pole, the magnetic center about which the extraneous world swung, and he knew it. A week before his birthday in 1866 he wrote to his wife: "I am the same as usual. Only one serious sickness is attacking me, and that is an evil without cure, the sixty years which I shall reach in eight days; but you must not believe that I am crushed or intimidated by that ailment. I see the years pass and I go my way. . . ." And if time could not touch him, what else could? "So, too, I see the protests of Ortega and little uncle Ruiz. All that they have accomplished so far is to make themselves ridiculous. The people keep on doing their work as I do and pay no heed to such heroes." He had grown stout, as if his very flesh were fed, as his spirit was, with the life of the losers. His spirit was charged with it. The mind which had thriven on adversity for so many lean years expanded when he looked forward to the end of his labors. "Great has been the calamity that has weighed on us in these last years," he wrote, "but we must console ourselves with the future, for me practically certain and close, when after this war the American Republics (I do not mean Washington, but Mexico at least) will be absolutely free of the triple yoke of a Religion of State, privileged classes, and onerous treaties with European powers. The recognition of the latter by the Emperor Maximilian has broken the pacts that reduced us to pupilage." He had lived long enough, and striven long enough, to see that day, and it could almost be said that intervention had proved a blessing in disguise. His enemies had served him well and Mexico stood to gain by the great conspiracy against it.

When he heard the first rumors of war abroad, he surveyed the broad pastures which the New World would offer to the Old, when the deluge was drained off. "I hope that the European war is a reality by now. It will co-operate in the prosperity of Mexico, which, within two years at most, will be in a position to give peace and guarantees of security to the sages, the wealthy, and the artisans who will be forced to flee the ravages of war and seek asylum where they can find peace and freedom." And when the rumors were confirmed, his heart leapt with fierce satisfaction. "You must agree with me that Bismarck is a mighty fellow, since he has succeeded in alarming and arousing the other wolves of Europe. God give him strength to persevere, so that the fire may not be extinguished but devour the very last oppressor in that part of the world!" Among the benefits of intervention, not the least were the new ties with the United States, which broke the bonds of the past and coupled the two countries in common interest. The influence of Washington had been brought to bear on the struggle with belated but powerful effect. Seward had assisted him parsimoniously but successfully, refusing to recognize any other government or pretender, forcing the evacuation of the French by a diplomatic pressure that increased steadily as Napoleon weakened, nudging his delays, nipping his repairs, frowning on the formation of a Foreign Legion, checking the sending of Austrian reinforcements by a peremptory note to Vienna, and reducing the American Emperor to his own resources; and it was due in no small measure to his management, acting as umpire and timekeeper, that the field was cleared for the final event and the principals were free to meet face to face for the crowning engagement.

With the ebb of evacuation the reoccupation of the precincts of the Empire proceeded rapidly. At the end of December the President arrived in Durango, and his family prepared to join him, delayed only by doubt of the best route, by land or sea. "The only advantage for me of going by way of Veracruz," his wife wrote him, "is that I would bring the bodies of our dead sons myself, which I could not do if I go by Monterrey."

The new year dawned brilliantly in Durango. "A magnificent reception was given the government," Juarez wrote on the first day of the year of fulfillment, "and this is natural, since the incoming Viceroy is not the same as the outgoing, as the saying goes." His reception was royal all along the way as he advanced toward the interior. In Zacatecas, where he arrived in the last days of January, he was welcomed with fireworks, balls, and festivities, and presented by public subscription with a walking stick worth two thousand pesos in money and a great deal more sentimentally; in his hands it was the rough equivalent of an Imperial scepter or a Marshal's baton, and he valued it as such. Four days after his arrival the town was attacked by Miramon, who fought his way in and forced the garrison to abandon it. Weary of official prudence and vicarious defense, the President remained with the troops until the last moment, when, breaking another custom, he abandoned his carriage and mounted horseback. To this hasty departure from his usual habit he owed his escape from capture. Miramon, seeing the presidential carriage racing down the road to Fresnillo, sent his cavalry in pursuit and discovered too late that the horsemen disappearing down the road to Jerez were Juarez and his ministers. The approach of Republican reinforcements forced him to abandon the town in turn, and a week later Juarez returned. The town had been sacked and his personal effects were lost, but an essential object was saved: he recovered the stick.

Writing to his family, he apologized for his temerity. "Though many persons thought that the government should withdraw from the city, and there were powerful reasons for doing so, I did not think it proper to follow their opinion and decided to share the fate of the troops. The well-nigh frantic enthusiasm with which these people received me, and the tremendous idea that my previous retreat might discourage the troops and the people strengthened me in my resolution. In short, my opinion was that if the town were lost, that misfortune should be the cause and not the effect of the retreat of the government. . . . At the moment that I left on the 27th Salome took my baggage to a house next to the Palace, which was subsequently searched by Joaquin Miramon and other bailiffs. Only my valise was saved and the stick that these people had just given me." The essential object was secured and the stick overruled all objections. His family regarded his conduct as a piece of foolhardy bravado, and he was obliged to revert to it a few weeks later. "I have received your sermon for what seemed to be a foolish fling in Zacatecas on the 27th of January. There are circumstances in life when one must risk everything if one wishes to go on living, physically and morally, and I was in those circumstances on the 27th. I came through safely and I am satisfied with what I did." It was too late to scold him, he was sixty, and he was tired of safety, tired of the necessary but inglorious role of a civilian directing the battle behind the lines; morally he could not go on living without having his fling before the end of the war. Physically he missed disaster by a narrow margin. Among the trophies taken from the enemy was an order signed by Maximilian a few weeks before, directing Miramon, if Juarez and his ministers were captured, to try and sentence them by court-marital, but to refer the sentence to him before executing it. A fatal ambiguity hung over that order and sealed the doom of its author. But whether Maximilian meant to ratify or reprieve, there was no doubt that Juarez would have been at his mercy, and it was that sovereign discretion which made the document damning: grace or the grave would have been equally disastrous to the President then. Of the forfeit which he barely escaped Juarez made no mention, however, to his family.

The reoccupation of Mexico was uncontested until the President reached Zacatecas. There the reconquest began. Retreating from the town, Miramon was attacked and routed by the advancing Republican forces at San Joaquin and fell back on Queretaro, where Maximilian, with Marquez and Mejia and some ten thousand troops, had established the front to protect the capital. Marquez referred sarcastically, at a public dinner, to his defeat; and morally Miramon was defeated in fact. After the battle of San Joaquin he wrote that the Republican forces were irresistible because they were defending the national cause, and recognized that, with that incentive, they were bound to succeed. Conviction there was none in the Imperial camp: it was a bare fight for survival. Men and money were raised by the usual methods—the one by forced levies, the other by forced loans. The lot of the ruined was run off by rote in random raids on the rich and the poor, and with the remains of such forces, mustered by extortion and abduction, Maximilian took the field as soon as the French left the capital. Abandoned to himself, he became consistent and accepted a situation which he knew to be untenable, because it was untenable; for of all the motives which prompted him to persist the most binding, and the one which fastened them all in a noose that nothing could slip, was the saving grace of redeeming his errors by expiating them honorably. He was in honor bound to tempt Providence, and by his honor he was wound, knowingly and without blindfold, in the thin web of illusions which his partisans wove about him for their own salvation. Divesting himself of the original sin of the invader, and reduced to his native resources, he set forth to meet Juarez on the same footing and naturalized himself finally for the last quarter of an hour in Queretaro.

Invested by the Republican forces under General Escobedo, Queretaro held out for almost a hundred days, from February 19 to May 15. Outnumbered in the open, Maximilian was blocked within the walls by his lieutenants. Trusting to his talents and the truth of the adage that a town besieged is a town taken, Miramon favored an attack on the besiegers before the city was completely encircled and cut off, but he was outgeneraled by Marquez, who persuaded Maximilian to remain on the defensive. By the fourth week of the siege the situation had become desperate, and Marquez made a dash through the lines with a large escort of cavalry to secure reinforcements from the capital. But he did not return. Whether this was due to deliberate desertion or military discretion remained a moot point: his subsequent conduct was equivocal. Entrusted with full powers as Lieutenant General of the Realm, he succeeded in squeezing succor from the capital and made a dash for Puebla, which was threatened by Porfirio Diaz, but Puebla was captured before he arrived and he fell back on the capital, where he shut himself up for a last stand. In diverting relief to Puebla, he took a direction which could be justified by military discretion, since the fall of Puebla cut the road of escape to the sea; so that a saving doubt covered his judgment. But there was no doubt of the fatal effect of his defeat on the siege of Queretaro, nor of his resignation to it in the six weeks that followed. Jealous of Miramon, detesting Maximilian, and Lieutenant General of the Realm himself, he exerted his brief authority in drumming up the citizenry for the fortification of the city without lifting a finger for the relief of the garrison in Queretaro even in the one way open to him. Maximilian had entrusted him with an act of abdication with instructions to publish it as soon as he fell prisoner; but Marquez, in the exercise of his discretion, saw fit not to betray his sovereign prematurely; so that he was loyal, after all, unto death.

Miramon, in the meanwhile, tried his tactics and made several belated sallies, which failed to break the lines but which sustained the spirit of the beleaguered garrison until May 15. A sally had been planned for that day, with small hope of success but with the promise of making a gallant finish at least in the field; but the end was mean. A traitor opened the town in the small hours of the morning, and Maximilian was captured with his entire staff. His conduct at the crucial moment was artless. He notified General Escobedo that he had signed his abdication and was no longer Emperor of Mexico, declared that he wished to be the sole victim, if a victim were necessary, and proposed that an escort be given him to leave the country forthwith, on his promise never to return. He was told that his request would be referred to the proper authorities; whereupon he surrendered his sword unconditionally, and all was over.

All was over, at least, in the mind of the Archduke, though even then he accepted his fate without finality. All was over, at last, in the light relief with which he rested from its unrelenting pursuit. All was over but the end of the tragedy which he had courted. The long agony of Empire was over, leaving behind it an incalculable score of wasted lives, ruined resources, social infection, national humiliation, and human bitterness that called for a full and final accounting; and since the real authors were beyond reach, it could only be a nominal one, and the expiation was all the more exacting because it was symbolic. Maximilian was held, with his lieutenants Miramon and Mejia, for trial by a military court. From this verdict he appealed to the President, who was in San Luis Potosi, in a note requesting a personal interview. The note was the logical corollary of his order to Miramon to hold Juarez for trial, if he were captured, but to suspend sentence. Of all the dangers with which that document was fraught, the greatest for Juarez was the risk of personal contact, with all its disarming human appeals, and now that their positions were reversed and Maximilian lay at his mercy, the peril was mortal and he eluded it with the instinct of self-preservation. The most sympathetic of enemies, Maximilian had sought a personal interview from the first day that he landed in Mexico as the solution of all his difficulties; their affinities demanded a face-to-face meeting; it was his supreme resource, but it failed him. His request was refused. He was referred to the court-martial for his defense, and he sent to the capital for legal advisers.

The conduct of his partisans at this moment was characteristic. The capital was subject to a double blockade, one by the army of Diaz beyond the walls, the other within them by the refusal of the authorities to admit the facts. The fall of Queretaro was concealed from the public, first by impenetrable silence, then by reports of imaginary successes and the imminent return of the Emperor. In the culminating mendacity and supreme meretriciousness of those days, Marquez and his accomplices attained the final triumph of the conservative mentality, trained by custom and creed perpetually to mistake title for truth, religion for the Church, stability for the State, society for self-preservation, appearance for substance, the name for the thing. To the end, the pseudo-Imperial government continued to lie away its last days of life; and it was only by the arrival of an emissary from Queretaro to find legal defenders for the ex-Emperor that the truth, officially stifled, transpired and his desperate pass was realized. Three lawyers responded, all of them Liberals, and one of them, Mariano Riva Palacio, an eminent advocate who was doubly qualified to plead his case, because of his own record as an uncompromising opponent of the Empire and because his son had fought brilliantly in the Republican ranks and had captured his client. With three foreign diplomats, they left immediately for Queretaro, where their several roles were distributed, one remaining with the accused to conduct his case, the others hurrying to San Luis Potosi to appeal to the government, where the only hope of defense lay, the outcome of the trial being a foregone conclusion by the mere institution of a military court.

The trial in Queretaro lasted three days, from June 11 to June 15, and was held, appropriately enough, in a theater, with the court and the accused on the stage and the public in front. Maximilian was absent, refusing to submit to that spectacular disgrace, and his codefendants alone were paraded across the boards to stand judgment as accomplices and suffer the fate of supernumeraries. Eclipsed by his absence, they disappeared in a perfunctory formality. One indeed had his moment of stigma and was condemned in his own right. Miramon, whose melancholy celebrity had been all but effaced by the shuffle of time, was recalled on his record, with a probing stress on the massacres of Tacubaya, and memory was meted out to him before he was relegated to oblivion. Mejia, who occupied the place which rightly belonged to Marquez, having no claim to criminal notoriety, was sentenced unnoticed. The third "M," the mute figure of the Imperial monogram, absorbed the whole attention of the court.

The case of Maximilian was defended by his advocates with more than perfunctory zeal or legal art, ardently, logically, boldly, in a large appeal to humanity and historical reason. They denied the competence of the court, explicitly, and the right of the government, implicitly, to try him as a rebel or, as the indictment read, as "a usurper of public power, an enemy of the independence and security of the nation, a disturber of order and public peace, and a violator of international law and individual rights"—sonorous phraseology, they said, fit for a newspaper column or a political club, but not for the considered judgment of mankind. Rebellion, they argued, differed from civil war both in kind and degree, and the legal code applicable to the one was too narrow to embrace the other, a great social schism having, by its nature and scale, acknowledged rights and corresponding wrongs to its account that varied inversely with its aims and success. A real case could be made for Maximilian along such lines, and his advocates approximated, though they did not fathom it. The fact that he was a foreigner magnified his trespass, but it also magnified the issue in dispute, which surpassed the simple prejudices of patriotism, and it was immaterial from the moment that he identified himself loyally with the land of his adoption. He had freed himself from the false position in which he was placed by French protection, and, by remaining at his risk and peril after their departure, he had vindicated his independence and was being tried, in fact, as a factional leader. Coming to Mexico at the call of one party in a civil war and seeking to rally and reconcile the other, whose faith and works he adopted, he conceived his role as that of a mediator and an arbiter. Force had been employed because force was indispensable, as he said in a speech that he made in Queretaro, "for without struggle and blood there is no stable success, no political development, no lasting progress." All the rights of humanity were achieved, in the last analysis, as all its wrongs were perpetuated, by force, and the legitimacy of force was determined by its results. The constituted authority under which he was being tried was itself of revolutionary origin and was legitimized by a disputed legal sanction and popular consent: Maximilian could claim the same measure of acceptance. The rights and wrongs of the *ultima ratio* depended on the interests that prevailed and were necessarily partial and relative; the methods were equally arbitrary, and where a people was engaged in civil war to make and unmake its own institutions, the accepted leaders were entitled to military,

not criminal treatment. The treatment of Jefferson Davis in the United
States was cited as a precedent accepted by civilized practice and as an
example to be emulated.

Such arguments were too real, however, for a military tribunal and
were dismissed by the court as a piece of legal decoration, like the classic
portico on the backdrop against which they sat. Conscious of what lay
behind them, they waved aside what lay ahead and saw only the damning evidence laid before them: they had no latitude to judge Maximilian in the perspective of history, no discretion to measure his transgression in terms of historical process. Late on the night of June 15 they
reached a verdict—a verdict directed both by the government that appointed the court and handed it the law, and by the dictates of the interests that had prevailed and that were represented by the army.

Execution was set for the next afternoon, and sentence was read to
the condemned late in the morning. Maximilian expected it. He had
formed his own judgment of a court composed, he supposed, of young
officers who could hardly read or write and whose eligibility to judge
him lay, he said, in their possession of presentable uniforms. Only a few
hours before he had received a report that Carlota was dead. The report was false, but never had an untruth been so bracing. "One more
link with life broken," he remarked. He made his preparations with
complete self-possession, dictated some letters, communed, confessed to
his physician that dying was easier than he imagined, and charged him
with a message for his mother that he had done his duty. The appointed
hour came and he met it punctually, but the courtesy of kings was not
reciprocated, and the hour passed as all hours pass in a land where time
meant nothing, even then. The delay was explained by the arrival of a
telegram from San Luis, granting the condemned a reprieve of three
days. He regretted it, having finished with the world, as he said, and
sharing none of the hopes which his friends read into that stay.

His friends in San Luis were active. Riva Palacio and his colleague
appealed repeatedly to the President, returned again and again to the
Palace, paced the anterooms and received indefatigably the same patient rebuff from Lerdo de Tejada, who guarded the inner sanctum
with the reason of state. The inmate of the sanctum received them and
explained himself. He sympathized with them. He realized, he said,
that they had suffered much in the discharge of their duty by the inflexibility of the government and could not understand the need of it
now nor the justice that dictated it: time would tell. "The government
acts by necessity on this occasion," Juarez explained, "denying the humanitarian sentiments of which it has given and will still give innumerable proofs. The law and the sentence are inexorable now, because
public safety so demands. It can also counsel the economy of blood, and
that will be the greatest satisfaction of my life. The tomb of Maximilian
and the others will be the redemption of the rest of the misled." And on

the way out the argument was paraphrased by Lerdo de Tejada, Iglesias, and all the sentinels of the inner sanctum.

After the lawyers came the diplomats. The Prussian Minister—no longer the uncle of the brass knuckle but Baron Magnus, who was of a different breed—wired ahead "in the name of humanity, in the name of Heaven," having no other credentials for a hearing, and descended on San Luis to intercede in person; and it was thanks to him that the reprieve was granted—a concession that Juarez regretted as soon as he made it, since it prolonged the agony needlessly, but the Baron meant well. Then came the women. The Princess Salm-Salm, whose husband was a prisoner with the Archduke, had been expelled from Queretaro for planning the escape of Maximilian and bribing his keepers, but she was received in San Luis with consideration and sympathy. When she asked Iglesias whether he would not have been glad had she succeeded, he assented with a smile; and though she was unable to wring the same avowal from the President, his manner conveyed the same impression; but she obtained only the reprieve already granted to Baron Magnus. On the night before it expired, she invaded the sanctuary again and, finding the President pale and suffering, flung herself at his feet and, clinging convulsively to his knees, refused to leave without a pardon. Carlota herself could have done no more. In her account of the scene the Princess recalled the laborious efforts which Juarez made to raise her—she had been a circus acrobat in early life—and his weary reply. If all the sovereigns of Europe were in her place, he could not spare Maximilian, he said. It was not he who took his life, but the law and the people; if he did not, they would, and his own as well. The excuse might have seemed insufficient, had it not been laden with his own conviction. The Law and the People! In those limitations lay the heart of his sanctuary; forced to function, he was forbidden to feel; but she brought tears to his eyes before she consented to leave, and Iglesias, who showed her out, assured her that the President suffered sincerely from the necessity of immolating so noble a victim as Maximilian and taking the lives of two of his countrymen. When she went out, a delegation of two hundred women went in, and when they withdrew the wife of Miramon was admitted with two small children; she was carried out unconscious. Then at last Juarez shut himself up and refused to see anyone for three days. Harrowing as the scenes were which he refused to spare himself, his conscience was clear, and the letters he wrote to his family during those days contained no trace of feeling, save for their return.

The ordeal, nevertheless, bore more heavily upon him than on Maximilian; he was not finished with the world, nor the world with him. In the month that elapsed between the capture and trial of Maximilian, the issue was agitated in every country, by every class of interest, every kind of mind, every type of character, and Juarez himself was on trial before the world. The sovereigns of Europe made concerted representations and addressed their appeals to Washington, which made a perfunctory gesture in their favor. More powerful, however, than the solidarity of sovereigns was the authority of ardent republicans, who also pleaded for the life of the prince. After the lawyers, the diplomats, the women, came the poets. Lamartine, who had lauded the Napoleonic idea, had the grace to be silent; but Victor Hugo, who had denounced it and whose fighting words had been posted in Puebla during the siege of 1863, was a partisan who had a right to be heard. "Let this Prince, who never divined that he was a man, learn that there is in him a meanness which is the King, and a majesty which is the Man," he wrote. "Never has a more magnificent opportunity presented itself. Act, Juarez, so that civilization may make an immense stride. Abolish the death penalty from the face of the earth. Let the Nation, at the very moment when it has annihilated its vanquished assassin, remember that he is a man and absolve him and say: You are the People, begone! This will be your second victory, Juarez. The first, in overcoming usurpation, is superb. The second, in forgiving the usurper, will be sublime. . . . Over all the monarchical codes dripping with blood open the Law of Light, and on the most sacred page of the Supreme Book let the finger of the Republic be seen resting on the command of God: Thou shalt not kill."

And yet more potent than the rhetoric of the poet was the appeal of the experienced coreligionist Garibaldi, whose prestige was immense in Mexico, where he was regarded by the Liberals as a blood brother; he also pleaded for the bloodless bond. But all these appeals suffered from two limitations—time and place. They came too late and they came from foreigners. It was no time for intervention from any quarter, on any grounds, no matter for what motives. A message from Seward, hinting that harsh measures "would not raise the character of the United States of Mexico in the esteem of civilized peoples," provoked a sharp reply. "The government, which has given numerous proofs of its humanitarian principles and its sentiments of generosity, is also obliged to bear in mind, according to the circumstances of cases, what is required by the principles of justice and its duty to the Mexican people." Garibaldi might have remembered his own motto—*l'Italia farà da se*—and Juarez mutely reminded him of it by his conduct. Victor Hugo was answered in the same way. Juarez, whose mercy was first and last for his people, made his decision the day that Queretaro fell. "The impatient are going to the devil," he wrote to his family then, "because they want everything to be over at once, although the great criminals will go unpunished, and the future peace of the nation will not be guaranteed; but the government, without heeding them, continues to make haste slowly with the firm determination to do what best befits the country, and without being influenced in its decisions by personal vengeance, misguided compassion, or any foreign threat. We have fought for the independence and autonomy of Mexico, and it must be a reality."

The outer world was remote during that trying month. The sole possibility of conducting an appeal lay with those on the spot, and they exhausted it. The lawyers, and those who followed them, testified that no vindictive sentiment was shown by the President or his ministers and that their intransigence was supported by reasonable motives. The reason of state was set forth succinctly by Lerdo de Tejada. "Weak peoples have no right to be generous," he said once; and again, more formally, "The civil war must and can end in a reconciliation of parties, but for this it is essential that the government remove the elements of probable disturbances." Baron Magnus sought to allay that apprehension by a formal pledge, on behalf of the monarchs of Europe, that neither Maximilian nor any of his associates would return to Mexico, if they were released; and a kindred offer was made by the Emperor Franz Josef, who gave the best guarantee of his good faith by waiving the Family Pact in favor of his brother. But no pledge, and least of all that of kings, could dispel the mistrust of the maimed. The fear was respectable, the caution legitimate, but it was still fear, the force that rules the world and perpetrates its variable violences and lineal retributions, and against which no reason avails.

Whether the fear was actually warranted was nonetheless questionable. The best guarantee against a repetition of intervention was the result of intervention itself, a warning far more forbidding than the forfeit of a figurehead. It was too soon, however, to see the result in historic perspective: here, too, time and place limited the long view. The government was hemmed in by the army, and the army was exasperated and inexorable. In Queretaro the officers demanded the head of Maximilian and the lives of all the adherents of the Empire, large and small: in the dining-room of the hotel a staff officer of Escobedo was heard to say that the body of Maximilian should be cut to pieces and distributed in every town in Mexico. The farewell letters to their mothers of two young patriots, Arteaga and Salazar, who perished under the sanguinary decree of October 3, were circulated to incense the public. Porfirio Diaz, personally the most moderate of soldiers, wrote to Juarez that if the Emperor were pardoned, he would not be master of the army besieging the capital. An implacable hatred of all foreigners fired the victorious patriots, and it exploded when the appeal made by Seward at the instance of the Austrian Government became known. The officers demanded a public defiance of the interference of Washington; and when the American Minister, who was waiting in New Orleans to proceed to his post, received a telegram from Seward urging him to seek out Juarez at once and plead for clemency to Maximilian and the other prisoners, he decided to disregard it rather than court an inevitable rebuff. The tension was too electric to touch. The compulsion un-der which the government acted was, as Juarez admitted, the throttling pressure of public opinion. How strong it was, and whence it came—whether from the army, or the extremists who surrounded him, or his own mind—and whether it was opinion or passion, these were also problematical factors; but the verdict was certainly anticipated. Neither Queretaro nor San Luis were propitious places, nor the morrow of tri-umph a favorable time, for cool judgment. Had the trial been post-poned and held in the capital by a court of recognized competence, many believed that temperate counsels would have prevailed. The trial was instituted to prevent the appearance of precipitancy, but its find-ings were a foregone conclusion, and the government, which had made haste slowly for five years, acted with extreme urgency at the end.

The reprieve expired on the morning of June 19. Maximilian main-tained his serenity to the last; during the final days of suspense, when the fictitious habits of life wore thin and the basic strains of breeding and character became transparent, he was sustained by his innate grace. The small motives of pique and pride which drove him to disaster were utterly purged away by the catastrophe. "I have no gall or bitterness in the bottom of my heart," he repeated more than once to an emissary of the French Minister who visited him in his prison; and he proved it. No word of recrimination passed his lips. On the day before the su-preme test he appealed once more for his comrades and asked that he be the sole victim. Though it was written that they should not meet, he wrote to Juarez, congratulating him on his triumph and adjuring him to benefit by his blood. "May my blood be the last to be shed, and de-vote that perseverance which you have shown in defending the cause that has just triumphed, and which I was glad to recognize and esteem in prosperity, to the nobler task of reconciling souls and founding peace in this unfortunate country." So, in spirit, he met Juarez at last.

The words were his parting bid for a good memory, and a good death gave him that power. Promptly at the appointed hour, three car-riages collected their cargo and lumbered through the streets of Quere-taro, followed by the harrowing scenes of popular sympathy that ac-company such occasions and that blotted out, on this one, the memory of countless other lives obscurely lost without benefit of pomp and cere-mony. The wife of Mejia stumbled after his carriage with maddening cries; the passing of the others was followed by the crowd with mute respect or expressions of compassion, of indignation, of dismay, of every sentiment except hostility. The facility of popular feeling accompanied the condemned, step by step, with the tolling of bells, to the Cerro de las Campañas, the hillside outside the city where Maximilian had been captured and where his progress ended. When he alighted, he had to support his father confessor, who was on the point of swooning. Scan-ning the dense crowd hemmed in by a square of four thousand troops, he asked if any friends of his were there and was assured that Baron Magnus was present. Divesting himself of a final privilege, he yielded the place of honor in the center to Miramon in tribute to a good soldier. Seeing some people weeping in the front row, he smiled at them, and when the captain of the firing squad asked his forgiveness, he thanked him and bade him do his duty. "I die for a just cause, the cause of the freedom and independence of Mexico," he said. "May my blood put an end to the misfortunes of my new country. Long live Mexico!" He had wished for a fair day to die, and he was not denied. It was a radiant summer morning, and the fresh hour before sunrise, when he looked his last on the town nestling in copses of green, and the broad valley, and the blue mountains about to be blessed with the sun. There was a volley, and the three figures shed their shadows on the lethal indifference of mother earth. His last words, as he lay expiring on the ground, were, "Man! Man!"

18

THE shadow which his life cast across Mexico was not dissipated by his death. A nominal accounting had been made, but the ringleaders remained at large, and Maximilian, dead, was judged with the posthumous indulgence due to a well-meaning and misguided accessory whose capital error was that he was caught. A tragic trifler with the destinies of nations, he had paid his fault in full. Mistakes in politics being crimes, his crime was that he was an amateur, but the atonement invested him with a compensating aura of martyrdom, and that aura cast a long shadow across the justice of Juarez.

The repercussions of the shots on the Cerro de las Campañas were world-wide, and the wisdom of the world which they shattered re-echoed them in reactions as various as the minds of men, and as permanent. The first reports reached France at an unfortunate moment: Paris was crowded with foreign visitors and crowned heads attracted by the Exhibition of 1867, and the catastrophe of an adventure which the government had every reason, as Douay said, to leave in shadow and silence provoked an outcry of guilty recrimination. Napoleon was profoundly affected by it and was dissuaded with difficulty from commemorating it by a funereal ceremony in Notre Dame, but he was induced to mourn Maximilian with discretion. The Empress was no less afflicted, but she was also irritated and, woman-like, she found relief in vital evasions. At one moment she approved the obstinacy of the victim in courting disaster. "He did well to remain," she said with spirit. "If I had been in his place I would have done the same; they are forsaking me, I would have said, I shall do them a bad turn. We have made mistakes, of course, but we should not bear the blame alone: the United States and the Court of Rome should bear a large share of it." Then, turning over the bad turn in her heart, she wept and said, "We are like people in a besieged town; we are hardly through with one trouble when another begins. If the Prince Imperial were eighteen years of age, we would abdicate."

Maximilian had carried tit for tat too far in getting himself killed to annoy them, and he managed to make them some trouble still in his grave. The Opposition unearthed it like ghouls in the Legislature. Jules Favre rehearsed the history of the whole expedition and concluded his arraignment by crying that, if France were a free country, the government would be on the bench of the accused. Thiers also capitalized on the sensation, lamenting the waste of energy in Mexico so badly needed on the Rhine and inveighing against the system of personal government, but he was considerate and tempered the wind to the shorn lamb. After recapitulating the record in turn and analyzing the history of Mexico, "which had to perform all at once all the revolutions through which Europe passed in three hundred years," and which was worn out by its triumph in 1860, he dodged the conclusion and hung the catastrophe upon Juarez. "The man in whose hands the government was then, and who had not yet imprinted an indelible stain on his name," he said, "that man, gentlemen, President Juarez, inspired some hope. Placed between good and evil, and not yet under the yoke of odious passions as he has fallen today, we believed that he might yet incline toward the good." His sententious sniff was greeted with cries of "Very good, very good," and as they were addressed to Adolphe Thiers, he preferred to be righteous rather than right. The historian who pursued his conclusions with relentless logic until they brought him up to date and smacked him in the face followed the popular line of the moment like the consummate opportunist and academic liberal that he was. The shock produced a revulsion of feeling even among those who had most bitterly blamed the expedition, and the government benefited by it. The press execrated the penalty paid at Queretaro as uprightly as Thiers. The official *Moniteur* gave the cue: "The assassination of the Emperor Maximilian will excite a universal sentiment of horror. This infamous act, ordered by Juarez, brands the brows of the men who call themselves the representatives of the Mexican Republic with an ineffaceable stain; the reprobation of all civilized nations will be the first chastisement of the government which has such a leader at its head." And the cue was picked up and carried by a chorus of pharisaical recrimination.

The reports of the *procureurs* emulated one another in echoing it: "The crime of Queretaro could not have excited more emotion had the victim been French." — "There has been but a single cry to brand the murder of the Emperor Maximilian." — "Men of all shades of opinion agree in abhorring this cruel act, this savage violation of international law." — "The note inserted in the *Moniteur* yesterday accurately echoes the unanimous sentiments of the population." — "There is but one voice to scourge this act of infamous and cowardly cruelty, the most odious ever recorded in history." — "Though it sets a funereal seal on our expedition, this crime legitimizes our unfortunate attempt in the opinion of many people, showing how incapable Mexico was of regenerating itself and how unworthy Juarez was of governing it." — Etcetera, etcetera.

All eyes and ears, the official eavesdroppers brought abundant balm to the wounded hearts in the Tuileries. For a month, for two months, Maximilian was the rage in Paris. Then his death became, as one of them said, "an historical event. A few men seek the causes of his fall, the majority no longer think of him. More than ever today, nations seem to be in a hurry to live and forget everything that does not have a present interest." The account was closed by another with a sigh of relief: "At the moment when the Universal Exposition cast its most brilliant blaze and our national pride, humiliated by the opposition of Prussia to the annexation of Luxembourg and the audacious aggrandizement of that Power rising from its wounds, saw the sovereigns of the greatest nations assembling in Paris as though to render solemn homage to the moral influence of France, the execution of the unfortunate Maximilian revived the painful memories of the expedition to Mexico. To the indignation of seeing treason and assassination accomplish with impunity their bloody work, there was coupled immediately, in all hearts devoted to the Emperor, another sentiment, the dread that the most ardent men of the Opposition might be so unjust as to trace the responsibility for this final disaster to His Majesty. That fear was only too well founded; but there has been but a single cry in all classes to protest against the violences of Jules Favre." Bazaine brought home evidence that Jules Favre had been in the pay of Juarez; Napoleon, who had begged for it three years before, tossed it into the fire. His dignity was as great as his grief; and while it lasted, no one could call him Napoleon the Little.

The abuse of Juarez lasted longer than the mourning of Maximilian. It was the abuse of an iconoclast. The wisdom of the world, which he mangled at Queretaro, denounced him as a vindictive barbarian who abused his victory over the invader. The disciples of the martyr arraigned him as a regicide who sacrificed Maximilian to his hatred of monarchy and profaned humanity to humble the mighty. The apologists of European civilization scolded him for preferring a brutal vengeance to the refined triumph of humiliating the Hapsburgs by a spectacular gesture of clemency. Political connoisseurs blamed the blunder more than the crime, and some republicans deplored the vindication of their principles in the bowels of a stray prince. But he was acclaimed as loudly as he was abused, and for the same reasons. Censure and sympathy were colored with class feeling, and humanity meant for each class what happened to it. The working class in their experience of the world claimed him for one of their own, and in a *Salutation from the French Republican Workers* their spokesmen coupled his name with that of Berezowski, a young Polish terrorist who had just attempted the life of the Tsar of Russia as he drove through the streets of Paris with Napoleon. "Your male vigor has surprised everyone, stunning some and electrifying others," they declared. "The lowly, the poor, the incapable Juarez has become the terrible, the barbarous, the savage Juarez. Yes, a savage was needed, American energy was needed, the Indian there, the worker here, to seize again the dagger and revive the spirit of Brutus, renew justice, and rekindle the month of June, which now has two happy dates! The old races and the old castes can perish. Make way for the new! Make way for the worker Berezowski! Make way for the Indian Juarez! Glory to the one who tried, and glory to the one who succeeded!" And they sent him revolutionary greetings from the veterans of 1848. "Ah! if we the civilized, the humane, the perfect souls of '48, instead of demolishing the gallows for a pretender, had had a little of your barbarism, you would not have had to execute one emperor and we would not have to execute another! What torrents of blood a single drop would have saved!"

Acclaimed, as he was abused, as a terrorist, he was mistaken by the most various types of mind, molded in their own image, and appropriated to their own purposes. The sentimental appeal of Maximilian infuriated doctrinaire radicals—a type well represented by Georges Clemenceau, on whose lips the bristles of the tiger were just beginning to grow. "How the devil could you suppose that you should pity the Maximilians and Carlotas?" he wrote to a woman, his mouth full and rabid with king-baiting. "My God! They are always charming, those people, I agree beforehand; for five or six thousand years it has always been so. They have the formula of all the virtues and the secret of all the graces. They smile—how delightful! They weep—how pathetic! They let you live?—what exquisite kindness! They crush you?—blame their unfortunate position! I have no pity for those people; to pity the wolf is to commit a crime against the lamb. His wife is mad, you say. Nothing more just: this almost makes me believe in Providence. Was it not her ambition that incited the fool? I regret that she *has* lost her reason and cannot realize that she killed her husband and that a people are avenging themselves. If Maximilian was a mere tool, then his role was all the more vile and not the less guilty. I am savage, you see, and what is worse, intractable, but I have no intention of changing. Believe me, all those people are alike, and they all support one another. Impossible though it is, if there were a Hell and no pit in it reserved for them, the good Lord would sink in my esteem. I doubt very much whether there is another atheist who suffers as much as I do from the want of a Providence: I would leave everything to Supreme Justice and feel myself dispensed from hating. But it is sad to think that all those wretches sleep the same sleep as the good." The range of minds that reflected the shadow was as broad as the parts in themselves were narrow, and as the shock which set them performing in a long tremor of typical attitudes.

Juarez himself rested his justice on the judgment of posterity, which remained suspended till kingdom come, the wisdom of the world disputing it in a lingering knell. The issue was settled only by the paling of time. The judgment of posterity was no more impartial than that of contemporaries, but its fallibility was tempered by mellow indifference; and in the meanwhile public opinion, the idol of democracy, continued to be a highly contentious court of appeal. The one thing that might have saved Maximilian was the surrender of the capital as soon as he was captured. The fall of the last stronghold might have facilitated the movement of moderate opinion and given time for temperate influences to commute the sentence, as they did later with the lesser convicts; but the prolonged resistance which Marquez maintained paralyzed every possibility of appeal and provided the best argument for a policy of rigor. The capital surrendered on June 21, when Diaz occupied it under the terms of a capitulation arranged with Baron Magnus, who brought back instructions from Maximilian to check the futile agony. Marquez disappeared in the confusion and, with that ability which never deserted him, made a miraculous escape from the country. Moderation entered the capital with the incoming government.

On July 13 Juarez arrived at Chapultepec. "Needless to say, my road has been a constant ovation, which the people rendered to the government until my arrival here," he wrote to his family. "The reception on Monday will be something extraordinary, judging by the preparations that are being made." It was. Diaz spared no expense to solemnize the occasion. Two days later the President drove into the city in sober republican state, amid the gala regalia of his martial homecoming, reviewed the troops from the balcony of the National Palace, and issued a proclamation in which, appealing for moderation, the closest approach which men could make to impartiality, he pronounced the last word on intervention and compressed its truth in a lapidary commonplace: "Among nations, as among individuals, respect for the rights of others is peace."

PART SIX

The Opposition

I

WHEN Juarez drove into the capital on July 17, 1867, he was at the apogee of his glory. The nature of that glory was easy to read; it was proclaimed on innumerable panels, placards, and arches of triumph along his passage, repeating a single inscription, *The People to Juarez*. He was the personification of the democratic revolution initiated ten years before and the collective hero of a people that had finally won internal freedom and national independence through his fortitude, his fearlessness, his faith, his vision, his tenacity, his integrity. His were the qualities which they had or wished to have, and they were grateful to have found at long last a man who had not failed them and who gave them for the first time in their history the conviction of incontestable success. No more was needed than that simple inscription to express the popular sentiment in Mexico. Abroad, his accomplishment was also recognized, and by no one better than by Emilio Castelar, a Spanish sympathizer who paid tribute to it twice, in the dusk of adversity and the meridian of triumph. Before Maximilian left Miramar, and when Juarez was being driven back on himself by Bazaine, Castelar wrote: "To be great with a great people, as Washington was, is easy. What is difficult is to be great where everything is small; persevering amid inconsistency; firm when heaven and earth are leagued against one man. Look at him, hunted, persecuted, without resources, with the forces of France against him, defying everything with his head high, illumined by the glow of conscience, while the somber shadows of remorse creep over the brows of the conquerors. We are sure that if Prince Maximilian goes to Mexico, the memory of Juarez will trouble his sleep a thousand times and he will understand that while there is a man so firm there democracy cannot die in America." And after the triumph: "There was nothing worthy or honorable in the expedition to Mexico, neither in its preparation nor its end nor in any of the persons who took part in it; what was very great and very honorable was the opposition that fought and overcame it, the divination and audacity of General Prim, the faith and strength of the Mexican people, and the imposing dignity and iron will of Juarez." The Spaniard merely paraphrased, a little grandiloquently, the simple and eloquent acknowledgment of the Mexican people.

Such was the general sentiment on that cloudless midsummer day in

1867 that saw the consummation of a decade of struggle. But thereafter a decline set in, slow, corrosive, and remorseless. Revolutions consume their offspring with saturnine appetite, and Juarez was no exception to the rule; his reputation suffered from the tarnishing of time, the aging of the man, and the triumph and deterioration of the revolution itself. The ravages of peace were deadlier than those of war, because they were pettier: the high morale of the struggle relaxed, and as the pulse of national life subsided to its normal level, there was an inevitable re-action in which the popular image of the war President, graven in great conflicts, was disfigured by small ones from which no one escaped in the descent to peace.

The source of these conflicts was various, but they were all latent in the struggle and had a common origin in the transition from war to peace. One month after his return to the capital, the President took steps to terminate his irregular tenure of power. General elections were called, but at the same time the government announced a program of Constitutional reforms which it proposed to submit to popular referen-dum. There was an immediate outcry. The proposed reforms, which included the veto power for the President, the creation of an upper house in Congress, qualification for Federal employees to stand for election to Congress, and suffrage for the clergy, were denounced in the press as an encroachment of the Executive on the Legislature, a con-spiracy to pack Congress with official jacks, and the opening wedge of a dictatorship; and the means of securing them as a circumvention of the Constitution, which provided for modifications of the national charter by act of Congress. In the ensuing controversy the Liberal party split and a vigorous opposition developed, insisting on strict construc-tion of the Constitution and assailing the attempt of the President to tamper with it. The issue was factitious, for exception was taken less to the reforms than to the means of introducing them, and the merits of the controversy could be judged by the fact that the Opposition was scandalized by a direct appeal to the people, but it provoked a heated discussion and brought up a genuine question. The proposed reforms were the fruit, the government explained, of prolonged meditation and mature experience. Save for suffrage for the clergy, they were technical repairs in the machinery of government intended to improve its effi-ciency. Of all the difficulties with which Juarez had to contend in ten years of civil and foreign war the most persistent, because the most deep-rooted in national custom and character, was the problem of au-thority. The Mexican, according to a popular adage, was a man who could not command and would not obey, and the truth of the adage had been brought home again and again to Juarez to his cost. "It is not possible to govern in these conditions, no one obeys, no one can be obliged to obey," he confessed to an intimate in 1861. During the civil war, and again throughout the war of intervention, he had been in-

vested with a power which, nominally unlimited, actually went no further than the voluntary co-operation of his subordinates and associates;
he depended on the good will of the governors for financial, political,
and military support, and on bargaining to be obeyed, and was always
at the mercy of their public spirit, their personal ambitions, and their
parochial patriotism; and the obstinate evasion of authority, or independent loyalty to it, was the congenital limitation under which the
struggle had been conducted and the liberation of Mexico achieved despite the independence of its patriots. These handicaps had been overcome by the pressure of necessity and his moral authority, but the miracle was abnormal, the chronic condition under which he labored was
a source of organic weakness too often attributed, even in normal
times, to his personal deficiencies as a leader, and in ten years only one
had been normal—the terrible year of 1861. War had disciplined the
national temperament and subdued it to the responsibilities of national
defense, but the invertebrate character of the conflict, which, in its later
phases, had been fought locally and spasmodically, had also fostered
the reliance of the scattered leaders on their own exertions and their
indifference to the formal authority of the civil government. These habits were not confined to the army, they extended to the civil administration, and they menaced the peace because they were profoundly
embodied in the political constitution of the country. The system of
Federalism, which guaranteed the autonomy of the states at the expense
of the central authority, and which was a cardinal dogma of the Liberal
party, seriously impaired the efficiency of the Federal power in periods
of crisis. Even Saligny, in a moment of sympathy, had noted the indifference of the states to the difficulties of the central government and
predicted the eventual disintegration of the country as a result of the
centrifugal pull of the parts away from the pole. Federalism was an
anachronism, originally adopted in the first days of the Republic as a
reaction against the centralization of power of the colonial and conservative regimes, and it created a loose federation of regional governments which corresponded to the psychology of the nation in its embryonic stage of development; the foreign war had stimulated national
sentiment and required a corresponding strengthening of the supreme
government. These tendencies were concentrated in Congress, which,
as the lawmaking power, exercised a strict Constitutional control over
the Executive; and as the amendments tended to increase the Constitutional power of the President and to divide and weaken that of Congress, they were bound to meet with an opposition there which could
be circumvented only by a direct appeal to the electorate. The need of
counteracting the loose political philosophy of Federalism and curbing
its decentralizing effects had been amply demonstrated by a decade of
experience and by the grant of emergency powers which Congress conferred upon the President for the defense of the country; but Cen-

tralism was associated with Conservative dictatorships and the proposed reforms were suspect in the eyes of an Opposition which saw in them the fruit—the rotten fruit—of the long latitude which Juarez had enjoyed and his emancipation from strict Constitutional practice in prolonging his tenure of power arbitrarily in 1865. He touched the ark of the covenant and was smitten by a superstitious outcry. Despite protests, warning, and rebuke, he persisted, but the result of the plebiscite was unfavorable, and he was obliged to acknowledge defeat and refer the reforms to Congress. The effect of his initiative was more damaging than its defeat, however, for in the course of the controversy a presumption was built up in the public mind of a design on the part of the President to usurp the Constitutional crown by a democratic subterfuge, and sedulously fostered by an Opposition that soaked up like a sponge every source of complaint, every sign of transgression, to swell its ranks.

The discussion aroused by the *Convocatoria* would have been entirely disproportionate to the intrinsic importance of the issue but for these underlying motives, and the effect of the agitation was reflected in the elections. The re-election of Juarez to the Presidency was a foregone conclusion for two reasons: first, as a debt of honor to the man; and, second, as a point of national pride, Napoleon having refused to recognize or treat with him. An effort was made, nevertheless, to build up his two formal competitors. Sebastian Lerdo de Tejada, who was one of them, was unpopular, the reforms being attributed to his influence, and his candidacy served merely to divide and weaken the strength of the government. A candidate of sufficient prestige to pit against the President was not easy to find, but the most favorable field was the military, and there the Opposition found their man in Porfirio Diaz. He had an enviable war record. He had distinguished himself in the two sieges of Puebla, he had defended Oaxaca against the French, losing it in 1865 and recovering it a year later, he had maintained the struggle in his own territory undaunted and unaided, raising money and men independently and loyally, he had retaken Puebla, he had captured the capital and won the gratitude of the population by the patient and bloodless siege which he laid to it and the discipline of his soldiery after he occupied it. The conspicuous services which he had rendered the national cause were entitled to recognition, and as the government gave him none, the Opposition made good the glaring omission by postulating him for the Presidency. He became the prototype of the deserving patriot neglected in the hour of triumph and the favorite of all those who had borne the brunt of the battle and who found no recognition, no gratitude, no berth in the budget at the close of the war. As the demobilization of the army cast on the country some sixty thousand men with scant means of livelihood and small hope of pensions, Diaz was in a position to command the dangerous support of postwar unemployment and inveterate militarism, and some of his friends urged him to seize power, but on the advice of an expert politician he resigned his command and retired to private life—a shrewd political play which heightened his popularity. He had been a close and trusted friend of the President, who referred to him as "our good Porfirio" until the close of the military and the opening of the political campaign, when their relations cooled. Though the change was commonly imputed to personal jealousy, it was due to sound political motives. During the siege of Queretaro, Diaz had sounded Escobedo with a proposal to form a triumvirate with himself and another general to assume power after the fall of the capital and elect one of their number to the Presidency. The proposal came to nothing, but it raised the question of who won the war: Diaz claimed the spoils for the soldier. The President had legitimate grounds to mistrust him and he did not conceal them. When he drove into the capital, it was noticed that Diaz, who had organized his reception and who met him at the gates, was not invited to ride in his carriage; he took his seat in the second coach with Lerdo de Tejada, and the procession visualized the precedence of the President very conspicuously. Diaz adroitly dispelled the impression that he was a danger to the civil power by his subsequent conduct. Correct, loyal, and disinterested enough to retire on the steps of the Capitol, he cut a handsome figure on very thin ice in the hour of victory. The lurking menace of militarism was eliminated, the election was waged on personal grounds, the issue was a competition of impeccables, and Diaz enjoyed the advantage over Juarez of being fifteen years his junior and, politically, an unknown and hence a faultless quantity.

It was not enough. It was not enough for Ortega in 1861, and it was not enough for Diaz in 1867. Juarez was re-elected by a broad plurality, which proved once again the preference of the country for the seasoned leader and the collective over the individual hero. To the Opposition, however, it proved something else. The result, they conceded, was a foregone conclusion, but not of spontaneous popular choice; it was the foregone conclusion of the influence, the fraud, and the force with which the government manipulated the elections. Such charges were impossible to prove or refute. They were the concomitant of every election in Mexico and the inevitable result of the right of universal suffrage bestowed on a people unprepared to exercise it responsibly. The mass basis of democracy in an electorate which in its overwhelming majority was illiterate, inert, and pliable to all the processes of the political machine, was necessarily a fiction: the reality was supplied by the process of natural selection provided by indirect elections. Droves of illiterate but schooled voters, herded to the polls and handed a prepared ballot by the local bosses and ward-heelers, created the college of electors with whom the actual decision lay and who were subject, in turn, to all the deals, the inducements, the pressures prevalent in more advanced stages of democracy. Under the conventional forms of free elections, what actually worked was the indigenous cacique system, the traditional control of a community by a local chief driving his flock in the immemorial patterns of primitive life, and producing a pretense of self-determination by a confederacy of professional favor and predetermined consent. The machinery invited at every stage, from the raw material to the finished product, manipulation and abuse, which the government was in the best position to exercise, although it held no monopoly of the controls, which were freely used against it. The election of 1861, when Juarez won an uncontested majority of five thousand votes without lifting a finger in his favor, was perhaps the single exception to the rule; but it was the exception that proved the rule. The common practices were accepted by general consent as a necessary evil; their prevalence, it has been said, made adulteration legitimate, since no government could be elected without them, and the function required by the Constitution could be performed only by violating the Constitution: a paradox produced by the ideological devotion of its framers to the democratic dogma of universal suffrage and its application to a people unfitted to practice it, for whom democracy was a forced growth and corruption an infantile disease in its development. Custom and convention were in conflict, and the result was an attack of periodic colic at every election. If the conditions were tacitly accepted, they were invariably protested, however, by the defeated party, and the government was attacked in the Opposition press, and the President excoriated by a tongue or two, for squandering the public revenues in wholesale bribery and carrying the country by intrigue, peculation, and bloodshed. The line between legitimate electioneering and palpable abuse was thin, and the losers were not apt to draw it exactly. When Congress convened and examined the credentials of the deputies, some were thrown out on the ground of irregularities; but in spite of this sop to the purists, the presumption persisted that the elections had been vitiated at their source and was added to the close accounting which the Opposition kept against the President. Whatever the method, the result would have been the same: his prestige was sufficient to insure his election, and his election to guarantee the integrity of his government and the functioning of democracy—political systems and institutions being worth no more, after all, than the men who run them, and his personal probity acknowledged and proven. Such was the retort of his supporters, and it satisfied the average citizen. The complaint was endemic and academic. The fact that it was made was nonetheless compromising; it had not been heard in 1861; and the doubts cast with the ballots of 1867 created a precedent, and a provocation, for the future.

After the elections Diaz retired to a farm in Oaxaca and abandoned public life definitely or indefinitely, depending upon his prospects. His conduct was exemplary—but of what? It was not the first time that a successful soldier and irreproachable patriot had gone down to defeat at the polls: Gonzalez Ortega had gone through the same experience before him and come out of it crushed; and his example was a case in point which the Opposition, defeated in Diaz, attempted to revive after the elections.

Since his arrest in January 1867 the pretender had languished in prison, forgotten by all but a few faithful friends. In protest against his prolonged incarceration, they elected him to Congress; but the election was ignored. Subsequently Congress was moved by Manuel Zamacona to order a judicial investigation of his case; but no action was taken. These evasions strengthened the contention of his partisans that he was a victim of political persecution. The emergency under which he was arrested and indicted having passed, no motive of public interest appeared to justify his further detention without trial: he was entitled to a hearing both on the charge of desertion and his claim to the Presidency, but the two were inextricably connected and the manifest reluctance of the government to prosecute the one or to investigate the other lent credit to the deduction drawn by Ortega and his defenders that the charge had been framed to foil the claim. "Who does not know that Ortega was imprisoned to prevent him from figuring as a candidate?" wrote the bitterest of the Opposition leaders, Ignacio Ramirez, who now turned his talents as an iconoclast on the popular cult of the President. The charge was ugly and the case equivocal enough to furnish the makings of scandal had there been any popular support for it; but there was neither sufficient sympathy for Ortega nor enough sentiment against the government to make a serious issue of it. The case was deferred by the government, first until the close of the war and then until after the elections, on the ground that the country was not sufficiently settled to allow of a calm consideration of its merits, but the time was indefinitely postponed, and to the Opposition the muffling of the case was conclusive proof that the Constitution had been violated both in the question of the succession and in the elementary rights of the accused, and that a government which professed to be the jealous guardian of legality was guilty of a flagrant abuse of power, aggravated by the compliance of Congress and the apathy of the public.

Technically, no doubt, this was true; but it was not the whole truth. Appearances were against the government, but the case was one in which appearances and realities were locked in conflict and deceptively confused. The country had long since pronounced judgment on the claims of Ortega to the Presidency and confirmed it by the re-election of Juarez: the question was dead, and it could be claimed with equal justice that the discretion with which the government buried it was dictated by a motive of public interest. To reopen a case already closed by the concensus of public opinion would have created a futile and gratuitous agitation, highly impolitic and inopportune at a time when the paramount task of the authorities was the restoration of peace and the return to normal conditions. Public sentiment was reluctant to prosecute one national hero and to embarrass another, or to ventilate a question which reflected on both, for the connection between the charge and the claim was such that one could not be raised without the other. Such was the view which the government, and Congress, and the country at large, took of a dilemma that was solved by a common sense which made the complaints of the Opposition, once more, academic. Congress chose the easy way out and, instead of a judicial investigation, disposed of the whole matter by judiciously ignoring it. If the solution was irregular, so was the situation from which it sprang; there are times and problems in which irregular solutions are the right ones, and this was clearly one of them. The triumph of expediency over principle reduced the snarl to its real importance; and though the sensible solution involved a serious injustice to Ortega, none but a few ineffectual champions of his Constitutional rights took it seriously. Muzzled and forgotten, he remained in custody until August 1, 1868, when after nineteen months of arbitrary imprisonment the government released him quietly and dropped the charge against him. Still unconvinced, still clinging to the rules and contesting the facts, still wrestling with the real and the literal, he continued to consider himself a victim of the reason of state and the ambition of Juarez, criminally abetted by a subservient Congress and a callous people who betrayed the faith for which he had fought; but he recognized the general indifference to his fate and resigned himself to it. Retiring to private life and burying himself in his books, he completed his political education without understanding it; and so in wisdom unawares his tragicomedy closed. His countrymen did him justice by forgetting both his rights and his wrongs and remembering him only as the hero of the past, and time, which he had always misjudged, preserved his glory by defeating his ambition.

His followers capitulated. Prieto, who had declared for him out of an honest conviction that the inviolability of the Constitution was more important than any motive of expediency adduced to suspend it, recanted. He had parted with Juarez at the time of the *coup d'état,* as the legalists called his prolongation of power in 1865, at the cost of an intense inner struggle. Not since his disillusionment in Degollado had he suffered such a shock to his ideals. "Do not believe for a moment that I plead for the person of Ortega," he wrote at the time to a friend. "I defend him because at this moment he is the personification of Law. Juarez has become an idol because of his virtues, because he was the sublimation of the law, because his strength was the law, and our glory, even in succumbing, was to succumb with the reason of society, which is the law. What is left of all that? Where are we now? Whom do we obey? Is there any difference really that yesterday it was Santa Anna, and Comonfort, and Ceballos, and today Juarez who is the suicide? Let us suppose that Juarez was necessary, sublime, heroic, immaculate in power—was he so by himself or by his titles? What is he worth without them? . . . I go so far as to suppose that this attempt at prestidigitation succeeds. Is it honorable to follow him? Must we assent to this scaling of power? Must we authorize by our tolerance of this fact others of the same kind which will not be long in following? I for one will not do it. I shall be so frank with you as to confess that what appalls me is not even the fear of breaking the Constitution, despite all that I have said; for our cause is so great, and so inaccessible would be the glory of the man who drove the French from our soil that I might be seduced to become an accomplice in this heroic aberration, because the reparation would be sublime. Reputation for the life of the country! Have I not given mine already? That does not frighten me. What frightens me is to see Juarez behaving like a revolutionist, inert, timid, evasive, minding a misreport or raising a mean personal vengeance to the rank of a question of state. Can you imagine Juarez as a revolutionist? . . . Do you realize what I have suffered?" His scruples, his doubts, his fears were dispelled, however, by 1867, and he came to his senses. Realizing finally the insignificance of the affair, and that his disillusionment had been an illusion pardonable in a pedant but not in a poet, he sought a reconciliation with the President. "Here I am," he said when they met. "Do what you will with me." Juarez embraced him tenderly, and their estrangement was never mentioned again.

The end of Gonzalez Ortega was not calculated to encourage other unrecompensed heroes, and Diaz bided his time. The bid for Constitutional reform, the election scandals, and the Ortega affair offered some fodder to the Opposition; their leaders labored these complaints to discredit the President, accusing him of going to the most unprincipled lengths to retain the power he had assumed by the *coup d'état* of 1865; but the respect which he commanded overpowered the Pharisees. Forced to pay lip-service to it themselves, they laid the irregularities of the *Convocatoria,* the elections, and the *coup d'état* to the influence of Lerdo de Tejada and, exonerating the President at the expense of his Prime Minister, drew a convenient distinction between Juarez and his alter ego, whom they labeled the Jesuit; but as Lerdo had been elected President of the Supreme Court and stood in lineal succession to the Presidency, they were indissolubly coupled in the public mind, and their association exposed them both to the attacks of an Opposition which went to the most unprincipled lengths itself to combat their prestige. With that facile solemnity so lightly assumed by propagandists for political effect, it was freely asserted that Mexico needed new men, that Juarez and Lerdo had outlived their usefulness, and that by refusing to recognize that their historical mission was completed they jeopardized the peace of the country to gratify their personal ambition for power, and that only the forbearance and discipline of the defeated prevented a return to the era of revolts and a relapse into the traditional disorders of the past. Minor grievances were labored with a great deal of loose talk; but the Opposition was as small as it was strenuous. Juarez was still too near to the heroic period of the war years to be successfully devaluated; and the image graven in the minds of his countrymen could not be disfigured overnight.

2

TO PROVE that the country needed new men it was necessary for time to pass and the heroic period to pale and recede and be forgotten. The demonstration was too difficult for the Opposition in 1867. Peace returned, despite confident predictions to the contrary in the foreign press, which echoed the forebodings of the native Opposition and expected the end of the war to be followed by chronic and incurable domestic dissension, according to Mexican custom. The morale of the war years, or the fatigue that followed them, forbade a relapse into the lawlessness of the past, and the future was assured for as long, at least, as those conditions prevailed. The period of recuperation was necessarily conservative, and as the government conformed to that spirit with a fidelity which guaranteed it against factional attack, the censors were deprived of any plausible fighting issue.

The state of the nation, as it was reflected in the address of the President at the opening session of Congress, was unquestionably sound. Foreign opinion was impressed, especially in France, where a gratifying tribute was paid to it by the leading independent paper, writing for the benefit of the Imperial Government. "When they read the words of the President of the Mexican Republic attentively, as we have done," the comment ran, "our readers cannot but ask themselves with surprise how we could ever have had for a single moment the idea of regenerating the people to whom such words were addressed. That savage Juarez with whom we refused to deal, that Congress whose members we pursued, what had we to teach them? Read over our

Blue Book, our diplomatic documents, our parliamentary archives, and we shall find there nothing more simple, or more lofty, than the message of the President of the Mexican Republic. Freedom, and not we, will regenerate Mexico." The message was sanity itself. After congratulating the country on its emancipation and the magnanimity shown to the vanquished—and with good reason, for besides the ringleaders shot at Queretaro, only three other lives were taken and the penalties paid by the defeated party were reduced to a reasonable minimum—the President abdicated his dictatorial powers, vindicated the liberty of the elections, and acknowledged his defeat on the disputed Constitutional reforms, referring them to Congress with exemplary republican discipline. Some disappointment the address inspired, indeed, in Mexico, among the close friends of the President, not on public but on private grounds. Serene and quiet in tone, Zarco detected in it, nevertheless, "a certain languor, a certain weakness, which leaves the impression of fatigue, the weariness of the traveler who, after a painful peregrination, reaches the last stage."

Symptoms of lassitude were discernible, however, only to the sympathetic eye. Of fatigue there was no trace in the diligence with which the President discharged his official duties; but after the rebuff of the Constitutional reforms, they were routine activities, and whatever slackening of his pace followed the peace was due to no flagging of his physical or mental power, but to the limitations of his Constitutional ones. Congress was quick to suspect and challenge any trespassing on its prerogatives, and the vigilance of the press tended to cramp the activity and to discourage the initiative, together with the independence, of the Executive. Strict construction of the Constitution was the dominant, if not the only political question of the day; the Argus eyes were unsleeping, a straight and narrow path was marked out for the President by the adverse result of the plebiscite, and a sound administration was the sole function left to his discretion. Within his own domain he remained master and exercised to the full his own prerogatives; with Congress he worked without friction, and the most systematic could find no fault with his Constitutional practice; yet even Zarco sounded a warning.

The return of Zarco to the *Siglo XIX* compensated the President to some extent for the defection of others of his old collaborators, such as Ramirez and Zamacona, who had joined the Opposition. His peculiar gifts, his ripe judgment, his equable sympathy, the superior poise which made it so easy for him to see things steadily and see them whole, provided the closest approximation to impartiality among his contemporaries and made him the acknowledged arbiter and moderator of public opinion; while his complete independence and disinterestedness fitted him to appreciate the same qualities in Juarez and to be his best interpreter and adviser. But Zarco was not immune to the mental climate of the postwar period: he too was affected by the neurotic suspicion that in the struggle against the monarchy the blood of the monster had dyed off on the dragon-killer and haunted by the irrational fear that the purest republican had been infected by some subtle and invisible poison of untrammeled power. Such were the psychological aftereffects of the *coup d'état* of 1865, which played havoc with the most sensible judgments.

In a zealous caveat Zarco warned the unwary that a sound administration might be the means of circumventing restraint and concentrating power surreptitiously in the hands of the Executive. In almost all countries governed by the representative system, he wrote, parties had grown up, not very numerous in themselves, which believed that to assure order and peace it was necessary to distract the attention of the people from public affairs and to remove them as far as possible from the exercise of their political rights, in order to allow the government latitude, while professing perfect respect for the Constitution, to act as it pleased; and as a warning example he cited Louis Napoleon, the professed heir of the revolution of '89, who had subverted the French Republic in the name of a sound administration: a formula which meant that the government must be everywhere and its influence felt in every branch, in finances, in justice, in material improvements, in elections, in political rallies, and in the press. "The government, to perform its providential and paternalistic mission, must have ample liberty of action and work without restrictions; it will not call itself a dictatorship, it will invoke the law and the fundamental charter of State, arranging beforehand for the necessary modifications in both dictated by experience; the liberal regime will not suffer, but the sum of the parts will be, nevertheless, a personal government and a disguised dictatorship." These tendencies, he added, had appeared in Mexico after every progressive revolution and might well emerge again "in the form of an administrative clutch entrusted to experienced mechanics—wise men whose skill must be taken at their own word as an article of faith, thanks to the efforts of the society for mutual admiration which they have formed for years among themselves." The mind was sore that could write such a sermon for Juarez. The suspicions which it expressed were singularly labored and strained, for nothing had happened to warrant them. But Zarco was hypnotized by the Constitutional fetish, and nothing showed more clearly than his pointless homily how prone the most level-headed were to the lingering prejudice of the pseudo *coup d'état*.

Had he pushed his probing a little further, Zarco might have divined psychological dangers, and more serious ones, in the political confinement of the President. The vision, the knowledge, the self-confidence, the seasoned handling of men and situations which Juarez had acquired in a decade of personal government under the most trying conditions, were now reduced to the compass of an efficient administration in which he was on the defensive, harnessed to a jealous Congress, hedged about by a captious press, paroled to public opinion, watched, warned, wasted, his initiative cut with his ambition, and his public spirit tamed in the traces of a public hack. He was stabled; and he was stalled. He atoned for the *coup d'état* by the most scrupulous submission to Constitutional precept, and the mistrust of power was repaid by the tarrying of enterprise. Acquiescing correctly in his legal limitations, he gave the country, if not the best that was in him, the service it required and the security that it wanted and became, in a word, once again the Governor of Oaxaca. He provided the State with the sound administration which first had brought him fame there, and repeated his record on a larger scale, but he was no longer a provincial official, he was the responsible head of a ruined nation that needed more than bureaucratic abilities for its recuperation and progress. But the nation was weary, its dynamic energies spent in self-defense, and craved repose. No initiative came from Congress, and no measure of moment except a concession and subsidy for the construction of a railroad running from Veracruz to the capital, which the government initiated and Congress ratified after a year of deliberation; and in the process of stabilizing the situation, the recovery of the country remained stationary.

It was too soon to rest. Peace returned, accompanied by a running counterpoint of occasional disturbances. The disbanding of the army cast on the country sixty thousand creditors of the nation, accustomed to adventure and soured for civilian life, many of them destitute, disabled, unpensioned, smarting with real or fancied grievances against the government which turned them loose to shift for themselves, and difficult to digest by an impoverished population; the country regurgitated enough of these superfluous patriots to swell the robber bands with a flow of social casualties that made the problem of brigandage as persistent and baffling as it had been to the French. On this residue of the wars it was as easy to graft political feuds as it had been to turn highwaymen into *guerrilleros;* and several such attempts were made during the year 1868 by ex-combatants taking as their tags whatever texts or pretexts happened to be current in the press at the time— the sanctity of the Constitution, the violation of the elections, the "despotism" of the President, the shabby treatment of Diaz, etc., etc. Diaz was urged to disavow the use of his name by these outlaws; but he declined to commit himself and dissociated himself from them only by his silence. On one occasion, however, he ventured to intercede for an old friend and companion-in-arms whose mutiny failed and whose fate lay in the hands of the President. The interview was brief and his memory of it long. As he told the story later: "I entered and was received by Don Benito standing. Don Benito was a man who never laughed and who inspired no confidence in anyone; very cold, very calm, very serious, very intractable. And we talked. 'How are you, Porfirio?' — 'Very well, Don Benito. And you?' — 'What can I do for you?' — 'Well, Don Benito, I have come to talk about poor Aureliano.' And I told him about Rivera and what he wanted. His features never moved. With that unbending look of his, and his eyes were like coals, he said, 'Tell Aureliano to present himself.' — 'To present himself? You mean that he is pardoned?' — 'The law will act. Tell him to present himself.' — 'But the law will shoot him, Don Benito.' — 'The law will act. Tell him to present himself.' — 'But, Don Benito, am I to tell him to come and be shot?' — 'The law will act; it is the only solution.' There was a pause, and seeing that it was useless, I rose and said, 'Well, Don Benito, I am sorry to have troubled you. I shall see what I can do for poor Aureliano.' He accompanied me to the door, shook hands with me, and said, 'We shall see what you will do for Aureliano.' And those words got me. God knows what influence they had in the decision which I took later! Those words got me. I shall never forget them." Despite the inflexibility of the President, Aureliano Rivera was subsequently reprieved, but not by the influence of Diaz. These sporadic uprisings were put down by the government promptly and without difficulty. The issues they paraded awoke no response, and public sentiment unanimously repudiated and outlawed any and every attempt to break the peace. They gave some comfort, however, to the detractors of the Republic abroad and were exploited for effect in France.

Technically the two countries were still at war; as the war had never been declared, neither was the peace, and hostilities of a covert and underhand kind continued. Napoleon did his best to live down the great idea of his reign; the order of the day was to ignore Mexico; but the thing would not down. The indebtedness, financial and political, had to be met, the Opposition called for an accounting; crops of books dealing with the misadventure by eyewitnesses stirred the public, the posthumous publicity which it received attracted the painters, and the disaster was crowned by a political, or at least a topical, trend in art. No less than thirty canvases portraying the execution of Maximilian were announced for the Salon of 1868, and one of them by Manet. In his case the authorities acted; the hanging of his picture was prohibited and prints of it were confiscated by the police. The most objectionable books were banned, but censorship was relaxed for the official press, which counteracted the morbid interest of the public in the Mexican tragedy by a running fire of comment on actual conditions in the lost colony. Multiplying the real revolts by the imaginary ones supplied by hearsay, surmise, and the proscripts who had fled their country, it was computed that in the fifteen months since the return of Juarez to the capital no less than ten mutinies had broken out against him. Ergo, the eagles could crow. What will they say to this, it was asked—those who for four years had accused French intervention of being the only obstacle to the reign of peace in Mexico? The Spartans, wrote *La Patrie,* taught their children temperance by showing them their drunken slaves to disgust them with the habits of helots; "to cure souls sick with republicanism, we have only to show them the republicans of Mexico, besotted with blood and crime." And so on. The Clerical press, insisting that intervention would have succeeded but for its liberal policies, took a new tack and harped on the growing conservatism of Juarez. Something unheard-of was happening: a reactionary movement was impending in Mexico, it was revealed on reliable authority, and Juarez himself had written to Rome offering to recognize the liberty of the Church; an emissary who had been his confessor, and Maximilian's as well, was on his way to the Pope, bearing the repentance and recantation of the surviving apostate—Canossa was just around the corner. And so on. The war of words went on unwearyingly; but it was one-sided. Something unheard-of, indeed, but not uncommon, was happening: the wild geese were flying in pursuit of the vultures. The Mexican press picked up these canards with little or no comment—they spoke for themselves. They were crippled outcries after the event, the distant campaign of the rear guard retreating into the night of time, and though the importance of calumny could never be exaggerated, as the bitter annals of intervention abundantly proved, its importance in 1867 lay in its impotence.

The Opposition in Mexico was stalled. The steady consolidation of peace deprived it of all controversy, argument, or grip on the government. The election of a new Congress in 1867 resulted in a fresh victory for the government, uncontested even by the routine charge of fraud—a fact which the Opposition explained by attributing it to the indifference of the public, convinced of the futility of bucking the official machine and refusing to vote. Zarco observed sensibly that the apathy of the public might be due to the absence of any political issue—to which there was no reply. The one notable feature of the election was the extension of suffrage to the clergy, the most debatable and the only one of the Constitutional reforms adopted by the outgoing Congress, and a concession that was neither questioned nor noticed.

Without political issues to agitate, the Opposition was reduced to personal ones and, not to die of inanition, fell back on steady sniping against the Ministry. Though these tactics were an indirect attack on the President, his person was still respected, and by a tacit convention of his critics he was represented as an irresponsible sovereign under the sway of his ministers and, in particular, of his prepotent partner, Lerdo de Tejada. As this propaganda developed, he was transformed from a puppet into a captive of the cabinet. and an unconscious prisoner of state, and his political obituary was prepared. "With Juarez isolated and at the mercy of the numerous agents of the ministerial police, who allow neither the persons nor the writing that might inform him of the state of opinion, public evils, and national needs to reach him, his reputation has suffered constantly from the formidable blows which the policy of his cabinet has dealt it. Juarez does not know it, because he has lost contact with the people. He is surrounded by Lerdo's friends, who say, Señor Juarez does not understand this matter, he is old and no longer concerns himself with affairs, let us see Don Sebastian, he is the man of the situation. Not content with casting a veil over the present," the complaint continued, "the ministerial policy reflects on the past of Juarez and destroys his antecedents: no opporunity is lost to bring charges of all kinds against the ministries over which Guzman, Ramirez, Zamacona, and even Zarco presided. When those ministries existed, Juarez was not sequestered from public affairs, as he is now. With them he governed. Whatever is said against them reflects, naturally, on the President who was not then, as he is today, a galvanized corpse. In presenting Juarez as a puppet today, and in his past as a stupid or criminal figure, the ministerial policy pursues, no doubt, two aims: first, to deprive him of all share in public affairs at present, and second, to destroy his popularity and prestige and make his candidacy impossible in the next presidential elections. Juarez was one of the great obstacles to the ambition of Lerdo, whose hypocritical policy has been destroying him little by little. Juarez was a great figure. It is sad to see him disappear behind the bonnet of a Jesuit." Well calculated to kill two birds with one stone, this attack was repeated persistently. The loyalty of the President to his Prime Minister was derided as "a mystery like that of the Holy Trinity: no one explains it, and everyone believes in it. It is an article of faith. Juarez is God, and Lerdo is his prophet. He who says Juarez says Lerdo, and conversely." But the bond remained unbroken.

The aims of this propaganda were too transparent not to be discounted by the common sense of the average reader. Nevertheless, deft fingers continued to ply the putty of public opinion and to remold the popular image of the President, deploring his decline as a melancholy law of life and presenting him, parenthetically to the current interests of 1869, as a respectable "has-been," atrophied in his official shell. Creating credulity by repetition and confident that calumny, however discredited, finally leaves some sediment, the artists of the Opposition agitated the weed, beseeching the seed, and their propaganda flourished in the absence of any response or refutation. Nail after nail was hammered into the casket, though the occupant refused to step into it. Waiting patiently for a false step, their hopes rose high when it was learned that despite the penury of the Treasury the President and his ministers had collected their salary in full, including the accumulated arrears of the war years. Juarez was paid off by a terrible tirade in the hostile press, which rehearsed his record then and now unsparingly. "The whole public knows and has condemned the fact that the Citizen President B. Juarez (and others) have had themselves paid not, as we mistakenly stated, ninety thousand, but almost two hundred thousand pesos, for having carried his position as President to El Paso del Norte, traveling constantly in all comfort and never exposing himself to any peril; for having cornered the national representation in the extreme confines of the Republic, where he was all but forgotten and believed to be dead, and consequently the noble, suffering, and resolute Liberal belligerents were declared bandits by the usurper; and lastly, for having on his own responsibility and contrary to the Constitution re-elected himself President and excited by this illegal act an ignoble conflict at a time when all ambition should have been subordinated to the danger of the country. No; the national representation is something that deserves respect; it could not follow a constant fugitive. The representation of the nation was always with those who scorned their lives for it, because it was necessary to breathe life into it and fire it to the fight. Do you want to know where the national representation was? Look for it first in the people, and then in Porfirio Diaz and so many other heroes who never evaded the struggle in the bitterest days nor abandoned their arms for a single moment. . . . In striking contrast, the Citizen President, who never suffered the privations and perils of the crude and highly dangerous war waged against the usurper, and who is not in poverty today, has had himself paid the considerable sum of two hundred thousand pesos, with full priority, and at a time when the Treasury is under the terrible threat of bankruptcy." The indictment was driven home deep and hard into the ears of the invalid. A cruel contrast was drawn between the patriotic thrift with which he cut his salary in 1861 and the callous privilege with which he collected it in 1869 as the measure of how far he had fallen in public spirit by rising in public esteem, fattening on popular favor, hardening with power, and settling into the selfish complacence of age. Zamacona rose on the floor of Congress to lament that "the power that rules the country is entering on the period of decrepitude and decadence which coincides in the individual with the period of egoism and greed, and no longer allows him the movements of generosity and abnegation of other days." Regret, reproach, indignation, and hope flared up; yet the public remained perversely unmoved. The debt of the nation to Juarez was not paid with his wages, and the attempt to collect damages for his services was the worse dud of all. The patriots of the Opposition were known for their own records, and few of them could boast; neither Zamacona nor Ramirez, the most ruthless censors of the President, had been as conspicuous in defending the country during the war as they were active in belittling him after it, and their bias was too obvious not to discredit their backbiting. The motives of the Opposition were many, but none was so glaring as the guilt of the weak glorying in an ungained morality and covering their records by catering to the military.

Mexico still knew too well who Juarez was, and he survived the collection of his salary. The shroud was measured and cut, it hung heavy and limp on the hands of the mourners. Something more important than personal nagging was needed to sap the solid reputation that defied opposition and blunted the blows of those who were bold after the battle. Other tacks were tried; but not until personal detraction was grafted on public complaints did the weakling war begin to gain weight. The consolidation of peace was an unquestionable fact, despite recurring disorders, but so was the poverty of the country, and this furnished the prosecution with a fresh lead. "Public misery is appalling," the hostile press complained. "Thousands of persons are seeking occupation and work without finding it. This pauperism, silently corroding society like a cancer, is felt especially and almost exclusively by the middle class. And can the Republic go on living like this? Impossible. Every violent situation creates a crisis. To civilize, to raise the indigenous race from their fatal prostration, and to combat pauperism in the middle-class, these are the two great needs of the Republic. Can our rulers do it? Do they want to do it? In reply to the first question, we do not hesitate to say that it is in their power to repair, or at least to attenuate, the evil. As for the second, it seems evident to us that they will do nothing."

This strategy placed the Opposition on higher and more solid ground. The consolidation of peace was a passive process of recuperation, and by 1869 the need for active methods of reconstruction was generally felt, to promote the prosperity which had been confidently expected to follow the period of convalescence and which was still conspicuous by its absence. After the second war of independence the nation faced the same problem as after the first—the pressing need of creating the economic independence essential to support its political emancipation. In one respect, the government was in a better position to meet that responsibility than any of its predecessors: for the first time since 1821 the nation was free to dispose of its full revenues. The government took the position that intervention and the recognition of the Empire automatically broke the onerous treaties which mortgaged its resources to foreign powers, and the political defeat of its creditors provided it accordingly with a clean slate; and though the repudiation was not absolute and an offer was made to negotiate new treaties, pending such settlements, the moratorium gave the government a breathing spell of which it took advantage to set its house in order.

Financial reorganization was begun by Matias Romero, who returned from Washington to put his patriotic zeal at the service of the Treasury—the most trying test to which it could be put—and by dint of hard work and economy he brought order out of chaos and introduced into that den of ancestral confusion, which had lured so many ministers to their doom, system and light; but the light was gloomy. During the lean years from 1863 to 1867, when the public revenues had been at their lowest, the budget had been balanced, but with the return to normal conditions, the familiar deficit reappeared, and on the eve of the congressional elections in 1869 the department suspended payment on the salaries of its employees, and the cry of impending bankruptcy was raised by the Opposition with plausible effect. The pinch was temporary and the alarm exaggerated, but the organic difficulties under which the department labored were persistent and acute. The customs were unfettered, but the volume of foreign trade was small under the best of conditions. The high protective tariffs maintained by the government made the use of foreign commodities prohibitive for a large portion of the population, to the detriment, as Romero explained, of the fiscal revenues, the public wealth at large, and the material advancement of the masses; exports were confined to the precious metals and a few products which commanded high prices abroad, and as the cost of transportation was high because of the broken configuration of the country, only articles of great value and comparatively small bulk could be profitably exported, while the wealthy alone could afford to consume foreign imports. These chronic difficulties were aggravated, of course, under abnormal conditions; during the French intervention foreign and domestic trade had shrunk to their lowest proportions, while the people raised only enough to meet their immediate needs, and a good crop was considered a calamity. The cure was a quandary in 1869. A reduction of the tariff was favored by Romero, but to tamper with the traditional livelihood of the government was regarded as too rash, and the idea was abandoned; and for the same reason he was unable to lower the interstate duties on which the Federal government and the states depended for internal revenue, and which hampered the circulation of domestic trade. The result was that the commercial community, representing roughly one-fourth of the total population, bore the burden of taxation almost exclusively; and as commercial relations were drastically reduced by the war, the impoverishment of the country, and the forbidding effect of the moratorium on foreign markets, the government which had entered into full possession of its resources still scraped bottom.

To broaden the base of contribution was recognized to be a pressing necessity. Good management and close thrift were negative methods of reconstructing the national economy; and as the improvement of communications was an essential prerequisite to opening new sources of revenue and increasing the capacities of production and consumption of the country, the government took the initiative and introduced into Congress measures for the extension of highroads and the construction of railways. Of these undertakings the line linking Veracruz to the capital was the most important. A subsidy of over a million pesos a year was voted for a term of thirteen years, and though it was generally agreed that no price was too high to pay for material progress, the Opposition managed to manufacture a bill of complaints on the score of extravagance and the fact that the contract was awarded to an English company. The subsidy, consuming one-eleventh of the budget, strained the resources of the government, the company ran into financial delays because of the difficulty of selling shares in London, and an agitation was set afoot to revoke the charter in favor of Mexican enterprise; but the weakness of native capital and the obvious risk of giving the country a bad name by a breach of contract checked the agitation, and the public utility of the venture outweighed both patriotic and pecuniary objections to it. Other projects were discussed and some of them started: a railroad across the northwestern corner of Mexico, a subsidy for an American shipping line to help the henequen trade in Yucatan, surveys for a Pacific port to be served by another line plying between California and Panama, and the Tehuantepec transit, which was revived, remarkably enough, without resuscitating the political panic of the McLane–Ocampo treaty. A pioneering will was at work, a sanguine vision of economic awakening, of potential improvements, of vital expansion and fusing contacts; but progress was slow, the returns of such undertakings were remote, poverty and unemployment in the meanwhile were pressing, and impatience with the present, the perennial present, was acute; and the Opposition turned its energy in another direction.

Financial reorganization and economic reconstruction could not be treated without touching the social question which lay at their core. Prodigious strides had been made by the political and religious reforms, the Opposition conceded, "but social questions have been treated very lightly. Not enough thought has been given to the fact that institutions are worth very little when they are applied to a society to which they are not well adapted. . . . The Constitution makes all Mexicans equal, but does that equality actually exist? . . . While the people are devoured by poverty and ignorance, is liberty possible? Certainly, democracy will be an illusion, morality a dream, and legal equality a sarcasm. . . . One of the great evils bred by this monstrous inequality of wealth and education is the system of robbery employed by the poor to satisfy the needs of those who, without work or education, must yet make a living. A small number of Mexicans own the territory of the Republic, the vast majority of citizens possess not an inch of land, almost every village is obliged to work for the landlord in return for a meager fare, the spirit of enterprise has been constantly stifled by disorder, industry is in its cradle struggling to break the bonds of ignorance, trade is lifeless, and the masses demoralized by the ambition of those who speculate in public misfortune and who are the real root of vandalism." This bill of complaints was legitimate and timely. Twelve years after Ponciano Arriaga had raised a lone voice in the Congress of 1857 and proclaimed the weak point of the Constitution, the necessity of agrarian reform was recognized as the revelation of experience, and here at least the criticism of the Opposition was constructive. Out of seven million inhabitants of the Republic, the writer pointed out, five million were Indians, who produced nothing and consumed nothing and were incapable of contributing to the upkeep of the State or to the increase of production by the two million who carried the burden of taxation. "What industry, what commerce, what speculation, can exist with a consumption as small as that of two million scattered through so vast a territory?" And the cure? Roads? Communications?—short cuts to bankruptcy under such conditions. Colonization? Immigration?—imported manpower could not be introduced soon enough or abundantly enough to replace those idle millions; and to dispossess the native, who was strong, tenacious, inured to hardship, and laborious, of his birthright would be to commit the crime of Cain. The aboriginal must be enabled to produce and consume; the problem was to leaven that inert mass, to knead that dumb matter, and to draw it into the national economy. "We believe that this would be possible by giving him the means of production; that is, a margin of labor and livelihood beyond the service required by his master, and good roads to market. There are properties in the territory of Mexico—and this may be said of almost all of them—of such extent that their owners cannot cultivate them, and consequently they are merely nominal values and practically unproductive; it should be noted, moreover, that while conditions remain as they are now, it would be useless and perhaps prejudicial to undertake labor for the product of which there would be no consumption, and which would only increase its costs. Would it not be possible, however, and without altering the present status of property, which might be dangerous, to give the native some share in the product and to provide consumption for such crops?" Or, if share-cropping proved impractical, why should not the government devote the abundant public lands at its disposal to the redemption of the peon?

By this approach the Opposition laid a line of political telepathy, capable of transmitting a circuitous but far-reaching shock to the solid popularity of the President. Was the man who had led the political and religious reforms to stop short of the social consummation of the movement? Was he to forget his own people and forego the one reform which, above all others, seemed to belong by right to him? Such was the point of a question which, for all its sincerity, was a skillful political snare. The Opposition raised the question, knowing the answer to it. The government needed no prodding. The public lands still at its disposal lay along the frontiers and the seaboard, far removed from the centers of population, and ill adapted to settlement under the conditions prevailing in 1869; but it met the challenge of the Opposition by a counterproposal. A project to tax uncultivated lands was submitted to Congress. By this measure it was expected that the great idle estates of the center, "virtually valueless at present for want of population, would centuplicate in price and importance through their subdivision into small properties and the increase of population"—an indirect approach to a problem of which the government no less than the Opposition recognized the dangers. "The government cannot," Romero explained, "without attacking the sacred right of property, limit the extent of land which any single proprietor may possess; but it does have a great interest in trying, since the good of society so demands, to secure the cultivation and exploitation of all such property as is susceptible of this improvement." Real estate, both rural and urban, was tax free throughout the Republic, with the exception of the Federal District, and "perhaps in the state of prostration in which a struggle of sixty years has left the nation, and in which commerce and agriculture are almost completely paralyzed, it would be unwise to decree a direct general tax on real estate, notwithstanding the urgent need of creating new sources of fiscal income"; but a light impost—twenty pesos a year on uncultivated property—could not be considered an unreasonable or a revolutionary demand, and it might lead to a voluntary release of surplus lands. A year later Romero repeated his recommendation, for Congress had taken no action on it.

The caution of Congress, the motion of the government, the proposal of the Opposition, were equally timid. They were unanimous motions, and nothing more. A common consciousness of the social question and a common reluctance to raise the issue of agrarian reform frankly and fully made the problem too sore to touch. The revolutionary impulse was exhausted; the political and religious reforms had consumed their authors and cost the country too violent a convulsion; one revolution was enough in a lifetime, and a new generation was needed to shoulder the next. In the meanwhile, the country continued to stagnate, and stagnancy was a fertile breeding ground for disillusionment, gloom, and unrest. The Opposition continued to labor the point. "It is indispensable to lend life and action and movement to the Republic, lest peace become a lethargy in the mouth of misery, and tranquillity the repose of the tombs. The people that does not progress perishes." The advantage of irresponsibility which the Opposition enjoyed was exploited to the full. The pall of poverty was a standing reproach to the President. The lapsing of his contact with the people was constantly lamented. The custody in which he was kept by Lerdo was incessantly stressed. The public was not allowed to forget that there was "a kind of *cordon sanitaire* around the President to prevent certain popular papers from reaching his hands. It is feared that the fiber in his heart, so sensitive in other times to everything that emanates from the heart of the people, may again vibrate." And the failure of the government to complete its historic mission became, in those practiced hands, the crushing proof that its day was finished.

Certainly the times were trying. The fruits of Reform were souring in 1869. With political independence achieved, and religious emancipation, the country continued to be governed by a colonial economy which was a permanent threat to national autonomy. If new men were not needed, it was necessary at least for the old ones to think in new terms, no longer of political systems and ideological rights, but of economic facts and philosophies, to forget the feudal past and attune their minds to contemporary capitalism, and to recognize that the progress made was partial and that emancipation from poverty was essential to national survival. The protracted slump, the paralysis of commerce and agriculture, the want of native industry, were pressing reminders that the country still depended on more advanced nations for its development; and it was necessary, therefore, to face the question of foreign relations frankly and fully.

The restoration of the Republic was followed by a period of prolonged isolation. Diplomatic relations had been severed with the powers that participated in intervention or that recognized the Empire—with the entire family of nations, that is, except the United States and the South American Republics—and no steps were taken to renew them until 1869. As a matter of dignity the Mexican Government refused to make the first move, and for the same reason the aggressors declined to make any overtures. The situation was abnormal, but diplomatic relations, as Zarco observed, were by no means indispensable; on the contrary, the country was relieved of a race of accredited meddlers who had consistently cursed it. Commercial relations languished, however. English firms in Mexico, and the bondholders in London, petitioned their government to renew official relations, but Lord John Russell found it easier to sue Juarez than to solicit him. Similarly the official press in Paris, without forgetting or forgiving, alluded to the possibility of official relations and rallied Juarez on his refusal to risk a rebuff. The Mexican Government, on its side, showed no signs of relenting until 1869, when the interdict was raised in favor of the North German Confederation, which, being a newcomer among the nations and born after intervention, was innocent as yet of original sin, and of Italy, which had always been regarded as a brother-in-arms. The ban on the major Powers remained unabated, however, and by 1869 the Opposition insisted that the time had come for the government to pocket its pride. In view of the domestic depression, autarchy was impossible. "What matter that Mexico can dispose of all kinds of materials, if it lacks the factories to elaborate them? What matter that its soil can produce everything, if it lacks the population to consume its products? What matter that its soil is so fertile, if the majority of its inhabitants lack the knowledge necessary to exploit it?" What matter, in short, that Mexico was free, if it was unfed? Why blink the fact that the umbilical cord with Europe could not be cut? Why refuse to recognize that the deadlock was merely a truce which must eventually be broken? Isolation was becoming more impolitic with every passing day. The security of Mexico lay in the very forces that had ruined it—the competing imperialisms of Europe and the United States. "Fortunately, those formidable forces almost cancel each other by their contrary tendencies. It does not serve the interests of Europe that Mexico should be absorbed by the United States, nor those of the United States that it should again become a colony of the Old World. From this mutual opposition results a state of equilibrium for Mexico that preserves its nationality and guarantees its independence." But "the interruption of relations with Europe favors American influences more and more every day, European capitalists are emigrating and forsaking their enterprises, the Americans are beginning to invade us on all sides," and it was imperative, therefore, to restore the balance without delay.

Relations with the United States had never been better. In 1867 the London *Times* and a section of the French press presented Mexico to its American patron with their compliments—an erratic genuflection which was read in Mexico to mean an irritated attempt to embroil the two republics and a peevish hope that Washington might inherit the difficulties that had defeated French intervention. Provocations of that kind were persistent in the foreign press, and as late as 1869 the *Bullionist* of London, warning the bondholders against any private settlement with the Mexican Government, which would yield nothing but "words, words, words," wrote: "The manifest destiny of Central America is to be absorbed by the great Republic. Mexico is even now little more than a distant province of the United States, and as the influence of the Washington Government contributed so greatly to defeat the efforts of European States to compel payment, it has incurred a moral obligation to make the fine promises of Juarez effective." *Telum imbelle sine ictu.* Mexico and Washington continued to maintain the same cordial relations as during the war and to preserve their friendship by keeping strictly apart. The only source of possible friction was the settlement of the debt, and when discussions were undertaken by the two governments, the foreign press followed the negotiations with sinister surmises that they involved territorial cessions and the penetration of American capital. These incitements produced some effect in Mexico, where they were echoed by the Opposition press, which attacked the Ministry for preparing the tutelage of Mexico by the recognition of a crushing debt which would wreck the recovery of the country or pave the way for American intervention.

The question was uppermost in the public mind when, in the closing months of 1869, Seward paid a visit to Mexico. He was received with conspicuous hospitality by the government and with intense suspicion by the Opposition, which insisted on seeing secret and sinister designs in what was merely the unofficial visit of a retired statesman. The hostility was so conspicuous, indeed, that the guest of the nation was moved to notice it, and at a banquet in the Palace he took occasion publicly to disavow the aggressive ambitions imputed to Washington and to expatiate on the new era of good feeling and disinterested solidarity inaugurated by both peoples in their common defense of republican principles. These professions were entirely trustworthy, so far as they went. The old statesman had undergone, if not a change of heart, the sobering effects at least of the civil war and the French intervention. In his sixty-eighth year he was convinced that the craving for territorial aggrandizement had sensibly abated in the United States and that his countrymen, as he said, had learned "to value dollars more and dominion less." The pressure of population and commercial expansion were sufficient, he had come to believe, to insure the course of empire. Manifest Destiny, of which he had once been the champion, was out of date, in its cruder forms; his ideas moved with the times, and it was only a matter of time—five, ten, or twenty years—before Mexico would open her doors to American immigration as cheerfully as Montana or Idaho; within thirty years Mexico City would become the seat of Anglo-Saxon power in the hemisphere. Such were the ideas which he was accustomed to confide to his intimates in the United States, and those which he expressed in Mexico were consistent with them. The gentlemen of the Opposition were not impressed. Although their spokesmen were not invited to dine at the Palace, they smuggled in reporters to study the platonic banquet, to lift the speeches, to look into the toasts, and to peer under the table for trouble. Seward did what he could to disarm mistrust. He paid tribute to his host. He placed Juarez in the pantheon of the American great; he ranked him with Washington, Lincoln, and Bolivar; at a public appearance in Puebla, before leaving the country, he described him as the greatest man he had ever known. The superlative, coming from one who had known Lincoln, was so startling that the American Minister, supposing he had been misquoted, felt it his duty to verify it: Seward repeated that it was his mature and considered opinion, and he stood by it. His efforts to foster good will were not fortunate, however. Foreign, and particularly American, favor was suspect, and the compliment was of dubious benefit, at that time, to the President.

Lincoln had died in time: Juarez had still to survive the test of reconstruction. Seward was confident that he would succeed—five years of peace, he computed, would put Mexico firmly on its feet—but the Opposition was impatient. At this moment another revolt broke out in the provinces and provided a fresh text for the prophets of doom. "The policy which we have been fighting for two and a half years has borne the fruits we foresaw. Isolation, poverty, immorality, and local disorders, and as the inevitable consequence of all this, revolution. Here is the work of the Lerdo Ministry. Here is the result of the criminal condescension of Juarez. . . . The policy of the Lerdo–Juarez dictatorship has employed disorder and violence to preserve power, and disorder and violence are turning against it today." The date was December 30, 1869.

The state of the nation in 1869 was no better and no worse than its state of mind. The psychological effects of isolation were unhealthy; seclusion deepened domestic dissension and distrust of the foreigner; the one was the corollary of the other, and both were fostered by the delusion of self-sufficiency. The solidarity and self-confidence won in the war with the French were sapped by the economic slump that followed it and gave way to a moral depression that despaired of independence, as the destiny of the nation, oscillating between Europe and the United States, seemed to offer only a choice of evils or the alternative of running down with the slackening momentum of national life to a complete halt. Xenophobia was one way out of the dilemma. Foreigners found it prevalent during these years and particularly pronounced against Americans. As the pull of economic gravitation drew the country toward the American orbit, the old ingrown antipathy to the nearest and most prepotent alien revived in a defensive reaction. The morbid sense of inferiority, which the American war created in 1847 and the visit of Seward quickened in 1869, was too deep-seated and undying to be eradicated in a score of years, and the Opposition played upon it precisely as the Reaction had done in the past, slipping unconsciously into a current of mind that carried it backward to the same fears, the same prejudices, the same mental rut of invalid nationalism. Inevitable as those fears were in a people prejudiced by experience and maimed by collision with the modern world, the propensity to nurse old grievances, to suckle the ulcer and feed on the past, was a pathological symptom and a stubborn impediment to recovery and progress; and the obverse of xenophobia was family friction. As the nation shrank into itself, the sore infection of infirmity turned inward and fed with sickly satisfaction on the steady depreciation and restless detraction of the national representatives. Had the state of the nation reflected the state of mind of the Opposition, the situation might have been alarming; but the Opposition was still a strenuous minority neutralized by the sensible majority. The Opposition press soaked up complaints like blotting paper, magnifying and blurring them; but also drew them like a poultice. The common sense of the country recognized in the sedulous propaganda against the government the studied confusion of men and conditions. If politics is the art of accomplishing the possible under a given set of conditions, the policies of the government achieved the feasible under the prevailing conditions that cramped it. Time was the cure for them; and time was, as it had always been, the best defense of the President. The same abilities which he had brought to the government of Oaxaca after the American war were manifest in his administration of the State after the French invasion: sound management, careful economy, public enterprise, the opening of communications, the spreading of education, the manuring of peace, the weeding out of revolts, roads and schools and police to bind and knit and brace the natural process of healing and progress; but his very success served to belittle him in 1869, because the times were rife with exaction and challenge, and the impossible was expected of the President of the Republic. He gave the country what it wanted and what it needed; no one could give it what it craved—the solution of the difficulties of the postwar period without the patience, the perseverance, and the co-operation to overcome them.

Zarco congratulated his countrymen on the possession of those qualities at the beginning of the year 1869. "The year 1868," he wrote, tearing the old leaf from the calendar, "records no resounding events in Mexico and no great cataclysms. One notes in the Republic something of the good practical instinct, the common sense of a man who on reaching mature years has the will power to repair the errors of his inexperienced youth." By the end of the year the state of mind of the nation might better have been compared to the reluctant common sense of a youth who, on attaining emancipation and maturity, finds himself foiled of a future; and precisely because the malaise was undefinable and unrelieved, it took the form of carping criticism and captious complaint of the practical paternal guidance of the government. The irritation of the Opposition was recognized to be unreasonable, but it was pressed on the public with an infectious persistence and a seasonable zeal that finally began to make an impression. Common sense is an uncommon quality in times of prolonged privation and depression; the doldrums were demoralizing; and by sheer force of repetition, magnifying the shortcomings and minimizing the achievements of the government, the minority multiplied and dissatisfaction spread. Then, just as detraction began to penetrate, an event occurred which restored the stature of Juarez and revived with fresh brilliance the fading glory of yore.

3

IN 1870 the crash came—not in Mexico, but in France. The Franco-Prussian war, the disasters of Sedan and Metz, the collapse of the Empire, the rebirth of the Republic—the repercussion of these events stirred the sluggish pulse of Mexico, revived the national pride in the President, and reminded the country of the magnitude of the services which he had rendered it. For until then something essential had been lacking. The scores of intervention had not been settled. Not until 1870 was it possible to appreciate the contribution which Juarez had made to the downfall of Napoleon by an indomitable resistance which weakened the position of the Emperor in Europe and created that rankling craving for *revanche* which led to the Franco-Prussian war. A French Republican paper recognized it and cited the example of his tenacity as a beacon amid the turmoil of the Prussian invasion. "May the conduct of that great Republican be a lesson to us!"—words which echoed with memorable resonance in Mexico.

Juarez himself was profoundly stimulated by these events. In the spring of 1870 his robust constitution began to fail. Shortly after his sixty-fourth birthday he was stricken by a cerebral congestion, and his life was in doubt for a few hours, but he recovered quickly, and he followed the unfolding of the crisis in France with the satisfaction of one who had been spared to witness the full and final consummation of his work. The chronicle would have been incomplete without the rout of the enemy for which he had been waiting; but his deepest relief was that the way lay open at last for a reconciliation of the two peoples. He was among the first to sign a message of sympathy to the French people from a group of Mexican republicans, and he forwarded it to a friend abroad with a request to give it the widest possible publicity. The message miscarried, but the accident was fortunate, for it prompted him to follow it by a long letter of his own, packed with personal reflections, political experience, and intimate revelations worth far more than the formal message.

"The message, which was dictated by the most cordial sympathy, and which I had the honor of being one of the first to sign," he explained, "was destined by its authors not only to transmit to the unfortunate French people the expression of our admiration and good wishes, but also, and above all, to dispel from their minds any doubt as to the fraternal sentiments which all true Mexicans feel for the nation to whom the sacred cause of liberty owes so much, and whom we have never confused with the infamous government of Bonaparte." Because the truth about Mexico had been brought home to France by the army, tired with defeat, prejudiced by patriotism, turgid with antipathy, the clear truth could be told only by contact of the two peoples, and in the affliction of the French Juarez was finally free to speak fraternally for his own. "Nevertheless, my dear friend," he continued, "to speak only of my own feelings, which are shared, I know, by our political world, just as the defeat of the bandit who sowed pillage and death across our fair land for five years gave me indescribable joy, and just as his fall, which was worthy of his elevation, at once tragic and grotesque, has filled me with satisfaction as a Republican and a Mexican, so, too, and in the same measure, have the continuation of the war by the Prussian King and its horrors saddened me profoundly. Yet, looking away from scenes of slaughter and devastation, if we can forget the anxieties of the present and scan and contemplate the infinite future, we must say that the appalling cataclysm which threatens to wreck France is, on the contrary, the signal for its ascension. For France is returning to its great political life without which a nation, no matter how much it may be worth in literature, art, and science, is only a human herd corralled in the barracks or the sacristy, those two secular dens of despotism which my friends and I have been trying to destroy in Mexico. But who can doubt the final triumph of France, if France wants to succeed, or rather if it knows how to want? If it *knows how to want,* I say; for though the reports from the invaded provinces reveal an admirable vigor and patriotism, fully equal to the circumstances, I cannot but feel serious dread when I think of the qualities and defects of the French soldier, so fond of fighting in regular battle where his fierce courage can be displayed before witnesses, but so little apt for guerrilla warfare, which is the only war of real defense, and the only effective one against a foreign invader." And he put his experience at the service of French patriots. "If I had the honor of directing the destinies of France now, I would act no differently than I did in our beloved country from 1862 to 1867 to destroy the enemy. No large bodies of troops that move slowly, that are hard to feed in a devastated land and easily demoralized after a reverse, but corps of fifteen, twenty, or thirty thousand men at most, connected by flying columns able to lend aid swiftly when necessary, harassing the enemy day and night, exterminating his soldiers, isolating and destroying his convoys, allowing him no rest, no sleep, no provisions, no munitions; wearing him out little by little in the whole occupied territory; and finally obliging him to capitulate, a captive of his conquests, or to save the battered remains of his forces by a retreat. This is, as you know, the whole history of the liberation of

Mexico. And if the despicable Bazaine, worthy servant of a contemptible Emperor, cares to employ the leisure which he has won by his odious
treason, he is the one best fitted to enlighten his countrymen as to the
invincibility of guerrilla bands when they are fighting for the independence of their country."

The prescription was peculiarly urgent for France because of the
turn which the war had taken after the collapse of the front and the
capture of the regular armies at Sedan and Metz. "But another question arises which seems terrible for so centralized a country as France.
Can Paris sustain itself until a relieving army raises the blockade? And
what will happen if Paris falls from hunger or is captured by force?"
And again he brought his experience to bear on a problem already tested
in Mexico. "Well and good! Suppose for a moment that Paris suffers
the fate of Sedan and Metz. What will follow? Is Paris France? Politically, yes, for the past eighty years. But today, when military considerations must prevail over all others, why should the fall of Paris necessarily entail the fall of France? And if the King of Prussia installs his
court in the Palace of the Tuileries, which is still saturated with the
contagious sickness of Bonapartism, why should this phantasmagoria
demoralize two or three millions of citizens armed for the defense of
their soil from one end of the country to the other? Maximilian was on
the throne of Mexico for four years, but this did not prevent him from
purging his crime on the Champs-de-Mars of Queretaro, while the national sovereignty returned in triumph to the city of Moctezuma. During those four years, when the only legitimate government went wandering like a fugitive from the Rio Grande to the Sacramento, many
who had been tempered in the struggle against adversity began to
nurse doubts of the efficiency of our efforts and to deny our future
liberation. As for me—and this is my only merit—aided by some indomitable patriots like Diaz, Escobedo, and Ortega, my faith never
wavered. Sometimes, when defection surrounded me as a result of
crushing reverses, my spirit was profoundly depressed, but I reacted
immediately. Recalling that verse of the greatest of poets, 'While one
remains afoot, not one has fallen,' I resolved then more than ever to
carry on the ruthless struggle and to be pitiless for the expulsion of the
intruder. God has crowned my efforts and those of so many brave men,
many of whom, alas, have paid with their lives for our common faith in
our country and in the Republic. I hope that the same will happen in
France. Her cause, since the fall of Bonaparte, has been the cause of all
free peoples. This truth has been so well understood by Mexican democrats that six hundred veterans of the struggle for Independence, the
same men who for five years carried on a just war against the troops of
Bazaine and Dupin, have thought it their duty to take ship at Veracruz
for New York. Armed and equipped at their own expense, they propose to sail from there to join the forces of the glorious Garibaldi. And

I am proud to proclaim it: the Mexican Legion is worthy of fighting and dying at the side of the regenerated French army for the sacred cause of the universal republic. With all my heart, Benito Juarez."

The letter sprang from his heart: nothing that ever came from his pen was written with a fuller or greater one. The liberation of France as the result of the liberation of Mexico—indirect, belated, but logical—crowned his life work with the final triumph, and he identified himself with the struggle in France with active sympathy, and the vicarious part which he took in it made it perfectly natural for him to write, "If I had the honor of directing the destinies of France now," for that was what, unwittingly, he had done for five years. The defeat of the French army in Mexico kindled the fuse which exploded its superiority and the security of the Empire in Europe. He had wrought better than he knew; and in a glow of self-consciousness he came to rest.

For there was no further to go. The Mexican Legion never reached Europe. The six hundred volunteers, who bore the message in their flesh and blood, were turned back by the armistice. To the crucial question whether Paris could hold out long enough for a relieving army to raise the siege the answer was the stoic resistance which the population opposed to the Prussians for four months, the strenuous attempts of Gambetta to muster an army in the provinces, and the Commune. The will to resist, concentrated in the people of Paris and invincible in the masses, was not shared by the authorities: the military commander called it a heroic folly, the Government of National Defense was determined to capitulate, but when the idea of an armistice was broached in mid-siege, the response was a popular uprising and a demand for the destitution of the government and the creation of the Commune of Paris to continue the defense. Compelled by popular pressure to continue a defense in which it had no faith, the Government of National Defeat drained Paris white for sixteen weeks by spectacular demonstrations, costly sorties, fatigue and starvation, and finally signed the armistice in February 1871.

What could Juarez have said to that defeatist Government of National Defense, which the Opposition organized after the fall of the Empire, and whose lions were Jules Favre and Adolphe Thiers? The former champions of freedom in Mexico were all on the side of surrender in France. But the armistice, far from concluding the struggle, merely transformed it, and a new phase began with the capitulation of Paris. A National Assembly, elected to make the peace and form a government, returned a majority of Monarchists from the provinces, the Republican deputies from Paris were insulted when they assembled at Bordeaux, and Paris, anticipating a reactionary *coup d'état,* organized to defend the Republic. Three weeks after the armistice Thiers, appointed provisional President by the Assembly, precipitated an insurrection in Paris by attempting to disarm the National Guard, the government fled to Versailles, civil war ensued, and the cause of democracy took a turn which split the country in social schism. Versailles became the focus of all the conservative forces released by the capitulation—the clergy, the Monarchists, the moneyed classes, and the army—which Thiers, with the help of Bismarck, who liberated the prisoners of war, assembled to crush the insurrection in Paris. For two and a half months the capital held out against a double blockade by the French and German armies and maintained against the internal enemy the indomitable defense of which it had been cheated against the foreign foe; and in the course of the struggle the bitterness of civil war developed into the fury of class war. The coalition in Versailles, haunted by the dread of revolution in the wake of defeat, identified the insurrection in Paris with the rising portent of socialism in Europe, and provoked a resurrection of the fevers of 1848 which it feared. When the insurrection started, it had a political but no social program. Manned by a militant proletariat and a middle-class menaced with ruin by two decrees passed by the Assembly, foreclosing on rents and credit, Paris proclaimed the Commune to save the Republic; but the Republic, seven years after the founding of the International, had come to mean for many of its champions in 1871 the universal republic of a socialist society, and in the elections for the Commune the International, the Labor Chamber, and the delegates of sixteen districts combined to issue a joint manifesto declaring that their candidates were presented in the name of a new world by the party of the disinherited, that the workers were entitled to a place in the coming reconstitution of France, and demanding the political advent of the proletariat and the fall of the government oligarchy and of industrial feudalism. Versailles replied by red-baiting and declared, without promising the Republic or consenting to discuss the issue, that its sole object was to suppress an insurrectionary committee, whose members professed communist doctrines, and who would sack Paris and destroy France. To insure their defeat, a dense curtain of calumny and propaganda was dropped about Paris. The press, the provinces, and foreign countries were flooded with lurid accounts of atrocities committed by the rabble in Paris, the Commune was outlawed, and prisoners shot; and when the Versaillese finally penetrated the city and massacred its defenders, the Commune retaliated and burned public buildings and shot hostages before it succumbed. The reprisals of the victors were savage and insatiable and cost the Commune over a hundred thousand victims, but Thiers was able to boast that the danger of socialism in Europe had been dispelled for a long time. The danger of a reactionary restoration was also dispelled, however, and the Republic, though not the universal republic for which so many of its martyrs died, was eventually restored. The faith and the fate of the Commune revealed the real nature of the civil war in France and opened a new vision of democracy for the future, but of that bloody and abortive revolt the terror, and the terror alone, was reported—the terror in Paris of the tricolor turning into the white flag of truce with the Prussian; the terror in Versailles of a revolutionary upsurge, turgid with outraged patriotism, and the red flag flying in Paris; the terror on both sides of civil war raising the leaven of national defeat, and class struggle sowing and reaping the whirlwind that swept away the Empire. The significance of the terror was suppressed with the insurrection itself. The issue was confused, the nation and the capital, class and country, embroiled in clashing claims of patriotism, and the accounts which crossed the ocean were heavily biased to blacken the Commune. In Mexico the meaning of the convulsion was clouded, and the fact was clearer than the truth—the fatal confusion, division, and defeat of France. The Mexican Legion could no longer have delivered its message. To whom was it to be addressed? To the indomitable French people in Paris?—but were they not called Communists? Or to the legal representatives of the nation in Versailles?—but could they be called patriots? Thiers and Favre and the Republican Opposition were all in Versailles, and the French army was engaged in stifling the universal republic in Paris. The situation no longer had any meaning for Mexico, save for the casual fact that among the hostages shot by the Commune figured a banker by the name of J. B. Jecker, who went to his death complaining that the Empire had fleeced him of his profits in Mexico.

The sole bearing which the disaster in France had for Mexico lay in the remote but providential connection between the catastrophe and the origin of the intrigue by which both peoples had been abused. The casualties which the collapse of the Empire left in its wake included what remained of the principal authors, agents, and accomplices of intervention, and a singular fitness marked their several fates. Napoleon, whose ambition to emulate the English led him to violate himself and his people by a fling at colonial empire for which neither was fitted—Napoleon was a refugee in England from his countrymen; the nephew of the uncle crossed the Channel and his fate, as a French republican paper said, was more ignominious than if he had fallen with his dupe at Queretaro. Bazaine, his trustworthiness warped by his treatment in Mexico, ended his career under the suspicion of treason at Metz: the neglected drudge falling in the habit of defeat and the harness of dishonor and surrendering an army without even destroying his munitions, as his best officers begged him to do in memory of Ortega at Puebla. The whole crew of the Empire, from the marshals who made their names in Mexico down to the drummers who lost theirs there, disappeared in the purge or reappeared for a brief moment of infamy to massacre their countrymen in Paris. The Mexican expatriates were not more homeless than their protectors and patrons; oblivion buried them all. In that year of reckoning other and more distant names were recalled for the part they had played in the tragic intrigue of intervention. Prim had repented in time and made ample amends by his outspoken championship of Mexico; and by a curious twist of fate it was Prim who precipitated the Franco-Prussian war by soliciting a Hohenzollern prince for the throne of Spain. The English partner had also withdrawn in time, but without reaping any benefit from the fiasco of intervention except the fall of Napoleon. The Pope was in a worse position. The French troops were withdrawn from Rome on the outbreak of the war, a few days after an ecumenical council had declared the infallibility of the Pope to be an article of faith. Rome became the capital of United Italy, and while his unlimited pretensions were recognized in the spiritual sphere, the secular authority of Giovanni Maria Mastai-Feretti was reduced to the extraterritorial rights of the prisoner of the Vatican.

Between the catastrophe in France and the expedition to Mexico the connection was casual in the temporal sphere, but neither fortuitous nor irrelevant in the region of first and last causes. Among the manifold causes of the crash in France, the Mexican misadventure was a contributing factor of delayed action but far-reaching effect; and as everything fell into perspective and everyone into place, the figure of Juarez loomed larger with the passing of time and the broadening background of his achievement. In the revivification of his glory he was honored in his own country and abroad. From foreign parts came tributes of the most various kinds. The range was broad, from the French nobleman who sent him a case of choice wines from the loot of the Tuileries—"It seems to me perfectly natural," he wrote, "that you who had the honor of being the first to rout the firm of Bonaparte & Co. should profit a little by the liquidation of that wretched association. Don Benito Juarez drinking the Madeira of Napoleon seems to me the last word to deride that disgraceful intervention which was to have been *the fairest page of my reign!*"—to the equally familiar and fervent but more solemn homage with which the secretary of Garibaldi apostrophized him as a son of the people and hailed him as a class comrade—"You who rose from a humble toiler in the Sierra of Oaxaca to become the great laborer of liberty, civilization, and progress; you who because of your deeds and your virtues have rightly been hailed the Lincoln of Mexico."

The comparison with Lincoln was frequent, and it was apt, but no analogy is accurate, and the affinities fell short of the differences. The most fitting tribute was to compare Juarez with himself; and for his misfortune that was what his countrymen did in the following years.

4

LINCOLN had died in time: Juarez survived his mission, and time was his assassin. The revivification of his glory, luminous as it was, was brief and fleeting—the reflected glory of other worlds, the evening glow of a day that was done, the lingering afterlight flushing the fading cumulus and towering shapes of the past with the radiant dusk of a vindicating but vainglorious vision; for the day was to end, after all, in clouds.

The morrow was gloomy. In the first days of 1871 Juarez lost his wife. Death, which had narrowly missed him nine months before, struck close the second time, for theirs had been a union of heart and mind so complete that it was a matter of common knowledge, and of public comment in the press, that he had lost the better part of his own life. The world honored her accordingly. The obituaries paid tribute to the most faithful of helpmates and celebrated the devoted wife, mother, and patriot who had shared both his private and public life with abnegation; extolling her as the model of the Mexican woman, blessed with the unassuming simplicity of fine breeding, bearing adversity and fortune with equal equanimity, never trespassing on public affairs, shunning the intrigues of the Palace, so discreet that she hardly knew the names of the ministers, so retiring that many of her admirers had never seen her, but always accessible to the needy and ministering to them with modest charity, and seconding her husband by a life so self-effacing that she was noticed only when she died. Such was her celebrity, and the accepted pattern of a President's wife. The domestic idyll was but one side of the medal, however, and these tributes told only half the truth. During her stay in the United States she had won the respect and admiration of Seward and Johnson, who paid her conspicuous attention in Washington at a time when such attention told politically, and Seward, associating her with her husband in the hour of triumph, placed an American warship at her disposal when she returned to the country which she had represented with exemplary courage and dignity in days of privation and hardship abroad. There was no reverse to the medal: it was the same figure on both sides, in high and low relief. The whole truth Juarez alone knew—the surpassing peace of perfect understanding, trust, and identity on which he had drawn for twenty-eight years and which had never failed him. He was twenty years her senior, and she called him Juarez and he called her "the little old lady," despite the disparity of their ages, for separation aged them both alike. She was barely forty-five when she died, and he was in the sere of life. Her death did him one last service. Hats were raised to him in unanimous sympathy. Taken on their sentimental side, the Mexicans responded to a man; there was a spontaneous outpouring of popular feeling, and political hostilities were suspended by common consent. The press without exception, and the Opposition papers most bitterly, mourned her passing. It was noticed that, though he bore the blow with his customary fortitude, he was profoundly shaken by it. When the time came to start for the cemetery, he mustered strength enough to lift her into the coffin himself, but he could not master his grief, and, groping his way back to the waiting-room, sank on a sofa, exhausted. It was noticed, too, as a sign of political truce, that two ringleaders of recent revolts, Aureliano Rivera and Miguel Negrete, whom he had pardoned, acted as pallbearers, and that one of them, turning his hand to a trade he had once practiced, soldered the coffin. These were significant symptoms; and so was the immense crowd that turned out to prove that the heart of the people still beat with his, as she was borne to the pantheon in which the national heroes rested to await his coming.

But the place of the one could not be taken by the many. The political truce was short-lived.

In 1871 his presidential term expired, and the year began ominously. The widower, whom the world pitied, was now reduced to the poor consolations of power, and he showed no inclination to relinquish the other life to which he had been wedded for thirteen years. On the contrary, he announced his candidacy for re-election. There was an outcry in the press, where all the motives of the past were recapitulated by the Opposition to cry halt. Re-election was attacked in principle as a breach of republican faith and a violation of the spirit, if not the letter, of the Constitution. In theory it was denounced as the abuse of an unwritten precept upon which the development of democracy depended, and in practice as the perpetuation in power of a person already prone to the dangerous notion that he was irreplaceable and indispensable to the welfare of the nation. To a doctrinaire generation, which had bled and died for its dogmas, the question of principle aroused genuine fears, which had been felt in 1867 and muffled out of respect for his reputation, but which now flared up without consideration for his person. He was reminded that in the thirteen years in which he had held power a generation had grown up, that 1856 and 1871 were different periods with different needs that wanted new men, and that no man, however great his ability, was apt for all situations. He had been elected in 1861, it was recalled, not for his labors but because the Reform was still infirm and required an uncompromising exponent; he had been re-elected in

1867 not as a recompense for his services, great though they were, but because the dignity of the Republic demanded a rebuke to the house-breakers after their rout; these reasons no longer existed, and no motive of public interest warranted yet another period in 1871. What motive, it was implied, could he invoke but personal ambition? What title, it was asked, could he produce for a fourth term? Four years of peace; but a peace of stagnation, breeding spleen and despondency and recurring disorders, while the country presented the paradoxical spectacle of loyalty to a government in which it was steadily losing confidence. What support could he claim but a bureaucracy of favorites, flatterers, and officeholders bent on retaining their berths without counting the cost to the country? To repeat, he was warned, would be to provoke revolution and raise the avenging arm of all oppressed peoples—the same arm that had stricken Santa Anna, Miramon, Zuloaga, Maximilian and, beyond the ocean, Napoleon. An apocalyptic election was predicted; the clamor was menacing, and it was not confined to the Opposition. The *Siglo* joined it. Zarco had just died—a sensible loss to the President—but his place was taken by a group of disciples schooled in sanity and trained to read the omens aright. The coolest counselors and his warmest friends urged Juarez to take counsel with his own heart, to consider his best interests, and not to tempt Providence. If he were elected, the charge of fraud would inevitably be raised; but they believed that he would be defeated, "and if this happens, what will remain of the already depleted prestige of Señor Juarez? He can still restore his name and his glory by an act of abnegation and real patriotism and avoid being confused with the vulgar ambitious after an ignominious defeat. We wish Señor Juarez to remain at the height at which he has placed himself, between Washington and Bolivar, those two glorious liberators of America. Like Bolivar to the Congress of Venezuela, let him say, 'Legislators, begin your labors, I have finished mine,' and posterity, and a grateful country, will place his name in the temple of immortality."

The augurs spoke, and echo answered them. Neither comparison with his peers nor with himself produced any perceptible effect on the President. He persisted, undeterred by opposition and protest, unimpressed by warning and alarm, unsuborned by flattery, unbribed by immortality. Inspired reports appeared that he had abandoned his candidacy and determined to retire to Ixtlan and the scene of his first childhood; but it also appeared that the reports were unfounded and that he was not the author of those ideas.

Ixtlan was as far from his mind as the humility with which he first assumed power in 1858 and the vow which he made then to lay down the burden as soon as he could be relieved of it. Something had intervened since then—something mightier than the French Intervention and the inevitable result of it—a settled self-confidence which had expelled any doubt of his right to power as finally as the world that had persistently challenged it and that he had spent so many years in mastering. He had not triumphed with impunity. His spirit, growing with the contest, was untamed; there was no turning back from the end for one who had not shrunk from the beginning. Public life had become second nature to him, and a habit which could no longer be broken, an indispensable, organic, physiological function, which continued to act automatically long after the need, or the demand, for it disappeared. Nay, the need deepened as the demand died, and a new sanction intensified the physiological craving, replaced the mandate that was wanting, and supplied the reason of state. Power was an anodyne for the loss of his wife. It was work, the harness that braced and relieved and gave him a reason for being; it was the solace of the solitary; and, lastly, it was his due. After a lifetime of abstinence, he was ambitious to be what he was. Ambition, after the fact, was the legitimate fruit of abnegation before it, the claim of nature for years of disinterested service and duty faithfully and fully performed. Another term, a fresh lease of life, was the vindication of his virtue, his vitality, his privations, his accomplishment. So, perhaps, an apologist might have explained his temerity; but the world could only wonder. What the motives were that drove him to defy the omens and ignore the augurs no one knew but himself. The augurs were not his spiritual confessors; they saw merely that his motives were no longer public ones, and that in his blind determination to vindicate his achievement he was doomed to destroy it.

The agitation continued unabated for nine months, and with growing bitterness as the day of election approached. The fluctuations of his fame had never been so violent in the spacious days of national strife as in that period, precisely because the agitation was compressed within the narrow limits of an election campaign. The campaign was waged with his principles against his person, and the issue was pressed with a condensed fury that threatened to explode in his face; but he conducted the experiment and tested the pressure which public opinion would bear with complete confidence in the common sense of the country. Politics, in the narrow professional sense, bore the same relation to reality as sport to war, a harmless outlet for the combative instincts, a sham battle fought with conventional sound and fury, which none of the players, for all the zeal that they put into it, took seriously. The objurgations of the Opposition were the hackneyed cant of partisan controversy, the objections to his re-election so flimsy that no one but their authors mistook them for genuine arguments. The game was dangerous, however, for though the arguments were factitious, they were loaded. His competitors were the same as in 1867, but not the conditions: Lerdo and Diaz had both been defeated before, and one of them was affected by the volatile gases that rose from the press. The fumes were deadly: day after day the alarm was raised, month after month the moral dinned into the minds of the credulous, revolution was the inevitable penalty of re-election; the mourners lamented the impending collapse, the gloom thickened, the pressure increased, and the authors of those dire predictions were the first to be shocked, and to recoil from the havoc they had wrought, when the explosion came.

On the eve of the elections a revolt broke out in the north, sweeping four states, seizing the port of Tampico, and compelling the government to undertake a regular military campaign to dominate it. The campaign was still in progress when the elections were held, and under such conditions that they were bound to be questionable. The charges of fraud and violence raised in 1867 were repeated with plausible effect in 1871. Diaz was cheated, according to the computations of his faction, of a vote double the combined poll of his opponents. The Opposition, definitely defeated by the elections, branded them a scandalous farce and a cynical formality. Everyone who cared to be quoted had a tale to tell, everyone knew the treatment meted out to him or to someone else, everyone had a list of victims, everyone could vouch, by personal experience or by hearsay, for the coercion and corruption that insured the victory of the President. His plurality at the polls was insufficient, however, and the election was thrown into Congress, which decided in his favor. A few days before the result was announced rebellion broke out in the capital. A mob, led by Aureliano Rivera, rioted in the main streets, the Governor of the Federal District was killed, and three hundred police opened the prisons and induced the convicts to join the uprising. The Minister of War being absent, the President himself took command and gave orders to attack the citadel, which had been seized by the mutinous garrison of the capital. The siege began at three in the afternoon, artillery was brought up, the defenses were smashed, the redoubt was rushed, and by midnight the mutiny was smothered. The courts-martial began to function immediately, and in the morning the executions were counted before they were confirmed. The Minister of War, interpellated by Congress, denied that there had been any shootings; an immense groan of incredulity rose from the galleries. Seventy were admitted on the following day, and the hostile press reckoned the total cost of the rising at close to a thousand lives. The score was multiplied by a chorus of mourning and checked by the computations of compunction. "Be it what it may, it is enough," wrote a neutral who implored the government to cry quits; "the councils of war are continuing; enough—enough—much blood has been shed, and it is Mexican!"

Congress ratified the re-election of the President on October 12, 1871. His prestige was vindicated at the cost of his popularity, and he was granted a new lease of life under lugubrious circumstances. The Opposition, conceding his victory with the conventional groan of "God save the Republic!" capitulated with the gloomy foreboding that "the revolution and, more yet, the sacred right of insurrection is about to be proclaimed." In the first days of November Diaz rose in revolt. Emerging from his farm in Oaxaca as the champion of the Constitution, he issued a plan that raised the cry and flung broad the banner of *No Re-election!* The response of the nation was overwhelming. The cry of *No Re-election!* was lost in the clamor of *No Revolution!* Public opinion unanimously, and the Opposition most loudly, condemned an appeal to arms, and the movement was not seconded by the general insurrection which Diaz expected. The sacred right was decried by the very press which had predicted the fatal result of the elections and which recoiled, appalled by the realization of its prognostic, and public feeling fully supported the vigor with which the government acted to suppress the revolt. Troops were put into the field, but battle was never joined, for the issue had already been settled, and Diaz, forsaken by his followers, fled into the Sierra and made his way northward to the remaining focus of rebellion and merged with it.

What happened to Diaz was what frequently happened to green politicians in Mexico who mistook the grumbling of the ignorant and the habit of the people of blaming all their ills on the government for a mandate to rebel, and who paid for their lip-reading by the ridicule and indifference which they reaped when they failed. These were immemorial Mexicanisms and poor support for an inexpert mind reader. The fumes of the press which elaborated and exploited those prejudices went to his head, and he evaporated with them. By delving in muddy waters, he succeeded merely in clearing them. The calm depths which he failed to fathom were revealed in the dense underlying determination of the country to bear any abuse but civil war. The abuse of the elections, which remained unproven and which was the familiar refrain of the defeated, was a lesser evil than the abuse of the public peace, and the common sense of the country absolutely repudiated the Opposition which had irresponsibly produced the crisis and which saved itself only by acquiescing in the verdict. The ease with which Diaz was routed was a triumph, however, as the press also pointed out, neither for the prestige of the President nor for the force of his arms, but simply and solely for the power of public opinion, and it was a pyrrhic victory. The aftermath of the test was turgid. The Opposition subsided sullenly, baiting the government on the responsibility it had incurred in risking the revolts which it crushed, and the foul advantage which it had taken of the popular instinct of self-preservation. Revolt was ruled out; but the fact remained that it had been provoked by the persistence of the President in seeking re-election, and he was not allowed to forget it. A single misstep at the end of the day was sufficient for his detractors to undo his life work, and the bitterest of them began to revise his reputation in the cloudy light of the elections of 1871. "The fools who commend Juarez as a necessary man do not have the sense to realize that by so doing they degrade themselves," railed Ramirez. "It is to have a very poor opinion of oneself, not merely as a Republican but even as a man, to suppose oneself incapable of doing what Juarez has done." Undoubtedly; but he had done it. The comforting thought was popular, however. "Juarez the savior of the Republic! The one thing that Don Benito did was to save his precious skin!" another head was raised to sneer. "Today it is not the Constitution that the government defends, since the government violates it; what is being defended is the presidential chair," a deputy protested in Congress. "To preserve himself in power, the present President of the Republic does not hesitate to sacrifice the independence and dignity of his country." The wrecking crew lowered the whole level of his life to a point at which they felt themselves finally equal to, and even with, him.

5

THUS, though with specious complaints and fallacious arguments, the Opposition succeeded at last in creating a real crisis in 1871. The revolt in the north was stubborn, and a prolonged and ruthless campaign was required to subdue it. Emergency powers, and the suspension of civil liberties accorded only in days of national danger, were demanded by the President; and while Congress debated, arbitrary measures were employed by the government to recruit forces. The forced levy reappeared, an odious system deplored by the government that employed it, abominated by the press, defended by no one, and dreaded above all by the working class, upon which it bore exclusively and which was becoming self-conscious and articulate in 1871. The pages of a small paper called *The Socialist* were filled with accounts of the curse on the artisans, fearful of walking the streets by night lest they be bagged by a raiding party and dragged off to the barracks or the vagrancy courts which fed the ranks, of their women flocking to the jails and searching for the missing in the common pool, of the terror in the countryside, where the peasants fled their fields and the Indians maimed themselves to escape the draft; all under the grim heading *Morituri, Caesar*. The cry was taken up by the sensational sheets and echoed sympathetically by the upper classes. The *leva* was the common bond, and the word gained a sinister celebrity. Flying from lip to lip, it was applied to any and every complaint and the most various types of publicity. The common cough called up the *leva,* the long capes of the ladies, and the style of their headdress was heightened, *a la leva:* everything and anything was fashioned to the popular stigma, and the tag carried a contagious propaganda. It was a warning, a censure, a rebuke to the government, but no refuge from it. The practice continued unchecked, and the unpopularity of the government grew with every concession made to its defense. Congress granted all the powers required by the President, the press vetoed, the public deplored them. The campaign in the north was pressed with great vigor, and with alternating reports of decisive successes and savage repressions, but the sedition eluded pursuit and remained unsubdued, and the mounting toll of lives deepened the disaffection, despondency, and disrepute that dogged the dismal inauguration of the fourth term of the President. His sixty-sixth birthday in 1872 was observed as a day of mourning by his monitors, and celebrated in a mingled strain of accusation and condolence. "Today is no day of rejoicing and hope, but an hour filled with bitter recollections of the years through which the uneasy existence of Señor Juarez has passed," the accusation read. "Before his eyes are the unburied remains of so many Mexicans who have fallen in fratricidal strife. . . . The prisons are filled with unfortunates accused of complicity in the revolutionary movements, and the trials move with a horrible slowness, while hunger and misery devour the prisoners. A terrible responsibility to rest on the head of a nation!" The condolence was more cruel. "More than ever today Señor Juarez feels the void left by the loss of his beloved wife. We evoke the shade which the unfortunate still feel on their brows, she will come with her white robe and her green palm of martyrdom, murmuring the words which will be heard in the depth of his soul by the man who today directs the destinies of the nation." But the guardian presence was gone, and the profane invaded his privacy in vain: their pleas made an impression only on themselves. The President continued to direct the destinies of the nation with the confidence and self-sufficiency of a veteran solitary. When he reported to Congress, a month later, on the state of the nation, his public appearance, rare and unfamiliar as it had become, brought out a full house and a harsh comment from the press gallery. A hush fell as he appeared in the hall, "with his immutable countenance, his turbid glance, and that smile which seems to have curdled on his lips for the last twenty years, and ascending lightly, despite his two-thirds of a century, the steps of the platform, took his place in the seat of honor of the Parliament. The murmur which arose at his entrance subsided as if by magic, and the voice of the first magistrate was heard perceptibly. He began by referring to the grave dangers which threatened the peace of the Republic, the efforts of his soldiers, the battles won over the revolution, the political tact of the Chamber in granting extraordinary powers to face it"—and he ended as he began. Attention strained to catch something more, some promise, some memory commensurate with the gravity of the situation; but that was all. It was the voice of a magistrate tone deaf to the tension about him, the report of an official who had long since delivered whatever message he had for the world, and who had nothing within him to add to it; and it was heard with a sinking heart.

Hopeless, stale, flat, and unprofitable as the destiny of the nation appeared to the Opposition, and Juarez as the most hopeless feature of it, there was no way out of the impasse. A point had been reached where the choice lay between disaster and a dead end. Peace was imperative at any price, and peace was preserved by stern discipline and a conscientious determination to sacrifice every consideration to public safety; but patience was strained to the limit. There was no promise for the future, nothing but the recurring pattern of the past, and the grim determination of the government to survive at all costs, which reduced it to the function of a police force and clothed it with the galling license of an indispensable dictatorship to maintain the peace of the sepulcher. The pragmatic sanction was granted, and the autocrat accepted as a necessary evil, unwanted and unaware that he was rotting, and the withered fruit becoming a fallow source of decay, which required pruning and which defied the knife. Day after day the end of the sedition was promised, and still it flourished and spread. The state of the nation, as it was reflected in the state of mind of the President, was summed up by the Opposition in four words—"I am the State"— and it was reflected in the thwarted routine of the mind readers as one of profound frustration. "How long? How long?" was the haunting refrain of the hostile press. The burden was borne; but not without murmur or relief. It was lightened by a toiling singsong, as slaves lightened their labor, and by bursts of bitter raillery. Satirists composed parodies, in the Aztec manner, of a primitive people paying tribute to His Majesty Benito I, or to the tribal deity Huitzilopochtli. The fall of a chandelier in the Palace was an accident missed—but not by the squibs:

> On Juarez if it had fallen,
> Now strike me dead, now strike me dead,
> The chandelier would have broken,
> But not his head, but not his head.

But derision and lament brought no relief. The taskmaster remained adamant, and deaf, and unabashed, a dense mass, a perpetual presence, a daily obsession, a dull incubus, a crushing weight that drove the Opposition underground, not to escape persecution, for there was none, but in search of deeper resentments. And from the depths of the underworld, where hopelessness turned to despair, voices rose prompting the assassination of the President. More than one paper called for a Brutus: "It being necessary to shoot Juarez out of the Presidency, we should resort to that method without delay." — "Julius Caesar was greater than Brutus, and everyone blessed Brutus for killing him." — "When a nation has no more hope than in the death of an individual, he is a hero who raises the knife, he is a demigod who saves his country, whatever the means. . . ." At that depth the Opposition touched the Reaction, which had gone underground and been buried for five years; but it recoiled from the contact. No Republican seconded the bid, and the incitement, like the instigation to civil war, was repudiated as soon as the source was recognized and before it could take effect. The pressure rose and fell; and the Opposition, falling back on its best argument, reverted to character assassination. Day after day, week after week, month after month, the comparison of the President with himself was labored. On June 18 the daily diet was served up for the last time. "We are in full retrocession. . . . Don Benito Juarez is the Messiah of the owls and the crows. He is moving backward with giant strides. He is returning to the past. And the past is reaction. Already the sinister hoots of the sacristy owls can be heard. The man of the black frock coat and the red bonnet has turned the bonnet into a nightcap. Don Benito Juarez, the perpetual President, was surrounded by pure Liberals in his period of triumph. Today he is calling the Moderates. Tomorrow he will be in the hands of the Conservatives. There is something in the atmosphere that reeks of death. The radicals are disappearing. Farewell to the Constitution; Farewell, Mamma Carlota!" The public was satiated, the copy was stale, the writers themselves weary of trumping up their work, and the drivel relaxed. Then death struck.

Early on the morning of July 18 the personal physician of the President was summoned to the Palace, where he found him in the final throes of angina pectoris. It was not his first attack, and the patient refused to believe that it was his last: though he suffered acutely, he dominated the regicidal knocking at his heart and received the blows, regally, on his feet. "The disease develops by successive attacks; he suffered them standing," the physician noted, almost convinced by that symptom that the patient was right. But the increasing force of the convulsions finally floored the stoic, and feeling the earth flee him he stretched himself out and waited on his back for the vertigo to pass. After each paroxysm he rose and conversed with the bystanders easily and naturally; four or five hours passed in this way; then another and more violent attack compelled him to take to his bed. The doctor applied an extreme stimulant. Boiling water was poured over the heart: the body responded in an involuntary spasm, the eyes opened, and the voice was heard observing, in the tone of one dimly aware of some blunder, that he had been burned. Deliberately, the doctor explained, and the mind responded immediately. Within a few minutes the heroic remedy took effect, and "the cadaver became once more what he habitually was, the well-bred gentleman, the amiable but energetic man," who revived the hopes of his familiars. The relief lasted for several hours and was so pronounced that the family retired to dine. Profiting by their absence, the President sounded the physician. Engaging him in conversation, he talked of his boyhood, of the protection he had received from his parish priest, letting his mind wander and leading his listener on and on until he caught him off guard with an abrupt question: "Doctor, is my disease mortal?" Assured that it was, he accepted the answer as casually as he put the question and resumed the narrative of his life where he left off; it was interrupted by another and yet more formidable attack, but the entire tale was told in the stamina with which he bore its final test. Tenacity, fortitude, and self-command were his to the last. The heroic remedy was applied again; this time he was prepared for it, and "with indifference and the most imposing calm—imposing because the pallor of his face, the flagging of his pulse, and his hard breathing announced that the end was approaching with giant strides—he lay down on the bed, bared his chest without haste and waited, unmoving, for the barbarous remedy." Only the automatic contraction of the muscles betrayed any feeling, the face "nothing! not a muscle moved; not the slightest sign of pain or suffering; the body remained rigid, although a swelling several inches thick rose from the scalded flesh when the water dried"; and the physician murmured the words of the confessor—"as if his body were not his but another's." The separation of spirit and flesh was complete, and throughout the throes of an agony that was prolonged by the repeated return of the enemy wrestling to part them, he who had been Juarez remained completely conscious, completely controlled, completely himself.

He was still Juarez: he would not say die. Word of his condition spread, but for obvious reasons its gravity was denied, and the world was not admitted to witness it. One of his ministers, however, who had been turned away, returned on the plea of urgent business and insisted on seeing the President. The President he saw; but not prostrate. Although he had been in excruciating pain for twelve hours, the dying man rose without complaint, wrapped himself in a shawl, seated himself in a chair, and received the Minister without betraying his condition, consulting his short breath and giving his decisions, while the doctor stood by, wiping the cold sweat from his forehead. The Minister retired, wishing him a speedy recovery from his rheumatism. An hour later the ordeal was repeated with a general who called for instructions for the campaign, and who received them from a bloodless brain that recalled clearly whom to trust and mistrust and that gave him names and dates and places to guide him. Then the grand business of dying was resumed at leisure. Once more he composed himself for the unseen struggle, and giddy death turning and returning to the attack knocked more and more faintly, in sinking and solitary spells, on the inaccessible seat of his power.

In the morning the world knew that he was dead; but no one saw him die. Not even the physician, who noted every stage of the bout, could say more than that the count stopped and the perpetual President passed on about midnight—at that late hour the doctor was nodding, after a hard day's work. Thus immortality. And immortality came in the morning, in hot pursuit and screaming extras. The press awoke abruptly and, shelving the routine attacks of the day, brought out the prepared obituaries instead. The shift was made in haste but without inconsistency. The rattling type released a mighty and unanimous chorus of eulogy, which testified, not to the specious nature of the attacks, but to the sporting instincts of the Opposition, which had won the sham battle by a fluke and was willing to cry quits and shake hands all around. They had meant no harm, and of the dead, naturally, *nihil nisi bonum*. So, while the cannon of the Palace thundered the end of his mortal term, unstinted tribute was paid to the passing of "the man who bore the standard of the Republic for so many years in his robust hand," and lavish homage to the leader of Reform and the patriarch of Independence who had finally "passed into the shining pages of contemporary history with the halo that hallows the great," and devout respect to a name that would be venerated by the whole world, "for Juarez was not merely a glory to his country, but a title of honor to humanity," and full admission was made of the perpetuity of his fame, and the dread that his death might be the beginning of great troubles, and the hope that the people might be spared that commemoration at least. For a day he occupied the front pages to the exclusion of every other topic, borne aloft by columns of solemn print and a parade of black borders. Then, relieved at last of the burden of greatness, the press returned to the pressing business of living.

The people invaded the Palace as soon as they learned of his death, but no one was permitted to enter his presence until he was fit to be seen. The many were invited to wait until he was embalmed. The favored few, who were allowed to look their last on him before the finishing touches were applied, informed the others through the *Official Gazette* that "the face of Juarez had lost its habitual severity and expressed the affable resignation with which the just die," and assured the curious that "they would hardly have found in his physiognomy the features that mark the man of political storm and stress." Then the doors were opened, and the One was seen by the many, lying in state, at one with himself. On the third day, when the funeral was held, he occupied less space in the press, which broke its columns to let him pass, along with the parade of officials, the hypnotic march of the people hugging the hearse, the bare heads and feet keeping pace with it, to the pantheon and his burial on the back pages, amid the interminable periods of the orators and many other items of current interest. Among these figured the cause of his death. In the crowd that assembled at the cemetery there were those who were not satisfied with the vague description that he was the victim of an instantaneous attack "in the regions of the heart." Waiting patiently to file by the bier, and working their way slowly forward, they advanced one by one and, looking their last on the box full of Juarez, drew their own deductions. The sentimental traced the development of the disease to the loss of his wife. The public-spirited declared that he died of Republican ingratitude. The disagreement of his friends excited the suspicions of his foes, and the one and the other met at the parting of the ways. In the absence of a satisfactory explanation, the sacristies supplied their own. Recalling the constant threats that darkened his last days, the cloth insisted that there was good reason to believe, in the absence of proof to the contrary, that the apostate had perished of poison administered by his Liberal enemies. The conflicting chronicle continued inconclusively. A crowd is a microcosm, and there were as many reasons for his death as men to feel them; and all were true; but they were the truths of contemporaries, all on their way to the cemetery. The ultimate truth was reserved for posterity and preserved in the death mask, which was cast in time to catch, together with the cosmic peace of death, the last glow of life hovering about the half-closed mouth, and to fuse them in a faint and knowing smile—the final, ineffable smile of the just.

6

HIS posthumous vitality was strong; for only one of his lives was laid down on July 18, 1872, and the other continued as long as men thought of him. His being had been blended so inseparably with that of his country that the contest between what he thought of himself and what others thought of him could not be extinguished by the urn and the pantheon. Immortality being a matter of memory, and of all human interests the most perishable, his semblance in afterlife was molded by the same interests which shaped his destiny before it; and while the glow lasted, and memory was fresh, justice was meted out to him in the same measure with which they received his.

The judgment of foreign opinion was as partial as that of his countrymen, which it reflected. In France the Republic, restored by the Commune, made amends for the Empire and recognized its debt to him afresh. "He taught us how to win, how to expel the foreigner, how to punish the usurpers; we gained no benefit from the lesson, but we must respect the man who gave it to us," was a rueful inscription to attach to the wreath, but the laurel was mixed with it. "It was that Indian, that lawyer, who dealt the first blow to the insolent fortune of the man of December, and the bullets that killed Maximilian at Queretaro, piercing the Imperial breast, struck the prestige of Caesarism that caught France in the toils of the *coup d'état*. When the Emperor surrendered to the King of Prussia at Sedan, he could give him only a fragment of his sword, for Juarez had broken it." — "Such was the Republican who put an end by himself alone to two emperors," another legend read. "We cannot love a man whose great qualities were directed against France; but whatever may have been his errors, we must honor the patriot who repelled the invasion, and of whom everyone says that we should not have lost Alsace and Lorraine if we had had a Juarez!" The wreath was redundant, but the reparations were as profuse as the abuse had been abundant. Across the Channel appreciation was cooler. The English recognized that they had a debt to collect, but not to pay: their partner had paid it for them. "Nothing is more certain than that the attempt to retrieve the humiliation in Mexico led to the war of 1870. Mexico was the Moscow of the Second Empire." Such was one way of settling old scores, and for humiliating the French Juarez received due credit, but with due discount as well. One epitaph went so far as to call Juarez the greatest statesman Mexico had produced since its independence; but the tribute was qualified by regret that ambition subverted his glory and that in his last phase he was "not far from Caesarism." The propaganda of the Opposition in Mexico served to cancel the national debt to him in England as well. That was one way of balancing accounts; and memory suggested many others. While one eulogist compared him to Cromwell, the London *Times* smugly nagged the Mexican regicide and dated his decline from the death of Maximilian. "We cannot determine how far the unfavorable judgment of the outer world contributed to weaken the foundation of Juarez' power, but it is certain that from the day of his triumph at Queretaro down to his death by a stroke of apoplexy Juarez had to cope with a series of revolts and conspiracies which were met with a determination that insured, indeed, a temporary success, but with an unscrupulous cruelty that disgraced even the Mexican name." Time had not told in that sacristy, and the old prejudices repaid his indisputable triumph by the providential troubles of his last years. Providence subscribed to the

Times, and its competitors copied it. "He was a great Indian, but, as far as we can understand his career, an Indian still, with a strain of unscrupulousness in his character which marred or destroyed his grandeur. Mexico will now probably be the scene of a savage civil war for the dictatorship in which the Indians will win." Many and various were the ways of writing off his death as a benefit for the British Empire; and none was missed.

The judgment of his contemporaries was colored by partisanship as long as his memory lingered among them, and his immortality, spun from the contentious substance of the quick, was such that generations were to pass before it became anachronistic. Posterity, continuing the chronicle, added its own bias to it, and the truth underwent fresh transformations in perspective. Asked for an inscription to place in an album of autographs, Juarez once wrote that he wished to be judged not by his words, but by his acts. The future took him at his word, and he was judged by generations to come with a double bias—both by what he had done and what he had left undone.

The first of his posthumous deeds was Diaz. By refusing to deed power to a successor during his lifetime, he supplied Diaz with a pretext and a precedent which produced political issue of far-reaching consequence. The brewing rebellion subsided with his death, and Lerdo, who succeeded him, proclaimed a broad amnesty to which Diaz was driven by abandonment to submit; four years later, however, when Lerdo was preparing his election for a second term, Diaz rose in revolt again and overthrew him and thereafter, with the exception of a single intermission filled by a proxy, the champion of *No Re-election* repeated his periods regularly and remained the undisputed master of Mexico for more than three decades.

Diaz developed, adulterated, and undid the work of his predecessor. The dictatorship succeeded because it provided the country with peace and prosperity. Something more than a politician and less than a statesman, Diaz was a self-made civil engineer who produced results by rule of thumb but who met the crying needs of the country; and for the sake of those securities the country accepted his rule without counting the cost. The cost was high. The halting experiment in Mexican democracy was arrested for thirty years—long enough for a generation to grow up in ignorance of it, and to develop a plutocracy that defeated it.

What Diaz achieved was the co-efficient of how he accomplished it. Capturing power on behalf of the veterans of the wars, he incorporated the military caste into the state and made it the cornerstone of his government. Power and peace—police power and praetorian peace—were preserved by a standing army, restored to regular pay and employment, supplemented by an organization of rural police which checked the common forms of lawlessness and gradually put an end to the inveterate plague of brigandage by the simple expedient of incorporating the brigands themselves into its ranks. Had he done nothing more, the country would have been grateful for such benefits; but he did much more. With peace guaranteed by the satisfaction of the troublemakers, Diaz built up a political machine which assured his control of the State and consolidated his personal power. A practical man, ignorant of principle and inexperienced in statecraft, he tinkered with the machine until he discovered the tricks that made it work. Dividing his enemies, shuffling his friends, and pitting his competitors against one another, he controlled the civil administration with the skill of an expert mechanic, eliminating friction by money, favor, position, intrigue, or suppression. Coercion and corruption made the government run; a scientific use of the spoils system filled every branch with loyal clients of the President; recalcitrants filled the prisons or faced the firing squads, and were rapidly reduced to a negligible minority of impractical idealists, incorruptible critics, self-seeking pretenders, or forgotten outcasts. Organized opposition disappeared after his first term. Organized government grew out of its grave. By the imposition of governors a system of state dynasties was created to buttress the central power and extend its authority through a hierarchy of local caciques, whose indefinite tenure of office established the machine in every part of the country; and by boss rule the looseness of Federalism was finally corrected and the centralized State firmly established. The centralized State prospered because it was based on the feed-bag and satisfied the two classes most likely to cause Diaz serious trouble. The military and the middle-classes combined to absorb all shocks to his regime, together with the bulk of its revenues. The growth of the bureaucracy assumed unprecedented proportions. In 1868 less than twelve per cent of the middle-class were employed in the civil service; eight years later the rate had risen to sixteen per cent, and by 1910 eighty per cent lived on the government. *Empleomanía,* militarism, and personal rule, the congenital infirmities of the infant Republic, reappeared in its maturity as flourishing symptoms of health, accepted by Diaz as the working conditions of his regime and the indigenous needs of an undeveloped people, proved and approved by peace and success.

Their weakness was his strength. The adaptation of government to the debility of a people and not to their capacity for progress—such was his political formula and such was his achievement. He conformed to native tradition and derived his support from it. The dictatorship developed parasitically by experiment, custom, and consent. It was not so much a deliberate enterprise as a natural growth. Coming to power as a rebel, he retired after his first term in favor of a trusted substitute, and though he resumed the Presidency uninterruptedly thereafter, he was careful to seek the sanction of popular consent at every re-election, and it was only as he secured it that he gained confidence to substitute

Diaz for democracy. The forms of the Republic were respected, but their virtue lapsed. Liberty was licensed, independence emasculated, conformity paid, opposition crushed or corrupted; the Constitution became a by-law, Congress an accomplice, and the press a mouthpiece for the Executive. In time even the formalities were waived. Congress was appointed by the President, elections were uncontested, public activity atrophied, the pretense of political life was abandoned, and custom consolidated his accomplishment. For the privation of political life ample compensation was provided. The driving power of the Mexican people, Diaz once said, was the dread of poverty—"not oppression, not servility, not tyranny, but lack of bread, home, and clothing" —and on the economic motive he built his power and won popular consent for it.

When he seized power in 1876 the government was crippled by chronic impoverishment, and the revenues of the State were severely strained to support the mercenaries who sustained his regime. The necessity of supplying them by fresh industry was recognized by General Manuel Gonzalez, the trusted lieutenant who replaced him for four years, and during his period a program of public works was promoted by which Diaz benefited and which he subsequently developed. Constructive measures of many kinds—railroads, port works, drainage systems, colonization schemes, land grants, agricultural and commercial enterprises—were undertaken, at great cost to the government in lavish concessions and extravagant subsidies and at greater cost to the country which these enterprises opened to the penetration and control of foreign capital. The revenues of the government were unequal to the task, and the fostering of foreign investment became the indispensable condition of material progress: prosperity ensued, but it was an imported prosperity from which foreign skill, foreign enterprise, and foreign investment reaped the profits, the native benefiting only by employment, commissions, and an example which he was unable to emulate. The national economy remained unchanged, and the national resources passed, together with vast tracts of public lands, into the hands of foreign capitalists who exploited the country as a market for raw materials and exported it for foreign consumers. The same parasitic process which established the dictatorship consolidated the control of foreign capital upon which it depended. Such was the economic compulsion of the dictatorship that Diaz, who bought the country for himself, was obliged to sell it abroad to save it from poverty. Serving as the middleman between producer and consumer, his government operated on margin, and the paucity of its real revenues and the obligation of feeding its supporters brought it more than once to the brink of ruin, and in 1893 to the verge of actual collapse; but a foreign loan averted the crisis, and by a fortunate coincidence new inventions and technical processes which enhanced the value of Mex-

ican mineral and metallurgical resources at that time initiated a boom
that raised the level of private and public wealth and allowed the
Treasury not only to overcome the chronic deficit, but to produce a
steadily increasing surplus that hallowed the regime with apparent
prosperity. By the end of the reign Mexico had been raised to the rank
of a free, independent, sovereign, and flourishing colony of international capital.

A corresponding social evolution accompanied the material progress
and political prostration of the country. The dictatorship, conducted
in the interest of the moneymakers, deepened the distance between the
privileged classes to which it catered and the proletariat which it exploited. Every protection was afforded to foreign capital—law and
order, security of communications and exploitation—and labor troubles were ruthlessly suppressed and unions smashed by the rural police. The same favors were extended to the large landowners, native
and foreign, who increased their holdings by the sale of public lands:
the abuses of land-grabbing, the expropriation of the communal lands
of the Indians, and the peonage system were amply protected by the
rural police, who impressed the dispossessed into the army or the slave
pens of the estates, the mines, and the factories. The poor grew poorer
and the rich grew richer under a regime committed for its own security to the protection of property, the cultivation of enterprise, and the
preservation of stability. The parvenus who benefited by the by-products of the boom, and the bureaucracy that fattened on official favor,
formed a plutocracy with aristocratic pretensions, sustained by foreign patronage. The proscripts of the past returned from exile, fully
reconciled to the new dispensation. The Church rallied to it and,
though the Reform Laws remained on the books, recovered sufficient
latitude to recoup, together with some of the property and privileges
it had forfeited, all of the authority and influence which it had never
lost. All these groups combined to create a new conservatism and to
produce a common mentality, alien to the past, satisfied with the present, flushed by the speculative prospects of the future, and devoted to
the adulation of Diaz. The fleshpots worked wonders: material progress carried the country to another dead end, but while the boom
lasted, it was dazzling. The dictatorship worked; it worked miracles:
the government was solvent; the American debt was met, the English
debt was recognized, and the foreign credit of the country, financial,
political, moral, rose to unprecedented heights. The regime accomplished what foreign intervention had failed to achieve, and Mexico,
a satisfied vassal of that economic imperialism which it had fought so
strenuously to escape politically, was finally recognized as a respectable
member of the family of nations. The interests served by the dictatorship united to convince the world that a beneficent despotism was the
natural destiny of Mexico and that Diaz was the redeemer of his peo-

ple, in whom the labor of generations had culminated and who consummated and surpassed the combined exertions of all his predecessors.

Juarez was eclipsed. In the gilded luster of the Diaz decades his name no longer had any glamor or meaning save in the minds of old men or in remote corners of the world—in a province of Brazil which bore his name, in a province of Italy where a boy was named in his honor Benito Mussolini. In his own country he was buried in peace and prosperity. His work having been liquidated, justice was done to it. He was the object of a patriotic cult and the subject of poems and statues; on stated occasions the rites were performed and the debt of honor paid; his birth and death were commemorated with official solemnities; and periodically, at the equinox and the solstice, he returned with the cycles of the passing years to receive his pension of immortality from the living. And so he rested, in hallowed obscurity, until controversy revived his vitality once more.

At the turn of the century, when the boom was at its height, an iconoclast rose in revolt against the conventional cult. In 1904 and 1905 two books by Francisco Bulnes demolished the consecrated image and kindled the old controversies anew. Basing himself on the verdict of the Opposition of 1872 and recapitulating the career of the *Benemérito* in the light of his end, Bulnes substituted for the accepted portrait of the great man the acid facsimile of a small one. The real Juarez, as he would have it, was an ambitious mediocrity who owed his fame to his collaborators and an impostor among the immortals who had never been found out: a bureaucratic hack harnessed to a movement which, far from leading, he hampered by weakness and inertia, and which succeeded in spite of him; a backward member of his race borne by the momentum of Reform beyond his depth; a reluctant renegade from the Church, a timid and expedient revolutionary, a passive and improvident patriot, and a friendless, inferior, and counterfeit hero whose true motives were his jealousy of his betters and his tenacity of power. The motives of Bulnes were ambiguous. He was both an opponent and a pillar of the Diaz regime, but whether he wrote to cater to it or to counteract it, or to flaunt his heresy out of sheer exhibitionism, the motives which dictated his attack did not include an honest search for the truth. A display of mental acrobatics and manual jugglery, garbled texts, twisted deductions, specious hypotheses, concocted proofs, and prejudiced interpretations was accumulated and manipulated to fit the purpose; and even the purpose was doubtful; for while the author compiled his damning tomes with one hand, with the other he dashed off an unqualified panegyric of his victim for a state occasion. But Bulnes was ambidextrous, and his interest in the truth was scientific only in the sense in which that word was applied to the *Científicos,* as the intellectual apologists of the regime were called. He was one of them, and his books were tracts for the times, the interest of which lay in their tendentiousness. In the shoddy era of Diaz, Juarez was no longer understood, or rather he was understood too well: another mentality had developed which had lost contact with the heroic period and which was yet aware that it had forfeited its heritage for the fleshpots and bartered its soul for the sham progress of the dictatorship, and it was that mentality which Bulnes expressed with brilliant sophistry. If he had been merely a pillar of the regime, his diatribe might have passed for a spectacular attempt to flatter Diaz by immolating his canonized rival to the reign of Mammon; but Bulnes was also a rebel at heart, who raged against the cult of false values of every kind consecrated by the creed and cant of success, and while he depreciated Juarez personally, he exalted the whole revolutionary movement to which he belonged and from which he dissociated him adroitly. Such psychological dodges were equally consistent with the sincerity of a dissident and the insincerity of a sycophant and betrayed the contradictory impulse of a mind working at cross-purposes with the past and the present. The anomaly was never resolved within himself, but he found a guilty relief, perhaps, in profaning the cult of the well-deserving dead and a perverse satisfaction in wrecking the reputation of a man who was a standing reproach to his posterity. The guilt motive, already recognizable in the attempts of the contemporary Opposition to belittle Juarez after the battle, grew in the gilded age of Diaz, which was a long convalescence from heroism and a melancholy epilogue to the Reform movement. Whatever the motives of Bulnes may have been, he served several interests at once, and among them those of Juarez himself. He made him once more a living issue. He wrote to shock, and he succeeded. The old friends and companions of Juarez, wounded to the quick, rallied to his defense, and a heated polemic ensued.

Thirty years after his death, the generation which had known him could judge him with some degree of detachment and perspective. The bias of Bulnes was so obvious, and his methods so meretricious, that his fabrications were easily demolished; but it was not so easy to destroy what was genuine in them. In belittling a national hero Bulnes betrayed a perverted form of national pride and a familiar failing in his fear that an inferior member of the family might be palmed off on the imagination of the world as an accepted representative of the nation. Here he touched a responsive chord. The champions of Juarez rose to the challenge and presented a solid front to the attack; but the charges which they refuted left an impression, and in the course of the controversy some concessions were made. The national hero was vindicated, but the limitations of the man were acknowledged, and when the dust settled, a balance was struck and a mean average established which passed into current tradition and was accepted by common consent. It was generally agreed that Juarez was intellectually inferior to his major collaborators: one of them, who had been closely associated with him over a long term of years, readily admitted that "neither his intelligence nor his erudition was first-rate." Juarez himself had always recognized his limitations, but he had the gift to evoke, and the intelligence to use, the powers of his helpmates to their mutual advantage; and he preserved an independence of judgment by no means common among the second-rate. Erudition and culture were second-rate tests of intelligence at best: the basic combinations of the human mind are so few that a little learning goes a long way and can readily dispense with its redundancies, and his knowledge of men was the better for not being blurred by too many books. But what counted in public life, as Ponciano Arriaga had said long ago, was character; this was the crux of the contest, and it was here that Bulnes drew blood. Faith, fortitude, tenacity, public spirit, personal probity—those virtues were incontestable; but one failing was admitted. More or less generally it was allowed that more or less legitimately the man was ambitious; but if he suffered, it was from the sin by which the angels fell. The hero was not whole, he was human, and his apologists met the charge frankly and served his best interests by removing him from the pedestal and restoring him to common humanity.

A good deal of bad blood was stirred by the controversy, but in the course of it Bulnes himself gave ground: in fact, he gave his whole case away and granted the cardinal issue by writing, between books, a remarkable testimonial to Juarez the Revolutionary. "Juarez was the revolutionary *par excellence,* worthy of admiration not only in America but in Europe. Since the day that he established the Reform, we have been really Mexicans and sociologically distinct from the Spaniards," he declared. "Adhesion to the memory of Juarez means belief in our dignity as free men." Our dignity as free men—that was the flaw in the dictatorship which made it so difficult to forget or forgive Juarez. The case of Bulnes *vs.* Bulnes, as the dispute turned out to be, was characteristic of the period: detraction and retraction, following each other as easily as breathing and as regularly as the inspiration and expiration of the heart, marked the normal pulse of the uneasy era of Diaz. The time was now ripe for a final reconciliation to crown the settlement, and the whole controversy was buried in another book by another *Científico.* In a large sumptuously printed and luxuriously written standard Life, Justo Sierra polished the golden mean, tacitly admitting and minimizing the points made by Bulnes, veiling them with pious discretion, diffusing the focus, blurring the protagonist in the crowd of his contemporaries, treating them all alike, and even the antagonists, with studied amenity, moderating the conflicts of past and present with bland impartiality, and producing a composition from which the sting and sense of life were completely extracted and a monument not of political, but of pure literature.

This phase of the avatar ended in the finished style of the accomplished eclectic who closed it. In a study of the social evolution of Mexico, however, Justo Sierra did justice to the unexceptionable contributions which Juarez had made to it, and in particular to the progress of popular education so conspicuously neglected by Diaz. In 1867 elementary education was made compulsory and gratuitous, and religious instruction was suppressed, anticipating both France and England in the three essential features of modern schooling. This law answered a question, raised by Bulnes, as to the religious convictions of Juarez. Bulnes portrayed him as a conventional but devout Catholic, who owed his emancipation to his association with Ocampo. If so, the emancipation was complete. In connection with Protestant propaganda in Mexico, Justo Sierra recalled that Juarez once said to him: "I should like Protestantism to Mexicanize itself and win the Indians: they need a religion that obliges them to read and that does not force them to spend their savings in tapers for the saints." His correspondence with his family abounded in like reflections. He was happy to learn that his daughters were learning to dance, "which will do them more good than praying and beating their breasts," and in the education of his sons he was careful to exclude "the sectary of any religion." Nevertheless, he was so far from bigoted unbelief or intolerance that, when his family returned to Mexico, he entrusted the education of his eldest son to a high prelate who, alone in the metropolitan chapter, had refused to swear allegiance to the Empire. The saving distinction was significant. His own creed was that of a conscientious agnostic. The need of relating human affairs to the universal perspective of religion was satisfied when he graduated from the Seminary. Once he had outgrown the organized ignorance of God which he learned there, he found his faith in his fellow men, the Creator in the created, and religion in the progress of human society and its binding power in the breaking of bondage; and his work bore witness to his faith.

The monument raised by Justo Sierra marked by its very title— *Juarez, His Work and His Times*—and by its polite treatment how remote the subject of it already was from his immediate posterity. The conventional cult of the immortal, modified by mutual agreement and reduced to reasonable proportions, continued to flourish unmolested, matter for imagination, matter for memory, but not for controversy. And abroad he receded even further than in the minds of his countrymen. In a history of the Second Empire by a Liberal Minister, he was recalled sympathetically, but no longer in terms of actuality. Emile Ollivier likened him to a character out of Plutarch. The phrase prospered, for it simplified the difficulty of defining him personally and placing him historically. It suggested the classic convention of character without personality and conveyed the impression of one of those abstract types composed in broad masses and simple planes, common alike to the literary and plastic portraiture of antiquity, and peculiarly appropriate to the generalized genius of Juarez; and at the same time it seemed to fit the figure of a primitive appearing in the middle of the nineteenth century and to compress in a word the antique virtue which distinguished him among his contemporaries and which set him apart from the finished mentality of *fin-de-siècle* European culture. But it relegated him to the museum. He became an antique, an anthropological find, a curious anachronism who belonged to the age in which he was cast by some obscure historical accident; and it became the fashion among historical curators and literary stylists to refer to him as a reincarnated hero, or simply a creation, of Plutarch or Tacitus. The fashion, originating in Paris, was copied in Mexico and incorporated into the cult; but, being a fashion, it became antiquated in turn with the changing seasons of the times.

The last word on that fashion was written by a critic who said: "The study of history is no longer the study of those details which entertained the ancients with the interest of legend, nor is it the depiction of men, traced in broad strokes and with strong tones of light and shade by the bold pens of Plutarch and Tacitus. . . . Yesterday there were great men; today there are only men who do great things." And because those accomplishments were achieved by the collective efforts of ordinary men, as Juarez himself faded, his memory gained greatness again as a medium for progress of the common man.

With the turn of the century new forces—or rather old forces reincarnated with fresh vitality—arose and remolded his immortality once more. In 1911 the Diaz regime and its ideals collapsed, and the perpetual President went into exile abroad. Liberty, and political life, and democratic progress, came into favor again; and for the next three decades another generation fought to reclaim the country from the mortgage of foreign imperialism and domestic dictatorships, which Diaz had fastened on it, ninety years after the declaration of national independence. New leaders arose to recover the national birthright and to steer the country back on the course upon which Juarez and his generation had set it. Madero and Carranza and Zapata and Calles and Obregon and Cardenas—a miscellaneous succession of militant amateurs and philanthropists and outlaws and politicians and apostles—lineal issue all of the Reform movement and of one another, following their several urges toward the goal, carried on the legitimate heritage of Juarez and fell into place, like him, in the long secular procession of temporary triumphs, leaving a fleeting mark and some substantial residue behind them. The freshening wind that rose with the century, sweeping away the stale haze of the Diaz era, uncovered the buried work of his predecessor and sifted it anew according to the needs of a new generation. The Constitution of '57 was discarded and replaced by a charter more consonant with the times; and the cardinal omission of the former became the cardinal conquest of the latter. The Constitution of 1917 added to the political provisions laid down sixty years before the social securities for which a few farsighted and premature prophets had cried in the wilderness of 1857 by guaranteeing the rights of labor and initiating agrarian reform. Although the theory was in advance of the practice, these liberties were steadily pressed forward by the Presidents who carried on the movement; and the advances which they achieved made the work of Juarez and his school once more obsolete. As a revolutionary, he was judged by what he had left undone. The one great measure which the Reform movement contributed to the economic emancipation of the country—the nationalization of Church property—had been conceived primarily as a political lever and had miscarried economically, serving inadvertently to promote the prosperity of the middle-class at the expense of the masses, legalizing the confiscation of the communal lands of the Indians by its provisions, which applied equally to civil and ecclesiastical corporations, favoring the feudal privilege of native and foreign landowners and the inveterate servitude of the peonage system, and creating a new secular conservatism as solid as the sacred plutocracy of the past. In some quarters Juarez was now decried, in retrospect, as a counterrevolutionary. "Juarez, the Indian of Guelatao, betrayed the Indians because his lack of political and economic vision placed them under a master, who may be Spanish or Yankee or French or Creole, but who is always the MASTER," the indictment ran. "The Reform was the political and economic movement of the Creoles to gain possession of the land. The Liberals were not wrong in enacting the law of June 25, 1856: it made them rich." And it made them wrong because the Reform of 1857, which contained the seed of the revolution of 1917, had not sown it. The judgment was summary, but the liberties lost and won were the connecting link between the new reformers and the old, and their sins of omission were counted against them by the radical progress and current prejudice of the time. The reformers of 1857 derived their philosophy of progress from the liberal middle-class developed abroad by capitalist democracy; the reformers of 1917 were informed by a strong ferment of incipient socialist sentiment, foreign-born but peculiarly congenial to conditions in Mexico at their period. Although Juarez gave some casual study to the utopian socialists of his day, he foresaw as little as his collaborators the determining force of socialism in the near future, seeping into Mexico to counteract the penetration of foreign imperialism and domestic capitalism, recasting the national Constitution within sixty years, dating his work and outmoding his cause.

The rising wind of the twentieth century was storm-laden, bearing in its wake world wars which united the Old and New Worlds and revolutions in the suction of which the ideology of the nineteenth century was profoundly transformed. The ideals for which Juarez had fought were forgotten in their fulfillment or obliterated by new forces which they developed and which eclipsed them. Republicanism and monarchy became obsolete issues, and the separation of Church and State an accepted principle of modern civilization. The formidable feuds of the past faded with the progress of freedom, and fresh conflicts were generated by its gains. Political liberty without economic equality exploded the delusion of democratic sovereignty, and republican institutions proved no panacea for the class struggle that produced them. The plutocracies which they begot and which controlled them became the real power of modern society, and the science of reconciling political liberty with economic privilege the test of self-determination for modern peoples. The sacred egoism of patriotism guaranteed no people against the world of which it was a part, and the fallacy of national freedom was exploded in turn by the promotion of economic empire which precipitated the general wars that disrupted and remolded the world and opened the way for the revolutions and counter-revolutions that regenerated or ruined modern civilization. To recite the seminal struggles of the nineteenth century today is to rehearse the evanescence of its gospels and the persistence of old forces in new forms. Republics, democracies, theocracies, monarchies, nay, nationalism itself—what remains of them now? National independence, no doubt, is still an indisputable dogma; but destined to become an international fiction when, as Victor Considérant said none too soon in 1866, "The field of wars and revolutions is no longer this or that country, nor even this or that continent: today, as the Apostle said, the field is the world." The fusion of the world is a fact after two world wars provoked by a paroxysm of nationalism that betrays its decay: its very violence caused by an insoluble ferment of social forces foreign to no country, and breeding a new consciousness of common humanity that makes nationalism obsolete; and while the collaboration of enemy nationals betrayed the solidarity of class interest during the battle, the reconstruction of the world after it is disputed by the kindred affinities of the class struggle, which marks the next stage of creative democracy. Democracy, divided against itself by the rise of the first socialist state, is dismembered, and the battle drawn for the universal republic among revolutionary, routine, and reactionary democracy everywhere. The issue, effacing national frontiers, embraces the common cause of humanity; and in that context Juarez assumes his true significance for posterity. The Opposition of Time, undoing what was transient, preserves what is imperishable in his life work. His immortality transcends the mutable accidents of time and place and is perpetuated by the progress that surpasses his because it is based on it. His work endures because it is unfinished, because it was progress and progress is unending, and he survives, like all the heroes of humanity, as part of the life stream of the race. Distant as his world may be, and dim his work, and the meaning of his ideals transmuted, the spirit that inspired them can never be anachronistic. He belongs to an age that is once again heroic, and the emancipator of Mexico is remembered today among the emancipators of man and numbered with those apostles of democracy who, suffering the persecution of their own time for the sake of the morrow with the same unfailing fortitude, prove themselves in their turn of divine stock.

In the re-creation of the world today the social mission which religion long ago forfeited to revolution of making us all members of one another calls once more for his faith, his religious faith, that, though the mind of God work like the mind of man in dynamic imperfection and cataclysmic revisions of original error, the captive divinity in man must finally triumph. That faith the future will always find in the past, and the past offers no better proof of it than the life of that obscure aboriginal who embraced so long an experience of the race in his brief span. Because he believed in the ability of man to become what he will, his posthumous vitality is perennial and as evergreen as the unhalting progress of humanity; and it is not in vain, then, that we return to San Pablo Guelatao in search of the man. The primitive world out of which he came, the feudal world which he overcame, the modern world which submerged him, are all one to him now; but there is no beginning and no end there where the statue stands, like the spirit of man himself, surveying the timeless solitude in which he was born; and the civilizations through which he passed are dust and the rumor of periods is still, and Juarez himself immutable bronze, forever oblivious to what has happened to him.

Bibliography

Bibliography

Alaman, Lucas. *Historia de México desde los primeros movimientos que preparon su independencia en el año de 1808 hasta la época presente.* Mexico: 1849-52. 3 vols.

———. *Semblanzes e ideario.* Ed. by Arturo Arnaiz y Freg. Mexico: 1939.

Altamirano, Ignacio M. *Obras.* Mexico: 1889. 1 vol.

———. *Biografía de Ignacio Ramirez.* Mexico: 1889.

Alvensleben, Baron Maximilian von. *With Maximilian in Mexico.* London: 1867.

Anonimo. *Apuntes biograficos del Ciud. Jésus Gonzalez.* Mexico: 1861.

Archivos privados de Don Benito Juarez y Don Pedro Santacilia. Mexico: 1928.

Arias, Juan de Dios. *Reseña historica de la formación y operaciones del cuerpo de Ejercito del Norte durante la intervención francesa, sitio de Querétaro y noticias oficiales sobre la captura de Maximiliano, su proceso integro y su muerte.* Mexico: 1867.

Arias y Ulna, Margil. *Apuntes historicos para la biografía del traidor Almonte.* Mexico: 1862.

Arrangoiz [y Berzabal], Francisco de Paula de. *México desde 1808 hasta 1847.* Madrid: 1871-72. 4 vols.

Ayala, Miguel de. *Benito Juarez, el indio sublime.* Santiago de Chile: 1939.

Aznar, Marcial. *Observaciones histórico-politicos sobre Juarez y su época.* Mexico: 1887.

Balbas, Manuel. *Los detractores de Juarez; refutación a la obra del señor ingeniero Francisco Bulnes titulada Juarez y las revoluciones de Ayutla y de reforma.* Mexico: 1916.

Bancroft, Hubert Howe. *History of Mexico.* San Francisco: 1883-88.

———. *Vida de Porfirio Diaz.* San Francisco: 1887.

Barail, Général François Charles du. *Mes Souvenirs.* Paris: 1869.

Basch S. *Maximilien au Mexique.* Paris: 1869.

Baz, Gustavo. *Vida de Benito Juarez.* Mexico: 1874.

Beals, Carleton. *Porfirio Diaz, Dictator of Mexico.* New York: 1932.

Belly, Félix. *A travers l'Amérique Centrale.* Paris: 1867. 2 vols.

Bencomo, Diego. *Juarez. Ensayo epico.* Mexico: 1875.

Beyens, Baron Napoléon. *Le Second Empire vu par un diplomate belge.* Paris: 1925-26. 2 vols.

Blairet, Louis. *Le Général Prim.* Paris: 1869.

Blanchot, Charles. *Mémoires. L'Intervention française au Mexique.* Paris: 1911. 3 vols.

Blasio, José-Luis. *Maximiliano íntimo, el emperador Maximiliano y su corte; memorias de un secretario particular.* Mexico: 1905.

Boulenger, Marcel. *Le Duc de Morny, prince français*. Paris: 1925.

Bourdeau, Colonel. *La Guerre au Mexique*. Paris: 1906.

Boussingault, Jean-Baptiste. *Conversation de J. B. Boussingault avec l'Empereur Napoléon III au sujet de l'expédition du Mexique*. Antibes: 1927.

Brioso y Candiani, Manuel. *La Evolución del pueblo oaxaqueño desde 1821 a 1855*. Mexico: 1939.

Buenrostro, Felipe. *Historia del primer congreso constitucional de la República Mexicana que funcionó en el año 1857*. Mexico: 1874.

Buffin, Baron Camille. *La tragédie mexicaine; les Impératrices Charlotte et Eugénie*. Brussels: 1925?

Bulnes, Francisco. *El Verdadero Juarez y la verdad sobre la intervención y el Imperio*. Paris: 1904.

———. *Juarez y las revoluciones de Ayutla y de reforma*. Mexico: 1905.

———. *La Guerra de independencia*. Mexico: 1910.

Burke, Ulick Ralph. *A Life of Benito Juarez, Constitutional President of Mexico*. London: 1894.

Bustamente, Carlos Maria de. *Diario histórico de México, 1822-1823*. Zacatecas: 1896.

Butler, Pierce. *Judah P. Benjamin*. Philadelphia: 1907.

Calañas, J. R. *El Dr. Mora. Homenaje*. Mexico: 1939.

Callahan, James M. *Evolution of Seward's Mexican Policy*. West Virginia University Studies in American History, Series I, nos. 4, 5, 6.

———. "The Mexican Policy of Southern Leaders under Buchanan's Administration," *American Historical Association Annual Report, 1910*. Washington: 1912.

Callcott, Wilfrid Hardy. *Church and State in Mexico, 1822-1857*. Durham, N. C.: 1926.

———. *Santa Anna*. Norman, Okla.: 1936.

Cambre, Manuel. *La Guerra de tres años en el estado de Jalisco*. Guadalajara: 1892.

Cañedo, Estanislao. *La Vérité sur la revolution actuelle au Mexique*. Paris: 1860.

Carriedo, Adalberto. *El Unico Juarez*. Oaxaca: 1904.

Case, Lynn M. (ed.). *French Opinion on the United States and Mexico, 1860-1867; extracts from the Reports of the Procureurs-Généraux*. New York: 1936.

Castex, Général. *Ce que j'ai vu*. Paris: 1902.

Castillo, José R. del. *Juarez y la intervención y el imperio*. Mexico: 1904.

Castro, Ana Maria. *Juarez*. Mexico: 1897.

Chavez Orozco, Luis. *El sitio de Puebla, 1863*. Mexico: 1942.

———. *Historia económica y social de México*. Mexico: 1938.

Chevalier, Michel. *Le Mexique ancien et moderne*. Paris: 1864.

[Considérant, Victor]. *Quatres lettres sur le Mexique*. Brussels: 1868.

Correspondance de Juarez et de Montluc, ancien consul général du Mexique. Publiée par M. Léon de Montluc. Paris: 1885.

"Correspondence Respecting the Affairs of Mexico," presented to both Houses of Parliament by Command of Her Majesty, 1862, in *Accounts and Papers* of Great Britain, Vol. LXIV.

Corti, Count Egon Caesar. *Maximilian and Charlotte of Mexico.* New York: 1928.

Cosmes, Francisco G. *El Verdadero Bulnes y su falso Juarez.* Mexico: 1905.

Cox, I. J. "Monroe and the Early Mexican Revolutionary Agents," in *American Historical Association Report, 1911.* Vol. I.

Creelman, James. *Diaz, Master of Mexico.* New York: 1908.

Cuebas, Luis G. *Porvenir de México, o juicio sobre su estado político en 1821 y 1851.* Mexico: 1851.

Cuevas, Mariano. *Historia de la nación méxicana.* Mexico: 1829.

D., E. A. *Los Indios quieren ser libres y lo serán.* Mexico: 1829.

Daran, Victor. *El General Miguel Miramon.* Mexico: 1887.

Dawson, Daniel. *The Mexican Adventure.* London: 1935.

Doblado, Manuel. *La Guerra de reforma segun el archivo de Don Manuel Doblado.* Ed. by Carlos E. Castañeda. San Antonio, Tex.: 1930.

Documentos de la Independencia. Publicación de la Secretaría de Educación. Tomo I. Mexico: 1928.

Documentos relativas a la intervención francesa. Papeles de la familia imperial encontrados en las Tuilerias. Traducidos por Gabriel Zarate. Mexico: 1873.

Domenech, Emmanuel. *Histoire du Mexique.* Paris: 1868.

———. *L'Empire au Mexique et la candidature d'un prince Bonaparte au trône mexicain.* Paris: 1862.

———. *Le Mexique tel qu'il est.* Paris: 1867.

Donaldson, Sir Stuart A. *Mexico Thirty Years Ago.* London: 1866.

Duchâtel, A. *La Guerre de 1870-1871.* Paris: 1889.

Dunbar, Edward E. *The Mexican Papers.* New York: 1860-61.

Elton, J. F. *With the French in Mexico.* London: 1867.

Estrada, Genaro. *Don Juan Prim y su labor diplomático en México.* Publicación de la Secretaría de Relaciones Exteriores. Mexico: 1928.

Figueroa, Francisco. *Biografía del benemérito Benito Juarez.* Mexico: 1906.

Flores, Jesus Romero. *Melchor Ocampo, el filósofo de la reforma.* Mexico: 1944.

Frias y Soto, Hilarion. *Juarez glorificado y la intervención y el imperio ante la verdad histórica.* Mexico: 1905.

———. *México y los Estados Unidos durante la intervención francesa.* Mexico: 1901.

Galindo y Galindo, Miguel. *La gran década nacional, o relación histórica de la guerra de reforma, intervención extranjera y gobierno del Archiduque Maximiliano, 1857-1867.* Mexico: 1904-1906.

Garcia, Genaro. *Juarez. Refutación a Don Francisco Bulnes.* Mexico: 1904.

———. *Documentos inéditos o muy raros para la historia de México.* Mexico: 1909 on. Tomos 1 al 34.

Garcia Granados, Ricardo. *La Constitución de 1857 y las leyes de reforma en México.* Mexico: 1906.

———. *Historia de México desde la restauración de la república en 1867 hasta la caída de Porfirio Diaz.* Mexico: 1923-28. 4 vols.

Garcia, Pedro. "Memoria sobre los primeros pasos de la independencia," in Colleción de documentos del Museo Nacional de Arqueología, Historia y Etnografía, Vol. IV; *Documentos de la Independencia,* Tomo I. Mexico: 1928.

Gaulot, Paul. *La Vérité sur l'expédition du Mexique d'après les documents inédits de Ernest Louet.* Paris: 1889-90. 3 vols.

Gobineau, Conde José Arturo de. *Ensayo sobre la desigualdad de las razas humanas.* Barcelona: 1937.

Gonzalez Ortega, José. *El Golpe de estado de Juarez, rasgos biográficos del general Jesus Gonzalez Ortega.* Mexico: 1942.

Gruening, Ernest. *Mexico and Its Heritage.* New York: 1928.

Guzman y Raz, Jesus. *Bibliografía de la reforma, la intervención, y el imperio.* Imp. de la Secretaría de Relaciones Exteriores. Mexico: 1930-33.

Hall, Frederic. *Life of Maximilian I, Late Emperor of Mexico.* New York: 1868.

Hans, Alberto. *Querétaro. Memorias de un oficial del Emperador Maximiliano.* Mexico: 1869.

Henestrosa, Andrés. *Benito Juarez, textos políticos.* Mexico: 1944.

Héricault, Charles d'. *Maximilien et le Mexique; histoire des derniers mois de l'Empire mexicain.* Paris: 1869.

Hidalgo, José-Maria. *Apuntes para escribir la historia de los proyectos de monarquía en México desde el reinado de Carlos III hasta la instalación del Emperador Maximiliano.* Paris: 1868.

Iglesias Calderon, Fernando. *El Egoismo norte-americano durante la intervención francesa.* Mexico: 1905.

———. *Las supuestas traiciones de Juarez.* Mexico: 1907.

Iglesias, José-Maria. *Revistas históricas sobre la intervención francesa en México.* Mexico: 1868.

Iturribarria, J. F. *Breve historia de Oaxaca.* Mexico: 1944.

———. *Historia de Oaxaca, 1821-1861.* Mexico: 1935-39.

Jecker, J. B. "La créance Jecker. Réponse à M. de Kératry," *Revue contemporaine,* 10 janvier, 1868 [Paris].

Juarez, Benito. *Exposiciones.* Mexico: 1902.

———. *Miscelánea.* Mexico: 1906.

Kératry, Comte Emile de. *La créance Jecker, les indemnités françaises et les emprunts mexicains.* Paris: 1868.

———. *L'Empereur Maximilien, son élévation et sa chute.* Paris: 1867.

Kollonitz, Paula. *The Court of Mexico.* London: 1868.

La France, le Mexique, et les Etats Confédérés. Paris: 1863.

La Gorce, Pierre de. *Histoire du Second Empire.* Paris: 1895-1905. 7 vols.

———. *Napoléon III et sa politique.* Paris: 1933.

Lalanne, Jesus. *Zaragoza y Puebla.* Mexico: 1904

Lally, Frank E. *French Opposition to the Mexican Policy of the Second Empire.* Baltimore: 1931.

Lano, Pierre de. *La Cour de Napoléon III.* Paris: 1895.

———. *Le Secret d'un empire. L'Impératrice Eugénie.* Paris: 1894.

Laurent, P.L.M. *La Guerre du Mexique de 1862 à 1866.* Paris: 1867.

Leal, José Roman. *México constitucional.* Mexico: 1886.

Lefêvre, Eugène. *Documentos oficiales recogidos en la Secretaría privada de Maximiliano; historia de la intervención francesa en México.* Brussels and London: 1869.

———. *Le Mexique et l'intervention européenne.* Mexico: 1862.

Lempriere, Charles. *Notes on Mexico in 1861; politically and socially considered*. London: 1862.

Leonardon, H. "Prim et la candidature Hohenzollern," *Revue historique* (1900), Vol. 74 [Paris].

Lerdo de Tejada, Sebastian. *Memorias*. Puebla: no date.

L'Expédition du Mexique. Paris: 1864.

Lissagaray, Hippolyte Prosper Olivier. *Histoire de la Commune de 1871*. Buenos Aires: 1944.

Loizillon, Pierre Henri. *Lettres sur l'expédition du Mexique*. Paris: 1890.

MacGregor, Genaro F. "La Ultima Aventura de Su Alteza Serenisima," *El Universal*, 7 de junio de 1943 [Mexico].

Magdaleno, Mauricio. *José-Maria Luis Mora, el civilizador*. Pachuca: 1935.

Mancisidor, José. *Miguel Hidalgo*. Mexico: 1944.

Manning, William R. *Early Diplomatic Relations between the United States and Mexico*. Baltimore: 1916.

——(ed.). *Diplomatic Correspondence of the United States: Inter-American Affairs, 1831-1860*. Washington: 1932-39.

Mariscal, Ignacio. *Juarez y el libro de Bulnes*. Mexico: 1939.

Marquez, Leonardo, *Manifiestos. El Imperio y los imperialistas*. Mexico: 1904.

——. *Refutación hecha al libelo de D. Manuel Ramirez de Arellano*. New York: 1869.

——. *Reminiscencias sobre el fusilamiento de Don Melchor Ocampo. Mentís al general Don Felix Zuloaga*. La Habana: 1800.

Marquez de Leon, Manuel. *Don Benito Juarez a la luz de la verdad*. Mexico: 1885.

Martin, Percy F. *Maximilian in Mexico*. London: 1914.

Marx, Adrien. *Révélations sur la vie intime de Maximilien*. Paris: no date.

Marx, Karl, and Engels, Friedrich. *The Civil War in the United States*. New York: 1937.

Masseras, E. *Un Essai d'Empire au Mexique*. Paris: 1879.

Metternich, Princesse Pauline de. *Souvenirs*. Paris: 1929.

Molina Enriquez, Andrés. *La Reforma y Juarez*. Mexico: 1906.

Monterde, Francisco. *Ignacio Ramirez, "El Nigromante."* Mexico: 1944.

Mora, José-Maria Luis. *Méjico y sus revoluciones*. Paris: 1836.

——. *Obras sueltas*. Paris: 1837.

Morelos y Pavon, José-Maria. *Documentos inéditos o poco conocidos*. Publicación de la Secretaría de Educación Publica. Mexico: 1927.

Muñoz, Rafael F. *Santa Anna, el que todo lo ganó y todo lo perdió*. Madrid: 1936.

Niox, Gustav Léon. *L'Expédition du Mexique*. Paris: 1874.

Ocampo, Melchor. *Obras*. Mexico: 1900. 3 vols.

Ocaranza, Fernando. *Juarez y sus amigos*. Mexico: 1939-42. 2 vols.

Ollivier, Emile O. *L'Empire libéral*. Paris: 1899.

Orellano, F. J. de. *Historia del General Prim*. Barcelona: 1871. 2 vols.

Palavicini, Felix F. *México, historia de su evolución constructiva*. Mexico: 1945. 4 vols.

Parra, Porfirio. *Estudio histórico-sociológico sobre la reforma en México*. Imp. Gaceta de Guadalajara. Guadalajara: 1906.

748 JUAREZ AND HIS MEXICO

Parthe, Ernst. *Die Intervention in Mexico und das neue Kaiserreich.* Leipzig: 1864.

Payno [y Flores], Manuel. *Memoria sobre la revolución de diciembre de 1857 y enero de 1858.* Mexico: 1860.

――――. *Mexico y el Señor Embajador Don Joaquin Francisco Pacheco.* Mexico: 1862.

Peña y Reyes, Antonio de la. *El Tratado Mon-Almonte.* Publicación de la Secretaría de Relaciones Exteriores. Mexico: 1925.

Pereyra, Carlos. *Juarez discutido como dictador y estadista a proposito de los errores, paradojas y fantasias del Señor Don Francisco Bulnes.* Mexico: 1904.

――――. *Téjas.* Mexico: 1935.

Perez, José T. *Bulnes a espaldas de Juarez.* Mexico: 1904.

Perez Martinez, Hector. *Juarez el impasible.* Madrid: 1934.

Peza, Juan de Dios. *Epopeyas de mi patria.* Mexico: 1904.

Planchet, Regis. *La Cuestión religiosa en México, o sea, vida de Benito Juarez.* Rome: 1906.

Poinsett, Joel R. *Notes on Mexico.* London: 1825.

Portilla, Anselmo de la. *Méjico en 1856 y 1857.* New York: 1858.

Praviel, Armand. *La Contre-guérilla au Mexique, souvenirs inédits.* Paris: 1931.

Prida, Ramon. *Juarez; como lo pinta el diputado Bulnes y como lo describe la historia.* Mexico: 1904.

Prida Santacilia, Pablo. *Siguiendo la vida de Juarez.* Mexico: 1945.

Prieto, Guillermo. *Lecciones de historia patria.* Mexico: 1901.

――――. *Memorias de mis tiempos.* Mexico: 1944.

――――. *Viaje a los Estados Unidos (1877) por Fidel.* Mexico: 1877-78.

Proudhon, P. J. *Napoléon III.* Paris: 1900.

Pruñeda, Pedro. *Historia de la guerra de México, 1861-1867.* Madrid: 1867.

Puig Casauranc, José Manuel. *Juarez, una interpretación humana.* Mexico: 1928.

Quinet, Edgar. *L'Expédition du Mexique.* London: 1862.

Rabasa, Emilio. *La Evolución histórica de México.* Paris: 1920.

Ramirez de Arellano, Manuel. *Ultimas Horas del imperio.* Mexico: 1903.

Ramirez, Ignacio. *Obras.* Mexico: 1889.

Ramos Pedrueza, Rafael. *La Lucha de clases a través de la historia de México.* Mexico: 1936.

Reinach-Foussemagne, Comtesse Hélène de. *Charlotte de Belgique, Impératrice du Mexique.* Paris: 1925.

Reyes, Bernardo. *Benito Juarez.* Monterrey: 1906.

Reyes, Rodolfo. *Benito Juarez, ensayo sobre un caracter.* Madrid: 1939.

Richardson, James D. *A Compilation of the Messages and Papers of the Presidents.* Washington: 1897.

Rippy, J. F. *The United States and Mexico.* New York: 1936.

Riva Palacio, Mariano, and Martinez de la Torre, Rafael. *Memorandum sobre el proceso del Archiduque Fernando Maximiliano de Austria.* Mexico: 1867.

Riva Palacio, Vicente. *México a través de los siglos.* Mexico: 1887-89. 5 vols.

Rivera, Agustin. *Anales mexicanos. La Reforma y el segundo imperio.* Lagos: 1891.

Rivera Cambas, Manuel. *Historia antigua y moderna de Jalapa y de las revoluciones del estado de Veracruz.* Mexico: 1869-71.

———. *Los Gobernantes de México.* Mexico: 1873.

Romero de Terreros y Vinent, Manuel (comp.) *Maximiliano y el Imperio segun correspondencias contemporaneas.* Mexico: 1926.

Romero, Matias. *Correspondencia de la Legación Mexicana en Washington durante la intervención extranjera, 1860-1868.* Mexico: 1870.

———. *Historia de las intrigas europeas que ocasionaron la intervención francesa en México.* Mexico: 1868.

———. *Mexico and the United States.* New York: 1898.

Rostovsky, S. N. *Nueva Historia de la America Latina.* Buenos Aires: 1940.

Ruiz, Eduardo. *Biografía del C. Melchor Ocampo.* Mexico: 1882.

———. *Historia de la guerra de intervencíon en Michoacán.* Mexico: 1940.

Rydjord, John. *Foreign Interest in the Independence of New Spain.* Durham, N. C.: 1935.

Salado Alvarez, Victoriano. *Refutación de algunos errores de Señor Don Francisco Bulnes.* Mexico: 1904.

Salomon, Henry. *L'Ambassade de Richard de Metternich à Paris.* Paris: 1931.

Sanchez, Juan. *Honor a Juarez.* Oaxaca: 1905.

Santibañez, Manuel. *Reseña histórica del cuerpo de Ejercito de Oriente, escrita con acopio de datos.* Mexico: 1892-93.

Santovenia y Echaide, Emeterio S. "Mexico y Espana en 1861-62," *Revista de historia de America,* diciembre de 1939, num. 7 [Mexico].

———. *Prim, el caudillo estadista.* Bilbao: 1933.

Schefer, Christian. *La Grande Pensée de Napoléon III; les origines de l'expédition du Mexique, 1852-1862.* Paris: 1939.

Schmit von Tavera, Ernst Ritter. *Geschichte der Regierung des Kaisers Maximilian I und die Französische Intervention in Mexiko, 1861-1867.* Vienna and Leipzig: 1902.

Schrynmakers, Arsène de. *Le Mexique; histoire de l'établissement et de la chute de l'empire de Maximilien.* Brussels: 1882.

Sender, Ramon J. *El Problema religioso en Méjico. Catolicos y Christianos.* Madrid: 1928.

Serra y Caussa, Nicolas. *Juarez, instantáneas y películas.* Mexico: 1912.

Sierra, Justo. *Juarez, su obra y su tiempo.* Mexico: 1905-1906.

———. *Mexico, su evolución social.* Mexico: 1901-1902.

Smissen, Baron A. L. A. G. van der. *Souvenirs du Mexique, 1864-1867.* Brussels: 1892?

Smith, Justin H. *The War with Mexico.* New York: 1919. 2 vols.

Sosa, Francisco. *Biografía de Don Benito Juarez.* Mexico: 1884.

Sprague, William F. *Vicente Guerrero, Mexican Liberator.* Chicago: 1939.

Strode, Hudson. *Timeless Mexico.* New York: 1944.

Teja Zabre, Alfonso. *Historia de México.* Mexico: 1935.

Teran, Jesus. *La Misión confidencial de Don Jesus Teran en Europa, 1863-1868.* Publicación de la Secretaría de Relaciones Exteriores. Mexico: 1943.

Testory, l'Abbé. *L'Empire el le clergé mexicain*. Mexico: 1865.

Thoumas, Général Charles Antoine. *Les Français au Méxique*. Paris: 1890?

Toledo y J., Domingo P. de. *México en la obra de Marx y Engels*. Mexico: 1939.

Toro, Alfonso. *La Iglesia y el estado en México*. Mexico: 1927.

Torres, Rafael L. *Estudio histórico sobre la traición de Querétaro*. Mexico: 1914.

Troncoso, Francisco P. *Diario de las operaciones militares del sitio de Puebla en 1863*. Mexico: 1909.

Tucé, Adrien de. *Cinq Ans au Mexique, 1862-1867*. Paris: no date.

Valades, José C. *Alaman, estadista e historiador*. Mexico: 1938.

Valdés, Manuel. *Memorias de la guerra de reforma*. Mexico: 1913.

Vallier, Emmanuel. *Historique des troupes coloniales, campagne du Mexique*. Paris: 1908.

Valori-Rustichelli, Prince Henri François de. *L'Expédition du Mexique, réhabilitée au triple point de vue religieux, politique, et commercial*. Paris: 1864.

Vanson, Emile. *Crimée, Italie, Mexique. Lettres de campagnes, 1854-1867*. Paris: 1905.

Vasconcelos, José. *Breve Historia de México*. Mexico: 1937.

Velazquez Bringas, Esperanza. *Hombres de la independencia*. Mexico: 1910.

Vicarte, Alberto. *Biografía de Benito Juarez*. Chihuahua: 1906.

Vidaurri, Santiago. *Correspondencia particular de Santiago Vidaurri, gobernador de Nuevo Leon (1855-1864)*. Prologada y anotada por el Lic. Santiago Roel. Monterrey: 1946. Tomo I.

Vigil, José-Maria. *México a través de los siglos*. Mexico: 1887. Vol. V.

Villaseñor y Villaseñor, Alejandro. *Obras*. Mexico: 1897-1910.

Viramontes, Leonardo. *Biografía popular del benemérito de América, Benito Juarez*. Mexico: 1906.

Ward, Sir Henry George. *Mexico*. London: 1829.

Wellesley, Sir Victor, and Sencourt, Robert E. *Conversations with Napoleon III*. London: 1934.

Weyl, Nathaniel and Sylvia. *The Reconquest of Mexico*. New York: 1939.

Yriarte, Charles E. *Les Portraits contemporains*. Paris: 1870.

Zamacois, Niceto de. *Historia de Méjico desde sus tiempos más remotas hasta nuestros dias*. Barcelona and Mexico: 1877-82.

Zarco, Francisco. *Comentarios de Francisco Zarco sobre la intervención francesa, 1861-1863*. Prologo de Antonio de la Peña y Reyes. Publicación de la Secretaría de Relaciones Exteriores. Mexico: 1929.

———. *Historia del congreso estraordinario constituyente de 1856 y 1857*. Mexico: 1857.

———. Miscellaneous articles in *El Siglo XIX*.

Zavala, Lorenzo de. *Ensayo histórico de las revoluciones de México desde 1808 hasta 1830*. Paris: 1831-32.

Zayas, Enriquez Rafael de. *Benito Juarez, su vide, su obra*. Mexico: 1906.

Zerecero, Anastasio. *Memorias*. Mexico: 1869.

MS. sources, Museo Nacional de Historia y Antropología, Mexico, D. F.
Newspaper files and periodicals in the Biblioteca de Hacienda, Mexico, D. F.

Index